LIFE

OF

ELIZABETH FRY.

COMPILED FROM HER JOURNAL,

AS EDITED BY HER DAUGHTERS,

AND FROM VARIOUS OTHER SOURCES.

BY

SUSANNA CORDER.

PHILADELPHIA:
HENRY LONGSTRETH,
No. 1336 CHESTNUT STREET.
1861.

Stereotyped by Slote & Mooney, Philadelphia.

Preface.

THE "Memoir of Elizabeth Fry," in two Volumes, edited by her daughters, has been extensively circulated in this and other lands; and rarely has any religious biography been perused with so general and so deep an interest. More *brief* notices of her life have also emanated from other pens: and it might seem superfluous again to depict her character, or to rehearse the circumstances which marked those arduous labours, in the service of Him who "went about doing good," to which, under the constraining influence of his love and power, she devoted every talent committed to her stewardship.

There are, however, many by whom a memorial of Elizabeth Fry, more compendious than that which has been published by her daughters, would, perhaps, be welcomed with pleasure and read with instruction. A work which might embrace more exclusively the records of her own experience, and of her religious and philanthropic engagements, appears, in the estimation of some of her most intimate friends, to be required, as filling up a chasm still left in the circle of readers, to whom the voluminous "Memoir" may not be conveniently accessible.

To venture on such an abridgment has not been contemplated without a serious conviction of the delicacy and importance of the task; and had not a special request from her daughters, (the Editors of her life,) in conjunction with other members of her immediate family, encouraged the Compiler of the following pages to undertake the work, it would not have been attempted.

But various considerations have *additionally* stimulated the Compiler to add another to the several sketches of the Life of Elizabeth Fry. A prominent one is suggested by the fact, that her character and sentiments have been represented by individuals, widely differing in religious opinion, both from her and from each other; and they have (in consequence of the varying mental complexion to which habit and circumstances impart a colouring peculiar to each) given, to their picture of Elizabeth Fry, a tinge which has prevented her from appearing, *as she was*, consistent in her language, her conduct, and demeanour, with the principles which, from conviction, she was early led to adopt, and to which, through life, she steadfastly adhered. This, it must be confessed, is calculated to induce the impression that, in Elizabeth Fry's life, there was evinced a compromise of principle; and it proves that whilst her ardent admirers exhibit a dazzling portrait of her piety, her loveliness, and her philanthropy, they fail, in degree at least, to depict her in the light of *truth*—in her meek and lowly garb of deep humility, treading with watchful circumspection and fear, the cross-bearing path of the blessed Redeemer.

Drawn by the attractions of heavenly love, her steps were directed into a course untried and new; and the service that was designed for her became gradually manifest, as she followed, in simple faith, the guiding light of the Holy Spirit: and whether it led her into the presence of monarchs, into association with princes, or into the company of the wise and learned,—whether she was brought into communion with fellow-disciples who, whatever might be the form of their Christian profession, were pursuing with her the same heaven-ward track, or surrounded by the votaries of a thoughtless world incapable of responding to the deep sympathies of her spirit, *in all situations*, and *under every circumstance*, she was enabled to maintain, with holy consistency, the dignified character of her high vocation, as a minister of Christ in the Society of Friends; adorning the doctrine of God her Saviour; being an example to the believers in faith, in patience, in meekness, and charity; raising in the hearts of thousands, among the varied classes of the people, a reverent acknowledgment of that divine influence, which constrained her to gather immortal spirits to the Fountain of life and peace. Yet how few, among the many who have extolled her deeds of mercy and love, were prepared to penetrate the veil that concealed, from the gaze of the world, the working of that heavenly power, through which alone she became instrumental in directing a resistless moral force against the dominion of sin and misery, which strengthened her spirit for the arduous combat, and armed her with those weapons that are "mighty through God, to the pulling down of" the "strong holds" in which Satan retains his government in the souls of the children of men.

To trace the operation of this invisible power—the mainspring of the wonderful machinery that became so effective in the counteraction of evil—will, to the spiritually-minded Christian, be the most instructive, and possibly the most interesting object that can result from a perusal of this Volume. For to the soul that is anxiously seeking deliverance from the corruptions inherent in our nature, as the frail children of Adam's fallen race, there is no feature of mental delineation more encouraging than that which is presented by a co-operation with "the grace of God which brings salvation." Through the regenerating and sanctifying influence of this grace, in the heart of Elizabeth Fry, the prophetic vision was in no small measure realised—that "instead of the thorn shall come up the fir-tree, and instead of the briar the myrtle-tree;" causing "the wilderness" of the human spirit to "become like Eden," and its "desert like the garden of the Lord; joy and gladness" to "be found therein, thanksgiving, and the voice of melody."

May the example, which this Volume exhibits, of constant and rigorous self-examination, of fervent love to God, and devotedness to promote the establishment of His kingdom of righteousness and peace, animate survivors to a like earnest endeavour to attain purity of heart, and to a diligent occupation with the talents bestowed on them: that so, when "their Lord cometh, and reckoneth with them," they may receive the sentence of "Well-done."

A serious responsibility rests on every individual member of the Church of God, by whatever name outwardly distinguished; for, to each has been given the one, the two, or the five talents; by the faithful dedication of which, according to the direction of the Holy Spirit, they may be instrumental in accelerating the advent of that most glorious era, when "the kingdoms of this world" shall "become the kingdoms of our Lord, and of his Christ, and He shall reign for ever and ever."

Contents.

CHAPTER I.

CHAPTER II.

CHAPTER III.

CHAPTER IV.

CHAPTER V.

CHAPTER VI.

CHAPTER VII.

CHAPTER VIII.

CHAPTER IX.

CHAPTER X.

CHAPTER XI.

CHAPTER XI.

LIFE OF ELIZABETH FRY.

Chapter First.

1780—1798. Birth—Parentage—Her Mother, her character—Memoranda by her—Removal to Earlham—Death of her Mother—Recollections by Elizabeth Fry, of her own early life—Sketch of female society—Circumstances of Elizabeth Gurney and her sisters—Her character and habits—Natural qualities as a young person—Absence of religious knowledge—Established principles requisite to happiness—William Savery comes to Norwich on a religious visit—Effects of William Savery's preaching—Description by himself—Account by one of her sisters—Her own journal.

Elizabeth Fry was born in Norwich on the 21st of the fifth month, 1780. She was the third daughter of John Gurney, of Earlham, in the county of Norfolk, and Catherine, daughter of Daniel Bell, a merchant in London; whose wife Catherine, daughter of David Barclay, was a descendant of the ancient family of the Barclays of Ury, in Kincardineshire, and grand-daughter of Robert Barclay, the well-known apologist of the Quakers.

John Gurney, of Earlham, the father of the subject of this memoir, was born in 1749, and was educated in the principles of the Society of Friends. As he advanced in life, his pursuits led to intercourse with persons of various denominations; this, with a naturally social disposition, induced an unusual degree of indiscriminate liberality of sentiment towards others. He was a man of ready talent, of bright, discerning mind, singularly warm-hearted, and affectionate, very benevolent, and in manners courteous and popular.

His marriage with Catherine Bell took place in 1775. They had twelve children—one of them died in infancy. Catherine Gurney was a person of very superior mind; and in her latter years, she became a serious Christian, and a decided *Friend*. All her children were, by nature, highly gifted, both with mental and personal endowments.

The usual residence of John and Catherine Gurney was in Norwich; but the summer months were spent at Bramerton, a pleasant village about four miles distant from the city.

This was a period when talent was frequently allied to scepticism, and the highest attainments in human learning were too often unaccompanied by soundness of religious faith. Many persons doubted; even more were indifferent to the great truths of Christianity; and so general was this state of things, that individuals of personal piety, who sincerely desired the prosperity of the kingdom of Christ, too little considered the opinions entertained by others, and associated freely with those whose religious belief was essentially at variance with their own. We cannot doubt that, to a certain extent, this was the case with John and Catherine Gurney, or that it had an injurious effect on their family, especially after the decease of their mother; who, in the inscrutable dispensation of an unerring Providence, was taken from them when her eldest child was seventeen years of age, her youngest only an infant.

Great indeed was the loss which they sustained by this deeply affecting event. The following extracts from her memoranda denote the pious care which she had exercised in the management of her household:—

"*Bramerton*, 1788.—In the morning endeavour, at first waking, to bring the mind into a state of silent waiting and worship, preparatory to the active employment of the day; when up, visit the several apartments of the children, and, if leisure permit, before breakfast read the Scriptures, if not, it should not be afterwards omitted; forget not the kindest attentions to my dearest companion before parting for the day. After walking with the little ones, and endeavouring to enjoy each individually, begin with the necessary instructions for Catherine and Rachel; then attend to the kitchen and all family regulations, and to the claims of the poor; again attending the nurseries before dinner; at which time forget not the excellent custom of grateful, pious acknowledgment for blessings bestowed. The introduction of the children after this meal, generally affords my dear husband and myself an opportunity of the united enjoyment of our domestic comforts. A short afternoon may either be devoted to the company of my dear husband, or to writing letters, reading, or instructing the children alternately; particularly in the knowledge of the Scriptures; and the few remaining hours of the evening to be devoted to the promotion of my husband's enjoyment, and, if possible, to blend instruction and amusement to the elder children, who are our constant companions till the time of rest. Then, being quiet and uninterrupted with my best friend, be not unmindful of the religious duties of life; which consideration may, I hope, lead to that trust in Providence that gives spiritual tranquillity and spiritual support.

Remember, that these desultory remarks are designed, first, to promote my duty to my Maker—secondly, my duty towards my husband and children, relations, servants and poor neighbours."

In the year 1786, John and Catherine Gurney had removed to Earlham Hall, a seat of the Bacon family, about two miles from Norwich: the three youngest sons were born after their settlement there.

The following memoranda were subsequently penned by Catherine Gurney.

"*Earlham*, 1792.—If, in conversation, we studied rather to avoid whatever may in its nature be reprehensible, than to search for approbation or admiration, would not associating with our friends become more innocent, if not more profitable? If our piety does not appear adequate to supporting us in the exigencies of life, and I may add, death; surely our hearts cannot be sufficiently devoted to it. It may be encouraging to the poor traveller through life to consider, that as he recedes from vice he approaches towards virtue; and as he despises the one, he will become enamoured with the other. Modern authors on religion and morality describe, perhaps very well, what human nature ought to be, but do they sufficiently point out the means of becoming so? Do they direct the inquirer to the still small voice within?

Books of controversy on religion are seldom read with profit, not even those in favour of our own particular tenets. The mind stands less in need of conviction than conversion.

As our endeavours in education, as in every other pursuit, should be regulated by the ultimate design, it would be certainly wise, in those engaged in the important office of instructing youth, to consider what would render the objects of their care perfect, when men or women, rather than what will render them pleasing as children. These reflections have led me to decide upon what I most covet for my daughters, as the result of our daily pursuits. As piety is undoubtedly the shortest and securest way to all moral rectitude, young women should be virtuous and good, on the broad firm basis of Christianity; therefore, it is not the opinions of any man or sect whatever, that are to be inculcated in preference to those rigid but divine truths contained in the New Testament."

The following are this tender mother's advices to her children on their first going to a place of worship:—

"Since we know that He, who gave us life, health and strength of body, has given us an understanding mind, which will show us what is reasonable and right to do, we ought to consider, whether it is not right to love and obey that excellent Being, who has certainly placed us here on earth, and surrounded us with blessings and enjoyments, that we may become as He would have us: that is, good; and that we should adore and love Him at all times; but as many things happen to lead the mind from this adoration and love of God, which is His due, and our truest enjoyment, it is necessary to retire with our friends and neighbours from hurry and business, that we may think of Him who delights to bless us, and will consider us as His children, if we love Him as a heavenly Father. Do not, then, my dear child, suffer thy thoughts to wander, or to dwell upon trifles, when thou art most immediately before Him, whom thou must strive to love, with all thy heart and soul."

The foregoing remarks of this judicious and pious mother give a lively impression of the greatness of the bereavement to this large circle of young persons, thus left destitute of maternal care.

In some recollections of her early childhood, recorded by Elizabeth Fry after arriving at mature age, are interesting allusions to this beloved parent.

"My mother was most dear to me, and the walks she took with me in the old-fashioned garden, are as fresh with me, as if only just passed.

My natural affections were very strong from my early childhood, at times almost overwhelmingly so; such was the love for my mother, that the thought that she might die and leave me, used to make me weep after I went to bed, and for the rest of the family, that notwithstanding my fearful nature, my childlike wish was, that two large walls might crush us all together, that we might die at once, and thus avoid the misery of each other's death. I seldom, if I could help it, left my mother's side; I watched her when asleep in the day with exquisite anxiety, and used to go gently to her bed-side to listen, from the awful fear that she did not breathe; in short, I may truly say, it amounted to deep reverence.

How great is the importance of a wise mother, directing the tastes of her children in very early life, and judiciously influencing their affections! I remember with pleasure my mother's beds for wild flowers, which, with delight, I used, as a child, to attend to with her; it gave me that pleasure in observing their beauties and varieties, that though I never have had time to become a botanist, few can imagine, in my many journeys, how I have been pleased and refreshed, by observing and enjoying the wild flowers on my way. Again, she collected shells, and had a cabinet, and bought one for Rachel and myself, where we placed our curiosities; and I may truly say, in the midst even of deep trouble, and often most weighty engagements of a religious and philanthropic nature, I have derived advantage, refreshment, and pleasure, from my taste for these things, making collections of them, and various natural curiosities, although, as with the flowers, I have not studied them scientifically.

My mother, as far as she knew, really trained us up in the fear and love of the Lord; my deep impression is, that she was a holy, devoted follower of the Lord Jesus; but that her understanding was not fully enlightened as to the fulness of gospel truth. She taught us as far as she knew, and I now remember the solemn religious feelings I had, whilst sitting in silence with her after reading the Scriptures, or a Psalm before we went to bed. I have no doubt that her prayers were not in vain in the Lord. She died when I was twelve years old; the remembrance of her illness and death is sad, even to the present day."

Elizabeth Fry entered life at a period marked, in the history of Europe, for great and almost sudden changes. The

French Revolution shook the surrounding nations to their centre, and deluged with blood the land which its originators had hoped to render free and happy—a natural consequence of the awful conflict between bigotry and tyranny on the one hand, and infidelity and unbridled licentiousness on the other. The theories, which in France had undermined the principles of religion, and had assigned to mere human reason the homage due only to the Almighty Creator, had become imbibed by many in *this* country, particularly by some who were conspicuously known as possessing superior natural and acquired talent. But no circumstance in the aspect of that remarkable era, was more striking than the impulse given to the education of females. Both in France and England a number of highly gifted women became known as authors of surpassing endowments. Previous to this time the education of girls had been much confined to needle-work and domestic employments, whilst those in the higher classes of society were accustomed to the frivolous, but fashionable amusements of the day—the mental powers of each being but little developed.

Whilst genius and science shone on some minds with the calm light of truth, they were too generally reflected in the glare of a false philosophy, which inculcated a most specious scepticism, and led to an utter rejection of the divine revelation granted to man through the medium of the Bible. Norwich had not escaped the contagion. It was noted for the talent and unbelief of the society of the town and neighbourhood. The daughters of John Gurney—especially the three elder ones—were exposed to frequent association with persons whose influence sapped the foundation of their religious faith. Left to their own resources, unaccustomed, since the decease of their mother, to the study of the Holy Scriptures, and with little opportunity of becoming correctly instructed, they were, for a time, permitted to stumble upon the dark mountains, seeking rest and finding none. Their father's occupations, both public and private, and his naturally trustful disposition, prevented his perceiving all the dangers to which they were subjected. They formed many acquaintances, and some friendships, with persons greatly gifted by nature, but fearfully tainted by the prevailing errors of the day. Great pain and bitter disappointment resulted from these connections. To the more dissipating gaieties of the world they were but little exposed—they were, however, accustomed to indulge in many amusements, such as dancing, singing, &c.—and none of the party appears to have entered into them with more zest than Elizabeth. But her pursuit of pleasure was often interrupted by delicate health. She was liable to severe nervous attacks, which frequently prevented her joining her sisters in their different occupations. She was, in her youthful days, very attractive: her figure tall, her countenance sweet and pleasing, and her person and manners dignified and lovely. She was gentle and quiet in temper, yet evinced a strong will.

In a letter, written before she was three years old, her mother thus mentions her:—"My dove-like Betsy scarcely ever offends, and is, in every sense of the word, truly engaging." The indisposition to which she was subject caused her no small suffering, and produced a great degree of timidity —a fear of being left in the dark—and a languor, both of body and mind, that rendered study irksome to her. This proved a serious disadvantage, her education consequently being defective and unfinished. But her mind was quick and penetrating, and for depth and originality of thought she was remarkable, even in her early years. In referring to her childhood, Elizabeth Fry said she thought that being *called* stupid really tended to *make* her so, and discouraged her efforts to learn. This was a natural result.

But whatever might be the effect of this physical hindrance to mental exertion, it was but temporary; her latent vigour of intellect became powerfully developed. She doubtless derived much advantage from the watchful care of her eldest sister, Catherine Gurney, who early evinced a thoughtful mind, a good understanding, and a thirst for instruction. She became an excellent person, manifesting, through life, an advancement in Christian principle; the blessed results of which shone brightly at its close.

Such were the circumstances, and such the characteristics of Elizabeth Gurney and her sisters, after the death of their mother: and years passed on, with few changes, but such as necessarily came with the lapse of time, and their advance in age. But He who had purposes of mercy towards them; in His own way, was preparing for them emancipation from their doubts, and light for their darkness. Wonderful is it to mark how, by little and little, through various instruments, through mental conflicts, through bitter experiences, He gradually led them, each one to a knowledge of the truth. The means by which they first became impressed with some abiding sense of the inestimable value of divine revelation, was remarkable. Among their numerous associates, was a gentleman who now became acquainted with the Earlham family, of high principle, and cultivated mind. With him the sisters formed a strong and lasting friendship. He addressed himself to their understandings, on the grand doctrines of Christianity; he referred them to the Holy Scriptures; he lent them, and read with them, books of a serious tendency. He treated religion, as such, with reverence; and although himself a Roman Catholic, he abstained from every controversial topic, nor ever used his influence, directly or indirectly, in favour of the peculiar views of his own church. There was another individual who proved an important instrument, in leading the sisters to sound views of Christian truth, though, on their first acquaintance, she was herself wandering in the wilderness of doubt, if not of error. This was Marianne Galton, afterwards Schimmelpenninck.* Being a highly educated person, of great mental power, and accustomed to exercise her abilities in the use of her reason,

*Authoress of a Tour to Alet and the Grande Chartreuse, &c., &c.

and in an honest search after truth; she acquired considerable influence over them. As the light of revelation opened upon her own understanding, and her heart became influenced by it, they shared in her advance, and profited by her experience. There were other persons with whom they associated, whose influence was desirable, but less powerful, than that of the two just mentioned.

They appear also to have derived advantage from the religious visits of Friends to Earlham. The family of John Gurney were in the habit of frequenting no place of worship, but that of Friends. The attendance of Elizabeth was frequently prevented by want of health, and it is difficult to know when the habit of absenting herself might have been broken through, but for her uncle, Joseph Gurney, who urged the duty upon her, and encouraged her to make the attempt. He had become a decided Friend, and had much influence with her, both then, and during her future life. She was ready, indeed, to essay anything, that might tend to satisfy her conscience, or meet the longings of her heart. The principles so early inculcated by her venerated mother, were rooted too deeply to be eradicated, though surrounded by influences unfriendly to their full unfolding. She commenced, at the age of sixteen, or perhaps earlier, the practice of recording her feelings and sentiments, by way of journal. From some of her first entries, the following selections exhibit a powerful struggle between light and darkness, the cravings of her spirit for something not yet attained, earnest desires after "virtue and truth;" strongly contrasted with the misgivings of a mind beclouded by doubts, and "stumbling" as on "the dark mountains."

"I am, at present, like a ship put to sea without a pilot—I feel my heart and mind so overburdened—I want some one to lean upon." "My mind is in so dark a state that I see everything through a black medium." "I see everything darkly—I can comprehend nothing—I doubt upon everything."

"Without passions of any kind, how different I should be! I would not give them up, but I should like to have them under subjection; but it appears to me (as I feel) impossible to govern them; my mind is not strong enough; as I at times think they do no hurt to others. But am I sure they will hurt no one? I believe by not governing myself in little things, I may by degrees become a despicable character, and a curse to society; therefore, my doing wrong is of consequence to others, as well as to myself."

In her Seventeenth Year.—"I feel by experience, how much entering into the world hurts me; worldly company, I think, materially injures; it excites a false stimulus, such as a love of pomp, pride, vanity, jealousy, and ambition; it leads to think about dress, and such trifles, and when out of it, we fly to novels and scandal, or something of that kind, for entertainment. I have lately been given up a good deal to worldly passions; by what I have felt I can easily imagine how soon I should be quite led away."

The reader will, doubtless, have already perceived that the children of John Gurney were allowed to mingle in the gaieties of life, and that they were not accustomed to observe that moderation in their costume, which is inculcated by the society of which they were nominally members. They did not use the correct grammatical language to which Friends adhere, and probably they would not, in any part of their external demeanor, have been recognised as belonging to this religious community.

Without a sketch of Elizabeth Gurney's life at its earlier period, marking the great change which, through the operation of divine grace, was wrought in her heart, and which became so strikingly conspicuous in her renunciation of the vanities of the world, this volume would be divested of much of its most interesting and instructive tendency. Further quotations from her journal, showing the habits of her youth, will therefore be proceeded with. The first of these indicates the injurious influence of association with persons whose sphere in life is unfriendly to the growth of virtue.

Prince William Frederick, afterwards Duke of Gloucester, was then with his regiment quartered at Norwich. And Elizabeth remarks, "I met the Prince—it showed me the folly of the world. My mind is very flat after this storm of pleasure."

"I love to feel for the sorrows of others—to pour wine and oil into the wounds of the afflicted. I love 'to look through nature up to nature's God.' I have no more religion than that, and in the little I have I am not in the least devotional, but when I admire the beauties of nature, I cannot help thinking of the source from whence such beauties flow. I feel it a support. I believe firmly that all is guided for the best by an invisible power, therefore I do not fear the evils of life so much. I love to feel good—I do what I can to be kind to everybody. I have many faults which I hope in time to overcome."

Thus, by contemplating the external creation, she was led to confide in an Infinite Being, although she had not yet beheld Him through the medium of divine revelation.

Monday, May 21st.—I am seventeen to-day. Am I a happier or a better creature than I was this time twelvemonths? I know I am happier; I think I am better. I hope I shall be much better this day year than I am now. I hope to be quite an altered person, to have more knowledge, to have my mind in greater order; and my heart, too, that wants to be put in order as much, if not more, than any part of me, it is in such a fly-away state.

(*Written on a bright summer's morning.*)

Is there not a ray of perfection amidst the sweets of this morning; I do think there is something perfect from which all good flows.

June 20*th*.—If I have long to live in this world, may I bear misfortunes with fortitude; do what I can to alleviate the sorrows of others, exert what power I have to increase happiness; try to govern my passions by reason, and adhere strictly to what I think right.

July 7*th*.—I have seen several things in myself and others, I have never before remarked; but I have not tried to improve myself, I have given way to my passions, and let them have command over me. I have known my faults, and not corrected them, and now I am determined I will once more try, with redoubled ardour, to overcome my wicked inclinations; I must not flirt; I must not ever be out of temper with the children; I must not contradict without a cause; I must not mump when my sisters are liked and I am not; I must not allow myself to be angry; I must not exaggerate, which I am inclined to do. I must not give way to luxury; I must not be idle in mind; I must try to give way to every good feeling, and overcome every bad; I will see what I can do; if I had but perseverance, I could do all that I wish: I will try. I have lately been too satirical, so as to hurt sometimes; remember! it is a fault to hurt others.

8*th*.—A much better day, though many faults.

10*th*.—Some poor people were here; I do not think I gave them what I did, with a good heart. I am inclined to give away; but for a week past, owing to not having much money, I have been mean and extravagant. Shameful! Whilst I live, may I be generous; it is in my nature, and I will not overcome so good a feeling. I am inclined to be extravagant, and that leads to meanness, for those who will throw away a good deal are apt to mind giving a little.

11*th*.—I am in a most idle mind, and inclined to have an indolent dissipated day; but I will try to overcome it, and see how far I can. I am well; oh, most inestimable of comforts! Happy, happy I, to be so well; how good, how virtuous ought I to be! May what I have suffered be a lesson to me, to feel for those who are ill, and alleviate their sorrows as far as lies in my power; let it teach me never to forget the blessings I enjoy. I ought never to be unhappy;—look back at this time last year, how ill I was, how miserable;—yet I was supported through it; God will support through the suffering he inflicts; if I were devotional, I should fall on my knees and be most grateful for the blessings I enjoy; a good father, one whom I dearly love, sisters formed after my own heart, friends whom I admire, and good health which gives a relish to all. Company to dinner; I must beware of being a flirt, it is an abominable character; I hope I shall never be one, and yet I fear I am one now a little. Be careful not to talk at random. Beware, and see how well I can get through this day, without one foolish action. If I do pass this day without one foolish action, it is the first I ever passed so. If I pass a day with only a few foolish actions, I may think it a good one.

25th.—This book is quite a little friend to my heart; it is next to communicating my feelings to another person. I would not but write in it for something, for it is most comfortable to read it over, and see the different workings of my heart and soul.

30th.—Pride and vanity are too much the incentives to most of the actions of men; they produce a love of admiration, and in thinking of the opinions of others, we are too apt to forget the monitor within. We should first look to ourselves, and try to make ourselves virtuous, and then pleasing. Those who are truly virtuous not only do themselves good, but they add to the good of all. All have a portion entrusted to them of the general good, and those who cherish and preserve it are blessings to society at large; and those who do not, become a curse. It is wonderfully ordered, how in acting for our own good, we promote the good of others. My idea of religion is, not for it to unfit us for the duties of life, like a nun who leaves them for prayer and thanksgiving; but I think it should stimulate and capacitate us to perform these duties properly. Seeing my father low this evening, I have done all I can to make him comfortable, I feel it one of my first duties; I hope he will always find in me a most true friend and affectionate daughter.

August 1st.—I have done little to-day, I am so very idle; instead of improving I fear I go back; my inclinations lead me to be an idle, flirting, worldly girl. I see what would be acting right, but I have neither activity nor perseverance in what I think right. I am like one setting out on a journey; if I set out on the wrong road, and do not try to recover the right one before I have gone far, I shall most likely lose my way for *ever*, and every step I take, the more difficult shall I find it to return, therefore the temptation will be greater to go on, till I get to destruction. On the contrary, if now, whilst I am innocent of any great faults, I turn into the right path, I shall feel more and more contented every step I take. Trifles occupy me far too much, such as dress, &c., &c. I find it easier to acknowledge my vices than my follies.

6th.—I have a cross to-night. I had very much set my mind on going to the oratorio, the Prince is to be there, and by all accounts it will be quite a grand sight, and there will be the finest music; but if my father does not like me to go, much as I wish it, I will give it up with pleasure, if it be in my power, without a murmur. I went to the oratorio, I enjoyed it, but spoke sadly at random; what a bad habit!

12th.—I do not know if I shall not soon be rather religious, because I have thought lately, what a support it is through life; it seems so delightful to depend upon a superior power, for all that is good; it is at least always having the bosom of a friend open to us, to rest all our cares and sorrows upon, and what must be our feelings to imagine that friend perfect, and guiding all and everything, as it should be guided. I think anybody who had real faith, could never be unhappy; it appears the only certain source of support and comfort in this life, and what is best of all, it draws to virtue, and if the idea be ever so ill-founded that leads to that great object, why should we shun it? Religion has been misused and corrupted: that is no reason why religion itself is not good.

15*th*.—For a few days past I have been in a worldly state, dissipated, a want of thought, idle, relaxed and stupid, all outside, no inside. I feel I am a contemptible fine lady. May I be preserved from continuing so, is the ardent prayer of my *good* man, but my *evil* man tells me I shall pray in vain. I will try. I fear for myself; I feel in the course of a little time I shall be all outside flippery, vain, proud, conceited; I could use improper words at myself, but my *good* man will not let me. But I am good in something, it is wicked to despair of myself, it is the way to make me what I desire not to be: I hope I shall always be virtuous; can I be really wicked? I may be so, if I do not overcome my first weak inclinations; I wish I had more solidity and less fluidity in my disposition. I feel my own weakness and insufficiency to bear the evils and rubs of life. I must try by every stimulus in my power, to strengthen myself both bodily and mentally, it can only be done by activity and perseverance.

19*th*.—Idle and relaxed in mind, greatly dissipated by hearing the band, &c. &c. Music has a great effect on me, it at times makes me feel almost beside myself.

30*th*.—"Come what, come may, time and the hour run through the roughest day." A very sad and trying day. Tried by being poorly, by others, and by myself; very far from what I ought to be.

Sept. 3*d*.—There is much difference between being obstinate and steady; I am obstinate, when I contradict for the sake of contradiction; I am steady, when I keep to what I really think right. I am too apt to contradict, whether I should or not. If I am bid to do a thing, my spirit revolts; if I am asked to do a thing, I am willing.

December.—A thought passed my mind, that if I had some religion, I should be superior to what I am, it would be a bias to better actions; I think I am, by degrees, losing many excellent qualities. I am more cross, more proud, more vain, more extravagant. I lay it to my great love of gaiety, and the world. I feel, I know, I am falling. I do believe if I had a little true religion, I should have a greater support than I have now; in virtue my mind wants a stimulus; never, no never did mind want one more: but I have the greatest fear of religion, because I never saw a person religious, who was not enthusiastic.

January, 1798.—I must die! I *shall* die! wonderful, death is beyond comprehension. To leave life, and all its interests, and be almost forgotten by those we love. What a comfort must a real faith in religion be, in the hour of death; to have a firm belief of entering into everlasting joy. I have a notion of such a thing, but I am sorry to say, I have no real faith in any sort of religion; it must be a comfort and support in affliction, and I know enough of life to see how great a stimulus is wanted, to support through the evils that are inflicted, and to keep in the path of virtue. If religion be a support, why not get it?

14*th*.—I think it almost impossible to keep strictly to principle, without religion; I don't feel any real religion; I should think those feelings impossible to obtain, for even if I thought all the Bible was true, I do not think I could make myself feel it: I think I never saw any person, who appeared so totally destitute of it. I fear I am, by degrees, falling away from the path of virtue and truth.

18*th*.—I am a bubble, without reason, without beauty of mind or person; I am a fool. I daily fall lower in my own estimation. What an infinite advantage it would be to me, to occupy my time and thoughts well. I am now seventeen, and if some kind and great circumstance does not happen to me, I shall have my talents devoured by moth and rust. They will lose their brightness, lose their virtue, and one day they will prove a curse instead of a blessing. Dreaded day!!

I must use extreme exertion to act really right, to avoid idleness and dissipation.

From the foregoing selections, we may perceive how earnest were Elizabeth Gurney's efforts at self-examination and self-control. The time was now at hand, when her mind was to be illumined by the beams of the "Sun of righteousness," and gradually delivered from the mists of scepticism. The appointed instrument of this blessed change was William Savery, a minister, well known and much beloved in our religious community. He had come from America to this country on a visit of gospel love, in the course of which he attended the usual Meeting at Norwich on first day, the 4th of second month, 1798. His preaching was very impressive: he was, through the power of the Holy Spirit, qualified, in no common degree, for the office of an ambassador for Christ, and many were the seals to his ministry amongst those whom he was instrumental in attracting to the pathway of life and peace. In his own published journal is this reference to the above-mentioned visit to Norwich.

"*Norwich, First-day, 4th of the month.*—Attended their Meeting: some not members stepped in, and there were about two hundred under our name; very few middle-aged or young persons who had a consistent appearance in their dress; indeed, I thought it the gayest Meeting of Friends I ever sat in, and was grieved to see it. I expected to pass the Meeting in silent suffering, but at length believed it most for my peace to express a little, and through gracious condescension was favoured to relieve my mind, and many were tendered. Had a Meeting in the evening, in a large Meeting-house, in another part of the town: there seem to be but few upright standard-bearers left among the members in this place, yet they are not entirely removed. Attended the Public Meeting, and the house, though very large, could not contain the people by several hundreds, but considering their crowded situation, many being obliged to stand, they soon became settled, and through mercy it proved a remarkably open, satisfactory Meeting, ending in prayer and praise to the Author of every blessing. The marks of wealth and grandeur are too obvious in several families of Friends in this place, which made me sorrowful, yet I saw but little opening to relieve my mind; several of the younger branches, though they are enabled through divine grace to see what the Truth leads to, yet it is uncertain whether, with all the alluring things of this world around them, they will choose the simple, safe path of self-denial."*

Elizabeth's sister, Richenda, thus describes this eventful day:—

On that day, we, seven sisters, sat as usual in a row, under the gallery at Meeting; I sat by Betsy. William Savery was there—we liked having Yearly Meeting Friends come to preach; it was a little change. Betsy was generally rather restless at Meeting; and on this day, I remember her very smart boots were a great amusement to me; they were purple, laced with scarlet.

At last William Savery began to preach. His voice and manner were arresting, and we all liked the sound; her attention became fixed; at last I saw her begin to weep, and she became a good deal agitated. As soon as Meeting was over, I have a remembrance of her making her way to the men's side of the Meeting, and having found my father, she asked him if she might dine with William Savery at the Grove,† to which he soon consented, though rather surprised by the request; we went home as usual, and, for a wonder, we wished to go again in the afternoon. I have not the same clear remembrance of this Meeting; but the next scene that has fastened itself on my memory, is our return home in the carriage. Betsy sat in the middle, and astonished us all by the great feeling she showed. She wept most of the way home. The next morning, William Savery came to break-

* William Savery's journal, published by Gilpin, 1844, pp. 27-8.

† The residence of her uncle, Joseph Gurney.

fast, prophesying of the high and important calling she would be led into. What she went through in her own mind, I cannot say, but the results were most powerful, and most evident. From that day her love of pleasure and of the world seemed gone.

How deep the impression, made upon the mind of Elizabeth, her own journal portrays.

Sunday, February 4th, 1798.—This morning I went to Meeting, though but poorly, because I wished to hear an American Friend, named William Savery. Much passed there of a very interesting nature. I have had a faint light spread over my mind, at least I believe it is something of that kind, owing to having been much with, and heard much excellence from, one who appears to me a true Christian. It has caused me to feel a little religion. My imagination has been worked upon, and I fear all that I felt will go off. I fear it now; though at first I was frightened, that a plain Quaker should have made so deep an impression on me; but how truly prejudiced in me to think, that because good came from a Quaker, I should be led away by enthusiasm and folly. But I hope I am now free from such fears. I wish the state of enthusiasm I am in may last, for to-day I have felt *that there is a God;* I have been devotional, and my mind has been led away from the follies that it is mostly wrapt up in. We had much serious conversation; in short, what he said and what I felt, was like a refreshing shower falling upon earth, that had been dried up for ages. It has not made me unhappy: I have felt ever since humble. I have longed for virtue. I hope to be truly virtuous; to let sophistry fly from my mind; not to be enthusiastic and foolish; but only to be so far religious as will lead to virtue. There seems nothing so little understood as religion.

On the 6th she had "a very serious ride" to Norwich, but meeting with some gay people "brought on vanity," and she says—

"I came home as full of the world, as I went to town full of heaven."

In hearing William Savery preach, he seemed to me to overflow with true religion, and to be humble, and yet a man of great abilities; and having been gay and disbelieving only a few years ago, makes him better acquainted with the heart of one in the same situation. If I were to grow like him, a preacher, I should be able to preach to the gay and unbelieving better than to any others, for I should feel more sympathy for them, and know their hearts better.

Sunday, 11*th*.—It is very different to this day week (a day never to be forgotten whilst memory lasts.) I have been to Meeting this morning. To-day I have felt all my old irreligious feelings—my object shall be to search, try to do right, and if I am mistaken, it is not my fault; but the state I am now in makes it difficult to act. What little religion I have felt has been owing to my giving way quietly and humbly to my feelings; but the more I reason upon it, the more I get into a labyrinth of uncertainty, and my mind is so much inclined to both scepticism and enthusiasm, that if I argue and doubt, I shall be a total sceptic; if, on the contrary, I give way to my feelings, and as it were, wait for religion, I may be led away. But I hope that will not be the case; at all events, religion, true and uncorrupted, is of all comforts the greatest; it is the first stimulus to virtue; it is a support under every affliction. I am sure it is better to be so in an enthusiastic degree, than not to be so at all, for it is a delightful enthusiasm.

15*th*.—My mind is in a whirl. In all probability I shall go to London. Many, many are the sensations I feel about it, numbers of things to expect. In the first place, leaving home, how truly I shall miss my best of friends, and all of them. (Meaning particularly her brothers and sisters.) In the next place, I shall see William Savery most likely, and all those plain Quakers. I may be led away, beware! my feelings are far more risen at the thought of seeing him than all the playhouses and gaieties in the world. One will, I do not doubt, balance against the other; I must be careful not to be led away; I must not overdo myself. I dare say it will not be half so pleasant as the Earlham heartfelt gaieties in the Prince's time; I must be very careful not to get vain or silly, for I fear I shall. Be independent, and do not follow those I am with, more than I think right. Do not make dress a study, even in London. Read in the Bible, when I can; but if I see William Savery, I shall not, I doubt, be over fond of gaieties.

16*th.*—We went to hear the band, which I am sorry for, as I cannot get courage to tell my father, I wish I had not gone; I will not go again without his knowing it beforehand.

Chapter Second.

1798-1800.—Visit to London, gaiety there—Return to Earlham—Becomes a decidedly religious character—Letter from William Savery—Gradual development of opinion—Journey into Wales and the South of England—Intercourse with Friends—Colebrook Dale—Increasing tendency to Quakerism—Return to Earlham—Attention to the Poor—Journey to the North of England—Becomes a decided Friend—Proposals of Marriage from Joseph Fry—Letters.

In this peculiar and awakened state of mind, Elizabeth, with the consent of John Gurney, visited London, that she might become acquainted for herself with those amusements and fascinations which the world offers to its votaries; that she might have the opportunity of "proving all things," and choosing for herself that which appeared to her "to be good." Her father took her to London; and there with an old and faithful attendant, left her for some weeks, under the protection and kind care of a relation. She was often interested and amused with the objects that were presented to her notice, but seldom satisfied or approving. The result was that she returned home entirely decided: a vain world rejected; her heart set upon heavenly things; and from that time, most steadily, though gently, did she continue to advance in the path, in which she believed it to be her duty to walk. But what a dangerous experiment was this search after pleasure! How calculated to dissipate every serious impression, which had been made on the mind of this young person! She attended the opera and the theatres,—engaged in the dance and other amusements,—mingled, in the gayest circles, with actresses, novelists, and others of a similar character,—yielded to vanities, from which her own good sense, now aroused to action by a regenerating power, revolted with disgust. "I went," she writes, "to Drury Lane in the evening. I must own I was extremely disappointed: to be sure the house is grand and dazzling, but I had no other feeling whilst there than that of wishing it over."

25th.—Although I told William Savery my principles were not Friendly, yet I fear I should not like his knowing of my going to the play. I think such religion as his must attract an atheist; and if there were many such Quakers as he is, the Society would soon increase.

Tuesday.—I went to the play at Covent Garden, I still continue not to like plays.

Wednesday, 28th.—We were out this morning; I felt proud, vain and silly. In the evening, we had a dance.

Thursday, March 1st.—I own I enter into the gay world reluctantly. I do not like plays. I think them so artificial that they are to me not interesting, and all seems so—so very far from pure virtue and nature. My hair was dressed, and I felt like a monkey. London is not the place for heartfelt pleasure, so I must not expect to find it.

That gracious Heavenly Parent, whose ever-watchful eye is upon them that fear Him, was providing something for her anxious mind, more soul-satisfying than pursuits of so frivolous a nature.

7th.—I went to Meeting in the evening. I have not enough eloquence to describe it. William Savery's sermon was in the first part very affecting, it was from the Revelations; he explained his text beautifully, and awfully, *most* awfully I felt it; he next described the sweets of religion, and the spirit of prayer. *How he did describe it!* He said, the deist, and those who did not feel devotion, looked at nature, admired the thunder, the lightning and earthquakes, as curiosities; but they looked not up through them to nature's God. How well he hit the state I have been in; I trust I may not remain in it; his prayer was beautiful; I think I felt to pray with him.

17*th.*—May I never forget the impression William Savery has made on my mind! as much as I can say is, I thank God for having sent at least a glimmering of light, through him, into my heart, which I hope with care, and keeping it from the many draughts and winds of this life, may not be blown out, but become a large brilliant flame, that will direct me to that haven, where will be joy without a sorrow, and all will be comfort. I have faith; how much to gain! not all the treasures in this world can equal that heavenly treasure. May I grow more and more virtuous, follow the path I should go in, and not fear to acknowledge the God whom I worship; I will try, and I do hope to do what is right. I now long to be in the quiet of Earlham, for there I may see how good I can be, and so I may here, for the greater cross the greater crown: but I there can reflect quietly and soberly on what has passed, there I hope to regulate my mind, which I know sadly wants it. May I never lose the little religion I now have; but if I cannot feel religion and devotion, I must not despair, for if I am truly warm and earnest in the cause, it will come one day. My idea is, that true humility and lowliness of heart is the first grand step towards true religion. I fear and tremble for myself, but I must humbly look to the Author of all that is good and great, and, I may say, humbly pray, that He will take me as a sheep strayed from His flock, and once more let me enter the fold of His glory. I feel there is a God and immortality; happy, happy thought! May it never leave me, and if it should, may I remember I have *felt* that there is a God and Immortality.

After being in London and its vicinity seven weeks, she returned home with her father, on the 16th of fourth month.

Thirty years afterwards, in 1828 she thus reviews this critical period of life.

"Here ended this important and interesting visit to London, where I learned much and had much to digest. I saw and entered various scenes of gaiety; many of our first public places; attended balls and other places of amusement. I saw many interesting characters in the world, some of considerable eminence in that day; I was also cast among a great variety of persons of different descriptions. I had the high advantage of attending several most interesting meetings of William Savery, and having, at times, his company, and that of a few other Friends. It was like the casting die in my life; however, I believe it was in the ordering of Providence for me, and that the lessons then learnt are to this day valuable to me. I consider one of the important results was, the conviction of these things being wrong, from seeing them and feeling their effects. I wholly gave up on my own ground, attending all public places of amusement, I saw that they tend to promote evil; therefore even if I could attend them without being hurt myself, I felt, in entering them, I lent my aid to promote that, which I was sure, from what I saw, hurt others; led many from the paths of rectitude and chastity, and brought them into much sin; particularly those who had to act in plays, or sing in concerts. I felt the vanity and folly of what are called the pleasures of this life, of which the tendency is not to satisfy, but eventually to enervate and injure the heart and mind; those only are real pleasures which are of an innocent nature, and used as recreations, subjected to the cross of Christ. I was, in my judgment, much confirmed in the infinite importance of religion, as the only real stay, guide, help, and comfort in this life, and the only means of our having a hope of partaking of a better. My understanding was increasingly open to receive its truths; although the glad tidings of the gospel of Christ were little, very little, if at all understood by me, I was like the blind man; although I could hardly be said to have attained the state of seeing men as trees. I obtained in this expedition a valuable knowledge of human character, from the variety I met with; this I think was useful to me, though some were very dangerous associates for so young a person, and the way in which I was protected among them, is, in my remembrance, very striking; and leads me to acknowledge, that at this most critical period of my life, the tender mercy of my God was marvellously displayed towards me; and that His all-powerful, though to me then almost unseen and unknown hand, held me up and protected me. Can any one doubt, that it was His Spirit which manifested to me the evil in my own heart, as well as that which I perceived around me? leading me to abhor it, and to hunger and thirst after Himself, and His righteousness, and that salvation which cometh by Christ."

But we return to her early journal:—

Earlham, April 20th, 1798.—To-day the children brought me a letter from William Savery: I cannot well express what I felt at receiving it. I do not know the course I am to run, all is hid in mystery, but I try to do right in everything. I feel he gives me a stimulant to virtue; but I fear by what I expressed in my letter, he suspects that I am turning plain Quaker. I hate that he should estimate me falsely. I must remember that on the foundation of the doctrine, I believe we agree. I must look to One higher than he; and if I feel my own mind satisfied I need not fear. Look up to true religion as the very first of blessings, cherish it, nourish, and let it flourish and bloom in my heart; it wants taking care of, it is difficult to obtain. I must not despair or grow sceptical, if I do not always feel religious. I have *felt* God as it were, and I must *seek*, to find Him again.

The letter referred to is as follows:—

"13*th of Fourth Month*, 1798.

"Dear Friend,

"As I left thee unwell, and without having it in my power to take thee affectionately by the hand, as I was much inclined to do; it gave me great pleasure to receive thy kind letter, which brings no complaint of thy present want of health; for, I assure thee, I feel interested in thy welfare and happiness every way. My attachment has not been more cordial or agreeable to any young Friend in England, and my heart leaped with joy to find thou art willing to acknowledge a state of hunger and thirst after righteousness, which, if thou cherish and dwell in, thou never need to doubt, my dear friend, will eventually be crowned with the enjoyment of the heavenly promise, 'thou shalt be filled.' Thou art favoured with amiable and benevolent dispositions, which I hope thou hast wisely determined shall not be eclipsed by a conformity to the god of this world; nor enslaved by its rudiments and maxims, its philosophy and vain deceit, but rather with a holy magnanimity, regardless of the world's dread laugh, thou wilt resolve to implore the Omnipotent Hand that formed thee for Glory, Immortality, and Eternal Life, to finish the glorious work He has begun, by creating thee anew in Christ Jesus unto every good word and work; bringing thee under the dominion of His own power and spirit, the fruit of which is love, joy, peace, long-suffering, gentleness, goodness, faith, meekness, temperance.

"I know, my dear, thou hast, and wilt have, many temptations to combat with; thou wilt, doubtless, be frequently importuned to continue, with thy gay acquaintance, in pursuit of that unsubstantial and false glare of happiness, which the world, in too bewitching and deceitful colours, holds out to the poor young, unwary traveller, which, if he be ensnared with, most certainly ends in blinding the intellectual eye, from discerning the uncontaminated source of soul-felt pleasure, resulting from an humble heart, at peace with its God, its neighbour, and itself. Thou asks my advice, my dear friend, and without any premeditation when I sat down, I find I have been attempting it; but it is very evident, thou art under the especial care of an infinitely better Instructor, who has already uttered his soft and heavenly voice, to teach thee that the first step towards religion is true humility; because, in that state only, we can feel the need we have of an arm, stronger than human, to lean upon, to lead us out of, and keep us from polluting things, which hinder our access to, and confidence in, that boundless source of purity, love, and mercy; who, amidst all the vicissitudes of time, is disposed to be our invincible Shepherd, Guardian, and Friend, in whom we may trust and never be afraid; but this blessed confidence is not, cannot be enjoyed by the gay, the giddy, proud, or abandoned votaries of this world.

"It is the peculiar privilege of those, who are sincerely endeavouring to wash their hands in innocency, that they may compass the altar of God availingly. I have experienced what it is to be under the imperious and slavish dominion of my own uncontrolled passions; and I know that such a state is abundantly mixed with the wormwood and the gall, and I have been, through adorable mercy, convinced there is an infinitely more happy one to be attained, even in this life; an enjoyment, under the perfect law of liberty, of that serene state of mind, wherein there is no condemnation, as Paul speaks, the law of the spirit of life in Christ Jesus setting the soul free from the law of sin and death. I do not pretend, my dear friend, to boast myself as having attained such an uninterrupted state, yet the transient foretaste which we partake of, in proportion to our obedience to revealed duty, is enough to inspire the soul of every Christian soldier, so to run, through God's mercy and grace, that we may obtain the full and complete enjoyment of it. There are many formal professors of religion, who think to obtain peace with God, by a critical exactness, and even rigid austerity in outward observances, and outside formalities, as well as many, who, from constitution or habit, are always exhibiting the dark and gloomy side of religion, not having, in my humble opinion, their minds sufficiently expanded by just conceptions of the adorable love and mercy of God; and both of these spread a discouraging report of the good land, or of the way which our Heavenly Father has appointed for us to obtain possession of it. I speak only my own experience, dear Elizabeth, when I say, that whenever I have found my way more than usually strewn with thorns, I have generally discovered, on a deep scrutiny of my heart, that it has been the fruit of some open or secret departure from the paths of obedience and virtue; so that I am confirmed that it is in our own ways we are corrected; but the ways of the Lord are ways of pleasantness, and all His paths peace. I know very well that the most virtuous, being children of frail humanity, and this world not designed to be the place of their undisturbed rest, but a school of discipline to prepare them for a better, are subject to afflictions, as well as others; still there is this difference in the midst of them all, that while the votary of this world is overwhelmed with murmuring and repining, and agitated with sorrow which worketh death, under the afflictive dispensations, that all, more or less, in the wisdom of Providence for our good must pass through in this life; the humble Christian, believing that even afflictions from His sovereign hand are mercies in disguise, and that all things shall work eventually for good to them that love and fear Him, is strengthened, through the Lord's love and mercy, to say, 'The cup that my Heavenly Father hath blessed, shall I not drink it?' 'for our light affliction, which is but for a moment, worketh for us a far more exceeding and eternal weight of glory, while we look not at the things which are seen, but at the things which are not seen, for the things which are seen are temporal, but the things which are not seen are eternal.' On the other hand, the temporal enjoyments of this life, being sanctified to us by the hand that gave them, and the world used without abusing it, the peace, comfort, and rational enjoyment of them is doubly tasted by the religious and grateful soul. My dear child, my heart is full towards thee, I have written a great deal more than I expected; but I fain would take thee by the hand, if I were qualified so to do, and ascend, as our

Heavenly Father may enable us, together, step by step, up that ladder which reaches from earth to heaven; but, alas! my weakness is such, I can only recommend both myself and thee to that good hand, that is able to do more abundantly for us than we can either ask or think; and bid thee, for the present, in much Christian affection, farewell.

"WILLIAM SAVERY."

April 21*st.*—I am so glad I do not feel Earlham at all dull, after the bustle of London; on the contrary, a better relish for the sweet innocence and beauties of nature. I hope I may say, I *do* look "through nature up to nature's God." I go every day to see poor Bob, (a servant in a decline, living at a cottage in the Park,) who I think will not live. I once talked to him about dying, and asked him if he would like me to read to him in the Testament. I told him, I felt such faith in the blessings of Immortality, that I pitied not his state; it was an odd speech to make to a dying man. I hope to be able to comfort him in his dying hours. I gave some things to some poor people to-day; but it is not there that I am particularly virtuous, as I am only following my natural disposition. I should be far more so, if I never spoke against any person, which I do too often. I think I am improved since I was last at home; my mind is not so fly-away. I hope it never will be so again. We are all governed by our feelings; now the reason why religion is far more likely to keep you in the path of virtue than any theoretical plan is, that you feel it, and your heart is wrapt up in it; it acts as a furnace on your character, it refines it, it purifies it; whereas principles of your own making are without kindling to make the fire hot enough to answer its purpose. I think a dream I have had so odd, I will write it down.

Before I mention my dream, I will give an account of my state of mind, from the time I was fourteen years old. I had very sceptical, or deistical principles. I seldom, or never thought of religion, and altogether I was a negatively good character; having naturally good dispositions, I had not much to combat with; I gave way freely to the weakness of youth. I was flirting, idle, rather proud and vain, till the time I was seventeen, when I found I wanted a better, a greater stimulus to virtue, than I had, as I was wrapt up in trifles. I felt my mind capable of better things; but I could not exert it, till several of my friends, without knowing my state, wished I would read books on Christianity; but I said, till I felt the want of religion myself, I would not read books of that kind; but if ever I did, would judge clearly for myself, by reading the New Testament, and when I had seen for myself, I would *then* see what others said. About this time, I believe, I never missed a week, or a few nights, without dreaming, that I was nearly being washed away by the sea, sometimes in one way, sometimes in another; and I felt all the terror of being drowned, or hope of being saved; at last I dreamt it so often, that I told many of the family what a strange dream I had, and how near I was being lost. After I had gone on in this way for some months, William Savery came to Norwich. I had begun to read the Testament with reflections of my own, and he suddenly, as it were, opened my eyes to see religion; but again they almost closed. I went on dreaming the dream. The day when I felt I had really and truly got true and real faith, that night I dreamed the sea was coming as usual to wash me away, but I was beyond its reach; beyond its powers to wash me away; since that night I do not remember having dreamed that dream. Odd! It did not strike me at the time so odd; but now it does. All I can say is, I admire it, I am glad I have had it, and I have a sort of faith in it; it ought, I think, to make my faith steady, it may be the work of chance, but I do not think it is, for it is so odd not having dreamed it since. What a blessed thought to think it comes from heaven! May I be made capable of acting as I ought to act; not being drowned in the ocean of the world, but permitted to mount above its waves, and remain a steady and faithful servant to the God whom I worship. I may take this dream in what light I like, but I must be careful of superstition; as many, many are the minds that are led away by it. Believe only in what I can comprehend or feel; don't, don't be led away by enthusiasm; but I don't fear. I feel myself under the protection of One, who alone is able to guide me to the path in which I ought to go.

29*th.*—The human mind is so apt to fly from one extreme to another; and why is not mine like others? I certainly seem to be on the road to a degree of enthusiasm, but I own myself at a loss how to act. If I act as they (meaning doubtless those around her) would wish me, I should not humbly give way to the feelings of religion; I should dwell on philosophy, and depend more on my own reason than anything else. On the contrary, if I give way to the religious feelings to which I am inclined, (and I own I believe much in inspiration,) I feel confident that I should find true humility, and humble waiting on the Almighty, the only way of feeling an inward sense of the beauties, and of the comforts of religion; it spreads a sweet veil over the evils of life; it is to me the first of feelings. I own my dream rather leads me to believe in, and try to follow the path I would go in. But I should think my wisest plan of conduct would be warmly to encourage my feelings of devotion, and to keep as nearly as I can to what I think right, and the doctrines of the Testament; not, at present, to make sects the subject of my meditations, but to do as I think right, and not alter my opinions from conformity to any one, gay or plain.

May 8*th.*—This morning, being alone, I think it a good opportunity to look into myself, to see my present state, and to regulate myself. At this time, the first object of my mind is religion. It is the most constant subject of my thoughts and of my feelings; I am not yet on what I call a steady foundation. The next feeling that at this present fills my heart, is benevolence and affection to many, but great want of charity, want of humility, want of activity; my inclinations lead me, I hope, to virtue; my passions are, I hope, in a pretty good state; I want to set myself in good order, for much time is lost, and many evils committed, by not having some regular plan of conduct; I make these rules for myself:—

First,—Never lose any time; I do not think that lost which is spent in amusement or recreation, some time every day; but always be in the habit of being employed.

Second,—Never err the least in truth.

Third,—Never say an ill thing of a person, when I can say a good thing of them, not only *speak* charitably but *feel* so.

Fourth,—Never be irritable nor unkind to anybody.

Fifth,—Never indulge myself in luxuries that are not necessary.

Sixth,—Do all things with consideration, and when my path to act right is most difficult, feel confidence in that power that alone is able to assist me, and exert my own powers as far as they go.

19*th*.—Altogether I think I have had a satisfactory day. I had a good lesson of French this morning, and read much in Epictetus. Saw poor Bob, and enjoyed the sweet beauties of nature, which now shine forth; each day some new beauty arrives. I love the beauty of the country, it does the mind good. I love it more than I used to do. I love retirement and quiet much more since my journey to London. How little I thought six months ago, I should be so much altered; I am since then, I hope, altered much for the better. My heart may rise in thankfulness to that omnipotent power, that has allowed my eyes to be opened, in some measure, to see the light of truth, and to feel the comfort of religion. I hope to be capable of giving up my all, if it be required of me, to serve the Almighty with my whole heart.

21*st*.—To-day is my birth-day. I am eighteen years old! How many things have happened to me since I was fourteen; the last year has been the happiest I have experienced for some time.

23*d.*—I have just been reading a letter from my father, in which he makes me the offer of going to London, what a temptation! but I believe it to be much better for me to be where I am, quietly and soberly to keep a proper medium of feelings, and not to be extravagant any way.

24*th.*—I wrote to my father this morning. I must be most careful not to be led by others, for I know, at this time, I have so great a liking for plain Friends, that my affections being so much engaged, my mind may be so also by them. I hope, as I now find myself in so wavering a state, that I may judge without prejudice of Barclay's Apology.

27*th.*—I must be careful of allowing false scruples to enter my mind. I have not yet been long enough a religionist to be a sectarian. I hope, by degrees, to obtain true faith; but I expect I shall lose what I gain if I am led to actions that I may repent of; remember and never forget my own enthusiastic, feeling nature. It requires caution and extreme prudence to go on as I should do. In the afternoon I went to St. Peter's, and heard a good sermon. The common people seemed very much occupied, and wrapt up in the service, which I was pleased to see; afterwards I went to the cathedral, then I came home and read to the Normans and little Castleton.

29*th.*—I feel weak in mind and body. If I go on approving revealed religion, I must be extremely careful of taking the idle fancies of the brain, for anything so far superior. I believe many mistake mere meteors for that heavenly light, which few receive. Many may have it in a degree, but I should suppose few have it, so as to teach others with authority.

June 1*st.*—I have been great part of this morning with poor Bob, who seems now dying. I read a chapter in the Testament to him, the one upon death, and I sat with him for some time afterwards. Poor fellow! I never saw death,

7

or any of its symptoms before; sad to see, it truly is; I said a few words to him, and expressed to him how happy we should be in expectation of immortality and everlasting bliss. Father of mercies, wilt Thou bless him, and take him unto Thee? Though my mind is flat this morning, and not favoured with Thy Spirit in devotion; yet I exert what I have, and hope it will prove acceptable in Thy sight. Almighty God, Thy will be done, and not ours. May I always be resigned to what Thou hast ordered for me; I humbly thank Thee, for allowing my eyes to be opened, so as even to feel faith, hope and love towards Thee. First and last of everything infinite, and not to be comprehended except by Thy Spirit, which Thou allowest to enlighten our hearts.

12*th.*—This evening I have got myself rather in a scrape; I have been helping them to beg my father for us to go to the Guild-dinner, and I don't know whether it was quite what I approve of, or think good for myself; but I shall consider, and do not intend to go, if I disapprove of it. How strange and odd! I really think I shall turn plain Friend; all I say is, search deeply; do nothing rashly, and I then hope to do right; they all, I think, now see it—keep up to the duties I feel in my heart, let the path be ever so difficult; err not at all if I can avoid it, be humble and constant. I do not like to appear a character I am not certain of being. For a few days past, I have at times felt much religion for *me;* humility and comfort belong to it. I often think very seriously about myself. A few months ago, if I had seen any one act, as I now do, I should have thought him a fool; but the strongest proof I can have that I am acting right at the present time is, that I am certainly a better, and I think a happier character. But I often doubt myself, when I consider my enthusiastic and changeable feelings. Religion is no common enthusiasm, because it is pure, it is a constant friend, protector, supporter, and guardian; it is what we cannot do well without in this world; what can prove its excellence so much as its producing virtue and happiness!

How much more solid a character I am, since I first got hold of religion! I would not part with what I have for anything; it is a faith that never will leave my mind, I hope most earnestly. I do not believe it will, but I desire always to be a strictly religious character.

The next entry is striking, giving us the first glance at her future course.

13*th.*—I have some thoughts of, by degrees, increasing my plan for Sunday evening; and of having several poor children, at least, to read in the Testament and religious books for an hour. I have begun with Billy; but I hope to continue, and increase one by one. I should think it a good plan; but I must not even begin that hastily. It might increase morality among the lower classes, if the Scriptures were oftener and better read to them. I believe I cannot exert myself too much, there is nothing gives me such satisfaction as instructing the lower classes of people.

24*th.*—I persevered in going to Meeting this afternoon. Coming home, I saw a scene that indeed interested me, my father jumping into the water at the New Mills, after a poor boy whom I thought drowned; my feelings were great indeed, both for my father and the boy. I believe I should have leapt in afterwards if my father had gone out of sight; he did it delightfully, with such activity and spirit, it was charming to see him. Poor little boy! I took him as soon as he was out of the water; it agitated me extremely.

July 9*th.*—How little is the mind capable of really feeling that we are all in the presence of God, who overlooks every action. Should we not tremble when we think of it? How many faults do we commit! It is impossible, without the assistance of His almighty power, to comprehend it. We could never be wicked, while we felt ourselves in the presence of the Almighty. Virtue alone can make this thought a happy one.

During the summer John Gurney and his seven daughters travelled into Wales, &c. Before quitting home, Elizabeth writes:—

20th.—I suppose we shall go off to-morrow on our journey. We expect the Opies and Bartlett Gurney to dinner. It is my wish to do my lesson with Le Sage, and the first thing afterwards to attend to my father; read to Mrs. Norman; see nurse Norman; walk to Colney about Billy; come home, set my things in the greatest order. Evening.—I have been confused by the thoughts of going and company. How much do I fear for myself this journey.

As they proceeded westward, stopping at many places, Elizabeth enjoyed the works of nature, and dwelt with pleasure on the beautiful scenery they passed through; but to the works of man, however imposing, she was comparatively indifferent. She visited cathedral cities; she beheld scenes of high historic interest; castles, whose walls could reveal dark tales of bye-gone days; but she scarcely mentions them, and if she notices them at all, it is but to draw some moral inference. In visiting the Dockyards, at Plymouth, and viewing one of the most striking instances of man's power and skill, a first-rate man-of-war, in perfect order, and equipped for sea, she considers the sad effects of war, and its evil influences on the human race. But by far the greatest interest, afforded her by this journey, was the prospect of seeing different Friends, and becoming better acquainted with them and their principles. The travellers paid a visit to Colebrook Dale, the residence of the well-known Christian philanthropist, Richard Reynolds, there she was left for some days with her cousin, Priscilla Hannah Gurney, cousin to the Gurneys of Earlham, by both their father and mother, her father being Joseph Gurney, and her mother Christiana Barclay. She was exactly the person to attract the young; she possessed singular beauty, and elegance of manner. She was of the old school; her costume partook of this, and her long retention of the black hood, gave much character to her appearance. She had early renounced the world and its fascinations; left Bath, where her mother and sister Christiana Gurney resided; became eventually a minister among Friends, and found a congenial retreat for many years at Colebrook Dale. The influence of this visit upon Elizabeth was very powerful. A place more likely to interest her, with persons more suited to her state of mind, could not perhaps have been found than Colebrook Dale, and the residents there. Richard Reynolds, at that time advanced in years, was a patriarch among his family, his friends, and dependents. He devoted a large proportion of a noble fortune, acquired by honourable industry, to objects of benevolence. His extensive iron-works were carried on with careful attention to the moral good of those employed in them.

Several other valuable Friends resided at Colebrook Dale, connected with each other in business, or by marriage, or by the stronger bond of religious fellowship.

The memoranda, penned by Elizabeth Gurney, during their journey, are interesting; some of them calculated to excite much sympathy, bespeaking, as they do, the temptations to which she was exposed.

Farnham, July 26th.—To-night I am much tired, quite fagged, body and mind, and the text comes strongly before me, "Blessed are they that mourn, for they shall be comforted," for though I feel weak in body, I have truly support in mind. God is a merciful Father, and when His children (though evil like me) mourn, He will comfort them, and preserve them, if they will exert their own powers also, to serve him in spirit and in truth. How often I fail! He is *never*-failing, no, *never!* He makes the sun to rise on the just and unjust, and we acknowledge not His blessings, but lament over the few clouds that shade its brightness: and sometimes murmur at the Lord that made us. Weak mortals! and I am weak indeed. But I feel I have to deal with a merciful Father.

Weymouth. 29th.—We dined here, and after dinner went on the sea. I always feel rather afraid when there, for I consider that if the least accident were to happen, I should be drowned; and I do not know if it be right, only for pleasure, to run the risk of one's life. I always feel doubtful of ever seeing land again; but I believe it to be partly unwise cowardice; if duty led me to it, I do not think I should fear. Some minds, by nature, are more cowards than others, and require more faith to overcome it. This evening, I am sorry to say, I feel a hankering after the world and its gaieties: but what real satisfaction is there in being admired! I am uncertain about going to the Rooms to-morrow. I should not object, I think, if no expense follow it; but if I can keep away, I will do so; I have been considering, and believe this subject requires real thought. I hear there is to be a ball, and I don't doubt we may go; if I go, I shall enter the world, and fall very likely into some of its snares. Shall I feel satisfied in going, or most satisfied in staying at home? I believe in staying at home. The worst of all will be, I shall have to contradict the will of all the others, (her sisters,) and most likely to disappoint my father by not going; there is the rub, if I don't go perhaps he will not let the others go. I think I shall leave it on these grounds; if I can stay at home in any way, do—but if I cannot without vexing my father I must go, and try not to be hurt by it.

Dawlish, August 3rd.—This morning Kitty came in for us to read the Testament together, which I enjoyed: I read my favourite chapter, the 15th of Corinthians to them. Oh! how earnestly I hope that we may all know what truth is, and follow its dictates. I still continue my belief that I shall turn plain Quaker. I used to think, and do now, how very little dress matters; but I find it almost impossible to keep up to the principles of Friends without altering my dress and speech. I felt it the other day at Weymouth. If I had been plain, I should not have been *tempted* to go to the play, which, at all events, I would not do; plainness ap pears to be a sort of protection to the principles of Christianity, in the present state of the world. I have just received a letter from Anna Savery, and have been answering it, and have written rather a religious letter, which I mean to show them, though it is to me a cross, as I say in it I think I am a Quaker at heart. I hope it will not hurt them; but it is better to be on clear grounds with my best friends, upon that which so nearly interests me. I know it hurts Rachel and John the most. Rachel has the seeds of Quakerism in her heart, that if cultivated, would grow indeed, I have no doubt. I should never be surprised to see us all Quakers.

4th.—I have been having such a morning with Chrissy Gurney, I do really love her; she makes me more of a Quaker than any one I ever was with. She certainly is the most interesting woman I ever met, quite one after my own heart: she is to me indescribable. It is odd to me, and I believe it is to herself, that she is not a Quaker. But she is good without it, not but what I think she would be happier with it. I have very little doubt I shall gain from her; I quite feel leaving this place.

Plymouth Dock, 8th.—After a good night, as soon as breakfast was over, we went to see the ropes made at the Docks, which was a most curious sight. How thankful I should be, that for all my constant erring from the path of truth, I am yet sometimes allowed to feel I have an Arm to lean upon, superior to human, that will support me in time of trouble. After leaving the Dock-yards, we went on board a ferry boat, and I felt rather afraid, to my shame. We then went to see a Review, which I felt rather uncertain if it were right for me to go to, as I so highly disapprove of war; but I believe whilst I appear as other people, I must act as they do, unless with the greatest difficulty. I do not alter from conformity, but from conviction. Afterwards we went to Lord Mount Edgecumbe's, a very fine place, but I was not in the mind for it. Am I right or not? An officer has come for us to hear a very famous Marine Band; and I do not go, because I have some idea it is wrong, even to give countenance to a thing that inflames men's minds to destroy each other; it is truly giving encouragement, as far as lies in my power, to what I most highly disapprove, therefore I think I am right to stay at home. I will now go on with an account of the day.. We went on board a man-of-war with Judd (their maid) and the men-servants; it was a fine but melancholy sight. I may gain some information by it, but it is not what I quite approve of, the same as the band; my heart feels most anxious this night that I may go right, for strait and narrow is the path that leadeth to eternal life, and broad is the way that leadeth to destruction. I must remark, before finishing this journal, that I feel much satisfaction attending my not going to the Review, a thing my heart is so much set upon as military music; as soon as I determined, in my own mind, to give it up, inclination vanished, and now would lead me to stay at home. If I look at it, my path is clearer than I think; for it ought to give me comfort and hope, that, in so small a thing, I feel so much satisfaction, it should help me forward in my journey to that haven, where alone comfort is to be found.

Surely no one can attentively trace the conflicts, fears, and doubt, which beset her mind, the obstructions which external circumstances placed around her, with so few to afford her counsel, or to assist her judgment, as she sought to advance in the path of life and peace, without feeling a deep and tender sympathy with her infant exercises, or without being impressed with the remarkable manner in which the Heavenly Shepherd graciously extended the crook of His love, to draw her spirit gently along to the fold of safety and rest.

Ivy Bridge, 9*th*.—The first thing we undertook this morning, was to see the Dock-yards, which is a sight too astonishing to describe. But after all the art, expense and trouble, that men put themselves to, what do they gain, but the destruction of their fellow-creatures? After that, we went by water to Plymouth, and saw many Friends; but one very plain, who was agreeable to us all, even interesting. As I left Plymouth, my mind felt deeply hurt on account of the poor sailors and women, of whom I have seen a sad number, and I longed to do them good, to try one day to make them sensible of the evil state they appear to be in. Just at that time, I read, or thought, of that passage in the Testament, where it says, we are to look upon all men as greater than ourselves. Christ truly taught humility, and I reflected that in all probability, if I had had the same temptations, I should have been equally wicked; for I am sorry, indeed, to say I fear I mostly give way to temptation, when it falls in my way. Ah! much, much have I to do, much to strive for, before I shall be able to feel that my house is built upon a rock. I know how weak is its present foundation; but this night my mind is cheered by the brightening light of religion.

The Christian solicitude, excited in her youthful heart, in behalf of the poor degraded population in the vicinity of the Dock-yards at Plymouth, made an impression that was not effaced during the long period of twenty-seven years—filled, as this period was, with important interests; and the reader may observe that, in the year 1825, Elizabeth Fry held a religious meeting with them at Devonport—more than fifteen hundred attending it—mostly of the lowest class—these being the chief objects of her concern.

Clifton, 15*th*.—This morning I have seen much beautiful country about Clifton. I think it very likely we shall go to the Welsh Half-Yearly Meeting, where I expect we shall meet most of the Colebrook Dale Friends, whom I quite long to see. We have been a pleasant excursion this afternoon to a Mr. Harford's; I had an interesting drive home, and thought about serious subjects. I often think of home with a longing heart, to set off once more quietly in my career.

Abergavenny, 18*th*.—We went one stage before breakfast

from Usk to Pontypool; as soon as we got there, we met two plain Friends, they both preached; my mind had some devotional feelings, which I felt a blessing. I remained and dined with them, and a little of that peculiar love I feel towards plain Friends, sprung up in my heart for them. Before the afternoon Meeting, I went with Mrs. B——— to call on Lady M———. I own I felt very uncomfortable, I felt as if I were too much a Friend with Friends, and too worldly with other people. I thought I should be acting a better part to say thee instead of you, to other people when I could, for I felt myself to-day, one minute saying thee, the next you; it appeared hypocritical. I had an argument in my own mind, which I will try to remember; I first thought how there could be any difference, in Christian virtue, in saying you or thee to people. I considered there were certainly some advantages attending it; the first, that of weaning the heart from this world, by acting, in some little things, differently from it. But I then thought, is it not better to be remarkable for excellence of conduct, than for such little peculiarities? I find that in a perfect state, such things would not signify, but we are in an imperfect state; and our virtue is hard to maintain, without some fortress, to support it; we must combat with imperfection, and, at times, be obliged to make great things of little things, and use them as arms to defend us from the many wiles and snares of the world.

Landaly, 21st.—A gentleman dined with us, to whom I did not attend, till I discovered he was Lord ———. Oh pride, how it does creep in upon me!

Aberystwith, 23rd.—Is dancing wrong? I have just been dancing; I think there are many dangers attending it, it may lead to vanity and other things. The more the pleasures of life are given up, the less we love the world, and our hearts will be set upon better things; not but that we are allowed, I believe, to enjoy the blessings Heaven has sent us. We have power of mind sufficient to distinguish the good from the bad; for under the cloak of pleasure, infinite evils are carried on. The danger of dancing, I find, is throwing me off my centre; at times when dancing, I know that I have not reason left, but that I do things which in calm moments I must repent of.

Caernarvon, 27*th*.—After a good breakfast, we set off on our journey. The first few miles I shall find very difficult to describe, for such a scene I had not an idea of; all surrounded with rocky mountains, lost in the clouds as they passed over them. Sometimes we were on the edge of a precipice, sometimes on the borders of a river, where the road was cut out of the rock, and high mountains on each side, now and then the wild goats straying over them. We were obliged to walk part of the way, which was trying to me, as I had the tooth-ache. Since I have been here, I have had a Welsh harper, which I was not quite sure was right, as it was giving, or at least causing money to be given, that might have been spent much better.

28*th*.—My mind is in an uncomfortable state this morning; for I am astonished to find I have felt a scruple at music, at least I could not otherwise account for my feelings; but my mind is rather uneasy after I have been spending time in it. These cannot be sensations of my own making, or a contrivance of my own forming, for I have such happiness when I overcome my worldly self; and when I give way to it, am uneasy; not but what I think feelings are sometimes dangerous to give way to; but how odd, yet how true, that much of human reason must be given up. I don't know what to think of it, but I must act somehow, and in some way; yet do nothing rashly or hastily, but try to humiliate myself to true religion; and endeavour to look to God who alone can teach me and lead me right; have faith, hope, and if little things are to follow to protect greater ones, I must, yes, I must do it. I feel certainly happier in being a Quaker, but my reason contradicts it. Now my fears are these, lately I have had Quakerism placed before me in a very interesting and delightful light; and is it unlikely that inclination may put on the appearance of duty? Now my inclination may, before long, lead me some other way; that is a sad foundation to build the fortress upon which must defend me through life; but I think I am wrong in one thing, though it is right to doubt myself; yet do I not make myself more uneasy, for fear I should be a ridiculous object to the world, and some of my dear friends. I believe I can give myself a little advice, not to promote anything leading to unquakerism; but try if it make me happy or not, and then take greater steps if I like.

Colebrook Dale, 31st.—Cousin Priscilla's room. This evening I am at Colebrook Dale, the place I have so much wished to be at. I had rather a comfortable drive here from Shrewsbury; read in the Testament, and got by heart one or two verses. I felt it a great pleasure to see cousin Priscilla. We have taken a long walk this afternoon. It brings me into a sweet state, being with plain Friends like these, a sort of humility. I expect to be here some days, which I delight in. I feel this evening in a calm, and rather religious state of mind. I am blessed a little to feel the existence of my Father who is in heaven; and I have some hope I may one day be confined in the sheep-fold, and not stray from the flock. I hope I shall, and I may; for thanks be to the Almighty, He has formed us for eternal glory, if we will be sufficiently melted down to be moulded into the right form.

September 2nd.—I cannot easily describe that which I would, for I know not in my own mind what my feelings exactly are. This morning, when breakfast was over, I had some talk with Priscilla, and then we sat down to read the account of a young woman of the name of Rathbone, to me striking and interesting; how well she was assured of Immortality, how clearly did she see her path to Heaven! Happy, happy woman; blessed, ah blessed is thy fate! may we also be permitted to accompany thee to glory, immortality, and eternal life, with our God and our Saviour; shall I ever be sensible of deserving immortal glory? too great a blessing, I fear, for me and my weak self ever to obtain. For hard is the task and narrow is the road that leadeth thereunto. We then went to Meeting, my mind was clouded, but now and then a small ray enlightened it. Between the two Meetings, I read again with cousin Priscilla, and all my sisters, that account of the young woman. Hard is the task of dedicating the heart unto God; I fear, yet I hope I may, with His assistance, one day so fortify it, as to become a defender of truth and religion. After the afternoon Meeting, we drank tea at Deborah Darby's; I felt much love towards her, and her friend Appleby particularly; I felt gratified when she said William Savery had mentioned me to her, and that Rebecca Young, who was out, was sorry she could not see me; there is little, ah, little indeed in me! When we came home this evening, my father took me aside, and gave me some good advice; to beware of passion and enthusiasm, which I hope I do most earnestly pray I may, for truly they are snares of the enemy.

3rd.—Got up late. Heard Deborah Darby was here, and went down; during breakfast, I felt my heart beat much; as soon as it was over, Deborah Darby preached in a deep, clear, and striking manner. First, she said, God would visit us all, and did visit us; that God was a father to the fatherless, and a mother to the motherless; my mind felt deeply impressed by it. She then addressed me in particular; I do not remember her words, but she expressed, first, I was, as I am, sick of the world; and looked higher, (and I believe I do,) and that I was to be dedicated to my God, and should have peace in this world, and glory everlasting in the world to come. Could more satisfaction be given? let me be thankful; I really cried, and I think never felt such inward encouragement. Let me be a worthy servant of my Master who is in heaven. May I, Oh! may I do right. My father has given me leave to stay till Fourth-day morning: kind he truly is. He spoke to me again this morning. I feel myself highly favoured, is all I can say; and may my heart bow before its Maker, now and evermore! After they all went, I came and wrote my journal, and sat with cousin Priscilla, and we read till dinner. After that, we sat again together with the children, and went on with some letters, interesting to me, from that young woman (E. Rathbone) to Richard Reynolds. This afternoon I was at the Darbys. I have felt, as it were, tinctured with the goodness of those I have been with; but little, I own. Oh, my inward temptations, shall I ever overcome you! Priscilla Gurney I feel my constant little friend, dearly indeed do I love her.

4th.—After tea, we went to the Darbys, accompanied by my dear friend Richard Reynolds, and still dearer Priscilla Gurney. We had spent a pleasant evening, when my heart began to feel itself silenced before God, and without looking at others, I found myself under the shadow of His wing, and I soon discovered that the rest were in the same state: I was persuaded that it must be *that* which I felt. After sitting a time in awful silence, Rebecca Young spoke most beautifully, she touched my heart, and I felt melted and bowed before my Creator. Deborah Darby then spoke; what she said was excellent, she addressed part of it to me; I only fear she says too much of what I am to be. A light to the blind; speech to the dumb; and feet to the lame; can it be? She seems as if she thought I was be to a minister of Christ. Can I ever be one? If I am obedient, I believe, I shall.

How wonderfully was Elizabeth Gurney, in after life, led, by an invisible hand, to fulfil the mission which was thus, under the inspiring influence of heavenly love, foreshadowed on the spirit of this nursing mother in Israel!

Merridon 5th.—I rose this morning about five o'clock: I did not feel so much as I expected leaving Colebrook Dale. There is a mountain for me to climb over, there is sacrifice for me to make; before I am favoured with faith, virtue, and assurance of immortality. I feel it would appear so like conformity to the opinions of others, to alter just after being with these Friends; but I think that it is a time to do so, for strength and courage have been given me. This day I have said thee instead of you; but still go on soberly and with consideration.

Coventry, 6*th*.—I rose in good time to write to Priscilla Gurney, and felt in a state of darkness and discouragement about my language, but I am happy to say my mind again feels clear. I dare not draw back. I hope to continue in the habit with spirit, and if by yesterday week I have kept up to it, and then feel discouraged, I may give it up. I felt saying thee very difficult to-day to Mrs.———, but I perceived it was far more so after I sang to them. I altogether get on pretty well, but doubts came into my mind this morning; yet were I not to persevere I should, I believe, feel unhappy in it. How shall I say thee to H—— in Norwich! It will, I think, make me lose all my dissipation of character, and be a guard upon my tongue.

Earlham, 9*th*.—My father, Kitty, and myself set out early this morning for Newmarket. When I was there, I saw Henry B——; my sensation was odd when I saw him, for I took to my heels and ran away. I thought I could not get courage to address him in the plain language; but after I collected myself, I did it without much difficulty. How easy it has been made to me! By what nice degrees I have entered it, but I believe the hardest part is to come; I have felt the advantage of it, though at times in a dark and discouraging state. It makes me think before I speak, and avoid saying much, and also avoid the spirit of gaiety and flirting.

It is evident that Elizabeth Gurney returned from this excursion with a mind strongly impressed by the conviction that the path of duty, designed for her by her Heavenly Father, was clearly marked, as that which involved her adoption of the habits and language of Friends. Had she resisted this conviction, she could never have been employed by the Lord, as an ambassador for Christ, declaring effectually the message of His salvation.

Earlham, 10*th*.—We arrived last night from our long, and in some respects, delightful journey. So far from hurting me, I hope it will act as a fresh stimulus to virtue and religion; at least it should; I have had some bright and clear times that should not be forgotten. I felt quite in a flutter, expecting H—— and Dr. Alderson to dinner: they came, and I had little difficulty in saying thee;—so do such evils vanish, if duty support us. In the afternoon, I had a very serious talk with Kitty about my being a Friend. She thinks that my judgment is too young and inexperienced to be able to keep up any particular opinions; she may be right. I am willing to give up the company of Friends and their books, if she request it; but I do firmly believe my mind will never be easy or happy unless I am a Quaker.

On being again settled at home, Elizabeth Gurney resumed her usual habits of self-occupation and usefulness to others; visiting and relieving the poor, both at Earlham and in Norwich, especially the sick, reading the Bible to them, and instructing their children. Her school, too, gradually increased from the small beginning of one little boy, to so great a number, that her teaching them in the house became inconvenient, and a vacant laundry was appropriated to this purpose. She had, at last, above seventy scholars, without assistance, without monitors, without even the almost countless books and pictures of the present day; how she controlled the wills, and fixed the attention, of so many unruly children, must ever remain a mystery to those who have not the gift which she possessed of influencing the minds of others.

Nor was her attention confined to the poor: where any little kindness seemed needed, there she delighted to offer it.

We have no exact knowledge of the time when she became a Friend in outward appearance. She was slow in adopting the costume; she first laid aside all ornament, then she chose quiet and inconspicuous colours, and had her dresses made with perfect simplicity. Her journal continues—

14*th.*—I know I am not able to judge, and all I pray for is, faith, humility and patience; and I hope, if ill or well, to do the will of God. May, oh, may I! is the inmost prayer of my heart. I must try not to fear; what will not faith do for us! It would lead us to all happiness; but works are required, and I believe true faith hardly attainable without them.

27*th.*—This evening I have been doing exercises, and singing with them; my mind feels very clear to-night and my body much better. I have been thinking about singing, I hope in that, as in everything else, to do what is right. I cannot say I feel it wrong to sing to my own family, it is sweet and right to give them pleasure. I do not approve of singing in company, as it leads to vanity and dissipation of mind; but that I believe I have no occasion to do, as dear Rachel does not request it, for she does not like it herself. I should be sorry quite to give up singing, as the gift of nature, and on her account; as long as it does not lead me from what is right, I need not fear.

29*th.*—I have much enjoyed the company of my dear boy Sammy this evening. I think we shall always feel much love for each other; young as he is, I love him particularly. Afterwards we received a letter from dear Priscilla Gurney.

October 5*th.*—In the evening a fiddler came, we all had a dance. I had the tooth-ache, and so far from its making me merry, it made me grave. I do not feel satisfaction in dancing.

6*th.*—This morning I awoke not comfortable, the subject of dancing came strongly before my mind. Totally declining it as a matter of pleasure, I do not mind, only as I am situated with the others I find it difficult; the question is, if these may not be scruples of my own forming, that I may one day repent of? The bottom of my heart is inclined to Quakerism, but I know what imagination can do. I believe the formation of my mind is such, that it requires the bonds and ties of Quakerism to fit it for immortality. I feel it a very great blessing being so little in the company of superior, fascinating Quakers; because it makes me act freely, and look to the only true Judge, for what is right for me to do. The next question I ask myself is, am I sufficiently clear, that dancing is wrong, to give it up? because I know much precaution is quite necessary. I believe I may, if I like, make one more trial, and judge again how I feel; but I must reflect upon it, determining to give it up, if I think right. I wish to make it a subject of very serious reflection, hoping, as usual, to do right; it will hurt them much I fear, but time, I believe, will take that off, if they see me more happy, and better for it. Let me redouble all kindness to them. Catherine seems to wish I would give up my correspondence with Anna Savery, which I think I may do. This day has been very comfortable in most respects, though I have not done much. I have finished my letter to my dear cousin Priscilla, and that to Mrs. ——; but I cannot feel quite easy to send it, without first speaking to my father, for I do believe it is my duty to make him my friend in all things; though I think it probable, he will discourage me in writing to my friend Sophy, yet never keep anything from him; but let me be an open, true, kind, and dutiful daughter to him, whilst life is in my body.

12*th*.—I have many great faults, but I have some dispositions which I should be most thankful for. I believe I feel much for my fellow-creatures; though I think I mostly see into the minds of those I associate with, and am apt to satirise their weaknesses; yet I don't remember ever being any time with one who was not extremely disgusting, but I felt a sort of love for them, and I do hope I would sacrifice my life for the good of mankind. My mind is too much like a looking-glass—objects, of all kinds, are easily reflected in it, whilst present, but when they go, their reflection is gone also. I have a faint idea of many things, a strong idea of a few; therefore my mind is cultivated badly. I have many straggling, but not many connected ideas. I have the materials to form good in my mind, but I am not a sufficiently good artificer to unite them properly together, and make a good consistence; for in some parts, I am too hard, in others, too soft. I hope and believe the great Artificer is now at work, that if I join my power to the only One who is able to conduct me aright, I may one day be better than I am.

17*th.*—My journal has not gone on well of late: partly owing to my going out, and having people in this room, now there is a fire; I dislike going out; what my mind wants, is peace and quiet. The other night, as I was alone in a carriage, a fine starlight night, I thought, what is it I want? how I overflow with the blessings of this world; I have true friends, as many as I wish for; good health, a happy home, with all that riches can give, and yet all these are nothing without a satisfied conscience. At times I feel satisfied, but I have not reason to feel so often. . . . This afternoon I have much to correct, I feel proud, vain, and disagreeable; not touched with the sweet humility of Christianity; nor is my heart enlightened by its happy doctrines. I have now two things heavily weighing on my mind—dancing and singing, so sweet and so pretty do they seem; but as surely as I do either, so surely does a dark cloud come over my mind. It is not only my giving up these things, but I am making the others miserable, and laying a restraint upon their pleasures. In the next place, Am I sure I am going upon a good foundation? if I am doing right, God will protect me and them also. If I am doing wrong, what foundation do I stand upon? None: then all to me is nothing. Let me try to take my thoughts from this world, and look to the only true Judge. I believe singing to be so natural, that I may try it a little longer: but I do think dancing may be given up. What particularly led me to this state, was our having company, and I thought I must sing; I sang a little, but did not stay with them during the playing. My mind continued in a state of some agitation, and I did not sleep till some time after I was in bed.

19*th.*—My mind feels more this morning, if anything, than it did last night. Can such feelings be my own putting on? they seem to affect my whole frame, mental and bodily; they cannot be myself, for if I were to give worlds, I could not remove them; they truly make me shake. When I look forwards I think I can see, if I have strength to do as they direct, I shall be another person: sorrow, I believe, will remove to be replaced by joy; then let me now act! My best method of conduct will be to tell Rachel how I am situated in mind, and then ask her what she would advise; and be very kind and tell her the true state of the case. Is it worth while to continue in so small a pleasure for so much pain? The pleasure is nothing to me, but it is a grand step to take in life.—I have been and spoken to Rachel, saying I think I must give up singing. It is astonishing the total change that has taken place; from misery I am now come to joy; I felt ill before, I now feel well—thankful should I be for being directed, and pray to keep up always to that direction. After having spoken to my darling Rachel where I fear I said too much, I rode to Norwich after some poor people: I went to see many, and added my mite to their comfort. Nothing I think could exceed the kindness of my dear Rachel. Though I have no one here to encourage me in Quakerism, I believe I must be one before I am content.

7*th December.*—I have had a letter to say my dear friend William Savery is arrived safely in America. Kitty and I have been having a long talk together this evening upon sects; we both seem to think them almost necessary. It is long since I have what I call truly written my journal;

writing my journal, is to me expressing the feelings of my heart during the day; I have partly given it up from the coldness of the weather, and not having a snug fire to sit by. I wish now, as I have opportunity, to look a little into the present situation of my heart; that is the advantage of writing a true journal,—it leads the mind to look inwards. Of late I do not think I have been sufficiently active, but have rather given way to a dilatory spirit. I have been reading Watts's Logic, it tells me how ill-regulated are my thoughts, they ramble truly! Regularity of thought and deed is what I much want; I appear to myself to have almost a confusion of ideas, which leads to a confusion of actions; I want order; I believe it difficult to obtain, but yet with perseverance attainable. The first way to obtain it, appears to me, to try to prevent my thoughts from rambling, and to keep them as steadily as possible to the object in view. True religion is what I seldom feel, nor do I sufficiently try after it, by really seeking devotion; I do not warmly seek it, I am sure, nor do I live in the fear of an all-wise Being, who watches over us; I seldom look deep enough, but dwell too much on the surface of things, and let my ideas float. Such is my state. I can't tell how I feel exactly:—at times all seems to me mystery; "when I look at the heavens, the work of Thy fingers, the moon and the stars which Thou hast ordained, what is man that Thou art mindful of him, or the son of man that Thou visitest him?" Thou must exist, oh God! for the heavens declare Thy glory, and the firmament showeth Thy handy-work.

8*th.*—Since dinner I have read much Logic and enjoyed it; it is interesting to me, and may, I think, with attention, do me good. Reading Watts, impresses deeply on my mind how very careful I should be of judging; how much I should consider, before I speak or form an opinion; how careful I should be not to let my mind be tinged throughout, with one reigning subject, to try not to associate ideas; but judge of things according to the evidence they give to my mind of their own worth. My mind is like a pair of scales that are not inclined to balance equally; at least when I begin to form a judgment, and try to hold the balance equally, as soon as I perceive one scale is at all heavier than the other, I am apt at once to let it fall on that side; forgetting what remains in the other scale, which, though lighter, should not be forgotten. For instance, I look at a character, at first I try to judge calmly and truly; but if I see more virtues than vices, I am apt soon to like that character so much, that I like its weaknesses also, and forget they are weaknesses. The same if evil may preponderate, I forget the virtues.

12th.—This day finished with a dance. If I could make a rule never to give way to vanity, excitement, or flirting, I do not think I should object to dancing; but it always leads me into some one of these faults; indeed, I never remember dancing without feeling one, if not a little of all the three, and sometimes a great deal. But as my giving it up would hurt many, it should be one of those things I part with most carefully.

30th.—I went to Meeting in the morning and afternoon; both times rather dark; but I have been a little permitted to see my own state, which is the greatest favour I can ask for at present; to know what I should do, and to be assisted in my duties: for it is hard, very hard, to act right, at least I find it so. But there is the comfortable consideration, that God is merciful and full of compassion, He is tender over His children. I had a satisfactory time with my girls and boys.

January 4th, 1799.—Most of this morning I spent in Norwich, seeing after the poor; I do little for them, and I do not like it should appear that I do much. I must be most guarded, and tell those who know I do charity that I am only my father's agent. A plan, at least a duty, that I have felt for some time, I will now mention. I have been trying to overcome fear; my method has been to stay in the dark, and at night to go into those rooms not generally inhabited; there is a strange propensity in the human mind to fear in the dark, there is a sort of dread of something supernatural; I tried to overcome that, by considering that, as far as I believed in ghosts, so far I must believe in a state after death, and it must confirm my belief in the Spirit of God; therefore, if I try to act right, I have no need to fear the directions of Infinite Wisdom. I do not turn away such things as some do; I believe nothing impossible to God, and He may have used spirits as agents for purposes beyond our conceptions; I know they can only come when He pleases, therefore we need not fear them. But my most predominant fear is that of thieves; and I find *that* still more difficult to overcome, but faith would cure that also, for God can equally protect us from man as from spirit.

8th.—My father not appearing to like all my present doings, has been rather a cloud over my mind this day: there are few, if any, in the world I love so well; I am not easy to do what he would not like, for I think I could sacrifice almost anything for him, I owe him so much, I love him so much.

I have been reading Watts on Judgment this afternoon; it has led me into thought, and particularly upon the evidence I have to believe in religion. The first thing that strikes me, is the perception we all have, of being under a power superior to human. I seldom feel this so much as when unwell; to see how pain can visit me, and how it is taken away. Work for ever, we could not create life. There must be a cause to produce an effect. The next thing that strikes me, is good and evil, virtue and vice, happiness and unhappiness—these are acknowledged to be linked together? virtue produces good; vice evil; of course the Power that allows this, shows approbation of virtue. Thirdly, Christianity seems also to have its clear evidences, even to my human reason. My mind has not been convinced by books; but what little faith I have, has been confirmed by reading the holy writers themselves.

27*th.*—I have had, in many respects, comfortable Meetings: only my thoughts too giddy, dwelling too much on what pleased me yesterday; they have, I am sorry to say, been occupied with old subjects, such as dress, and a little flirting, I fear. I have enjoyed my little party as usual, who are now, when complete, fifteen in number. What path I shall go in life, is hidden from my view. May I go in that in which I ought to go! Do not forget how much more tempting it is to choose the easiest, and yet do not enter difficulties for difficulty's sake. Try to be led by no person, but by my own conscience.

29*th.*—I am in a doubtful state of mind. I think my mind is timid, and my affections strong, which may be partly the cause of my being so much inclined to Quakerism; in the first place, my affections were worked upon, in receiving the first doctrines of religion through a Quaker; therefore it is likely they would put on that garb in my mind. In the next place, my timidity may make me uncomfortable, in erring from principles that I am so much inclined to adopt; so far I should be on my guard, and I hope not to forget what I have just mentioned. But yet, I think the only true standard I can have to direct myself by, is that which experience proves to give me the most happiness, by enabling me to be more virtuous: I believe there is something in the mind, or in the heart, that shows its approbation when we do right. I give myself this advice: do not fear truth, let it be ever so contrary to inclination and feeling.

February 7*th.*—I read much this morning in St. Basil, which is to me excellent, interesting, and beautiful. He advises a constant thanksgiving for the many blessings we enjoy, and that we should not grumble at the evils we are subject to; how much more cause have I for thankfulness than sorrow! I seldom give thanks for the many blessings that surround me. St. Basil beautifully says, "we should not eat, we should not drink, without giving thanks to God."

14*th.*—I hope I have from experience gained a little. I

am much of a Friend in my principles at this time, but do not outwardly appear much so; I say "thee" to people, and do not dress very gay, but yet I say "Mr." and "Mrs.," wear a turban, &c., &c. I have one remark to make; every step I have taken towards Quakerism has given me satisfaction.

18th.—I feel I must not despair: I consider I first brought sceptical opinions upon myself, and it is only what is due to me that they should now hurt me. I hope I do not much murmur at the decrees of the Almighty: and can I expect, who am so faulty, to be blessed with entire faith? Let me once more try and pray, that the many evil roots in my own mind may be eradicated. I had altogether a pretty good day, rather too much vanity at being mistress at home, and having to entertain many guests.

24th.—What feeling so cheering to the human mind as religion! what thankfulness should I feel to God! I have great reason to believe Almighty God is directing my mind to the haven of peace, at least I feel that I am guided by a Power not my own. How dark was my mind for some days! How heavy! I saw duties to be performed that even struck me as foolish. I took courage and tried to follow the directions of this voice; I felt enlightened, even happy. Again I erred, again I was in a cloud; I once more tried, and again I felt brightened.

25th.—This time last year, I was with my dear friend William Savery, at Westminster Meeting. I can only thank fully admire, when I look back to about that time, the gentle leadings my soul has had, from the state of great darkness it was in; how suddenly did the light of Christianity burst upon my mind. I have reason to believe in religion from my own experience, and what foundation so solid to build my hopes upon; may I gain from the little experiences I have been blessed with, may I encourage the voice of truth, and may I be a steady and virtuous combatant in the service of God. Such I think I may truly say is my most ardent prayer. But God, who is omnipresent, knows my thoughts knows my wishes, and my many, many feelings; may conclude with saying, "cleanse thou me from secret faults.'

28th.—We have had company most part of the day. I have had an odd feeling. Uncle Joseph, and many gay ones, were here; I had a sort of sympathy with him. I feel to have been so much off my guard, that if tempted, I should have done wrong. I now hear them singing. How much my natural heart does love to sing: but if I give way to the ecstacy that singing sometimes produces in my mind, it carries me far beyond the centre; it increases all the wild passions, and works on enthusiasm. Many say and think it leads to religion; it may lead to emotions of religion, but true religion appears to me to be in a deeper recess of the heart; where no earthly passion can produce it.

March 1*st.*—There is going to be a dance—What am I to do? As far as I can see, I believe, if I find it very necessary to their pleasure, I may do it, but not for my own gratification. Remember, don't be vain, if it be possible, dance little.

I began to dance in a state next to pain of mind; when I had danced four dances, I was trying to pluck up courage to tell Rachel I wished to give it up for the evening; it seemed as if she looked into my mind, for she came up to me at that minute in the most tender manner, and begged me to leave off, saying she would contrive without me; I suppose she saw in my countenance the state of my mind. I am not half kind enough to her, I often make sharp remarks to her, and in reality there are none of my sisters to whom I owe so much; I must think of her as my nurse; she would suffer much to comfort me; may she, oh God! be blessed; wouldest Thou, oh wouldest Thou, let her see her right path, whatever that may be, and wilt thou enable her to keep up to her duty, in whatever line it may lead. Let this evening be a lesson to me, not to be unkind to her any more. I think I should feel more satisfaction in not dancing; but such things must be left very much to the time. How very much do I wish for their happiness; that they may be blessed in every way, is what I pray for to the Great Director; but all is guided in wisdom, and I believe, as a family, we have much to be thankful for, both for bodily and mental blessings.

4*th.*—I hope the day has passed without many faults. John is just come in to ask me to dance in such a kind way,—oh dear me! I am now acting clearly differently from them all. Remember this, as I have this night refused to dance with my dearest brother, I must, out of kindness to him, not be tempted by any one else. Have mercy, oh God! have mercy upon me! and let me act right, I humbly pray Thee; wilt Thou love my dearest, most dear brothers and sisters, wilt thou protect us? Dear John! I feel much for him, such as these are home strokes, but I had far rather have them if indeed guided by Supreme Wisdom; for then I need not fear. I know that *not* dancing will not lead me to do wrong, and I fear dancing does; though the task is hard on their account, I hope I do not mind the pain myself. I feel for them, but if they see in time that I am happier for it, I think they will no longer lament over me. I will go to them as soon as they have done, try to be cheerful and to show them I love them, for I do most truly, particularly John. I think I might talk a little with John, and tell him how I stand, for it is much my wisest plan to keep truly intimate with them all; make them my first friends. I do not think I ever love them so well as at such times as these. I should fully express my love for them, and how nearly it touches my heart, acting differently to what they like. These are truly great steps to take in life, but I may expect support under them.

16*th.*—I know I want correction, for these few days past I have not gone on well, a sort of coldness, darkness, and uncertainty, that will sometimes take possession of the mind; it is I believe much owing to a want of vigilance and activity on my part, and it does not always please the Almighty to enlighten us equally. I am a very negligent being. If, as Deborah Darby said to me, I will do as far as I know to be right, I may one day be a light to the blind, feet to the lame, &c., &c. Shall such a state ever be mine? If there be any chance of such a thing, I should labour for it. I think the time I spent at Colebrook Dale one of the happiest, if not the happiest time of my life. I think my feelings that night, at Deborah Darby's, were the most exalted I ever remember. I, in a manner, was one of the beginners of the Meeting; suddenly my mind felt clothed with light, as with a garment, and I felt silenced before God; I cried with the heavenly feeling of humility and repentance. Then, when I was in this awful state, there were two sermons preached, one telling me to get the pearl of great price; and the other telling me what I might expect, even happiness in this world, and everlasting happiness in the one to come. But that silence which first took possession of my mind, exceeded all the rest.

At this time, Elizabeth adopted the numerical style of dates.

Fourth Month, 6th.—I have not done a great deal to-day, and yet I hope I have not been idle: I try to do right now and then, but by no means constantly. I could not recover the feeling of being hurt at rejecting, I suppose, the voice of my mind, last night, when I sang so much; they were not, I believe, feelings of my own making, for it was my wish to enjoy singing without thinking it wrong.

7th.—I have hopes the day may come when Norwich Meeting will prosper and be enlivened again, from a state of cloudiness. In the afternoon, I went with them to hear a person preach at the Baptists' Meeting: I felt afraid of setting my own opinions up, and being uncharitable. It did not seem to suit me like our silent method of worship, and the prayers and sermon did not make their way into the heart, as those of our Friends do; but it is likely I should feel that, as I have much love for my own Society. Uncle Joseph was here in the evening, and he seemed rather surprised at my going to hear Kinghorn. I had an interesting time with my young flock, I fear I might say rather too much to them; mayst Thou, oh Father! preserve them, for without Thy aid my efforts are ineffectual; mayst Thou make me an instrument in leading them to true virtue, and may the day come when Thou wilt call them to everlasting joy.

15th.—I had, for my poor wandering thoughts, a satisfactory Meeting; partly owing to being nervous, for it leads me to cast my care upon the Lord. I went to Bedlam, and felt glad to see the poor Melton woman going on well. If comfort be once permitted to enter her heart, it will be a cause of true pleasure to me, and I hope of gratitude to the All-wise Director; but He knows better than I what is for her good. To-day, at Meeting, I felt such a relief in the thought that God knows all our thoughts, all our temptations, and that He knows also how much power we have to overcome them: for I felt I could not have a just estimate of my own self.

22nd.—I have read a good deal of Lavater's journal, and have felt sympathy with him. I like the book, as it reminds me of my duty. I hope that I shall have more steady reliance upon God; more regularity of mind; less volatility of thought. To have my heart pure in the sight of Thee, who knowest and seest all my weaknesses, all my defects; God have mercy on me, I pray Thee! mayst thou find in me a faithful servant, abounding in good works; may my whole heart say truly, "Thy will be done!" may I ever, with all my heart, say the Lord's prayer. Thou knowest my wishes, oh God; Thou knowest them!

24th.—I awoke with good resolutions, wishing to obtain that peaceful state of mind, of feeling myself humbly trying to do the will of the Almighty; I took good resolves, but my nature seems not in the mind to act up to them. I feel to have too much volatility of thought to keep that watch so necessary about my thoughts, words, and actions. I do not think this has been a bad day; part of it very satisfactory, particularly teaching three little girls. How little the feelings of my heart seem under my own power; I feel them like my body, under another power; yet mankind do not seem willing to allow that God is the Governor and Director of the heart, though they mostly acknowledge, it is He who guides all outward circumstances; we find we have inward and outward evil to combat, but we have a power within ourselves, that will much alleviate the many evils we are subject to.

28*th.*—I then had a very satisfactory evening with my dear Sam; how do I love that dear boy—may he do well! I am inclined to think the day will come, when we shall see him a religious character.

Fifth Month, 1*st.*—Even acting right will sometimes bring dissensions in a family, as it says in the Testament; we must not be discouraged even when that is our lot, for whatever may be our situation, if we strictly adhere to that which we believe to be our duty, we need not fear, but rest steadily upon Him who can and will support us. I often observe how much weakness of body seems to humble the mind; illness is of great benefit to us, as I have found from experience, if we try to make good use of it; it leads us to see our own weakness and debility, and to look to a stronger for support. So I believe it may be with the mind; dark and gloomy states are allowed to come upon it that we may know our own insufficiency, and place our dependence upon a Higher Power.

16*th.*—I have not done much to-day, partly owing to taking a walk to Melton, and company this afternoon. I am sorry to say, imperceptibly my mind gets wrapped up in the Election. I must take care, or I think I shall be off my guard, and I do think if I become so warm in it, I shall find it better to go out of the way; and may perhaps go to London Yearly Meeting. But why not try to command my mind at home? I intend to try, but in such cases as this, it is difficult to act a negative character; for even such a body as I am, might, I believe, get many votes amongst the poor: but yet I feel as if it were giving to the poor with an expectation of return from them to ask for their votes. Still, if the cause be such, as may be of use in tending to abolish the war (for every member in the House carries some weight), is it not right to be anxious to get any one, who opposes war, into it? "Many a little makes a mickle."

27th.—At last this long-wished-for, expected day has arrived; it has been one of real bustle. Before we went to Norwich, I was much affected to hear of the death of poor Betty Pettet, and it moved me. Let death come in any way, how very affecting it is! We went to Norwich, and then entered its tumults. I have not been so very, very much interested; I might have acted pretty well, if pride, vanity, and shame had not crept in; we lost the Election, which is certainly a very great blank, but we soon get over such matters, and it convinces me, the less public matters are entered into the better, they do not suit us; keep to our own sphere, and do not go out of its bounds.

Seventh Month, 12th.—This day has not been idle, but not religious. I was most part of the morning at Norwich; in the afternoon, I settled accounts; and in the evening, cut out clothes for the poor. I don't think I have looked into the Testament, or written my journal to-day; it leads me to remember what uncle Joseph said to me the other day, after relating or reading to me the history of Mary, who anointed our Saviour with the precious ointment, and His disciples said she might have sold it, and given to the poor, but Christ said, "The poor ye have always with you, but me ye have not always;" now I thought, as uncle Joseph remarked, I might this evening have spent too much time about the poor, that should have been spent about better things.

In the Seventh Month, John Gurney travelled into the

North of England, accompanied by his daughters Elizabeth and Priscilla, and his son Samuel. They attended the General Meeting at the school at Ackworth: this interested Elizabeth, from bringing her into communication with several Friends.

The travellers afterwards visited Sheepwash, an estate on the beautiful banks of the Wanspeck, at that time belonging to John Gurney; they extended their journey to Edinburgh, and returned home, paying a few visits on their way.

On the day when they set out on this tour is the next entry in Elizabeth's journal.

Lynn, Seventh Month, 28th.—This was one of the very bustling mornings, to which Earlham is subject, on any of the family leaving home. We had a quiet sort of a journey here, and though I felt sorry, yet I am now glad to be away from home, as we have lately had so much bustle, and I know I have so little cultivated or encouraged a religious state of mind; indeed I have been in a darkish state of late, sadly erring from the path of right; and I appeared to have gone so far out of it, that I could not get into it again, till temptation was a little lessened, which I hope it will be this journey. I think it probable, I shall be more stimulated in the right, than in the wrong path.

Peterborough, 29th, First-day.—We went to Meeting this morning: and since have been travelling.

30*th.*—We had a long day's journey; I hope it has been my object, at least, to try to act right. The propriety of saying "thou" has lately struck me: if I think it right to say it, I hope I shall be able, though any alteration of speech is very difficult to make.

Ackworth, Eighth Month, 1st.—To-day what is called the General Meeting began; we first had a Meeting of worship, which was rather agreeable: after which we dined with a very large party in the boy's dining-room at the School; as I was wandering about in the bustle, I went into the plain Friends' room, (which I often did,) where I had not been very long, before I felt myself fall into silence before God, which the rest of the party appeared to do also; we had not sat long before a ministering Friend began to preach to me. I was much affected; then a dear aged minister also said something to me; may I profit by such refreshing times. At four o'clock, the Women's Meeting met; I, amongst a great number, was chosen one of the Committee to examine the children, school and household: —— (a female preacher from America) appeared to me to hold rather too high a hand. After Meeting, we examined the bed-rooms, which I thought in good order, and talked a little to —— (the preacher just alluded to.)

2nd.—I arose about six to go to the School to hear the girls spell, which I was pleased with, but should have liked to have questioned them more myself. After that, we breakfasted; then met in the Committee, to fix a little the plans we should go upon. I and Sarah Cockfield were mentioned to go and attend to the Grammar School; I said that I had only a slight knowledge of grammar. We then went to the Grammar School; the writing, ciphering, working, mending, spinning, knitting, and sewing, all which I liked much, and thought, upon the whole, they did very well indeed; we then examined parts of the house; after which we dined, and at three o'clock met to hear the report of the Committee; I forgot that before dinner, we met at twelve o'clock to draw up the report of what we thought of the proceedings of the School. It was some time before any one would speak; Friends were begging the Committee to say what they thought, but in vain, till I think —— broke the ice, and encouraged the young people to say what they thought; for they had been requested before. As it appeared to me it was delaying the Meeting, I took courage (as I thought it was more right than wrong) to speak; and said what I thought of the grammar and ciphering; I felt glad I had done it, though I trembled at doing it, not a little. Towards the latter part of the sitting, I was pointedly asked what I thought of their spelling, which I said; and also that I did not think they attended to the words of one, so well as to those of many syllables. After the Meetings, I was encouraged in what I had done, by salutations from the Friends, H. B. and E. C. After dinner, we met again and heard the report they had written to bring into the men. I thought the Meeting paid rather too much deference to H. B., in delaying the Meeting, because she was not come in. We took the report to the men; I own my body and mind longed impatiently to have Meeting over. After tea I entered into talk with ——. I mentioned dear William Savery: we went and sat in the Doctor's room, where was Thomas Scattergood, whom, though I do not think he spoke, yet I liked.

3rd.—I arose in a bustle and hurried about till the "cold victuals" were given to the poor, which plan I did not much like, as it seemed like showing off. —— preached to them agreeably, after which Thomas Scattergood called us aside, and in a little Meeting expressed the great love he felt for me yesterday, which made it appear to me, as if there were a sympathy of soul, and we both were guided by the same spirit; he expressed how much he felt for me at the time I came into Doctor Binns' room, and had then felt it on his mind to say something to me; I also had felt a silent inclination to hear. We then set off on our journey to York. I have not sufficiently dwelt on the kindness of some Friends to me, during our stay at Ackworth. First, dear Christiana Hustler and her daughter; Friend Messer, and many others. May I really profit by this time. We arrived at York to a late dinner, and drank tea at Lindley Murray's, whom, though I hardly spoke to, I really loved; there was also B—— F——'s daughter, who seemed sweetly under the guidance and influence of religion; she was to me truly interesting, but I think I was too forward with her; I felt my own inferiority.

4*th.*—This morning we walked about York and saw its wonders. The Minster is a beautiful building; how much people spend about a pious building! would they spend as much time and trouble about their own souls? We got to Darlington to-night. This morning, I was much pleased by a note and present from Lindley Murray, of one of his English Readers; it renewed my feelings of love towards him.

5*th.*—We were at both Meetings at Darlington to-day; I was much pleased with the Friends there, and their appearance of unity and hospitality. We reached Durham to-night; I was interested with the beautiful scenery on entering the town.

6*th.*—Arrived at Newcastle in a hard rain. Was in a bad storm of thunder and lightning, at the Glass-houses; altogether my mind was calm.

7*th.*—Much bustle and fatigue in walking about Newcastle, seeing different sights; we arrived at Sheepwash to-night.

8*th.*—This morning, we spent in riding about my father's estate, which is a beautiful place; I had rather an exertion of courage in riding an unruly horse.

9*th.*—Walked with R—— C—— to Broom Park. I must beware of my proud, vain self.

10*th.*—We spent the day, till about five, at Broom Park; I do not like myself in that sort of company, I am almost sure to lose ground by a sort of foolish wish to please every body; I do not absolutely deviate from my character; but I enter, as far as I can, into the character of those I am with, and unintentionally give up more than I should. We went from thence to Alnwick Castle, belonging to the Duke of Northumberland, a very magnificent place; but seeing such places never leads me to wish for high life, for, after all, are the possessors happier, if so happy as others? the only true and lasting source of happiness is an easy conscience.

Edlington, Scotland, 11*th.*—We saw to-day a very beautiful view, Peese Bridge, nature and art are so finely united; there is sea, land, wood, waterfall, mountain, valley, and a bridge, I should say more than two hundred feet high.

Shields, 19*th.*—I am sorry it is so long since I wrote my journal. We have been to Edinburgh, which is a city well worth seeing for its beauty and curiosity. There was an American Friend who put me much in mind of dear William Savery. We again went to Broom Park, where we were most hospitably received. On Second-day evening, on our way from Edinburgh, I was rather nervous. I feel, I am sorry to say, little progress in the path of virtue: keeping up that watch and dependence upon God is so difficult; it is hard work to look only to the true source in our hearts, we are so apt to wish to save ourselves that trouble, and to look to inferior sources. I believe talking much on the subject has not a good effect, for it leads us to an outward rather than deeply inward feeling; it is hard work really to dig deep; I seem to have so many faults or errors encamped round about me, they are out of my power to overcome alone; but can I not do it with looking to God for assistance?

Earlham, 29*th.*—On Third-day evening, we arrived safely at home, after altogether a pleasant journey.

Ninth Month, 13*th.*—This morning I awoke with a cloud over me, and so I must expect both to wake and sleep, if I do not try more completely to do the will of God. I dare not take resolutions, as I know now I cannot keep up to them.

17*th.*— I feel a comfortable state of mind, not so inclined to be off my guard as sometimes, I know it is not owing to myself; but being so, should be a cause of gratitude.

This evening I did a thing I felt I had to repent of, but it has at least made me clear upon the subject; as they were singing and playing, they begged me to sing, and I did it, but I felt far more pain than pleasure from doing it. A really uneasy mind was my portion the rest of the evening.

18th.—This morning I went to Meeting, and fully felt my weakness; but I have found myself to-day and yesterday a little under the influence of religion, which is a blessed thing. I had much palpitation at the Meeting of Discipline, because I saw some things so clearly, but being mentioned by others, I thought I might get off giving an opinion. I was proposed to be representative, and said I had no objection, indeed I felt no objection on my own part, because though I know how weak I am, yet even the weak should not fear to exert the little power they have: and I do feel interested for the Society, and, for the most part, approve its principles highly.

Tenth Month, 1st.—I feel in a state of much mental weakness, real and true discouragement; I have little faith, and little hope, and almost fallen, so as not to be able to rise. But if there be a God and a Saviour I need not fear; for though I know and find my state of corruption, yet I believe the warmest wish of my heart is, to do the will of God, and to act right: I do most truly hunger and thirst after righteousness. I find one thing very hard to overcome, which is pride and vanity in outward religious matters. True religion, I believe, will not admit of pride and vanity. Another temptation is, that I have too much formed in my own mind what I think I am to be; which may outwardly encourage me in a path, that nothing but the dictates of conscience should lead me into. I am really weak in faith, and in works; I believe, at least I have a hope, that if I exert the little power I now have given me, the day will come when I shall feel the power of God within me.

13th.—Narrow is the path that leadeth unto life eternal, and few there be that find it. There are many called, but few chosen—for though we are blessed with being called, yet if we follow not when we are called, and that strictly, we do not deserve to be called the children of God, for, as it says in the Revelation, "He that overcometh shall inherit all things, and I will be his God, and he shall be my son."

24th.—I feel this morning, as I have felt lately, quite in a hurry about what I have to do; and I do not think that that is the way to do it well; it is better to go soberly and quietly to work about it, and not to flurry and bluster. I think this day has not been quite so idle, and I hope in a little degree I may have done well. I put some things in proper order, read history and grammar, wrote letters and worked. I feel in rather a flat, silent state of mind. May I be thankful that opportunity is offered me to spend my time in doing something. May pride and vanity be cast far from me. May doing Thy will, be my constant object, oh God! I see Thee not, for Thou art invisible, yet I have reason to believe, I am not invisible to Thee; therefore look upon my weakness with pity, and deign to strengthen my lukewarm faith.

26th.—I am rather in a volatile mind this morning, and that state which requires care. I still feel as if I could not act really and minutely well; a sort of lukewarmness that leads to forgetfulness; and a flying off from the centre in my inmost heart. But weak as I am, if I exert my powers, and in times of need pray for more, and try to turn out worldly ideas, till I receive strength by waiting in stillness upon God, to let His will be done in me; I then shall find if the arm of the Lord be sufficient for me. But I feel and know it is much easier to write than practise; for it is hard, a very hard matter, to wait quietly upon God; it is for the time, giving up the world to follow Him. For though I seldom, or ever, have found more than darkness in my own endeavours to wait, (and how seldom I do it!) yet remember, "Ask, and it shall be given thee, seek and thou shalt find, knock, and it shall be opened unto thee." If I continue steady in seeking, and will try and pray to seek more and more, the day will come when I shall find,—let me remember this. I believe, at times, the door has been in mercy opened, when at the moment, I have not been knocking, for I have now and then tasted the beauties of holiness; but it appears as if it had mostly been through others, or with others, I have felt it. But how humbly thankful should my soul be, that my path of conduct has so far been shown me, when I sought after it, and that I have had my eyes anointed to see the difference of right and wrong in my conduct; that, perhaps, is enough for me for the present; may I be sufficiently thankful for it, for does it not show that the Most High has not forsaken me?

Eleventh Month, 17*th*, *First-day*.—In the evening, with my children, I had in some respects a very comfortable time; it was, at least, my wish to act right with them. In part of one of the chapters, I seemed carried through to explain something to them in a way I hardly ever did before. It was striking the difference in my power this evening, and this day week. This day week I tried, and tried to explain, and the more I tried the more I seemed to blunder; and this evening I was determined not to attempt it, unless I felt capable, and *that* I did, suddenly and unexpectedly to myself; I had a flow of ideas come one after another, in a sweet and refreshing way. The rest of the evening was principally spent with Hannah Scarnell, talking about my poor mother, who died this day seven years.

26*th*.—Towards the latter end of yesterday evening I had some uncomfortable mental feelings, and this morning they really amounted to pain of mind. I believe they were deep and inward temptations of the imagination; silent waiting upon God seemed my only resource, and it was difficult to do so; it was like a trial in my mind between the two powers. My imagination, I think, was partly set at work by being nervous, rather more so than usual: and it requires spiritual strength to overcome the painful workings of a nervous imagination. There are few temptations, I believe, so hard to overcome, as those that try to put on the appearance of duties. They are willing to represent the Spirit of truth in our hearts; at such times before I act, try quietly to wait upon God; look to Him for help, and when things at all appear in the light of duties, the thought of which produces agony to the soul, it requires much deliberation before we act.

Twelfth Month, 11*th.*—In the afternoon I was rather industrious. I was uncertain whether to go to the Grove or not, but at last I fixed to do so. In going there, I observed the sweet states I had experienced for being obedient. My path seemed clear, and my heart acknowledged, "I have sought, and have found, I have knocked, and it has been opened unto me;" it also appeared to me in how beautiful a manner things work together for good. After all this, again myself got the victory, and I came home with a degree of remorse, for saying upon some subjects more than I should have said; how great a virtue is silence, properly attended to!

At this time, Elizabeth Gurney had adopted the costume and language of Friends; this added to her comfort, and spared her many difficulties. Of the truth of their principles she had been long convinced, and had deliberately chosen Quakerism as the future religious profession of her life.

Her mind being thus established on matters of the first importance, was the more prepared to entertain a subject which now claimed her consideration—proposals of marriage from Joseph Fry; at that time engaged with his brother, William Fry, in extensive business in London. Her timid, sensitive nature shrunk, at first, from so momentous a question, and for a time she seemed unable, or unwilling, to encounter the responsibility. But, on the subject being again brought before her, whilst on a visit in the neighbourhood of London, it claimed her serious consideration. The prospect of religious association in Joseph Fry's family, and of residing among Friends, offered great and strong inducements to her to yield to his solicitations.

The following entry in her journal evinces her anxious desire to be rightly guided in this important concern.

Twelfth Month, 12*th*.—I believe the true state of my mind is as follows. I have, almost ever since I have been a little under the influence of religion, thought marriage at *this* time, was not a good thing for me; as it might lead my interests and affections from that Source in which they should be centered, and also, if I have any active duties to perform in the church, if I really follow, as far as I am able, the voice of Truth in my heart; are they not rather incompatible with the duties of a wife and a mother? And is it not safest to wait and see what is the probable course I shall take in this life, before I enter into any engagement that affects my future career? So I think, and so I have thought. But to look on the other side. If Truth appears to tell me I may marry, I should leave the rest, and hope whatsoever my duties are, I shall be able to perform them; but it is now at this time the prayer of my heart, that if I ever should be a mother, I may rest with my children, and really find my duties lead me to them and my husband; and if my duty ever leads me from my family, that it may be in single life. I must leave all to the wisdom of a superior Power, and, in humble confidence, pray for assistance both now and for evermore, in performing the divine will.

First Month, 1*st*, 1800.—This has not been one of the clear and bright days of life: little has been done, and that little as in a nightmare; not feeling able to get forward, and discouraged. None but one Being knows how I spend my time, and how little I really do in the service of God; but I cannot quite judge myself, and I feel I have complained too much to-day, of the burdens of life, to other people. My uncle Joseph was here, and I felt my own weakness by his side. I had my children, and found them a great burden; at least, I thought that I was making more show than reality. So are my down-sittings, and my uprisings. Have mercy on

12

me, if Thou existest, oh God! forsake not one who does wish to trust in Thee, and to be Thy servant, in the way Thou mayst see meet for her.

7th.—This morning, at Meeting, I had rather a trying time in some respects, at least I fully felt the disobedient state of my own heart. I think, as far as I can judge from past experience, my feelings were not those of imagination. I felt, supposing it was my duty to speak in that Meeting, what would it not be to me? and I don't think I felt perfectly clear of that awful duty; not that I now believe it will be, at this time, required of me, but it appears to me a devotion of heart that I must try to attain; or else my lamp will not be prepared, that I may go when my Master calleth. I have felt, and still feel, "I cannot do it," when required of me. Almost as much as that: though I yet believe, if I were sure it was required by God, it should be done, if I had power; but in our present state of weakness, we are to see so far, and no farther, and we can only act as far as we, in our great weakness, think is the best way for us. My faith is as a grain of mustard-seed. But we may all judge from experience; and I think I may truly say, that when I have followed the direction of this Voice in my heart (those feelings that may be enthusiasm, or what else,) yet I never have failed to feel content in doing so; even to be amply rewarded, and never to have repented following its dictates, but the more I have been wholly and humbly given up to obey, the more I have found my foundation a stable one; and trying as it has been sometimes, yet after I have gone through the trial, reason and inclination and all have applauded. But reason and inclination often leave us in the day of trouble. However, to go on with my tale. I continued most of the Meeting in this state, not clear of this awful duty, and yet by no means seeing it right to act; but as for that, I believe I would hardly let it come into my mind, and into my thoughts; I wished William Crow to preach, as I do sometimes, and when he rose my heart seemed to feel it was right for him to do so. He began to speak of the state of some one present, and did take me surprisingly home to mine; he mentioned how the ministry had come before that mind; but seemed to think it was not an immediate duty, but was to be tried. So I leave it. I am unwilling to think any thing of the kind would be at present required of me. I believe it would be a greater trial than I can describe; my whole appearance being so different from those who are generally ministers among us. But yet I hope, if ever duty really requires it of me, I may do it, let it be early or late.

At this time she thus writes to a young Friend:—

True religion seems a subject of that great importance, that we must not play with it, either mentally or in word; perhaps thou wilt think it odd, but at seasons I am not a friend to too many religious thoughts; for thoughts are apt to wander, and border on imagination. Religion is a deep inward working of the feelings, and of the heart; we must not look too much for bright light on the surface of things, but we must humbly and quietly try to seek deep; attending to the day of small things, trying to be faithful in the little, or we cannot expect to be rulers over more. Seek for these little feelings of the heart; watch, that thou mayst know truly the voice of thy Shepherd. I feel this advice may be received by us both; I cannot tell how thou findest it, but this voice has at times led me into trials; but where I have followed, truly I may say I have had my reward; where I have not, then I have felt the good part within me weakened. I believe our temptations may be different, but the deeper I dig in my own mind, the clearer I see how I am surrounded with them; I can hardly bear to feel them, and to observe them; but that light, which I deeply sought, has shown me the danger; and, as a friend of mine wrote to me the other day, "in vain is the snare laid in the sight of the bird." By thus seeking, may we truly find the road that leadeth unto salvation. Fare thee well!

Second Month, 9*th*.—In the evening, my father brought two Friends with him and Lawrence Candler. As I was reading to my children in the laundry, my father brought them all in; when I had finished reading in the Testament we were all silent, and soon John Kirkham knelt down in prayer, and we all rose up; it was a very solemn time; my heart was not much moved, but I believe many of my dear children were much affected by it; he then preached to them, and it was surprising to me to see how much it seems the same Spirit that works in all; and how solemn a thing it is to preach and pray only from authority, and how very different an effect it has on the mind to other advice; however, it was an encouraging thing, and I hope it will not be passed over by me, or the children.

11*th*.—How much I wished, almost prayed, I may one day be a perfect sacrifice, wholly given up to the service of God.

18*th*.—Time will tell, if what "Friends" have told me will be true, that I shall one day be different from what I am; indeed, taste of the beautiful comfort and support of true religion, and not only receive myself, but be an instrument in giving to others; and that my own beloved family will feel support in me, and in a degree do as I may have done, or that my principles will spread. None but One knows my heart, and my most deep wishes, nay, I may almost say prayers, that I may, in whatever way it may be, do to my utmost the will of God; may I not faint in the day of trial and tribulation; and may self not be exalted in the day of prosperity.

At this time Elizabeth Gurney's attention was seriously fixed on the proposal that had been brought under her consideration, in reference to the most important change in her external circumstances. And the following letter, addressed by her to her much valued friend and relative, Joseph Gurney Bevan, marks her deep solicitude to attain best direction:—

Clapham, *Fourth Month*, 1800.

My dearest Cousin,

It is not pleasant to me, having a subject that now is of no small importance to me, unknown to thee, for I feel thee to be, and love thee as my kind friend. Some time ago, Joseph Fry, youngest son of William Storrs Fry of London, paid us a visit at Earlham, and made me an offer of marriage. Since our stay in this neighbourhood, he has renewed his addresses. I have had many doubts, many risings and fallings about the affair. My most anxious wish is, that I may not hinder my spiritual welfare, which I have so much feared, as to make me often doubt if marriage were a desirable thing for me at this time, or even the thoughts of it; but as I wish (at least I think I wish), in this, as in other things, beyond every thing else, to do the will of God, I hope that I shall be shown the path right for me to walk in. I do not think I could have refused him, with a proper authority, at this time. If I am to marry before very long, it overturns my theories, and may teach me that the ways of the Lord are unsearchable; and that I am not to draw out a path of right for myself, but to look to the One who only knows what is really good for me; but the idea of leaving my station at home is to me surprising, as I had not thought that it would have been the case, and perhaps it may not now happen, but it does not seem improbable. How anxiously do I desire I may through all, strive after the knowledge of God, and one day, if it be right, obtain it. Excuse this hasty scrawl, and believe me, my dear cousin, thy very affectionate,

E. GURNEY.

Earlham, Fifth Month, 30*th*.—I have written lately many melancholy journals, and I seem rather inclined this morning gratefully to mention the calm and sweet state I feel in.

Even if the feelings be but for this time, it is a blessing to have them. My feelings towards Joseph are so calm and pleasant, and I can look forward with so much cheerfulness to a connexion with him.

Sixth Month, 6*th*.—I felt rather nervous and weak this morning. I wrote to Eliza Fry, and worked and talked. I might talk too much. I received a letter I liked from Joseph, and answered it this afternoon. I felt unwilling to represent my own faults to him, although I told him how faulty I was, yet it is much more unpleasant to acknowledge any real fault committed, than the natural inclination to faults.

9*th*.—I have been busy to-day without doing much. They all went out about twelve. I then put my poor people's things in a little order, and cut out linen till dinner, and from dinner till tea. I am slow in what I do. I have thought seriously upon becoming mistress of a house. I look in that, as in other things, that principle may be my support, for it leads and supports even in the smallest occurrences of life. The preparations of clothing, &c., &c., as they lead me into the little things for which I have a taste, if I do not take care may hurt me, and yet they are both pleasant and interesting to me.

17*th*.—My state is a truly comfortable one this morning, such peace of mind and body. I seem to have at present no cloud over me—so calm, so easy—partly owing to having lately felt so much bodily pain, ease and rest are peculiarly pleasant; let it be an encouragement to me, next time pain or sorrow surrounds me, that even when heavily clouded, the sun may not be far off; may enjoying this sort of peace lead me to long for a more durable and lasting one, and may it stimulate me with more vigour to seek after it, by more frequent, patient waiting upon God, and may I experience an increasing willingness to take up the cross when called to do so.

Eighth Month, 4*th*.—This has been a comfortable day to me. I have been busy, and a little gone on in my old plans;

I have great hopes of leaving all things in good order, which is a relief to me. It is a blessing indeed to feel thus healthy in mind and body; for I think we are subject to mental diseases, that are not in our power any more than bodily ones, and that require our patience; although it is our duty in both mental and bodily maladies, to do our utmost to overcome them.

13th.—This morning the Fellowes were here; nothing particular happened till evening, when all my poor children came; it was rather a melancholy time to me. After having enjoyed themselves with playing about, I took them to the summer-house, and bade them farewell; there were about eighty-six of them; many of them wept; I felt rather coldly when with them, but when they went away, I shed my tears also; and then my desires took the turn of anxiously longing for the spiritual welfare of all of us, as a family.

Chapter Third.

1800—1809. Marriage—First visit to Plashet—Settlement in London—Letter to a Friend—Yearly Meeting—Birth of the eldest child, 1801—Journey into the North of England—Second daughter, born 1803—Birth of eldest son, 1804; illness and journey to Bath—Her second son, born 1806—Death of her mother-in-law—Birth of her fifth child, 1808—Letter to John Gurney and his wife—Death of the latter—Death of her father-in-law.

THE marriage of Joseph Fry and Elizabeth Gurney took place on the 19th of Eighth Month, 1800, at Friends' Meeting House in Norwich; her own description of the day is:—

I awoke in a sort of terror at the prospect before me, but soon gained quietness and something of cheerfulness; after dressing, we set off for Meeting; I was altogether comfortable. The Meeting was crowded: I felt serious, and looking in measure to the only sure place for support. It was to me a truly solemn time; I felt every word, and not only felt, but in my *manner* of speaking *expressed* how I felt; Joseph also spoke well. Most solemn it truly was. After we sat silent some little time, a female Friend knelt down in prayer, my heart prayed with her. I believe words are inadequate to describe the feelings on such an occasion; I wept good part of the time, and my beloved father seemed as much overcome as I was. The day passed off well, and I think I was very comfortably supported under it, although cold hands and a beating heart were often my lot.

Leaving the home of her childhood was a great effort to

her. Driving through Norwich for the last time, as a residence, "the very stones of the streets seemed dear" to her.

On the 31st of the same month, she says:—

We arrived at Plashet about three o'clock; it was strange to me. I was much pleased with the place, and admired the kindness of its inhabitants.

Her home, however, was for some years, to be in scenes far less congenial to her early habits, than Plashet House, in Essex; then the residence of her husband's parents. It was a much more prevailing custom in that day, than it is now, for the junior partner to reside in the house of business, in conformity with which, Joseph and Elizabeth Fry prepared to establish themselves in Mildred's Court, in the city of London. The house was large, airy, commodious, and what, in the city, is a still more rare advantage, quiet; and continued to be an occasional residence of different members of the family, till it was pulled down in consequence of alterations in London.

Elizabeth Fry was, by her marriage, brought into completely new circumstances; her husband's family had been members of the Society of Friends, since an early period after its foundation. In this it resembled that of the Gurney's; but unlike her own parents, her father and mother-in-law adhered strictly to the habits of Friends, and she was surrounded by a large circle of new connections and acquaintance who differed from her own early associates, in being almost exclusively of the same decided class. This, for a time, brought her into occasional difficulty, and even trial, from the incongruities of the parties assembled at her house; formed of her own tenderly beloved family and near connections (few of whom were inclined to walk in the same path as that into which *she* had been led), and the members of the Society to which she had become so closely united in religious profession; and earnest were her desires to be preserved from, in any degree, swerving from the line of duty.

George Dilwyn, a Friend from America, who was engaged in religious service in London, as a minister of the Gospel, became their guest on the 7th of the Eleventh Month, only a few days after the young married pair had arrived at their home; he remained with them for several weeks, and his company appears to have been useful and agreeable to them; although his presence brought the bride into difficulty, on a point that, at the present time, seems almost inconceivable, that of reading the Holy Scriptures aloud in the morning. Family devotion, amongst all persuasions, was much less common at that period than it is now; and the habit of assembling the household at a stated hour daily, for this religious duty, had not been observed at Mildred's Court. The servants of that establishment were not, until some years afterwards, partakers of this privilege; and Elizabeth Fry, whilst believing it to be incumbent on her to introduce the practice, shrunk from attempting it, especially in the presence of one like George Dilwyn, to whom she looked up with a degree of fear.

Mildred's Court, Tenth Month, 30th.—After breakfast, my husband and I set off from Plashet in my father's coach, with nurse Barns, for Mildred's Court. I felt rather low at the prospect before me, and more so when I saw the state of the house; confusion in every part. I had a bed-room turned into a sitting-room, put in order, and then went and put myself in order for dinner; our brother William dined with us. I spent rather a pleasant afternoon, which is to me quite a rarity. Joseph and I had a comfortable evening. Both, I believe, feeling the true comfort, I may say blessing, of being, at last, quiet in our own house. All seemed to shine upon us. May we mutually endeavour to hold all in subservience to that Being, to whom all our thoughts, wishes, and actions, are known. I sometimes feel the self-interestedness of wishing to be good, for, after all, what earthly enjoyment is like it? may we not stop short in our career, but try to run the race that is set before us.

Eleventh Month, 7th.—George Dilwyn came to-day; I feel almost overcome with my own weakness, when with such people.

11*th.*—After breakfast, I believed it better to propose reading in the Bible, but I felt doing it, particularly as my brother William was here; not liking the appearance of young people, like us, appearing to profess more than they who had lived here before us. However I put off, and put off, till both William and Joseph went down; I then felt uneasy under it, and when Joseph came back I told him, as I did before, what I wished; he, at last, sat down, having told George Dilwyn my desire. I began to read the 46th Psalm, but was so overcome that I could hardly read, and gave it to Joseph to finish.

12*th.*—I rather felt this morning it would have been right for me to read the Bible again, and stop George Dilwyn and Joseph reading something else. Now stopping G. D. was a difficult thing; for a person like me to remind him! however I did not fully do as I thought right, for I did not openly tell G. D. we were going to read, but spoke to my husband, so as for him to hear; then he read, I knowing I had not done my best.

14*th.*—I again felt some difficulty at reading the Bible; however I got through well. George Dilwyn encouraging me, by saying, he thought I portioned the reading well. After a little bustling we set off for Hampstead. I was there told by ——, he thought my manners had too much of the courtier in them, which I know to be the case, for my disposition leads me to hurt no one, that I can avoid: and I do sometimes but just keep to truth with people, from a natural yielding to them in such things as please them. I think doing so in moderation, is pleasant and useful in society. It is amongst the things that produce the harmony of society; for the truth must not be spoken out at all times, at least not the whole truth. I will give an instance of what I mean. Suppose any one was to show me the colour of a room, that I thought pretty, I should say so, although I thought others more so, and omit saying that; perhaps I am wrong, I do not know if I be not, but it will not always do to tell our minds. This I have observed (and I am sorry for it), that I feel it hard, when duty dictates, to do what I think may hurt others. I believe this feeling of mine originates in self-love, from the dislike of being myself the cause of pain and uneasiness.

15th.—George Dilwyn said, for our encouragement this morning, that he had seen, since he had been with us, the efficacy of reading in the Bible the first thing,—he thought it a good beginning for the day.

19th.—Dear Kitty and Priscilla came this afternoon; I felt a good deal at seeing them. How dear they are to me! George Dilwyn came home this evening; and it was rather odd, but we fell into unusually interesting conversation.

22nd.—I think I have tried to do better to-day, and a bad cold has prevented my saying much, which is so often a stumbling-block, for that little member, the tongue, is very hard to command; until the root be mended, I cannot expect the branches to flourish, or to bring forth much fruit. Thoughts, words, and actions, appear to spring from a corrupt source. I feel my sisters a lesson to me, they seem so much more virtuous.

Twelfth Month, 1st.—We dined at the Barclays' to-day; I felt it pleasant being at Clapham, although the change of society I have, is at times a trial; it requires much strength to be on one's guard.

5th—To-day, we had the W——s and C——s, to dinner. We provided handsomely, but I much disapprove of a luxurious table; as superfluity at table appears to me as bad, if not worse than other things.

8th.—I value being alone with my husband; it is a quiet

that I have not lately enjoyed, and it does seem to me, at this time, one of the great blessings of life; talking of blessings, am I not ungrateful, when thus surrounded with them, to be wishing for more? it is a pity!

9*th.*—Anna Savery drank tea here; we had not sat long after tea, before we fell into silence. During the time, I first felt a sort of anxiety for the welfare of us young travellers, and it came strongly across my mind, Is it not my duty openly to express it? this put me into an agitation not easily to be described; and I continued in this state, which was a truly painful one, nearly feeling it my duty to pray aloud for us; oh, how hard it did seem! I tried to run from it, but I found the most safety in trying to wait upon God; hoping, if it were imagination, to overcome it; if it were duty, that I might be obedient. Towards the latter end, I felt *more* inclined towards obedience. But what an obstacle is my not holding my will in subserviency to that of my Maker; for perhaps, after all, it was only a trial of my obedience, that would not have been called for, but to show me how far I was from a resigned state of heart. I felt oppressed the rest of the evening.

10*th.*—I awoke in a burdened state of mind; I thought it better to relieve it to my dear husband, and found comfort in doing so; he warned me against imagination. I must try to trust in the Lord, and I hope to find safety. I felt quite in a state of agitation till we went to Meeting; it made me feel almost ill in body, both last night and this morning; however my mind was sweetly calmed in the Meeting, and I felt vastly relieved from my terrors, and a little love and trusting in the Heavenly Master. I was almost ready to do whatever might be right for me. Oh! may I give up to what is called for at my hand, and may I not be deceived, but follow the true Shepherd, for my feet seem much inclined to wander!

14*th.*—I attended both Meetings as usual, and, as usual, I came from them, flat and discouraged. To attend our place of worship, and there spend almost all the time in worldly thoughts, is, I fear, too great a mark of how my time is mostly spent; indeed, my life appears, at this time, to be spent to little more purpose than eating, drinking, sleeping, and clothing myself. But if we analyze the employment of most, what do they more than, in some way, attend to the bodily wants of themselves or others? What is our work, the good we do to the poor, &c., &c., but for the body!

In reply to the letter of a Friend, Elizabeth Fry, at this period, thus describes her own state of mind, and anxiety for spiritual advance:—

Mildred's Court, *First Month*, 1801.

In referring to thy former letter, I remembered thou there hailed me as a fellow-traveller towards a better country; and I remember feeling encouragement from it: I am doubtful how far thou couldest now do so, but I trust, although I see little, and feel hardly anything of good in my own mind, that I am not yet quite forsaken, as one dead to good works. I am at times ready to feel, what shall I do? for if I were sure this state was out of my own power, I needed only quietly rest, hoping for better times: but my fear is, that, from want of more watchfulness, I am so continually devoted to things of this world, as to blind my spiritual sight from observing things belonging to the other. There are times when my anxiety for good is great indeed, and for a short time, it is my endeavour to seek strength where I hope to find it; but alas! my good wishes and good endeavours are of short, very short duration. I often remember that part of Scripture (more particularly at Meeting) where our Saviour says to Simon, "Couldest not thou watch with me one hour?" I feel able to draw some consolation from what I here read, when I see that others so great and good have found it hard to do so; but I experience the force of the question. I have, at times, great fears that I may be led astray in matters of the first importance, for there is a power that will, at times, deceive the unwary mind, for we may remember it can even put on the appearance of an angel of light. It was my lot, in very early life, to be much in company with Deists, and to be rather a warm advocate of their doctrines. I now, in many shapes, feel myself touched with these early imbibed opinions; for it appears to be that, unless I be, by a very superior power, really lifted above these opinions, my poor weak nature is apt to doubt almost everything. How poor is the enjoyment, how dark is our prospect, when the enlightening rays of true religion are taken from us! I did not expect thus to have opened my heart to thee, but one thing led on to another. I now and then remember a remark of thine, and thou believed a soul was still living to that which is good, whilst it partook of that unity, that the poor travellers Zion-ward are favoured to feel towards each other; I have sometimes hoped, when thinking of it, that I am not yet quite dead to such things; as I feel my heart nearly drawn towards some of those whom I believe to be truly making progress in this blessed journey, and while I, at times, so peculiarly love the disciple, I hope I am not an enemy to the Master.

First Month, 11*th*, 1801.—I attended both Meetings; what wishes I had at moments for good! and how surprisingly ineffectual they were!

15*th*.—I set off early for Newington, to see J. G. Bevan, who I heard was poorly. I think my visit answered. I met with a very kind reception, and he appeared pleased to see me. He proposed to me reading with the family on First-day evening; which is what I have often thought of, but do not wish to practise, until my husband and I are unitedly clearer on the subject.

Second Month, 3*rd*.—This morning, after writing notes, &c., &c., I walked out and went to see a poor woman whom I half like, and half do not, as there is something in her very odd; however, I spent much time about her. I then read the letters from home, which were comfortable and satisfactory. I was just dressed for company; we had a rather pleasant visit, but I think, of late, I more and more dislike society of every kind, I really wish for a more retired life; my present constant liability to company seems too much for my weak mind.

4th.—I went to Meeting as usual: Sarah Lynes mentioned to the Meeting the manner in which she had accomplished her late journey, and the feelings of reward she experienced; her account struck me very much; her influence was, on me at least, truly pleasant and satisfactory. She afterwards named her concern to visit some Meetings in the City of London, which was also done with remarkable simplicity, and I may say, almost humility. I longed for her continued good, and almost prayed she might be kept in a state of humility. For striking is it how liable, at all stages, we are to fall. I almost longed for the good of the religious, as of some far distant from me. Before the Monthly Meeting finished, Mary Bevan got up and addressed herself to the young women, saying we were not to be discouraged at not being called like her (Sarah Lynes), but that all who endeavoured to perform their duty, should and would equally meet with their reward. I felt much, and longed for good. I think myself at this time on rather dangerous ground, for retirement of mind, or that necessary watchfulness which keeps us poor mortals out of danger, is what I am nearly a stranger to; and in a state of deadness to religion, that has lately been my experience, I am also tried by great fears about what duty may call me to. If these be fears of my own imagination, how much is truth wanted to overcome them. Seek, seek, until I find, and do not give up till the last!

Third Month, 15th.—I felt really better this morning (alluding to previous indisposition) and went to Meeting, but all my small efforts to quiet my thoughts were ineffectual;

the same in the afternoon; it is very serious. Really when I awake in the morning I feel a flatness; when I find my great object of the day no longer appears to be even to wish to do the will of my Creator. But I am as one who has, in some measure, lost his pilot, and is tossed about by the waves of the world. But I trust that there is yet a power that will prevent my drowning: I draw some consolation from my dreams of old, for how often was I near drowning, and yet at last saved.

17*th.*—Mary Ann Galton arrived to-day, every room in our house was full, and altogether, with the tooth-ache, I have hardly had spirit to go through it comfortably.

18*th.*—We had a large dinner-party; I felt unusually poorly and nervous at dinner, being fagged with tooth-ache and the numbers around me.

21*st.*—This morning I proposed to my father to take us to Richmond Hill, as we had never been there. After some doubting we agreed to go, and we set off; before we left London it rained violently, but we persevered,—I was fully of the mind it was better to do so; but hardly expressed it enough, for I make myself appear almost weak by my fear of other people. I feel, with my father, almost always a difficulty in boldly doing what I think right. One great pleasure in the day has been being so much with him, and I have quite enjoyed his company. The views and country were delightful; it appeared to do me good once more to look at the beauties of nature, and to see the little lambs, and all was very pleasant.

25*th.*—I feel almost overcome with the multiplicity of visitings and goings out.

Fourth Month, 9*th.*—We set off this morning on our journey to Norfolk. I felt leaving my dearest husband. The beauties of nature were striking—violets and primroses quite decorated the hedges.

Fifth Month, 8*th.*—Of late I have been cumbered with the little things in life that are not worth being worried about.

I have fixed dinners for the Yearly Meeting with Jane King.

During the fortnight occupied by the Yearly Meeting, Mildred's Court was, according to a very general custom among the Society, an open house for the reception of the Friends assembled in London on that occasion, from all parts of the kingdom: some were inmates there during the time, whilst the parties at dinner were generally very numerous.

Fifth Month, 15th.—We went in the evening to see a Friend (Joseph Lancaster), who kept a school for poor children. I felt a wish that the young man might be preserved in humility; for I know, from experience, it is a hard matter, when we have the apparent approbation of many, and more particularly of those whom we esteem.

16*th.*—I was rather busy this morning. After dinner, our dear cousin Priscilla arrived; I felt seeing her, I love her very much; being with such, has a great effect on me, where they interest me as she does; but may I not be led by man, but by his Maker.

27*th.*—I went to Gracechurch Street Meeting this morning, and to the Meeting of Discipline in the afternoon, which tired me.

29*th.*—After dinner, we attended our Women's Meeting, at four o'clock, which lasted till nearly eight o'clock, it was to me very long and very tedious; indeed it may be, and I doubt not is in great part my own weakness; but to hold fast my faith, I found in this Yearly Meeting, no instrument ought to be looked to. I am afresh come to this conclusion, that only the clear dictates of duty should lead us to act, even in matters of religion; that we should be very careful in expressing even a religious sentiment, without great clearness, and more particularly where others are concerned. How exceeding cautiously should religious advice be given to others! it should not be done, without strong and clear feelings of duty, for I know from experience, such things are apt, even if they be given as encouragement, to discourage or weaken the feeble mind, if out of place; I believe it better to do too little than too much in them. Notwithstanding the many remarks that I have made, I trust I shall, in the end, be better for this time, for I have seen much to love and admire in the instruments, and I trust the principle is not weakened within me. May it lead me to seek deeply to serve my Maker in singleness of heart, for that appears the only way to rectitude of conduct; and not to forget the numerous rocks there are to split upon, on every side. These observations should teach me the necessity of keeping a constant watch and dependence on my Creator.

Sixth Month, 5th.—I had most of this morning in quietness, which was quite a treat to me; I wrote my journal, settled my accounts, and was not destitute of a wish to do right: we had many to dinner, which rather vexed me, as I had set my mind on quiet.

15*th.*—If I can, with truth, acknowledge it to be my first wish to do my best, although I may not feel the sensible gratification of doing my duty, I may yet be really doing it. If I do all I can, I have no occasion to fear sooner or later meeting with my reward. I was rather disappointed at our having company, indeed we have now little time alone: it is quite a serious thing, our being so constantly liable to interruptions as we are. I do not think, since we married, we have had one-fourth of our meals alone. I long for more retirement, but it appears out of our power to procure it; and therefore it is best to be as patient under interruptions as we can, but I think it a serious disadvantage to young people setting out in life.

Plashet, Seventh Month, 9th.—We are so much from home, and in such continual bustles, that really when I am here, I feel at a loss for regular employment. I just have time enough to keep things in order; engagement follows engagement so rapidly, day after day, week after week, owing principally to our number of near connections, that we appear to live for others, rather than ourselves : our plan of sleeping out so often, I by no means like, and yet it appears impossible to prevent it; to spend one's life in visiting, and being visited, seems sad. Joseph Lancaster came in after breakfast, I had some talk with him about poor people; he enlightened me about his school plans, but not generally about the poor.

10*th.*—I had to fix with Jane King about the nursery, and to reprove a servant for something I did not approve, which kept me in a state of agitation for some time, it is so trying to me to reprove any one; it is so very trying to my natural disposition, partly I suppose from a feeling of self-love that does not like being the cause of pain; partly I suppose from feeling for others. I mostly feel satisfaction when I take courage to act the mistress; as it is so much out of my nature.

11*th.*—It now and then strikes me to how little end are all these employments that occupy us; we seem principally occupied in clothing, feeding, and taking care of our bodies, and yet I trust if even that be done in a right spirit, we still are doing our duty, and it is in these actions about our bodies that our minds and principles act also, if it be our object to do all things to the glory of God. But we are apt rather to do things in subserviency to our own will, rather than the will of our Maker; we therefore devote ourselves to these outward and bodily things. Now, when such things are done, which I believe they may be, under a devotional spirit, we are not injured by being occupied with such trifles.

Eighth Month, 5th.—I feel that when I do my part towards really performing my duty, it sheds a sweet and sober colouring over all my occupations; but when I do not, it appears to cast a mist that I am obliged to find my way as well as I can, without my guide.

15*th.*—I have had an interesting talk with my dear sister

Rachel: she appears to me to have perceived that which will direct her steps. But how hard it is deeply, strictly, and for a long time together, to have our first object to serve our Creator—for at first there is a natural glee, as for something new, and then we feel we have to pass through lukewarmness, which is a dangerous state; I believe one, where many are lost. May I be carried through it!

It is evident that the circumstances in which Elizabeth Fry was placed at Mildred's Court, were too fatiguing for her, then approaching her first confinement, so as to depress, not merely her bodily powers and her natural energy, but also, in a degree, her spiritual liveliness. In anticipation of this event, her active mind had already occupied itself in forming nursery arrangements.

Her eldest child was born in the Eighth Month, and to this event succeeded the pleasures and anxieties of a young mother; upon which, perhaps, no one could have entered with a more lively sense, either of their enjoyment or responsibility.

My thoughts, she says, are now very often in my nursery, fixing plans for children. I am very full of castles about my good management; but all must be, should be, held in subserviency to a great and divine Power, who alone knows what is best for them and us; and it is to be hoped He will, in His mercy, guide the hands of the parents to lead them in the right path in every way. I am a great friend to close and constant attention to early education, even the very first years of a child's life.

Ninth Month, 12th.—I have hardly had time or strength, as yet, to describe the events I have lately passed through. I did not experience that joy which some women describe, when my husband first brought me my little babe, little darling! I hardly knew what I felt for it, but my body and spirits were so extremely weak, I could only just bear to look at those I loved. I felt the dear baby at first a quiet source of pleasure, but she early became a subject for my weakness and low spirits to dwell upon, so that I almost wept when she cried; but I hope, as bodily strength recovers, strength of mind will come with it.

20th.—I have now pretty much recovered. I was at Meeting this morning; there appears great cause for my being thankful to have got through so great a trial, and to have a dear little living girl; but we are not always sensible of the blessings we enjoy.

23rd.—Certainly I am ignorant about the management of such young infants, but I do not feel uneasy about the charge of her body; from my self-confidence I fear; but I believe if we endeavour to do our duty, even in such things, we shall find the way. I much wish to avoid my mother-in-law's very "cotting" plan, for a degree of hardiness I think most desirable—I think being too careful and tender really makes them more subject to indisposition.

Tenth Month, 1st.—My present feelings for the babe are so acute as to render me at times unhappy, from an over anxiety about her, such an one as I never felt before for any one. Now it appears to me, this over anxiety arises from extreme love, weak spirits and state of health, and not being under the influence of principle, that would lead me to overcome these natural feelings, as far as they tend to my misery. For if I were under the influence of principle, I might trust that my dear infant indeed was under the care and protection of an infinitely wise and just Providence, that permits her little sufferings for some good end, that I know not of. How anxiously do I hope this poor dear baby may be held in resignation by me to the Divine will. Oh! that I might feel dependence on that Almighty arm about her, and about other things. Beyond every thing else, I wish to do my duty, idle and relaxed as I am, in performing it.

Mildred's Court, 10th.—I here sit hearing the great noise and bustle of the Illumination for Peace; my husband and the rest of the party are gone out to see it; my dearest babe is sleeping in the room. This evening I am very tired, and the noise of the mob nearly makes my head ache. This is the way in which they show their joy! it does not seem to me the right manner of showing our gratitude, as it appears to lead to drunkenness and vice. I think true gratitude should lead us to endeavour to retain the blessing, or to make good use of it, by more virtue in ourselves, and encouraging others to the same.

Joseph and Elizabeth Fry visited Norfolk, taking their little treasure, the lovely infant; and E. F.'s journal continues:--

Earlham, 21*st*.—We have had a comfortable journey; meeting them at Thetford was very pleasant, they appeared so delighted to see us. I altogether entered this place in much agitation, our reception was delightful; my father and all so much admired our little darling, and seemed to love her so dearly, that it was delightful to me: it was indeed a striking sight to see them all meet her, so much real interest was shown. Yesterday I went once more to Norwich Meeting,—my reception was very warm.

Mildred's Court, *Eleventh Month*, 25*th*.—My cough has been so poorly that my husband called in Dr. Simms. I asked his advice about our little one being inoculated; he strongly recommended the cow-pox, and said that he would undertake the care of her if we liked: I think highly of his judgment, and I believe it to be our duty to avoid evil, both bodily and mentally. So trifling a complaint as the cow-pox, being likely to prevent so dreadful a disease as the small-pox, at least it appears justifiable to try it; although the idea is not pleasant, it almost looks like taking too much on ourselves to give a child a disease. But I altogether was easy to do it. I felt a good deal about the operation, which was very little and easily performed. What a wonderful discovery it is, if it really prevent the small-pox.

30*th.*— I went to see a poor woman: it is always a cross to me leaving my child, but going over the bridge I enjoy; the air, sky, and water look so sweetly.

Twelfth Month, 5th.—I was up in pretty good time, dressed by eight, and after reading, settled my great housekeeping accounts. I wrote to cousin Priscilla, my uncle Barclay, and my father. This evening I feel very flat, rather in a low state, partly perhaps bodily weakness. I feel almost ready to pant after the courts of the Lord.

First Month, 26th, 1802.—It is more than a month since I wrote my journal; I am sorry for it, but I have been Martha-like, and so much engrossed in the affairs of this life, that little time has been spent in reviewing my conduct; indeed, I appear very much to have taken my flight from spiritual things. It is not my feeling bereft of the comforts of religion that alarms me, it is my not sufficiently seeking after them, I fear; for I hardly ever am on the watch for the Master's coming. I may say my heart has now and then been full, almost to prayer, for my husband, child, and myself; particularly for my little infant, that we may not prove stumbling-blocks in its way to salvation; if it please God it should live to an age of understanding. I believe it would be better for me, if I were in a more constant habit of daily retirement; for it would afford me time for self-examination, which I am so unaccustomed to, and if I only sit quietly, I believe I may find it useful, although I feel of myself I can do nothing.

28*th.*—I do heartily enjoy our being alone, and falling into some plans: not being interrupted, I appear naturally to fall into employment; and it is so sweet to have quiet plans at my own dear home. How much I think my marriage tends to my outward comfort; it is wonderful to me to observe how every act of mine has prospered, that has been done under the anxious wish of serving my Creator in it.

Second Month, 13*th.*—My poor baby has been so poorly, that we took her to Dr. Willan's; she has had a cough and is really unwell. I felt much tired, and longed for resignation and patience.

20th.—I felt our dearest child in great danger, as did many besides me, indeed I believe all of us. This was indeed a trial, but I was supported with some resignation of soul, feeling the weight of that part of the prayer, "Thy will, and not mine, be done."

21st.—As the morning advanced, my little infant began to change from a very feverish state to an almost deadly languid one, that I believe most present thought might be the beginning of a more awful change. She sat on my lap, I happened to be also very faint at the time; I think I may say, I felt resigned to the all-wise dispensations of Providence, which was a great blessing; my mind felt depending on that Power that alone can support in the day of trial. I desire to feel that of myself I can do nothing, and that I may remember the blessing of being able to say, "Thy will, and not mine, be done."

23d.—Our little one appears mending, although very poorly, faint, and weak: her recovery seems more than I can enter into, at present, with a joyful heart. But I feel rather as if quietly waiting for the will of her Maker to be done. Some would perhaps call me insensible to the blessing. May I continue to look to the all-merciful Fountain of Good, and hold my submission to His will, and properly estimate the numerous blessings afforded me: and may I be thankful for my little one. My prayer seems to have been heard, that whether she lived or died she might not suffer much.

Fourth Month, 19th.—Oh! may my obedience keep pace with my knowledge at this time; my knowledge of good appears small; my longings to be better are only known by a Superior Power, who I trust will, in time, have mercy on me. I have this day prayed, that, in this day of darkness, I may not prove an obstruction in the way of others; truly a South Land is my portion,—I only long for the wells of living water.

Fifth Month, 18th.—The sight of my uncle Joseph this morning rejoiced me; he is to me, in every point of view, so dear; I love him as a religious character, and as my near and dear relation. We had many Friends to dinner, and many to supper.

19*th.*—This day Yearly Meeting began generally. I was in my usual lukewarm, flat state, full of the wanderings of imagination; but I believe, as a spectator, Meetings were more satisfactory than last year. We had a very large number to dinner.

31*st.*—Yearly Meeting is now, I am happy to say, finished. I attended all the Meetings but one. In some of them I was much more interested than last year, and felt for the interests of the Society. We have seen a good deal of Friends, and I think I admire them more than I did last year. I have had a few more serious feelings than usual: I have been always devoted to the world, except now and then, when my heart has anxiously hoped for something better. I have felt very much how we are all surrounded with continual temptations, and how very hard it is to hold fast that which is good; I see so many faults in myself, that I fear there are many I know nothing of, from not sufficiently seeking for them; for I observe faults in others who are better than myself, that I believe they know nothing of.

During the autumn of this year, Elizabeth Fry took a long journey into the North of England with her husband; a few entries respecting it are presented to the reader.

Coventry, Tenth Month, 2nd.—We were up in good time, and went to see Shakspeare's monument, at Stratford-upon-Avon; a sweet country churchyard; in the church we saw the monument. We breakfasted at Warwick, and saw the castle and church; the outside of the castle I liked very much, the inside pretty well. We are at an unpleasant inn here; but I have learnt one lesson—that I do not think in travelling we are sufficiently cautious in our behaviour to inn servants, but hurry them and worry them too much: I hope to be more cautious in future. I went to see D——

L—— and his wife, and by accident went to the wrong house; I made several droll blunders, and became confused.

Wolverhampton, 6th.—During our journey here, I was very low and anxious on account of our little baby, who appeared uneasy, and in much pain. She seemed suddenly really unwell. I wish my heart not to be too much set on her, or her health; for I should endeavour to remember, she is taken care of by One infinitely wiser than I am. All medicine, gum-lancing, &c., is one of my trials, for I do not like or approve putting children to unnecessary pain, unless I have good ground for believing it right to do it; and yet I fear my cowardice improperly preventing my doing it.

Rock Ferry, 10th.—We admired Chester,—the town is so extraordinary; from the walks on the walls the country is beautiful. We could not prudently go over to Liverpool on account of the rain, therefore we remained here, which I believe we all enjoyed; the quiet within was so pleasant, when the storms without were so violent, and I enjoyed my beloved husband's company; what earthly pleasure is equal to the enjoyment of real unity with the nearest of all ties, husband and children.

Liverpool, 12th.—Our patience was rather tried, by waiting from breakfast time till twelve o'clock, for a passage over. My fears of the water are surprisingly gone off, I hardly felt any fear, although the wind was high, and we sailed. I believe as we grow older, and have greater and more serious things to occupy us, those little feelings go off; I do not think I am nearly such a coward about some little things, as I was before I married.

Manchester, 17th.—We drank tea at John Thorp's; I really admire and love that man: I think we seldom see so much of good, united with a cultivated understanding, and the sweet simplicity of religion, as in him. I long for help to penetrate the clouds that surround me, for I feel that of myself I can do nothing.

Keswick, 25th.—This morning we went in the rain to see

a very fine waterfall, it was a grand and beautiful sight; but I do not much like this country, at this time of the year, it looks so barren and dreary. This evening I went with Joseph on horseback to see some fine waterfalls. There is too much water in this place, and about here, to please my taste,—too much lake, and too much of barren mountain; too little snugness, and too few fine trees.

26th.—This would have appeared to me, some time ago, rather a fearful day; we first took a long ride, part of it over rather frightful roads, on the edge of a precipice, without any wall or guard to it. This evening, my husband and I climbed Skiddaw; when we arrived at the top, after some pain and fatigue, we were almost in a whirlwind, and so extremely cold and damp, being in the midst of a cloud, and the wind so violent, that it appeared almost impossible to stand against it: however we got down safely.

Mildred's Court, Eleventh Month, 18*th.*—We have had a prosperous journey, and have at last arrived at our comfortable home. It really looks quite sweet and nice; it is a great thing to have gone so far, and returned home safely.

Their family was at this time increased by her brother Samuel Gurney's coming to London, to learn the details of business there. He resided some years at Mildred's Court. The shelter of such a residence, in that great and depraved Metropolis, can hardly be too highly estimated; but beside this, he had the advantage of his sister's close and watchful care. She had been much attached to him, when young; and it was an interest and pleasure to her to have him for an inmate. Her labours were eminently blessed to him—and, in his faithful love through life, she reaped a rich reward.

First Month, 5*th,* 1803.—I feel hardly willing to begin this year without observing how very numerous my blessings are; as far as outward blessings go, I believe I want nothing: may I endeavour to be aware of it, and may it stimulate me afresh to strive to serve that Power which has conferred them on me. My secret trials and temptations are known by no man, that inclination to lukewarmness of mind, and also forgetfulness of what is good, are powerful temptations. They do not, like some others, make a very conspicuous appearance; but they undermine our strength, for want of sufficient effort and sufficient watchfulness; I look forward with much hope, that I may be supported in the day of expected trial. But if I seek so little for a close acquaintance with what is good; if I cannot now endeavour humbly to place my confidence in the Power that alone can deliver, is it likely that, in such emergency, I shall be able to do it? I believe if rightly influenced, I might in some small measure rejoice, if I could feelingly believe that these afflictions, which are but for a moment, work for us a far more exceeding and eternal weight of glory. Suffer we must in this world, and the less we kick against the pricks the happier for us.

She thus records the birth of her second child, which took place in Third Month.

Fourth Month, 12th.—My heart abounded with joy and gratitude, when my dear little girl was born, perfect and lovely. Words are not equal to express my feelings, for I was most mercifully dealt with, my soul was so quiet, and so much supported.

Plashet, Fifth Month, 21st.—I have been long prevented writing my journal, by a severe attack of indisposition. It is difficult exactly to express what I have gone through, but it has been, now and then, a time of close trial; my feelings being such, at times, as to be doubtful whether life or death would be my portion. One night I was, I believe, very seriously ill; I never remember feeling so forcibly, how hard a trial it was in prospect, to part with life. Much as my mind, as well as body, was then tried in this emergency, still I felt forcibly an inward support, and it reminded me of that text of Scripture, "Can a woman forget her sucking child, yea they may forget, yet will I not forget thee." And then I told those around me, that I was so ill, I could almost forget my child; but that I felt the existence of a Power that could *never* forget. I have gone through much since, in various ways, from real bodily weakness, and also the trials of a nervous imagination: no one knows but those who have felt them, how hard they are to bear, for they lead the mind to look for trouble, and it requires much exertion not to be led away by them; nothing, I believe, allays them so much as the quieting influence of religion, and that leads us to endeavour after quietness under them, not looking beyond the present. But they are a regular bodily disorder, that I believe no mental exertion can cure or overcome, but we must endeavour not to give way to them.

Mildred's Court, Sixth Month, 5th.—Since I last wrote, I have been gradually becoming better, but still I feel not in usual health; my nerves are in an irritable state, I am soon overcome and overdone. I have been at Meeting, and am now once more entering upon my usual occupation: I fear I am not so much benefited as I ought to be, by the illness I have lately gone through; for I have so forcibly felt—What am I, without a hold on something beyond this life?

Soon after this she visited Norfolk with her husband, taking also her children.

Earlham, Seventh Month, 30th.—I went to Norwich this morning with my husband, and when there, we received a letter from William, expressing a desire for Joseph's immediate return. The account rather tried me; and also the apprehension about the French coming, cast a gloom over the party; John came in the evening, and it was truly pleasant, all twelve of us, and the two children being here together. But partly owing to circumstances, the uncertainty of human events so deeply impressed me, that I could not avoid feeling the doubt of our all meeting again.

The fear of an invasion of the French, and the daily expectation of their landing, caused such general alarm at this time, that Joseph Fry was summoned by his brother, "to be at his post." On his return, he found preparations had been made for flooding the marshes of the river Lea, and breaking down the bridges on the Essex road; whilst his father-in-law was also prepared, so soon as the French should land, to convey his daughters into the Isle of Ely; still regarded by the East Anglian portion of England as a "camp of refuge."

Mildred's Court, Eighth Month, 22nd.—My brother William came to town in haste, to say my mother was come home very ill. I went with Dr. Willan to Plashet to see her. I was quite sorry to find her so ill, and felt real love for her. My time is very much occupied with other people, indeed I find it has a very dissipating effect; and it is difficult to keep my mind in its right centre, when it is so often diverted from it.

Tenth Month, 4th.—After reading a little, I went some way off to see a poor woman. After searching a long time in one of the disagreeable parts of London, I could not find her, but I was directed to another poor person who lived near the place, and although I believe the first woman had deceived me, it led me to serve two others that I have reason to think really wanted. I felt quite in my element serving the poor, and although I was much tired with looking about, it gave me much pleasure; it is an occupation my nature is so fond of; I wish not to take merit to myself beyond my desert, but it brings satisfaction with it more than most things.

Upton, Third Month, 15th, 1804.—Since I last wrote, I have more closely witnessed the scene of death, than I ever did before. Last First-day morning, about three o'clock, my mother died; I was with her, at times, on Seventh-day; and although I have every reason to believe she died happily, I did not experience those awful, sweet feelings, I should have looked for at so serious a time. On First-day morning, I went into the room, and sat some time with the corpse; it was very affecting to me to see it, and I was a good deal overcome, and felt it much. I have been surprised how little this event has led me into a serious state of mind, I fear it has not had so profitable an effect upon me as it ought.

The death of her mother-in-law, a woman of powerful mind and understanding, united Elizabeth Fry still more closely with her husband's father; to whom she had been always much attached. From the time of her marriage, he had treated her with uniform kindness and attention: and now, in his affliction, it was her pleasure, as well as her duty, to unite with his own children in soothing his declining years; more time was consequently passed at Plashet with him, and his only daughter, Elizabeth.

At this period of her life, the poor shared much of her attention, and notwithstanding the impediments offered by a great Metropolis, to a young and delicate woman personally visiting them, she persevered occasionally in this habit, until withdrawn from it, by residence in the country, and the increase of more important duties. Her energy and courage in pursuing this object were great, as is proved by the following anecdote.

One cold winter day she was accosted by a woman asking charity in the street, with a half naked little child in her arms, very ill with the hooping-cough; grieved at the appearance of the child, and her suspicions excited by the evasive answers of the woman, Elizabeth Fry offered to accompany her home, and there relieve her necessities: this the woman tried to elude, but determined on her purpose, she succeeded in following her into a low, back street, where, in a wretched, filthy house, the melancholy spectacle presented itself, of a number of sick and neglected infants, not only without comforts, but with the aggravations of misery. The next day, when the medical attendant of her own children went, at her request, to assist the little sufferers, the room was empty, woman and children gone, nor was any trace ever found of them. On inquiry among the neighbours, it was discovered that these were parish children, put to this woman to nurse, who kept them in this condition, not merely to assist her purposes of mendicity, but with the intention of shortening their lives, and then, by concealing their death, receiving the pittance allotted for their maintenance.

It has already been shown, that in 1801, her attention was called to Joseph Lancaster, who, struggling under difficulties and embarrassments, had assembled around him a large school of very poor children, in an upper chamber in Southwark.

She had also formed some valuable friendships with superior and excellent persons. Of this number was her cousin Joseph Gurney Bevan, her father's early friend, whom she especially esteemed; John Hull of Uxbridge, and Rachel Smith, a friend living in London; all judicious counsellors, and her frequent companions.

During several succeeding years, she was permitted to pass through many illnesses and much suffering; but her spirit bowed in meek submission under the refining process; deep conflict was often her portion, until her bonds were broken, and she was enabled "to rejoice in the Lord, and joy in the God of her salvation." Earnest desires for the religious welfare of others, animated her soul.

The impression which, during the early stages of her religious course, had been made on her mind, that if faithful to her God, she would be required to advocate His holy cause as a minister of the Gospel of Christ, continued deeply to impress her. This was indeed an awful prospect, from which her whole nature recoiled.

Seventh Month, 10th.—Since I last wrote I have gone on pretty comfortably in most respects; at times a degree of lowness, but I have altogether been much more encouraged than I was, and feel, at present, able to leave my fears; trusting in the mercy of Him who may afflict. Oh! may I be ready to bear! I have had many desires after good, and I think reading a little of "No Cross, no Crown," has been rather a stimulus to me, to endeavour after more strictly attending to that voice, that instructs us how to take up the daily cross, in overcoming our natural propensities. I was reading in Jeremiah to-day, "Cursed be they who serve the Lord deceitfully," and I hoped that might not be my case. What I long for is, to serve the Lord with strict integrity, keeping self-love in subserviency.

Her eldest son was born in the Seventh Month of this year; her confinement was followed by a trying and tedious illness.

Bath, Ninth Month, 24th.—Since I last wrote, I have been very unwell, and passed through great suffering, owing to great sickness, faintness, and nervous irritability: however, each trial has had its alleviation; I have not once quite sunk; I have experienced, that though at times it has been rather hard to bear, I do not think it has been too much for me; for although I have felt the wounding hand, yet I have also soon found that the same Power could, and did, make whole.

Mildred's Court, First Month, 14th, 1805.—A new year begun—one of my first desires upon waking was, that I might improve in it.

Plashet, Second Month, 5th.—Since I last wrote, I have been much occupied with many things: rather more than usual about the poor. I have been desirous that attending to them as I do, may not prove a snare to me, for I think acting charitably leads us often to receive more credit than we deserve, or at least to fancy so; it is one of those things that give my nature pleasure, therefore I believe I am no further praiseworthy than that I give way to a natural inclination. Attending the afflicted is one of those things that so remarkably brings its reward with it, that we may rest in a sort of self-satisfaction which is dangerous; but I often feel the blessing of being so situated, as to be able to assist the afflicted, and sometimes a little to relieve their distresses.

11*th.*—We ought to make it an object in conversation and in conduct, to endeavour to oblige those we are with, and rather to make the pleasure of others our object, than our own; I am clear it is a great virtue to be able constantly to yield in little things; it begets the same spirit in others, and renders life happy.

Fifth Month, 7th.—Yesterday, my sister Eliza Fry was here; we were saying something about the children's dress; and she remarked that for the sake of others, (she meant the fear of not setting a good example,) she would not do so and so. I said it struck me that those who do their duty with integrity, are serving others as well as themselves, and do more real good to the cause of true religion, than in looking much outwardly, either to what others do or think. I believe that conscience will sometimes lead us to feel for others, and not act so as materially to hurt a weak brother; but I believe we should seldom find that we hurt those whose opinion would be worth caring for, if we kept close to the witness in our own hearts. If I were going to do a thing, I should endeavour to find whether it appeared to me in any way wrong, and whether I should feel easy to do it; looking secretly for help, where it is to be found; and there I believe I should leave it; and if it led me to act rather differently from some, I should probably be doing more good to society, than in any conformity, merely on account of others, for if I should be preserved in the way of obedience in other things, it would, in time, show from whence such actions sprang; and I think this very spirit of conforming in trifles to the opinion of others, leads into forms, that may one day prove a stumbling-block to the progress of our Society; whereas, if we attend to the principle that brought us together, it will lead us out of forms, and not into them.

Earlham, Sixth Month, 7th.—There is quite a change since I last wrote, I have passed through much illness among the children; the Yearly Meeting, and since that, coming here. After my return from Plashet, dear little Rachel was very poorly, and poor John; all these things tried me, but I endeavoured to bear them with patience and cheerfulness. The Yearly Meeting was very interesting to me, I felt a good deal about it; in the first place, I am struck afresh with the beauty of our principles: but so am I also with the great want of simplicity and integrity in us who profess them; for I am willing to believe, that if we more closely attended to them, there would be more unity, more clearness, and more promptness in our manner of attending to the business of the Society. I used to fear that a selfish principle frequently rose up amongst us, rather than the simple love and fear of God, which spirit I think alone should rule, in the management of the discipline intended to protect our religious principles. The dread I had over me, in Plaistow Meeting, of saying something, impressed me in most of the Meetings. I had such clear ideas in some of the Meetings; but I did not believe it necessary for my salvation to do it, and I believe hardly any motive short of that, could induce me. Once, in hearing the queries answered, that many were negligent in attending Week-day Meetings, it struck me, it arose from allowing the business of the world to stand too much in competition with the things of God, and of how much more importance one was than the other; for a right attention to religious duties, enables us much better to perform our temporal ones.—I have enjoyed coming here, and being with them.

Seventh Month, 3rd.—It appears to me, that we, who desire to be the servants of Christ, must expect to do a part of our Master's work; which, no doubt, is to bear with the weaknesses and infirmities of human nature; and if we be favoured to feel them, and not sink under them, we may be enabled in time to help others to bear *their* burdens; and it appears to me, that all Christian travellers must expect to pass through, in their measure, the temptations and trials their Master did on earth.

Mildred's Court, 19*th*.—Yesterday, and the day before, I have been driven from one thing to another, and from one person to another, as is usual in this place. I have feared my attention being quite diverted from good. But I have also thought that doing our duty is most effectually serving the Lord. May I therefore endeavour to do mine, and not be impatient at my numerous interruptions, but strive to centre my mind in an humble desire to do the will of my Creator, which will, through all, bring a degree of quietness.

Mildred's Court, Second Month, 15*th*, 1806.—I have been confined nearly all this week with a bad cough, and still continue poorly. I have particularly felt the vacancy of all outward help, or consolation, or protection; neither reading good books, writing journals, nor anything else, will, or can do; but placing our dependence on the Power, that calls us out of darkness into light, and that alone can lead us, and point out to us the rocks on which we are likely to split, for though we may certainly profit by the experience of others, yet there is a new way, as it were, for each to tread in: and they are not the same temptations which assail all travellers Zion-ward, but different natures are differently tried: all must first seek for light to guide them (individually), that will teach them in the right time what to do, and what to leave undone, and prove in the end their strong tower, and preservation from all harm.

Earlham, Third Month, 8*th*.—These words of Haggai strike me, chap. i. 5, 6, "Now, therefore, thus saith the Lord of Hosts; consider your ways. Ye have sown much, and bring in little; ye eat, but ye have not enough; ye drink, but ye are not filled with drink; ye clothe you, but there is none warm; and he that earneth wages, earneth wages to put them into a bag with holes." Whether they may not be applied to myself and some others, who go on as it were, saving seed not of the best sort, too much mixed with our own desires, our own gratifications, and therefore we bring forth little.

Fifth Month, 13*th*.—There is One only who knows my heart, and its great wants. To Him then I look, even to Him who has borne our infirmities. Teach me Thy way, lead me in the paths of righteousness for Thy name's sake; give me strength in weakness, if Thou seest meet, O Lord! that I may overcome temptation. O Lord! teach me to do Thy will towards those nearly connected with me: may I be a faithful steward of what may be committed to my trust.

Elizabeth Fry, having been appointed by the Friends of Gracechurch-street Meeting, a visitor to the school and workhouse belonging to the Society at Islington, entered upon the employment with no little interest, as congenial to her former tastes and habits. She visited the establishment as often as her other engagements would permit, always to the general pleasure of the children, who soon learned to appreciate her interest in them, and desires for their good.

Fifth Month, 15*th*.—Yesterday I went to the workhouse to spend the evening with the children; a prospect I have had in view some time, almost ever since I have been on the appointment. I took them things for tea: I dreaded going on many accounts, fearing I should not feel at liberty to make any remarks I might wish to the children, during their reading, which it was my principal object in going to attend. I did not exactly see my way; however, I thought I would *make* my way. I found, after tea, they did not read till nearly eight, and I could not remain later than a little past seven. I spoke to the governess about it, and she was quite willing to alter the hour, and so was the stewardess. I proposed reading a little pamphlet that has lately come out, by

Frederick Smith, to children. There was a solemnity during reading it, so that Ann Withers was in tears most of the time, and some of the children were disposed that way; afterwards, when we had finished, I endeavoured to weigh whether I really had anything to say to them, or not; I thought that I had, and therefore took up the book, as if to explain it; making my own remarks, which appeared to affect the children and the governess, so that those who were on the point of tears really wept. Now this event has made me feel rather odd; it is marvellous to me how I got courage to do it before Ann Withers. I have felt so desirous not to stamp such a thing too highly; for I am ready to believe, though the party appeared to feel what I said so much, it was principally owing to their great tenderness, as that which I said seemed rather to flow naturally from my heart and understanding, than anything really deep from the living fountain. I have desired that this little event may not encourage me too much, for hard things seemed made quite easy. Oh! that in anything like a religious duty, I may never go beyond the right Guide, nor ever give self the praise. Keep me humble, and dependent on Thee, O Lord! even if self suffer in being so.

Mildred's Court, 21*st*.—The Yearly Meeting has been begun for us for some days, as we have had company here very often since Seventh-day. On Second-day, we had rather a choice party to dinner, and, to me, a very solemn opportunity after: I can hardly describe what passed, but it was of that nature, that I considered it as an increase of talent committed to our charge; and ought indeed afresh to stimulate to seek after, and depend upon Him, who alone can protect us. How much I desire that Friends may, at this time, get beyond the natural part, that is indeed corruptible; and get down to the spiritual part, that will unite us in the love of Christ, and lead us to endeavour, in meekness and forbearance one towards another, to come at the right thing. I know well the harmony of Friends is great; but my fear is lest the natural part should be disposed to take a part in spiritual things, and sometimes lead us to judge, from externals, one of another, and so mar that spiritual beauty that would otherwise show itself, and perhaps beguile some into the way of godliness.

Her fourth child was born Sixth Month, 1st, 1806.

Sixth Month, 8th.—This day week I was confined with a sweet boy. How much do I now desire, that I may be able to leave all things to the All-wise Disposer of events, trusting in his wisdom and mercy ; so far indeed I have abundant cause for thankfulness ; and though my poor mind has, at times, passed through a little of the depths, yet I have felt the delivering power near at hand : may I hope that, in the right time, it will again come to my help.

Seventh Month, 6th.—It struck me this morning at Meeting, that in states when we appear to have no power of our own, no energy, and no capability to do any good thing, our cry is heard, and our petitions come in a more acceptable form, than sometimes when full of power, vigour, and life. How much do I desire that above all things, I may have a life in doing the will of my Creator. I am ready to believe that I had rather suffer affliction to be what I ought to be, than to enjoy the pleasures of life, if less profitable.

Mildred's Court, Eleventh Month, 10th.—I have received a very sweet and encouraging letter from my beloved cousin J. G. Bevan. This led me, for many hours in the day, to be in a craving state for spiritual food, and to anxious desires that the work might be perfected in me, and that nothing of the creature may ever stand in competition with the will and the work of the Creator.

Early in the Twelfth Month, Joseph and Elizabeth Fry went to Earlham, to be present at the marriage of her sister Louisa, to Samuel Hoare, Jun., of Hampstead, Middlesex.

Earlham, Twelfth Month, 26th.—On Fourth-day morning, the 24th, our dear Louisa was married at Tasborough Meeting. A very serious and interesting time to us all. My father, all of us eleven, my husband and Samuel Hoare. The Meeting was very solemn, and did, to me, sweetly license them in their solemn engagement; it was like a seal set to it. There was testimony upon testimony, and blessing upon blessing, from the ministers present; and, what was better than all to me, a sweet inward covering over the Meeting. All appeared unity and love; rather remarkable to see so large a family all so nearly sympathising, and closely united. My dear brother John was sweet indeed, and deeply feeling; may it last in him, and may he truly find the pearl of great price.

Newmarket, Twelfth Month, 31st.—The last day of this year, looking forward to the next. Thou, who knowest what our trials and temptations are, keep us faithful unto Thee; preserve us from the snares of the enemy; be with us all as a family; and bless the dispensations of Thy Providence to us, by drawing us nearer to Thyself through them!

First Month, 6th, 1807.—My dear brother John, I believe this morning will marry our dear cousin Elizabeth Gurney; may they truly prove blessings to each other, and to both families.

The following letter was written shortly before this event.

My very dear John and Elizabeth,—

I leave off writing my journal, to write to you; for whilst I was expressing in it my feelings, the love I then felt, and now feel for thee, dear John, came so powerfully before me, that instead of writing it in my journal, I wish to express it to you both. My interest and sympathy is great in your present undertaking; and my desire, sincere, that in your union you may indeed obtain the Divine blessing. What is the Divine blessing, but in the first place to be cleansed from our sins and weaknesses so fully, that we may, in innocency, compass the altar of God availingly. And secondly, to live under the protection of Him, who is able to save us from every hurtful thing, and turn all the circumstances of our lives to good account; so as in them to bless us, and draw us nearer to Him, who can do all things for us, both inwardly and outwardly.

It is hardly likely that I shall see you before, or soon after you marry; you have, you know, my good wishes for your prosperity in every way, but you must expect some bitter mixed with the sweet cup; for without it we should rest too much in the enjoyments of life. I think you will be a very devoted couple to each other; therefore I advise you to be on your guard, and to remember that all natural things, and natural affections amongst the rest, are corruptible. That there is something better that must be loved first, and that we must hold all things in subjection to this Power, that alone must be worshipped, and that alone can sanctify all other things to us, and so make them partake of the enduring, powerful, heavenly nature. This is what I desire all my affections to be tinged with; that I may love those who are near to me, not alone with my own natural feelings, but that a better love may be felt in me towards them; a love that is not affected by the separations and trials of life.

Mildred's Court, First Month, 27th.—Do with me as Thou wilt, only let me be Thine! This is in measure my desire this morning, and that whether it be in heights, or depths, I may spend my life to Thy glory.

Elizabeth Fry again travelled into Norfolk, to attend the wedding of her sister Hannah.

She was married at Tasborough Meeting, to Thomas Fowell Buxton, afterward Sir T. Fowell Buxton, Bart.

Fifth Month, 20th.—I have been deeply interested in my beloved Hannah's marriage, which was satisfactory; I desire their good every way. Now I am again entering Yearly Meeting; this leads me to various feelings, and some desires after the good of the whole body, more particularly that we may rest in no form, and not make too much of it. How very poor I feel, but I admire at the merciful hand that still appears extended to help me.

Sixth Month, 22nd.—To-day I have been to try to draw a poor young woman from her evil course. I felt my own incapability to help her, and my own lukewarmness. But I desire that if it be right, I may receive a little help, and be enabled in some measure, to assist in drawing a poor sinner into a better path, and if such should be the case, may I give the glory where it is due.

Plashet, Seventh Month, 20th.—I have been, I think I may say, very ill, with something of an intermittent fever. I desire to express a little, what I have gone through. I have certainly, at times, been very closely pressed, bodily and mentally: but for all that, I have no cause to complain, but indeed to give thanks. I very soon found I had but one place to fly to, but one sure place of refuge, and that was humbly to endeavour with all my power, wholly to give myself up to God, knowing His dispensations were all-wise: as for my poor soul, I could only look to His mercy and forgiveness; for He can pardon in mercy, little as I deserve it. I could offer few words on behalf either of soul or body, but the desire was to be wholly given up to Him, who could do all things for me; I desired to leave all. Oh, how do I crave that I may, in sickness and in health, and under every dispensation, be wholly given up, body, soul, and spirit, and no longer falter as between two opinions.

Eighth Month.—At Meeting, Richard Phillips spoke on the necessity of faith, I felt tendered and refreshed, and so well altogether, that health appeared quickly returning; but, not unlike the events of life, the next morning I awoke ill; in a suffering state, and very faint. I had two days of considerable trial from such very deeply painful feelings of bodily weakness and sinking, then a day of comparative rest. The next day a return of my old complaint, the fever, and one more since then. It was of a very suffering nature to me whilst it lasted; but still I may say with truth, I once more have only cause to give thanks, for the burden did not appear too hard, and there was a merciful and healing power open to my cry, for I was helped, and my prayers appeared to be granted. But I found that looking back to the help that I had before experienced would not do; the manna of yesterday was not for to-day!

Questions for Myself.

First,—Hast thou this day been honest and true, in performing thy duty towards thy Creator in the first place? and secondly, towards thy fellow-creatures; or hast thou sophisticated and flinched?

Second,—Hast thou been vigilant in frequently pausing in the hurry and career of the day, to see whom thou art endeavouring to serve; whether thy Maker, or thyself? And every time that trial or temptation assailed thee, didst thou endeavour to look steadily to the Delivering Power; even to Christ, who can do all things for thee?

Third,—Hast thou endeavoured to perform thy relative duties faithfully: been a tender, loving, yielding wife, where thy own will and pleasure were concerned; a tender, yet steady mother with thy children, making thyself quickly and strictly obeyed, but careful in what thou requirest of them: a kind, yet honest mistress, telling thy servants of their faults, when thou thinkest it for *their*, or *thy* good, but never unnecessarily worrying thyself, or them, about trifles: and to every one endeavouring to do as thou wouldest be done unto?

Mildred's Court, First Month, 1st, 1808.—A new year begun—and to me, with some weight at my heart; oh, for my beloved's welfare, as well as my own and our dear lambs, spiritually. May none of us prove an injury to the principle we profess; and may we, in all our undertakings, that originate in evil, be marred and stopped in our course. Oh! I can say, if Thou seest meet, lead us not into temptation, but deliver us from evil. I know how frail we all are, may we not be utterly cast off; may we, in the end, prove our integrity, and all be given up to follow the good alone, in the newness of life. How grievous to serve the evil one; and how sweet to follow Him, the Shepherd of Israel; and lead others, in ever so small a measure, to do so. O Lord! I pray for mercy, give us not up to the will of the enemy: may we live to show forth Thy praise! I am favoured in some small measure to hope in the Lord, and to rejoice in the power of His salvation; for indeed He can deliver from evil.

15*th.*—I yesterday felt a good deal about Mary Ann —— coming to teach the children and live here, fearing for the peace of our nursery establishment; and I did desire that I might, in those matters, receive the Divine Blessing: for to me it is no light matter to direct my household and children; and I feel in that, as in all other things, without Divine assistance what can I do?

Second Month, 18*th.*—Oh, that my faith fail not, but that I may be enabled to look to the right place for support!

Her fifth child was born in the Second Month. In the Fifth Month following, Elizabeth, wife of her eldest brother John, died, after a lingering illness. She was cut off in the bloom of youth, and the height of human prosperity, at a period when the large family of which she was a member, were in the enjoyment of this world's brightest prospects.

Fifth Month, 27*th.*—Since I last wrote, I have gone through much trouble. Last Seventh-day week, an account was received of the death of our much loved sister, Elizabeth Gurney. I felt it deeply; during her illness my heart cried unto the Lord for mercy, and that He would take her unto Himself, and that her transgressions might be blotted out. Being still so much inclined to trying, nervous feelings, made me feel it in a more painful way. Not finding any rest away from them all, Joseph and I went to Lynn—an afflicting time. On Third-day morning, I had a most affecting meeting with dear John, yet felt myself far too weak, poor, and in too painfully nervous a state, to afford him comfort; but rather needed it myself. It was a very melting interview. The remainder of the day, being spent in the house with the dear remains, was really sweet to me; I had comfort in my sorrow. Fourth-day, we left Lynn for Earlham. The next morning was the funeral at Norwich, and poor I, hardened, and almost entirely devoted to my own nervous feelings. This was a trial to me, when I had hoped to have been enabled to seek after the best help for the dear afflicted; and also to feel on account of our much loved lost Elizabeth. But I desired that this humiliating dispensation might be for my good.

Earlham, Eighth Month, 20th.—I have been married eight years yesterday. Various trials of faith and patience have been permitted me; my course has been very different to what I had expected, and instead of being, as I had hoped, a useful instrument in the Church Militant, here I am a careworn wife and mother, outwardly, nearly devoted to the things of this life. Though, at times, this difference in my destination has been trying to me, yet, I believe those trials (which have certainly been very pinching) that I have had to go through, have been very useful, and brought me to a feeling sense of what I am; and at the same time have taught me where power is, and in what we are to glory; not in ourselves, nor in anything we can be, or do, but we are alone to desire that He may be glorified, either through us, or others, in our being something, or nothing, as He may see best for us. I have seen, particularly in our spiritual allotments, that it is not in man that walketh to direct his steps;

it is our place, only to be as passive clay in His holy hands; simply and singly desiring, that He would make us what He would have us to be. But the way in which this great work is to be effected, we must leave to Him, who has been the Author, and we may trust will be the Finisher of the work: and we must not be surprised to find it going on differently, to what our frail hearts would desire.

I may also acknowledge that, through all my trials, there does appear to have been a particular blessing attending me, both as to the fatness of the land and the dew of Heaven; for though I have been at times deeply tried, inwardly and outwardly, yet I have always found the delivering Arm has been near at hand, and the trials have appeared blessed to me. The little efforts, or small acts of duty, I have ever performed, have often seemed remarkably blessed to me; and where others have been concerned, it has also, I think, been apparent in them, that the effort on my part, has been blessed to both parties. Also, what shall I say when I look at my husband and my five lovely babes? How I have been favoured to recover from illnesses, and to get through them without material injury in any way. I also observe, how any little care towards my servants appears to have been blessed, and what faithful and kind friends to me, I have found them. Indeed, I cannot enumerate my blessings; but I may truly say, that of all the blessings I have received, and still receive, there is none to compare to believing that I am not yet forsaken, but notwithstanding all my deviations, in mercy cared for. And (if all the rest be taken from me) far above all, I desire, that if I should be led through paths I know not of, which may try my weak faith and nature, I may not lose my faith in Thee; but may increasingly love Thee; delight to follow after Thee, and be singly Thine; giving all things up to Thee, who hast hitherto been my only merciful Protector and Preserver.

Again, sickness and death were permitted to enter her immediate circle. Henceforward, Elizabeth Fry was frequently called upon to witness the last moments of some, and largely to sympathize in the afflictions of others. She was now to partake personally in the solemn scene of death, on occasion of the decease of her father-in-law, William Storrs Fry; this event took place at Mildred's Court, where she had nursed him assiduously during some weeks' illness. To the latest period of her life, she dwelt with pleasure on the satisfaction and privilege of having been permitted to be a comfort and assistance to him during his passage through the dark valley. He was a man of piety and of an amiable disposition, and had endeared himself to her by gentleness and affectionate attention. His decease produced an important change in her circumstances, causing the removal of the family to Plashet.

Mildred's Court, Tenth Month, 17th.—We have had my poor father Fry here for five weeks, very ill indeed; and last Seventh-day morning, at a little before two o'clock, he died. This was to me a very affecting time, not so much so on his own account, as we had reason to hope and believe it was well with him; but the awful sight of death was very overcoming to me, never having witnessed such a scene before. But I often had very sweet and refreshing moments by his bed-side: and from his own expressions, we had great reason for hope—at one time he said, he had no fear, and indeed it appeared a well-grounded feeling. During the first part of his illness, while at Mildred's Court, death appeared to him in an awful, and almost dreadful point of view; he desired life for a little longer to prove his further dedication; this he often expressed. After he was confined up stairs, he seemed more to feel the necessity of an interest in that Power which can alone do all things for us, and prove indeed our salvation, for it is only through the redeeming power of Christ, we can look for salvation. He said, he felt himself, "a poor repentant nothing;" and "alone depended on mercy." Some days after that, he said he had "no fear:" and one morning when we thought him dying, he said, we "need not be afraid, for he was comfortable, comfortable, comfortable." I, with many others wept, I believe with thankfulness. I felt little less than joy, as I did at one or two other times in the room. There was such sweetness attending him. It is certainly an encouraging consideration, for it shows to me that it does not much signify what talent is committed to us, if we be but faithful with it. My dear father-in-law was not one that had great things required of him, apparently; but being faithful in the little, we need not doubt, he now possesses more. I loved him very dearly, and his memory is sweet to me; I have a pleasure in considering I was able to nurse him in his last illness. There is one remark I make, that I believe it is through Christ we are saved, but I would not have *that* lessen our diligence to work out our own salvation, for I believe those who endeavour to follow Him, are enabled to have faith, and have an interest in that power that can save.

Eleventh Month, 10th.—I have hardly settled at home since my dear father's death. Last First-day, I was sent for to see my dear sister Hannah, who was very poorly; it proved to be the scarlet fever, and being the only sister at liberty, I have nursed her. This I consider a great privilege to be able to do; though I have felt it a very serious thing, with a young babe, and the mother of so many little lambs, to enter so catching a disorder. I have desired that I might not enter it in my own will, or simply to gratify inclination, which leads me to enjoy nursing those I love so dearly: circumstances appeared to bring me into it, indeed I had hardly an option, as I was in the first instance brought into it, not knowing what the complaint was; and in the second, there was no one else that I thought proper to fill my place, as my sister Louisa was prevented. I have desired that what is really best for me may occur, even if it be to pass through trouble. But if my merciful Creator sees meet to preserve me and my family, from any further suffering on this ac-

18

count, may I be enabled to give the praise where it is due, and may it afresh stimulate me to seek with renewed vigilance, to dedicate myself, and all that belongs to me, to Him whom my poor, weak, unworthy soul loves; I could think beyond everything; though I know the world has a strong hold, and perhaps my heart is more devoted to it, than to its Creator. I feel thankful for my beloved sister being better.

Plashet, 20th.—Though I have been but very delicate in my health the last week, yet I have been favoured with sweet and precious moments. I have felt sweet peace, not exactly the peace arising from any act of obedience in particular; but unmerited, unlooked for quietness of soul, so that I could say, my peace flows as a river! not that my natural spirits have been high, far from it; but there has, at times, been an enjoyment in the low valley, far above any feeling of exhilaration; and I have been reminded of that text, "Thou wilt keep him in perfect peace, whose mind is staid on Thee." Though, as I said before, I am conscious that this is quite an unmerited state; and also how little I have done, towards trying to stay my mind in the right place. No one, as yet, has taken the complaint of my sister, which I consider a great outward blessing; may I be enabled to give thanks, and to prove my thankfulness, by more and more endeavouring to give up body, soul, and spirit, to the service of my beloved Master; if I dare say so of Him, whom my soul delights to serve.

Fragment that occurs at this part of the Journal.

Children should be deeply impressed with the belief, that the first and great object of their education is, to follow Christ, and indeed to be true Christians: and those things on which we, the Society of Friends, differ from the world in general, should not, I think, be impressed on them, by only saying, as is often done, "because Friends do it;" but singly and simply as things that the Christian life appears to us to require, and that therefore they must be done. They should also early be taught, that all have not seen exactly the same; but that there are many, equally belonging to the church of Christ, who may, in other respects, be as much stricter than ourselves, as we are than they in *these* matters. But this does not at all lessen the necessity of *our* employing a simple mode of expressing ourselves, who are permitted to see the consistency and propriety of it.

(Signed) ELIZABETH FRY.

30*th*.—At this time there is no set of people I feel so much about, as servants:—I do not think they have generally justice done to them; they are too much considered as another race of beings, and we are apt to forget that the holy injunction holds good with them, "Do as thou wouldest be done unto," and I believe that, in striving to do so, we shall not take them out of their station in life; but endeavour to render them happy and contented in it, and be truly their friends, though not their familiars, or equals, as to the things of this life; for we have reason to believe the difference in our stations is ordered by a wiser than ourselves, who directs us how to fill our different places; but we must endeavour never to forget, that, in the best sense, we are all one, and though our paths here may be different, we have all souls equally valuable, and have all the same work to do; which, if properly considered, should lead us to great sympathy and love, and also to a constant care for their welfare, both here and hereafter.

Mildred's Court, Second Month, 14*th*, 1809.—The thought of forming a new establishment at Plashet, with servants, &c., is, to me, a very serious one. I find it so difficult fully to do my duty towards them, and even when I do, to give them satisfaction. My mind is often much burdened on this subject; I long to make them my friends, and for us all to live in harmony and love. We greatly (I mean servants and their heads in general) misunderstand each other; I fully believe partly from our different situations in life, and partly from our different educations, and the way in which each party is apt to view the other. Masters and mistresses are greatly deficient, I think in the general way, and so are most servants towards them: it is for both to keep in view strictly to do unto others, as they would be done unto; and also to remember that we are indeed all one with God.

Oh, that I may keep watchful and near my Guide; and that if it be consistent with the Divine will, I may be enabled to say, "As for me, and my house, we will serve the Lord," and delight to do His commandments.

Chapter Fourth.

1809—1813. Removal to Plashet, enjoyment of the country—Birth of her sixth child, 1809—Summons into Norfolk—Death of her father—Extract from the journal of Rachel Gurney—Commencement of her public ministry—Funeral of her cousin Anna Reynolds—Letter to a distant friend—Visit to Earlham—Journey into Gloucestershire—Birth of her seventh child, 1811—Acknowledged as a minister by Friends—Attention to the Poor, School, &c.—Norwich Bible Society—Death of a little niece—Journey with Henry Hull and her sister, Priscilla Gurney—Visit to the Meetings of Friends in Norfolk—Extract from a letter to her cousin, J. G. Bevan—Letter to Edward Edwards—Death of a domestic servant—Death of Eliza Shepherd—Birth of her eighth child, 1812—Letter to her cousin, J. G. Bevan—Removal to London for the winter—Religious visit to Friends of the London Quarterly Meeting—For the first time goes to Newgate—State of that prison.

In the spring of 1809, Joseph and Elizabeth Fry removed to Plashet.

This change, from the smoke and din of a crowded city, to the calm tranquillity of the country was most delightful. It was a renewal of early tastes and pleasures, not the less appreciated because years of vicissitudes had passed over her, leaving traces of hard-earned experience. She had remarkably the talent of throwing aside graver objects, and, for short intervals, divesting herself of care. She would enjoy her garden and flowers, generally with some of her children about her, and then as quickly resume her employments. Although these occupations appeared different, there was unity of purpose in the whole. She desired to serve God in the fulfilment of her daily duties; she offered to Him the sacrifice of thanksgiving, by the spirit in which she accepted and enjoyed His beauties in creation. Her brow would relax, and her countenance beam with intelligence, as she explained to her children the wonders of the Heavenly bodies, the structure of an insect, or the growth and beauty of a flower.

In the dealings of God with man, there is a marvellous adaptation to the respective powers and circumstances of each individual. When he requires unusual service, or peculiarly active devotion to the cause of religion upon earth, He frequently bestows with it, a power in proportion, of receiving refreshment and delight from the outward blessings of life. That many refuse to enjoy, and deny themselves the good things that He has provided for His children, proves nothing against the bounty and indulgence of the hand which proffers them. After the deepest conflicts of spirit, amidst heavy and peculiar sorrows, she, whose character we desire to portray, would turn with a thankful heart to the blessings granted; her courage raised, her faith strengthened, by thus dwelling on His wonderful goodness to the children of men.

Plashet, Third Month, 8th, 1809.—My dearest little Rachel has been seriously unwell for some time past, so as to make me very low at times; but I have not suffered much from painful anxiety, as, in mercy, I may say I have been screened from that feeling. I desire, with regard to my dear lambs, to be ready to give them up, if called for at my hand; for we know not what is best for them; and I believe we should seek to look upon them, as charges committed to our stewardship, and not as our property.

Plashet, Sixth Month, 13*th.*—After having gone through so much since I last wrote, it is difficult for me to express all, but more particularly from rather unusual and repeated causes of thankfulness, in having experienced the Divine Arm held out for my encouragement and help. I had one or two very striking times during the Yearly Meeting, as if meant to confirm my poor, feeble faith. Once, when dear Ann Crowley and John Hull dined with us; before a word was spoken, or the cloth was removed from the table, my soul was brought from a dry, flat, insensible state, to be humbly prostrate before Him, whom it has at times desired to serve. So much so, that I felt that this was enough, without words from others: but it was not long before dear Ann Crowley had to express the same, and told me the very thoughts and feelings of my mind and heart. It was indeed a wonderful confirmation; almost like seeing face to face in a glass. What a blessing to be under such a living ministry, that speaks to, and reveals the innermost soul! Since the Yearly Meeting, I have been greatly helped and supported through the trial of my dear sister Elizabeth Gurney's confinement, which, at one time, I felt no strength to encounter; but power and courage were given me sufficient for the day.

Seventh Month, 3rd.—I have, as usual, to acknowledge many mercies received by me; I have been greatly occupied in attending my sister Fry, who had been dangerously ill, from breaking a blood-vessel. I have felt her patient conduct an example to me.

Ninth Month, 13th.—Time runs on apace. I desire my imagination may not dwell on that which is before it. Every outward thing appears nearly, if not quite ready; and as for the inward preparation, I cannot prepare myself.

Her sixth child was born on the 20th of this month.

23*rd.*—On Fourth-day, my lovely boy was born. I had to acknowledge present help in trouble, so that I could only give thanks; indeed I have renewed cause for thankfulness and praise, which my poor, unworthy mind has felt little able to render since, being weak at times, tempted and tried; but I desire to abide near, and cling to that Power, that can pardon and deliver.

Tenth Month, 5th.—Yesterday I was much affected by an

account of poor dear nurse at Earlham, being dangerously ill of scarlet fever, at Lynn, and not likely to live. Sweet love and unity I have towards her, accompanied by a feeling belief that it will be well with her, in life or in death; for I could almost say, she bore the mark of her high calling, being a living example in the house; not a talker, but a doer of the work; at least so she appeared to me. This awfully brings death home, which indeed I feel hardly able to look at in my own power, but it is one of those subjects upon which I do not desire often to dwell, I had rather look to the work of each hour as it comes: and oh, when it please the Master to call me hence, may He find me watching!

6*th.*—The account of dear nurse's death arrived yesterday; in her, we have all lost a most valuable friend.

Her father's health appeared failing, and she thus alludes to it:

Tunbridge Wells, 16*th.*—Since I last wrote, I have had much to feel on account of my dear father: dearest Priscilla has also had the scarlet fever. I have felt all these things: but not in a distressing way, having more hope than fear, and both of them going on well has been a comfort to me. With regard to myself, my health has altogether continued finely; a little more nervous trial the last day or two. But I desire to be submissive and quiet if I can, under whatever may come, if it be right that I should be tried. Having no Meeting here, we yesterday sat silently together in the family; and I have to relate what has pained me with regard to myself. There appeared, on our first sitting down, so solemn a covering, but, notwithstanding all my covenants, and all my good desires, I flinched in spirit, and turned my mind from it, instead of feeling, "Speak, Lord, for thy servant heareth;" my great fear was, lest I should have to acknowledge, that I believed the promise was verified with us, "where two or three are met together in My name, there am I in the midst of them."

Now, I think it very likely I should not have found myself thus called upon: but my fear was so great, that I dare not ask whether it were the right call or not, but turned from it. This has renewedly led me to see what I am, and humbly to desire, feeling my own extreme weakness and rebellious heart, that He, who has in mercy begun the work in me, will be pleased still to carry it on, and to grant ability to do that which he may require at my hands. I could almost have said, yesterday, "Let not Thine hand spare, nor Thine eye pity, until thou hast made me what Thou wouldest have me to be;" and yet, afterwards, I was more disposed to say, "Be pleased to mix mercy with judgment." I had a sweet little encouragement during my confinement; being one morning rather remarkably led to feel for a young woman whom I believed to be devoted to the world; and that very person calling a few hours afterwards, though I did not know she was coming, I was enabled to express what I felt to her, and had to experience the truth of that text, "in the day of my power my people shall be made a willing people:" it appeared as if this were granted to help me through it, in my very weak state: may I show my gratitude by further obedience, when power is less manifested.

Earlham, 30th.—I hardly know how to express myself:—I have indeed passed through wonders. On the 26th, as we were sitting quietly together, (after my dear sister Richenda had left us, and my soul had bowed on my beloved father's account, of whom we had daily very poor reports,) an express arrived bringing Chenda back, saying our most dear father was so ill, that they did not expect his life would be spared. Words fall short to describe what I felt, he was so tenderly near and dear to me. We soon believed it best to set off for this place, on some accounts under great discouragement, principally from my own bodily weakness, and also the fever in the house; but it did not appear as if we could omit it, feeling as we did; therefore, after a tender parting with my beloved flock, my dearest Joseph, Chenda, and I with the baby, set off.

We arrived at Mildred's Court the first night, where our dear sister left us, in hopes of seeing our parent alive. In very great weakness I set off the next morning, and had, at times, great discouragements; but many hours were comforting and sweet. Hearing on the road, at the different stages, that my dearest father was living, we proceeded till we arrived at Earlham, about twelve o'clock that night. We got out of the carriage, and once more, saw him who has been so inexpressibly dear to me through life, since I knew what love was; he was asleep, but death was strongly marked on his sweet, and to me, beautiful face. Whilst in his room, all was sweetness, nothing bitter, though how I feel his loss is hard to express: but indeed I have had abundant cause to rejoice on his account. *After very deep probation*, his mind was strikingly visited, and consoled, at last, in passing through the valley of the shadow of death. He frequently expressed that he feared no evil, but believed that, through the mercy of God in Christ, he should be received in glory; his deep humility, and the tender and loving state he was in, were most valuable to those around him. He encouraged us, his children, to hold on our way; and sweetly expressed his belief, that our love of good (in the degree we had it) had been a stimulus and help to him.

The next morning he died, quite easily; I was not with him, but on entering his room soon after it was over, my soul was bowed within me, in love, not only for the deceased, but also for the living, and in humble thankfulness; so that I could hardly help uttering (which I did) my thanksgiving and praise, and also what I felt for the living, as well as the dead. I cannot understand it: but the power given was wonderful to myself, and the cross none—my heart was so full that I could hardly hinder utterance.

She repeated the passage from the Revelation which she afterwards uttered at the funeral, " Great and marvellous are Thy works, Lord God Almighty; just and true are thy ways, thou King of saints." Her sister Rachel thus describes it—"Dear Betsy uttered thanksgiving, and a song of rejoicing, for mercy that had been so richly extended to our beloved father; and a prayer, that it might be continued to us all."

I have desired since to leave this event; but it was a glorious time, such an one as I never before passed through, all love, all joy, all peace, or the nearest I think to that state, that I ever experienced. I had the first night of coming, a few nervous and painful moments about the scarlet fever, on account principally of my beloved flock at home; and a fear, whether in my weak state of body, it might not be too much for me. But love so powerfully drew me to them, that I believe I could not properly have staid away; and indeed I have felt in my place, as far as I could tell. Should I forsake my beloved family in the day of trouble? I hope, and believe not! we have had most valuable and sweetly enlivening times together; all love; I believe each of our hearts quickened, to feel fresh and renewed desire to be dedicated to His service, who has thus shown Himself in mercy to our beloved father. What can we render for all these benefits?

Eleventh Month, 3*rd*.—We attended our beloved father's funeral. Before I went, I was so deeply impressed at times, with love to all, and thanksgiving, that I doubted whether it might not possibly be my place to express it there; but I did, the evening before, humbly crave not to be permitted to do so, unless rightly called to it. Fear of man appeared greatly taken away. I sat the meeting under a solemn quietness, though there was preaching that neither disturbed nor enlivened me much: the same words still powerfully impressed me, that had done ever since I first entered the room where the corpse was. Upon going to the grave this still continued; under this solemn quiet calm, the fear of man appeared so much removed, that I believe my sole desire was, that the will of God might be done in me. Though it was unpleasant to me, what man might say, yet I most feared it was a temptation, owing to my state of sorrow; but that, I fully believe was not the case, as something of the kind had been on my mind so long; but it had appeared more ripe the last few weeks, and even months, I had so often had to "rejoice in the Lord, and glory in the God of my salvation;" that it had made me desire, that others might partake, and know how good he had been to my soul, and be encouraged to walk in those paths, which I had found to be paths of pleasantness and peace. However, after a solemn waiting, my dear uncle Joseph spoke, greatly to my encouragement and comfort, and the removal of some of my fears. I remained still, till dearest John began to move to go away; when it appeared as if it could not be omitted, and I fell on my knees, and began, not knowing how I should go on, with these words, "Great and marvellous are thy works, Lord God Almighty, just and true are all Thy ways, Thou King of Saints; be pleased to receive our thanksgiving;" and there I seemed stopped, though I thought that I should have had to express, that I gave thanks on my beloved father's account. But not feeling the power continue, I arose directly; a quiet, calm, and invigorated state, mental and bodily, were my portion afterwards, and altogether a sweet day, but a very painful night, discouraged on every side, I could believe, by him who tries to deceive. The discouragement appeared to arise principally from what others would think, and nature flinched, and sank, but I was enabled this morning to commit myself in prayer. May I be preserved in future, if my life be spared, from taking Thy holy name in vain; enable me, if Thou seest meet, to follow hard after Thee, that I may know Thy voice, Thou Shepherd and Bishop of souls, and be as one of Thy sheep! It was my prayer this morning, to be able to turn from the subject, as my poor, weak mind felt hardly able to look at it, which was in some measure the case. This day has altogether been a comfortable one, though very low at times, and having to walk in the valley; may I be enabled, if it be right for me, to trust, and not to fear. I have greatly felt my beloved father's loss to-day, and yesterday; though calm, yet I suffered much on his account; he was in some things, like my heart's delight; I so enjoyed to please him, and was so fond of him, that to hear of the sufferings he passed through, before he came to a state of reconciliation, greatly affected me to-day; but I have had more comfort on his account, [than anything else. The great love and kindness I have received from them all, and from my uncle Joseph, has been encouraging to me; and my husband has been a true helpmate, and sweet counsellor.

Some account of this scene of bereavement, and yet of great consolation, is extracted from the journal of her sister, Rachel Gurney, and is as follows:—

"*Monday, October 23rd*, 1809.—To-day my dear father expressed to me his conviction, of the necessity of preparing for another world, whilst health and strength were ours; he said, that he trusted mercy would be extended to him, for all his past errors, and infirmities; and acknowledged thankfully how he had been blessed with spiritual support; although discouragement and heaviness had been, at times, his portion.

"A paroxysm of pain, attended with *great anguish of mind*, caused him to speak despondingly of his condition; and the text, 'If any man say he is without sin, he is a liar, and the truth is not in him,' recurred painfully to him, until reminded of the ensuing verses, 'If any man sin, we have an Advocate with the Father, Jesus Christ, the righteous,' &c., which gave him some comfort, although his mind was burdened, and his spirit oppressed, by the remembrance and consciousness of sin. My sister Catherine pointed out to him the precious promise, 'To him who forgave much, shall much be forgiven,' as applying particularly to his case. This was to him a beaming consolation, and he replied, 'Few men, have, I believe, forgiven more than I have.'

"On Monday night, a very interesting conversation took place. My dear father spoke of the purity of the law laid down by our Saviour, extending even to the thoughts and desires, and lamented his frequent failings, and short-comings. He acknowledged that the love of religious truth, and the conscientious practice which characterized his children, had been the means of blessing and instruction to him; and he sought their prayers in the present hour of extreme trial.

"I was composedly observing a holy peace shedding its radiance on his countenance, as he sank that night to rest; and I sat by his bed-side, in the full assurance of faith, that the Lord was present with him, notwithstanding the doubts and fears which had oppressed him. Tuesday was a mournful day. Deep probation of spirit, and grievous depression from bodily illness were his portion, but he wrestled with God in prayer, and grace and help were given him. On Wednesday morning, his mind shone forth in wonderful brightness, and although the spasms of pain which he endured were agonising, grace appeared to triumph, and his spirit seemed to rise out of the fiery furnace, purified by the Great Refiner. With simplicity and ardour he laid hold on the hope set before him; trusting only in the satisfaction that has been made for sinners, by the blood of Christ. The consolation attendant upon this change in his mind was the greater, from the sore conflicts he had had to pass through in his illness, and the anguish of mind he had endured.

"He was comforted by the presence of his children, who had assembled around him, and expressed to us with tenderness and humble thankfulness, his deep and grateful sense, that he owed more to us than he had been able to give us, and that we had indeed been to him a strength and stimulus in all good things. He continued in the possession of joy and peace until his death, which took place on Saturday morning, the 28th of October, when he entered (we humbly trust) that region, where the redeemed ones rejoice in the view, as well as feel the influence, of their God."

Plashet, Eleventh Month, 16th.—We arrived here on Third-day evening; though plunged into feeling before I arrived, I felt flat on meeting my tenderly beloved little flock. I was enabled, coming along, to crave help; in the first place, to be made willing either to do, or to suffer, whatever was the Divine will concerning me. I also desired that I might not be so occupied with the present state of my mind, as to its religious duties, as in any degree, to omit close attention to all *daily* duties, my beloved husband, children, servants, poor, &c.; but if I should be permitted to enter the humiliating path, that has appeared to be opening before me, to look well at home, and not discredit the cause I desire to advocate. Last First-day morning, I had a deeply trying Meeting, on account of the words, "Be of good courage, and he will strengthen your hearts, all ye that hope in the Lord," which had impressed me towards Norwich Meeting before I went into it; and after I had sat there a little time they came with double force, and continued resting on my mind until my fright was extreme; and it appeared almost as if I must, if I did my duty, utter them. I hope I did not wholly revolt, but I did cry in my heart, for that time to be excused, that like Samuel, I might apply to some Eli to know what the voice was that I heard; my beloved Uncle Joseph, I thought was the person; on this sort of excuse or covenant, as I may call it, a calmness was granted the rest of the Meeting, but not the reward of peace. As soon as the Meeting was over, I went to my dear uncle, and begged him to come to Earlham to see me. The conflict I had passed through was so great, as to shake my body, as well as mind, and I had reason to fear and to believe, I should have been happier, and much more relieved in mind, if I had given up to this little service; I have felt since like one in debt to that Meeting. My dear uncle came, and only confirmed me, by his kind advice, to walk by faith, and not by sight: he strongly advised a simple following of what arose, and expressed his experience of the benefit of giving up to it, and the confusion of not doing so. How have I desired since, not to stand in the fear of man; but I believe it is the soul's enemy, seeking whom he may devour; for terrible as it was, as then presented to me, and as it often had been before, yet, when some ability was granted to get through, that same enemy would have had me glory on that account. May I not give way either to one feeling or the other, but strive to look to the preserving power of God.

Twelfth Month, 4th.—When I have given up in the morning, only to make an indifferent remark to the servants, on our reading, sweet peace has been my portion; but when it has been presented to me, and I have not followed, far different has been the case. In Meeting, it is such an awful matter, for the sake of others as well as myself. If it be Thy work in me, be pleased, O Lord! to grant faith and power, sufficient for the needful time; I long to serve Thee, and to do Thy commandments, and I believe if I be faithful in the little, Thou wilt be pleased to make me ruler over more.

9th.—Soon after sitting down in Meeting, (on Fourth day,) I was enabled to feel encouraged by these words, "Though the enemy come in like a flood, the Spirit of the Lord will lift up a standard against him." This appeared my experience, for soon the storm was quieted, and a degree even of ease was my portion. About eleven o'clock, these same words, that had done so in Norwich meeting, came feelingly over me—"Be of good courage, and He will strengthen your hearts, all ye that hope in the Lord." And that, which had hitherto appeared impossible to human nature, seemed not only possible, but I believe I was willing; simply desiring that, in this new and awful undertaking, I might not lose my faith, and that the Divine will might be done in me. Under this sense and feeling, as if I could not omit, I uttered them. Though clearness still continued, nature, in a great measure, seemed to sink under the effort afterwards, and low feelings and imaginations to have much dominion, which, in mercy, were soon relieved, and I have gone on sweetly and easily since, often even rejoicing.

11th.—Surrounded with numerous outward occupations, weak in body, and at times tossed in mind, so that the wall of preservation appears almost broken down, yet my heart says, I will not fear but that I shall, at last, praise Him, whom I desire to be "the health of my countenance, and my God." I feel a wish, and great necessity of pressing hard after Him, who alone can preserve me, for when the enemy appears, to whom can I flee, but to Him, whom I desire to call Father? and who has hitherto proved my merciful Protector. Be pleased to keep me in this hour; make me, O Lord! what Thou wouldest have me to be; enable me to become passive in Thy holy hand: mayst Thou be glorified, even if it be through my suffering; and preserve me from ever taking, what is only Thy due, to myself.

22nd.—Again, on Fourth-day, I have dared to open my mouth in public: I am ready to say, What has come to me? Even in supplication—that the work might be carried on in myself and others, and that we might be preserved from evil. My weight of deep feeling on the subject, I believe, exceeded any other time; I was, I may say, brought into a wrestling state, that the work of the ministry in me might, if right, be carried on, if not, stopped short. I feel of myself, no power for such a work; I may say, wholly unable; yet, when the feeling and power continue, so that I dare not omit it, then what can I do?

23rd.—Giving up, to make a little remark after reading to the servants, has brought sweet peace; indeed so far, it has appeared to me, that prompt obedience has brought me the most peace. The prospect of the Meetings next week, more particularly the Quarterly Meeting, already makes me tremble, I can hardly say why, but it is very awful to be thus publicly exposed, in a work that I feel so little fitted for; yet, I believe, it is not my own doing, nor at my own command.

Plashet, First Month, 1st, 1810.—It is rather awful to me entering a new year, more particularly when I look at the alterations the last has made—most striking the last three months, or a little more! First, a child born; second, the loss of nurse; third, my beloved father's death; fourth, my mouth being opened in Meetings. My heart says, What can I render, for having been so remarkably and mercifully carried through these various dispensations of Providence? I think I never knew the Divine Arm so eminently extended for my comfort, help, and deliverance; and though of late, I may, in a degree, have had to pass through the valley of the shadow of death, yet it has not lasted long at a time, and oh, the incomings of love, joy, and peace, that have, at other periods, arisen for my confirmation and consideration! But the manna of yesterday, I find, will not do for to-day.

9th.—In the evening of First-day, I expressed what I had long on my mind to the servants, on entering a new year, which brought sweet peace. Yesterday, we dined at my brother and sister Samuel Gurney's—we met there my brother and sister Hoare, and my brother Fowell Buxton; I felt afterwards, as if I had not been enough on my guard, in conduct and conversation, indeed I awfully feel my conduct with regard to others, as well as to myself; for it appears strange for those to preach, who do not practise. Oh! for a double watch over thought, word, and deed!

11th.—It has been strongly impressed on me, how very little it matters, when we look at the short time we remain here, what we appear to others; and how far too much, we look at the things of this life. What does it signify, what we are thought of here, so long as we are not found wanting towards our Heavenly Father? Why should we so much try to keep something back, and not be willing to offer ourselves up to Him, body, soul, and spirit, to do with us what may seem best unto Him, and to make us what He would have us to be? O Lord! enable me to be more and more, singly, simply, and purely obedient to Thy service!

Second Month, 5th.—The first part of last week I was much occupied in arranging my new household; at least, two new servants, housekeeper and cook. I much felt the weight of filling my place rightly towards the servants, whom I may say, I love; how did I desire to help them, in the best sense, and that I might feel, that, as for me and my house, we will serve the Lord; I may say, there is nothing I desire so much; and the more I know, and the more I wish to follow Him in the way of His requirings, the more sweet do I find the path, and the more desirable does it appear.

19*th.*—Yesterday was an awful, and to me instructive day at Plaistow Meeting. I had not sat very long, before I was brought into much feeling desire that the darkness in some minds might be enlightened; however, no clearness of expression came with it, but under a very solemn covering of the spirit of supplication, a few words offering, I, after a time gave way to utter them; but that which appeared greatly in the cross to me, was having some words presented, to speak in testimony (ministry) afterwards, which I did, I believe, purely because I desired to serve my Master, and not to look too much to the opinion of my fellow-servants; and there was, to me, a remarkable solemnity, and something like an owning, or accepting, of this poor little offering. I have desired, and have been in a degree enabled, to feel a little on that sure foundation; that although the wind may blow, and the rain may descend, yet whilst I keep on this Rock, they will not be able utterly to cast me down. What a mercy, amidst the storm, to feel, ever so slightly, something of a sure foundation! Thus much I know, that, even if I be mistaken in this awful undertaking, my desire is to serve Him in it, whom my soul, I may truly say, loves and delights to please O Lord! I pray Thee, preserve Thy poor handmaid in the hour of temptation; and enable me to follow Thee in the way of Thy requirings, even if they lead me into suffering, and unto death.

31*st.*—My little —— has been very naughty; his will I find very strong; oh, that my hands may be strengthened rightly to subdue it. O Lord! I pray for help, in these important duties! I may truly say, I had rather my dear lambs should not live, than live eventually to dishonour Thy great cause; rather may they be taken in innocency, but, if Thou seest meet, O Lord! preserve them from great evils, and be pleased in Thy abundant mercy to be with them, as Thou hast been, I believe, with their poor unworthy parents; visit them, and revisit them, until Thou hast made them what Thou wouldest have them to be. Oh, that I could, like Hannah, bring them to Thee, to be made use of as instruments in Thy Holy Temple! I ask nothing for them, in comparison of Thy love; and above all blessings, that they may be vessels in Thy House; this blessing I crave for them, that they may be employed in Thy service, for indeed I can bow and say what honour, what joy so great, as in ever so small a measure, to serve Thee, O Lord!

Mildred's Court, Sixth Month, 1*st.*—Yesterday I attended the funeral of our beloved Anna Reynolds, whose death has been deeply felt by me. We had, I think, I may truly say, a glorious time, for the power of the most High, appeared to overshadow us: a belief of her being in safety, has bowed my soul prostrate, in humble thankfulness, and renewedly led me to desire to prove my gratitude for such unspeakable mercy, as has been showed my near and beloved relations, by my love and entire dedication. I uttered a few words in supplication, at the ground; my uncle Joseph, my cousin Priscilla, and many others beautifully ministered; after Meeting, I might truly say, my cup ran over, such sweetness covered my mind. After a solemn time in the family, with dear cousin Priscilla, and Ann Crowley, I ventured on my knees, praying, that His Holy Hand would not spare, nor

His eye pity, until He made us what he would have us to be; only I craved, that He would not forsake us, but, let us be made in some small measure sensible, that He was with us, and that it was His rod, and His staff, that we depended upon. Through heights, and through depths, through riches, and through poverty; may it alone be my will, to do the will of the Father!

Plashet, 2d.—I have found it pleasant and refreshing, being again with my beloved family in this sweet place. I have desired that the time spent in the Yearly Meeting, and what I have received there, may return as bread cast upon the waters.

To an early friend, and guest at Mildred's Court, she writes, describing her outward circumstances, and mental exercises, about this time.

Plashet, *Seventh Month*, 1810.

My beloved Friend,

As I have been much with thee in mind this morning, I feel inclined to tell thee how sincerely I love thee; I believe in that love which neither time nor distance can affect. Looking back to some account of what I passed through when thou wast at our house long ago, and how nearly I felt united to thee, has brought thee to my remembrance. I have often felt disposed to write to thee, since thou left England, but did not feel my letters worth sending so far; many changes have taken place, since we were together, perhaps more remarkably to me; we have now six little children, three girls and three boys, all well and lovely, and much enjoyment they give us, though at times in looking to their best interest, we are ready to tremble for them: may we do our part, so that we can in faith and humble confidence, look to Him who can alone bless our endeavours. All our beloved parents are taken from us, the loss of my own father, as thou mayst suppose, was a close trial, but I am ready to believe and hope, it brought its blessings to many of us; the great mercy he received at last, from his having a sweet hope and confidence, that, through the mercy of his Redeemer, it would be well with him, proved to my mind, I think, the strongest excitement to gratitude I ever experienced, so much so, that it appeared to break the ice for me, and on my knees I publicly expressed my thankfulness. This matter of publicly exposing myself, in this way, has been for many years struggling in my mind, long before I married, and once or twice when with thee, in London, I hardly knew how to dare to refrain. The past I must leave, but I am ready to think extreme unwillingness to give up to this matter, has kept me longer than I need have been, in a lukewarm, and at times wilderness estate; however, since a way has thus been made for me, it appears as if I dare not stop the work; if it be a right one, may it go on and prosper, if not, the sooner stopped, the better. I can hardly doubt, if I am only enabled to cling fast to Him, whose work I believe it is, that I shall experience preservation, though I find my state a new one: I do not understand myself, and I find I must walk by faith, and not by sight; at times I am permitted to abound, and to feel power that I cannot but believe to be beyond myself, at others, brought very low, poor, weak and almost miserable; my faith tried as to a hair's breadth; yet through all, I have found abundant cause for thanksgiving and praise.

Eighth Month, 10*th*.—I have thought this morning, I may in a measure adopt the language of the blessed Virgin, "My soul doth magnify the Lord, and my spirit hath rejoiced in God my Saviour." May my being led out of my own family, by what appear to me duties, never be permitted to hinder my doing my duty fully towards it, or so occupy my attention, as to make me, in any degree, forget or neglect home duties. I believe it matters not where we are, or what we are about, so long as we keep our eye fixed on doing the great Master's work, and that whatever we do, may be done to His glory. When I feel as I do to-day, what a glorious service it is, (though we may have, at times, to pass through great trial and poverty,) and remember how in these little religious services, I have been helped and carried through, and that, as I expressed before, my soul hath, in a measure, been able to magnify the Lord, and my spirit to rejoice in God its Saviour, I fear for myself, lest even this great mercy should prove a temptation, and lead me to come before I am called, or enter service I am not prepared for; but in all these things, I have but one place of safety, to take refuge in. Be pleased, then, O Lord! Thou who knowest my heart, and all its temptations; be pleased to preserve me, and enable me, if Thou seest meet, to do Thy will, in strength and in weakness, when it leads to the hardest crosses, as well as into the way of rejoicing.

Earlham, Ninth Month, 1st.—Yesterday I had much conversation with my beloved sisters Rachel and Richenda, upon their religious experience, and present belief. At the time, I felt very fully strengthened, to express my mind, and not to shrink; and I believe I did no hurt; but I have felt, and still feel very low; much pressed down; why, I cannot tell; they represent their case clearly, but can I, after what I have felt, known, and experienced, doubt the truth of this blessed principle, the sensible and constant direction of the Spirit of God in man? The head and judgment of man is most frail, or it would not twist so many ways; the work of religion must be in the heart, and if that become sanctified by the great "I am," and brought low before Him, and our wills be brought into subjection to the Divine will, and He become our all in all; then the great work, appears to me accomplished in us.

Plashet, 10th.—I desire gratefully to acknowledge my being once more returned home to my beloved family, my little ones appearing to have prospered in my absence, and I hope all going on well. And also I think, with abundant cause to be grateful, that on leaving Earlham, and my tenderly beloved brothers and sisters, my mind felt very clear, trusting that I had been enabled to accomplish that which came to hand to do amongst them; and I hope without hurting the great cause. How very near and dear they are to me. On First-day, I attended Ipswich and Colchester Meetings; I believe I was helped in the ministry, in both; if any praise be due, may it be given, both by me and others, to the great Author. Spent an interesting evening, with dear old John Kendall.

13*th.*—It is my great wish, that being engaged in these awful and important duties, may not, in any degree, lessen my attention to the smaller concerns of life; but rather prove a stimulus to do all well: I wish if right, still to feel a life in them, and not have my mind so occupied by the greater, as not to enter with spirit into the smaller. How much does gratitude call for at my hands at this time.

Tenth Month, 5*th.*—I had yesterday a very narrow escape of my life, from falling out of a whiskey upon my head, owing to a violent jolt; if it had gone on, I believe it must have gone over my head; many have been either killed, or materially injured by such a fall. I was, at the time, favoured with clearness, and knew what to do, and by immediately applying cold water to my head from a pond just by, my suffering was, in a great measure, relieved. I wonder I have not felt this event more seriously, but I did not, even at the time, feel much frightened, or overcome: I believe I was thinking, only about a minute before, that in case of my sudden death, I had nothing to look to but mercy.

24*th.*—I feel self-love and pride are hidden, very, very deep in me, and may sometimes rise, under specious appearances: I cannot root them out myself; but may I more often than the day, look to Him, who can do it for me.

26*th.*—This day year, a day I think never to be forgotten, whilst memory lasts, my beloved father died! and I first opened my mouth as a minister.

30*th.*—I crave to be, in all things, doing the will of Him, whom I desire to feel my Master; this is at times hard to come at; I do not feel by any means, a ready and willing servant: still not willing either to speak a word before meals, or after our reading. My very frequent speaking in Meeting, is very awful to me. Be pleased, O Lord! still to be with Thy poor child, preserve her, if Thou seest meet from right hand, as well as left hand errors: increase my faith, and renew a right spirit within me. May neither heights nor depths; riches nor poverty; health nor sickness; be permitted to overcome me, and separate me from Thy love; and be pleased, O Lord! to enable me always to give Thee the glory, and not to take it to myself. May I more faithfully do my duty towards Thee, towards my neighbour, and towards myself: when called upon publicly to advocate Thy cause, be pleased to grant me faith sufficient! Create in me a more willing mind, to express whatever may arise, as in the newness of life; whether in public or in private, that the short time of my continuance here, I may in life, conduct, and word, live to thy glory. Amen, saith my poor soul.

In the Twelfth Month she travelled into Gloucestershire, taking three of her children, to visit William Fry and his wife; the latter was in seriously delicate health. They were residing at that time at Rodborough, a very beautiful place which W. Fry had hired, hoping that his wife might derive benefit from the air.

Rodborough, Twelfth Month, 22nd.—I enjoy being here, and the company of those I am with. I trust not in myself, in my own weak and disobedient heart, but I trust in Thee, O Lord! before whom the mountains skip like rams, and the little hills like lambs.

Plashet, 28th.—I may indeed acknowledge that a way has been, to me, wonderfully made, for even my disobedient heart has been brought down, and made willing to submit; may I never forget it, or to whom the power and praise belong; who capacitated me to do, what to human nature felt impossible, on First-day, at Nailsworth. When evening came, after passing through little short of distress of soul, I was enabled, after their reading, to kneel down and offer my little sacrifice, which I felt abundantly helped in, both as to power and utterance; my beloved sister Eliza seemed to feel it extremely, so much so, that I was afraid it might overcome her, and make her ill; but she soon revived, and told me how much she had felt it, and united with me, which was sweet and encouraging. I was enabled to leave that place with a clear and peaceful heart, knowing of no burden.

Plashet, First Month, 5th, 1811.—I find it no easy matter to serve the poor, I desire to do right towards them; but it is very difficult either to turn them away, or to give to all, without doing as much hurt as good. I desire a right spirit about them, and ability to know what is best to be done.

6*th.*—In the evening the servants and children read with us, and much in the cross to human nature, I believe I may say, my will was subdued for me, and power given to crave a blessing upon us and our household; I was abundantly helped, and a sweet feeling has been my portion since; like abiding under the shadow of His wing, whom I desire to be my Lord, and my God, my all in all.

11*th.*—Felt very low yesterday evening, rather unusually so for me, partly from the children being naughty and trying. I also feel how poorly my duties are performed towards all. If I be clearer in one description of duty than another, I think it is towards servants; but in that I often have to mourn over my defects. I have felt a little encouragement this morning, and am at times brought to leave others, and their interests, and to look and depend upon Him, who can help them, and even listens to the cry of His little ones. As for my beloved children, I had rather they should not be, than have them live to go greatly astray; but let me not forget that if they, like myself, should go astray for a time, there is that power which can bring them back. Oh, that this may be the case; may they eventually become redeemed from the world, and advocates or valiants in the great cause! It is almost my single desire for them; all others are small in comparison—and as for my beloved husband, oh! that we may be preserved, going hand in hand, and bowing before the Holy One in sweet unity; not turning aside to any other gods, or making to ourselves graven images, and worshipping them.

Second Month, 7th.—Yesterday was, to me, an awful and affecting day; there came up a minute from the men, desiring the women to meet them after the next Monthly Meeting, to consider the subject of acknowledging me as a minister. Friends felt so kindly for me, as to call me out of Meeting to tell me, lest hearing it should overcome me; this was unnecessary, for though I felt and feel it deeply, that was not likely to be the case. It brings me prostrate before the great "I am;" but I have little or nothing to say for myself: certainly, it is cause of humble gratitude, to believe my little offerings in the ministry have not burdened, but been acceptable to the church. O Lord! if it be Thy will to preserve my life, yet a little longer, and to continue me in this service, preserve me, even if it be through chastisement, from ever hurting Thy great and holy cause, and enable me to walk worthy of the vocation whereunto I am called.

Her seventh child, Elizabeth, was born on the 20th of Second Month.

Mildred's Court, Second Month, 26th.—Though confined to a lying-in-room, and not actively engaged, may I seek, in all things, to be acting in conformity to the Divine will; for this state has its temptations. May the day's work, whatever it be, keep pace with the day.

The Meeting, of which she was a member, feeling unity

with her engagements as a minister, acknowledged her at this time, in that character.

In reference to it, she says:—

This mark of their unity is sweet, and I think strengthening, and I believe will have advantages, as well as trials, attending it. I feel, and find, it is not by the approbation, any more than by the disapprobation of man, that we stand or fall; but it once more leads me only to desire, that I may, simply and singly, follow my Master in the way of His requirements, whatsoever they may be. I think this will make a way for me in some things, that have been long on my mind.

Plashet, Sixth Month, 3d.—Yearly Meeting is finished: I have renewed evidence that there yet remains a God, hearing prayer; as my inward cries, as well as outward, appear to have been, in some instances, rather remarkably heard and granted. I have also had renewed evidence, that there yet remains a Gospel ministry, as I have been ministered to, and have known the same with others, and have been, I believe, enabled a little to minister myself, I could almost believe from the living Source. I have not had much to do in this way, but a little at times, in private and public. I find it an awful thing to rise, amongst a large assembly, and unless much covered with love and power, hardly know how to venture.

19th.—I feel, at times, deeply pressed down, on account of my beloved children. Their volatile minds try me; but, amidst my trials, I have a secret hope concerning them, that all will end well; and a blessing attend them, if they bow to the blessed yoke, (for so I feel it,) in their youth. May you, if ever you read this, my beloved little ones, hearken to the advice of your tenderly affectionate mother. Submit to the cross of Christ, in small matters and in great,—there is no way like it; the crown is, in a measure, partaken of, even here. That no enemy of your souls be permitted to overcome you, or turn your feet into another path, is the sincere desire, nay, prayer of her, who feels your souls' welfare very near to her own; may we all so live, that when time to us here shall be no more, we may unite, and sing praises in eternity. Look at it,—what folly, for the sake of self-gratification for a few years, to forfeit even the chance of such a prospect! ah, my children, press forward through all opposition; walking by faith, rather than by sight, for in that alone you will find strength and safety; looking too much out, loses time and creates confusion, whilst humbly looking within, with the eye of faith, and following whatever that may lead into, or out of, tends to confirm, stablish, and strengthen. May the God of peace be with, bless, and preserve you, saith my soul. Amen. O Lord! be pleased to have mercy on them, win them over to Thy love, and teach them that there is no way like Thy way, no joy like Thy joy.

Earlham, Seventh Month, 21st.—I am come with my beloved husband, to attend my dear uncle Gurney's funeral. I cannot easily express my feelings this day; the state of the souls of the family is so deeply interesting to me. My soul has been laid low, and brought very prostrate, feeling for the various conditions of my beloved family, who are brought together on this awful occasion; desiring for those who have at times to advocate the great cause, that we may get deep enough, and not speak from outward knowledge and observation, but alone move in the great service, as the pure life may lead us into it: may we be enabled to say enough, and preserved from saying too much. Be pleased, O Lord! to grant us tongue and utterance, to show forth Thy praise, that those afar off, may be induced to come, taste, and see, how good Thou art. Be pleased also to anoint their eyes, and their ears, both to hear and see for themselves, that there is none like unto Thee; but that Thou art worthy both now and for ever, to be praised and exalted above all. Amen.

Plashet, Eighth Month, 23rd.—We had three clergymen and their wives, besides another neighbour and his wife, here yesterday; I believe good men, and I hope good women also; I felt love, and I think that sort of unity with them, that I have with good Friends. From a great fear of hurting others, I feel, though I believe it is not very apparent, a bowing to their opinions, and not openly professing my own, which tries me. There are, no doubt, advantages, as well as disadvantages, in associating with people of different descriptions: especially, in being with the Good, we are increasingly led to estimate the good in all, and also to observe, how the mercy of our heavenly Father is extended towards us, and how he sees meet to accept us, in our different ways. But, at the same time, there is safety in keeping within our narrow enclosure, more particularly for young people not established in principle. It may induce to make the example of others, a plea for more liberty, instead of rightly stimulating them to look at home, and examine how far they are doing the work committed to them, which should be the effect of seeing others zealously pursuing their course. It is also important, as children become marriageable, with whom they associate, and parents should in this, as in other things, keep on the watch, and seek the best direction how far to go, and where to stop. But my feelings of love would lead me almost to encourage an intimacy with one of these clergymen and his wife: but I desire to be rightly directed, and if we are likely to lose more than we gain, by not holding fast the profession of our faith without wavering, then I hope not to encourage it; I leave it, thinking it will make its own way, which I trust will be the right one, but Friends being so much united with others, and brought so forward in works of benevolence, may prove a snare by flattering them, and taking them off their guard. It is on account of schools that we have been thus brought together.

On being settled at Plashet, Elizabeth Fry had formed various plans for the benefit of her poorer neighbours, which she gradually brought into action. One of her early endeavours, was to establish a girls' school for the Parish of East Ham; of which Plashet is a hamlet.

A young woman named Harriet Howell, who was much occupied at that time in organizing schools on the Lancasterian system, came to Plashet. The clergyman of East Ham (alluded to in the journal) with his wife united with Elizabeth Fry in the object. A school of about seventy girls was established, and, although afterwards removed to a more central situation, continues to the present day.

The bodily wants of the poor, especially in cases of sickness or accident, claimed her careful attention. There was a depôt of calico and flannels always ready, besides outer garments, and a roomy closet well supplied with drugs. In very hard winters, she had soup boiled in an out-house, in such quantities, as to supply hundreds of poor people with a nourishing meal. Nor was her interest confined to the English poor in East Ham. About half a mile from Plashet, on the high road between Stratford and Ilford, the passer-by will find two long rows of houses, with one larger house in the centre, if possible more dingy than the rest. At that time they were squalid and dirty. The windows generally stuffed with old rags, or pasted over with brown paper, and the few remaining panes of glass refusing to perform their intended office from the accumulated dust of years; puddles of thick black water before the doors; children without shoe or stocking; mothers, whose matted locks escaped from the remnants of caps, which looked as though they never could have been white; pigs, on terms of evident familiarity with the family; poultry sharing the children's potatoes—all bespoke an Irish colony.

It was a pleasant thing to observe the influence obtained by Elizabeth Fry, over these wild, but warm-hearted people.

One clear frosty morning, she called her elder children to accompany her on a visit to one of these cottages. A poor woman, the mother of a young family, had died there; she had been well conducted as a wife and mother, and had long shown a desire for religious instruction; the priest, a kind-hearted man, liberal in his views, and anxious for the good of his flock, thought well of the poor woman, had frequently visited her in her illness, and was in that, as in many other cases, very grateful to Elizabeth Fry, for the relief and nourishment she had bestowed, and which it was not in his power to give.

On the bed of death lay extended the young mother, her features, which were almost beautiful, stiffened into the semblance of marble. Her little children were on the floor, the husband, in a corner, leaning on a round table, with his face buried in his hands. A paper cross lay on the breast of the corpse; the sun shone into the room, and lighted the dreary scene. The apartment was close, from the fumes of tobacco, and the many guests of the wake, which had been held during the night. Elizabeth Fry spoke soothingly to the husband; she reminded him of his wife's desires for his good, and for that of his children; she slightly alluded to the uselessness of the cross as a symbol, but urged the attention of those present, to the great doctrine of which it was intended to remind them. Again, she offered solace to the mourner, promised assistance for his little ones, and left the room.

Some of the scenes in Irish Row were very different. She enjoyed giving pleasure, it was an impulse, as well as a duty with her, to do good. Gathering her garments round her, she would thread her way through children and pigs, up broken stair-cases, and by narrow passages, to the apartments which she sought; there she would listen to their tales of want or woe, or of their difficulties with their children, or of the evil conduct of their husbands. She persuaded many of them to adopt more orderly habits, giving little presents of clothing as encouragements: she induced some to send their children to school, and with the consent of the priest, circulated the Bible amongst them. On one occasion, when the weather was extremely cold, and great distress prevailed, being at the time too delicate herself to walk, she went alone in the carriage, literally piled with flannel petticoats for Irish Row ; the rest of the party walking to meet her, to assist in the delightful task of distribution. She made relieving the poor a pleasure to her children, by the cheerful spirit in which she did it ; she employed them as almoners, when very young ; but expected a minute account of their giving, and their reasons for it. After the establishment of the Tract Society, she always kept a large supply of such Tracts as she approved, for distribution. It was her desire never to relieve the bodily wants of any one, without endeavouring, in some way, more or less directly, to benefit their souls. She was a warm advocate for vaccination, and very successful in performing the operation ; she had acquired this art from Dr. Willan, one of its earliest advocates and most skilful practitioners. At intervals, she made a sort of investigation of the state of the parish, with a view to vaccinating the children. The result was, that small-pox was scarcely known in the villages over which her influence extended.

In a green lane, near Plashet, it has been the annual custom of the Gipsies to pitch their tents, for a few days, in their way to Fairlop fair. The sickness of a gipsy child, inducing the mother to apply for relief, led Elizabeth Fry to visit their camp ; from that time, from year to year, she cared for them whenever they came into her neighbourhood ; clothing for the children and people, and a little medical advice she invariably bestowed ; but she did far more than that, she sought to influence their minds aright, she pleaded with them on the bitter fruits of sin, and furnished them with Bibles, and books the most likely to arouse their attention.

But though thus abounding in labours for the good of all around her, self was not exalted. Her spirit was preserved in a state of deep humility and godly fear.

Ninth Month, 5th.—I have lately been so much hurried by an almost constant change of company and employments, as to be at times a good deal tried, and I am fearful my temper will be made irritable by it. I think I may truly say, my desire is, to do my duty fully and faithfully to all connected with me, nearly and remotely, rich and poor. Be pleased, O Lord! to bless the small, feeble endeavours of Thy poor child, to do her duty to others; for, without Thy blessing, they are ineffectual, and with thy blessing, I need not doubt but they will tend to my own good, and to the good of those whom I desire to serve, more particularly at home. With my dear little ones I often feel myself a poor mother, but my hope is not in myself; for I am sensible I do not apparently manage them so well, as many others do their children; but, O Lord! Thou knowest my heart, and its desires for them, and that I may not be found wanting towards them. I neither ask health nor riches, nor anything for them in comparison with this, that as they grow in years, they may grow in favour with Thee, and with those who love Thee, by walking in humility, and in Thy fear. My feeling of my own great deficiencies towards them and others, at times leads me to take great comfort from the shortness of life, if I be but ready, and have done faithfully the work committed.

In the Ninth Month, Elizabeth Fry visited Norfolk: whilst there, she attended the first Bible Meeting held in Norwich.

Earlham, Ninth Month, 10th.—I think a more deeply exercised state, that has at times bordered on distress of soul, I hardly ever remember, than I feel this morning going to Meeting; in the first place, with the Edwardses and my own family, in their various states; in the next place my prospect of going into the men's Monthly Meeting; and in the last, an idea having passed my mind, whether I may not have, amongst the very large companies who are likely to be here, consisting of many clergymen and others, to say something, either before meals, or at some other time. The words that (I believe) have arisen for my encouragement, are these, "The Lord is my Shepherd, I shall not want." Yes, I will try not to fear, for if God be with me, who can be against me?

12*th.*—What can I render for all his benefits? In the first place, I went to the Meeting for worship with the Edwardses: I had not long been there, before I felt something of a power accompanying me, and words arose, but my exercise of mind was so great, that it seemed like being "baptized for the dead:" though not, that I know of, from any particular fear of man; I was helped (I believe I may say), as to power, tongue, and utterance. That Meeting might be said to end well.

Yesterday was a day indeed:—one that may be called a mark of the times. We first attended a General Meeting of the Bible Society, where it was sweet to observe so many, of various sentiments, all uniting in the one great object, from the good Bishop of Norwich (Bathurst), for so I believe he may be called, to the dissenting Minister, and young Quaker (my brother Joseph). We afterwards, about thirty-four of us, dined here. I think there were six clergymen of the Establishment; three dissenting Ministers; and Richard Philips, besides numbers of others. A very little before the cloth was removed, such a power came over me of love, I believe I may say, *life*, that I thought I must ask for silence after Edward Edwards had said grace, and then supplicate the Father of mercies for His blessing—both of the fatness of the earth, and the dew of Heaven, upon those, who thus desired to promote His cause, by spreading the knowledge of the Holy Scriptures; and that He would bless their endeavours, that the knowledge of God and His glory might cover the earth, as the waters cover the sea; and also for the preservation of all present, that through the assistance of His grace we might so follow Him, our blessed Lord, in time, that we might eventually enter into a glorious eternity, where the wicked cease from troubling, and the weary are at rest.

The power and solemnity were very great. Richard Philips asked for silence, I soon knelt down, it was like having our High Priest amongst us; independently of this power, His poor instruments are nothing, and with His power, how much is effected! I understood many were in tears, I believe all were bowed down spiritually. Soon after I took my seat the Baptist minister said, "This is an act of worship;" adding that it reminded him of that which the disciples said, "When He walked with us, did not our hearts burn within us?" A clergyman said, "We want no wine, for there is that amongst us, that does instead." A Lutheran minister* remarked, that although he could not always understand the words, being a foreigner, he felt the Spirit of Prayer, and went on to enlarge in a striking manner. Another clergyman spoke to this effect; How the Almighty visited us, and that neither sex, nor any thing else, stood in the way of His grace. I do not exactly remember the words of any one, but it was a most striking circumstance, for so many, of such different opinions, thus all to be united in one spirit; and for a poor woman to be made the means, amongst so many great, wise, and I believe good men, of showing forth the praise of the great "I am." After reading last evening, the dear Lutheran minister, Dr. Steinkoff, said a few words in prayer. This morning, my desire, indeed I may say prayer, is, that this may not degenerate into a form amongst us, and I should not be surprised, if I had to express as much; however, that I leave. Be pleased, O Lord! still to preserve me on the right hand, and on the left, and let me in no way do contrary to Thy will; and if called upon to testify that I can only unite in prayer, where I apprehend Thy Spirit leads into it, enable me, I beseech Thee, to do it so as to strengthen, rather than weaken the love, that I feel so sweetly to unite me with those who differ from myself.

In a letter from Joseph Hughes, one of the Secretaries of the Bible Society, this occasion is thus described:—

* Dr. Steinkoff.

"On the Monday after my return, I proceeded with my excellent colleagues for Norwich, where a numerous and respectable meeting was held on Wednesday, in a very spacious and commodious hall; the Mayor presided; the Bishop spoke with great decision and equal liberality; and the result of the whole was, the establishment of the Norfolk and Norwich Bible Society; about £700 was subscribed, and one happy, amiable sentiment appeared to pervade the company. My colleagues and myself adjourned to Earlham, two miles from Norwich, where we had passed the previous day, and where we had witnessed emanations of piety, generosity, and affection, in a degree that does not often meet the eye of mortals. Our host and hostesses were the Gurneys, chiefly Quakers, who, together with their guests, amounted to thirty-four. A clergyman, at the instance of one of the family, and I presume with the most cordial concurrence of the rest, read a portion of the Scriptures, morning and evening; and twice we had prayers, I should have said thrice, for after dinner on the day of the Meeting, the pause encouraged by "the Society of Friends," was succeeded by a devout address to the Deity, by a female minister, Elizabeth Fry, whose manner was impressive, and whose words were so appropriate, that none present can ever forget the incident, or ever advert to it, without emotions, alike powerful and pleasing. The first emotion was surprise; the second, awe; the third, pious fervour. As soon as we were re-adjusted at the table, I thought it might be serviceable to offer a remark, that proved the coincidence of my heart with the devotional exercise in which we had been engaged; this had the desired effect. Mr. Owen and others suggested accordant sentiments, and we seemed generally to feel like the Disciples, whose hearts burned within them as they walked to Emmaus.

"The days passed in this excellent family, were opened with joy, and closed with regret; few such days will occur again; yet when devotion shall cease to be measured by days, pleasure far more intense, shall spring up for ever fresh; and all the members of the vast *Household of Faith* shall behold each other, in a scene where purity is unblemished, and harmony uninterrupted, and bliss complete and everlasting.

"'When shall I wake and find me there?'"

Plashet, Tenth Month, 3rd.—In the evening, after reading at Earlham, I was greatly helped in prayer for my brothers and sisters, who were all present; it was in thanksgiving and prayer; acknowledging our many blessings; particularly, that of being so united with each other, which blessing I craved might increase; that we might increasingly dwell in God, and He in us. I also prayed for our little ones, that they, with us, might have the knowledge of God, and of our blessed Lord Christ Jesus; that we might eventually obtain a habitation not made with hands, eternal in the heavens. It was a very solemn time, many, I believe, wept, and I trust all felt it, and united in prayer. I think I may say I went away rejoicing, which appeared marvellous to me, my season of discouragement had, at times, whilst there, been so great; but I believe these things tend to keep me low, and preserve me, or I might, when so uplifted, be tempted to take my flight. I find, on my return, much cause for gratitude.

Shortly after Elizabeth Fry's return home, her baby became seriously ill: scarcely had it recovered, ere another event claimed her tenderest sympathy, the death of her sister Buxton's infant.

Plashet, Tenth Month, 17th.—I was enabled, on First-day evening, to pray for my dear children in their presence; since then, I have felt more cheerful and easy about them, having committed them to *His* keeping, who alone can protect them. I am but a poor instrument in His holy hand. His they are, though He may have appeared to give them to us, my heart's desire and prayer is, that, like as Hannah with Samuel, they may all be lent unto the Lord. My dear baby is poorly, I desire not to be too anxious about her; but that the Divine will may alone be done in all things, and that I may be enabled to commend her to His holy keeping; not that I feel compunction for naturally desiring her life, and that she may be saved from much suffering.

21st.—Much occupied night and day, by the illness of my sweet babe; I was so low in the night, that I shed many tears; a mother's feelings are strong in me;—Oh, that I may be granted a submissive and resigned spirit, and that imagination may not colour the dark side: may I, in all my various allotments, be enabled to bow in faith, before Him, who orders all things well; even amidst the risings of natural feeling, which, rightly modified, I do not believe to be wrong. I desire, above all, that not my will, O Lord! but Thine be done. Amen, saith my soul.

25th.—My dear babe much better; it appears as if my prayer had been heard.

Eleventh Month, 18th.—(The day of the funeral of her little niece.)—To whom can I go in moments of trial, but to Him who hath hitherto helped me? Be pleased, O Lord! to be with us, and bless the present occasion to us; may it draw us nearer to Thee, and make us increasingly willing to become Thy servants, and Thy handmaids; if anything should, as a minister, come to my hands to do, may I be helped by Thy power, and anointed by Thee, who can alone savingly help us. May the state of my heart be such, that I may with truth say, here am I, Lord, do with me what Thou wilt, only make me what Thou wouldest have me to be. May this event be of lasting benefit to us all; but more particularly to the dear parents. Grant me, O Lord! wisdom and power to proclaim Thy power and Thy praise, that if made use of at all, others as well as myself, may be drawn nearer to Thee, and wholly give Thee praise, never taking, or giving, that glory to the creature, which alone belongs to the Creator.

Afternoon.—The funeral of dear little Susannah Buxton has taken place to-day. The event of her death has been very affecting to me, and most unexpected to us all. This day week, she only appeared to have a cold; she was one of the loveliest, sweetest, and most lively of little babes. She appeared to suffer little in her illness. I was not there at her death, but comfort was then near to her dear mother, and faith that strengthened her to believe it was well, and that her spirit had ascended unto God, who gave it. This was very much the case with me when there after her death; but naturally, it has been a close stroke, the child was very dear to me, but consolation has been near.

We have had to-day a very solemn, and, I trust, in the best sense, an encouraging time, the remembrance of it is sweet and reviving to me. I was helped in prayer, greatly as I think, and in a few words afterwards; but may self pass unobserved, for there was a better than man present with us. Words fall very short of expression: Oh, that all would come, taste, and see, how good the Lord is; for blessed is the man that trusteth in Him,—although, like others, he may be afflicted!

Henry Hull, a valuable Friend and Minister from America, was at this time frequently a guest at Plashet. Early in the winter, Elizabeth Fry believed it her duty to unite with him in a religious visit to some of the Meetings near London. Her sister, Priscilla Gurney, accompanied them.

Twelfth Month, 28th.—My heart is very full this morning, at the prospect of this journey; the tears rise in my eyes, for it appears probable that we shall be out longer than I at first expected. I have something of a confidence that my beloved family will be cared for in my absence. My prayer for myself is, that I may not run without being sent; and if the gift in me grows and increases with exercise, may I ever be preserved from decking myself with the Lord's jewels.

Plashet, First Month, 13th, 1812.—I returned safely home yesterday, and to my great comfort found all my beloved children well and good. My beloved husband is gone into Wales; all my household appears in very comfortable order; and so far from having suffered in my absence, it appears as if a better blessing had attended them than common. Thus much for them, now for myself—I may, I trust, with gratitude acknowledge, that I have, in my religious duties, experienced the Lord to go before me, and to prove my rear-ward; I have naturally been in a low estate, much felt my absence from home, and have not been well in my health. I have also, in a spiritual sense, been often brought low, under a peculiar feeling of some of my infirmities, and great fear of the power of the tempter. I have felt much increased value and love for Henry Hull, and dear Priscilla has been a sweet, kind, and valuable companion; may our union be farther cemented. My desire for myself on my return is, that I may walk within my house with a perfect heart.

Second Month, 1st.—On reading over my old journals yesterday, it has led me to admire how some of my early prayers and desires have been answered; how gradual has been the arising and opening of Divine Power in my heart. How much has occurred to strengthen my weak faith, and doubting, fearful heart; how much has been done for me, and how little have I done myself; how much have I rebelled, except in the day of power; how often unwatchful; yet in mercy, how has help been administered, even a willing heart, which I consider an unspeakable gift; but I think I should have flourished better, and grown stronger by this time, had I more fully and more faithfully followed the Lamb whithersoever He goeth. My heart's desire and prayer for myself, above everything else, is, that this may be more entirely done by me. O Lord! be pleased still to carry on Thy own work in me, until Thou hast made me what Thou wouldest have me to be; even entirely Thy servant, in thought, word, and deed! Thou only knowest my weakness and fear of suffering; when in Thine infinite wisdom, Thou mayst see meet to afflict, be pleased to mix mercy with judgment, and uphold me by Thine own power; I thank Thee for all Thy benefits towards me, and desire to prove my gratitude by my love and good works. O Lord! enable me so to do! Amen.

3rd.—The prospect I have had for some months, of going into Norfolk, to attend the Monthly and Quarterly Meetings, is now brought home to me, as I must apply to my next Monthly Meeting for permission. It is no doubt a sacrifice of natural feeling, to leave the comforts of home, and my beloved husband and children; and to my weak, nervous habits, the going about, and alone (for so I feel it in one sense without my husband) is, I have found from experience, a trial greater than I imagined; and my health suffers much I think, from my habits being necessarily so different. This consideration, of its being a cross to my nature, I desire not to weigh in the scale; though, no doubt, for the sake of others, as well as myself, my health being so shaken is a serious thing. What I desire to consider most deeply is this:—Have I authority for leaving my home and evident duties? What leads me to believe I have? for I need not doubt that when away, and at times greatly tried, this query is likely to arise. The prospect has come in that quiet, yet, I think, powerful way, that I have never been able to believe I should get rid of it; indeed hitherto I have hardly felt anything but a calm cheerfulness about it, and very little anxiety. It seems to me as if, in this journey, I must be stripped of outward dependences, and my watchword appears to be,—"My soul, wait thou ONLY upon God; for my expectation is from Him."

6th.—My beloved little ones have been ill with a severe cold, and my sweet babe has so very serious an attack, and one that has now lasted some days, that I believe her life is thought to be in danger. I have suffered a good deal, the most in the night; my desire for myself is, to be enabled to submit to the dispensations of Almighty wisdom, and that faith may be granted me, to drink the cup, whatever it may be, as coming from the Lord's holy hand; nothing doubting that it will be ordered in infinite wisdom and mercy. Natural feelings I do not desire to be without, for I had rather have them, if under proper subjection. Jesus wept, may not we? I feel much gratitude that her sufferings appear comparatively small, and rather to decrease; if I could have a prayer on her account outwardly, it would be that she might be spared much suffering; but I desire and pray above all things, that I may leave all to Him, who has dealt with me and my little ones, in unspeakable mercy, that He will yet watch over us for good, and not permit us to suffer more than is best for us. How much better to have her life cut short in innocency, than for her to live to that state, in which her sins should have separated her from God. Be pleased, O Lord! to grant Thy poor servant and her little one, strength sufficient for the day, and whether mourning or rejoicing be my portion, may it work together for my good, and make me a better servant to Thee. Amen, and Amen.

7th.—A few hours after I last wrote, a change took place in the dear babe for the better, and the amendment has been gradual since. I desire to receive it as from the blessed hand that makes sore and binds up, that wounds and makes whole

20th.—My sister, Elizabeth Fry, means to go with me into Norfolk: my uncle Joseph is likely to go another way: it appears as if I could not mind much who is to go with me. But I feel disposed to a very single dependence, and if I be rightly put forth to this service, may He who puts me forth, be with me; if I have to administer food to others, may it be that which is convenient for them, and which will tend to their lasting nourishment. I have often thought that, in this little prospect, I must go like David, when he went to slay the giant. I am ashamed of the comparison; but I only mean it in this respect, I go, not trusting in any power or strength of my own; I feel I dare look to no helper outwardly. I feel young and a stripling, without armour, yet I trust the Lord will be with me, and make the sling and stone effectual, if He please to make use of His poor child, to slay the giant in any one.

Earlham, Third Month, 14th.—Have I not renewed reason for faith, hope, and confidence in the principle which I desire to follow? In the night, I had to acknowledge that the work must be Thine, O Lord! and that it is to me wonderful. My fears and causes of discouragement were many; for some little time before I set off, my own poor health, and my little ones; then my lowness and stupidity. In the first place, my health and the dear children's improved so much, and I inwardly so brightened, that I left home very comfortably. As I went on my way, such abundant hope arose, that light, rather than darkness, appeared to surround me. I have now attended the Monthly Meetings, and three other Meetings. I have also had frequent opportunities of a religious nature, in families; the most remarkable were, one in a clergyman's family, in supplication for him and his house, and another, where he had to supplicate for my help. May I ever remember how utterly unfit I am, in myself, for all these works: unto me alone belongs abasedness. I can take nothing to myself. As Thou hast seen meet, O Lord! Thou, who art strength in weakness, thus to make use of Thy poor hand-maid, as an instrument in Thy service, be pleased to keep her from the evil, both in reality and appearance, that she never may, in any way, bring reproach upon Thy cause!

16*th.*—I expect my beloved brother, John, will be here to-day; may I be enabled to walk before him in humility and godly fear, (not the fear of man,) that he, at least, may be enabled to believe that I am not following cunningly devised fables, or imaginations of my own, but rather seeking to follow a crucified Redeemer, in the way in which He leads me.

In a letter to her cousin, Joseph Gurney Bevan, she alludes to the duties in which she was engaged:—

May I now be enabled to attend to my own vineyard, and after having been made instrumental, thus to warn and encourage others, may I not become a cast-away myself. I hardly understand what Friends mean by reward for such services, for I do not feel the work mine, and no reward is due; as for reward, is it not enough to feel a Power, better than ourselves, influencing and strengthening us to do the work that, we humbly trust, is His own? for what honour, favour, or blessing so great, as being engaged in the service of Him whom we love, in whatever way it be, whether performing one duty or another, and having a little evidence granted us, that we are doing His will, or endeavouring to do it? I peculiarly feel, in ministerial duties, that I have no part, because the whole appears a gift,—the willing heart, the power, and everything attending it; the poor creature has only to remain as passive as possible, willing to be operated upon.

Plashet, Third Month, 28th.—I will first mention how it was with me in the Norwich Quarterly Meeting. I went, looking to Him who has hitherto helped me; my beloved uncle Joseph said a few words, as a seal to what I had expressed, and it was, I believe, a peculiarly solemn and favoured time: much blessed in a few words of supplication, at the Grove, before dinner. In the adjourned Meeting, I felt it safest to go to the Men's Meeting, where I had to bid them farewell in the Lord; after I had been helped with a few words of tender love and encouragement, Sarah Bowly said a little, and then my dear sister Elizabeth arose, and said, "She hoped what had passed that day, would not be attended to as a tale that was told, but as everlasting truths;" which appeared to me to bring great solemnity and sweetness with it. In the Women's Meeting, we also had a very solemn time at parting, in which I bade them farewell; desiring that we might all ascend, step by step, that ladder which reaches from earth to heaven. Before we set off, I had, after reading, in heart-felt and heart-tendering supplication, to pray for the preservation of the family, and our support in the day of trial; and amidst all the various turnings and overturnings of the Holy Hand upon us. Here I once more am, surrounded by outward blessings, and well in health; yet I hardly know how to return thanks, or to rejoice in Him who has helped me, being poor, low, stripped, the tears come into my eyes. Though cast down, I love the Lord above all, and desire, through the saving, redeeming power of Him, who came to save that which was lost, and has, I believe, proved a Saviour to me *in part*, that I may draw nearer and nearer to the most high God, and become in all things more completely His.

The reader will, perhaps, be struck with the expression "in part," as applied to the Saviour's work; an extract from a letter which is here introduced, written to a clergyman, Edward Edwards, explains that her use of these words arose, not from any mistrust of the saving power of Christ, but from her consciousness that the great work of sanctification in her heart was incomplete and unfinished.

My beloved Friend,

Thy letter is one I do not desire lightly to answer, as I wish to receive it and attend to it, with the seriousness it deserves, as coming from one, who I believe desires the prosperity of truth, individually and generally; and in this desire, has with love addressed me, for my own good, and also the good of the body to which I belong. I hope to profit by it; I am spiritually but a child, "I think as a child, I speak as a child, and I understand as a child." I do not believe that the great mysteries of the gospel are, by any means, fully opened to me; but my dependence is on Him who has so far opened my eyes, that He will, in His own time, further enlighten, confirm, settle, and strengthen me in that faith, which is the substance of things hoped for, the evidence of things not seen. Thus far I believe, from having experienced what it is to feel alienated or separated from my God, no doubt by corruptions and sin. I experienced the state of being under the law; I may truly say, "I know that in me, that is, in my flesh, dwelleth no good thing; for to will is present with me, but how to perform that which is good, I find not; for the good that I would I do not; but the evil which I would not that I do." Thus I have experienced and do yet experience, that it is not in me, or my fleshly nature, to do or to will any good thing. Then how naturally do these words arise, "O! wretched man, (or woman,) that I am, who shall deliver me from the body of this death?" Then comes the Saviour, then comes the Deliverer, to whom can I go, but to Him, who alone has the words of eternal life? I feel ashamed of now bringing my experiences forward, as it is with humility and confusion of face, that I may acknowledge that I have also felt what it is, in a measure, to be in Christ Jesus; "for the law of the spirit of life in Christ Jesus, maketh us free from the law of sin and death; for what the law could not do, in that it was weak through the flesh, God sending his own Son in the likeness of sinful flesh, and for sin, condemned sin in the flesh, that the righteousness of the law might be fulfilled in those who walk not after the flesh, but after the Spirit." I have thus quoted Scripture, because I know no other way of so clearly expressing my own faith, and experience in measure, and also what I believe to be the faith of the body, (though there may be unbelievers amongst us as well as others,) that we lay aside all our own works, and believe we neither will, nor do, of ourselves, but that it is God, or the saving power of Christ, that worketh in us to will and to do; that we desire alone to give all the glory to Him, of whatever is done to his praise, believing Him to be the author and finisher of our faith, and our only hope of glory. The work of regeneration is a gradual one, and I feel, if alive at all, only a beginner, therefore do not understand that I feel free from the law of sin and death; but I believe if the Spirit of Christ in us be permitted to operate, and is not resisted by our wills, we may experience a being made free from the law of sin and spiritual death, even here below.

Fourth Month, 4th.—Since I last wrote, I have been afflicted inwardly and outwardly; I have had a more serious attack of illness than I have had for many months. It led me to consider, if taken hence, where would be my hope? To feel an operative faith, of being accepted through the mercy of God in Christ, is a gift which we cannot command. Oh! that my soul may be more deeply anchored in this faith, that nothing may be permitted to shake it: I also find, that without the present gift of faith, I cannot commit my beloved husband and children to His holy keeping, who can alone preserve them.

16*th.*—I am poorly, and I believe five of my dear children have the whooping-cough; but all now appears light, nay, more than light; such sweetness has covered my mind, little short, at times, of joy and peace, as if no alloy were permitted to take hold: so are we dealt with, not according to our merits, but to His mercy, who careth for His poor dependent ones, and enlivens them when He seeth meet.

This letter to her brother, John Gurney, undated, was obviously written during this spring, not long after her Norfolk journey.

My dear John,

I feared thou wouldest almost think me forgetful of thee in not having expressed my near interest in thy welfare for so long; but feeling very low this morning, to whom can I write better than to one who mourns, and can sympathize with me, though our causes for suffering may be different? I hope my last letter did not hurt dear Catherine and Rachel. I have felt fearful how far it was right for me to touch upon their present state, lest I should hurt the cause I most desire to advocate; I am, therefore, cautious of saying much, but I very deeply feel the state of the family, believing it not unlikely they will leave a path that has to me appeared a remarkably blessed and safe one! and not only to so weak an instrument as I am, but surely there have been many in our family, that, in the same path, have done credit to the Christian cause. However, I desire to leave it, if in ever so small a degree my tears and prayers, (when enabled to offer them,) may prove effectual in desiring preservation for you all, that after trying all things, you may indeed be enabled to hold fast that which is good, even if it lead you into a different path from me; but I acknowledge it has been sweet to me, whenever I have had a hope that the day might come, when we should fully unite in spiritual things; but if it never should, may true charity and love be our portion; I mean that spirit of charity that comes from above, and unites all true and sincere travellers Zion-ward. I should much like soon to hear from you; with regard to thee and Rachel I have no fear about your love for me, for I could believe, much as we have differed, we have never been separated; indeed, dear John, when thou lived to the world, how did my soul pant after thee, what tender solicitude have I felt on thy account, and now I do indeed rejoice in thy experience. I cannot think, if when we felt so very differently, we loved so much, that now when we desire to be following the same Master, and to be devoted to the same cause, we shall be separated—I believe it cannot be.

Plashet, Fourth Month, 24th.—To whom can I go when brought into straitened places, but to Him who has hitherto succoured me, in His own way? Snares are apt to beset me on every hand; for there are left, as well as right hand errors.

I expected to remain pretty quietly at home, but I have been four times to Meeting this week. Seldom have I had to move much more in the cross, than on Third-day; how did I naturally flinch, how did I recoil, at a prospect which came unexpectedly upon me, of going into the Men's Meeting at Plaistow. In the Meetings for Discipline, I sought Him to whom power belongeth, and in His power, His people are made a willing people; I believe my prayers were heard; and may I, as need to be the case with all pilgrims, who seek to go Zion-ward, not turn from anything, from unwillingness and impatience. May we rather seek Him, who "giveth power to the faint, and to him that hath no might He increaseth strength."

Sixth Month, 16th.—It now appears too late to give much account of the Yearly Meeting. The prospect of going into the Men's Meeting, naturally was so awful, nay, almost dreadful, that as I sat at breakfast, fears arose lest my understanding should fail; however, though in great measure taken from me, upon first sitting down in Meeting, yet after a time the concern arose with tranquillity, and with a powerful, though small voice, at least with power sufficient to enable me to cast my burden upon the Meeting; this brought, I thought, great solemnity; I appeared to have the full unity of Friends: dear Rebecca Bevan went with me; I felt myself much helped when there; matter, tongue, and utterance were all given in testimony and supplication. I think the calm frame I enjoyed, upon returning into the Women's Meeting, must almost be a foretaste of that rest which the soul pants after.

During this annual assembly, which, as usual, occupied the concluding twelve days of the Fifth Month, a circumstance occurred that filled many hearts, of every class amongst those who were privileged to convene on the solemn occasion, with deep and tender sympathy. A beloved messenger of the gospel, who had crossed the Atlantic, in order to pay a visit of christian love to his brethren and sisters in religious fellowship, in Great Britain, &c., was introduced into a dispensation of sorrow of no common character. He had, as a father in the church, been instrumental in nurturing many, especially among the younger members. They shared his affliction; but it became the interesting duty of Elizabeth Fry, at whose house he was an inmate, to extend to him those affectionate and soothing attentions, and to minister to him those consolations, which she was so peculiarly qualified to offer, and which his bereaved spirit so greatly needed. After the close occupations of this mournful period had a little subsided, she writes:—

Sixth Month.—My press of engagements has been very great; in the first place, the deep affliction of our much-loved friend, Henry Hull. He having received letters, to say, that his wife, son, mother, and brother-in-law, were all dead of a contagious fever, and the lives of the rest of the family very uncertain; much as he suffered, he bore it like a man, and a Christian, so as to encourage, rather than try my faith; it of course took up my time and attention, to wait upon, and care for him. We have had a very large family party, my brother and sister Fry, three children and servants; my sister Elizabeth, and cousin Sarah, besides many Friends, backwards and forwards: with much illness in the house, my sister and her nurse, and also her baby, very dangerously ill. These have all been objects of care, and interest, so that I am sorry to say, I have been, at times, so weighed down, and panting for rest, that I have been almost irritable, and I fear not enough estimated the value of their company, or the comfort of being able to serve them; but I hope my health may be some excuse for me, for they are very dear to me. I think my temper requires very great watchfulness, for the exercises of my mind, my very numerous interests, and the irritability excited by my bodily infirmities, cause me to be in so tender and touchy a state, that the "grasshopper becomes a burden."* In this, as in all my infirmities, I have but one hope; it is in the power of Him, who has in mercy answered my prayers, and helped me in many of my difficulties, and I humbly trust yet will arise for my deliverance. As to the ministry, I have been raised up, and at times cast down, but my heart and attention have been mostly turned to rigidly performing my practical duties in life, which is my object, by night and by day. I have felt, as if I could rest in nothing short of serving Him whom my soul loves, but I desire to watch, and am fully aware that with regard to myself, I have nothing to trust to, but mercy; but leaving myself, I long whilst permitted to remain in mortality, not to be a drone, but to do every thing to the glory of God. I think I desire to do all things well, more for the cause sake, than for the sake of my own soul, as my conviction of the mercy and loving kindness of Him who loveth us, and who is touched with a feeling of our infirmities, is so great, that whilst my heart is seeking to serve Him, (full as I am of defects,) I am ready to trust that, that mercy which has hitherto compassed me about, will be with me to the end of time, and continue with me through eternity. The fear of punishment hardly even arises, or has arisen in my mind; it is more the certain knowledge that I have, of the blessedness of serving our Master, and the very strong excitement of love and gratitude, and desire for the promotion of the blessed cause upon earth. Through all my tried states, I have one unspeakable blessing to acknowledge; and that is, an increase of faith.

Seventh Month, *3rd.*—We have, for the last week, been alone, which appears greatly to have recruited soul and body; I much wanted this time with my dear husband and child-

* In reference to this allusion to irritability, her family, and those who were her most constant attendants, have expressed much surprise at the entry—as nothing approaching to improper temper was ever apparent to those around her.

ren, it has enabled me to turn my attention to my home duties, and I trust I may rest pretty easy in believing things are generally in good order, as to servants, children, &c., &c. The poor may want a little further investigation; I feel thankful in thus being enabled to stop and examine the state of my family and house. How much I have to be thankful for, though all may not be quite what I wish; how many valuable dependents I have: those who I believe love us, and that which is good; some I hope will remain our friends for life. My beloved children, who are come almost to an age of understanding, I long to see more under the Cross of Christ, and less disposed to give way to their own wills; I sometimes indulge them too much when young, I mean when very little, and perhaps their nurses do so too. I could desire, though it appears asking a great deal, as to things temporal, that, if right for us, we may be able, through life, to live in the open, liberal way we do now, endeavouring to make all around us comfortable, and that we may be able to continue generous friends to the poor. I fear that to be much limited, would be very difficult to me: I desire that my attention being so much turned to things temporal, may not hinder my progress in things spiritual; I do not believe it injurious to have the natural part occupied in natural things, provided all be done under subjection, and with a single eye to the service of our great Master.

Plashet, Eighth Month, 14th.—Eighteen, in addition to our own family, slept here last night; we passed a comfortable, and, I hope, not an unsatisfactory day. When surrounded by many of my own family, I desire to be preserved from the spirit of judgment, but I find it difficult not to be on the watch with those who have been outwardly baptized; how far the living baptism shines forth in them, and enables to renounce the devil and all his works, the pomps, lusts, and vanities of this present world. Surely, saith my soul, there is but one saving baptism, even that which redeems from the world; and I more and more think I see the danger of the outward form or ordinance, lest any should deceive themselves (into thinking) that they are baptized into Christ, when in reality they know little about it; not that I judge those before alluded to, but there is need of further washing, I believe, in them, and in me.

Ninth Month, 2nd.—This morning our poor servant, who has for some weeks kept his bed very seriously ill, died. I feel that I have cause for humble gratitude, in having been, at the awful time, strengthened by faith, and I believe, I may say, having experienced the Divine presence near; I have often sat and watched by his bed-side, desiring to know whether I had anything to do, or say, as to his soul's welfare. I found neither feeling, faith, nor ability, to say or do much more, than endeavour to turn his mind towards his Maker, but I think never more than once, in anything of the anointing power. Yesterday morning I found him much worse, a struggle upon him that appeared breaking the thread of life, and his sufferings great, mentally and bodily. The first thing I found in myself was, that a willing mind was granted me, and in sitting by him, the power and spirit of supplication and intercession for him arose, to which I gave way; it immediately appeared to bring a solemn tranquillity, his pains and restlessness were quieted; his understanding, I believe, was quite clear: he thanked me, and said, "God bless you, ma'am," as if he felt much comfort in what had passed. Faith, love, and calmness, were the covering of my mind. He had, I believe, only one or two more slight struggles after I left him; after that I was sent for, and found that the conflict appeared over, and he breathed his last in about a quarter of an hour. There was peculiar sweetness, and great silence and solemnity in the room. I had to acknowledge that I believed the mercy of our Heavenly Father was then extended towards him, and to express a desire, that it might, in the same awful moment, be extended towards us, feeling how greatly we stood in need of mercy. The rest of the day passed off as well as I could expect; I feared lest the servants and others should attribute that praise to me, with which I had nothing to do, for I could not have prayed, or found an answer to prayer, without an anointing from the Most High. It led me to feel it a blessing to be entrusted with this sacred and precious gift; for though ministers may have much to pass through, and many crosses to take up, for their own good and that of others, yet, it is a marvellous gift when the pure life stirs, operates, and brings down strongholds. My nerves were rather shaken, so as to make me naturally fearful, at times, the rest of the day. I have a great desire, that this event may be blessed to the household, more particularly the servants, that it may humble and bow their spirits, that they may live more in love, and grow in the knowledge of God, and of our Lord and Saviour Jesus Christ.

The funeral of the servant was fixed for the following First-day: as the time approached, Elizabeth Fry felt an earnest desire arise in her heart, that the occasion might be one of benefit to others, as several of his friends were to be present; some from the immediate neighbourhood.

She proposed that, in the evening, all the assembled guests should be invited to attend the family reading with her own household, but before the hour arrived for the performance of a duty, which was to her exceedingly weighty, she was summoned to visit Eliza, the newly married wife of her cousin, James Sheppard, who was rapidly sinking into the grave. The afflicted husband and sister were deeply needing the skilful tenderness, with which she could meet such exigencies. At Meeting, in the morning, her heart had been strengthened, and apparently prepared, for the duties of the day. By the bed of languishing, we find her, waiting for that unction, without which she was sensible that her services could avail nothing; and on the same evening, in her own dwelling, when surrounded by about forty, besides her children, she speaks in exhortation and prayer. Her address was closely suited to the state of some persons present, and unflinchingly did she impress upon them, that the "way of transgressors is hard." The occasion was long remembered by individuals who were there, and who attributed their permanent improvement to the solemn truths they then heard; and for the first time, effectively received into their hearts. Her own journal of the day, written the following morning, portrays the workings of her mind.

Plashet, Ninth Month, Second day.—Yesterday was rather a remarkable day. I rose very low and fearful: my spirit appeared overwhelmed within me, partly I think from some serious outward matters, but principally from such an extreme fear of my approaching confinement, feeling nothing in myself to meet it, and knowing that it must come unless death prevent it. I went to Meeting, but was almost too low to know whether I should go or not; however, being helped in testimony to show the blessedness of those who hope in the Lord, and not in themselves, appeared to do me good, as if I had to minister to myself, as well as to others; I had a trust that my help was in the Lord, and that therefore I should experience my heart to be strengthened. A message came requesting my immediate attendance on poor dear Eliza Sheppard, who appeared near her end. Of course I went. These visits are very awful; to sit by that, which we believe to be a death-bed; to be looked to by the afflicted, and others, as a minister from whom something is expected, and the fear, at such a time, of the activity of the creature arising, and doing that which it has no business to do. After sitting some time quiet, part of which she appeared to sleep, and part to be awake, a solemn silence covered us, the words of supplication arose in due time; when I believed her to be engaged in the same manner, by her putting her hands together; I knelt down, and felt greatly helped; but had not so much to pray for her alone, as for all of us, there present with her. I had a few words also to say, in taking leave; the visit appeared sweet to her by her smiles, and her whispering to her sister, expressing this. Thus ended this solemn scene, her husband, her own sister and brother, and dear Elizabeth Gurney were present; dear Eliza Sheppard's mind appeared in a truly calm, resigned state. I returned home in rather more than an hour, when the prospect of the evening felt very serious to me. After poor John's funeral, I wished the servants, and those who attended it and were disposed to do so, to be present at our reading. The party were in all about forty, many young people, and others. We first read two chapters in Matthew: after a pause I knelt down, and had to supplicate, first, for all the party; afterwards, for our own household, more particularly for the servants; in all which I was helped, and a very solemn silence followed. The party broke up; I think I found myself strengthened, rather than weakened, by the day's work, mentally and bodily, though my own great weakness soon returned upon me, and it appeared striking that such an one should have been so engaged; but painful as these feelings of depression are to bear, I know "it is well," as it keeps me humble, at least I hope so, lowly and abased. Oh! saith my soul, after thus ministering to others, may I not become a cast-away myself, and neither in trouble, nor rejoicing, bring discredit on the cause that I love, or on His name, whom I desire to serve.

Plashet, 10*th*.—A hopeful, and I trust thankful frame of spirit. May the praise be wholly and entirely ascribed where the praise is due, for neither in myself, nor in any outward thing or person, can I at times receive consolation, unless the Divine blessing attend. Enable me, O Lord! to rejoice in Thee, and to give Thee thanks, that Thou hast so far seen meet to relieve me from my fearfulness, and the captivity I have been in. Oh! it is a blessed thing to know that there yet lives a Saviour, ready to help our infirmities: blessed be His holy name for ever. In Him lo I trust, not in myself; be pleased, O Lord! to confirm, establish and strengthen my feeble heart, that I may rightly and fully ascribe glory, honour, and power to the Father, Son, and Holy Spirit; yet feeling all as one, and but as mighty parts of the same eternal, invisible, and invincible power. Whatsoever be taken from me, may this faith live, grow, and increase abundantly.

Her eighth child was born in the Ninth Month, 1812. Writing very soon afterwards to her cousin, Joseph Gurney Bevan, she thus records her thankfulness.

Plashet, *Fourth day.*

My beloved Cousin,

I am safe, and I have a sweet little girl. What can I render? My heart feels this morning rather overwhelmed within me. I hope not without love to the great Master; but how sweetly has it flowed towards many, whom I believe to be more or less His followers. I have particularly felt it towards my much-loved Friends in Gracechurch-street Meeting. My spirit has felt amongst you; I hope you do not forget me, for I do not forget you; with what love have you, as a body, been brought to my remembrance; many individually. May we each fill our respective ranks, none drawing back, but stepping forward in the cause of righteousness. Though I have been long out of sight, yet I trust I am not quite out of the minds of many, but I desire the prayers of the church, for preservation, and more full dedication and resignation, in all things, to the Divine will. It would be very pleasant to see thee, or any of those whom I feel so near (though so unworthy of it, yet I could hope) in the covenant of life. My heart has also been so filled with love towards the Friends of my own Quarterly Meeting, that I could have written them a letter of love.

17*th.*—It appears due for me to acknowledge the tender mercies and loving-kindness of a long-suffering God, in my late safe deliverance, though, at times, tried by various feelings of weakness, yet I have been permitted to find the healing virtue near, keeping soul and body, the calming influence of which has, at times, been very sweet; at others, my heart has had to flow with love towards many. No doubt my late confinements have been precious seasons, wherein the love of the Father has been present with me; though occasionally at others, brought very low, and tried by bodily and mental infirmities. Enable me, O Lord! to render all the praise to Thee, and yet to trust and not be afraid.

Plashet, Ninth Month, 28th.—When my spirits are low, I am apt to feel leaving the country, which is proposed for the winter. I am almost surprised at myself, the tears have often risen; very few, indeed I believe none, know how sweet the quiet and the beauties of the country have been to me; it takes hold of some of my tender feelings.

Mildred's Court, Eleventh Month, 24th.—I arrived here last evening to settle for the winter, after a very encouraging Public Meeting, with dear William Forster, at Plaistow, which I believe did me good; I felt the Power near, it appeared to cover us and the assembly, though I passed through much in the Meeting, so as to shake me very much; but truth appeared to me to come into dominion, which was cause for humble gratitude. May I be enabled to perform my duties, at home and abroad.

Mildred's Court, First Month, 12th, 1813.—At last I have been enabled to accomplish my desire, in having the greater part of our family here, present at the Scripture reading in the morning: it has been to me a very humbling thing, and I may say trying; the difficulty, reluctance, and lukewarmness about it, that appeared to exist, so that I was obliged to beg my beloved husband to ask it for me. It was very exercising on the First-day morning, when we met; but through all, unusual peace has been my portion, in giving up to it. It has been entered into more by faith, than by sight, as it appeared so very discouraging; others not uniting in what seems to me so important a duty: but I have a secret hope and belief, that good will come of it, if the Lord will be pleased to bless and strengthen me in it. Oh! saith my soul, may it tend to our sanctification and redemption. Be pleased, O Lord! so to bless it, that it become not a dead form, but may it enliven our hearts towards Thee; and enable Thy poor handmaid to be a faithful minister of Thy word amongst them, so as to be made instrumental in drawing some nearer to Thee. I am thankful, for having been so far helped on my way, and for a little peace within, when discouragement was without.

Mildred's Court, Second Month, 5th.—The subject of visiting the Monthly Meetings, has been very present with me. Grant, O Lord! I beseech Thee, strength and ability to do Thy will, and promote Thy cause in the hearts of others; I know I am little and weak, yet Thou canst cause one to chase a thousand, and two to put ten thousand to flight. I feel little doubt but that my way will be made in this matter, and that this concern is not of my own appointment. Let me commit myself, as much as I can, into better hands, there leaving it, seeking in all things, a humble mind and resigned will. I have felt and still feel, if the armour of the Lord be put on, which I humbly trust it will be, that I shall be enabled to fight valiantly. Be with me, O Lord! then I need not fear, what any man, or any power can do unto me. See, and cleanse me, if there be any wicked way in me, and lead me in the way everlasting: make this visit instrumental of still more closely uniting me, in Gospel love and fellowship to all scattered here about; yet preserve the poor creature from ever being exalted, or taking that glory that is not its due.

Mildred's Court, 11th.—I feel fresh cause for thankfulness, in being helped through yesterday at our Monthly Meeting, in mentioning my concern to Friends, to visit the Monthly Meetings, &c., of our Quarterly Meeting; I was unusually exercised in doing it, it appeared such a very pressing matter, as if I must do it, though some of my best and most valued friends advised me against it, thinking that I might safely go without any minute, which I did not feel to be the case, as I apprehended the concern to be more extensive than it at first appeared. I have seldom experienced greater relief in any thing. I could hardly help rejoicing yesterday, with the feelings of thankfulness, that the thing was got through so much to my satisfaction and comfort. Oh, how I loved my friends, I even felt it sweet their participating with me, as I believe they did, though little was said, in what I have felt so awful and important, yet, enough was said to satisfy me, and even in one instance, in stronger terms than I quite approved, more than I dared myself say of the concern. I felt a fear yesterday, and also feel it to-day, of taking anything like my rest in this sweet feeling that has attended me, and so becoming unwatchful, not devoted and circumspect enough. I believe I may truly say my desire is, that this event may be blessed to me, and be instrumental in making me better in all things.

Mildred's Court, Second Month, 15*th.*—My fear for myself, the last few days, is, lest I should be exalted by the evident unity of my dear friends whom I greatly value; and also my natural health and spirits being good; and being engaged in some laudable pursuits, more particularly seeing after the prisoners in Newgate. Oh, how deeply, how very deeply, I fear the temptation of ever being exalted, or self-conceited. I cannot preserve myself from this temptation, any more than being unduly cast down, or crushed by others. Be pleased, O Lord! to preserve me: for the deep inward prayer of my heart is, that I may ever walk humbly before Thee: and also before all mankind. Let me never, in any way, take that glory to myself which alone belongs unto Thee, if, in Thy mercy, Thou shouldst ever enable one so unworthy, either to do good, or to communicate.

16*th.*—Yesterday we were some hours at Newgate, with the poor female felons, attending to their outward necessities; we had been twice previously. Before we went away, dear Anna Buxton uttered a few words in supplication, and very unexpectedly to myself, I did also. I heard weeping, and I thought they appeared much tendered; a very solemn quiet was observed; it was a striking scene, the poor people on their knees around, in their deplorable condition.

Thus simply and incidentally, is recorded Elizabeth Fry's first entrance upon the scene of her future labours, evidently without any idea of the importance of its ultimate results.

From her early youth her spirit had often been attracted, in painful sympathy, towards those who, by yielding themselves to the bondage of sin, had become the victims of human justice. Before she was fifteen years of age, the House of Correction at Norwich excited her feelings of deep interest, and by repeated and earnest persuasion, she induced her father to allow her to visit it. She referred, many years afterwards, to the impressions which had then been received, and mentioned to a dear and venerable father in the truth amongst us, that it had laid the foundation for her engagement in prisons.

In the First Month of this year, four members of the Society of Friends, all well known to Elizabeth Fry, had visited some persons in Newgate, who were about to be executed. Although no mention is made of the circumstance in the journal, it has always been understood that the representations of these Friends, particularly those of William Forster (one of the number), first induced her personally to inspect the state of the women, with the view of alleviating their sufferings, occasioned by the inclemency of the season.

At that time, all the female prisoners in Newgate, were confined in that part, now known as the untried side. The larger portion of the Quadrangle was then used as a state prison. The partition wall was not of a sufficient height to prevent the state prisoners from overlooking the narrow yard, and the windows of the two wards and two cells, of which the women's division consisted. These four rooms comprised about one hundred and ninety superficial yards, into which, at the time of these visits, nearly three hundred women, with their numerous children, were crowded: tried and untried, misdemeanants and felons, without classification, without employment, and with no other superintendence than that given by a man and his son, who had charge of them by night and by day. In the same rooms, in rags and dirt, destitute of sufficient clothing (for which there was no provision), sleeping without bedding, on the floor, the boards of which were in part raised to supply a sort of pillow, they lived, cooked and washed.

With the proceeds of their clamorous begging, when any stranger appeared amongst them, the prisoners purchased liquors from a regular tap in the prison. Spirits were openly drunk; and the ear was assailed by the most terrible language. Beyond that which was necessary for safe custody, there was little restraint over their communication with the world without.

Although military sentinels were posted on the leads of the prison, such was the lawlessness prevailing, that even the governor entered this portion of it, with reluctancy. Fearful that their watches would be snatched from their sides, he advised the female Friends, (though without avail,) to leave them in his house.

Into this scene, Elizabeth Fry entered, accompanied only by Anna Buxton. The sorrowful and neglected condition of these depraved women and their miserable children, dwelling in such a vortex of corruption, deeply sank into her heart, although at this time, nothing more was done than to supply the most destitute with clothes. She carried back to her home, and into the midst of other interests and avocations, a lively remembrance of all that she had witnessed in Newgate; which, within four years, induced that systematic effort, for ameliorating the condition of these poor outcasts, so signally blessed by Him, who said, "That joy shall be in heaven over one sinner that repenteth, more than over ninety and nine just persons who need no repentance."

When we contemplate the enormous evils existing in this receptacle of vice and wretchedness, the query naturally suggests itself, how could an enlightened Christian government, and a well organized, municipal corporation, like that of our great metropolis, have so long overlooked, or passively tolerated, a system so fraught with misery and moral contamination? The problem can only be solved by recalling the events of that and the antecedent period of our national history, when public attention was so continually absorbed, by the vicissitudes and the calamities of wide-spread warfare, that but few were at liberty, and yet fewer were inclined, to direct their attention to internal improvements. The great work of Prison Reform was commenced when a happier era was dawning on Europe, and a sentiment was becoming diffused, that breathed, "Peace on earth, and good-will towards men."

Chapter Fifth.

1813—1818. Letter to Edward Edwards—Summer at Plashet—Illness during the spring—Her ninth child born, 1814—Illness and death of her brother John Gurney—Letter to her family—Death of Joseph Gurney Bevan—Illness of her babe—Journey into Norfolk—Earlham, party assembled there—Visit to Kingston Monthly Meeting—Death of one of her children—Extracts from letters—Attends Dorsetshire Quarterly Meeting—Her tenth child born, 1816—Leaves her four elder children in Norfolk—Letters to her daughters—Removal to London for the Winter—Attends the funeral of her cousin Joseph Gurney, Jun.—Places her two elder sons at School—Letter to her sister—General state of Prisons—School in Newgate—Case of Elizabeth Fricker—Newgate Association—Description from Buxton—Sophia de C——'s Journal—Vote of thanks from the City—Letters from Robert Barclay, &c.—Notice in newspapers—Marriage of her brother, Joseph John Gurney—Extracts from Letters—Examinations before House of Commons—Capital Punishments—Case of Skelton—Duke of Gloucester and Lord Sidmouth—Queen Charlotte's Visit to the Mansion House—Letter to Countess Harcourt.

Not only did a considerable space of time elapse, after Elizabeth Fry's first visits to Newgate, before she renewed them, but, in the interim, many events occurred of deep import to herself. He "who sits as a Refiner and Purifier of silver," saw meet to exercise her in the school of affliction, before raising her up for the remarkable work which she had to perform. Long and distressing indisposition; the death of her brother John Gurney, that of her paternal friend Joseph Gurney Bevan; the loss of a most tenderly beloved child; considerable decrease of property; separation, for a time, from all her elder children, were among the means used by Him, who cannot err, more entirely to prepare her for His service.

Mildred's Court, Second Month, 19*th.*—I feel very unworthy this morning, though the day appeared to begin well, in a few words of solemn supplication. After reading, yesterday, I think I was too much off my watch, and did not keep that bridle over my tongue, which is so important; too much disposed to bow the knee of my soul to mortals, rather than to the living God alone. In consequence, I felt this morning at reading, unwilling to take up the cross. In how very many ways is my soul beset! no mortals know, or I believe, even suspect, how much so; at times my hands appear ready to hang or fall down. Alas! may it not be so.

To Edward Edwards.

Mildred's Court, *Third Month,2nd,* 1813.

My dear Friend,

I have been questioning whether to write to my dear sister Richenda or thyself, for my heart is full towards you; but as I had thought of writing to thee before, I think thou hast the first claim. Words fall short of expression when the heart is very full; this is my case at present. I feel you all very near and dear to me, and there are times when I cannot help longing to have all differences and distinctions done away, that we may have one heart and be of one mind; this was brought home to me by the desire I have for your sympathy and prayers in my steppings along, that you may be able, as it were, to go with me heart and hand; I feel this because you are so near to me (I trust) in the covenant of love and life, but amidst these cogitations, a sweet thought has arisen, that although, in time, we may not experience all walls of separation to be broken down, yet we may look forward to a blessed eternity, where with one accord and one heart, we may join the heavenly host, in ascribing glory and honour, wisdom and power, unto our God, and the Lamb for ever.

Even here the sweet love and unity of which we at times are permitted to partake, appears like a foretaste of that which is to be enjoyed. If any of you should feel disposed to write me a few lines, I hope you will do so; and if any hint or caution arises, I beg you will freely give it; for it is well to watch over one another for good. The sense of my own weakness, infirmity, and utter insufficiency to promote the glorious cause, also a natural flinching from such an exposure, and so far taking up the cross, at times make my heart feel sick, and my spirit ready to faint within me; then again arises for my help and consolation, a faith in Him who gives power to the faint, and to him who has no might increases strength; indeed my confidence is not in myself, but in the power of a Saviour and Redeemer. My desire is, through the ability given, or grace afforded, that I may attend to the blessed injunction of "Continue ye in my love. If ye keep my commandments, ye shall abide in my love, even as I have kept my Father's commandments and abide in His love." May it be under the constraining influence of this love, that I ever dare to advocate His cause, and may I be preserved from my own willings and runnings. I find, my dear friend, thou hast lately been afflicted and tried: unto such how many precious promises are offered, yet there are times when the heart feels unable to receive them, and we can hardly believe ourselves of the number to whom they apply. Is this ever thy case? perhaps we can sympathize in the feeling of, at times, walking in darkness, and having no light; may we then "trust in the Lord, and stay ourselves upon our God." My dear love to thy wife, dear Richenda, and my brother, D—— G——, and remember me affectionately to our friends, the Hankinsons. Believe me thy affectionately interested friend,

ELIZABETH FRY.

Mildred's Court, Third Month, 22nd.—Began the day poorly, by not doing what came to hand at our family reading; and now, I am going to set out to visit the sick and sorrowful belonging to Westminster Meeting. O Lord!

have mercy on me, and pardon my transgressions, and enable Thy poor unworthy one to speak a word in season to the afflicted and tried. Thou only knowest my heart and its many fears; preserve me from evil, and keep the gift pure, I beseech Thee, and unalloyed by the dross of my nature, as I fear for it, lest being so very often called forth, I should ever stir in my own strength; help Thy poor, dependent child, O Lord! I pray Thee have mercy on me, be with me in the way that I should go, preserve me from undue fear of man, yet keep me open to caution, reproof, or advice of those further advanced; keep me humble, lowly and obedient, walking in Thy fear, and in Thy love. Amen. Enable me to walk before Thee this day, with a watchful, circumspect, and faithful heart. Thou hast blessed, be yet pleased to bless!

Plashet, Fourth Month, 8*th.*—Yesterday I gave up my minute. I was helped to acknowledge how it had been with me, that way had been made for me inwardly and outwardly, to accomplish that which I had in view; and although I before had deep humiliation to pass through, and had to bear the cross greatly in some things, also to feel much abased, under a sense of my own infirmity and unworthiness, yet that I had experienced a power, better than myself, helping me; even that which I believed to be the power of an endless life, strengthening me to do things which I could not of myself have done; I had learned afresh that, to the creature, nothing belongeth but confusion of face, but to the Holy Helper, who alone is worthy,—glory, honour, power, thanksgiving, and praise. Sweet quietness and peace, was felt after this acknowledgment to the women and men. I also expressed my desire, that whenever weakness or infirmity had shown itself, it might be laid to the creature, but whenever good, however small, had appeared, that it might by myself and others be attributed to the Creator.

Plashet, 28*th,*—Dear Edward Edwards and his wife are staying here, which has been pleasant to me.

Fifth Month, 1st.—So one month passes away, and another comes. A sweetness and power enlivens my heart this morning. I pray Thee, O Lord! Thou who hast hitherto helped me, be with me this day, preserve me humble and lowly in spirit, enable me to do Thy will; if Thou grantest ability to Thy poor handmaid to speak in Thy name, enable her, and all, to give wholly unto Thee the glory and honor of Thy own work. We had a very striking time yesterday evening, before our dear friends Edward and Anne Edwards left us, when sitting with them, my sister Priscilla, and some others. Dear Edward Edwards knelt down, and to my feelings, expressed himself in a very lively manner; others were led to speak, both in testimony and supplication; afterwards, I had to pour forth a little of my soul; there appeared to flow a current of life and love, as if we were owned by the Most High; I felt my own like a song of praise.

Sixth Month.—I am likely to attend dear Mary Dudley, to the families of this Monthly Meeting, which appears a suitable opening for me, and one which seems lively and desirable to my spiritual sight.

Plashet, 24th.—Enabled publicly, after reading, to cast my case upon my Holy Helper, and I have since found much comfort and relief to my before tried mind, so as to know a degree of that precious feeling of my peace flowing as a river, and being in measure enabled to do that which I have to do, as unto the Lord.

Plashet, Tenth Month, 15th.—My original intention in writing this journal, has been simply and purely the good of my own soul; but, if, after my death, those who survive should believe that any part of it would conduce to strengthen others in the faith, and to encourage them in righteousness, by manifesting the loving-kindness of the Almighty to His unworthy child, or to the comfort of any mourner in Zion, I am willing that it should be exposed, even if my weaknesses are acknowledged; so long as they lead to the love of Him, who has, in tender mercy, manifested Himself to be strength in my weakness, and a present Helper in every needful time.

Eleventh Month, 12*th.*—I am likely to set off early to-morrow without my husband, to go into Norfolk; this prospect I feel pleasant and painful; pleasant, the idea of being at Earlham; painful, leaving home, and more particularly my husband. May I be enabled there faithfully to do my duty, in whatever way I may be led, in Meeting, or out of Meeting; may the time spent there be to our mutual comfort and edification, and may those left be cared for and preserved, soul and body, by Him who careth for us; this I humbly trust will be the case. Amen.

Plashet, 25*th.*—I returned safely home to my beloved family, on Second-day evening, the 22nd, I trust I may say, in thankfulness of heart, finding all well, and going on altogether very comfortably. I returned by Ipswich, accompanied by my sister Priscilla and my brother Joseph, and spent all First-day there; but I was unusually low, almost distressed, on account of little Betsy, as I heard she was unwell, and knew not the extent of it; so that my natural impatience to get home was great; but I felt kept there, and as if I could not go away, and thus deeply tried in myself, was greatly helped from one service to another, during the day, being variously and often engaged. It was a day of natural tribulation as far as fears went; and may I not say almost of spiritual abounding? So it is! and so I often have found it, that I have to be brought as to the dust of the earth, before I am greatly helped. Out of the depths, we are raised to the heights. Dear Priscilla, before we parted, prayed for my safe and speedy return home, which prayer has been remarkably granted. Third-day, my beloved husband, with our children, attended the Monthly Meeting, where our certificate was received.

This was from Gracechurch-street Meeting to that of Plaistow; their removal to Plashet having brought them within the compass of the latter.

I should say, the day was begun by returning thanks in my own family, amongst my children, husband, and servants, to my peace; the rest of the day passed in much domestic comfort with my husband at home. This was one of the very bright days of life; blessings are abundantly granted, and sometimes even a blessing upon the blessings, that makes all feel sweet and lovely!

Plashet, Twelfth Month, 13th.—I do think, at times, that it is by far my first desire, to be brought into conformity to the Divine will, but at other times, I am ready to fear that I deceive myself; but I am thankful in believing that the secret intents and purposes of my heart are known, though at the same time I am sensible that there is much infirmity, and evil propensity which must also be known; yet even of that I am glad, for it is well the physician should know the extent of the malady, as he alone can rightly apply the remedy. Thou knowest me, O Lord! much better than I know myself; Thou knowest the intents and purposes of my heart; bring *that* under, which, in any way, opposes itself to Thy will being done in me, by me and through me; be with me unto the end, O Lord! I pray Thee, and, in Thine own time, subdue all that rebels against Thee; do for me that which I cannot do for myself; even carry on Thine own work in me, to Thy own praise; make me willing at all times, to speak in Thy name, when it is according to thy will; yet more and more manifest Thine own power, in Thy poor unworthy child.

First Month, 24th, 1814.—I feel affected by the distresses of the poor, owing to the very sharp weather; and hardly know how to serve them, but I mean to go after them, and desire a blessing may attend my small efforts to relieve them, for it appears very little we can do, so as thoroughly to assist them; but I trust a better than ourselves is near to help and support them under their many trials.

Plashet, Second Month, 4th.—I am low, under a sense of my own infirmities, and also rather grieved by the poor. I endeavoured to serve them, and have given them such broth and dumplings as we should eat ourselves; I find great fault has been found with them, and one woman seen to throw them to the pigs: however, I truly desire to act in this with a Christian spirit, still persevering to do my utmost for them, and patiently bear their reproach, which may be better for me than their praises.

Third Month, 20th.—The craving of my soul for preservation is almost past expression: feeling as I am permitted to do at times, the goodness of the Lord, how fervent is my desire, how inexpressible my prayer, that I may ever be His, in and through all things; that I may dwell nearer in spirit to my Redeemer, that increased humility, watchfulness, patience and forbearance, may be my portion; that I may not only be saved myself, but that I may not stand in the way of others' salvation, more particularly in that of my own household and family; that I may, if consistent with the Divine will, be made instrumental in saving others. Now, in the time of my retirement from the world, from being unwell, my soul craves in deep prostration, preservation from Thee, O God! There are seasons of deep prostration, when my soul is overwhelmed within me, under the feeling of Thy goodness, Thy power, and in love towards Thyself, Thy ever blessed cause, and those that fear Thy name. This morning my heart commends numbers, who are assembled for the solemn purpose of worshipping Thee, to Thy grace and good keeping; animate them by Thy love, keep them in Thy fear; yet be with, and keep Thy poor, unworthy handmaid; be it unto her according to Thy will, or Thy word: yet, in Thy abundant mercy, permit her soul to magnify Thee, O Lord! and her spirit to rejoice in God her Saviour, which she has been permitted to do of late, even in seasons of deep humiliation, or when coming out of the depths.

25th.—May I spiritually and temporally this day be enabled to give myself up to my Master, not looking upon myself as my own, or feeling anxious as to what I suffer, or may suffer, but rather resigning myself unto Him who knows what is best for me: but this is not in my own power. Keep me, O Lord! near unto Thyself, and Thy own preserving power, and let me not wander from Thee, either in word, deed, or desire, or be over anxious as to what may await me, but strengthen me, if consistent with Thy will, to trust in Thy mercy towards one so poor, so weak, and so frail.

Fourth Month, 30th.—In great weakness and infirmity. Gracious and Almighty Father, permit Thy poor child to come unto Thee, her God and Saviour, that, if consistent with Thy holy will, she may once more be healed and revived, through thy Almighty, saving power; give her not over to the will of her soul's enemies, and permit not temptation or weakness to overcome her, but in Thine own unspeakable and unmerited mercy, be Thou yet unto her, her Lord and her God, her Saviour and her Redeemer, her present help in trouble, and her only hope of glory. Amen.

Plashet, Fifth Month, 24th.—My soul followeth hard after Thee, O Lord! enable Thy poor child to follow after Thee, preserve her from letting in want of faith, mistrust, or fear, but enable her to cleave very close unto Thee, and through all her trials, that nothing may, in any degree, separate her from Thy love.

Plashet, Sixth Month, 13th.—Though clouds may be permitted to overshadow me, before the real trial comes, yet I cannot but have a hope that help will marvellously be extended in the needful time. Help, dearest Lord, or I perish; permit me neither to let go my hold in times of trial, nor deny Thee in thought, word, or deed; but acknowledge Thy goodness to thy very greatly favored, but unworthy child. These words arise; "be still, and thou shalt see the salvation of God." Be it so, saith my soul.

The birth of her ninth child took place on the 14th of Sixth Month.

Plashet, 20th.—As I lay this morning, these words occurred to me, Lackest thou anything? The answer of my heart was, Nothing, Lord! Thy mercies abundantly overflow; only enable me and mine to keep a still closer covenant with Thee, and to remember Thy commandments to do them; and may my soul ever make her boast in Thee, her God and Saviour; and never, no never, take *that* to herself, that in no degree belongs to her. Under a fear of too freely approaching Thy sacred footstool in word, as Thou, Lord, knowest my heart, and its secret purposes, do that for me that I cannot do for myself; and may I, day by day, yet experience Thy grace to be sufficient for me, whether in mourning, or in rejoicing.

21st.—My soul cannot help feeling greatly bowed in gratitude for the many and great benefits received; thanksgiving is the voice of my heart, though something of anxiety and disquietude has been my portion, more particularly on account of my beloved husband and children. I also desire to settle my household aright, to walk before them with an upright, humble, and perfect heart, fulfilling the Law and the Gospel. I desire to be scrupulously nice as to my conduct towards servants. I thought, if not saying too much for myself, that I have wept, as between the porch and the altar, on their account, and on that of my beloved family altogether; I feel it cause for much thanksgiving, so far to be restored to them again, but my natural spirits, at times, are overcome. Grant wisdom and grace, O Lord! I pray Thee, to Thy poor child, to order her steps aright before them all, being wise as the serpent and harmless as the dove.

Elizabeth Fry was, at this time, tenderly affected by the critical illness of her beloved friend and relative, Joseph Gurney Bevan.

And, as soon as her health was sufficiently restored to admit of it, she took a journey to Earlham, to see her brother John Gurney, who was then rapidly declining.

Plashet, Eighth Month, 15*th.*—Once more arrived at my sweet home, and truly thankful in having finished my visit to my much-beloved brothers and sisters with satisfaction. I feel most tenderly for all, and I humbly trust, all are pressing Zion-ward, though I cannot say that I fully understand, or enter into, the activity of the creature appearing to show itself so much in things belonging to the soul's salvation: but this I know, inasmuch as it is of God, it will stand; but inasmuch as it is of man, it will fall. It is not for a poor unworthy fellow-mortal, like myself, to say what is of God, and what is not; though I may apprehend that there is a mixture, not only in them, but in myself, and in us as a body; though our belief and profession is, that nothing short of the Holy Spirit can really help forward the cause of righteousness on the earth, whether it be immediately, or instrumentally; and that we can only do good when influenced by this Spirit, and therefore desire to wait for its stirrings. I parted from my beloved sister Rachel, who has, for months past, been to me a tenderly beloved friend, a most watchful and valuable nurse, and a most loving sister; I felt parting from her a good deal.

Plashet, 29*th.*—My heart has been much affected by the accounts of my beloved brother, who appears sinking into the grave, step by step; but his soul most mercifully cared for, and also his body greatly shielded from suffering.

Earlham, Ninth Month, 9*th.*—I trust I have been enabled to do what I ought, in this matter; after writing the above, a letter arrived, that quite confirmed me in the propriety of making ready to set off early on the Third-day morning, but I could not feel easy to do it till that time. I felt bound in spirit to offer up my family to the care of a protecting Providence publicly, after our reading in the morning, before I set off, which I was enabled to do; and also to pray for my beloved brother, that in passing through the valley of the shadow of death, he might fear no evil; (this prayer appeared fully answered). I left home, after this, with a peculiarly happy, may I not say cheerful mind? I mean free from burden. I have seldom had a more comfortable journey; in small things as well as great, I saw the kind hand of Providence.

On the day after her arrival at Earlham, the spirit of her beloved brother was released from the bonds of mortality, of which she thus writes to her family.

Earlham, *Ninth Month, 8th,* 1814.
(by the remains of my beloved brother.)

My much loved Husband and Children,

Believing you will feel with me, in what so nearly concerns me, and not only me, but you also, I sit down to tell you, as nearly as I can, what has happened since I came here. I believe you know that I arrived about four o'clock yesterday morning. I was then led into the room where my tenderly beloved brother lay in bed; he was awake, but some feared he would not know me, instead of which, upon seeing me, his words were, "My dear sister, come and kiss me;" then he expressed his great pleasure at our being together—he looked very sweet, quite easy, may I not say, like one redeemed. After staying some time by him, I went to bed; but I did not rest much, feeling low, burdened, and rather poorly. My dear sister Priscilla came to me a little past nine o'clock, and advised me to come, he was so very bright, his powers of mind appearing much clearer than any dying man I ever witnessed, except our poor servant John. Upon going into his room he kissed us each again, and again said, he wished for all his sisters together, appearing clearly to recollect each, for upon one saying, "Now there is no exception, all the sisters are with thee," he at first misunderstood, and said, "Did you say there is one exception, for there is not," or to that effect: he said it was delightful, how we loved one another. It appeared my place to return thanks for such unspeakable blessings. He then said, "What a sweet prayer!" and afterwards, "I never passed so happy a morning; how delightful being together, and loving one another, as we do." As the day further advanced, he said, "What a beautiful day this has been!" My dear uncle and aunt Joseph, came a little before dinner: Charles Brereton, William Wilkinson and his wife, Hannah Scarnel, nurse Norman, and his own man, were our companions. Dr. Alderson called in the morning, and D. Dalrymple, each much affected, he expressed himself so kindly to them; he desired his love to Amelia Opie; he enjoyed our dear sister Richenda, singing hymns to him; he took leave of most of the old servants; to one whom he used not much to like, he spoke the most kindly, said he was glad to see him, and shook him warmly by the hand, and bade him "farewell;" he appeared deeply impressed with his many blessings, and the mercy shown him. About half an hour after it was over, we had once more to approach the sacred footstool (for ability) to bless the Sacred Name, both for His giving and taking away. Thus closed such a day as I never passed; may we not say, "Blessed are the dead that die in the Lord?" Oh, my beloved children and husband, may we not only feel, but profit by this striking event. . . . . .

Earlham, Ninth Month, 13th.—My heart feels very full; my body I believe has trembled, ever since I rose, to meet the party now assembled, and likely to assemble here. My own corrupt dispositions, I found showed themselves to myself yesterday, which I believe tended to lay me very low; may I not say, the feeling of my heart is, that I am lying prostrate in the dust? I have been greatly tendered in spirit with love to those here, whom I believe to love the *Lord;* united to them in a manner inexpressible, in my inmost heart—all barriers being broken down. Yet I feel it needful to be very watchful, very careful; to be faithful to the testimony that I apprehend myself called upon to bear, not only for my own sake, but also for the sake of the younger ones about me; Lord, be pleased to help me, to guide me, to counsel me, that from my own will and prejudice, I wound not a beloved brother or sister in Christ, but so keep me in Thy fear, in Thy love, and under a sense of Thy presence; that I act in these most awful and important duties, according to Thy most holy and blessed will. During these few days, when so surrounded by many of various descriptions, keep my eye, I fervently pray Thee, single unto Thyself, doing whatever Thou wouldest have me, either to do, or to suffer,—not bowing the knee of my heart to any mortal, or seeking to gratify, or even satisfy self—but, O Lord! let Thy will be done in me, by me, and through me; permit our souls to be united in sweet and precious unity with all who fear Thy name, and not only those; even animate the hearts of others, who may not yet know Thee, that they also may be touched by Thy love, and united together in Thy fear. Let Thy good presence be with us, that the feeble be strengthened, the discouraged animated by hope, the lukewarm stimulated, and the backslider turned from the error of his ways, even so, if consistent with Thy holy will. If thou seest meet to make use of Thy unworthy children to speak in Thy name, be unto them tongue and utterance, wisdom and power, that through Thy grace, and the help of Thy spirit, sinners may be converted unto Thee. Amen, Amen.

Plashet, 22nd.—My beloved brother's funeral was a very solemn and humbling day to me; whilst we sat at Earlham round the body, my uncle Joseph, my sisters Catherine, Rachel, and Priscilla, and I, each had something to say; also Edward Edwards. I had to finish the sitting with these words, "There are different gifts, but the same Spirit. And there are differences of administrations, but the same Lord. And there are diversities of operations, but it is the same God which worketh all in all. But let us earnestly covet the best gifts." It certainly was a striking occasion. Were not all, in a measure, leavened into one spirit? It was a very solemn time at the ground, and I trust an instructive one, very affecting to our natural feelings, thus to leave the body of one so tenderly beloved, to moulder with the dust. Upon my return, I heard of the sudden death of my long-loved cousin, J. G. Bevan. My spirit was much overwhelmed within me, but there was a stay underneath; blessed be the name of the Lord. I bid them all farewell, at Earlham, in near unity. Oh, may my children love as we love—this has been the prayer of my heart!

30th.—Another month nearly gone, how much has passed in it; how awfully has death been brought to my view. I have felt it a good deal, on my own account: and cannot say that, at present, death appears to have no sting for me, or the grave no victory. May that blessed state ever be mine, of knowing the sting of death to be altogether removed.

Extract from a letter to her cousin, P. H. Gurney.

Plashet, *Tenth Month, 19th,* 1814.

My beloved Cousin,

I regret not answering thy letter before, but almost constant engagements have prevented me. I believe few can more feelingly sympathize than myself, in thy great loss in this our tenderly beloved cousin, Joseph Gurney Bevan.

He was indeed a true friend, a wise counsellor, and is an inexpressible loss to me; I feel a real and great deprivation, and a vacancy that I know not who can fill. Dear John Hull's state is also very affecting, but he yet remains not only alive, but lively in spirit. I have once been to see him, and may be thankful that he is yet spared to us, but it is a blessing I do not expect long to enjoy; dear Rachel Smith's loss is also present with me. Now for my tenderly beloved brother; words fall very short of expression. I do not know that I can feel grateful enough on his account; we may truly say that his end appeared blessed indeed, love, joy, and peace were the covering of his spirit, "Blessed are the dead that die in the Lord." No evil or sorrow appeared to be permitted to come near him, no pain, mind, or body, that we could perceive,—what a fav ur! He was buried in the Friends' Burying Ground at Norwich, by his wife.

Plashet, Eleventh Month, 2nd.—My beloved husband and girls returned from France, on Second day; my heart was rather overwhelmed in receiving them again. I also had to feel the spirit in which some persons took my having allowed them to go, making what appeared to be unkind remarks. Oh, how do I see rocks on every hand; thus almost all persons, who appear to pride themselves upon their consistency, are apt to judge others; whilst some, who no doubt yield to temptations, greatly suffer, and weaken themselves by it. How weak, how frail are we on every hand; my heart was much overwhelmed, seeing the infirmities of others, and feeling my own.

Elizabeth Fry exercised a watchful care, never, unless *duty* required it, to oppose the wishes of her husband; and it could not reasonably be expected that she would prevent his taking his two elder girls on this excursion. But her solicitude on account of her family became increasingly great. She found as her children advanced in age, and the corrupt propensities of the natural mind developed themselves, that she often failed in her attempts to control the unyielding will, and to subdue the vain inclination—and, from external circumstances, she did not receive the co-operation requisite, rightly to govern their volatile temperament: but earnest were her efforts to guide them into the way of peace, and fervent her prayers that they might be gathered to the fold of the good Shepherd.

Mildred's Court, First Month, 16th, 1815.—We came here for a little change of air, on account of our poor babe, who has been, and continues seriously ill. Instead of her sweet smile, her countenance mostly marks distress; the cause appears greatly hidden; my mind and heart are oppressed, and my body fatigued, partly from losing so much sleep. I have felt my infirmity during this affliction, and also having betrayed it to others, which I have, I apprehend, to judge by my touchy feelings; but, I trust, I repent. Oh, what am I? very poor, very unworthy, very weak, but through all, I trust that the Lord will be my stay; and even when brought thus low, I have known a little of being, at seasons, clothed with that righteousness which cometh from God: I found it was well so feelingly to have been brought to a knowledge of what I am, *in myself*, as I could more fully testify from whence the good comes, when brought in measure, under its calming, enlivening, and loving influence. Preserve me, O Lord! from hurting the little ones, more particularly those before whom I have to walk; and permit me yet to encourage their progress Zionward.

25th.—A time of anxiety about things temporal has lately been my portion, but much deliverance has so far been granted; my sweet baby is much better: though other matters are still pressing, yet it appears, as to things temporal, that prayer has been heard and answered. From one cause or another, how much my heart, mind, and time have, for more than a year past, been engaged with the cares of this life; alas! may the pure seed not be choked.

Second Month, 27th.—I have a religious concern in prospect, which I am likely to lay before Friends to-morrow; but believing that to be the Lord's work, I am enabled to leave it, trusting in Him.

This entry in Elizabeth Fry's journal, alludes to some Meetings which she attended on her way into Norfolk. She spent a few days at Earlham, before her return home.

Erith, Third Month, 23rd.—Yesterday morning commenced our little journey, our friends the Steinkopffs and Rebecca Christy with us, as I did not like the Steinkopffs should leave as, believing them to be fellow-disciples. My heart felt very full, with my husband, children, and household around me: it almost overwhelmed me. I had cast my whole care upon my holy and blessed Helper, who has hitherto kept me, and cared for me and mine. Oh, saith my soul, may He preserve us, now separated, as well as together. I have had to speak to them all, in testimony, in these words, "If ye love me, keep my commandments," believing that we poor, fellow-mortals might address that language to each other. Then, upon sitting down to breakfast, I had to return thanks for bread being broken to us, spiritually and temporally, and to pray for more. I deeply felt parting, most particularly with my sweet, dear, little babe; but I believe we parted under the canopy of divine love, and blessing. We travelled well, and comfortably here, but in the night I had a deep plunge, making me exceedingly low and nervous. The enemy seemed to come in like a flood; I sought after quietness and patience, and in due time, felt a standard to be lifted up against him, for which mercy may I not say, "Bless the Lord, oh, my soul, and all that is within me, bless his holy name." I believe baptisms are necessary for our preparation and refinement for such awful services, therefore I desire not to flinch, but to pray that if consistent with the Divine will, fears may not have dominion over me. Oh, for preservation on every hand; and be pleased, righteous Father, to be with, and bless my husband and children, as well as Thy poor, unworthy handmaid; enable her so to keep the word of Thy patience, that Thou mayst keep her from the hour of temptation. Amen, and Amen. Be with us, O Lord! this day and night, that we may know our poor bodies and souls to be a little strengthened, if consistent with thy holy will.

Towards the end of the summer, which had been passed in tranquil enjoyment at Plashet, she believed it her duty to join her friends William Forster and Rebecca Christy in a visit to the families of Kingston Monthly Meeting.

Plashet, Ninth Month, 9th.—I think I may acknowledge, that although much stripping and deep poverty has at times been my portion, during my visit to the families of Kingston Monthly Meeting, with dear William Forster and Rebecca Christy; yet power, consolation, and sweetness have also been felt at times, and I think our way has been remarkably made in the hearts of those we have visited. I came home with the feeling, that he who waters is also watered. The prospect of not having finished, and of leaving home again, is serious; but oh, for preservation and strength to do the will of God, at home and abroad.

15*th.*—I returned home last evening, having just finished my engagement with William Forster and Rebecca Christy. Being at home again, and having some heavy clouds, a little, indeed a good deal, dispersed, is a great comfort and relief. We have been much favoured in our goings along; help being granted from season to season, much unity of the Spirit, and general sweetness and openness amongst others. But I have felt since my return, this morning, in our frail state, how difficult it is, even when engaged in religious services, to prevent our infirmities creeping in and showing themselves, something like the iniquity of our holy things. Great as is the honour and favour of being employed in the Master's service, and the peace and consolation which attend the remembrance of it; yet I am so much aware of the evil seed not being eradicated from my own heart, that my present feeling is this, "Who can understand his errors? cleanse Thou me from secret faults, keep back Thy servant also from presumptuous sins, let them not have dominion over me;" and how anxiously do I desire that I may not only be as a vessel, washed and cleansed from impurities, contracted in being used, but also if these have shown themselves, that the most precious and blessed cause of truth and righteousness, may not have been hurt by me, but that our little labours of love may be blessed to ourselves and others; and now that I am come home, oh, may I labour and not faint.

Tenth Month, 14*th*.—I have been of late principally occupied at home, which has its peculiar exercises, as well as being abroad; having to govern such a large household, where the infirmity and evil propensity of each one, old and young, too often show themselves, and deeply try me in many ways. It confirms me in a feeling of my infirmity; it humbles me; yet I trust through all, the discipline of the cross may be found amongst us, and through its subjecting influence, the wrong thing in measure is kept under. However, I have my consolations, and *great* consolations, but I find, I am not to rest even in the ruling and order of my household. Many changes in our family circle, among others, my dear sister Richenda is likely to marry Francis Cunningham.

Elizabeth Fry had known many trials during the two preceding years, but an acute sorrow, and one unlike any which she had hitherto experienced, now awaited her. The death of her little Elizabeth, the seventh child. She was lovely, and of much promise; with her mother's name she possessed much of her nature, and more of her general appearance, effect, and manner, than any of her other children.

Plashet, Eleventh Month.—It has pleased Almighty and Infinite Wisdom, to take from us our most dear and tenderly beloved child, little Betsy—between four and five years old. She was a very precious child, of much wisdom for her years, and I can hardly help believing much grace; liable to the frailty of childhood: at times she would differ with the little one, and rather loved her own way; but she was very easy to lead, though not one to be driven. She had most tender affections, a good understanding; for her years, a remarkably staid and solid mind. Her love was very strong, and her little attentions great to those she loved, and remarkable in her kindness to servants, poor people; and to all animals, she had much feeling for them; but what was more, the bent of her mind was remarkably towards serious things. It was a subject she loved to dwell upon; she would often talk of "Almighty," and almost every thing that had connection with Him. On Third day, the 21st, after some suffering of body from great sickness, she appeared wonderfully relieved, and I may say raised in spirit; she began by telling me how many hymns and stories she knew, with her countenance greatly animated, a flush on her cheeks, and her eyes very bright, a smile of inexpressible content, almost joy—I think she first said with a powerful voice,

> "How glorious is our Heavenly King
> Who reigns above the sky."

And then expressed how beautiful it was, and how the little children that die stand before Him, but she did not remember all the words of the hymn, nor could I help her; she then mentioned other hymns and many sweet things; she spoke with delight of how she could nurse the little ones and take care of them, &c., her heart appeared inexpressibly to overflow with love. . . . In her death, there was abundant cause for thanksgiving; prayer appeared indeed to be answered, as very little, if any suffering seemed to attend her, and no struggle at last; but her breath grew more and more seldom and gentle, till she ceased to breathe. During the day, being from time to time strengthened in prayer, in heart, and in word, I found myself only led to ask for her, that she might be for ever with her God, whether she remained much longer in time or not, but that if it pleased Infinite Wisdom, her sufferings might be mitigated, and as far as it was needful for her to suffer, that she might be sustained. This was marvellously answered beyond anything we could expect. I desire never to forget this favour, but, if it please Infinite Wisdom, to be preserved from repining, or unduly giving way to lamentation, for losing so sweet, so kind a child. . . My loss has touched me in a manner almost inexpressible; to awake, and find my much and so tenderly beloved little girl so totally fled from my view, so many pleasant pictures marred. As far as I am concerned, I view it as a separation from a sweet source of comfort and enjoyment, but surely not a real evil; abundant comforts are left me, if it please my kind and Heavenly Father to give me power to enjoy them, and continually in heart to return Him thanks, on account of His unutterable loving-kindness to my tenderly beloved little one, who had so sweet and easy a life, and so tranquil a death; and that, in her young and tender years, her heart had been animated with love and desires after Himself, and also that, for our sakes, she should so often have expressed it in her childish, innocent way.

Extract from a letter of Richenda Gurney's, to her sister Rachel at Rome, dated "Plashet, November 26th:"—

"I never witnessed stronger faith, more submission, more evidences of the power of grace, in any one, than in our beloved sister at that time; I felt it a mercy to be a humble sharer in the rich portion granted her in that hour of need; never was I more impressed with the blessedness, which is experienced by those who have served the Lord Jesus, who have preferred Him above all things, who have been willing to take up their daily cross to follow Him. He is not a hard Master; He never leaves nor forsakes His own, and will show himself strong, in behalf of those whose hearts are perfect towards Him. After a few minutes, we retired with our dear sister into the next room. She was desirous that children and servants, (especially the nurses,) and all her friends who had been present, should come to her; when thus surrounded, as she lay upon the sofa, she poured out her heart in thanksgiving and prayer, in a manner deeply affecting and edifying; for myself, I felt it highly valuable, and would not but have been there for a great deal. Whilst memory lasts, I think and hope I never shall forget the scene, or the impression it made."

Plashet, Eleventh Month, 27th.—Man is not to live by bread alone, but by every word of God. It appears now my case, in my deep sorrow; I am not, indeed, to live by bread alone, but to be nourished, and kept alive by that inward, powerful word, that cometh from God, and by every word being renewed in the needful time; I feel no other sure source of consolation. Abundant mercy has indeed been shown me; my weaknesses met, and my prayers answered, even about smaller things. Although it pleases my Heavenly Father thus to chastise me, yet I am permitted to feel that He doth love those whom he chasteneth. I feel His love very near, and, like a tender parent, that may see right to inflict the rod, rather, perhaps, than spoil the child; yet the same hand administers the salve to the wound, and cherishes the more tenderly after it; and makes manifest to His poor child, that, although a deep wound, it is in mercy, and to the unspeakable gain of one most tenderly beloved, having taken her from the conflicts of time, and (I humbly trust) permitted her an entrance into the enduring joys of eternity; and that, through the blood and power of her Redeemer, she has been washed and made clean. Though, from her tender years, and good and innocent spirit, we believed her remarkably ready, still I saw and felt need of a Saviour, even for such a little child; for, of course, she had some childish transgressions, or little deviations, but I believe that they were all washed away, and that indeed reconciliation was obtained, as far as there ever had been any separation. So I cannot help hoping that she was ripe for glory.

Plashet, Twelfth Month, 1st.—I have been enabled in measure to arise and attend to the business of life, but a cloud appeared to rest over me, in remembrance of what we have lost; but, when enabled to view her with her Heavenly Father, and out of the reach of all harm, then I can go more cheerfully on my way, and enjoy my remaining blessings; particularly my children; though every thing of the earth has been made, I think, increasingly to shake, in my view.

But I desire that this feeling my increase in my mind, she cannot return to me, but I may go to her. Ah! may I not say, how hast Thou helped her that is without power! How savest Thou the arm that has no strength! May I be more willing to be faithful in the gift at all times, in all places, in weakness and in strength.

Plashet, 2nd.—I am brought into some conflict this morning, respecting my attending the Dorsetshire Quarterly Meeting. I had looked to it before the illness of our dear lamb, and not feeling clear of it, and yet not much light shining upon it, my poor soul is tried within me; for under my present circumstances, I appear much to want the help of faith, to leave my other sweet lambs; but ought I not rather to feel renewed stimulus, seeing how short time is, to do what comes to hand, and after all that I have experienced, should I not rather trust than be afraid, for was the hand of Providence ever more marked, even as it related to outward things? I believe I am fully resigned to go, if it be the Lord's will: for I do believe, for all my many and great infirmities, my flinching nature, my want of faith and patience, yet it remains my first desire, to do or to suffer, according to the Divine will. If consistent with Thy holy will, dearest Lord, if I ought to go, be pleased to throw a little light upon the subject, and if not somehow make it manifest; and if Thou shouldst think fit to call Thy poor child into Thy service, be pleased to be with her in it, and bless her labours of love, where her lot may be cast, that others may be made sensible how good a God Thou art, how great is Thy tender mercy and loving-kindness, and that these may be encouraged yet to serve Thee more, with the whole heart; also be pleased, dearest Lord, if Thou shouldst order it that I go, to keep my beloved husband, children, and household in my absence, that no harm may come to them spiritually, or bodily. Thou hast, in abundant mercy, regarded the weak estate, and infirm condition of Thy handmaid, and hitherto answered her cry, and even met her in her weakness; that, if not asking in her own will, she could supplicate Thee, that their poor bodies as well as their souls, may be preserved from (much) harm in her absence; but, dearest Lord, let me not go, if my right place be at home; but if Thou callest me out, be pleased to grant a little faith, and a little strength, that I may go forth in Thy power, trusting in Thee, as it relates to them, as well as to myself. Be pleased also, if I be called from home at such a time, not to let it try or weaken the faith of others; but rather may it tend to confirm and strengthen it.

Plashet, 11th.—Truly I went forth weeping; and my sweet Louisa being poorly, much increased my anxiety; and it's difficult to say the fears and doubts that crept in, on my way to Shaftesbury, though, through mercy, the enemy's power appeared limited, and my fears gained no dominion over me, but they were soon quieted, and I had mostly quiet, comfortable nights, though it was wading through deep waters, and in great weakness; yet help was, from season to season, administered.

Plashet, 14th.—It is the opinion of medical men that the scarlet fever, in a mild form, is the complaint in the house; it is most probable that it will appear again amongst us, but that I desire to leave. They also think our dear Rachel has a very serious hip complaint, but this I also feel disposed not to be very anxious about. With regard to my tenderly beloved little Betsy, she is in my most near and affectionate remembrance, by night, and by day; when I feel her loss, and view her little (to me) beautiful body in Barking burying-ground, my heart is pained within me; but when, with the eye of faith, I can view her in an everlasting resting-place in Christ Jesus, where indeed no evil can come nigh her dwelling, then I can rest even with sweet consolation; and I do truly desire that when her loss is so present with me, as it is at times, that I cannot help my natural spirits being much overwhelmed, that I may be preserved from anything like repining, or undue sorrow, or in any degree depreciating the many blessings continued; particularly so many sweet, dear children being left us; for through all, I feel receiving them a blessing, having their life preserved a blessing, and in the sweet lamb who is taken, I have felt a blessing in her being taken away; such an evidence of faith has been granted that it is in mercy, and at the time such a feeling of joy on her account. It is now softened down into a very tender sorrow, the remembrance of her is inexpressibly sweet, and I trust that the whole event has done me good, as I peculiarly feel it an encouragement to suffer whatever is appointed me; that being (if it may ever be my blessed allotment) made perfect through suffering, I may be prepared to join the purified spirits of those that are gone before me; and having felt so very deeply, I am almost ready to think has a little prepared my neck for the yoke of suffering.

Plashet, First Month, 11*th,* 1816.—The turning a new year I felt very much, more particularly the change in the last, in our beloved Betsy being taken from us. I little expected, so soon upon entering this, to have one, so deeply beloved as my brother Samuel, so seriously ill; I have, from his early years, prayed for him, and interceded, with strong intercession of spirit, that he might not be hurt by evil. I hardly knew how to give him up, and my soul has craved, that if right, he may live, to continue to be a blessing to his family, an ornament to the Church, and to show forth the praise of his Great Lord and Master.

Plashet, Third Month, 10*th.*—I returned home, after being at Stamford Hill for change of air; but my cough, &c., &c., continue very poorly, but through abundant mercy, a calm, and not unfrequently a cheerful spirit, is my portion; though I do not feel dwelling so evidently near the fountain and source of all good, as I desire; at least, fears arise for myself; though it appears due to acknowledge, that the fountain and source of all good dwells near me, so that some things which would, at times, have ruffled and troubled me a good deal, have passed quietly, nay, comfortably by; as if, in this time of weakness of body, I was shielded, in degree, from the storms. My views of these trials continue at times to be rather unusually calmed, at least not often so dreadful as at some former periods. I feel, although I expect to get through my approaching confinement, my life more concerned in my present lung complaint, than it often has been in more painful and trying attacks; but at present, unworthy as I am, this does not excite uneasiness, though perhaps it might, if I believed it more serious than I do; but at times I have that hope in my Redeemer, not in myself, but in Him who has already visited and cared for me, in Him whom my soul has loved, and at seasons rejoiced in, in Him to whom, in weakness, I have sought to prove my love, by serving him through His own help, that I am ready to believe, nay to trust, that He will be with me to the end; that He will not leave, nor forsake his unworthy one, that He will yet sustain her, in doing, and in suffering, as far as He may be pleased to call into either; that after carrying her through all the remaining conflicts of time, He will even continue to be with her to all eternity; and where He lives and reigns, there she expects to find everlasting rest and peace. Thou hast, gracious Lord, been a merciful God to me; granted me help and strength, in the name of Thy beloved Son: Thou hast visited and anointed my unworthy soul.

Plashet, Fourth Month, 3rd.—Since writing the last journal, much feeling of illness and lowness of spirits have been my portion; but how much do I desire quietness and patience, in this straitened place, where the waves and billows are in measure permitted to pass over my head. It is indeed like a cloud resting over the tabernacle, so that I cannot perceive clearly the comforts and blessings that surround me. I felt a little ray of comfort this morning, in these words, "My King and my God," for however tried, however afflicted, however clouded, we may be, in this there is indeed hope and consolation, (if it please Almighty loving-kindness to permit us to see it,) even to feel that the Most

High is our King and God; that he hath in abundant mercy manifested Himself to be so, and that now and then, through the help of our Redeemer, we have been enabled to prove that we have sought to serve Him, and desired that He alone should be our King and our God. Dearest, kindest Lord! Thou, who hast regarded me, and dispersed many clouds for me, be pleased yet to regard me, whatever be my state; however low I may be brought before Thee; and, in Thine own time, disperse my clouds, let the sun arise, as with clear shining after rain; and, if consistent with Thy Holy Will, let not fear or irritability gain dominion over me; but be Thou my King, and my God, from season to season, scattering all mine enemies before my face, that they overcome me not; and, if consistent with Thy Holy Will, permit no conflict, either before, at, or after my confinement, really to overcome body, soul, or spirit; but as my day is, so may my strength be. I believe my present indisposition may be increased by my long confinement to two rooms for my cough, now nearly a month; and not a little from sorrow and distress. I have known much this winter; the loss of my lovely child—the frequent illnesses in the house amongst the family—loss of property—my own long cough; yet I know hardly any trial, except indeed real evil, that appears so greatly to undermine comfort outwardly and inwardly, as a nervous state of body and mind; it calls for watchfulness on the part of those who have it, not unduly to give way to it; though I believe few things are really less in our power.

15*th.*—I was favoured to feel much relieved and comforted yesterday, in pouring forth my soul in supplication, before my family after dinner; a sweet calm followed, help appearing to be very near. After all other remedies fail, what a stronghold is prayer; how have my poor soul and body been helped in answer to my supplications, more particularly those called for before others; it is, I think, a very striking evidence that such sacrifices are acceptable in the Divine sight, and called for at His hand, even in publicly committing ourselves to Him. Oh, that I were not so faithless, but more believing; then I think fear never would take the place it does; yet this is my infirmity, perhaps permitted for my good, that I may more and more know what I am, and what the Power is, that we alone desire to rest upon us.

Her tenth child was born on the 18th of Fourth month.

Fourth Month, 27th.—Thanks, I may say, be unto my God, who has proved Himself an all-sufficient Helper. A heavy cloud passed over—but fears now arise for my spiritual preservation; and my desire is great, in word and in deed, to be enabled to testify of the gracious goodness of my Holy Helper. Family cares also come upon me, which my great weakness hardly knows how to encounter. The remembrance of my little Betsy has been very present with me, by night and by day. Be Thou pleased, O Lord God Almighty! yet to look down upon us, and bless us; and if Thou seest meet, to bless our loved infant, to visit it by Thy grace, and Thy love; that it may be Thine in time, and Thine to all eternity: we desire to thank Thee for the precious gift. I have also had a fresh trial in the dangerous illness of my beloved brother, Daniel, since his return from the Continent.

In the Sixth Month, her children went to Pakefield, for the benefit of sea air, where they were under the care of their aunt Cunningham. Their parents followed them, and for a short period remained with them. It was a new position for her to be the guest of an active, devoted clergyman, and that clergyman her brother-in-law. She remained some weeks in Norfolk, and at last returned without her four elder children. Joseph and Elizabeth Fry had determined upon passing the ensuing winter in London, a situation in many respects so disadvantageous for her daughters, that she left them with her beloved relatives. She deeply felt their being thrown among those who were not Friends, but the advantages of the wise care and oversight of her sister Rachel

Gurney, and the privilege of associating with the brother who invited them to be his guests, overcame her objections.

Her boys remained at Earlham till near the close of the year, when their parents had arranged to send them to school; her two children, the next in age, became inmates with their uncle and aunt, Samuel and Elizabeth Gurney, and joined the school-room party at Ham House.

Earlham, Sixth Month, 27th.—Much has passed since writing the above,—dear John Hull's death, a matter of real importance to me,—the children all gone to the sea-side, except the baby—but home was sweet to me, though much hurried by business there. We attended Barking Meeting, to visit the grave of our beloved little Betsy: it brought many tears, but I afresh remembered she was not there, but is indeed utterly gone from this transitory scene. I often pant after a resting-place with her—may it in due season be granted me, but I also, at present, feel strongly tied and attached to life, and have much to endear it to me.

Seventh Month, 4th.—I have been at Pakefield with my beloved brother and sister; my soul has travailed much in the deeps, on many accounts; more particularly while with them, that in keeping to our scruples respecting prayer, &c., &c., the right thing might be hurt in no mind. Words fall very short of expression, of how much my spirit is overwhelmed within me for us all: our situation is very peculiar, surrounded as we are with those of various sentiments, and yet, I humbly trust, each seeking the right way; to have a clergyman for a brother, is very different to having one for a friend; a much closer tie, and a still stronger call, for the sake of preserving sweet unity of spirit, to meet him as far as we can, to offend as little as possible by our scruples, and yet, for the sake of others, as well as ourselves, faithfully to maintain our ground, and to keep very close to that which can alone direct aright.

This letter to her two eldest daughters, Katherine and Rachel, was written after her almost solitary return to Plashet.

Plashet, *Ninth Month,* 1816, *Evening.*

My dearest Girls,

After drinking tea alone in your father's little dressing-room, and taking a solitary walk, and sitting in the rustic portico at the end of the green walk, I am come to write to you, as I cannot have your company. Only think! this evening I have neither husband nor child to speak to, little Hannah being gone to tea at the Cottage. I found it even pleasant to go and stand by poor old Isaac and the horse, and the cows and sheep in the field, that I might see some living thing to enliven poor Plashet. The grounds look sweetly, but the cherry tree by the dining-room window is cut down, which I think quite a loss. The poor little school children, when I see them, look very smiling at me, and I suppose fancy they will soon see you home. Poor Jones's little boy is still living; such an object of skin and bone I have hardly ever seen. I fear she is greatly distressed. Our house looks charmingly, as far as I think a house can—so clean neat and lively—but it wants its inhabitants very much.

Your most nearly attached mother,

E. F.

Early in the Twelfth Month, Elizabeth Fry went into Norfolk, in consequence of heavy affliction befalling the family of her uncle Joseph Gurney, in the death of Joseph, his only surviving son. She staid at Earlham, where her two eldest boys, under the care of their aunts, were pursuing their education. She then visited her brother Daniel Gurney at North Runcton, with whom her daughters were residing. Whilst conscious of the literary advantages enjoyed by her children, she feared the probable effect of their circumstances, and of the influences to which they were subjected.

Mildred's Court, Twelfth Month, 13*th.*—I returned yesterday from attending poor dear Joseph's funeral at Norwich, the son of my uncle Joseph Gurney. I have gone through a good deal, what with mourning with the mourners, the ministry, &c., &c. I think I was, in this respect, at the funeral, helped by the Spirit and the Power that we cannot command; though I left Earlham with a burdened mind, not having any, apparently, suitable opportunity for relief, hurrying away, to my feelings prematurely, of which I find even the remembrance painful; my sweet dear girls and boys I much feel again leaving, seeing their critical age and state. What I feel for the children I cannot describe. Oh! may they be sheltered under the great Almighty wing, so as not to go greatly astray.

First Month, 1*st,* 1817, *Evening.*—This has been rather a favoured day, the commencement of another year,—so far sweet and easy, and enabled to commend us and ours to the best keeping, which brought consolation and comfort with it. Afterwards, a very comfortable Meeting at Gracechurch-street; indeed it is like being at home returning there, and I cannot but hope that I am here in my right place.

Second Month, 13*th.*—I yesterday left my dearest boys, John and Willy, at Josiah Forster's school; it has been a very important step to take, but I trust it is a right one, as we could not comfortably see any other opening for them. I was enabled to commend them in supplication to the Lord for His blessing and providential care. It is, indeed, a very serious thing to me, thus permitting them to enter the world and its temptations, for so I feel it; it caused me great lowness at first, but afterwards, having committed them to the best keeping, my soul was much comforted and refreshed, and much enlarged in love towards them, as well as the kind friends whose house I was at. Oh may it please Almighty Wisdom to bless the boys, and keep them by His own preserving power from any great sin, and may He pardon the follies of their youth!

She wrote, and gave to each of these sons, some "Rules for their strict observance while at school," from which the following excellent precepts are selected:—

"I advise thy faithfully maintaining thy principles, and doing thy duty; I would have thee be very careful of either judging or reproving others; for it takes a long time to get the beam out of our own eye, before we can see clearly to take the mote out of our brother's eye. There is, for one young in years, much greater safety in preaching to others by example than in word; or doing what is done in an upright, manly spirit, unto the Lord, and not unto man. I have observed a want of strict integrity in school-boys, as it respects their schoolmasters and teachers, a disposition to cheat them, to do that behind their backs which they would not do before their faces; and so having two faces. Now this is a subject of the utmost importance—maintain truth and strict integrity upon all points. Be not double-minded in any degree, but faithfully maintain, not only the upright principle on religious grounds, but also the brightest honour according even to the maxims of the world."

Three years had now elapsed since Elizabeth Fry first visited Newgate; but her spirit had, from time to time, been led into deep and solemn feeling on account of the degraded inmates of that prison: and a conviction became gradually impressed on her mind that she was required by Him, to whose service she had been enabled to dedicate herself, as an unquenched coal on His sacred altar, to labour, as He might see meet to open her way and to direct her steps, for the moral reformation, and above all, for the spiritual conversion and help, of the most depraved and miserable of her sex. Nothing but the constraining love of Christ, could have induced this tender and delicate woman thus to surrender domestic comfort and personal ease, and even to risk her own reputation, to follow what she believed to be the call of her Divine Master, leading her into labours most arduous and painful, from which her nature recoiled with dread. Yet was the unction of holy love so abundantly poured out upon her spirit, that she willingly yielded to the appointment of that compassionate Saviour, who, through her instrumentality, was thus graciously extending His hand of mercy, in order to rescue from the pit of destruction, those who were sunk in vice and wretchedness.

The course, which was henceforth to be marked out for Elizabeth Fry, was a very remarkable and peculiar one, little anticipated either by herself, or by others; but it was eminently blessed to the arousing of many from the sleep of sin, to the encouraging and strengthening of fellow-disciples of the same Lord, and to the exaltation of His holy name.

Mildred's Court, Second Month, 24th.—I have lately been much occupied in forming a school in Newgate, for the children of the poor prisoners, as well as the young criminals, which has brought much peace and satisfaction with it; but my mind has also been deeply affected, in attending a poor woman who was executed this morning. I visited her twice; this event has brought me into much feeling, attended by some distressingly nervous sensations in the night, so that this has been a time of deep humiliation to me, thus witnessing the effect and consequences of sin. This poor creature murdered her baby; and how inexpressibly awful now to have *her* life taken away! The whole affair has been truly afflicting to me; to see what poor mortals may be driven to, through sin and transgression, and how hard the heart becomes, even to the most tender affections. How should we watch and pray, that we fall not by little and little, become hardened, and commit greater sins. I had to pray for these poor sinners this morning, and also for the preservation of our household from the evil there is in the world.

Extract from a letter to her sister Rachel Gurney:—

Mildred's Court, *Third Month, 10th and 11th.*

My heart, and mind, and time, are very much engaged in various ways. Newgate is a principal object, and I think until I make some attempt at amendment in the plans for the women, I shall not feel easy; but if such efforts should prove unsuccessful, I think that I should then have tried to do my part, and be easy. My own Monthly Meeting, though absent from it, is rather a weight, and Gracechurch-street I am also much interested about. I have gone, besides, to only one London Meeting, all the time that I have been here. The poor occupy me little more than at the door—as I cannot go after them with my other engagements; the hanging at Newgate does not overcome me as it did at first, and I have only attended one woman since the first. I see and feel the necessity of caution in this respect, and mean to be on my guard about it, and run no undue risk with myself.

I have felt, in thy taking care of my dearest girls, that thou art helping me to get on with some of these important objects, that I could not well have attended to, if I had had all my dear flock around me.

From the notice before inserted, of the visit paid to the prisoners in Newgate, by Elizabeth Fry and Anna Buxton in 1813, the reader will be prepared for a report of the disgraceful state in which many of the prisons of the British empire were found, thirty years ago. We naturally seek to account for the continuance of so crying an evil.

That the sceptical philosophy which prevailed towards the end of the last century, was unfavourable to questions of moral and religious reform, we cannot doubt. Whether the startling events of the French Revolution—the tremendous wars that followed it—the rise and fall of empires—had so engrossed the attention and drained the resources of the English nation, that improvement at home was neglected; or whether looking to a still deeper source, it may be attributed to that tendency to degenerate, inherent in all human institutions, the fact is indisputable. Howard, and his humane exertions, appear to have been forgotten, and Acts of Parliament to have become a dead letter; some, if not all the provisions of those acts, being, in the vast majority of gaols, openly violated. For Counties as well as Boroughs, an old gate-house, or the ancient feudal castle, with its dungeons, its damp, close and narrow cells, and its windows overlooking the street, often formed the common prison of offenders of either sex, and of all grades of crime. The danger of escape was provided against, by heavy irons and fetters. Dirt and disease abounded: and even where the building contained wards and yards, the women were imperfectly separated from the men, whilst idleness, gambling, drinking, and swearing, were habitual amongst them. These evils were magnified by the crowded state of the prisons; for crime had enormously increased, and convictions more than doubled within the ten preceding years. Of the prisons for the counties, those of Bury, Ilchester, Gloucester, with a few others, formed honourable exceptions to the general rule; and in the Metropolis, the Penitentiary at Millbank, which had been recently erected.

The moral contamination produced by the disorderly state of prisons, was beginning to be perceived, and the necessity for stricter discipline and better regulations, to be acknowledged.

In the United States of America, and in a few instances on the continent of Europe, the experiment had been tried, and with such success as to establish the principle, that classification, employment, and instruction tended to the reformation of the criminal, and to the decrease of crime. A deputation of the Gaol Committee of the Corporation of London, was appointed in 1815, to visit several gaols in England, especially that of Gloucester, with a view to the amelioration of those under their own jurisdiction. From this resulted some improvements in Newgate. The women, from that time occupied the whole of the quadrangle, now called the women's side;" including what were formerly the state apartments: mats were provided for them to sleep on. Double gratings, with a space between, were placed to prevent close communication with their visitors, who were of both sexes, and many of them as vile and as desperate as themselves; but to overcome the difficulty thus presented, in receiving the contributions of those whose curiosity brought them to the spot, wooden spoons fastened to long sticks were contrived by the prisoners, and thrust across the intervening space. Notwithstanding these improvements, they remained in an unchecked condition of idleness, riot, and vice of every description. They were of the lowest sort—the very scum both of the town and country—filthy in their persons, disgusting in their habits, and ignorant, not only of religious truth, but of the most familiar duties of common life.

At the suggestion of her brother-in-law, the late Samuel Hoare, Elizabeth Fry had, in the interval between 1813 and 1816, accompanied him on a visit to the women in Cold-Bath-Fields House of Correction, whose neglected state had much impressed him. S. Hoare, with another of her brothers-in-law, (the late Sir T. F. Buxton,) and some of her personal friends, were, at this time, occupied in forming a society for the reformation of the juvenile depredators, who infested London, in gangs. This object led them into different prisons, where their attention was soon attracted to the subject of prison discipline. Although not originating in this cause, it may be presumed, that the conversation and influence of these gentlemen would tend to keep alive in the mind of Elizabeth Fry, the interest, awakened in 1813, for the female prisoners in Newgate. As in that instance, so at this time, her journal fails to convey any explicit information respecting her visits there. We are indebted to other sources for the fact, that they were recommenced about the close of the year 1816.

On her second visit, she was at her own request, left alone amongst the women for some hours; and on that occasion, she read to them the parable of the Lord of the vineyard, in the 20th chapter of Matthew, and made a few observations on the eleventh hour, and on Christ having come to save sinners, even those who might be said to have wasted the greater part of their lives estranged from Him. Some asked who Christ was; others feared that their day of salvation was passed.

Their children, who were almost naked, were pining for want of proper food, air, and exercise. Elizabeth Fry, on this occasion, particularly addressed herself to the mothers, and pointed out to them the grievous consequences to their children, of living in such a scene of depravity; she proposed to establish a school for them, to which they acceded with tears of joy. She desired them to consider the plan, for without their steady co-operation, she would not undertake it; leaving it to them to select a governess from amongst themselves. On her next visit, they had chosen as schoolmistress, a young woman, named Mary Connor, recently committed for stealing a watch. She proved eminently qualified for the task, and became one of the first-fruits of Christian labour in that place; she was assiduous in her duties, and was never known to infringe one of the rules. A free pardon was granted her about fifteen months afterwards; but it proved an unavailing gift, for a cough, which had attacked her a short time before, ended in consumption. She displayed, during her illness, much patience and quietness of spirit; having, as she humbly believed, obtained pardon and peace, through our Lord and Saviour. She died in the hope of a blessed immortality.

Elizabeth Fry's views were received with cordial approbation, by the Sheriffs of London, the Ordinary, and the Governor of Newgate; although they looked upon the experiment as almost hopeless. An unoccupied cell was, by their permission, appropriated for the school-room. On the day following this arrangement, she went to the prison accompanied by her friend, Mary Sanderson, (afterwards the wife of Sylvanus Fox,) and (with the poor prisoner Mary Connor, as mistress,) opened the school, for the children and young persons under twenty-five years of age; but from [illegible] size of the room, they had the pain of being obliged to refuse admission to many of the women, who earnestly entreated to be allowed to share in their instructions. Mary Sanderson then visited a prison for the first time, and her feelings were thus described by herself to Sir T. F. Buxton:—

"The railing was crowded with half-naked women, struggling together for the front situations, with the most boisterous violence, and begging with the utmost vociferation. She felt as if she were going into a den of wild beasts, and she well recollects quite shuddering when the door closed upon her, and she was locked in with such a herd of novel and desperate companions."

Something similar must have been the effect on that faithful co-adjutor in this work, Elizabeth Pryor, at rather a later period, upon seeing the women, "squalid in attire, and ferocious in countenance, seated about the yard." From the prison door one issued, "yelling like a wild beast;" she rushed round the area, with her arm extended, tearing everything of the nature of a cap from the heads of the other women. The sequel too is important: for this very woman, through the grace and mercy of God, became humanized under the instruction of these Christian visitors. After having obtained her liberty, she married; and for years came occasionally to see Elizabeth Pryor, who considered her a well-conducted person, her appearance being always most respectable.

A few other ladies gradually united themselves to those already engaged in the work, and the little school in the cell of Newgate continued, for many weeks, their daily occupation.

"It was in our visits to the school, where some of us attended almost every day, that we were witnesses to the dreadful proceedings that went forward, on the female side of the prison; the begging, swearing, gaming, fighting, singing, dancing, dressing-up in men's clothes; scenes too bad to be described, so that we did not think it suitable to admit young persons with us."*

The visitors thought some of the existing evils could be remedied by proper regulations; but in the commencement of the undertaking, the reformation of the women, sunk as they were in every species of depravity, was scarcely thought of, much less anticipated. By degrees, however, the heroic little band became convinced that good might be effected, even amongst these, for intercourse with the prisoners had inspired them with confidence. The poor women were earnest in their entreaties, not to be excluded from the benefits, which they began to perceive would result to themselves, from improved habits. But whilst Elizabeth Fry and her fellow-labourers were thus encouraged on the one side, every sort of discouragement presented itself on the other. The officers of the prison, as well as the private friends of the visitors, treated the idea of introducing industry and order into Newgate, as visionary. Even some, who were most interested in the attempt, apprehended that it would fail, from the character of those for whose good it was intended, from the unfavourable locality, in the midst of a great metropolis; and from the difficulty of obtaining a sufficiency of labourers for such a work. It was also urged that, even if employment could be procured, the necessary materials for work would be destroyed, or stolen. In recalling this period, one of those engaged in it, thus writes: "But amidst these discouraging views, our benevolent friend evinced that her heart was fixed; and trusting in the Lord, she commenced her work of faith and labour of love."

How aptly did the poet Crabbe, in reference to this undertaking, describe Elizabeth Fry—

* Elizabeth Fry's evidence before the House of Commons.

One, I beheld! a wife, a mother, go
To gloomy scenes of wickedness and woe;
She sought her way through all things vile and base
And made a prison a religious place:
Fighting her way—the way that angels fight
With powers of darkness—to let in the light.
Yet she is tender, delicate and nice,
And shrinks from all depravity and vice;
Shrinks from the ruffian gaze, the savage gloom,
That reign where guilt and misery find a home:
Guilt chained, and misery purchased, and with them
All we abhor, abominate, condemn—
The look of scorn, the scowl, th' insulting leer
Of shame, all fixed on her who ventures here:
Yet all she braved; she kept her steadfast eye
On the dear cause, and brushed the baseness by,—
So would a mother press her darling child
Close to her breast, with tainted rags defiled.

Mildred's Court, Third Month, 7th.—My mind and time have been much taken up with Newgate and its concerns. I have been encouraged about our school, but I find my weak nature and proneness to be so much affected by the opinions of man, brings me into some peculiar trials and temptations: in the first place, our Newgate visiting could no longer be kept secret, which I endeavoured that it should be, and therefore I am exposed to praise that I do not the least deserve; also to some unpleasant humiliations—for in trying to obtain helpers, I must be subject to their various opinions; and also, being obliged to confer at times with strangers, and men in authority, is to me a very unpleasant necessity. I have suffered much about the hanging of the criminals, having had to visit another poor woman, before her death; this again tried me a good deal, but I was permitted to be much more upheld, and not so distressed as the time before. May I, in this important concern, be enabled to keep my eye singly unto the Lord, that what I do may be done heartily unto Him, and not, in any degree, unto man. May I be preserved humble, faithful, and persevering in it, so far as it is right to persevere. And if consistent with the Divine will, may the blessing of the Most High attend it, that it may be made instrumental in drawing some out of evil, and leading and establishing them in the way everlasting, where they may find rest and peace.

The recurrence of these distressing scenes impressed on the mind of Elizabeth Fry an increasing disapprobation of the dreadful penalty of death. She often visited the cells of condemned criminals on the day or night preceding their execution; she marked the agony of some, and the obduracy of others, and she traced the hardening effect of such punishments on the fellow-prisoners of the sufferers, as well as on the lower orders of the public in general.

With what self-sacrificing love, with what yearnings of Divine compassion, did she encounter circumstances of the most appalling character, yielding her spirit in willing sympathy with the utmost depths of human misery, ministering to the wretched victims of sin a word of hope, pointing to the door of mercy, opened through Jesus Christ to every truly penitent soul. Awfully impressive were the opportunities when, in the gloomy dungeon of the condemned criminal, her prayers were poured forth in fervent solicitude, that the power of that Almighty Saviour, who "was manifested that He might destroy the works of the Devil," might snatch even these brands from the burning, and impart ability to look upward from the gulf of despair to the Deliverer, who "is exalted at the right hand of God, to give repentance and remission of sins."

The woman alluded to in the last extract from the journal, was Elizabeth Fricker; she was executed for robbing, or being accessory to robbing, in a dwelling-house. The following memorandum was written by Elizabeth Fry, Third Month, 4th, 1817, the day preceding the execution.

I have just returned from a most melancholy visit to Newgate, where I have been at the request of Elizabeth

Fricker, previous to her execution to-morrow morning, at eight o'clock. I found her much hurried, distressed, and tormented in mind. Her hands cold, and covered with something like the perspiration preceding death, and in an universal tremour. The women who were with her, said she had been so outrageous before our going, that they thought a man must be sent for to manage her. However, after a serious time with her, her troubled soul became calmed. But is it for man thus to take the prerogative of the Almighty into his own hands? Is it not his place rather to endeavour to reform such; or restrain them from the commission of further evil? At least to afford poor, erring, fellow-mortals, whatever may be their offences, an opportunity of proving their repentance, by amendment of life. Besides this poor young woman, there are also six men to be hanged, one of whom has a wife near her confinement, also condemned, and seven young children. Since the awful report came down, he has become quite mad from horror of mind. A strait waistcoat could not keep him within bounds—he had just bitten the turnkey; I saw the man come out with his hand bleeding, as I passed the cell. I hear that another, who had been tolerably educated and brought up, was doing all he could to harden himself, through unbelief, trying to convince himself that religious truths were idle tales. In this endeavour, he appeared to have been too successful with several of his fellow-sufferers. He sent to beg for a bottle of wine, no doubt in the hope of drowning his misery, and the fears that would arise, by a degree of intoxication. I inquired no further, I had seen and heard enough.

In a published letter, by "the Honourable H. G. Bennett," addressed to the Common Council and Livery of London, on the abuses existing in Newgate, he says, in allusion to Fricker's case:—

"A man, by the name of Kelly, who was executed some weeks back for robbing a house, counteracted by his conversation, and by the jest he made of all religious feelings, the labour of Dr. Cotton to produce repentance and remorse amongst the prisoners in the cells; and he died as he lived, hardened and unrepenting. He sent to me the day before his execution; and when I saw him, he maintained the innocence of the woman convicted with him, asserting, that not Fricker, but a boy concealed, opened the door, and let him into the house. When I pressed him to tell me the name of the parties concerned, whereby to save the woman's life, he declined complying without a promise of pardon; I urged as strongly as I could, the crime of suffering an innocent woman to be executed to screen criminal accomplices; but it was all to no effect, and he suffered, maintaining to the last the same story. With him was executed a boy of nineteen or twenty years of age, whose fears and remorse Kelly was constantly ridiculing."

Mildred's Court, Third Month, 11th.—My mind too much tossed by a variety of interests and duties—husband, children, household, accounts, Meetings, the Church, near relations, friends, and Newgate—most of these things press a good deal upon me. I hope I am not undertaking too much, but it is a little like being in the whirlwind, and in the storm; may I not be hurt in it, but enabled quietly to perform that which ought to be done; and may it all be done so heartily unto the Lord, and through the assistance of His grace, that if consistent with His Holy will, His blessing may attend it, and if ever any good be done, that the glory of the whole work may be given where it is alone due.

19*th.*—I yesterday applied to our Monthly Meeting for liberty to join William Forster in paying a religious visit to the families of Gracechurch-street Meeting; I think I had reason to be encouraged, from the solemn covering over us, and also the unity expressed by Friends. I thought it a great mercy and favour to have the unity of all; but I desire not to place undue dependence even on this, though it is sweet, and I esteem it a great blessing to have it. My dear sister Elizabeth was particularly favoured in what she said. If permitted to enter this service, may the Lord be with us in it, and bless us. I have not at present, felt much burdened by the prospect; I consider it an honour, favour, and blessing, to be engaged in the service of our great Master, even if humiliations, trials, and crosses attend it.

20th—Thou Lord, who knowest my heart and my wants, be pleased to help me under them; also permit Thy poor child to ask Thee, yet to look down upon her husband, children, brothers, and sisters, for good, upon all those most near and dear to her, and particularly those who are in trial.

Fourth Month, 12*th*.—I have found, in my late attention to Newgate, a peace and prosperity in the undertaking, that I seldom, if ever, remember to have done before. A way has very remarkably been opened for us, beyond all expectation, to bring into order the poor prisoners; those who are in power are so very willing to help us: in short, the time appears come to work amongst them. Already, from being like wild beasts, they appear harmless and kind. I am ready to say, in the fulness of my heart, surely, "it is the Lord's doing, and marvellous in our eyes;" so many are the providential openings of various kinds. Oh! if good should result, may the praise and glory of the whole, be entirely given where it is due, by us, and by all, in deep humiliation and prostration of spirit.

In the Fourth Month, 1817, the wife of a clergyman, and eleven members of the Society of Friends, formed themselves into "An Association for the Improvement of the Female Prisoners in Newgate." The object they had in view is stated to have been, "To provide for the clothing, the instruction, and the employment of the women; to introduce them to a knowledge of the Holy Scriptures, and to form in them, as much as possible, those habits of order, sobriety, and industry, which may render them docile and peaceable whilst in prison, and respectable when they leave it." On comparing these intentions with the existing state of things. it is easy to believe that the scheme was viewed, by those in authority, as very desirable, but almost impracticable. Still, to their honour be it spoken, they promised and gave their warmest co-operation.

The concurrence of the sheriffs and city magistrates was asked and obtained. But the doubt still remained, how far the women would submit to the restraints, which it would be needful to impose upon them, in order to effect this change. To ascertain this, the sheriffs met the members of this "Association" on a First-day afternoon at Newgate; the women were assembled, and in their presence, as well as that of the ordinary and governor, they were asked by Elizabeth Fry, whether they were willing to abide by the rules, which it would be indispensable to establish amongst them, for the accomplishment of the object so much desired by them all. The women, fully and unanimously, assured her of their determination to obey them strictly. The sheriffs also addressed them, giving the plan the countenance of their approbation; and then turning to Elizabeth Fry and her companions, one of them said, "Well, ladies, you see your materials."

How they used these "materials," and the blessing permitted to attend their exertions, is demonstrated by a letter received in 1820, from one of the prisoners, who had shared in the benefit of this earliest attempt to reform these unhappy women. The writer, as will be perceived, had been sent as a convict to New South Wales.

To Mrs. Fry.

"Paramatta, New South Wales, *July* 10*th*, 1820.

"Honoured Madam,

"The duty I owe to you, likewise to the benevolent Society to which you have the honour to belong, compels me to take up my pen to return to you my most sincere thanks, for the heavenly instruction I derived from you and the dear friends, during my confinement in Newgate.

"In the month of April, 1817, how did that blessed prayer of yours sink into my heart; and, as you said, so have I found it, that when no eyes see, and no ears hear, God both sees and hears; and then it was that the arrow of conviction entered my hard heart; and in Newgate, it was that poor Harriet S——, like the prodigal son, came to herself, and took with her words, and sought the Lord; and truly can I say with David, 'Before I was afflicted I went astray, but now have I learned Thy ways, O Lord!' and although affliction cometh not forth of the dust, yet how prone have I been to forget God, my Maker; who can give songs in the night; and happy is that soul that, when affliction comes, can say with Eli, 'It is the Lord,' or with David, 'I was dumb, and I opened not my mouth, because thou didst it;' and Job, when stripped of every comfort, 'Blessed be the Lord who took away, as well as gave'—and may the Lord grant every one that is afflicted, such an humble spirit as their's. Believe me, my dear madam, I bless the day that brought me inside of Newgate walls, for then it was that the rays of Divine truth shone into my dark mind; and may the Holy Spirit shine more and more upon my dark understanding, that I may be enabled so to walk, as one whose heart is set to seek a city whose builder and maker is God. Believe me, my dear madam, although I am a poor captive in a distant land, I would not give up having communion with God, one single day, for my liberty; for what is the liberty of the body, compared with the liberty of the soul? and soon will that time come, when death will release me from all the earthly fetters that hold me now, for I trust to be with Christ, who bought me with his precious blood. And now, my dear madam, these few sincere sentiments of mine, I wish you tc make known to the world, that the world may see that your labour in Newgate has not been in vain in the Lord. Please give my love to all the dear friends, and Dr. Cotton, Mr.

Baker, Simpson and all, the keeper of Newgate, and all the afflicted prisoners; and although we may never meet on earth again, I hope we shall all meet in the realms of bliss, never to part again. Please give my love to Mrs. Stennett, and Mrs. Guy.

"And believe me to remain,
"Your humble servant,
"HARRIET S——."

The remainder of the history will be better described by an extract from the "Enquiry whether crime and misery are produced or prevented by our present system of Prison Discipline. By T. F. Buxton."

"Having succeeded so far, the next business was to provide employment. It struck one of the ladies, that Botany Bay might be supplied with stockings, and indeed all articles of clothing, of the prisoners' manufacture. She, therefore, called upon Messrs. Richard Dixon and Co., of Fenchurch Street, and candidly told them, that she was desirous of depriving them of this branch of their trade, and stating her views begged their advice. They said at once, that they should not in any way obstruct such laudable designs, and that no further trouble need be taken to provide work for they would engage to do it. Nothing now remained but to prepare the room; and this difficulty was obviated, by the sheriffs' sending their carpenters. The former laundry speedily underwent the necessary alterations, was cleansed and white-washed, and, in a very few days, the Ladies' Committee assembled in it all the tried female prisoners. One of the ladies, Mrs. Fry, began by describing to them the comforts to be derived from industry and sobriety, the pleasure and profit of doing right; and contrasted the happiness and peace of those who are dedicated to a course of virtue and religion, with that experienced in their former life, and its present consequences; and describing their awful guilt in the sight of God, appealed to themselves, whether its wages, even here, were not utter misery and ruin. She then dwelt upon the motives which had brought the ladies into Newgate ; they had left their homes and their families, to mingle amongst those from whom all others fled ; animated by an ardent and affectionate desire to rescue their fellow-creatures from evil, and to impart to them that knowledge, which they, from their education and circumstances, had been so happy as to receive.

"She then told them, that the ladies did not come with any absolute and authoritative pretensions; that it was not intended they should command and the prisoners obey, but that it was to be understood, all were to act in concert; that not a rule should be made, or a monitor appointed, without their full and unanimous concurrence; that for this purpose, each of the rules should be read and put to the vote; and she invited those who might feel any disinclination to any particular, freely to state their opinion. The Rules were then read.

"And, as each was proposed, every hand was held up in token of their approbation. In the same manner, and with the same formalities, each of the monitors was proposed, and all were unanimously approved. When this business was concluded, one of the visitors read aloud the twenty-first chapter of St. Matthew, the parable of the barren fig tree, seeming applicable to the state of the audience; after a period of silence, according to the custom of the Society of Friends, the monitors, with their classes, withdrew to their respective wards in the most orderly manner. During the first month, the ladies were anxious that the attempt should be secret, that it might meet with no interruption; at the end of that time, as the experiment had been tried, and had exceeded even their expectations, it was deemed expedient to apply to the Corporation of London. It was considered that the school would be more permanent, if it were made a part of the prison system of the City, than if it merely depended on individuals. In consequence, a short letter,

32

descriptive of the progress already made, was written to the sheriffs.

"The next day an answer was received, proposing a meeting with the ladies at Newgate.

"In compliance with this appointment, the Lord Mayor, the Sheriffs, and several of the Aldermen attended. The prisoners were assembled together; and it being requested that no alteration in their usual practice might take place, one of the ladies read a chapter in the Bible, and then the females proceeded to their various avocations. Their attention, during the time of reading, their orderly and sober deportment, their decent dress, the absence of everything like tumult, noise, or contention; the obedience and respect shown by them, and the cheerfulness visible in their countenance and manners, conspired to excite the astonishment and admiration of their visitors. Many of these knew Newgate, had visited it a few months before, and had not forgotten the painful impressions made by a scene, exhibiting, perhaps, the very utmost limits of misery and guilt.

"The magistrates, to evince their sense of the importance of the alterations which had been effected, immediately adopted the whole plan as a part of the system of Newgate, empowered the ladies to punish the refractory by short confinement, undertook part of the expense of the matron, and loaded the ladies with thanks and benedictions. About six months after the establishment of a school for the children, and the manufactory for the 'tried side,' the committee received a most urgent petition from the untried, entreating that the same might be done among them, and promising strict obedience. In consequence, the ladies made the same arrangements, proposed the same rules, and admitted, in the same manner as on the other side, the prisoners to participate in their formation. The experiment has here answered, but not to the same extent. They have had difficulty in procuring a sufficiency of work, the prisoners are not so disposed to work, flattering themselves with the prospect of speedy release; besides, they are necessarily engaged, in some degree, in preparation for their trial. The result of the observations of the ladies, has been, that where the prisoners, from whatever cause, did no work, they derived little, if any, moral advantage; where they did *some* work, they received some benefit, and where they were *fully* engaged, they were really and essentially improved."

A gentleman well known to Elizabeth Fry, who was desirous of seeing and judging for himself of the effect of this singular experiment, visited Newgate just one fortnight after the adoption of the new rules. We give his own words.

"I went and requested permission to see Mrs. Fry, which was shortly obtained, and I was conducted by a turnkey to the entrance of the women's wards. On my approach, no loud or dissonant sounds, or angry voices, indicated that I was about to enter a place, which I was credibly assured, had long had, for one of its titles, that of 'Hell above ground.' The court-yard, into which I was admitted, instead of being peopled with beings scarcely human, blaspheming, fighting, tearing each other's hair, or gaming with a filthy pack of cards for the very clothes they wore (which often did not suffice even for decency) presented a scene where stillness and propriety reigned. I was conducted by a decently-dressed person, the newly appointed yards-woman, to the door of a ward, where, at the head of a long table sat a lady belonging to the Society of Friends. She was reading aloud to about sixteen women prisoners, who were engaged in needle work around it. Each wore a clean-looking blue apron and bib; with a ticket, having a number on it, suspended from her neck by a red tape. They all rose on my entrance, curtsied respectfully, and then at a signal given, resumed their seats and employments. Instead of a scowl, leer, or ill-suppressed laugh, I observed upon their counte nances an air of self-respect and gravity, a sort of consciousness of their improved character, and the altered position in which they were placed. I afterwards visited the other wards, which were the counterparts of the first."

Encouraged by many concurring circumstances, the newly formed Ladies' Committee, now for the first time, introduced a matron into Newgate. The prisoners were divided into classes, and placed under her superintendence. She was eventually paid in part by the Corporation; and received in addition twenty pounds a-year from the funds of the "Ladies' Association." They furnished the rooms appropriated to her, and she was regarded as their servant. The yards-woman was also appointed and paid by them.

Previous to the appointment of the matron, and until she was thoroughly established in her office, some of the visitors spent the whole day in the prison amongst the women: taking a little provision for themselves in a basket, or remaining without any; and for a long time afterwards, one or two of them never failed to spend some hours daily in this important field of labour.

From the manuscript journal of one of their number, Sophia de C——, we present to the reader some extracts descriptive of this period:—

"*Fifth Month*, 1*st*, 1817.—After nearly a sleepless night, spent in anticipation of the scenes of the morrow, I called on Dorcas Coventry, who had promised to introduce me to inspect the important labours which the Ladies of the Prison Committee had engaged in, for the reformation of the women in Newgate, for some time past. We proceeded to the felons' door, the steps of which were covered with their friends, who were waiting for admission, laden with the various provisions, and other articles which they required, either as gifts, or to be purchased, as the prisoners might be able to afford. We entered with this crowd of persons, into an ante-room, the walls of which were covered with the different chains and fetters, suspended in readiness for the culprits: a block and hammer were placed in the centre of it, on which the chains were rivetted. The room was guarded with blunderbusses, mounted on moveable carriages. I trembled, and felt sick, and my heart sunk within me, when a prisoner was brought forward to have his chain lightened, because he had an inflammation on the ankle. I spoke to him, for he looked dejected, and by no means ferocious. The turnkey soon opened the first gate of entrance, through which we were permitted to pass without being searched, in consequence of orders issued by the sheriffs. The crowd awaited until the men had been searched by the turnkeys: and the women, by a woman stationed for that purpose in a little room by the door of entrance. These searchers are allowed, if they suspect spirits, or ropes, or instruments of escape to be concealed about the person, to strip them to ascertain the fact. A melancholy detection took place a few days ago. A poor woman had a rope found upon her, concealed for the purpose of liberating her husband, sentenced to death for highway robbery, which sentence was to be put into execution in a few days. She was of course taken before a magistrate, and ordered into Newgate to wait her trial. She was a young and pretty little Irish woman, with an infant in her arms. After passing the first door into a passage, we arrived at the place where the prisoners' friends communicate with them; it may be justly termed a sort of iron cage; a considerable space remains between the gratings, too wide to admit of their shaking hands. They pass into this from the airing-yard, which occupies the centre of the quadrangle, round which the building runs, and into which no persons but the visiting ladies, or the persons they introduce, attended by a turnkey, are permitted to enter. This door is kept by a principal turnkey, and was opened to our attendant by his ringing a bell. A little lodge, in which an under turnkey sleeps, is also considered necessary to render the entrance secure. This yard was clean, and up and down it, paraded an emaciated woman, who gave notice to the women of the arrival of their friends. Most of the prisoners were collected in a room newly appropriated for the purpose to hear a portion of the Sacred Scriptures read to them, either by the matron, or by one of the Ladies' Committee; which last is far preferable. They assemble when the bell rings, as near nine o'clock as possible, following their monitors or wardswomen, to the forms which are placed in order to receive them. I think I never can forget the impression made upon my feelings at this sight. Women from every part of Great Britain, of every age and condition, below the lower middle rank, were assembled in mute silence, except when the interrupted breathing of their sucking infants informed us of the unhealthy state of these innocent partakers in their parents' punishment. The matron read; I could not refrain from tears, the women wept also; several were under the sentence of death. Swain, for forging, who had just received her respite, sat next to me; and on my left hand, sat Lawrence *alias* Woodman, surrounded by her four children, and only waiting the birth of another which she hourly expects, to pay the forfeit of her life; as her husband had done for the same crime, a short time before.

"Such various, such acute, and such new feelings passed through my mind, that I could hardly support the reflection, that what I saw was only to be compared to an atom in the abyss of vice, and consequently, misery of this vast metropolis. The hope of doing the least lasting good, seemed to vanish; and to leave me in fearful apathy. The prisoners left the room in order. Each monitor took charge of the work of her class on retiring. We proceeded to other wards, some containing coiners, forgers, and thieves; and almost all these vices were ingrafted on the most deplorable root of sinful dissipation. Many of the women are married; their families are in some instances permitted to be with them, if very young; their husbands, the partners of their crimes, are often found to be on the men's side of the prison, or on their way to Botany Bay.

"Some of these poor women are really beautiful, and healthy, and even modest-looking; their figures fine, and their countenances not disfigured by the expression of sin. The greatest number appeared to me Irish, a very few Scotch; the former are always ignorant, and preserve the peculiarities of their national character, even in this abode of sorrow and captivity; for to them privation and hardship are well known, and their Roman Catholic profession places their responsibility to God, in the keeping of their priests, so that life is deprived of its heaviest burden, and they expect to be finally happy, if they attend, even in that place, to the private ceremonies which their form of worship enjoins. I felt much more interested during my momentary glance, for some of these poor creatures, than for others. I was warned by my friend not to place too much dependence on expression of countenance, or on what they might say, as deception is the ruling temptation while here, and without much care, would produce mischief and injustice. They appear to be aware of the value of character, to know what is right, but to forsake it in action; finding this feeling yet alive, if properly purified and directed, it may become a foundation on which a degree of reformation can be built. In appealing to this statement in their breasts, and cultivating their own knowledge of it, many of the causes of former misbehaviour are crushed. Thus they conduct themselves more calmly and decently to each other, they are more orderly, more quiet, refrain from bad language, chew tobacco more cautiously, surrender the use of the fire-place, permit doors and windows to be opened and shut, to air or warm the prison, reprove their children with less violence, borrow and lend useful articles to each other kindly, put on their attire with modesty, and abstain from slanderous and reproachful words.

"It is to be hoped that by and by, a deeper and purer sense of the truths of religion may be found the cause of a real reformation. None amongst them was so shocking as an old woman, a clipper of the coin of the realm, whose daughter was by her side, with her infant in her arms, which had been born in Bridewell; the grandfather was already transported with several branches of his family as being coiners. The old woman's face was full of depravity. We next crossed the airing-yard, where many prisoners were industriouly engaged at slop-work, for which they are paid, and after receiving what they require, the rest is kept for them by the Committee, who have a receipt book, where their earnings and expenditure may be seen for any time, by the day or week. On entering the untried wards, we found the women very different from those we had just left; they were quarrelling, and very disorderly, neither knowing their future fate nor anything like subordination amongst one another. It resembles the state of the women on the tried side, previous to the formation of the Visitors' Committee; not a hand was employed, except in mischief. One bold creature was ushered in for committing highway robbery. Many convicts were arriving just remanded from the Sessions House; and their dark associates received them with applause,—such is the unhallowed fellowship of sin. We left this revolting scene, and proceeded to the school-room, situated on the untried side of the prison, for want of room on the tried. The quiet decency of this apartment was quite a relief; about twenty young women rose on our entrance, and stood with their eyes cast to the ground.

"A young woman of respectable appearance, named Mary Connor, had offered herself as mistress, for keeping the young children in order; who were separated from their parents' wards, and placed in this room. I gave those who wished it, permission to read to me; several could both read and write, some could say their letters, and others were in total ignorance; they wept as I asked them questions, and I read to them the parable of the prodigal son, as being peculiarly applicable to their present situation; they then resumed their needle-work. We next proceeded to the sick ward, (it was in good order,) and took a list of the additional clothes wanted there, and read a chapter from the New Testament; we then bade adieu to this dismal abode.

"*2nd.*—Rose early and visited Newgate (accompanied by Elizabeth Pryor,) where most of the Committee met to receive the Lord Mayor, the Sheriffs, several Aldermen, among whom were Sir William Curtis, Atkins, and some of the Gaol Committee, who had visited Elizabeth Fry the preceding day, in order to learn what had been done, what remained to be improved, and to lend the assistance deemed needful in this important work. The wisdom and integrity of her purpose were made apparent to them, and the plans gradually expanded before each of them; nothing was precipitated, caution marked every step, and even the irritable state of City politics does not interfere with this attempt at improvement. The women were assembled as usual, looking particularly clean, and Elizabeth Fry had commenced reading a Psalm, when the whole of this party entered the already crowded room. Her reading was thus interrupted for a short time. She looked calmly on the approaching gentlemen, who, soon perceiving the solemnity of her occupation, stood still amidst the multitude, whilst Elizabeth Fry resumed her office, and the women their quietude. In an impressive tone she told them, she never permitted any trifling circumstance to interrupt the very solemn and important engagement of reading the Holy Scriptures; but in this instance it appeared unavoidable from the unexpected entrance of so many persons, besides which, when opportunity offers, we should pay respect to those in authority over us, those who administer justice; she thus, with a christian prudence, peculiar to herself, controlled the whole assembly, and subdued the feelings of the prisoners, many of whom were but too well acquainted with the faces of the magistrates, who were themselves touched and astonished at thus being introduced to a state of decorum so new within those walls, and could not help acknowledging, how admirably this mode of treatment was adapted to overcome the evil spirit which had so long triumphed there. The usual silence ensued after the reading, then the women withdrew. We could not help feeling particularly glad that the gentlemen were present at this reading; the prisoners crowded round the Lord Mayor and Sheriffs, to beg little favours. We had a long conference with these gentlemen relative to this prison and its objects, the wisest regulations for Prison Discipline, and the causes of crime; indeed we could not have received more kind or devoted attention to what was suggested. Elizabeth Fry's manner seemed to awaken new trains of reflection, and to place the individual value of these poor creatures before them in a fresh point of view. They talked of building a school-room, but as it would encroach on the area of the yard, the scheme was unanimously abandoned. Regulations for cooking, washing and dining, were promised; but everything at present that involves expense to the city is relinquished. Economy, not parsimony, was the theme of the Lord Mayor; private benevolence has up to this time supplied every extra expense, besides what is termed the Sheriff's Gift. The Sheriffs came to our Committee-room, they ordered a cell to be given up to the Committee, for the temporary confinement of delinquents; it was to be made appear as formidable as possible, and we hope never to require it.

"12*th*.—The soldiers who guarded the interior of Newgate, were, at our request dismissed; they overlooked the women's yard, and rendered them very disorderly.

"23*rd*.—I found poor Woodman lying-in, in the common ward, where she had been suddenly taken ill; herself and little girl were each doing very well. She was awaiting her execution at the end of the month. What can be said of such sights as these?

"24*th*.—I read to Woodman, who is not in the state of mind we could wish for her, indeed so unnatural is her situation, that one can hardly tell how or in what manner to meet her case. She seems afraid to love her baby, and the very health which is being restored to her produces irritation of mind."

The visit paid by the city authorities, as described above by Sophia de C., was highly satisfactory to them. They had themselves experienced insurmountable difficulties in the attempt to control, or introduce order amongst the women in Newgate, and appear to have relinquished the task as hopeless. When, therefore, this new system and its unlooked-for success was exhibited before them, they did not start aside, mistrustful of the agency, or the novelty of the proceedings, but, without hesitation, gave to these efforts the weight of their influence and authority, without which, the benefit would probably be of short duration, and of comparatively unimportant results.

The different arrangements made by the visitors, together with the purchase of clothing for the prisoners, entailed considerable expenses; which soon proved beyond their private resources; a subscription was therefore opened to meet them, to which the Sheriffs added the sum of eighty pounds. Elizabeth Fry, at an after period, related to one of her coadjutors, that at this time she applied to some of her own relations for assistance in this object, for she perceived the work before her to be great, and the opening for usefulness beyond her expectation, but that to follow it up, she required the command of more money, than she could conscientiously ask from her husband. Her application was most cordially responded to by them; especially by her cousin, Hudson Gurney, and her uncle, Robert Barclay; they gave her help, and encouraged her to persevere in her important objects, desiring her to apply freely to them, whenever their aid was required.

But far beyond any other assistance was that which she received from her own brothers; who not only entered warmly into her objects of interest, but were unfailing in the generous support which they afforded them. From that time, until her labours of love were ended upon earth, not one year elapsed in which they did not most liberally contribute, as occasion required, to her various purposes of benevolence, leaving the division to her own judgment. Thus did He, who had called her to this work, open the hearts of persons in various circumstances, each to contribute of that which he had, some in personal exertion, and cheerful consecration of time and strength; some the countenance of their authority and official dignity, whilst others poured in the needful supplies of silver and gold.

We return to the journal.

Plashet, Sixth Month, 16*th.*—I found the prison going on in a very encouraging manner, so much quietness and order, quite like a different place to what it used to be. We may humbly trust from the fruit produced, that the blessing of the Most High has given the increase to the scattered seed.

On the eleventh of Sixth Month, 1817, she writes to her two eldest daughters; who, for nearly a year, had been the guests of their uncle Daniel Gurney, at North Runcton, under the maternal care of their aunt Rachel.

My dear children, remember, if you wish to be real helpers to me, and to your dear father, you must take heed to yourselves; and seek to keep your eye single to Him, who can alone enable you to do your duty towards yourselves, or towards us. For I am more and more convinced, that unless what we do, is done heartily unto the Lord, it profiteth little and availeth nothing. I cannot tell you,—for I have not language to express it,—the longing that I have, that you, my sweet, dear children, may go on in the right way. How far before all other things do I ask it for you. That whilst here, you may be "guided by His counsel, and afterwards received into glory."

ELIZABETH FRY.

Plashet, Sixth Month, 20th.—My dearest boys are returned from school, and the girls I expect this evening. To be once more surrounded by our sweet flock, is pleasant, and appears cause for much thankfulness. May a blessing attend us amongst them, so that in word, and in deed, we may preach Christ; and O, gracious Lord! be pleased so to let Thy blessing attend our labours of love, that they may all grow in grace, and in the knowledge of Thee, and Christ Jesus whom Thou hast sent.

Seventh Month, 21st.—I seem kept almost always, by night and by day, going again and again to the mercy-seat; I can hardly express what I have felt at times—groanings unutterable, for the children upon their getting out of childhood, in their many temptations; some seem more beset than others; but I do trust in Him, who has done marvellous things for *me*, and I humbly believe will do so also for *them;* this is the language of faith in my heart, so that I can hardly help consoling myself with the hope that, sooner or later, it will be verified, "I will pour my Spirit upon thy seed, and my blessing upon thy offspring, and they shall spring up as among the grass, as willows by the water-courses. One shall say, I am the Lord's; and another shall call himself by the name of Jacob; and another shall subscribe with his hand unto the Lord, and surname himself by the name of Israel."

Eighth Month, 4th.—My having been brought publicly forward in the newspapers, respecting what I have been instrumental in doing at Newgate, has brought some anxiety with it; in the first place, as far as I am concerned, that it may neither raise me too high, nor cast me too low, that having what may appear my good works, thus published, may never lead me or others to give either the praise or glory where it is not due. And that being brought thus forward in a way I do not like, and by a person whom I do not quite approve; I may in this, and in all other things, experience preservation, for indeed, I cannot keep myself, and that this labour, if consistent with the Divine Will, may continue to be blessed, and to make progress. And for myself, that I may be kept humble, watchful, faithful, and persevering.

The change that had taken place in Newgate, was noticed, for the first time, in the public journals, during the autumn of this year, by a man who has since been distinguished for his wild and theoretical views, Robert Owen, of New Lanark. This was, to Elizabeth Fry and her companions, a painful and unpleasant circumstance, notoriety being far from agreeable with their inclination. It immediately arrested public attention, Prison Discipline having become an object of general interest.

Plashet, Eighth Month, 28th.—I was yesterday at Newgate with Sheriff Brydges, &c., &c. I have felt of late, fears, whether my being made so much of, so much respect paid me by the people in power in the city, and also being so publicly brought forward, may not prove a temptation, and lead to something of self-exaltation, or worldly pride. I fear, I make the most of myself, and carry myself rather as if I were somebody amongst them ; a degree of this sort of conduct appears almost necessary—yet oh ! the watchfulness required not to bow to man, not to seek to gratify self-love ; but rather, in humility and godly fear, to abide under the humiliation of the cross. Lord, be pleased so to help and strengthen me in this, that for Thine own cause' sake, for my own soul's sake, my beloved family's, and the Society's sake, I may in no way be a cause of reproach ; but in my life, conduct, and conversation, glorify Thy great and ever excellent name. In all my perplexities be pleased to help me, and make a way where I see no way.

In the Ninth Month, her brother, Joseph John Gurney, of Earlham, married Jane, daughter of John Birkbeck.

Plashet, Ninth Month, 19th.—I returned from attending my dearest brother Joseph's wedding, with Jane Birkbeck, yesterday; they were married on the 10th; a Meeting very conspicuously owned by the great and good Shepherd of Israel, so that we could but look upon it as a token for good; the ministry flowed; but the immediate visitation of Divine love was still better. My brother said a few words in supplication, to my great comfort and refreshment, not doubting but that the Holy anointing was poured upon him; therefore I believe that he will be a great instrument in his Heavenly Father's hand, if he only keep very near to His guidance in heights and in depths; but I could *naturally* feel fears for his very sensitive and tender mind—the conflicts necessary for the service are so great and deep. His dear wife I believe will prove a true helper to him. I saw them afterwards settled at Earlham.

The following touching letter proves that her spirit was, in no degree, exalted by the applause of the world; the deep and hidden sorrows, of which she so feelingly speaks, caused her path to be one of much tribulation.

To HER BROTHER, JOSEPH JOHN GURNEY.

Plashet, *Tenth Month*, 16*th*, 1817.

My dearest Joseph,

It is rather odd to myself that I should not have written to thee before, who hast been the frequent subject of my most tender interests. My heart has been raised for thy support and preservation under every circumstance.

Perhaps, my dear brother, thou wilt like to hear a little of me, though thou hast so much to occupy thy heart and mind. Few, perhaps, can acknowledge more of the abundant loving kindness of the Almighty, who, in a remarkable way, has dealt with me. But in blessing, He has been pleased, at times, to permit some deep sorrows in the cup; some known to my fellow-mortals, and some remarkably hidden; but this, I doubt not, has been for good. At times, even though there are so many whom I love, so many near and dear to me, "I watch, and am as a sparrow alone upon the house-top," like "the owl in the desert, or the pelican in the wilderness;" but I believe "when no man seeth me, God seeth me, and when no man pitieth me, God pitieth me." I have felt also what the blessing is of having Him on our side; how doth He comfort those that mourn, and administer to all our wants. In short, though cast rather down in some things, I have felt much raised up in others, as if the power of the Endless Life shone strong in me through all; so that I may say, "though sorrowing, yet always rejoicing." This is a most private letter, as such an acknowledgment is almost like boasting, but I believe I may say it is not so, for all I desire to convey is, that amidst all my cares, sorrows, and perplexities, through His gracious power who strengthens me, I do rejoice.

Let me hear from you soon, and believe me, in near and tender love, thine and thy dear Jane's

Very affectionate sister,

E. F.

Mildred's Court, Twelfth Month, 17th.—A remarkable blessing still appears to accompany my prison concerns; perhaps the greatest apparent blessing on my deeds, that ever attended me. How have the spirits both of those in power, and the poor, afflicted prisoners, appeared to be subjected, and how has the work gone on! most assuredly the power and the glory is alone due to the Author and Finisher of every good work: things in this way thus prosper, beyond my most sanguine expectations; but there are also deep humiliations for me. My beloved children do not appear sufficiently under the influence of religion. I am ready to say, oh! that I could prosper at home in my labours, as I appear to do abroad. Others appear to fear for me, that I am too much divided; but alas! what can I do, but follow the openings? I think that I do also labour at home; but He who searcheth the heart, who knoweth all things, He knows my faith, my goings out, and my comings in; He knows the desires of my heart towards Himself—indeed the deep, inward travail of my spirit has been unutterable and indescribable; but my humble trust and strong confidence is, that He who hears and answers prayer, listens to my cry, hearkens to my deep inward supplications for myself, my husband, children, brothers, sisters, and household, my poor prisoners, and all things upon which I crave a blessing; and that being breathed in the faith, and I humbly trust through the power of the Redeemer, access will be granted them, and that He who has been with me, will be with me even unto the end. Amen, and Amen, saith my unworthy, sorrowful, and yet in another sense, rejoicing soul; as I do, at seasons through all, in a marvellous manner, in all my sorrows and cares, greatly and unspeakably rejoice in God my Saviour, my Redeemer, and my only hope of glory.

Mildred's Court, 23*rd*.—My spirit is much overwhelmed within me, this morning, but may I be enabled to look to the Rock that is higher than I. O Lord! I beseech thee, sustain me, and grant me cheerful resignation to Thy will, whatever Thou mayst be pleased to do with my little one who is sick; either in life, or in death, may she ever be Thine, and be comforted by Thy love, and life-giving presence. Amen.

Mildred's Court, 1818.—Lord, be pleased to grant the blessing of preservation which is above every blessing. It is very striking and wonderful to me, to observe how some things have been verified, that, in times of great lowness and unutterable distress, I have been led to believe would happen; in reading the 142nd Psalm, these words particularly, "The righteous shall compass me about, for Thou shalt deal bountifully with me." Has not this been, and is it not now, remarkably verified, by those filling almost the highest stations in life, to the lowest; by persons of almost all denominations, have I not been compassed about? My prison concerns have thus brought me, a poor and very unworthy creature, into public notice, and I may most humbly adopt this language in the 71st Psalm, "I am as a wonder unto many; but Thou art my strong Refuge. Oh! let my mouth be filled with Thy praise, and with Thy honour all the day;" but, O Lord! merciful and gracious, Thou who knowest the heart and its wanderings, and also its pantings after Thyself, be pleased yet to manifest Thyself to be a God hearing and answering prayer. Thou hast, in times of deep adversity, and of great affliction, when the heart of Thy handmaid has been ready to say, Refuge failed her, Thou hast then been her Stronghold, her Rock, and her Fortress; so that she has not been greatly moved, nor overcome by her soul's enemy. Be pleased, most merciful and gracious Lord God Almighty, now to keep her in the day of prosperity, when the righteous compass her about, that she may be, for a time, even as a wonder unto many. Keep her, O Lord! even as in Thine own Almighty hand, that no evil befall her, nor any plague come nigh her dwelling; and as Thou hast so far, in Thine abundant mercy and loving kindness, delivered her soul from death, Oh, be pleased to keep her feet from falling; hold up her goings in thy paths, that her footsteps slip not; but increasingly enable her at all times, under all circumstances, in heights and in depths, in life and in death, to show forth Thy praise, to walk faithfully and circumspectly before Thee, obeying Thee in all things, in Thy fear and in Thy love; abounding in the true faith, as it is in Jesus; ever giving Thee, O Lord God on High, with Christ Jesus our Lord, and Thy Holy Spirit our Comforter, one God, blessed forever, the glory due unto Thee, now in time, and in an endless eternity. Amen, Amen.

During the winter of 1817-18, Elizabeth Fry received many letters of inquiry from different parts of the country, in relation to the system pursued in Newgate. Ladies wished to form similar associations. Magistrates wished to improve the state of prisoners under their control, &c., &c.: all which required minute and carefully-considered replies. Some of the most distinguished and influential persons in the kingdom were anxious to witness, for themselves, what had been done in the prison, and a part of almost every morning was spent in accompanying such parties thither.

Many were asking for counsel, others for employment, which they supposed Elizabeth Fry could obtain for them; and almost constant applications from the poor, who thought her purse as inexhaustible as her good-will, "humbly praying" for assistance. Her benevolent feelings would hardly suffer any of these to pass unheeded; and her daughters, the eldest of whom was in her seventeenth year, proved efficient helpers in answering the demands.

A person who visited the prison infirmary, found a woman very ill; she spoke most feelingly of the kind attentions of the ladies, adding, "All the comforts around me, and all the consolation of my mind, are owing to them."

The prisoners who were sent from Newgate to the Penitentiary, were remarkable for the propriety of their conduct; and, as opportunities occurred, the manner in which they would ask after the health and welfare of the "Ladies' Committee" was highly interesting. A visitor said, "I never heard more minute or more affectionate enquiries, or more grateful acknowledgments. Mentioning Elizabeth Fry, I asked if she had done them any good? The answer of one struck me much, but more from the manner than the language:—'God bless her, and the day she came to Newgate! She has done us all good, and we have, and shall always have, reason to bless her.' This prisoner had been in Newgate previously, as well as subsequently, to the introduction of the Ladies' Committee; and she gave me a striking picture of the contrast between the two periods."

During the former, it had been the practice for convicts, on the night preceding their departure for Botany Bay, to pull down and break or burn everything within their reach; and to go off shouting with the most hardened effrontery. But when the last set went out, they took an affectionate leave of their companions, and expressed the utmost gratitude to their benefactors, and the next day entered their conveyances peaceably; and their departure, in the tears that were shed and the mournful decorum that was observed, resembled a funeral procession; and so orderly was their behaviour, that it was deemed unnecessary to send more than half the usual escort. As a proof that moral and religious instruction had produced some effect upon their minds, when these poor creatures were going, those who remained entreated that their share of the profits (a little fund they were allowed to collect for themselves, kept in a box under the care of the "Ladies' Committee") might all be given to those who were about to leave them.

In ten months after the working-system was introduced, the women had made nearly twenty thousand articles of clothing, which had been supplied principally by the slop-shops; and their knitting produced from sixty to a hundred pairs of socks and stockings every month. Their earnings averaged about eighteen-pence per week for each one.

Elizabeth Fry was informed that some were still gaming in the prison. She went alone, assembled the prisoners, and told them what she had heard,—that she feared it was true; dwelt upon the sin of gaming, its evil effect upon their minds, the interruption it gave, and the distaste it excited to labour; told them how much the report had grieved her, and said "she would consider it a proof of their regard, if they would have the candour and kindness to bring the cards to her." She did not expect they would do it, as it would be betraying themselves. But soon after she had retired to the "ladies' room," there was a gentle tap at the door, and in came a trembling girl, who, in a manner that indicated real feeling, expressed her sorrow for having broken the rules of so kind a friend, and presented her pack of cards. She was soon followed by another and another, until Elizabeth Fry had received five packs, which she burnt in their presence; assuring them, that so far from its being remembered *against* them, she should "remember it in another way."

A few days after this, she took with her some presents of clothing, and calling the first one, gave her a neat muslin handkerchief. To her surprise the girl said she hoped Elizabeth Fry would excuse her being so forward, but if she might say it, she felt exceedingly disappointed. She had hoped that Elizabeth Fry would have given her a Bible with her own name written in it, which she would value beyond anything else, and always keep and read it. This was irresistible. The treasure so much desired was brought, and Elizabeth Fry assured a friend that she never gave a Bible which was received with so much interest and satisfaction, nor one that she thought more likely to do good.

This had been one of the worst of girls, and had behaved very badly upon her trial; but she conducted herself afterwards in so amiable a manner, that she appeared "almost without a flaw," and it was hoped "would become a valuable member of society."

One of the prisoners had said, it was "more terrible to be brought up before Mrs. Fry than before the judge." This was mentioned, when Elizabeth Fry was giving her evidence before the Committee of the House of Commons, on which she remarked:—"I think I may say we have full power among them, though we use nothing but kindness. I have never proposed a punishment, and yet I think it is impossible, in a well regulated house, to have rules more strictly attended to than they are."

"Our habit is constantly to read the Scriptures to them twice a day—many of them are taught, some can read a little themselves. It has had an astonishing effect; I never saw the Scriptures received in the same way. When I have sometimes gone and said it was my intention to read, they would flock up stairs after me as if it were a great pleasure I had to afford them."

When asked by the committee if the ladies confined themselves to the reading of the Scriptures, without inculcating any peculiar doctrine, Elizabeth Fry replied,—"We consider, from the situation we fill, as it respects the public, as well as the poor creatures themselves, that it would be highly indecorous to press any peculiar doctrine of any kind,—any thing beyond the fundamental doctrines of Scripture."

The Committee had obtained a pardon for one poor woman, of whom Elizabeth Fry said, "We taught her to knit in the prison. She is now living respectably out of it, and in part gains her livelihood by knitting."

"One poor woman, to whom we lent money, comes every week to my house and pays two shillings. We give part and lend part, to accustom them to habits of punctuality and honesty."

A man, who was executed, left his wife in the prison, under sentence of death. They had eight children. On being asked respecting her, Elizabeth Fry replied,—"I heard her state to a gentleman, that it had been a very great blessing to her to be at Newgate, and I think there has been a very great change in her. Her case is now before Lord Sidmouth,"—hoping for a pardon.

On rewards, Elizabeth Fry replied,—"We divide our women into classes, with monitors."—"They not only have the earnings of their work, but we endeavor to stimulate them by a system of marks; for a certain number of good marks at a fixed period, they are rewarded with such prizes as we think proper—articles of clothing, or Bibles and Testaments." The matron superintends the classes.

The committee inquired if some prisoners had not suffered

from want of clothing? Elizabeth Fry said, "I could describe such scenes as I should hardly think it delicate to mention." —A woman had been brought in recently, with "hardly a covering, no stockings, and only a thin gown. We provided clothing immediately for the woman, and for her baby, which was born a few hours after she came in."

When asked if she thought any reformation could be effected without employment, she replied—"I should believe it impossible. We may instruct as we will, but if we allow them their time, and they have nothing to do, they naturally must return to their evil passions."

Elizabeth Fry closed her evidence before the Committee of the House of Commons, with the following remarks:—"I will just add, that I believe, if there were a prison fitted up for us, which we might visit as inspectors—if employment were found for our women, little or no communication allowed with the city, and room given to class them, with female servants only—if there were a thousand of the most unruly women, they w uld be in excellent order in one week. Of that I have not the least doubt."

This examination took place on the 27th of Second Month, 1818, ten months after the "Ladies' Association" had been formed. In the report of this Parliamentary Committee, the following sentence occurs: —"The benevolent exertions of Mrs. Fry and her friends, in the female department of the prison, have indeed, by the establishment of a school, by providing work and encouraging industrious habits, produced the most gratifying change. But much must be ascribed to unremitting personal attention and influence."

Crimes of almost every grade and description were then punishable with death. In regard to forgery, a case was hardly to be conceived in which it was not made a capital crime; and the law recognised no distinction between the systematic forger and the foolish lad or confiding female who, misled by others, became their dupes and victims. So sanguinary a law, if carried fully into effect, would have exacted an average of more than four executions per day, exclusive of First-day, in Great Britain and Ireland. To lessen this fearful sacrifice of human life, every possible expedient was adopted. The police often connived at the escape of those whom they pretended to seek; jurors often seized with avidity extenuating circumstances, to satisfy their consciences in returning a verdict of "not guilty;" and judges often leaned to the side of mercy, granting respites and reprieves, when cases of those under sentence of death were considered in council.

"A Society for Diffusing Information on the Subject of Punishment by Death" had been formed in 1808, when William Allen convened a little band of seven patriotic men at his own house, who organised a committee on capital punishments; and Sir Samuel Romilly, whose attention had been directed to the severity of the criminal code, determined to attempt an amelioration of it, and to begin with the act of Queen Elizabeth, which made it a capital offence for one to steal privately from the person of another. He was supported in this by Lord Holland and the Marquis of Lansdowne. Sir Samuel Romilly renewed his attacks upon this code, though almost single-handed, every succeeding session,—changing his plan of operation as circumstances required,—until his humane exertions were terminated by death, in 1818. His bill to remove the penalty of death for shoplifting, in 1810, was rejected by the Peers, when the following protest was presented:—

"*Dissentient.*—1st. Because the statute proposed to be repealed appears to us unreasonably severe, inasmuch as it punishes with death the offence of stealing property to a very inconsiderable amount, without violence or any other aggravation.

"2dly. Because, to assign the same punishment for heinous crimes and slight offences, tends to confound the notions of right and wrong, to diminish the horror atrocious guilt ought always to inspire, and to weaken the reverence in which it is desirable that the laws of the country should be held.

"3dly. Because severe laws are, in our judgment, more likely to produce a deviation from the strict execution of justice than to deter individuals from the commission of crimes; and our apprehension that such may be the effect, is confirmed, in this instance, by the reflection, that the offence in question is become more frequent, and the punishment, probably on account of its rigour, is seldom or never inflicted.

"4thly. Because the value of money has decreased since the reign of King William, and the statute is consequently become a law of much greater severity than the legislature which passed it ever intended to enact."

This was signed by the Dukes of Sussex and Gloucester, Lord Holland and the Marquis of Lansdowne.

On the 17th of Second Month, 1818, two women were executed for forgery. At six o'clock in the morning, one of them addressed the following letter to Elizabeth Fry:—

"Honoured Madam:—As the only way of expressing my gratitude to you, for your very great attention to the care of my poor soul, I feel I may have appeared more silent than perhaps some would have been on so melancholy an event; but believe me, my dear madam, I have felt most acutely the awful situation I have been in. The mercies of God are boundless, and I trust, through His grace, this affliction is sanctified to me, and through the Saviour's blood my sins will be washed away. I have much to be thankful for. I feel such serenity of mind and fortitude. God of His infinite mercy, grant I may feel as I do now in the last moments! Pray, madam, present my most grateful thanks to the worthy Dr. Cotton and Mr. Baker, and all our kind friends the ladies, and Mrs. Guy. It was a feeling I had of my own unworthiness made me more diffident of speaking as was perhaps looked for. I once more return you my most grateful thanks. It is now past six o'clock. I have not one moment to spare. I must devote the remainder to the service of my offended God.

"With respect, your humble servant,

"CHARLOTTE NEWMAN."

She added, that Mary Ann James (who was to be executed with her) felt, as she hoped, all that she had expressed.

Those under sentence of death for forgery were apt to consider themselves "more sinned against than sinning,"—that they were the victims of a harsh and cruel law, which made property of more value than human life,—and thus, being the injured parties, they were to die more as martyrs than as criminals. On the same day that brought poor Newman's letter, Elizabeth Fry received one from William Wilberforce.

"Kensington Gore, 17*th Feb.*, 1818.

"My dear Madam:—I think I need not assure you that I have not forgotten you this morning. In truth, having been awake very early, and lying in peace and comfort and safety, the different situation of the poor women impressed itself strongly on my mind.

"I shall be glad, and Mrs. Wilberforce also, I assure you, to hear that your bodily health has not suffered from your mental anxiety, and I will try to get a sight of you, when I can, to hear your account and remarks on the effects of the last few days, both on the poor objects themselves and their prison companions.

"With real esteem and regard, I am, my dear madam,

"Yours very sincerely,

"W. WILBERFORCE."

The circumstances at Newgate, which had been wont to pass unheeded, and almost unknown, save to a few heart-stirred philanthropists, now attracted the attention and excited the interest of great numbers among the varied classes in society. During the spring of this year, executions had become so frequent, that they were made subjects for investigation, and for public as well as private discussion.* The sanguinary provisions of the penal code were beheld with a sentiment of disapprobation, and even abhorrence, before unfelt. The wretched tenants of the "condemned cells," after having received the sentence of death at the Old Bailey, awaited, with mingled hope and fear, the decision of the Council, by whom some were selected for mercy, the others to suffer the extreme penalty of the law. No reasons were assigned by the Council for this distinction; each one, therefore, hoped to escape the dreadful doom Among those who were waiting in this state of terrible suspense, was a young woman named Harriet Skelton. There was something peculiarly touching in the case of this poor creature. "A child might have read her character in her countenance—open, confiding, affectionate, possessing strong feelings, but neither hardened in depravity, nor capable of cunning." Under the influence of the man whom she loved, she had been induced to pass some forged notes: "thus adding another to the dismal list of those who, with the finest impulses of our nature, uncontrolled by religion, have been lured to their own destruction." Skelton was ordered for execution; the sentence was unlooked-for; "her deportment in the prison had been good, amenable to regulations, quiet and orderly. Some of her companions in guilt were heard to say, that they supposed she was chosen for death, because she was better

* The heart sickens at the thought how, even in the last generation, human life was recklessly sacrificed. Persons convicted of comparatively small crimes paid the forfeit of life; some of them might, unquestionably, have become reformed and useful. The late Charles Wesley, in a letter to his friend John Fletcher, vicar of Madely, dated "June 30th, 1776," says, "*A fortnight ago I preached the condemned sermon to above* 20 *criminals. Every one of them, I have good grounds to believe, died penitent.* 20 *more must die next week!!* See *Memoir of Elizabeth Mortimer*, p. 101.

prepared than the rest of them." Elizabeth Fry was vehemently urged to exert herself on behalf of this unhappy woman. She made various attempts—one through the Duke of Gloucester, who with other dwellers in palaces and lordly halls, visited the poor convict in Newgate; and "his former companion in the dance" led the Duke through the gloom and darkness of that most gloomy of prisons—a new scene indeed to him, and to many others, who, through life, had been "nursed on the downy lap of ease," in luxurious abodes, that strangely contrasted with the "dark vaulted passages—the clanking fetters—the offensive smell—the grating sound as the heavy key was turned—the massive bolts drawn back—and the iron-sheathed door forced reluctantly open," unaccustomed, and as if unwilling, to admit such guests.

The Duke of Gloucester made a noble effort to save Skelton, by an application to Lord Sidmouth; he also accompanied Elizabeth Fry to the Bank Directors: but all entreaties were in vain. Lord Sidmouth was annoyed by Elizabeth Fry's earnest solicitations, and highly offended at some disclosures which involved a degree of censure on the Bank Directors. There were, in the case, circumstances of collusion, on the part of some who were concerned in bringing this unfortunate creature to the gallows, of which Elizabeth Fry might perhaps have spoken with a degree of freedom that exceeded the limits of strict prudence: but who can read the tale without a strong and sympathetic interest in her humane appeal for mercy? or without deep regret, as well as surprise, that this appeal could have been regarded in the light of an offence? and how does the emotion acquire intensity, when we contemplate the dreadful severity of an enactment, which, within a few years afterwards, was, through the aroused and resistless force of public opinion, expunged from the statute-book!

The claims of *mercy* had rendered it very important to Elizabeth Fry that she should have access to the Secretary of State. She had been wont to intercede with Lord Sidmouth on behalf of those whom his decision might either consign to an untimely and ignominious death, or award a further term of earthly probation. But now her influence with him was lost. She endeavoured, by a personal interview, to remove the unfavourable impressions which he had imbibed, and to convince him that, although she might have erred in judgment, her intentions had been upright, and her desire sincere not to oppose his wishes. But all was in vain: his heart was steeled against remonstrances, and nothing but pain resulted from the interview. Elizabeth Fry had been accompanied in this unsatisfactory visit by the excellent Countess Harcourt, one of the ladies of the Court; and under her special care and protection had, on the same day, reluctantly, and with a heavy heart, to mingle in a very different scene, and to encounter objects of a remarkably opposite character. The aged Queen Charlotte, who, through a lengthened life, had appeared little moved by questions of a philanthropic character, her interests being much confined within the sphere of her court and its cold formalities and etiquette, had heard of the wonderful changes in Newgate and elsewhere, wrought through the instrumentality of Elizabeth Fry, and had become impressed by the evidences of an awakened and powerfully religious feeling, which had begun to operate on the minds of some persons of rank and influence, who had witnessed the labours of this devoted woman; and, on the occasion of a public examination of the children of some large metropolitan schools in the Egyptian Hall of the Mansion House, the Queen intimated her desire to be present, and requested that Elizabeth Fry would also attend on the occasion. This was an injunction that could not, with any degree of propriety, be disregarded; and accordingly, though as she says against her will, Elizabeth Fry, in company with the Countess Harcourt, repaired thither. It had been intended that she should be presented to the Queen in the drawing room—this would have been much more select and agreeable—but, through some misunderstanding, Lady

Harcourt and Elizabeth Fry were conducted to the hall, and placed on the side of the platform, which was crowded with waving feathers, jewels, and orders; several of the bishops standing near her, the great hall lined with spectators, and in the centre hundreds of poor children from the different schools. Elizabeth Fry was an object of general attraction. After a time the Queen perceived her, and advanced to address her. It was a striking scene, and painted by an artist—the diminutive stature of the Queen, covered with diamonds, but her countenance lighted with an expression of pleasure and of the kindest benevolence,—Elizabeth Fry's tall figure, clad in her simple Friend's dress, her countenance a little flushed, but preserving her wonted calmness of look and serious dignity of manner. The spectators of this remarkable interview, with a murmur of applause, hailed the scene before them, as the meed of approval offered by royalty at the shrine of mercy and good works.

The fatigue of the day proved too much for the Queen's declining bodily powers. In the succeeding autumn she finished her earthly course. It was a cause of much satisfaction to the many who cherished an interest in her eternal well-being, that the power of religion increasingly influenced her mind, as she approached the confines of a never-ending state of existence. During her last illness, in the Ninth Month of this year, the Countess Harcourt, in a letter to Elizabeth Fry, says,—

"We are at present in great anxiety on account of the poor Queen. I wish she had had the advantage of knowing you earlier, and more intimately. But I believe her opinions on religious subjects, are what you would highly approve, and Mrs. Bendorff who never leaves her, reads and prays with her constantly, and has done so, at all periods. The conduct of the two Princesses is most exemplary, but I much fear Princess Augusta's health is declining, and her nerves are very much shook. If the Duke of Gloucester had not kindly suffered the Duchess to remain, and share this painful duty with Princess Augusta, she must have sunk under it. Princess Sophia is also very ill, at Windsor, from her extreme anxiety. The distressed state of the Royal Family should prove, that there are none of those circumstances, that are called advantages, that can even alleviate, much less exempt the possessors from the misfortunes common to mortality. The lesson is a useful one, and so is the patience and resignation with which the Queen bears her sufferings, and her family bear their sorrows. I am told the Queen shows a particular gentleness and gratitude to all around her, making no complaints, even when in agonies of pain. Her strength of constitution, which is very great, is probably the cause of the protraction of her sufferings, and the period may still be prolonged some days, or it may terminate in a moment."

Chapter Sixth.

1818—1823. Engagements in the Prison—Convict ships—The Maria —Visitors to Newgate—Letter from Lady Mackintosh—Lord Lansdowne's speech—Scotch journey—Letter from the Countess Harcourt —Takes her sons to school—Illness—Journey in consequence—Letter to prisoners—Letters to her sons and Priscilla H. Gurney—Affliction in her family—Scripture readings in Newgate—Female convicts in New South Wales—Journey into the North of England—Letters to her daughter, Walter Venning, &c.—Foreign Prisons—Death of her sister Priscilla Gurney—Capital punishments—Mackintosh's Motion—Buxton's speech—Prison Discipline Meeting—Marriage of a daughter—Visits to several Meetings—Death of a sister-in-law—Letter to the Princess Royal of Denmark—To J. J. Gurney—Sale of prisoners' work—Convict ships—Interesting visit to one of them —Letter from the Duchess of—— —Attends Bristol Quarterly Meeting, &c.—Reflections.

After the arduous exertions and interests of the winter of 1817–18, it was no small relief to Elizabeth Fry and her family, to return to Plashet: and she writes—

Plashet, Fourth Month, 29th.—May we more evidently *live* in the best sense, even unto God. Since I last wrote, I have led rather a remarkable life; so surprisingly followed after by the great, and others in my Newgate concerns; in short, the prison and myself are become quite a show, which is a very serious thing, in many points. I believe, that it certainly does much good to the cause, in spreading amongst all ranks of society a considerable interest in the subject; also a knowledge of Friends, and of their principles: but my own standing appears critical in many ways. In the first place, the extreme importance of my walking strictly, and circumspectly, amongst all men, in all things; and not bringing discredit upon the cause of truth and righteousness.

In the next place, after our readings there, the ministry is a most awful calling, thus, publicly amongst men, to be in season and out of season. I desire to live, (more particularly in these things,) in the fear of God rather than of man, and that neither good report, nor evil report, the approbation nor disapprobation of men, should move me the least, but my eye should be kept quite single to the great and good Shepherd and Bishop of souls; this is my continual prayer for myself.

That the desire for preservation, so continually raised in her heart, was graciously answered, we have many evidences. We observe, in the journal of William Allen, the following notices of these important engagements at Newgate, of which she so feelingly speaks.

"*Second Month*, 8*th*, 1818.—Went with E. J. Fry and Cornelius to Newgate. About one hundred women prisoners were collected, and behaved in a most exemplary manner. E. J. Fry read the seventh chapter of Luke to them in a solemn manner, and made some comments upon it very sweetly. I thought a precious degree of power attended. I also ventured to address them, and felt peace."

"*Fifth Month*, 27*th*.—Professor Pictet and his son Charles Vernet went with me to Gracechurch-street Meeting. I afterwards accompanied them to meet E. J. Fry at Newgate. The Duke of Leinster and the Swedish Ambassador were there. It was a solemn time. E. J. Fry read a psalm, and was afterwards engaged in prayer. Hannah Field also supplicated, and Mary Sanderson spoke in ministry."

"*Seventh Month*, 14*th*, 1820.—I accompanied the Marquis Pucci to Newgate. E. J. Fry read to about sixty female prisoners. They seemed in excellent order. The reading was followed by a solemn pause, and supplication from E. J. Fry."

Similar memoranda of the religious opportunities that often occurred in the prison, might be multiplied from the pens of many excellent persons; and, frequently, the visitors of *every* class, and the prisoners themselves, were equally affected. A near relative of the Duke of Wellington said he was "*amazed at the reverence* of Elizabeth Fry in reading the Scriptures, and at the attention of the prisoners." His heart melted into tenderness while he listened to her faithful and compassionate addresses to her serious congregation: he had never before seen anything like it. He was an officer in the navy, and it was remarked by one who was present, "When Elizabeth Fry kneeled down and offered prayer in the blessed name of our great High Priest, Jesus Christ, as our only Mediator and Advocate with the Father, for the Divine mercy, and pardon, and grace, to rest upon all present, for their salvation and eternal glory, the captain was overcome: he burst into tears and wept like a child."

A fresh object of interest now opened upon the attention of the "Ladies' Newgate Association." The removal of the female convicts for transportation: and the circumstances under which those whom they so anxiously desired to benefit, were to pass the long and dreary months of confinement on ship-board.

Previous to the commencement of those efforts which produced such a marvellous change in the conduct of these unhappy women, it had been usual, on their departure for the convict ships, to have them conveyed from the prison to the water-side in open waggons, generally amidst assembled crowds,—the prisoners and those who surrounded them being alike riotous and noisy, the disorder being maintained on the road and in the boats. Elizabeth Fry prevailed on the Governor to consent to their being moved in hackney coaches. She then promised the women, that if they would be quiet and orderly, she and others of the visitors would accompany them to Deptford, and see them on board the *Maria* convict ship; accordingly, when the time came, no disturbance took place; the women in hackney coaches, with turnkeys in attendance, formed a procession, which was closed by her carriage, and the women behaved well upon the road. When on board the ship, Elizabeth Fry and her co-adjutors were distressed to see so many women and children herded together below deck. They were to be divided into messes of six each, and as each woman must, of necessity, associate the most with those of her own mess, it seemed to be a good opportunity to class and number them. This was no sooner proposed, than accepted by all concerned in the arrangement; they were divided into classes of twelve, including the monitor, chosen from the number by the women themselves. As far as possible, those whose ages or criminality were similar were placed together, each class contained two messes. The superintendence thus became as complete, as the nature of the case would permit. There were one hundred and twenty-eight convicts, besides their children.

Employment and instruction were still wanting; the women complained of having nothing to do. To procure work for a hundred and twenty-eight persons, during so long a voyage, appeared to be a hopeless endeavour; and even if it could be obtained from Government or individuals, that it would be useless to give it to them, with no responsible person to take charge either of its execution or appropriation. The visitors were told that patchwork and fancywork found a ready sale in New South Wales. They accordingly made it known that they required little pieces of coloured cotton, for this purpose; and in a few days, enough were sent from the different Manchester houses in London, fully to supply them with work, aided by some knitting. The time and ingenuity required in patchwork, rendered it a particularly suitable occupation; and as the convicts were to have the things when done, to sell for their own profit on arrival, it was evidently their interest to turn their skill to the best account. By this means, another important good was effected; for at that time, no factory or barrack of any description existed, for the reception of the women when landed in the colony; not so much as a hut in which they could take refuge, so that they were literally driven to vice, or left to lie in the streets. The proceeds of their industry on board ship, though small, would enable such as desired it, to obtain shelter until engaged as servants, or until they could find some respectable means of subsistence. A fact that occurred the following year, in the *Wellington* female convict ship, showed the correctness of this opinion, and how well patchwork had answered the intended purpose; for when that ship touched at Rio de Janeiro, the quilts made by the women were there sold for a guinea each. Bibles, prayer-books, and religious tracts, were placed under the care of each monitor, for the use of her class; arrangements were also made, that those who could not read and wished to learn, should have an opportunity of doing so.

But though some provision was thus made for the necessities of the women, the poor children were still in misery and in ignorance, fourteen of them were of an age to receive instruction; with some difficulty, a small space of the vessel was set apart for a school: there, during the greater part of the day, the children were taught to read, knit, and sew; one of the convicts undertook to be school-mistress, for whom a reward was placed in the hands of the captain, provided she persevered in her duties to the end of the voyage. During the five weeks that the ship lay in the river, some members of the "Association" devoted much of their time to making these arrangements. The expense of £72 10*s*. was incurred in working materials, aprons for the women, and additional clothing for the most destitute. The good effects of these regulations were speedily seen, but none were sanguine as to their continuing in force after the ship had fairly put to sea, and there would be no longer any stimulus or inducement to persevere. The captain, a very respectable man, died suddenly at Calcutta, on the voyage home, which prevented its being ascertained with certainty, how long, or to what extent the plans were beneficial. The only person who could give or enforce an order, was the surgeon-superintendent, appointed by Government to the care of the women. In this instance, the appointment had fallen on a man who did not take even the least interest in the moral organization of the convict ship. The last time that Elizabeth Fry was on board the *Maria*, whilst she lay at Deptford, was one of those solemn and interesting occasions that leave a lasting impression on the minds of those who witness them. There was great uncertainty whether the poor convicts would see their benefactress again. She stood at the door of the cabin, attended by her friends and the captain; the women, on the quarter-deck facing them. The sailors anxious to see what was going on, climbed into the rigging, upon the capstan, or mingled in the outskirts of the group. The silence was profound—when Elizabeth Fry opened her Bible, and, in a clear, audible voice, read a portion from it. The crews of the other vessels in the tier, attracted by the novelty of the scene, leaned over the ships on each side, and listened apparently with great attention; she closed the Bible, and after a short pause, knelt down on the deck, and implored a blessing on this work of Christian charity from that God, who, though one may plant and another water, can alone give the increase. Many of the women wept bitterly, all seemed touched; when she left the ship, they followed her with their eyes and their blessings, until her boat having passed within another tier of vessels, they could see her no more.

But we return to her own journal.

Plashet, Seventh Month, 1st.—Since I last wrote, much has happened to me; some things have occurred of an important nature. My prison engagements have gone on well, and many have flocked after me, may I not say of almost all descriptions, from the greatest to the least; and we have had some remarkably favoured times together in the prison. The Yearly Meeting was a very interesting one to me, and also encouraging. I felt the unity of Friends a comfort and support. I had to go into the Men's Meeting, which was a deep trial of faith, but it appeared called for at my hand, and peace attended giving up to it. The unity which the women expressed at my going, and the good reception I found amongst the men, were comforting to me; but it was a close, very close, exercise. Although I have had much support from many of my fellow-mortals, and so much unity expressed with me, both in and out of our Society—yet I believe many Friends have great fears for me and mine; and some, not Friends, do not scruple to spread evil reports, as if vanity or political motives led me to neglect a large family. I desire patiently to bear it all, but the very critical view that is taken of my beloved children, grieves me much.

From the very diverse habits of thought in different individuals—habits engendered by education, by pre-conceived notions, and by the influences of association and natural temperament—the opinions of men will ever widely vary—most especially on subjects with which, from their novelty, they may be but slightly acquainted. It was thus, in reference to the calling and engagements of the excellent person whose course is described in this volume. She was, at times, heavily oppressed under the effect of conflicting views; yet, sustained by the evidences, often vouchsafed, that an Almighty Helper was her Friend and Guide, she was enabled, with singleness of purpose, to pursue her efforts for the welfare of her fellow-creatures, and for the reconciliation with God of spirits alienated from Him by wicked works. His blessing rested on her labours, and *some, at least,* were brought to a *saving* knowledge of their gracious Redeemer. And unto *Him* she ascribed *all* praise.

8*th.*—My heart is too full to express much; yesterday, I had a very interesting day at Newgate, with the Chancellor of the Exchequer, and many other persons of consequence; much in the cross to myself, I had to express a few words in supplication before them, but the effect was solemn and satisfactory. After this I felt peaceful and comforted; sometimes

I think, after such times, I am disposed to feel as if *that* day's work was *done*, and give way to cheerful conversation, without sufficiently waiting for the fresh manifestations of the Spirit, and abiding under the humiliations of the Cross.

It is needful now to revert to the excitement produced in the public mind, as the circumstances of the remarkable transformation effected in Newgate, became generally known. The visits of Elizabeth Fry were the theme of conversation among all ranks, and the accounts circulated of the interesting scenes which were to be witnessed there, brought a strange variety of persons to that abode of sorrow. It would be too much to say that all, who then, or in after times, attended the readings in Newgate, were actuated by high and holy feelings in desiring admittance; but if a list of the names of the visitors could be published, it would prove how strong was the simpathy felt among the nobly born, and richly endowed with intellectual, as well as worldly, wealth.

Sir James Mackintosh became, in Parliament, a powerful advocate for the reform of the penal code. A letter from Lady Mackintosh to Elizabeth Fry (published by special permission), is strikingly interesting, as a testimony to the effect of the arduous labours in the prison. We give an extract:—

"I have had a note from Sir James, in which is the following passage, I cannot resist copying it, in the hope of your pardon for doing so. 'I dined Saturday, June 3d, at Devonshire House. The company consisted of the Duke of Norfolk, Lords Lansdowne, Lauderdale, Albemarle, Cowper, Hardwicke, Carnarvon, Sefton, Ossulston, Milton, Duncannon, &c. The subject was Mrs. Fry's exhortation, to forty-five female convicts, at which Lord ——— had been present on Friday. He could hardly refrain from tears in speaking of it. He called it the deepest tragedy he had ever witnessed. What she read and expounded to the convicts, with almost miraculous effect, was the 4th chapter to the Ephesians. Coke (of Norfolk) begged me to go with him next Friday; I doubt whether, as that is the day of my motion,* I shall be able to go, and whether it be prudent to expose myself to the danger of being too much warmed by the scene, just before a speech in which I shall need all my discretion.'

"As the above extract was only intended for my eye, I am sure you will so consider it. My motive for submitting it to you is twofold; that you may not be ignorant how much your great work of mercy contributes to inspire good feelings, and to supply pure and edifying subjects of conversation at the tables of the most illustrious persons in the country, for rank and talents."

Among the visitors were to be found persons, who, as friends of humanity, came to ascertain the truth of all that they had heard; actuated by the same motives, bishops, clergymen, and other ministers of religion resorted thither. It will at once be seen how the concurring testimony of individuals, distinguished in such various ways, must have influenced public opinion in favour of a mode of treatment which, in the course of a few weeks, had struck at the root of the more glaring evils, so lately existing in the principal metropolitan prison of England. Nor can it be doubted that the influx of visitors, objectionable as it must be considered in itself, and injurious as it would be, in a well-ordered prison, was then an important means of spreading knowledge and exciting interest, and thus assisting to prepare the way for the improvements in Prison Discipline subsequently effected. It appears highly probable that the rapidity and ease with which legislative enactments on these subjects were afterwards carried, may be chiefly attributed to what had been seen and heard in Newgate.

* For the revision of the Penal Laws.

On the Third of Sixth Month, 1818, the Marquis of Lansdowne moved an address to the Prince Regent, on the state of the prisons of the United Kingdom. In his speech, after stating appalling facts as to the increase of crime within the preceding ten years, attributing it to various causes, especially to the vicious and deplorable condition of the prisons themselves, he made this observation in reference to Newgate:

"It was impossible from the manner in which it was constantly crowded, to apply any general system of regulations. There, it was necessary to place several felons in the same cell, and persons, guilty of very different descriptions of offences, were mixed together. The consequences were such as might be expected, notwithstanding all the efforts of that very meritorious individual (Mrs. Fry), who had come like the Genius of Good into this scene of misery and vice, and had, by her wonderful influence and exertions, produced, in a short time, a most extraordinary reform among the most abandoned class of prisoners. After this great example of humanity and benevolence, he would leave it to their lordships how much good, persons similarly disposed, might effect in other prisons, were the mechanism, if he might use the expression, of those places of confinement better adapted to the purposes of reformation. The institution of the great Penitentiary-house was likely to be attended with great advantages, though he did not approve of all the regulations. That establishment was a great step taken in the important work of reformation. He was aware there were persons who considered all expense of this kind as useless, who thought that all that could be done was to provide for the safe custody of prisoners, and that attempts to reform them were hopeless. Let those who entertain this notion, go and see what had been effected by Mrs. Fry and other benevolent persons in Newgate. The scenes which passed there, would induce them to alter their opinion. There were moments when the hardest hearts could be softened and disposed to reform."

After reading this sentence, delivered in the house of Lords, and published in all the journals of the day, it causes no surprise, to find that admittance into Newgate was sought with eager curiosity by all sorts of persons; to many of whom, admission could not, with any propriety, have been refused by either magistrates, officers, or ladies. Inconveniences arose from it, but at this juncture, of prison reformation, they were greatly outweighed by its effects in diffusing information and calling attention to the subject.

The members of "the Ladies' Committee" had, at this time, effected several minor arrangements to lessen the temptations, and increase the reasonable comforts of the prisoners. There had been a great consumption of beer amongst them. In order to prevent this evil, they engaged a sub-matron or gate-keeper, who assisted in the lodge, and amongst other duties, superintended a little shop, which had been established, as it is quaintly expressed in their minute-book, "between gates," where tea, sugar, a little haberdashery, and other equally harmless articles, were sold to the prisoners. The communication between them and their acquaintances outside the prison, being so much restricted, lessened their supplies from that quarter, and the prison allowance being scarcely sufficient, this plan was resorted to, in order to meet their necessities, and ensure their portion of the earnings being expended in a proper manner.

But, amidst all her interests of a public nature, how great was Elizabeth Fry's solicitude respecting her own children, and for the blessing of preservation to herself!

Plashet, Seventh Month, 24th.—I have many causes of deep anxiety at this time. What to do with our boys, for the best, has occupied much of my consideration, and at present I see no other way than continuing them at school; but I do not acknowledge too much, if I say that it is the prayer of my heart that a kind Providence may open the way for their going to the best place for them, wherever it may be, and deep is the craving of my spirit, that they may, in the end, go on well. O Lord! I beseech Thee, whatsoever Thou mayst be pleased to do with them, whether to grant them health or sickness, riches or poverty, long life or short life, oh, for Thy beloved Son's sake, give them not over to the will of their enemies, but establish their goings in Thy paths; put a new song into their mouths, even praises to Thee, their God. And seeing, gracious Lord, that in a very marvellous manner, Thou hast been pleased to make a way for Thy child and servant, where she could see no way—how, in a wonderful manner Thou restored her in early life, showed Thyself to be on her side, when spiritually her enemies appeared ready to overcome and destroy her, and how also in many and various seasons, "Thou hast made darkness light before her, and crooked paths straight," how Thou hast been pleased to raise her from season to season, from the bed of languishing; how Thou hast temporally cared for her, and answered her prayer, when it appeared likely even that she would be scarcely provided for, how Thou hast helped her in spirit, at seasons, to do Thy will, to see into the glorious mysteries of Thy kingdom, how Thou hast aided her in her weakness, and enabled her to overcome the extreme fear of man; and to declare Thy doings amongst the people, and to show Thy marvellous works to the children of men, even from princes and prelates, to the poorest, lowest, and most destitute; so as, in a remarkable manner, to bring to pass what she saw for herself in early life, though as through a glass darkly, which others more clearly saw for her, and had to declare unto her; and seeing, gracious Lord, and almighty Saviour, how Thou hast been pleased to deal with Thy unworthy servant, to increase in her even, at seasons, mightily and powerfully the knowledge of Thee her God, and Christ Jesus her Lord.——Be pleased to help her in the like precious faith, and preserve her from the many snares of the enemy; let not the spirit of the world, or its applause, ever entangle her; nor the reproach of any, not even of the good, unduly discourage her; but let her be increasingly Thine own, and at all times, at all seasons, and in every place, by whomsoever surrounded, give unto Thee the Glory due unto Thy name, and worship Thee in the beauty of holiness: and let neither heights, nor depths, life, nor death, nor any other thing, ever separate her from Thy love: but enable her, O Lord! at all times, and at all seasons, and in every place, and by whomsoever surrounded, to glorify Thy great and ever excellent name, with Thy beloved Son, Christ Jesus our Lord. And with regard to her beloved family, be unto them, what Thou hast been unto her; even their Guide, and their Guard, their God and their Saviour; and make a way for them, where their poor mother sees no way for them. Amen, says my unworthy soul; cast down, but not destroyed; afflicted, but not in despair; at times almost comfortless, but not forsaken; at other times abounding in the joy and blessing of my God.

In the Eighth Month, Elizabeth Fry left home to visit Scotland, and the North of England, accompanied by her brother Joseph John Gurney, his wife, and one of her own daughters.

Belford, Northumberland, Eighth Month, 25th.—For some months I have looked to attending the General Meeting in Scotland, but it appeared almost impossible, my home-claims being so very strong—indeed, the Monthly Meeting before the last, it came with great weight so as to frighten me; but I neither saw outward way for it, nor did I feel the heart made willing; but as I have so often found when there is a real "putting forth," way is made within and without; so it has been now, all my sweet flock are, I trust, carefully provided for; not only outward way has been made, but the willing heart also granted, and I had remarkably sweet peace and relief in being willing to give up to it; such an evidence that I think it remains undoubted in my mind. Friends appeared to feel much unity with me, which was a help. My beloved brother Joseph, and sister Jane, joining me, has been much cause for humble thankfulness; it has made, what would have been very hard to flesh and blood, comparatively sweet and easy; we are a united band in spirit and in nature; Joseph a very great help in the ministry. I think he is, and will yet be more abundantly, an instrument of honour in his Master's hand. We have sat four Meetings, visited several families of Friends, and inspected many prisons, which is one of our objects. In our religious services, our gracious Helper has appeared very near; we have gone on in them with much nearness and unity; we know the blessed truth that, as we abide in Christ, we are one in Him. I have felt, at seasons, as leaving all for my Master's sake, and setting out without much of purse or scrip: but how bountifully I am provided for, internally and externally; the Great Shepherd of the sheep has been near to me in spirit, as strength in my weakness, riches in my poverty, and a present helper in the needful time; I may say,—

"Are these Thy favours day by day,
To me above the rest?
Then let me love Thee more than they,
And try to serve Thee best."

Conflicts have attended, and no doubt will attend me; but I look upon it as an honour, a favour, and a blessing, even to suffer in the Lamb's army, if we may but be of the number of his soldiers, who fight the good fight of faith, and are, in any degree, permitted to promote the cause of truth and righteousness upon earth.

Aberdeen, 29th.—I have felt low upon arriving here; five hundred miles from my beloved husband and children; but a good account of them is cause for thankfulness, still it is a deeply weighty thing, and I have to try my ground again and again. In almost every new place, the language of my spirit is, Why am I here? At this place we find several other Friends, also travelling in the ministry, which makes me feel it the more; but as my coming is not of my own choice, or my own ordering, I desire to leave it; and to commit myself, my spirit and body, and all that is dear to me, absent and present, to Christ my Redeemer. We visited the old Barclay seat, at Ury, where our mother's forefathers once lived. How great the change from what it once was!

Stonehaven, Ninth Month, 2nd.—We left Aberdeen this afternoon, having finished our services there, and at Kinmuck, where several Friends reside. Other Friends besides ourselves being at Aberdeen, certainly tended to increase my exercise, for fear of the ministry not going on well, or by not keeping in our ranks; but I think that we were enabled to do so, and although much passed, yet we had cause for thankfulness, inasmuch as there appeared to be harmonious labour for the advancement of truth, and the spreading thereof. Our General Meeting at Aberdeen was ended under a feeling of quiet peace; but fears crept in for myself, that I had fallen away a little as to life in the truth, and power in the ministry, for I did not experience that overflowing power which I have sometimes done at such seasons; still gracious help was granted me from season to season. The day after the General Meeting, we went to Kinmuck, about fifteen miles north of Aberdeen; a short time after our arrival there, before I went to Meeting, such a feeling of suffering came over me as I can hardly express; it appeared only nervous, as I was so well in body, that I could not attribute it to that; it continued exceedingly upon sitting down in Meeting, and led me into deep strong supplication, that the enemy might by no means deceive us, or cause our ministry to be affected by anything but the holy anointing. I feared if this awful state had to do with those present, that I should have something very close to express; if only with myself, I considered that it might be a refining trial. However, Joseph knelt down, in the beginning of the Meeting, as well as myself, and afterwards he spoke as if he felt it necessary to warn some to flee from their evil ways, and from the bondage of Satan. This tended to my relief; but it appeared as if I must follow him, and rise with these words, "The sorrows of death compassed me about, the pains of hell gat hold upon me;" then enlarging upon the feeling I had of the power of the enemy, and the absolute need there is to watch, to pray, and to flee unto Christ, as our only sure refuge and deliverer; I had to show that we might be tried and buffeted by Satan, as a further trial of faith and of patience, but that if we did not yield to him, it would only tend to refinement. After a time I felt greatly relieved, but what seemed remarkable was, that neither Joseph nor I dared to leave the Meeting, without once more bowing the knee for these dear Friends; but after all this very deep and remarkable exercise, a solemn silence prevailed, really as if truth had risen into dominion; and after my making some such acknowledgment in testimony, that our low estate had been regarded, that our souls could then magnify the Lord, and our spirits rejoice in God our Saviour, that light had risen in obscurity, and darkness had, in measure, become as the noon-day, and the encouragement it was for us to run with patience the race that was set before us, &c., the Meeting concluded; and I think upon shaking hands with the Friends, there hardly appeared an eye that had not been weeping amongst those that were grown up. This whole exercise was very remarkable, in a nice little country Meeting, and the external so fair; but afterwards we heard of one or two painful things, one in particular; we visited nearly all the families, were pleased with some of them: their mode of living truly humble, like our cottagers. The next day we had a Meeting with a few Friends in Aberdeen, where the exercise was not very great, and the flow in the ministry sweet, and I trust powerful. We parted from our beloved old friends, John and Elizabeth Wigham, their children, and children's children, and are now on our way to Edinburgh.

Hawick, 13*th*.—I may thankfully acknowledge being so far on our way, but our journey through life is a little like a common journey; we may, after a day's travelling, lie down and rest, but we have on the morrow to set off again upon our travels: so I find my journey in life, I am not unfrequently permitted to come, for a short time, to a sweet, quiet resting-place; but I find that I soon have to set forth again. I was glad and relieved in leaving Aberdeen, and then a fresh work began in Edinburgh; on Seventh-day, we visited the prisons, accompanied by some gentlemen, the Lord Provost and others. Here we were much interested. On First-day, we went in the morning to Meeting, and were favoured to do well, many were not Friends; and what were my feelings in the evening, to find a considerable number of people, quite a Public Meeting. It gave me a great deal of alarm, but we had a good Meeting, and I trust the cause was exalted. The morning before we came away, about eighteen gentlemen and ladies came to breakfast with us, amongst them Sir George and Lady Grey, good people, whom I have long wished to know: we had, after breakfast, a solemn time. Alexander Cruickshank read, and afterwards I knelt down, and I think we were drawn together in love and unity of spirit. We arrived at Glasgow that evening, and the next day visited the prisons, and formed a Ladies' Committee. We visited some families the next day, and accompanied by several gentlemen, magistrates, and others, we again went to the Bridewell and Prison, where I had to start the Committee in their proceedings; it was awful to me, having to bow the knee for a blessing, before so many who were strangers to our ways, but blessed be the Lord, the power of truth appeared to be over all, so that I remembered these words, "Rejoice not that the spirits are made subject unto you, but rather rejoice that your names are written in heaven." We had two Meetings, one in the morning for Friends, but many others came, and one, to my deep humiliation, in the evening, for the public; awful work as it was, we were favoured to get through well, and to leave Glasgow with clear minds. We have since travelled through great part of Cumberland, attended many Meetings there, some very important ones, and some highly favoured by the Presence and the Power of the Most High; thence to Kendal.

At Liverpool was the next Meeting we attended, it was a large public one, and so it has been in many places. I deeply felt it, I hardly dared to raise my eyes because of the feathers and ribbons before me; however, best help was afforded, to my very great relief and consolation; truth appeared to be in great dominion. After a sweet uniting time with the Benson family, we left Liverpool for Knowsley, the seat of the Earl of Derby, as we had a pressing invitation from Lady Derby; we were received with the utmost kindness and openness by all this very large household; a palace was now our allotment; a cottage has been so during our journey. My internal feeling was humiliation and self-abasement.

Knowsley, 24*th.*—Here we are, all the family about to be collected for a religious opportunity; Lord, be pleased to be with us, to own us by Thy life-giving presence, and help us, by Thy Spirit, for it is a very awful time. Make us, Thy unworthy children, fit for Thy service, and touch our lips as with a live coal from Thy altar, for we are unworthy to take Thy great and ever-excellent name into our mouths; Thou, Lord, only knowest the state of Thy unworthy servant: help her infirmities, blot out her transgressions, and enable her to show forth thy praise, if consistent with Thy Holy Will, that all may be more abundantly converted unto Thee, and brought into the knowledge of Thy beloved Son, Christ Jesus our Lord!

Sheffield, 26*th.*—After writing the above, I was summoned into the dining-room, where the family were assembled—I should think, in all, nearly a hundred. My beloved brother read the third chapter of John; there was then a solemn pause, and I found it my place to kneel down, praying for a blessing upon the house and family, and giving thanks for the mercies bestowed upon them; particularly in the time of their affliction, in having been supported by the everlasting

Arm; and prayer arose for its being sanctified to them. The large party appeared humbled and tendered—then dearest Joseph arose, and was greatly helped by the power of the Spirit—I followed him with a few words. Many of the party were in tears; some exceedingly affected. Joseph then knelt down, greatly helped; the service principally fell upon him. After he rose, I reminded them of the words of our blessed Redeemer, "that whosoever giveth a disciple a cup of cold water in the name of a disciple, shall receive a disciple's reward;" this, I said, I humbly trusted would be their case. I also alluded to their servants' kindness in the same way. Thus ended this memorable occasion. It was like what we read of in Friends' journals formerly, when the power appeared to be over all in a very extraordinary manner. I remember in John Richardson's journal some such an account. So it is,—and this is not, and cannot be, our own work; surely it is the Lord's doing, and marvellous in our eyes!

Earlham, Tenth Month, 6th.—Once more arrived at this interesting place, that has so long been a home to me. I will go back to where I left off. Our visit to Sheffield was an important one; I had so deeply to feel for a beloved Friend, who has long been a mother in Israel, under heavy family affliction. Oh, what I felt for her in Meeting, and out of Meeting, I cannot describe; my spirit was in strong intercession for her preservation and support, under these deep tribulations. We had a favoured meeting in the morning, though I had indeed to go through the depths before I ascended the heights. By the desire of my dear brother, we had a Public Meeting in the evening, which was well got through, but not without suffering. We then proceeded to York; I can hardly express how deeply I felt entering that Quarterly Meeting; "fears gat hold upon me," still hope arose underneath, that this end of our services, as to our northern journey, would crown all—and so I think it proved—not only from service to service, and from Meeting to Meeting, did the holy, blessed, anointing Power, appear to be abundantly poured forth upon the speakers, but upon the hearers also; that where I feared most, I found least to fear; such unity of spirit, such a flow of love and life, as quite refreshed, encouraged, and comforted my soul. I was much rejoiced to find so many fathers and mothers amongst them. "Bless the Lord, O my soul! and all that is within me bless His holy name."—"Praise and exalt Him, above all for ever," might then have been the language of my soul.

We travelled on to Lynn, and there my brother with his dear Jane left me. At the Meetings there, I felt as if I had to minister almost, without the power, and yet that I must yield to the service; but I was so fearful and weak, at both Meetings, that truth did not appear in dominion, perhaps I found the change after York, and I missed my dear brother Joseph. I often minister as if in bonds, this is very humbling—so many fears, so many doubts arising; this was the case in nearly all my services during the day.

In the course of this northern journey, J. J. Gurney and his sister had visited the prisons of the several towns through which they passed. They found them to be generally in a condition of the most disgraceful neglect—and the hardships, and even cruelty, endured by the inmates, were harrowing in the extreme to the tender nature of Elizabeth Fry.

But the cases of the poor lunatics, confined in some of those abodes of misery, made above all a most powerful impression on her heart, and induced a sympathy, with such as were afflicted with this heaviest of physical maladies, that continued deeply to influence her feelings through life.

The results of their observations were published in a pamphlet—"Notes on a Visit to Prisons, &c., by J. J. Gurney and Elizabeth Fry.

To such persons as were interested in Prison Reform, this

book afforded much matter for reflection. Whilst they deplored the evils described, they rejoiced that they should be brought to light—as the first step towards their being remedied.

The voice of Elizabeth Fry was heard, and her appeals were promptly responded to. Her brother, in writing of this northern journey, says: "She exhibited a perfect tact and propriety in her transactions;" she well knew, "when in the pursuit of such objects, how to soothe all asperities, influence all parties, and overcome the greatest difficulties." In confirmation of which, some passages may be quoted from a letter, written by a Scotch lady, who attended Elizabeth Fry when she visited the prisons at Glasgow:—

"She found our prisons very badly managed," &c., and "has left a letter for the magistrates. She had an interview with them, and this evening a number of ladies met at the Bridewell. She told them, with much simplicity, what had been done at Newgate. She entered into pleasant conversation with every one, and all were delighted when she offered to speak a little to the poor women. But the keeper of the Bridewell said he feared it was a dangerous experiment; that they never, but by compulsion, listened to reading, and were generally disposed to turn any thing of the kind into ridicule. She said that she was not without fears of this happening, but she thought it right to attempt it. The women, about a hundred, were then assembled in a large room, and we went in, misdoubting and anxious. She took off her bonnet, and sat down on a low seat fronting the women; then looking at them with a kind, conciliating eye, yet an eye that met every eye there, she said, 'I had better just tell you what we are come about.' She told them, she had to deal with a great number of poor women, sadly wicked, and in what manner they were recovered from evil. Her language was scriptural,—always referring to our Saviour's promises, and cheering with holy hope these dissolute beings. 'Would not you like to turn from that which is wrong? Would not you like for ladies to visit you and speak comfort to you, and help you to become better? Surely you would tell them your griefs; they who have done evil have many sorrows.' As she read to them the

'*Rules*,' asking them, if approved, to hold up their hands, all hands were upraised, and, as soon as she spoke, tears began to flow. One very beautiful girl near me had her eyes swimming with tears, and her lips moved, as if following Mrs. Fry. One old woman, who held her Bible, we saw clasping it with emotion as she became more and more impressed. The hands were ready to rise at every pause, and these callous and obdurate offenders were with one consent bowed before her. Then she took the Bible, and read the parables of the *lost sheep*, the *piece of silver*, and the *prodigal son*.

"It is impossible for me to express to you the effect of her saintly voice, while speaking such blessed words. She often paused, and looked at the poor women with a sweetness that won their confidence, applying with beauty and taste all the parts of the story to them, and in a manner I never before heard, and particularly the words 'His father saw him when he was yet afar off.' A solemn pause succeeded the reading. Then, resting the large Bible on the ground, we saw her on her knees before them. Her prayer was devout and soothing, and her musical voice, in the peculiar, sweet tones of the Quakers, seemed like the voice of a mother to her suffering child.

"In the prison of Glasgow, the emotions were much more varied than at Bridewell—astonishing repugnance, and, in some instances, obstinate resistance to listen; in others, anxious desire to accept her aid. She read and conversed with them, and the proposal of work, was, in general, greedily received. How different were the impressions in the varied figures before her! One old woman, with the appearance of a menial servant and hardened features, said, 'No! no use work!' But these rugged lines were at length relaxed, and I saw a tear fall over the brown visage. But it was not the prisoners alone: for there was not a man in the room unmoved."

J. J. Gurney and Elizabeth Fry received many letters after the "Notes" were published—many opinions and suggestions were offered—some objections were raised—but there were individuals, and they were not few in number, nor unimportant in influence, who simply encouraged them in their researches, and expressed warm desires for the eventual success of the cause they espoused. Among these letters, one from the Countess Harcourt may be cited, as showing the impression made on persons who possessed much of the power needful to apply remedial measures.

"My dear and most respected friend,

"It is impossible to have read the excellent publication, giving an account of your tour with Mr. Gurney, without being most anxious to express the satisfaction Lord Harcourt and I received from the work. He read it to me, and there was scarcely a page at which we did not stop, to exclaim our admiration of the justness of the remarks, and our earnest wishes that they might prove the means of ameliorating the system of our prisons. We felt that each word gave conviction to our minds; and the beauty of the style, certainly added to the gratification of reading it. Oh! my good friend, what a blessed tour you have made, and may Heaven reward your wonderful exertions, by making them effectual to the purpose intended.

"I ought not to use the word envy, but I cannot help feeling the great difference between the manner in which your life is spent and my own. You ought indeed to be thankful that it has pleased God 'to put into your mind good desires,' and to have given you health to go through such arduous undertakings."

The Countess Harcourt then proceeds to mention several of the Royal Family, to whom copies of the "Notes" were sent by her; and the desire of the Princesses to receive a visit from Elizabeth Fry.

Mildred's Court, First Month, 17*th*, 1819.—I returned home yesterday from leaving my dearest boys at Darlington. My journey was certainly a favoured and an encouraging one. The situation for my beloved boys appears very safe and desirable. I had abundant kindness and unity shown me, particularly by my dearest sister Rachel. I came home to many troubles and anxieties, also certainly to many comforts and blessings; but ah! gracious Lord, be pleased to conduct me safely through the difficulties that surround me, and give neither me, nor mine, over to the will of our enemies.

The great and varied exertions, to which the duties of Elizabeth Fry subjected her, proved too much for her physical strength; and her health became seriously affected: she was, in consequence, under the necessity of yielding to the wish of her family and friends, by spending some weeks in Sussex, chiefly at Brighton.

On becoming somewhat recruited in strength, she wrote as follows:—

Brighton, Fourth Month, 8th.—I have once more been to Meeting—on First day morning, on Third day, the first meeting of the Quarterly Meeting on Fourth day, and also to the Monthly Meeting. It was sweet and refreshing, to assemble with some of the outward church. In abundant mercy, strength was granted in my great weakness, yet once more to show forth the praise of Israel's Shepherd; deep as my late conflicts have been, all appears intended renewedly to stimulate and encourage myself, as well as others, to run with fresh diligence the race that is set before us. The language of my heart is, "Though he slay me, yet will I trust in Him." A wonderful calm has been granted me after a very awful, and to my fearful nature, terrible storm. I have through unmerited mercy, had such a sweetness and serenity over me, that the cares and sorrows of life have been almost hidden from my view, and I have hardly felt able even to look at them. These are the dealings of a kind Providence to an unworthy child. He has shown His power in casting down and raising up, in wounding and making whole, blessed be His name for ever. And oh! dearest Lord, whenever Thou mayst be pleased to lay me low again, lift up, I beseech Thee, a standard against the enemy of my soul, that he overcome me not; and when I cannot help myself, be Thou my help and my strength. And I reverently return Thee thanks, that Thou, gracious Lord, hast manifested Thyself to be my deliverer, that Thou hast once more broken my bonds asunder, brought my poor soul out of prison, and not given me over to the will of my enemies; but in Thine abundant mercy, delivered me from my fears, and I humbly trust, established my goings, and put a new song in my mouth, even praises to Thee, my God; Amen, and Amen.

During her stay at Brighton, Elizabeth Fry had the gratification of receiving from the female prisoners in Newgate some very satisfactory letters, bespeaking much grateful feeling, and she wrote the following answer:—

Brighton, *Fourth Month, 4th*, 1819.

To the female prisoners in Newgate, more particularly to those who are likely to leave their native land, perhaps never to return to it.

Although it has pleased the Almighty, that for some time I should be separated from you by illness, yet you have often been in my affectionate remembrance, accompanied with anxious desires for your good. I am fully sensible that many of you claim our pity and most tender compassion, that many have been your temptations, many your afflictions, and what we may most pity you for, is, that in the time of temptation you have yielded to what is wrong, and so given yourselves over to the will of the enemy of your souls! But mournful as your state is, yet you may have hope, and that abundantly; if you only seek to repent, to return from the error of your ways, and live unto God. Remember these words, "Christ came into the world to save sinners," and that "He is able to save to the very uttermost those who come unto God by Him, seeing that He ever liveth to make intercession for them." Therefore, let me intreat you before it is too late, to come unto Christ, to seek Him with your heart, and to submit yourselves unto Him and His righteous law—for He knows all your thoughts and all your desires, and is willing and ready to receive you, to heal your backslidings, and to love you freely. He was said to be the Friend of sinners, and those will indeed find Him their friend, who look to Him and obey Him—He will enable such to forsake the evil of their ways, and to do that which is acceptable in His sight. Do you not remember in the parable of the Prodigal Son, that when he was yet *afar off*, the Father saw him, had compassion on him, and even went out to meet him. So I doubt not, you would find it, even some of you who are now afar off from what is good, if you are only willing to return; you would find yourselves met by your Lord, even with great compassion, and He would do more for you than you could ask or think. I feel much love for you, and much desire for your own sakes, for the sake of others, and for our sakes, who are willing to do what we can to serve you, that you would thus in heart seek the Lord, and prove your love to Him, and your repentance, by your good works and by your orderly conduct. I was much grieved at the little disturbance amongst you the other day, but I was pleased with the letter written me by those who were engaged in it, and I quite forgive them. Let me entreat you, whatever trying, or even provoking things may happen, to do so no more, for you sadly hurt the cause of poor prisoners by doing so, I may say all over the Kingdom; and you thus enable your enemies to say, that our plans of kindness do not answer, and therefore, they will not let others be treated kindly. Before I bid you farewell, I will tell you that I am not without a hope of seeing you before long, even before the poor women go to the Bay, but if I do not, may the blessing of the Lord go with you when on the mighty deeps, and in a strange land. What comfort would a good account of you give us, who are so much interested for you, and in case I should not see you, I have two things particularly to mention to you and guard you against—things that I believe have brought most of you to this prison. The one is giving way to drinking too much, the other is freedom with men. I find I can most frequently trace the fall of women to these two things, therefore let me beseech you to watch in these respects, and let your modesty and sobriety appear before all; and that you may grow in these and every other Christian virtue and grace, is the sincere desire and prayer of your affectionate friend, and sincere well-wisher,

ELIZABETH FRY.

We return to the journal.

Ninth Month, 6th.—Since I last wrote, I parted from my beloved boys for school, John, William and Joseph. I felt a good deal in giving them up, but, at the same time, believing it to be a right thing, I humbly trust that the blessing of the Most High will be with them. My dearest sister Priscilla has been very dangerously ill, raising blood from the lungs, which has brought me into great feeling and conflict. As I mostly find the case in nursing, it has caused me afresh to see my own unworthiness; so little do I feel able to administer spiritual help, so hard is it to my nature, particularly when under discouragement, to wait upon my gift, or to give it its free course; but I may thankfully acknowledge, that I appeared to be a great comfort, help, and strength to her, indeed her dependence was so close upon me, that I could not leave the house night or day, for any length of time. Her state appeared to be indeed a bright and a very blessed one; so calm, so gentle, so humble, and so much resigned to live, or to die. Since I have left her sick room, sorrow and deep discouragement have been my portion, from the extreme difficulty of doing right towards those most near; it does appear, at times, impossible for me, but most likely, this arises from want of more watchfulness, and more close abiding in the Light and the Life of our Lord. When I exercise a watchful care from seeing the dangers that attend some, it seems to give the greatest pain, and so causes me the deepest discouragement. Still, yesterday, in the great, in the bitter sorrow of my heart, I found, in a remarkable manner, the power of my Redeemer near, even helping by His own good Spirit and presence. When I felt almost ready to sink—and my footsteps indeed ready to slip—then the Lord held me up. In the first place, after a very little while, from having been deeply wounded, my heart overflowed with love and forgiveness towards the one who had pained me; I felt what would I not do for the individual? and a most anxious desire, if I had missed it, to make it up by every thing in my power. Thus, when I had feared discouragements would have almost overwhelmed my spirit, there was such a calming, blessed, and cheering influence came over my heart, that it was like the sick coming to our Saviour formerly, and being immediately healed; so that I was not even able to mourn over my calamity. It appeared as if "the Holy One who inhabiteth Eternity" would not give me over to the will of my enemies.

Perhaps few will read the preceding extract, without perceiving something of the deep and hidden sorrow, which often weighed down the spirit, and preyed also on the bodily frame, of this precious follower of the Lamb. It is not needful to attempt to penetrate the veil that conceals, from the eye of the stranger, the circumstances that rendered her path of life a tribulated one: it is enough to know that her perplexities and distresses were endured with meek submission, and a degree of forbearance, that could only be the effect of that state of watching unto prayer with all perseverance, in which she was so remarkably preserved; and by which she was kept, through all her mental vicissitudes as in a region of love.

Mildred's Court, Tenth Month, 23rd.—Re-entering our London life is certainly a serious thing. Much as I have to attend to, and very numerous as my calls are, yet I have believed that these words should be my motto, Phil. iv. 6, 7, "Be careful for nothing; but in everything by prayer and supplication and thanksgiving let your requests be made known unto God. And the peace of God, which passeth all understanding, keep yonr hearts and minds through Christ Jesus." Now though I may have many trials of faith and patience, the more I can be without too much carefulness, and cast all my care on my Lord and Redeemer, the better I believe it will be for my body and soul; and the better also for all those with whom I have to do. Dearest Lord, I pray Thee, help me to abide in this state, that I may dwell near to Thee in spirit, and amidst all the perplexities of life, that I may feel Thee to be my Helper, my Comforter, my Guide and my Counsellor. Amen.

The weighty responsibilities of Newgate did not preclude other objects of public interest, to some of which Elizabeth Fry devoted much attention. Among these, was a "nightly shelter for the houseless." During the rigorous winter of 1819-20, the sufferings of homeless wanderers called for prompt relief,—the heart of this Christian philanthropist was deeply touched by some affecting cases,—in one instance a little boy, who had in vain begged at many houses for the few halfpence required to procure admittance to some passage or cellar, was found frozen to death on the step of a door! An asylum was immediately provided. It was well warmed, nutritious soup was prepared night and morning, with a ration of bread for each of the inmates, who were also furnished with beds. Employment, in various ways, was procured; and the bounty of the public flowed in to encourage the hearts and to strengthen the efforts of benevolent persons, who united in labouring for the management and success of the establishment. Many hundreds were, night after night, admitted—great numbers, who could not be accommodated at the "Shelter," were supplied with food, clothing, and the means of procuring lodgings elsewhere. The females were placed under the care of a "Ladies' Committee," with Elizabeth Fry at their head.

She now wrote the following to her sons at school:—

Mildred's Court, *First Month*, 19*th*, 1820.

My dearest John, William and Joseph,

I am sorry that I have not written to you before, to tell you how much I rejoice at your father's excellent account of you. I believe no words can express the deep interest I take in your welfare, and how pleasant it is to me to have such good accounts of your conduct and learning. I cannot help hoping that my sons will be my comfort, and may I not say by their goodness and learning, that they may become my glory. My London life is now a very busy one, it is almost like living in a market or a fair; only that I have not merchandize to sell. We see a great variety of company, principally people who are interesting and occupied by subjects of importance. We lately had an East Indian Missionary, who told us many particulars about the poor Indians: I think in one province, about seven hundred poor widows burn themselves every year, when their husbands die. We expect soon to see the Persian Ambassador, and I mean to give you an account of him. Believe me, your nearly attached mother,

E. Fry.

To her Cousin, Priscilla Hannah Gurney.

Mildred's Court, *Second Month*, 23*rd*, 1820.

My very dear Cousin,

I have for some time past wished to write to thee, but it is very seldom that I can get any quiet opportunity. I wish much to hear particulars of thee; I feel that confidence in our near tie to each other, that I believe communication is not necessary to keep it up, but I cannot help sometimes regretting that I have not more opportunity of opening my heart to one, whom I feel so particularly near and dear to me, and who I am sure so tenderly sympathises in all my sorrows, and joys also. I have been favoured with health this winter, except being at times a little overdone, and having some cough. My engagements, as usual, are very numerous. I have, from being on a committee of our Quarterly Meeting, visited some of our Monthly Meetings, but I have had no other engagements of that sort. Our prisons continue to prosper, and Newgate goes on well; it does not require much of my time, though the many things it introduces me into, occupy me a good deal. And now for my beloved family; I think that they are going on much the same as when thou left us; I long to see more of the advancement of the blessed Truth amongst us, but I still hope, that that day will come. I anxiously desire to be enabled to do my part, and to walk before my household with a perfect heart, but this is a great attainment, almost too much for so weak and unworthy a person to look for.

After mentioning the great comfort she had derived from hearing good accounts of her boys, then at school, she asks of her cousin "a little favour."

The children and myself are collecting English shells, and as my aunt made so fine a collection, we want to know what is the best book for us to procure, to direct us in our search, and where, and from what coast, we are most likely to procure the finest. We have written to know whether we cannot buy some in Devonshire. I think this such a good object for the children, and nice amusement for us all in London, where we have not the garden and flowers to enjoy, that I endeavour to cultivate it.

'The flowers of the garden; the shells of the ocean;
The coralline branches, which sea-weeds entwine;

The stars that gleam o'er us;
The light forms before us,
That flit in the sunbeams--all, Father, are thine;
All tell us of Thee, and for Thee claim devotion.'

Thy nearly attached Cousin,
ELIZABETH FRY.

After the arduous exertions, and varied interests of this winter, it was no small relief to Elizabeth Fry to be again with her family in the retirement of Plashet; although her enjoyment was soon to be clouded by peculiar and affecting family sorrows, as well as by domestic solicitudes. Her much valued brother and sister Buxton, were plunged into deep affliction, through the removal by death of four lovely children, within the short space of five weeks; this most touching event called forth Elizabeth Fry's tenderest sympathy, and her unwearied exertion in nursing these darling objects of affectionate care.

Plashet House, Fourth Month, 26th.—My time has been so exceedingly occupied as to prevent my writing, but I have gone through a great deal. My dearest brother and sister Buxton being so heavily afflicted, has brought me into very deep conflict, in short almost inexpressible; still, through all, we may acknowledge that we have found the Lord to be gracious, for assuredly He has been very near to help and support. Dearest Lord, we pray Thee, continue to have mercy upon us all; and at this time of great sorrow, to regard us in our low estate, and to increase our faith, according to its trial. Amen.

Fifth Month, 3rd.—Hard, very hard, as this trial has been, and is, yet there is abundant cause to bless, praise, and magnify the great and excellent name of our Lord, both for having given these precious children, and then taking them through His redeeming love into His kingdom of Light, Life, Peace, and Glory. But what a proof, that our hearts must not be set upon any temporal things.

The visits to the prisoners, and the labours for their reformation, were continued with undiminished assiduity, and the impression made on the public mind became even increasingly intense. The Scripture readings were still frequented by great numbers. Many persons have described these occasions; perhaps none more graphically than the writer of the following interesting narrative, which has been kindly sent to the Compiler, with the subjoined notice by the Lady Elizabeth Waldegrave:—

"Account of a visit to Newgate, June 2d, 1820, written by the late Hon. Mrs. Waldegrave, for her mother, lady Elizabeth Whitbread, on whose death, in 1846, it was sent to me.

"ELIZABETH WALDEGRAVE, Jun.

"4, Harley Street, London,
March 2*d*, 1852."

"*June* 2*nd*, 1820.—We reached Newgate at half-past ten, and waited with the rest of the company in a small room up stairs; in the way to it we passed through several wards, in which the most perfect stillness prevailed; these were the former scenes of all the riot and confusion of which we had heard so much.

"After waiting a short time, Mrs. Fry entered, saluting everybody in the most dignified manner. The female convicts, forty in number, came in upon a bell being rung, and took their seats at one end of the room with perfect order—the monitors sitting on the first bench, and the others in classes behind; each had her work, at which she employed herself till Mrs. Fry began reading. They had ivory tickets round their necks with numbers on them.

"Mrs. Fry arranged a large old Bible on her desk, and sat down—her voice was so gentle that we wondered we could hear what she said, but remarkably mild and sweet. She began by requesting their *attention*.—'I am desirous that your attention should be, as much as possible, undivided—notwithstanding our being subject to-day to the interruptions of company, it is equally important that your minds should be fixed on what I say—praying that the Holy Spirit may enlighten your understanding. I am going to read the 4th chapter of Paul's Epistle to the Ephesians.' They all laid aside their work, most of them fixed their eyes on the ground, and we could not observe that more than two or three looked about afterwards till she had done reading. She read the chapter slowly and impressively—the 6th, 28th, and 32nd verses appeared to affect them deeply—every word that she uttered seemed to be written in her own heart. She then turned to the book of Psalms. After a moment's pause, she turned back to the chapter which she had been reading, and said, 'I was going to read a Psalm, but I thought I should be best satisfied to say a word on the chapter I have been reading; the greater part of it is so simple and clear, that a very little endeavour on your part will enable you to understand it; but there is one expression which perhaps may be obscure: 'One Lord, one Faith, one Baptism.' If you look only at the external, you might say, so many different opinions prevail, people are so divided as to what they think ought to be believed, how can they be said to have one faith? I have always viewed it very differently: 'One Lord,'—yea, and have not all Christians the same Lord, which is Christ? and while we acknowledge him our Master, look to him for our justification, follow his precepts, obey his commandments, love him, serve him,—he is our Lord—he is the 'one Lord' of all who *thus* acknowledge him their *head.*—Again, 'one Faith'—there is a diversity of opinions, but only one true and saving Faith, the Faith which lives in the heart; and becomes evident by its fruits, which lays hold of the promises, which actuates to all godliness, and produces the blessed effects of a holy life. This one true, saving faith, is common to *all* Christians—how exceedingly soever they may seem to differ. So also, 'one Baptism': Christians may differ as to the manner of administering the Baptism of water, nay, though some even dispense with *that* altogether, yet there is one spiritual baptism of the heart,—the Spirit of God, sanctifying and renewing the heart, and creating it after God, in righteousness and true holiness. In this manner we have all 'one Lord, one Faith, one Baptism; one God and Father of all, who is above all, and through all, and in you all.' What a sweet bond of unity is this, where we are not only brethren in this world, but may hope to meet in Heaven, there to give glory to Him with one accord, for ever and for evermore.'

"Mrs. Fry then read the 86th Psalm, at the end of which, a brother Quaker said a few words of exhortation to all present, to join in Prayer on behalf of the poor sufferers contained in these walls, and not to be unmindful that all were sinners, all under one condemnation.

"She then knelt down, and prayed so beautiful a Prayer,—with such fervency, so rich a flow of ideas, and such perfect command of Scripture language to clothe them in, that it is impossible to convey an idea of its beauty—the *chaunt*, in which the Quakers recite their prayers, gave it a very singular, but very impressive effect; for her voice is good, and when exerted, very strong and clear. This, after a few words from one of the company, concluded the service—the women retired in perfect order, each class separately, with its monitor from the front row; all making courtesies as they left the room. Mrs. Fry, in the course of some conversation with Lord Albemarle, said, that she believed the coolness she had experienced from Lord Sidmouth, to have originated in too anxious a desire on her part to save the life of a condemned woman; which had induced her to speak to the Duke of Gloucester on the subject, after Lord Sidmouth had refused to interfere; by which she believed that she had given offence, that she thought they had been wrong and had urged it too far; that at first they had free communication with the Secretary of State's office, but that it had been closed for some time.

"She said that her success surprised herself as much as it did others—that a very remarkable Providence had attended all her efforts—she had never seen the Bible received as it had been there. 'Ten years ago,' said she, 'when it occurred to me to make trial, I went with a young Friend into one of the wards, in which the greatest riot and confusion prevailed. I went in with my Bible in my hand, and told them I was come to read the Scriptures; they all flocked round me, and I am convinced many had never heard them before—it seemed to be glad tidings to them—all were attentive. I had been warned to take off such things as could possibly be stolen, but no attempt of the kind was made; if I dropped anything, it was picked up and brought to me. I felt rather alarmed at first, at the idea of being shut up with these poor creatures, but I was preserved through it.'

"She said that some remarkable things had happened for her encouragement: one, which occurred lately she related,—'A woman, who was one of the lowest of the low—a thief, a drunkard, and in every way as bad as possible, was committed to Newgate. On the first day that she attended (the reading) I happened to read the parable of the prodigal son; she was much affected by it, and the next day, I received from her a letter, (she could write,) in which she expressed her thankfulness to God that, through our instrumentality, a new way had been opened before her—that she was like the prodigal son, and it seemed as if God had seen her afar off—that she prayed to be enabled to hold fast the hope she felt—all in this strain. We made her our school-mistress, and during the whole term of her imprisonment, I never knew her break one rule, or be guilty of the smallest impropriety of speech or behaviour. When they quit Newgate, we support them from our fund, till they are otherwise provided for—in consequence of illness, *she* remained for some time dependent on us. We received a message from her, requesting that we would, if possible, obtain her admittance into some workhouse, where, if we could furnish her with a little tea and sugar, she should be much happier than now, for that she was miserable at the idea of diminishing *that fund*, which might be the means of rescuing other poor creatures from the state she had herself been in. We got her into a workhouse, where she lately died, one of the most peaceful, happy deaths; the only pain she experienced was, from none of us being present, that she might have expressed to us her gratitude for the benefit she had derived through our means. Another young woman, too, of the same character, is lately dead; she lived well, and died well.'

"We went afterwards through part of the prison, but in a very unsatisfactory manner, owing to the number of persons present. She said that one proof of essential good being done, was, that, whereas the returns used to be 30 per cent., they are now less than 4."

The readers of this volume will doubtless contemplate with interest, such engagements in the prison as that which has just been described; but they will not easily conceive the astonishment excited in many an actual spectator of the scene. Evidences of the Christian philanthropy and devotedness of woman, had rarely been wont to arrest popular attention; and the English people, as they now are performing their part on the stage of life, can but faintly imagine the state of public feeling, as it existed at the time when Elizabeth Fry commenced her arduous work. A mighty change has passed over the religious sentiments of the nation since the close of the last century. That was a time when, notwithstanding that witnesses for the truth were preserved among the different Christian communities—as "the salt of the earth"—the sceptical principles of French philosophy had become, under the influence of the grand agent of evil, who transforms himself into the semblance "of an angel of light," the means of dazzling the minds of great numbers, particularly of the democratic class, and of plunging many into the vortex of infidelity, whilst those who moved in the more fashionable walks of life, were generally immersed in dissapition, or devoted to politics and war. Few comparatively, of this class were disposed to listen to the claims of the gospel; and when a Porteus, a Wilberforce, and some other excellent men, uttered a serious appeal to the public mind, on the high importance of its truths, and on the solemn responsibility that rested on all to obey its practical injunctions, the truly patriotic effort was too often met by cold indifference, or even by ridicule. The writings of Hannah More, though frequently little regarded by many to whom they were especially addressed, and who, by this vain world, would be estimated as the great and noble, were, however, beginning to exercise a salutary influence on the more thoughtful amongst the different ranks of the people; and the present century dawned on the nation with the sunshine of hope; and many persons were becoming impressed, not only with the importance of individually accepting the truths of Divine revelation, but with the duty of extensively using them, as being, under the direction of the Holy Spirit, the only weapon that could be effectually wielded in the counteraction of evil: the organization of the Bible Society was the result of this conviction; and a gradual, but sure revolution was effected in public opinion. Even from those circles where vice and debauchery had reigned triumphant, an influence was seen to emanate, that proclaimed itself on the side of virtue: and the manner in which the religious labours of Elizabeth Fry, for the conversion of sin-degraded souls, were hailed by all classes, more especially by persons of the highest rank and intelligence, evinced the increase of power to appreciate the relative value of those objects that belong only to this transitory state of existence, compared with the infinitely important interests of immortality. And, whilst the deep impression, made on many hearts, through the instrumentality of this divinely-gifted woman, bespoke the onward progress of that regenerating principle, which alone can secure the happiness and well-being of man, her heaven-directed efforts gave, to the operation of this principle, an impulse, which powerfully stimulated many awakened minds to "seek those things which are above, where Christ sitteth at the right hand of God."

In pursuing her engagements at Newgate, Elizabeth Fry had gradually learned many particulars of the Penal Colony of New South Wales. She found through a communication from Samuel Marsden, the chaplain there, that all labours of her co-adjutors, and her own, all systems of Prison Discipline, all efforts to reform the offender, were absolutely null and void, and but a wasteful expenditure both of time and money, so long as the female convicts were without shelter, without resource, and without protection, on their arrival in the land of exile. Rations, or a small allowance of provisions, sufficient to maintain life, they certainly had allotted them daily: but of any place to sleep in, or the means to obtain one; or necessary clothing for themselves, and when mothers, for their children, they were entirely destitute. It was worse than useless; it was only an aggravation of their misery to inculcate morality, and to raise the tone and improve the tastes, of these unhappy ones, and above all to impress on them the solemn truth, that, "without Holiness no man can see the Lord," whilst they were placed in circumstances where existence could be maintained only at the price of virtue.

Much of this was learned from the prisoners themselves, but every inquiry made upon the subject, confirmed their statements; and, in order to induce the government to provide a suitable home, and proper employment for these exiled convicts, much renewed exertion was entailed on Elizabeth Fry and her companions in the work.

Plashet, Eighth Month.—I may indeed say, dearest Lord, help me in all my difficulties, regard me in my low estate, and let me see the lightings up of Thy countenance on my beloved children. Though I am deeply sensible that, in bringing to the knowledge of Thyself, Thy ways are not our ways; and that Thou mayst even permit the poor mind to wander in darkness and in unbelief for a season, that it may be more fully prepared to see the beauty of Thy light, to rejoice in the appearance of the day-star from on high, and to feel the excellency of faith; yet, oh! that in Thy tender mercy and compassion, Thou wouldst permit Thy unworthy one to see some fruit of the working of Thy Spirit in her children, that she might still rejoice and be glad in Thee; but above all, Lord, strengthen and enable her to cast all her care upon Thee, and to commit herself, and those most near and dear to her, to Thy grace and good keeping. I desire not to forget all Thy benefits, which are many and great, naturally and spiritually; we are all of us favoured with health, still, day by day provided for, and some desires spiritually raised in our hearts after Thyself; and I am also thankful that Thy blessing is, in so remarkable a manner, resting on the prison cause, and on our labours for these poor destitute creatures, that have come under our care. O Lord! be pleased to bless the work of our hands, even in these things establish Thou it, and if consistent with Thy holy will, be pleased to bless the labours of Thy poor child at home, as well as abroad. Amen.

It may be observed that entering in her journal a record of her thoughts, her desires, her sorrows, and, at times, her varied and almost opposite reflections and feelings, continued to afford relief to her spirit; and was still, as she described it to be when but a girl, *like opening her heart to a friend*—and, at this date, she adds to the last notice, the following:—

I think before I conclude this journal, I should express amongst my many blessings, how much I am enabled to take pleasure in the various beauties of nature, flowers, shells, &c., and what an entire liberty I feel to enjoy them; I look upon these things as sweet gifts, and the power to enjoy them as a still sweeter. I am often astonished, when my mind is so exceedingly occupied, and my heart so deeply interested, how I can turn with my little children to these objects, and enjoy them with as great a relish as any of them; it is a wholesome recreation, that I fully believe strengthens the mind. I mention it as a renewed proof that the allowable pleasures of life, so far from losing their zest by having the time and mind much devoted to higher objects, are only thereby rendered more delightful.

19*th.*—I have this day been married twenty years; my heart feels much overwhelmed at the remembrance of it—it has been an eventful time. I trust that I have not gone really backwards spiritually, as I think I have in mercy certainly increased in the knowledge of God, and Christ Jesus our Lord; but this has been through much suffering. I doubt my being in so lively a state as ten years ago, when first coming forth in the ministry; but I believe I may say, that I love my Lord above all—as far as I know, far above every natural tie; although, in His infinite wisdom and mercy, He has been pleased, at times, to look upon me with a frowning Providence. If I have lately grown at all, it has been in the root, not in the branch, as there is but little appearance of good, or fruit, as far as I can see. In the course of these twenty years, my abode has often been in the valley of deep humiliation; still the Lord has been my stay, and I may say through all, dealt bountifully with me; assuredly He has raised me up from season to season, enabled me to speak well of His name, and led me to plead the cause of the poor, and those that are in bonds, naturally and spiritually.

Ninth Month, 2nd.—Since writing my last journal, I have had a Minute from my Monthly Meeting, and have been visiting the Essex Monthly Meetings. I have passed through deep exercise and travail of spirit in doing it, but thanks be unto my God, I found help in the needful time, and when least expected, in unmerited mercy, the holy anointing oil was once more freely poured forth upon me, so that I was enabled boldly to declare His doings amongst the people, and to show forth His marvellous works to the children of men. I am to-day likely to set out again—Lord, be with us, I pray Thee! help us, guide us, strengthen us, uphold us and comfort us, and enable me to leave all with peace and comfort at home. We are now likely to break up house-keeping here, for many months; how, and when, we shall meet together again in this place, and whether ever—our Lord only knoweth.

4th.—I returned yesterday from finishing visiting the Monthly and Quarterly Meetings in Essex. I was carried through the service to my own surprise; I felt so remarkably low, so unworthy, so unfit, and as if I had little or nothing to communicate to them, but I was marvellously helped from Meeting to Meeting; strength so arose with the occasion, that the fear of man was taken from me, and I was enabled to declare Gospel truths boldly. This is to me wonderful; and unbelievers may say what they will, it must be the Lord's doing, and is marvellous in our eyes—how He strengtheneth them that have no might, and helpeth those that have no power. The peace I felt after the services for some days, seemed to flow like a river, for a time covering all my cares and sorrows, so that I might truly say, "There is even here a rest for the people of God." I am sure, from my own experience, there is nothing whatever in this life, that brings the same satisfying, heart-consoling feeling. It is to me a powerful internal evidence of the truth of revealed religion, that it is indeed a substantial truth, not a cunningly devised fable. My sceptical doubting mind, has been convinced of the truth of religion, not by the hearing of the ear, but from what I have really handled, and tasted, and known for myself, of the word of life, may I not say of the power of God unto salvation? I visited my most dearly beloved brothers and sisters at Earlham, towards whom I feel united by bonds inexpressible. My sweet, dear sister Priscilla, continues very seriously ill, which much melted my heart, but her establishment on Christ, the Rock of Ages, consoled us under every sorrow.

The Newgate Association having become established, and three years having tested the success of the plans pursued there, a Corresponding Committee was formed to answer inquiries and communicate information. "Ladies' Associations" were established in several places, and in others one or two individuals undertook the work of prison visiting; but some degree of classification, employment, and moral influence, were all that their unassisted endeavours could effect. To carry out Elizabeth Fry's views, solitude by night, complete classification, unceasing superintendence, compulsory occupation, regular instruction, and religious influence were necessary, to produce reformation of character; and to obtain these advantages, larger prisons, embracing more extensive districts, and conducted on a system of strict surveillance, were required.

But Newgate had proved that something might be effected even under the most unfavourable circumstances. As applications for information became more numerous, and her interest in the subject increased, Elizabeth Fry undertook a journey in the Ninth Month of this year, with the view of visiting many of the most important prisons in England. She was accompanied by her husband, and their two elder daughters.

She had generally letters from official persons, or private

friends, to the Visiting Magistrates of the prison which she desired to see. There she would go, accompanied by the officers of the prison, any magistrates who were disposed to accompany her, or private individuals interested in the cause. She would pass from yard to yard, from one ward to another, addressing the most minute inquiries to the jailor or turnkey; and calculating the capabilities of the building for the greatest possible degree of improvement. The result of her observations she almost always stated afterwards, in a letter addressed to those of local authority. Besides this, she endeavoured to form a Committee of Ladies, to visit the female prisoners, or she strove to induce, at least, one or two to undertake this Christian duty. She convinced the judgment of some—she touched the feelings of others—but seldom failed to bring to her purpose, such of her own sex as she had selected, as being, in her opinion, suitable for the undertaking.

This journey led to important results, from the increased experience and knowledge it gave her, and also tended to the diffusion of both interest and information on the subject of Prison Discipline.

She thus notices the events of this journey:—

Southend, Darlington, Ninth Month, 5th.—I left home, after parting with my sweet Chenda, and dearest little ones, last Sixth-day week. I had much weighty service in Nottingham, and established a Ladies' Association for visiting prisoners. Numbers followed me, particularly to Meeting, but I was helped through, finding grace sufficient in time of need. I was called away from Sheffield, to attend the funeral of dear little Jonathan Backhouse, who died rather suddenly —a sweet boy, about eight years old; a great and deep trial to his father and mother; but their Lord has been their stay, and I think I may say, we have had to rejoice together in Him, whose tender mercies are over all His works; indeed the more we see, and the more we know, may we not say, "blessing, and glory, and honour, and power, thanksgiving and praise, belong unto God, and the Lamb, for ever and ever," and this, in times even of deepest sorrow and privation naturally, when helped by the influence of the Spirit.

Swinton, near Hackfall, Yorkshire, 29th.—We are here staying at a beautiful place, with a brother of Lady Harcourt's. He and his wife, and all the family, are exceedingly kind to us; they indeed make too much of us. However much such visits may be to the taste, they always bring me into considerable exercise of mind; in the first place, for fear of not faithfully standing my ground in Christian humility, simplicity, and faithfulness; and in the next, from the fear of not making proper use of such providential openings for promoting the blessed cause of truth and righteousness. O dearest Lord! if Thou callest for anything at my hands, I pray Thee open my way outwardly, and strengthen me spiritually.

Letter to two of her Daughters.

Mildred's Court, *Twelfth Month*, 13*th*, 1820.

It was pleasant to hear of your safe arrival at Earlham, after your journey with your dear uncle. Our London life is so very busy, and one event puts another so much out of mind, that it is difficult to relate exactly how time passes; but I will try to tell you, as far as I remember, how we have been engaged. On Seventh-day morning, I was much occupied till about one o'clock, in settling accounts. So one more year is passed, and have we wanted any needful thing or indulgence? Afterwards, I visited the eight poor men under sentence of death, their wives, some of their families and friends; and a very affecting time it was. We read together, and appeared to be under the merciful influence of that blessed Spirit, that manifests itself to be from Him who remains to be "Lord God on high, mightier than the noise of many waters." On Third-day, I went to Sophia Vansittart, and had a satisfactory interview with her; she is willing to join a Ladies' Committee in Westminster, and to visit Tothill-fields prison, if way can be made in it.

The interest of Elizabeth Fry was not confined to the prisons of her native country. She opened a correspondence with the late Walter Venning of Petersburg, who devoted himself to visiting and instructing the prisoners in that city. The Princess Sophia Mestchersky, and other ladies, had formed themselves into a committee, with highly satisfactory results, to visit the women confined in the five prisons of that capital. In a letter written by the Princess to W. Venning, on the 2nd of Eighth Month, 1820, she says:—

"Though I acknowledge myself completely unable to write in English, as you wish me to do, for to show your friends in England the state of our prisons, such as the Ladies' Committee found it to be in the beginning, and such as it is now, eight months after the establishment of the society; yet when you told me it would prove a token of our regard and high esteem for Mrs. Fry, and her fellow-labourers, I readily comply with your request, and shall try to overcome all the difficulties which ignorance of your language and the novelty of the subject, present to me. Not I alone, Sir, but all the Ladies of our Committee, expressed a hearty wish that something of our public exertions, and of our efforts to follow the example which that lady gives us, might be communicated to her, as a proof that her labours are blessed from above, and that a spark of that love which animates her generous heart, has also reached our distant country, and influenced many hearts with the same Christian feelings for suffering humanity. May this prove a comfort to her soul, and a new encouragement for her to continue her labours in that large and important field of usefulness, in which she is called to serve our Lord. We will all endeavour to follow her according to the strength and abilities granted us, looking for help and hoping for success to and from Him, from whom we receive every blessing, and whose 'strength is made perfect in weakness.'"

Extract from a letter from Elizabeth Fry to the late Walter Venning of Petersburg.

Respected friend,

Though personally unknown to thee, I am confident, from the interest we both feel in one cause, that thou wilt excuse the liberty I take in writing to thee, to express my heartfelt satisfaction at the interesting and important accounts thou hast given my brother Hoare of the proceedings of the Gentlemen and Ladies' Prison Associations in Petersburg. Most warmly do I desire their encouragement in this work of charity and utility, for the more I am acquainted with the subject, and the more extensive my observation of the effects of prison discipline is, the more confident I feel of its importance; and that although the work will be gradual, yet through the Divine blessing, its result will be sure. Not only that many will be stopped in their career of vice, but some truly turned from their evil ways, and the security and comfort of the community at large, increased, by our prisons, that have been too generally the nurseries of vice, and scenes of idleness, filth, and debauchery, being so arranged and so attended to, that they become schools where the most reprobate may be instructed in their duty towards their Creator and their fellow-mortals; and where the very habits of their lives may be changed.

It will be found in this, as in every other good work, that some trials and some discouragement will attend it; but the great end in view must induce those engaged in it to persevere, and use increased diligence to overcome them, doing what we do to the Lord, and not unto man, and then we shall do it well.

We continue to have much satisfaction in the results of our efforts in Newgate—good order appears increasingly established, there is much cleanliness amongst our poor women, and some very encouraging proofs of reformation in habit, and what is much more, in heart. This, in a prison so ill-arranged, with no classification, except tried from untried, no good inspection, and many other great disadvantages, is more than the most zealous advocates of prison discipline could look for.

I lately had the pleasure of seeing the Duchess of Gloucester, who is our Patroness; she desired me to express how much gratified she was with thy account of what you are doing in Petersburg, and her wish that the ladies may be encouraged in their good work.

It is now more than three years since we first began our operations in Newgate, and how encouraging it is, that the experience of every year should increase our hopes, and diminish our fears, as to the beneficial result of these exertions. Indeed it is wonderful to observe the effects of kindness and care, upon some of these poor forlorn creatures —how it tenders their hearts, and makes them susceptible of impression. I am of opinion, from what I have observed, that there are hardly any amongst them so hard, but that they may be subdued by kindness, gentleness, and love, so as very materially to alter their general conduct. Some of the worst prisoners have, after liberation, done great credit to the care taken of them. In two particular instances, young women who had sunk into almost every depravity and vice, upon being liberated, conducted themselves with much propriety, as far as we know, and after long illnesses, died peaceful deaths. They were striking instances; through a blessing upon the care taken of them, they, in a remarkable manner, were turned from Satan unto God, and we humbly trust, through the mercy of Redeeming love, they are received into glory. Some are settled in service, others, we hope, are doing well in different situations. We wish it were in our power to attend more to the prisoners upon leaving the prisons, as we think this an important part of the duty of such associations; but in London the numbers are so very great that it is almost out of our power to do it, as we desire, though we endeavour to extend a little care over them.

How delightful it is to hear of the interest that the Emperor Alexander, Prince Galitzin, and ladies of high rank, take in the cause of the poor prisoners. May the best of blessings rest upon them, for thus manifesting their care over the destitute of the earth.

We also feel gratefully sensible of their kindness to our friends William Allen and Stephen Grellet. I hope thou wilt let us know before long how you go on. I am much obliged for the book thou kindly sent me; and believe me, with much regard and esteem,

Thy friend,

ELIZABETH FRY.

After the death of Walter Venning, the correspondence thus commenced, was long continued with his brother, John Venning; whose labours, in reforming the criminal, and in relieving the suffering inmates of asylums, prisons, &c., were unwearied, and greatly blessed of the Lord. He stated that the letters which he received from Elizabeth Fry were "invaluable as regarded the treatment and management of both prisoners and insane persons. It was the fruit of her own rich practical experience, communicated with touching simplicity, and it produced lasting benefits to those institutions in Russia."

After he had presented to the Emperor Nicholas a statement of the defects of the Government lunatic asylum, the dowager empress and her son visited the asylum together, and being convinced of the necessity of a complete reform in the management of the insane, the emperor requested his mother to take it under her own care, and to appoint John Venning the governor of it. An order was soon given to purchase, of one of the princes, a palace-like house, having above two miles of garden, and a fine stream of water running through the grounds. A plan of this great building was sent to Elizabeth Fry, for her inspection and hints for improvements. Two extensive wings were recommended for dormitories. The wings cost £15,000: in addition to this sum from the government, the emperor gave £3000 for cast-iron window-frames recommended by Elizabeth Fry; as the clumsy iron bars in the old institution had drawn from many a poor inmate a sigh, with "Sir, prison! prison!"

Elizabeth Fry recommended that all, except the violent lunatics, should dine together at a table covered with a cloth and furnished with plates and spoons. The empress was delighted with this plan, and, when the arrangements were completed, requested John Venning to invite them to dinner. Sixteen came and took their seats. The empress approached the table, ordering one of the upper servants to sit at the head of it and ask a blessing. When he arose to do this, they all stood up. The soup, with small pieces of meat, was then served, and as soon as they had dined, they all rose up spontaneously, and thanked her for her motherly kindness. She was deeply moved, and turning to John Venning, said, "My friend, this is one of the happiest days of my life." The next day the number at table was increased, and the day following was still greater.

A letter from Elizabeth Fry, on "the great importance of supplying the lunatics with the Scriptures," which John Venning said "deserved to be written in letters of gold," and which he sent to the imperial family, was received with marked approbation. The court-physician, Dr. Richl, a devoted philanthropist, requested a copy of it. This letter removed all difficulties on the subject, and John Venning was requested to furnish them in their various languages. It was considered, by some, "a wild and dangerous proceeding;" but he soon found them collected in groups, and quietly listening, while one of their number was reading the New Testament; and instead of disturbing their minds, it produced a soothing influence. A Russian priest, a lunatic, collected a number together, and read to them. And John Venning found a poor Frenchman in his bed-room, during a lucid interval reading the New Testament, with tears rolling down his cheeks.

Whenever John Venning received a letter from Elizabeth Fry, he would write it out in French for the empress, and was pleased to see, as soon as she had read it, with what alacrity she ordered one of her secretaries to translate it into

Russian, to be entered into the journal at the asylum, for immediate adoption. One contained a list of fourteen rules, which were all confirmed by the empress the same day. And they introduced very important arrangements, viz., "treating the inmates as far as possible, as the sane persons, both in conversation and manners towards them; to allow them as much liberty as possible; to engage them daily to take exercise in the open air; to allow them to wear their own clothes, and no uniform prison dress; most strictly to fulfil whatever was promised them; to exercise *patience, gentleness, kindness* and *love* towards them; and to be exceedingly careful as to the characters of the keepers appointed to watch over them."

Petersburg was not the only continental city, with which communication on the subject of ladies visiting prisoners had now been opened.

At Turin, La Marquise de Barol née Colbert was assiduously occupied in this important work. This lady was a Roman Catholic, and had entered upon it, from a sense of duty. Francis Cunningham, when travelling through that place, had obtained permission to see the prison, had there become acquainted with her, and opened a correspondence for her with his sister-in-law Elizabeth Fry, which was maintained for many years. Letters were also received from Amsterdam, where those interested in the cause, were endeavouring to form a Prison Discipline Society, and Committees to visit the prisoners.

Mildred's Court, First Month, 1*st*, 1821.—Having poured forth my soul in prayer, and having exhorted my household to live in the love and fear of the Lord, I have obtained some relief upon entering a new year, and finishing another. I opened my Bible at these words, so consonant with the feelings of my heart, I quote them here, "Hear my prayer, and be merciful unto thine inheritance; turn our sorrow into joy, that we may live, O Lord, and praise Thy name.'

In the way which was consistent with His holy will, did the Beloved of her soul answer this petition of His servant. He saw meet to dispense the bitter cup, but it was sweetened by His mercy and love. She had become much affected in the Ninth Month of the preceding year, by the alarming illness of her beloved sister Priscilla.

From 1792, the year of Catherine Gurney's decease, her daughters had continued an unbroken band; but now, upon the youngest of the seven, the hand of disease was making a fatal impression, and she was evidently declining under the influence of pulmonary consumption. She was singularly lovely and attractive in mind and person. To her maternal sister, Elizabeth Fry, she was peculiarly endeared, and the bond that so closely united their spirits, was a high and sacred one; they had both been led to embrace the principles of the Society of Friends, and both were engaged in the holy vocation of the Gospel ministry. Priscilla Gurney was a diligent labourer in the cause of Christ, and was highly esteemed by her fellow-professors, for her work's sake; and greatly beloved by many pious and excellent persons of other Christian communities; and it may be truly said that she did, in word and ministration, and in conduct, adorn the doctrine of God her Saviour. She was revered in the domestic circle, even by those who did not unite in her distinctive religious views.

Earlham was her residence with her other unmarried sisters and brothers; nor did it cease to be their home, at the marriage of their brother, Joseph John Gurney, in 1817. His adoption of the principles of Friends had been a great satisfaction and support to her, in her own course.

From the Isle of Wight, where she had passed the winter preceding, on account of her declining health, she wrote, in 1820, to her beloved sister E. J. Fry.

"Thou hast been much in my thoughts lately, my beloved sister, and I can hardly describe to thee, the flow of love and of deep interest which sometimes arises towards thee: there is a certain understanding which I feel with thee, that I can hardly feel in the same way with any other mortal, except, perhaps, it may be with our dearest brother Joseph. We three do, I believe, intimately understand one another's paths—we know one another's conflicts—we have partaken in the same depths—we have been mercifully permitted, according to our different measures, (for I feel my measure small indeed compared with thine,) to partake of the same kind of spiritual consolations, and of the same deliverance from depths into heights. What a support, and stay, and refreshment, in short, what a mother, hast thou been to us both! I must confess my heart often turns towards thee with joy and with thankfulness, though thy path has been strewed with many crosses and many afflictions, yet so in proportion has, I firmly believe, been the victory, which has been given thee through Christ our Saviour, to the great comfort and encouragement of many, as well as to thy own present, and may we not humbly trust, eternal peace and salvation! how fervently do I desire, that the blessing which has so eminently attended thee, may be in all things thy crown, thy rejoicing—that it may prosper thee in all thy ways!"

The summer of that year was passed by Priscilla Gurney at Earlham. As the autumn advanced, she was removed to Cromer Hall, then the abode of her brother and sister Buxton; and with them she passed the few remaining months of her life, nursed, with the most assiduous care, by her sister Rachel, who had been devoted to her through the latter stages of her prolonged decline. Here Elizabeth Fry visited her, and writes in her journal:—

Cromer Hall, Second Month, 9th.—Here I am, with my dear brother Samuel Gurney, come to visit our dearest sister Priscilla in her declining state. The sweet and peaceful state of her soul is cause for much thankfulness and rejoicing, but the low valley is my own abiding place; and my desire for myself and mine, I may say, my prayer is, O dearest Lord! give us not over to the will of our enemies. My feeling for my dearest brothers and sisters is,—in the first place, thanksgiving, particularly for their spiritual state;

and secondly, desire that grace may be found sufficient for them, and that no snare of the enemy, however gilded by apparent holiness, may ever hurt or ensnare them; and for my dearest sister Priscilla,—O Lord! Thou who hast been with her, be with her to the end, and in Thine own time burst all her bonds asunder, and bring her into the abundant and glorious liberty of Thy children. And also permit Thy unworthy child, through all her trials, to acknowledge how truly marvellously Thou hast provided for her, and abundantly loaded her with benefits. Cause us, dearest Lord, to hear, to feel, and to acknowledge Thy loving kindness and Thy tender mercies, not only now, but for ever. Amen.

Cromer Hall, Third Month, 11*th, First day.*—Dearest Priscilla said to this effect, that the experience of her illness had greatly confirmed and deepened her in the foundation and principles of Friends, more particularly as it respected the ministry; though she most truly found her boundaries enlarged towards all; and upon my saying "Thou feelest all one, if in Christ," "Yes," she said, "just so." She expressed how entirely she felt her dependence on the Lord alone, and how little she felt the want of outward ministry, though what came in the life was refreshing and sweet. She yesterday expressed her love for silence, how she found it tended to strengthen body, as well as soul, and it was one reason she wished to be alone at night. She also expressed this morning a great desire for the *Friends* of the family, that they should hold fast their principles.

To her husband and one of her daughters, she wrote:—

Cromer Hall, *Third Month, 25th,* 1821.

About nine o'clock this morning the scene closed, and our most tenderly beloved sister went to sleep in Jesus. The conflict of death was long upon her; I think it may be said from Third or Fourth-day, to this morning. She has been sensible, evidently so, till late last evening, and her calm, quiet, and patient state continued. I think every day her conflict diminished; she had nearly lost the power of speech; but when we were all collected round her, last evening, about nine, she was heard to say, "Farewell, Farewell," several times. Some one heard her add, "My love is with you," and the last thing we could hear was, "O Lord!" In the morning, she appeared very full of love—put out her hand to several of us—showed much pleasure in your uncle Buxton's being here, and tried to speak to him, but could not be understood—expressed her wish for reading, and from her feeling of love and fondness for the chapter, and some signs, we believed she meant the thirteenth of 1st Corinthians, and we had a very sweet, animating time together, and afterwards our dear brother Fowell spoke very sweetly to her; and besides the Bible, she appeared to have some satisfaction in hearing other books read, as it had been her habit during her illness, just like mine when ill. She appeared to have finished her work, and to have nothing to do but to die; her sweet spirit was quite at liberty to pass away the time in reading, and having, I believe, no headache, she could bear it, though she confined it to religious books, yet many of an interesting nature; her hymns* interested her much—she liked Samuel Scott's Diary—Piety Promoted—Accounts of the Missions—Watts and How—and many other books of that description. I write thus particularly, because I thought you would wish to hear. I think her object in reading was gentle amusement, and at times edification—she was very particular not to read the Bible except she felt herself in rather a lively state. We were all by her when her prepared spirit left the body, and a sweet time it was; no struggle. After commending her to her Lord, and, for His name's sake, into glory, my brother Joseph quoted these words—

Selection of Hymns, by Priscilla Gurney.

"One gentle sigh the fetters breaks,
We scarce can say they are gone,
Before the willing spirit takes
Its station near the throne."

Catherine expressed her firm belief that she was one of the blessed who died in the Lord.

Rachel after a time, uttered a few words in thanksgiving for her, and prayer for us who remain.

Thy letter, my dearest ——, gave me much satisfaction, and my opinion is, though death loses its sting of sin to the righteous, yet they equally, or very nearly so, have the natural conflict to pass through ; and death certainly is a very great conflict, generally speaking; but it has struck me again and again, what this would have been to a sensitive mind, feeling at the same time the sense of condemnation and the sting of sin ; but my beloved child, there is much in thy remarks, and I think the death of the righteous is often represented as too easy ; for human nature is the same in all, and how much did our blessed Lord go through, who took upon Himself our nature. Ah ! my ——, I think of thee and thy birth-day. May the Lord be with thee in it, opening thy eyes to behold the beauty of holiness, and enlarging thy heart, by His own power, to make thee willing "to lay aside every weight and the sin that may so easily beset thee, and to run with patience the race that is set before thee, looking to Jesus, the Author and Finisher of our Faith." In much near and dear love, farewell,

ELIZABETH FRY.

First day, Fourth Month, 14th.—I returned from Norfolk —my second visit, after being from home about six weeks, where I had attended my much-loved sister to the last, almost constantly devoted to her in the day, for four weeks before her death, and then staying to her funeral, &c. For the first fortnight, tenderly as I felt for my beloved sister's sufferings, yet there was so much sweetness in being with her, such inexpressible unity with her spirit in its redeemed state, that it was not a distressing time. I was also greatly favoured with excellent health, as the sea air appeared to revive me so much; but the last fortnight, my health sunk a good deal, and my beloved sister's great reduction, with, no doubt, some suffering, was almost too much for me; still, I may acknowledge, that rather marvellously, every day help, strength and sufficient consolation, have been granted. I was certainly impatient at my darling sister being so long passing through the valley of the shadow of death; but how did I perceive my folly when I saw how gentl y he was led through it, and how I might observe the kind hand of Providence making her way naturally and spiritually; and I do believe, deeply as we felt for her, it was to herself greatly sweetened, and a renewed cause for us to return thanks on her account.

Elizabeth Fry's return from Norfolk was shortly followed by interests, new and very different from those which had occupied her, by the death-bed of her sister. The subject of Capital Punishments was attracting increased attention, opinions differed, and opposing views were entertained; but it was no longer looked upon with indifference.

The Society "for the Improvement of Prison Discipline, and Reformation of Juvenile Offenders," was also actively at work. Many persons of influence had joined it, and zealously supported the plans of the Committee. Elizabeth Fry's experience at Newgate was considered as an exemplification of the effects of religious instruction, and moral discipline and control, combined with Christian kindness. She believed it to be her duty to use the influence this circumstance gave her, to the utmost of her power, and to avail herself of every right opportunity for communicating the results of her personal observation. Nor was her attention confined to this branch of the subject; she was too keen an observer not to know, that her experiment, though successful, could not be universally tried, and that nothing short of a complete change in the spirit and practice of the criminal legislation of the country, carried on by systematic government regulation, could effect permanent and general good. She considered that the religion which we profess to obey, that the humanity implanted even in the natural heart of man, should induce individuals suited for the office, to visit prisons, hospitals, and other public institutions; although this was, to her mind, a matter wholly independent of their construction and arrangement. In a letter on the subject of female convict ships, in which she urges the necessity of certain measures being adopted by government, she adds:—

"I am anxious that a few things which would greatly tend to the order and reformation of these poor women, and protect their little remaining virtue, should become established practices, authorised by government, and not dependent upon a few individuals, whose life and health, and everything else, are so uncertain."

Few persons have possessed so little speculativeness of character, combined with such extraordinary quickness of perception, as Elizabeth Fry. She saw, that whereas the greater number of persons had hitherto been content to take no heed to passing circumstances, and to allow abuses to continue, scarcely recognizing their existence, the time was come when the rights of humanity would make themselves heard. Men of reflection had begun to investigate the causes, and the probable results, of the facts around them. Enormous errors were committed, incalculable mistakes made, as must ever be the case, when finite man leans to his own finite understanding; yet the good preponderated; and where philosophy had learned in the school of Christ, undeniable truths were proclaimed, and peace and good will extended to mankind.

Elizabeth Fry perceived that light had dawned, she was persuaded that it could never be again extinguished; but she saw, that to direct the mental energies of the people aright, general education, combined with scriptural instruction, and the unlimited circulation of the Holy Bible, was requisite.

On the 23rd of Fifth Month, Sir James Mackintosh brought forward his motion, "for mitigating the severity of punishment in certain cases of forgery and the crimes connected therewith." Sir Samuel Romilly had, with the exception of Lord Nugent, and a very few others, stood almost unsupported in the Lower House; now, the contest had become nearly equal, and Sir James Mackintosh's Bill was lost by a very small majority. It was on this occasion, that T. F. Buxton delivered his admirable speech upon Capital Punishment. Many had gone that night, doubtful as to the expediency of the measure proposed, but were convinced by his arguments, based as they were upon incontrovertible facts, varied calculations, and unquestionable evidence. Some had taken their seats indifferent as to the question at issue; his warm appeal to their humanity, and the responsibility of legislating for the lives of thousands, without having weighed the merits of the case, or considered the practical effects of punishment, aroused them from their apathy; others from a dread of change, and a certain sort of adherence to the opinions of party, unconnected with the merits or demerits of the opinions themselves, were startled by the delicate irony, with which he showed the impracticability of the laws, and the strange devices resorted to, to evade their literal fulfilment. Excellently did he generalize the subject, when he said, "There is no one who will deny, that the laws of the land ought to be congenial with the feelings of the people. There was a time, we may suppose, in which this happy sympathy prevailed. But that period is long passed. During the last century, they have each fled from this point of concurrence; the law in its enactments, and the people, in the tenor of their feelings. The people have made enormous strides in all that tends to civilize and soften mankind, while the laws have contracted a ferocity, which did not belong to them in the most savage part of our history, and to such extremes of distance have they proceeded, that I do believe there never was a law so harsh as British law, or so merciful and humane a people as the British people. And yet, to this mild and merciful people, is left the execution of that rigid and cruel law!"

Although Sir James Mackintosh's bill was lost, yet it was a defeat so nearly approaching to victory, as to afford Elizabeth Fry heartfelt satisfaction. She had again cause to rejoice, when early in the following Sixth Month, she witnessed the Freemason's Hall filled, on occasion of the Meeting for the Improvement of Prison Discipline, and the Reformation of Juvenile Offenders. The *Times* of the 4th of that month, in an account of the meeting, states that she was mentioned by many of the speakers in terms of high eulogium, and was loudly applauded, when she quitted the Hall; but no allusion to this is made in her journal, or in any letters that have been found.

The Duke of Gloucester presided, supported by Lord John Russell, Lord Stanley, (the late Earl Derby,) Lord Belgrave, (Marquis of Westminster,) Lord Calthorpe, the Bishop of Gloucester (Ryder), Sir James Mackintosh, Sir Thomas Baring, and many other individuals of rank and talent. Nobly was the cause advocated which had brought them together. Lord John Russell was almost prophetic in expectation, when he concluded a short, but brilliant speech, by expressing his belief, that our country was about to "become distinguished for triumphs, the effect of which should be to save, and not to destroy;" and that "instead of laying waste the provinces of our enemies, we might begin now to reap a more solid glory in the reform of abuses at home, and in spreading happiness through millions of our own population."

Plashet, Eighth Month, 29th.—My beloved daughter Rachel, was married last Fifth-day, the 23rd, at Runcton, by my brother-in-law, Francis Cunningham.

Plashet, Ninth Month, 3rd.—I doubt not but that my late tendency to depression of spirits is caused, not only by the sorrow which I certainly feel, and great disappointment, from a child not keeping to the principles that I have brought her up in, and also from the deep sense I have of their intrinsic value; but, moreover, that I have to bear my conduct in the affair being misconstrued by others. Yet, I have certainly met with much kindness, great love and sympathy, and from quarters where I should have least expected it, also particularly from the Friends of my own Monthly Meeting.

I am very much absorbed at home, where many things deeply occupy my heart and head. To do right in my many relative duties is very difficult; how deeply I feel my short-comings in them! and yet I fervently desire to do my best. —— has my prayers much more often than the day. Lord, help this dear child by Thy Spirit, guide him by Thy counsel, and save him by that salvation that cometh by Christ. And for my sweet, dear William, so visit him, and influence him by Thy anointing, that he may become a vessel of honour, calculated and prepared to show forth Thy praise. Ah! dearest Lord, bless the lads; above all things I ask of Thee, far above all temporal good, sanctify them, and fit them to exalt and magnify Thy great and ever-excellent name.

Plashet, Tenth Month, 18th.—I have lately been called into various engagements. I attended the Quarterly Meeting of Kent to much comfort and satisfaction, surprised to find so much openness, so little obstruction in the way, and not a little consoled to feel the anointing, afresh and fully poured forth to my great relief; and I believe I may say, enabled to declare the word, in that power that tendered and refreshed many minds. Afterwards visited Lord and Lady Torrington, at Yotes Court; Maidstone Barracks and Gaol, and the Noëls at Barham Court, to satisfaction. The love of the Gospel appeared much over us towards all amongst whom our lot was cast; our dear sister, E. Fry, was with us throughout. Since this, I attended the Quarterly Meeting for Sussex and Surrey, but not to the same relief and satisfaction.

I had one very important Meeting at Brighton, so many came that it rendered it a Public Meeting; it was a fearful time, but the best help was granted, to my peace and consolation, and a hope that it was not without good to others. Since my return home, last Seventh-day, the 13th, I have been enabled to enjoy and estimate my blessings, particularly my delightful, quiet home, garden and little children.

Plashet, Second Month, 21st, 1822.—Yesterday, we attended the wedding of Cornelius Hanbury and Mary Allen. It was a very solemn and comforting day.

Third Month, 9th.—Since I last wrote, we have visited almost every family belonging to Ratcliff Monthly Meeting, Elizabeth Copeland, my sister Elizabeth Fry, and myself. I may say that we have found what we believed to be the best help near us, as we went from house to house, enabling us to speak well for our Master, and to encourage the feeble travellers in their way to Zion. Some of the visits were poor and low times, with such as appeared to have their hearts more in present things than in those that are to come, which produces great flatness; but we were rejoiced to find many, who, we could not doubt, were humble-minded Christians, seeking to dwell near the Spirit of truth in their hearts. How do I rejoice in the prosperity of Zion, and the enlargement of her borders! (the true church, under all denominations, may be called Zion,) and in our small body, I love to see it spiritual and consistent with our high profession. I have felt it an honour and favour to be once more thus engaged in my dearest Master's cause, it has, at times, brought that sweet peace with it, that nothing else can give.

Plashet, Fifth Month, 2nd.—I am favoured with general health of body, and cheerfulness of mind; a good deal occupied by temporal things, though I trust not resting in them.

My readings in Newgate at this time of the year, are peculiarly exercising to me, so many attend, and often such a variety; and some of such high rank, I should think so little accustomed to hear the truth spoken. The prospect of them is sometimes really awful to me, and if I know the desire of my heart respecting them, it is this—that the cause of truth and righteousness may be exalted, my Lord glorified, and living faith in Him promoted; and for myself and those engaged in the work, that we may dwell low before Him who hath helped us, abide in His fear, and not the fear of man; seek His pleasure, and not our own pleasure, and if, in unmerited mercy, He is pleased to help us and to own us by His presence, that we may ever remember, that to us belongs nothing but confusion of face, but to Him alone, glory, honour, power, thanksgiving and praise. Amen, Lord, be pleased to bless these seasons, that we have been brought into, we humbly trust, by the ordering of Thy providence; so that they may tend to good, and that they may be to some, as "bread cast upon the waters, that will return after many days."

Plashet, 28th.—Since writing the above, I have had fresh cause to raise up my Ebenezer; help having been granted, and to my own feelings way marvellously made for me, in things that I exceedingly dreaded. In the first place, I felt very low, and peculiarly under discouragement, partly from my sense of weakness both of body and mind, and partly from the idea that Friends might not feel unity with me after my child's marriage. In the first place, I had, in the Meeting of Ministers and Elders, to pray for direction and help for myself and others during the Yearly Meeting, which appeared as if owned by the Great Head of the church. The next thing was our Ladies' Prison Meeting, which I dreaded, and had many misgivings about; however, this was got through quite beyond my expectation: the accounts of many instances of reform from different prisons were truly encouraging and comforting, and the whole feeling was as if a blessing were in it; dear Mary Dudley prayed, and several of us had to acknowledge the kindness of the Most High in it, and to Him alone, in all things, did we desire to give the glory. This Meeting gave me a little hope and encouragement; still, when I found that my awful concern to visit the Men's Meeting remained, fear was indeed my portion, and such a dread lest I might not know the voice of the great and good Shepherd; however, I found amidst all my fears, no way of relief for my mind, but in laying my views before the Women's Meeting; they were met with much unity and encouragement, quite beyond what I expected. My beloved sister, Elizabeth Fry, went with me, Sarah Benson, and my aunt Jane Gurney. We entered the Men's Meeting trembling. What an awful service it is for a poor weak woman to go amongst so many hundred men. After being seated, I soon found the spirit of prayer poured forth; I knelt down, and found myself greatly strengthened to offer up my supplications for ourselves, and for the body then present; Elizabeth Fry then spoke, in much calmness and power, which I doubt not would deeply impress those who heard her; I followed her, and it was marvellous to me the unction that I felt to deliver what opened to me, principally to the young people, and to the sorrowful and perplexed, especially from outward causes; there was great solemnity over the Meeting, and very many appeared to be in tears; therefore what can we say, but that our merciful God was on our side, and He became our Helper? Surely it is the Lord's doing, and marvellous in our eyes.

Much comfort and satisfaction were expressed after Meeting, by different Friends, and so my fears vanished. May this afresh lead me, in doing and in suffering, to commit my cause to my most Gracious Helper, Saviour, and Redeemer, and fully trust in Him.

Sixth Month, 10th.—Obliged to go to town to meet the Prince and Princess of Denmark, at the Borough Road School; afterwards received a very poor account of dearest Jane. A low day.

Plashet 13th.—Accounts came that our dear sister Jane, the wife of my much-loved brother Joseph, died at Earlham on Second-day the 10th, a little before six o'clock, and that my dearest brother, thanks be to Him who helped him, was enabled to give her up with a resigned spirit. Heavenly love and support were very manifest to them both: and she appeared greatly prepared for it, notwithstanding the short notice she had. She was, I believe, one who loved and feared the Lord, and who proved her love by her humble dedication, and watchful, circumspect conduct; she was an excellent wife, mother, daughter, and sister, a great friend to the poor, and remarkably generous. May her loss be fully made up to our poor brother, by that gracious Power that has thus bereaved him of one so dear and so lovely to him.

Earlham, 16th.—After weighing the matter the best I could, such were my inexpressible drawings of love to Joseph and the others, that I believed it best for my body and mind to come here, though I left home really poorly; but I found the change of air useful, till last evening after arriving here, when I felt very unwell, which took sad hold of my nerves, and I had a painful night. Still I may acknowledge my true and deep consolation in seeing my dearest brother Joseph, my aunt Birkbeck, and the rest of the family so greatly, even marvellously, supported.

Earlham, 21st.—Day by day strength is granted to us, to my beloved brother and his poor mother-in-law, though the late afflicting event cast a cloud over all temporal things: some of the party appear wonderfully raised in spirit and strong in faith. I rejoice and am glad for them; for myself I feel particularly unworthy, and as if far behind some others in spiritual advancement, and true dedication; I am ready to be reminded of that text, "The first shall be last, and the last first." Still I trust there is a following on to know the Lord, amidst many infirmities.

Earlham, 22nd.—I feel brought low before the Lord; what can I say and what can I do, but beseech Thee, oh, our Lord! to care for us, present and absent, to undertake for us, to show us the sufficiency of Thy grace, and the power of Thy salvation? We beseech Thee, through Him that hath loved us and given Himself for us, that Thou wouldest draw us all, whether now far from Thee, or near unto Thee, by the powerful cords of Thy loving-kindness, out of darkness into Thy marvellous light, that we may ever dwell in Thy light and in Thy love, and know the fulness of Thy power, Thy glory, and Thy majesty. Amen.

We were favoured to get through the first Meeting of the Quarterly Meeting to great satisfaction, the truth arose even into something of dominion; many of the Lord's servants had to minister in His name, and even I, unworthy as I am, was greatly helped.

Plashet, Seventh Month, 1st.—I was just set off for town, when I had to return, to receive the Princess of Denmark; it was a satisfactory visit. Several Italian noblemen and others to dinner. My brother and sister Hoare, and many besides, slept here. My fatigue great.

Eighth Month, 20th.—Yesterday was our wedding-day, we have been married twenty-two years; how many dispensations have I passed through since that time, how have I been raised up, and cast down! How has a way been made in the depths, and a path in the mighty waters; I have known much of good health, and real sickness; great bodily suffering, particularly in my confinements, and deep depression of spirits.

I have known the ease of abundance of riches, and the sorrow and perplexity of comparative deprivation; I have known to the full, I think, the enjoyment of domestic life; even what might be called the fullness of blessing, and also some of its most sorrowful and most painful reverses. I have known the abounding of the unspeakable, and soul-satisfying joy of the Lord; and I have been brought into states, when the depths had well nigh swallowed me up. I have known great exaltation amongst my fellow-mortals, also deep humiliation. I have known the sorrow, of some most tenderly beloved, being taken from me by death; and others given me, hitherto more given than taken.

What is the result of all this experience? It is even, that the Lord is gracious and very merciful, that His compassions fail not, but are renewed every morning; and may I not say, that His goodness and mercy have followed me all the days of my life? Though he has, at times, permitted me, amidst many and unspeakable blessings, to pass through unutterable sorrows; known only to the full extent by Him and my own soul, yet He hath been an All-sufficient helper; His right hand hath sustained me and held me up, blessed be His name for ever; He hath never forgotten to be gracious, nor hath He shut up His tender mercies from me. May I not indeed raise up my Ebenezer, and acknowledge that there is "no God like our God," and that it is a most blessed thing to serve Him, even if it be by the way of the cross, for He is indeed worthy to be served, worshipped and obeyed, now and for ever. Above all, I pray for myself, that whatever dispensations I may yet pass through, nothing may separate me from His love, or hinder me from His service, but that I may be increasingly and entirely devoted to Him in heart, mind, and spirit; through the help of my most dear and blessed Redeemer.

Plashet, 16*th*.—I believe it right once more to make an acknowledgment of the mercy of my God. Although I feel in a very sensitive state of mind and body, yet my soul is in great mercy kept calm, quiet, and generally cheerful, before the Lord; I speak thus because, through the grace and free mercy of my God, I feel, in measure, living unto Him; and as if His power and His presence were near, to calm the storms that would naturally arise, and also as if what I did, I was enabled to do in reference to His will. Most assuredly He is no hard Master; how truly can I speak to this! although, in wisdom, He has led me by the way of the cross, very greatly so, to flesh and blood, both in doing and in suffering; yet there is abundant liberty in the gospel. How do I, at times, find that the very same Spirit leads into rest, and refreshment, and consolation—how far from requiring what we are not able to perform! May those, for such there are, I do believe, even tender ones, who desire to do right in the sight of the Lord; who, from their own activity, go beyond His requirings, and therefore misinterpret His word inwardly and outwardly, and make religion appear a gloomy and rigid path,—may these be brought to feel the rest, refreshment, and even right liberty (not in evil) which the gospel of light and salvation really brings into. I think I know what it is when a fearful mind, or looking to the opinions of others, or a judgment of myself, has led to a sort of self-denial, that the best witness in my heart has neither warranted, nor led into, though I most fully acknowledge also that too great laxity is my more prevailing temptation, as it respects myself and others—but enough do I know of the true liberty of the gospel, however, at seasons, we may indeed have to bear our cross in doing and in suffering—enough do I know of it, to long for all to be brought into it, from the most worldly to the most rigid formalist, under every denomination; for such I believe there are amongst all; and though I feel for these, in what appear to me bonds of their own making, yet I doubt not, but that, in tender mercy, they are accepted, and that their state is safe indeed, compared with that of the worldly-minded.

Elizabeth Fry now mentions meeting Dr. Chalmers. They mutually helped each other in plans of benevolence.

On the 1st of Eleventh Month, her youngest child was born, and on the same day her eldest grandchild.

Plashet, Eleventh Month, 7th.—Words fall utterly short of expression of the unmerited mercy which has been shown us. On the night of the 30th, I had to pass through a very deep conflict of spirit, comfort appeared to fail, deep discouragement and great fear took hold of me; I felt I had a baptism to be baptized with, and how was I straitened until it was accomplished, (if the servant dare allude to drinking even, at seasons, of the cup the Master drank of,) but after a time the conflict ceased, sweetness, trust, love and confidence, took place of it. I felt bound to have my husband, children, my dear sister Gurney, and Susan Pitchford, besides such of the maids as liked to join us, collected together, when, after reading I poured forth my soul in fervent prayer, for my dearest Rachel and myself in our time of conflict, for help spiritually, and naturally for tender mercy. And how striking to me it was, in little more than twenty-four hours—only fourteen hours apart—Rachel and myself had each a darling boy born. Both of us very graciously and wonderfully helped.

Plashet, 13*th*.—I write this journal in the midst of my lying-in with my eleventh child, in a very tender, delicate state of body, and unworthy state of soul, after having (of late peculiarly) received many and great blessings, spiritually and naturally. I cannot feel thankful enough for all my many blessings; so weak has been my state that the very grasshopper has become a burden, and I think I have shown my infirmity to others, as well as felt it myself, though I may say that I have sought after a quiet and patient spirit. In a serious and trying attack of spasms in my side, I found, in tender mercy, that Power to be near, which helped me; although I was seriously alarmed about myself, I felt my pleasant pictures marred, and was even much affected at the idea, that perhaps I should be taken from my beloved family, still I think it was principally nervous fear; for when such a call really comes, strength will be given for the need, and the same help administered, that has so marvellously been displayed in many of the deep conflicts of time.

My soul feels utterly unworthy, and deeply prostrate before Thee, dearest Lord, at my utter inability fully to return Thee thanks for all Thy benefits. Make me fit to receive them; enable me to acknowledge them; strengthen me to walk more circumspectly before Thee in thought, word, and deed. Thou knowest that I love Thee, that, above all things, I believe my desire is, to serve Thee, love Thee, and obey Thee. Thou hast manifested, and canst manifest Thyself to be all-sufficient, to be "strength in weakness, riches in poverty, and a present helper in every needful time." Grant a little help, if Thou seest meet, to bring me again into life; that I may serve Thee better, love Thee more, and as a wife, mother, mistress, and member of Thy church, and of society at large, may more perfectly keep my eye single unto Thee, and do all to Thee, and through Thee, to the praise of Thy Holy name. And continue to grant, if it please Thee, a blessing on those labours of love, that Thou hast permitted me to be brought into in the prisons, and that the work may not stop till much more be accomplished in it. Amen.

First-day, 17*th*.—My body recovering, though weak. My spirit tendered before the Lord, for His great and unspeakable benefits. My naturally too insensible heart softened before Him, who I may say is the delight of my soul, my Lord and my God, my Saviour and Redeemer. I remember those that are worshipping, as worshipping with them, and my spirit feels sweet unity with the Church Militant, and perhaps, though utterly unworthy of it, with the Church Triumphant, as if I could unite with both, in the everlasting song of high praises, even to our God, and to His Lamb, who hath shown such tender mercy towards us, and made Himself manifest to us, as our Saviour and Redeemer. Blessed for ever be His name.

27*th*.—Peace and sweetness appear to rest upon me in entering life. Oh! for my sweet infant, if life be granted him, may he be indeed devoted to the Lord. We neither circumcise nor baptize, but may he be baptized by the saving baptism of Christ! and be in spirit circumcised unto the Lord! I have (perhaps in weakness) much set my heart upon this child, rather expecting he may be a comfort to us in our old age, and not only so, but above all, that he may prove a devoted servant of Christ. May this blessed work not be hindered by any false indulgence in us; but may it be truly promoted by example, precept, and the true discipline of love and wisdom.

Twelfth Month, *2nd*.—Yesterday, at Meeting, the Truth rose into much dominion, blessed be the name of the Lord. I was enabled to supplicate and minister to my own relief, and I trust to the refreshment of others, also my dearest brother Joseph, Rebecca Christy, and my sister, Elizabeth Fry, in prayer. It appeared a solemn time. The day, generally speaking, a favoured one; but in the night I was deeply brought to a sense of my own weakness. If the beautiful garments spiritually were put on in the morning, surely they were taken off at night. What are we but instruments, however, for a season decorated with our Lord's ornaments; self cannot boast, when left to ourselves, and our decorations taken off! How wonderful is the work of the Spirit—how it heals, and raises up body and soul, when they are to be brought into service; none can tell, but those who have experienced something of it, how the anointing is poured forth from on high. It is an honour I am unworthy of, to be thus helped spiritually, particularly in the ministry. But how deeply doth my spirit crave that I may also be aided in all the practical duties of life.

14*th*.—I yesterday went to London, and visited Newgate. My greeting there was warm from the prisoners, the committee, and others. I felt peaceful there, and afresh sensible that the work was not our's, that we had first been *brought* there; and I had to crave a blessing upon our labours, and also to acknowledge the tender mercy of our God as our Saviour and Deliverer. I was low in myself, but felt renewedly the great importance of the prison cause; and if those who espouse it are enabled to persevere, what good may be done, in preventing much crime that has been both plotted and perpetrated in prisons.

In this year (1822) the late John Randolph, while American Envoy to this country, visited Newgate—he gave a description of the scene to a friend who thus recites the particulars of the narrative: "Suddenly, Randolph rose from his chair, and, in his most imposing manner, thus addressed me: 'Mr. Harvey, two days ago I saw the greatest curiosity in London—aye, and in England, too, sir—compared to which Westminster Abbey, the Tower, Somerset House, the British Museum, nay, Parliament itself, sink into utter insignificance! I have seen, sir, Elizabeth Fry, in Newgate, and I have witnessed there, miraculous effects of true Christianity upon the most depraved of human beings! And yet the wretched outcasts have been tamed and subdued by the Christian eloquence of Mrs. Fry! I have seen them weep repentant tears while she addressed them. I have heard their groans of despair, sir! Nothing but religion can effect this miracle; for what can be a greater miracle than the conversion of a degraded, sinful woman, taken from the very dregs of society! Oh, sir, it was a sight worthy the attention of angels! You must, also, see this wonder.

During this year the Prince and Princess Royal of Denmark visited England. They inspected many charitable and public institutions, and evinced a lively interest in objects that conduced to the moral and religious welfare of mankind. Early one morning Elizabeth Fry received information that the Princess wished, on that day, to breakfast with her. She came accordingly; the visit was a very satisfactory one, and from that time an association commenced with this excellent Princess, that continued until E. Fry's decease.

We find her, soon afterwards, addressing the following letter:—

To the Princess Royal of Denmark.

Plashet House, *Eleventh Month*, 23*rd*, 1822.

Dear and respected Friend,

Allow me to call thee so, for such I feel thee, as thou art truly both loved and respected by me. According to thy kind and condescending wish, expressed when here, I take up my pen to inform thee, that upon the first of this month, through the tender mercy of my God, I was safely delivered of a sweet boy, and to add to our cause of joy and thanksgiving, my dear daughter had also one born on the same day, so that twenty-four hours added a son and grandson to our already numerous family; we have, both of us, with our infants, been going on well, and with the exception of some illness, that I passed through in the early part of my confinement, and my habitual delicacy at such times, I am as well now as I can expect to be.

I have often thought of thy kind visit with deep interest, and strong desires are raised in my heart for thy welfare and preservation in every way, that the God of Peace may be with thee continually, guiding thee by His counsel, helping thee by His Spirit, comforting thee by His love, during thy continuance here; and afterwards, when he may be pleased to take thee hence, to be seen of men no more, through His mercy in Christ Jesus, receiving thee into glory. I also feel real interest and best desires for the Prince Royal,—may you both be encouraged in every good word, and work. I remember the words of Paul, in the 15th chapter of the 1st of Corinthians, 58th verse: "Be ye stedfast, unmoveable, always abounding in the work of the Lord, for as much as ye know that your labour is not in vain in the Lord."

It would give me great pleasure and satisfaction to hear from thee, or if that be asking too much, perhaps the lady whom we had the pleasure of seeing here, will let us know many particulars respecting your welfare, and how you go on in Denmark, as it respects the prisons, schools, and other works of charity and love. I should also be pleased to know whether the books and the other things which we sent to Count Moltke, and also some of the work of the prisoners, ever came safely to thy hand, as we were prevented sending them quite so soon as we hoped to have done. I should be glad to be very respectfully and affectionately remembered to the Queen, and also to the Prince Royal, thy consort: and believe me, with much respect and regard,

Thy attached and obliged Friend,

ELIZABETH FRY.

Plashet, First Month, 2nd, 1823.—"Our years pass away as a tale that is told." Upon concluding one, and beginning another year, my heart has been brought low before the Great I am; and I have desired, after a renewed searching of heart, to see how my accounts stand spiritually, and in what I can more fully serve my Lord, and bear the fruits of the Spirit. I have inwardly prayed for help, as well as vocally for myself, my family, my household, and those most near and dear to me; above all, that there may be known amongst us more of the light, life, and spirit of religion; and beyond every other blessing, more knowledge of the truth as it is in Jesus.

Amongst the interests of the opening year was the marriage of Elizabeth Fry's youngest brother Daniel Gurney of North Runcton, to the Lady Harriet Hay, one of the daughters of the Earl of Erroll. The contrast of his circumstances of prosperity, with those of his brother, Joseph John Gurney, treading the lonely path of widowhood, touched her closely; and after writing to one brother, she addressed the other.

The following is an extract from her letter to her brother Joseph John Gurney.

Plashet, *First Month*, 8*th*. 1823.

My dearest Joseph,

Having just written to one dear brother, feeling and expressing my sympathy in his joys; I think I shall better conclude my morning's work, by also telling thee how much I have been with thee in mind in thy low estate. I feel for thee and sympathize with thee, but if a poor fellow-mortal feels so tenderly for another, how must it be with Him, whose love, pity, and tender compassion are unbounded. Surely thy Lord and His Comforter, will be found very near to thee, in His own time healing thy wounds. I believe, as we may rejoice and return thanks for our dear brother's present fulness of enjoyment, so we may also for thee in thy privations; because all is permitted in tender mercy and loving-kindness. I doubt not that thou hast many pains to bear, by night and by day, as the desolation produced by thy loss would naturally occasion; but I trust patience will have its perfect work, and so tend further to purify, and redeem, and fit thee for thy Master's work.

Plashet, First Month, 8*th*.—A deep feeling of infirmity has been my portion. Yesterday, my mind was so much engrossed in temporal things, that I did not get rid of them, even at Meeting; and the day before some inattention in a servant annoyed me too much in mind, which in degree was shown, so as to be followed by condemnation, and being thus brought, through my omissions and commissions, to the feet of Jesus, the prayer of my heart is to Him for justification, and purification, that I may know my transgressions to be forgiven, and that I may be afresh fitted and prepared by His Spirit, for a more watchful and circumspect walk before Him, whom my soul loves and pants after; and I believe desires, above all things, to serve, worship, and obey.

22*nd*.—On the 16th, I was sent for to Hampstead, to my beloved sister Hoare, (who was ill). Such seasons are to me times of real conflict spiritually and naturally: spiritually to know what, in the way of religious service, may be required at my hand, and also close sympathy with those in trouble, naturally, from my acute sense of suffering, and my great love for my sisters. I know few things that occasion me a deeper feeling of impotence and unworthiness, than attending the sick. I may say, it always brings home to me very deeply the unworthiness of my own heart; indeed, I do not much think nursing is my allotment, though often in it, for my acute feeling for those near to me is such, that however I may maintain a cheerful countenance, my heart is affected so as painfully to affect my nerves.

The sentiments here expressed, respecting her services for the sick, are very different from those entertained of her by such as received or witnessed her attentions. She displayed, in cases of illness, great presence of mind, a quick perception of the changes taking place in the patient, a singular readiness in expedients to meet them, much judgment and skill in the administration of remedies, and the whole combined with a quiet, cheerful manner, and most tender sympathy, so as to inspire complete confidence and dependence on herself in the sufferer, as well as the assistants.

During the present month she writes in her journal—

I attended Westminster Meeting, which I have looked to for some time, as well as others of our Quarterly Meeting. I believed when there, that if I were well carried through that, to the relief of my own mind, and if best help then felt near, I should have to visit most of the Meetings in our Quarterly Meeting, held on First-day Mornings. It so proved that I felt help very near, so that the language of my spirit was, "It is the Lord's doing, and marvellous in my eyes." In nothing has the work of grace been so marvellous to me as in the ministry; it surely is not my own work; —I know enough of myself to believe it to be quite impossible. Oh, what an unction I now and then feel, it is as much to be felt strengthening the soul, as the body is felt to be refreshed after wholesome good food. The work of the Spirit is a wonderful work, and, to my naturally doubting and sceptical mind, astonishing. I have been permitted to know more of it than I could have either asked or thought. I believed it best to lay my prospect of a general attendance of these Meetings, before our dear friends at the Monthly Meeting yesterday, which was to my peace; sweet unity and sympathy were expressed in it, and my beloved sister E. F. proposed to join me, which is a comfort to me. It is cause of much thankfulness to have such a companion.

Plashet, Second Month, 13*th*.—I attended Tottenham Meeting on the 2nd. I went low and under deep exercise of mind; I returned in measure relieved, though naturally upset with many fears; I hardly ever remember being engaged in a service where doubts and fears beset me to an equal extent. On First day the 9th, we were at Devonshire House; it was an extraordinary Meeting. I desire, in more simplicity of faith, to attend the other Meetings. I think I have been too anxious, too fearful; if the work be not our's, why worry and perplex myself about it?

19*th*.—Since writing the above, I attended the Peel Meeting, on First-day, which was to the great relief of my mind: since that time my bonds have appeared wonderfully broken, my spirit has had to rejoice and be glad, and my fears have been removed, so that I can indeed say, how marvellous is the work of the Spirit!

On Second-day, I dined at the Mansion House, with my husband; a change of atmosphere spiritually; but if we are enabled to abide in Christ, and stand our ground, we may, by our lives and conversation, glorify God, even at a dinner visit, as well as in more important callings. Generally speaking, I believe it best to avoid such occasions, for they take up time, and are apt to dissipate the mind; although it may occasionally be the right and proper calling of Christians, thus to enter life; but they must then keep the eye very single to Him, who, having placed them in the world, can alone keep them from the evil.

24*th.*—We were helped through the service yesterday at Ratcliffe Meeting. It really appeared a favoured time, and peculiar harmony and power in the ministry generally prevailed, with great solemnity in the silence. I may say that I had afterwards a cheerful, peaceful day, with my family.

Third Month, 5th.—I have lately been remarkably full of occupations, and yet they have appeared right, and almost unavoidable. On First-day, I attended Southwark Meeting; mercy and peace eventually accompanied it. On Fifth-day, I went to town, to meet the Secretary of State (Sir Robert Peel) and the Speaker of the House of Commons at Newgate, with my brother Fowell Buxton, and my husband; I trust the time was blessed to the good of the cause.

Sixth-day in town again to Newgate, one of the bishops and many others there; it was a solemn time—a power better than ourselves seemed remarkably over us. I visited another prison, and then returned home; besides these out of door objects, I am much engaged in nursing my babe, which is a sweet employment, but takes time; the rest of the children are comfortably settled in with dear Mary Ann Davis, who is now once more with us. Upon sitting down to write, and looking round me, surrounded as I am with my family, supplied with so many temporal comforts, spiritual blessings not withheld: for I trust that there is rather an increase than decrease of the best thing amongst us; I thought, as the query arose in my heart, "Lackest thou any thing?" I might indeed say, "Nothing, Lord," except a further establishment for us all, in the ever blessed truth, as it is in Jesus. What can I render to Thee for all thy benefits? Grant, dearest Lord! in thy child and servant, a heart fully and entirely devoted to Thee and Thy service. Amen.

29*th.*—Since I last wrote, I have attended Winchmore Hill Meeting to satisfaction, together with my dear sister

Elizabeth, William Allen, and my brother Samuel, whose company I enjoyed. My husband has engaged Leslie, the painter, to come and take likenesses of him and me, to which, from peculiar circumstances, I have appeared *obliged* to yield; but the thing, and its effect on the mind, are unsatisfactory to me; it is not altogether what I like, or approve; it is making too much of this poor tabernacle, and rather exalting that part in us which should be laid low, and kept low; I believe I could not have yielded the point had not so many likenesses of me already appeared, and it would be a trial to my family, only to have these disagreeable ones to remain. However from one cause or another, this has not been a satisfactory week, too much in the earth and the things of it, too little in the spirit; though not without seeking to take up my cross, deny myself, and follow my Lord and Master. I feel particularly unfit and unworthy to enter again upon my religious engagement: we propose going to Uxbridge this evening. My only hope is in Him, who can alone cleanse, fit, strengthen, and prepare for his own work; under a deep feeling of my short-comings, may I not say, dearest Lord, undertake for me!

Fourth Month, 7th.—We went to Uxbridge, though naturally rather a low time, yet it ended to my real comfort. The Morning Meeting was a very solemn one, a deep feeling of good, and the anointing of the Spirit appeared freely poured forth. The Evening Meeting was satisfactory; and in several religious opportunities in the families, my heart was enlarged in much love to the dear Friends there, whom I think I may say, I love in the Lord.

12*th.*—Since I last wrote, we have been engaged in various ways, particularly in the sale of work done by the poor prisoners in Newgate; this has been a considerable public exposure, but I trust not without profit. I deeply felt upon entering it, the danger of the pollutions of the world, and the desire that we, who are seeking in this way to promote the cause of truth and righteousness, might maintain the watch on this point. I trust no harm was done; but I feel, after being with so many, much brought down in myself, under a feeling of great infirmity. I think, in looking back on the last two days, I do not feel condemned, but rather that I have been in my right place, and that some good may result from the whole thing.

Since the *Maria* had been visited in 1818, as each successive season brought the sailing of a female convict ship, the subject obtained a large share of Elizabeth Fry's attention. Amongst those who assisted her in her efforts to improve the condition of these ships, the late Elizabeth Pryor was one most especially devoted to the work; *with the exception of one ship* (the *Amphitrite*,)* she visited every transport which sailed from England with female convicts, until prevented by the sickness, which terminated in her death, in 1841.

This was not done without much fatigue and inconvenience; frequent exposure to weather in open boats, and occasionally to danger. On one occasion, Elizabeth Pryor and Elizabeth Fry were placed in a situation of considerable alarm, from which they were relieved, by the interposition of the present Harbour Master at Ramsgate. His narrative will interest the reader:—

"It was on a fine sultry day, in the summer of 1821, that I was racing up the river Thames, in the command of the Ramsgate Steam Packet, *Eagle*, hoping to overtake our Margate competitors, the *Victory* and *Favourite* steamers, and bring them nearer to view as we rounded the points of the Reach of the river. It was in the midst of this excitement, that we encountered one of those sudden thunder

* This vessel was wrecked off Boulogne. One hundred and twenty female convicts, many of whom had been objects of care and instruction in Newgate, together with a large number of children, also the captain, officers, and nearly all the crew, were lost. Neither Elizabeth Fry nor any of the Committee ever visited this ship.

squalls, so common in this country, and which passing rapidly off with heavy rain, leave behind them a strong and increasing northerly gale. I was looking out a-head, pleasing myself with the reflection that we were the fastest vessel against a head wind, and should certainly overtake our Margate friends; when upon entering Long Reach, about two miles below Purfleet, I saw a boat labouring with very little effect against the gale, and with a whole ebb-tide just making, to add to their difficulties; in this boat were two ladies, in the close habit of the Society of Friends, evidently drenched with the heavy shower which had overtaken them. I was then a dashing high-spirited sailor; but I had always a secret admiration of the quiet demeanour of that Society, and occasionally had some of them passengers with me, always intelligent and inquiring, and always pleased with any information a seaman could extend to them. Well, here was a dilemma! To stop, would spoil my chase, in which most of my passengers were as eager as myself, but to go on, and pass two ladies in such a situation! I passed the word softly to the engineer; desired the mate to sheer alongside the boat carefully; threw the delighted rowers a rope, and before the passengers were fully aware that we had stopped the engines, the ladies were on board, the boat made fast astern, and the *Eagle* again flying up the Thames. I have those two persons strongly, nay, indelibly stamped upon my mind's eye. The one I had last assisted on board, still held my hand, as she thanked me, with dignified, but beautiful expression: 'It is kind of thee, Captain, and we thank thee. We made no sign to thee; having held up our handkerchiefs to the other packets, we did not think we should succeed with thee.' I assured them that I could not have passed them under such circumstances, and called the stewardess to take them below into the ladies' cabin and see to their comfort. They had been well cloaked, and had not suffered so much as I had anticipated.

"The gale had cleared away the rain, and in a very short time they came upon deck again, one of them was Mrs. Fry, and she never lost an opportunity of doing good. I saw her speaking to some of my crew, who were looking very serious as she offered them tracts, and some of them cast a side glance at me, for my approval or otherwise. I had some little dislike to sects then, which, I thank God, left me in riper years,—but who could resist this beautiful persuasive, and heavenly-minded woman? To see her, was to love her; to hear her, was to feel as if a guardian angel had bid you follow that teaching, which could alone subdue the temptations and evils of this life, and secure a Redeemer's love in eternity! In her, you saw all that was attractive in woman, lit up by the bright beams of philanthropy devoting the prime of life, and health, and personal graces, to her Divine Master's service; and I feel assured that much of the success which attended her missions of mercy, was based upon that awe which such a presence inspired. It was something to possess a countenance which portrayed, in every look, the overflowing of such a heart, and thus, as a humble instrument in the hands of Divine Providence, she was indeed highly favoured among women.

"She told me that her companion, Mrs. Pryor, and herself had been down to Gravesend to take leave of the unfortunate women (convicts) on board a ship bound to the settlements, and gave me so touching a description of their behaviour, that I volunteered to take charge of any thing for her at any time, or render her any service in my power, in my voyages. When about to land, her anxiety to make some pecuniary recompense was very great, but I would not allow her to do so. Mrs. Fry never forgot me when she came near our locality; I saw her from time to time, the earthly tabernacle failing, but the same spirit lighting up with animation her untiring energies. It was an honour to know her in this world; may we follow her to the society of the accepted and blessed, in that which is to come.

"K. B. MARTIN.

"Ramsgate, *February*, 1847."

On another occasion, Elizabeth Fry reached Deptford late in the afternoon of a very tempestuous day. A female convict ship was under sailing orders for the next morning, and it being after office-hours, she went to the private house of Admiral Young, to request him to send her off to the ship. By the time she returned on shore, it was quite dark, and the wind and rain to which she had been exposed, seemed to make a little rest and refreshment almost indispensable, before she set off homewards. But she resisted all the invitations of Admiral Young and his family to remain with them; assigning, as a reason, that she had left one of her children seriously ill, to whom she was anxious to hasten back. This little incident left a deep impression on their minds; "that such a claim on a mother's heart, had not been permitted to interfere with that, to which she had pledged her best energies and powers."

Thus, did this tender and delicate woman willingly encounter personal suffering and exposure, in obeying the dictates of divine love, which led her to follow in the footsteps of Him, "who came to seek and to save that which was lost."

It was not for the sinners and outcasts alone that Elizabeth Fry pleaded; whatever she believed likely to promote the real good of the people, and the cause of religion upon earth, found in her a ready advocate. To the poor and needy her ear was always open, and she would "humble herself," for so she felt it, to ask that for them of her family and friends, which it was not in her own power to bestow. Her brothers gladly responded to every call on their benevolence, and she enjoyed from this source, the high gratification of being able to supply the streams of blessing, in many and varied channels.

But it was not only to the poor—to those who moved in the humbler walks of life—that she was the messenger of consolation and help. She was frequently introduced into circumstances, that called forth her deep religious sympathy with persons of exalted worldly rank, whose piety derived strength and encouragement from association with her.

The following letter received at this time, exemplifies this fact.

THE DUCHESS OF———TO ELIZABETH FRY.

"*June 28th*, 1823.

"You, dear madam, were so kind as to call upon me some days ago, I was most unfortunately out, and missed you; will you not have the kindness to try again? I cannot express in writing, half the pleasure your last visit gave me. The poor are not the only beings to whom you bring hope and comfort, whom you strengthen, when you hope they are in the right; and whom you would assist to recover the way of life, did you see (which their own feelings, prejudices, temper or sufferings, might blind them to,) that they were going wrong. If you would let me have a line, to tell me when I might hope to see you, I would take care not to be again disappointed. I leave town the last week in July.

"Believe me, your most truly obliged,

"————."

Plashet, Seventh Month, 31st.—Since I last wrote, I have passed through a scene of deep affliction, in attending dear Mary Hanbury. I was called to her on Third-day, the 6th; after great illness, she died on the 16th, leaving her beloved father (William Allen), husband, and helpless infant. I had to drink the bitter cup with the afflicted, in an unusual degree, so as to bring me very low in myself, out of which state I have not fully risen, but am rather sunk in mind and body. I have, however, the consolation of believing, that I was a help and comfort to my sweet and dear young friend, whose remembrance is precious to me, so was her company, I think I may say to the last, her spirit appearing to overflow with love, joy, and peace. She having, I believe, kept the faith, finished her course, and fought the good fight. I have since attended great part of the Yearly Meeting, and the Prison Meeting, in all, to me, a low time.

Plashet, Eighth Month, 7th.—We have lately had much company, which leads to handsome dinners, and that sort of excitement which I feel painful on account of my family; but I find it very difficult to act rightly under some of these circumstances. Oh! for more ability, in the power, and in the spirit, to maintain the standard of truth and righteousness in my own house, in all things; so that *others* may be induced to do the same.

Earlham, Tenth Month, 1st.—My beloved husband left

me this morning for London, and I am here, with nine children and my little grandson. Since I last wrote, the face of things brightened. I went to Bristol to attend the Quarterly Meeting there, accompanied by my brother, Joseph John Gurney, and my sister E. F.; we left home on Sixth-day, the 11th of last month, and returned on Fifth-day, the 17th. In this short time, we travelled about two hundred and eighty miles, visited the Meeting at Bath, and the Bristol Quarterly Meeting; held two Public Meetings, visited the prison, attended to the magistrates and committee; visited Hannah More, my cousin Priscilla H. Gurney, and several others. The last few days my husband and I have been at Cromer, and paid an interesting visit to my much-loved brothers and sisters there. I was at different times, engaged religiously amongst them, and help was granted me in these services. I feel unworthy and unfit, and find that there is need of close, cleansing, baptisms of spirit, to make me, in any degree, ready thus to espouse the best of causes. I am much struck in having all my children, but one, now here; several of them grown up; what marvellous changes have I witnessed since I first knew this place; wonders, indeed, have been done for me, spiritually and naturally—how have I been raised up, as out of the dust! I am surrounded by a numerous, fine, and healthy offspring; one only taken from me, and that one with a peculiar evidence of going to an everlasting and blessed inheritance. Spiritually also, how has mercy been shown me; has not the beloved of my soul said, "live?" and how has He been with me in many tribulations, and sanctified many blessings. Indeed, I have found that my Lord is a wonder-working God, and has manifested himself to be to my soul, "Wonderful, Counsellor, the Mighty God, the Everlasting Father, and the Prince of Peace." What can I render for His unspeakable benefits? Lord, in Thy unmerited mercy, continue to be with, and bless Thy servant, whose hope is in Thee. Grant also Thy grace to her children, to love, serve, and obey Thee, that *her* God may be *their* God, *her* Saviour *their* Saviour, and *her* Comforter *their* Comforter. Be with, visit, and bless her husband, brothers and sisters, and children's children yet unborn, as well as the sweet grandchild, now granted her. Amen.

Chapter Seventh.

1824–1829. Journey to Worcester—British Ladies' Society—Establishment of Manor Hall Asylum and School of Discipline at Chelsea—Brighton—District Visiting Society there—Books for Preventive men, near Brighton—Letter from Dr. Steinkopff—Dagenham—Visit to Brighton—Return to Plashet—Death of her aunt Gurney—Goes into Norfolk—Letter to her family—Marriage of her eldest son—Autumn at Dagenham—Journey into Cornwall and Devonshire—Letter from Hannah More—Convict Ships—Visit to Ireland—Illness at Waterford—Return home—Illness and death of Rachel Gurney—Birth of a grandson—Journey into Norfolk and Derbyshire—Marriage of a daughter—Heavy sorrows—Leaves Plashet—Winter in London—Settlement at Upton-lane.

Early in this year, Elizabeth Fry paid a religious visit to some of the Midland Counties. She was accompanied by her brother, Samuel Gurney. She returned home in feeble health.

Plashet, Third Month, 29th.—We reached home last Fifth day, having accomplished the duty we had in prospect, to our own peace, and I trust to the edification of those amongst whom our lot has been cast. I continued very unwell the whole journey, and what with exercise of mind, and real illness of body, I think I have seldom known such a time; nor do I ever remember being so helped through the different services that I was brought into. Visiting gaols, attending two Quarterly Meetings, and many not Friends; one occasion in Worcester gaol; one large Public Meeting, the first I ever appointed of that description; and many other Meetings: but the way I was raised up, as from the dust, was wonderful to myself; enabled to speak with power, and in the Quarterly Meetings to go from service to service. It was indeed a remarkable evidence, that there is, in man, something beyond the natural part, which, when *that* is in its lowest, weakest state, helps and strengthens; none can tell what its power is, but those who submit to it. I now feel fully called to rest. I gratefully remember the abundant kindness shown me upon my journey. Greater enlargement of my heart in love do I never remember, or to have met more from others. I have been permitted to feel, throughout this illness, at times, very sweet consolation. A state of rest, as if the sense of pain and sorrow was taken away from body and mind, and, now and then, almost like a peep into the joys of the Kingdom.

First-day, 15*th*.—Yesterday, after a very weak and faint morning, I attended our "Ladies' British Society" Meeting; it was surprising, even to myself, to find what had been accomplished! How many prisons are now visited by ladies, and how much is done for the inhabitants of the prison-house, and what a way is made for their return from evil. It is marvellous in my eyes, that a poor instrument should have been the apparent cause of setting forward such a work.

The necessity for asylums, for the reception of discharged female prisoners, now claimed the attention of Elizabeth Fry and her fellow-labourers.

In 1822, a small house for receiving some of the most hopeful of the discharged prisoners was opened in Westminster, under the name of Tothill-Fields Asylum. It owed its existence to the Christian benevolence of one truly valuable member of the committee, Caroline Neave. She has consecrated her time and purse to this important object, which was first suggested to her mind during a drive with Elizabeth Fry, thus related by herself:—"A morning's expedition with dear Mrs. Fry made me at once resolve to add my help, if ever so feebly, to the good cause. I distinctly remember the one observation made. I can call to mind at this moment, the look, and tone, so peculiar, so exclusively her's who spoke—'Often have I known the career of a promising young woman, charged with the first offence, to end in a condemned cell! Was there but a Refuge for the young offender, my work would be less painful.' That one day's conversation upon these subjects, and in this strain, laid the foundation of our prisoners' home."*

The inmates at first, were only four in number; in 1824, they had increased to nine; after a few years, under the name of "The Royal Manor Hall Asylum," it contained fifty young women.

There was another class of persons who claimed the attention of the ladies of the British Society at this meeting. The vicious and neglected little girls, so numerous in London, early hardened in crime, who, whether they had, or had not, been imprisoned, had no chance of reformation at home; yet were too young to be placed with advantage in any existing asylum. Before the next anniversary, a School of Discipline, for the reception of such children, was opened at Chelsea, where, withdrawn from their former associates, they might be trained to orderly and virtuous habits. The idea first occurred to Elizabeth Fry, when conversing in the yard at Newgate, with a friend, on the extreme difficulty of disposing of some very juvenile prisoners about to be discharged.

Brighton, Fifth Month, 18th.—We arrived this evening, my health continuing very delicate. I have been induced to come here, partly by finding my weakness increase, and

* In addition to this excellent Institution, which continues very prosperous, a similar one, for the reception of discharged female prisoners who appear likely to prove themselves to be reformed characters, is now established at Hackney, and, under the designation of the "ELIZABETH FRY REFUGE," is effecting much good. Both these Asylums are liberally patronized by our beloved Queen, and they have a very strong claim on the benevolence of the public.

partly to oblige my husband, and others; although it is, on many accounts, much to my regret, leaving my dear children. I have also much felt leaving my dear Friends at the Yearly Meeting; still I trust we have done right in coming, and I can, now, only commend myself, and my all, absent and present, to Him who alone can keep and preserve us; and if it please Him to bless this measure for my recovery, may thankful hearts be our portion.

First-day, 23*rd*.—I am once more away from Meeting on this day; but my strength does not appear sufficient, to venture to sit one. . . . . I felt this morning as I sometimes have before, about the time that people generally assemble to worship, (when I have been sitting in solemn silence poorly, and alone,) *peculiar unity* with, and sweet love for, the members of the Church of Christ, not only that part of it to which I belong, but to others also. I do believe there is a communion of spirits, that neither separation of person, nor difference of sentiment, can obstruct, if we abide in a watchful, waiting state, and that so many of the members of the living Church, being engaged in waiting upon and worshipping our God, through Christ Jesus our Lord, spreads a good and refreshing influence, which extends even to those who are absent.

During her stay at Brighton, Elizabeth Fry was often distressed by the multitude of applicants for relief. This was not confined to beggars by profession, who infested the streets, following carriages and foot-passengers, with clamorous importunity, but extended to the resident poor, many of whom had acquired the habit of asking assistance at the houses, not only of the inhabitants, but of the visitors to the place. It was difficult for the former, but almost impossible for the latter, to discover their true condition, whether their poverty was real or assumed; and if real, whether caused by improvidence and idleness on their own part, or whether the result of misfortune and providential infliction.

Brighton appeared exactly the field for working a District Visiting Society. There was no lack of benevolent feeling, and abounding affluence was to be found there ; but the former was frequently misdirected, and the latter misapplied. A Provident Society had been in operation some years, but this touched only one part of the evil.

It was no easy matter to unite in the same object, persons wholly different in opinion, especially in religious matters; but without co-operation the desired end could not be effected, and after some delays, and much discouragement, she succeeded in getting the "Brighton District Society" established. The Earl of Chichester became its President. Its objects were—the encouragement of industry and frugality among the poor, by visits at their own habitations; the relief of real distress, whether arising from sickness or other causes; and the prevention of mendicity and imposture, together with "a system of small deposits, upon the plan of Savings' Banks, which was encouraged by a present premium, in order to induce the labouring classes to try to lay by a little store for their own necessities." To accomplish the desired ends, visitors were found, or offered themselves, to go from house to house, and become acquainted personally with the character and circumstances of their occupants.

"The smallest pittance, as a deposit for rent, or clothing, or fuel, by being often repeated, may prove to the poorest, that it is within their power effectually to help themselves, by such habits of frugality and resolution." The personal intercourse of the visitors with the poor, is a most important branch of the subject, it tends to good-will on both sides; it induces order and cleanliness amongst the visited, and a feeling of kindness and interest in the heart of the visitor.

In the course of Elizabeth Fry's illness at Brighton, she was liable to distressing attacks of faintness, during the night and early morning; when it was frequently necessary to take her to an open window, for the refreshment of the air. Whether, through the quiet grey dawn of the summer's morning, or by the fitful gleams of a tempestuous sky, one living object always presented itself to her view on these occasions; the solitary blockade-man* pacing the shingly beach. It first attracted her attention, and soon excited her sympathy; for the service was one of hardship and of danger, and was one that entailed much privation, both on officers and men; the stations were often placed in dreary and inaccessible places. From the very nature of the service, they were precluded from communication with the inhabitants, amongst whom it was exceedingly unpopular; constantly harassed with nocturnal watching, exposed to danger, both from weather and affrays with smugglers, they might almost be said to be in a state of blockade themselves. What Elizabeth Fry heard, only confirmed her desire to do something for their moral and religious good. The lieutenants in command of several of the neighbouring posts warmly seconded her views. Considering the nature and regulations of the Coast Blockade, almost the only thing that could be done, was to supply the people with Bibles and useful books. In furtherance of this purpose, she applied to the Bible Society, whose liberal response was conveyed in the following letter from one of its Secretaries, Dr. Steinkopff.

Savoy, *July* 12*th*, 1824.

"My Esteemed and Dear Friend,

"I have received your truly kind and affectionate letter this morning, and immediately communicated its contents to the Printing Sub-Committee of the British and Foreign Bible Society, which happened to meet at Earl-street. They have unanimously resolved to transmit fifty Bibles and twenty-five New Testaments to the Brighton Auxiliary, with a request to place them at your disposal, for distribution among the men employed in the Preventive Service. In general, we have found cheap sale preferable to gratuitous distribution, but if, in consideration of all the peculiar cir-

* Now called the "Coast Guard," or "Preventive Service," for the detection of smuggling.

cumstances of the above-mentioned men, you should judge it most desirable to present the copies as a donation to them, you are at liberty so to do."

The distribution of these books was a welcome office to her, to whom it was intrusted; it brought her into agreeable and interesting communication with some of the officers, as well as men, stationed in the neighbourhood of Brighton. Her endeavours to serve them were received with openness, and responded to with the warmth and simplicity of the sailor character. Communications, a few months afterwards, proved that the benefit was likely to be lasting.

After quitting Brighton, Elizabeth Fry passed about two months at Dagenham, a secluded village on the banks of the Thames. The rest and retirement were very beneficial to her health, and she greatly enjoyed the fine air and beautiful scenery that surrounded her. Few persons have evinced a higher relish for the varied productions of nature, or for the quietness of a country life, than she did. During her stay there, she writes :—

Dagenham, Seventh Month, 30th.—We left Brighton last Sixth-day, the 23rd, and after what I passed through in suffering, and afterwards in doing, in various ways, I may acknowledge that I have no adequate expression to convey the gratitude due to my merciful and gracious Lord. I left it, after a stay of nearly ten weeks, with a comparatively healthy body, and above all a remarkably clear and easy mind; with a portion of that overflowing peace, that made all things, natural and spiritual, appear sweet, and in near love and unity, not only with Friends there, but *many, many* others. I felt as if, although an unworthy instrument, my labours there had not been in vain in the Lord, whether in suffering or in doing. It has not been without a good deal of anxiety, fatigue, and discouragement, that this state of sweet peace has been attained as I am apt to suffer so much from many fears and doubts, particularly when in a weak state of health. The District Society, in which I was interested, I left, I trust, in a way for establishment; and likely to be very useful to the poor and to the rich. Also an arrangement to supply the Blockade men on the coast with Bibles and other books: and I hope they will be put in the way of reading them, instead of losing their time. Some of the poor Blockade men seemed much affected by the attention paid them, as also did their officers; and I am ready to hope that a little seed is scattered there. In Meetings, I passed through much, at times going when I feared I should faint from weakness; but I found that help was laid on One who is Mighty, and I may indeed say, in my ministerial services, that out of weakness I was made strong. The Meetings were generally largely attended by those not Friends, of course without invitation, but I trust that they were good ones, and that we were edified together. This was through deep humiliation, and many, many fears. It certainly calls for great care and watchfulness in all things that we enter, to find that they be not of ourselves, but of our Master, whose servants we are; for He alone should point out our work. The end, in an uncommon manner, appeared to crown all.

26th.—I returned from a short expedition to Brighton last evening. A very interesting, and I trust not unimportant one. My object was the District Society that I was enabled to form there, when I was so ill, or rather recovering from that state. Much good appears done, much more likely to be done; a fine arrangement made, if it be but followed up; and I humbly trust that a blessing will attend the work, and has already attended it. I feel that I have not time to relate our interesting history, but I should say that the short time we spent there was a mark of the features of the present day. A poor unworthy woman, nothing extraordinary in point of power, simply seeking to follow a crucified Lord, and to co-operate with His grace in the heart; yet followed after by almost every rank in society, with the greatest openness for any communications of a religious nature; numbers at Meeting of different denominations, also at our own house, noblemen, ladies in numbers, clergy, dissenters, and Friends. We had most satisfactory religious opportunities together, where the power of an endless life appeared to be in great dominion. Our dear Lord and Master himself appearing remarkably to own us together. William Allen was there, a great helper; we were at dear Agatha and Elizabeth Barclay's, whose kindness, love, and sweetness, were abundant towards us. Two of my daughters were with me.

Third Month, 3*rd*, 1825.—I hope I am thankful for being really better, though delicate in health. I wish I did not dread illness so much; it is a real infirmity in me; may grace be granted to overcome it. I think, strange to say, I felt, and I fear appeared to those about me, to be irritable. Certainly, I had some cause to be so; but after what I have known of the power that is able indeed, to help us, I never ought to give way to anything of the kind; all should be meekness, gentleness, and love. Perhaps I said too much about some pictures and various ornaments that have been brought from France for us; much as I love true Christian simplicity, yet if I show a wrong spirit in my desire to maintain it in our house and furniture, I do wrong and harm the best of causes. I far prefer moderation, both from principle and taste, although my experience in life proves two things; first, that it is greatly for the good of the community, to live according to the situation in which we have been placed by a kind Providence, if it be done unto the Lord, and therefore done properly; then, I believe that by so doing we should help others, and not injure ourselves. Second, I have so much seen the extreme importance of occupation, to the well-being of mankind, that many works of art, that tend to our accommodation, and even the gratification of our taste, may be innocently partaken of, may be used and not abused, and kept in their proper places; as by so doing, we encourage that sort of employment that prevents the active powers of man from being spent in things that are evil.

In reference to the foregoing paragraph, and others in this volume that allude to some feeling of irritability of temper, her daughters bear the following testimony:—

"The contrition so frequently expressed in the course of Mrs. Fry's journal, for *irritability of temper*, is calculated to *mislead* a stranger, who would naturally suppose that it must occasionally *have betrayed itself in conduct.* To those who intimately knew the never-failing gentleness, forbearance, and Christian meekness of her deportment, that *such* feelings ever ruffled her mind, is almost *inexplicable.* Those most closely connected with her, in the nearest and most familiar relations of life, can unhesitatingly bear their testimony to the fact, that they *never* saw her in what is called a pet, or heard an angry, or passionate expression of displeasure, pass from her lips. Her tender conscience, and fear of offence towards God and man, can alone account for these outpourings of the hidden evils of her heart."

Yet surely they can scarcely be termed *evils.* Sin does not consist in being *tempted.* The Apostle says, "Blessed is the man who endureth temptation, for when he is tried he shall receive a crown of life." There is abundant evidence that, if a temptation to any feeling of irritability of temper ever presented itself to the mind of this meek servant of Christ, it was resisted and overcome, through His grace. Her husband has recently given to the Compiler a full assurance of this, in the following words:—"I never knew her do an act, and never heard her utter a word, that, in her most solemn moments, she could have wished to recall."

Plashet, Fourth Month, 6th.—The delightful weather and season; the innumerable beauties of nature, now showing themselves, have, I may say, refreshed my soul, and led it to "look through Nature, up to Nature's God." To my mind the outward works of creation are delightful, instructive, and edifying. I am, I hope, thankful for so much capacity to admire and rejoice in them. How important to cultivate this taste in youth! It is an advantage through life, in many ways.

Plashet, Fourth Month, 21st.—My occupations are just now multitudinous. The British Society, and all that is attached to it, Newgate as usual. Forming with much fear, and some misgivings, a Servant's Society, yet with a hope, and something of a trust, that it will be for the good of this class of persons for generations to come. I have felt so much for such, for so many years, that I am willing to sacrifice some strength and time for their sakes. It is, however, with real fear that I do it, because I am sensible of being, at times, pressed beyond my strength of body and mind. But the day is short, and I know not how to reject the work that comes to hand to do.

Plashet, 25th.—I have had some true encouragement in my objects since I last wrote. The British Society Meeting was got through to much satisfaction. To myself, (the poor, humble instrument amongst women in this country,) it is really wonderful what has been accomplished in the prisons during the last few years. How the cause has spread, and what good has been done, how much evil prevented, how much sorrow alleviated, how many plucked like brands from the burning; what a cause for deep thanksgiving, and still deeper humiliation, to have been, in any degree, one of the instruments made use of to bring about these results. I have also received a delightful account of the effects of my labours for the poor at Brighton; it appears that the arrangements made, have greatly prospered amongst both rich and poor; also for the blockade men on the coast. This is cause for fresh thankfulness of heart. I may say, that I there sowed in tears, and I now reap in joy.

The Servants' Society appears gradually opening, as if it would be established according to my desire. No one knows what I go through in forming these Institutions,—it is always in fear.

Fifth Month, 23rd.—I think that I am under the deepest

exercise of mind that I ever experienced, in the prospect of a Meeting to be held this evening, for all the young people assembled at the Yearly Meeting. It is held at my request, my brother Joseph uniting in it. In a remarkable degree it has plunged me into the depths, into real distress; I feel so unfit, so unworthy, so perplexed, so fearful, even so sorrowful, so tempted to mistrustful thoughts, ready to say, "Can such an one be called to such a service?" I do believe that "this is my infirmity;" and I have a humble hope and confidence, that out of this great weakness I shall be made strong. As far as I know it has been in simple obedience to manifested duty, that I gave up to this service, and went through the ordeal of the Yearly Meeting. If I know my own deceitful heart, it has been done in love to my Lord and to His cause. Lord, preserve me through this depth; through this stripping season! If it should please Thee to grant me the garments of Thy salvation, and the help of Thy Spirit, further enable me wholly to give unto Thee the glory, which is due unto Thy name. If thou makest use of Thy handmaid to speak in Thy name, be Thou Thyself her help and her strength, her glory, and the lifter up of her head. Enable her to rely on Thee, on Thy might, and on Thy mercy; to commit her whole cause unto Thee, and keep in the remembrance of Thy handmaid, that the blessed cause of truth and righteousness is not *her's*, but *Thine.*

Plashet, Sixth Month, 2nd—The awful and buffetted state of my mind was, in degree, calmed as the day advanced. I went to town with my beloved brother Joseph, who appeared to have been in something of a similar depth of unusual suffering—we went into the Meeting together; the large Meeting-house was soon so crowded, that no more could get in; I suppose from eighteen hundred to two thousand persons, principally youth. All my children were there, except little Harry. I heard hundreds went away who could not get in. After going in and taking my seat, my mind was soon calmed, and the fear of man greatly, if not quite, taken away. My beloved brother Joseph, bowed the knee, and poured forth prayer for us. I soon after rose and expressed what was on my mind, towards the assembly: First, that all were acceptable who worked righteousness and served the Lord. Secondly, that the mercies of our God should induce this service, as a debt due to him. Thirdly, that it must be done by following a crucified Lord, and faithfully taking up the cross. Fourthly, how important, therefore, to the church generally, and to our religious Society, for us so to do individually, and collectively; so that if this were done, there would be, from amongst that company, those who would be as lights to the world, or as a city set on a hill that cannot be hid; I had to conclude with a desire that an entrance might be abundantly ministered unto them, into the everlasting kingdom of our Lord and Saviour Jesus Christ. I then sat down, but did not feel to have fully relieved my mind. Joseph rose, and stood more than an hour; he preached a very instructive and striking sermon on faith and doctrine. Then, my dear sister Elizabeth Fry, and my uncle Joseph, said something. Afterwards, I knelt down in prayer, and thought I found no common access to the Fountain of all our sure mercies; I was enabled to cast my burden for the youth, and my own beloved offspring amongst the rest, upon Him who is mighty to save and to deliver. I had to ask for a blessing upon our labours of love towards them, and that our deficiencies might be made up; that the blessing of the Most High might rest upon them, from generation to generation, and that cross-bearers and standard-bearers, might not be wanting from amongst them. I felt helped in every way, the very spirit and power appeared near, and when I rose from my knees, I could in faith leave it all to Him, who can alone prosper His own work. A few hints that impressed me I afterwards expressed, which were to encourage the youth in the good works of the present day; but to entreat them, when engaged in them, to maintain the watch, lest they should build up with one hand, and pull down with the other. Secondly, that it was never too soon to begin to serve the Lord, and that there was nothing too small to please Him in. Then, commending them to His grace, and bidding them farewell, the Meeting concluded in a very solemn manner; it lasted about two hours and a half, and general satisfaction appears to have been felt. When it was over, I may say we rejoiced together, I hope, in the Lord; so that my soul did magnify the Lord, and my spirit rejoiced in God my Saviour.

Plashet, 6th.—The death of my dear aunt Gurney, obliges me to go into Norfolk; I therefore set off to day, accompanied by my sister Elizabeth. I propose also attending the Essex Quarterly meeting in going, and the Suffolk in returning. It has been a sacrifice giving up to go, but I desire to do it in simplicity of faith, as unto my Lord; trusting that it will prove for edification and refreshment.

EXTRACT FROM A LETTER TO HER FAMILY AT HOME.

Earlham, *Sixth Month, 11th*, 1825.

I wonder almost that I have not written to you before, but my engagements have been, I think I may say, hourly and constant. On Fifth-day, the funeral, and yesterday, Norwich Monthly Meeting; we dined at the Grove. I have felt a good deal in this visit. The changes that take place in these parts are very affecting. I paid a quiet visit to the grave-yard the other morning, and there sat, first upon my mother's, then my father's, then Priscilla's, and John's graves; and, as you may suppose, wept at their sweet remembrance. I could not but meditate upon the probability of all our heads being, before very long, placed under the "green grass turf." These were my cogitations, and I trust not without some of a higher nature; it is a fearful thing not to be ready, for the change may come very unawares; but I may say, as it respects my own, I have felt an increasing hope that "all will be well."

Plashet, 18th.—I am returned home after attending my dear aunt's funeral, and two Quarterly Meetings. I paid a very interesting visit to Earlham. I have passed through much deep feeling, and been, in various ways, much engaged as a minister, of which service I am wonderfully unworthy; but, out of weakness, I often experience help and strength, to my own admiration.

Since I returned home, a great press of company every day, Lord Bexley and Sophia Vansittart, Lord Suffield, Lord and Lady Torrington, and many others. Lord, grant a little help, quiet and enlighten my heart, that I may see what to do, and what to leave undone, and that which I find to do, enable me to perform in simplicity of faith, unto Thyself, and Thy glory; and, Lord, be pleased to keep Thy very frail and unworthy servant, on the right hand, and on the left, that evil overcome her not.

A storm prevailed in the commercial world, during the latter part of 1825, it subsided as 1826 advanced; but it did not pass away without leaving fearful traces of its course. Many mercantile houses were entirely overthrown; whilst others were so shaken, as never to recover the shock. These things made it a very anxious time to Elizabeth Fry, and called forth much of her sympathy towards the sufferers. In reflecting on this event, she wrote—

The principle of justice cannot be too deeply impressed upon the youthful mind, also, the great uprightness in all money transactions. How do I desire for myself that, however it may be my duty to be occupied about temporal things, my treasure be not in them, but that my heart and soul may be raised above them. This morning, I think I have had a glimpse of those possessions that cannot be shaken by the ups and downs of life.

In reply to a slight request, about that time addressed by Elizabeth Fry to Hannah More, she received this kind reply:—

"My dear Friend,

"Any request of yours, if within my very limited power, cannot fail to be immediately complied with. In your kind note, I wish you had mentioned something of your own health, and that of your family.

"I look back with no small pleasure to the too short visit with which you once indulged me, a repetition of it would be no little gratification to me. Whether Divine Providence may grant it or not, I trust through Him who loved us, and gave himself for us, that we may hereafter meet in that blessed country, where there is neither sin, sorrow, nor separation.

"Believe me, my dear friend, with true esteem and warm affection to remain your's sincerely.

"H. MORE.

"Barley Wood, 15*th of April.*"

Elizabeth Fry entertained a high appreciation of the character of Hannah More, and of the benefits which she had conferred upon her contemporaries, especially upon her country-women. She always referred with great pleasure to her visit to Barley Wood, and the impression made upon her by the mingled sweetness and dignity of Hannah More's countenance and manner.

In a copy of her "Practical Piety," given by Hannah More to Elizabeth Fry, is this inscription:

TO MRS. FRY.

Presented by HANNAH MORE,
As a token of veneration,
Of her heroic zeal,
Christian charity,
And persevering kindness,
To the most forlorn
Of human beings.
They were naked and she
Clothed them;
In prison and she visited them;
Ignorant and she taught them,
For *His* sake,
In *His* name, and by *His* word,
Who went about doing good.

Barley Wood, June 17*th*, 1818.

Dagenham, Eighth Month, 10th.—On Fifth-day, the 4th of this month, my dear eldest son was married. Upon the previous evening, with a few of the family present, I was enabled to commend him to his God, for direction, and for protection; it was a very serious time. The next morning, we all, in our wedding garments, proceeded to London; my beloved husband and myself alone in the chariot, deeply feeling the weight of the occasion. Upon our arrival at the Meeting House, in Westminster, we found the party generally assembled. Soon after our sitting down in the Meeting, there was *that* which quieted our spirits, and said, "Peace, be still." We sat more than half an hour, when dear Rebecca Christy knelt down, and, in a powerful manner, prayed for the young people, that a blessing might be with them; above all, a spiritual blessing; my heart went with her, and I poured forth my tears before the Lord on their account; there was a very solemn feeling over us, a little as if the Master owned the wedding company by His presence. I had to offer fervent petitions for their good, naturally and spiritually, and for grace for them to keep their solemn covenant with each other, and to make fresh covenant with their Lord. We had an elegant and hospitable entertainment afterwards; my dear uncle Barclay was there; he is grandfather to the bride, and great uncle to the bridegroom.

A period of rest and refreshment at Dagenham was preparatory to fresh exertion. Elizabeth Fry again believed it her duty to leave home, and travel into Devonshire and Cornwall, accompanied by her sister-in-law, Elizabeth Fry.

Dagenham, 21st.—Yesterday, we laid our concern before our Monthly Meeting. I believe we had the sympathy, unity, and near love of our Friends, which was really encouraging and comforting. How truly do the living members of the militant church help one another; surely it is well, now and then, to have their feeling for each other excited.

I was enabled in the Meeting, to commend those who go, and those who stay, to the keeping of the unslumbering Shepherd, and found near access to Hím in prayer, being strengthened to cast my care upon Him on whom help is laid. I have felt happier since.

On arriving at Kingsbridge, Elizabeth Fry believed it right to appoint a Meeting; she says—

It has cost me a good deal to give up to it; but I am more comfortable since I have done so; although I feel very unfit for such services. Ah! dearest Lord, anoint us with fresh oil for this service, that it may tend to the exaltation of Thy name, and the unity, edification, comfort and strength of Thy people of every denomination.

Plymouth, Tenth Month, 1st.—I trust that I am thankful to be able to say that the Meeting (at Kingsbridge) was very satisfactory, and to my feelings, brought almost unspeakable peace. I thought we were favoured, in a remarkable manner, to feel sweet unity of spirit, with those present, of various descriptions, and we might say, like the disciples formerly, "Did not our hearts burn within us as He talked with us by the way?" At first, deep poverty of spirit, with many fears on my own account beset me, but as the Meeting advanced, power increased, these were allayed, and we might rejoice in the feeling, that the Lord God Omnipotent reigneth, God over all, blessed for ever.

Liskeard, 8th.—Another week is now past, and much has been gone through. At Plymouth, we attended several Meetings; but one was important to me; it was one that I had appointed at Devonport. I first felt the concern when a girl travelling with my father, I then believed that, if ever I became a minister, I must hold a Meeting there;* and the time now appeared come for it. My attraction was to the

* The concern on behalf of the people at Devonport, was first im pressed on her mind, in the summer of 1798.

lowest and worst classes. It was indeed an act of faith; I have a feeling of unfitness and unworthiness for such services beyond what I can express. The day passed tolerably, I attended two regular Meetings, but, as the time for this Meeting drew near, my heart was ready to fail; fears got hold of me, and almost had dominion over me. On entering the assembly, I hardly dared to look up, when I did, I thought there must be fifteen hundred people present, mostly poor; I may I think say, it was, before it ended, a glorious time; much solemnity prevailed amongst us, the power of the great and good Spirit appearing to reign over all. I cannot help humbly trusting that the fruit will remain. We had an interesting Meeting with the youth, and another the next morning at a wedding; we were much united to many dear friends. We have since visited three Meetings in Cornwall. The beautiful country delights me, when my mind is at liberty.

Sixth Month, 3rd, 1826.—Our Yearly Meeting concluded yesterday. I can hardly express the sweetness of the remembrance of the time. We have, at seasons, I may truly say, rejoiced together in the Lord, and partaken of that, which as evidently comforts and delights the soul, as outward refreshment does the body, when hungry, thirsty, and faint. I have been really refreshed in spirit.

Plashet, Sixth Month, 24th.—(*First day morning.*)—The commencement of this day always feels weighty to me; another week begun, the awful and responsible situation of a minister of the gospel in the services of the day, at home and at Meeting; all weighs upon me. Grant, O Lord! I pray Thee, a little help, that whatever Thy unworthy servant does, in word or in deed, may be done, as in the name, so through the power, of Christ her Saviour. Bless this day, I pray Thee, O Lord! not only to our house and family and to our religious body, but to thousands and tens of thousands; that however outwardly separated, Thy servants may unite in magnifying Thy name, and that their spirits may rejoice in Christ their Saviour.

Dagenham, Seventh Month, 24th.—Yesterday was so very wet and windy, that we spent a quiet First-day here. Serious as it is, not to attend our places of worship, yet it is not without its advantages, to find, that the same worship can be performed in private as in the public assembly; and that it is not the place, or the people, but (if in a right spirit) an acceptable worship may be offered every where. All our family assembled twice in the day, I think to real edification, so that it proved neither dull nor unpleasant, though we were all shut up, for a long day, in this little house.

The return of the season had brought with it the interest of the annual transportation of female convicts. During this year, five ships had been employed for that purpose. A young lady—the daughter of an Admiral—has often recurred to a farewell visit to a female convict-ship, on the point of sailing, in which she accompanied Elizabeth Fry. In allusion to this visit, she says:—

"I could scarcely look upon her as any other than an angel of mercy, calmly passing from one to another of the poor wretched beings around her, with the word of counsel, comfort, or reproof, that seemed suited to each individual case, as it presented itself to her notice. With several kind assistants, she was arranging work for them during the voyage; in itself no trifling matter. But many a point of deepest interest and anxiety, brought to her ready ear, met with such response as could only be looked for from a devoted follower of Him, who 'went about doing good.'"

On the mind of this young person the circumstances was strongly impressed, of accompanying her father, on another occasion, to the female convict-ships, lying off Woolwich, to meet William Wilberforce and Elizabeth Fry.

"On board one of them, between two and three hundred women were assembled, in order to listen to the exhortation and prayers of, perhaps, the two brightest personifications of Christian philanthropy that the age could boast. Scarcely could two voices, even so distinguished for beauty and power, be imagined united in a more touching engagement—as indeed was testified by the breathless attention, the tears, and the suppressed sobs, of the gathered listeners. All of man's word, however there heard, heart-stirring as it was at that time, has faded from my memory; but no lapse of time can ever efface the impression of the 107th Psalm, as read by Mrs. Fry, with such extraordinary emphasis and intonation, that it seemed to make the simple reading a commentary; and, as she passed on from passage to passage, struck my youthful mind, as if the whole series of allusions might have been written by the pen of inspiration, in view of such a scene as was then before us. At an interval of twenty years, it is recalled to me as often as that Psalm is brought to my notice.—Never, in this world, can it be known to how many hearts its solemn appeals were, that day, carried home, by that potent voice."

Elizabeth Fry believed herself called to visit Friends in Ireland, and to attend to some other duties of a more public character. She was accompanied by her brother J. J. Gurney, and her sister E. Fry.

Twelfth Month, 27th.—Last Third-day week, I believed it my duty to lay my concern to visit Ireland, before my Monthly Meeting; at the close of the Meeting for worship. We told our dear friends what we had in view, and, feeling the great weight of leaving my family, made me doubt a little, whether Friends could unite in my going; but for all these things, I think I hardly ever felt a more solemn covering over a Meeting, both before and after we spoke; and a very unusual number expressed their sympathy, unity, and desire to encourage us; not only the elders and ministers, but the very babes in Christ. There was testimony upon testimony. I felt uncommon peace and relief afterwards, as if the thing was right; many expressed a belief that the Lord would be with us, and preserve us, that He would be our shield and exceeding great reward, that He would go before us, and be our rear-guard.

Dear W. Allen believed "that those who stayed by the stuff would partake of the spoil." I never remember feeling the blessing of Christian love, and unity of spirit, more than at this time, and how truly the members of the Christian Church "bear one another's burdens, and so fulfil the law of Christ."

Yesterday, we laid it before our Quarterly Meeting. The certificate having been signed on First-day, to my rejoicing, by all those who I thought might possibly have been somewhat against it, as well as those who I knew heartily united with us. I had, in both the Men and Women's Quarterly Meeting, to express something, particularly to the youth, that, notwithstanding the humiliations and deep baptisms attending it, I considered it an honour and favour that I was unworthy of, to be thus made use of in my Master's service; for I could in deed and in truth testify, that there are no ways like His ways, no service like His service, and no joys to be compared to the joys of His salvation. I also addressed the wives and mothers amongst us, on parting from our women Friends; asking not only their sympathy, but their prayers; as "the prayers of the righteous availeth much:" and not only for me, but in a particular manner for those who stayed behind. To-day my mind feels lightened and peaceful, and I have a confirming hope that this calling is of the Lord, utterly unworthy as I know I am, to do the least thing for such a Master; as for the outward sacrifices attending this step, I count them as nothing, if I may but humbly trust that my most gracious Lord and Master will, through His own power, and His own mercy, keep those who stay, as well as those who go, near to Himself. The pain of leaving my most tenderly beloved family, my comfortable and commodious home, with my delicate bodily frame, is a sacrifice most willingly made by me, if those left do not suffer harm by it. I believe I must go in faith, nothing doubting;

trusting all to Him, who knows the deep, earnest petitions of my heart, for them and for us, and who can work with or without instrumentality.

Extracts from her own letters, furnish not merely the history of her journey, but an account of her natural fears, and her spiritual consolations—the difficulties that appeared before her, and the power by which she was enabled to surmount them.

She was accompanied as far as Melksham by her husband. Thence she proceeded with her brother, J. J. Gurney, by Worcester, Colebrook-dale, &c., to Holyhead; where, joined by her sister, Elizabeth Fry, they sailed for Dublin. There, a great variety of weighty engagements occupied them closely. They inspected several asylums, four jails, the Bridewell, House of Industry, also a Nunnery; formed Prison Committees, had important interviews with persons in authority, visited many Members of our own religious Society, and attended several large Meetings for worship, some of them peculiarly favoured ones.

They pursued their journey, being similarly engaged in many places—particularly in Armagh, and Monaghan,—to Lisburn, where the Quarterly Meeting was held. The concluding Meeting for worship was, she says, "one of the most solemn and striking I ever attended. The good power and anointing distilled as the dew amongst us, to the great refreshment, I believe of all present. May my husband, children, brothers, sisters, and all near and dear to me, partake of this joyous, glorious, full salvation."

The travellers visited a Moravian settlement near Lough Neagh; and afterwards, on their route, the Giant's Causeway. Of this grand specimen of the operations of an Almighty Hand, *designed* doubtless to be *viewed* by intelligent beings, in the spirit of adoration and reverent awe of the Infinitely Wise and Omnipotent Creator, Elizabeth Fry says, in writing to her children,—

Walking over rocks, and at the edge of cliffs, we opened upon this wonderful work of nature; like an unfinished building, formed of stones fitted into each other, being concave and convex, and so rising in pillars of different heights, some with three sides, some as many as nine, of various colours. I am glad we saw it, as a fresh proof of the wonderful and various works of God.

After visiting many other places—being closely occupied at all the principal towns in the same round of services as already described—they reached Waterford on the 12th of Fourth Month. But the great fatigue and exposure to which they had been subjected had caused each of the travellers to become, in the course of their journey, considerably indisposed; but at this time Elizabeth Fry was *seriously ill*, and more than a week's careful nursing was requisite to restore her exhausted frame.

Her brother J. J. G., in a letter to a sister, remarked on this circumstance; "It was no small trial of faith and patience to be detained at Waterford day after day, and there was a considerable flatness in it." For a time the dear invalid had much fever, and it excited no small alarm: but it proved to be of a low intermittent character, and was at length subdued by quinine, so as to admit of their proceeding on the 19th to Clonmel, where the Quarterly Meeting convened on the 21st. Elizabeth Fry, though still very unwell, was able to attend some of the Meetings held on that occasion, and thence to go forward to Dublin to the Yearly Meeting.

After arriving at home, she writes—

The great numbers that followed us, almost wherever we went, was one of those things that I believe was too much for me, no one can tell but those who have been brought into similar circumstances, what it is to feel as I did at such times; often weak and fagged in body, exhausted in mind, having things of importance to direct my attention to, and not less than a multitude around me, each expecting a word, or some mark of attention. For instance, on one occasion a General on one side, a Bishop on the other, and perhaps sixty other persons, all expecting something from me. Visiting Prisons, Lunatic Asylums, and Infirmaries; each institution exciting feeling and requiring judgment. I endeavoured to seek for help from above, and for a quiet mind, and my desire was, that such times should not be lost upon those persons; they ended frequently in religious opportunities, and many came, in consequence, to our Public Meetings; however these things proved too much for me, and tired me more than any part of our service.

There were some, I believe, who feared my exaltation, and if they judged from outward appearances, I do not wonder at it; but a deep conviction of my own unworthiness and infirmity was so living with me, that these things appeared more likely to cast me into the dust, than raise me up on high. We went on thus, from place to place, until we reached Waterford; we had visited Limerick, Cork, and other places. I felt completely sinking, hardly able to hold up my head, and by degrees became seriously ill. Fever came on and ran very high, and I found myself in one of my distressing, faint states; indeed a few hours were most conflicting; I never remember to have known a more painful time; tried without, distressed within, feeling such fears lest my being thus stopped by illness, should try the faith of others, and lest my own faith should fail. My pain too in being from home was great. We were obliged to stop all the Meetings that we had appointed for days to come; however, much as I suffered for a short time, I had most sweet peace afterwards, my blessed Saviour arose with "healing in his wings," delivered me from my fears, poured balm into my wounds, and granted me such a sense of having obtained full reconciliation with my God, as I can hardly describe. All was peace. I no longer hankered after home, but was able to commit myself and those nearest, to this unslumbering, all merciful, and all powerful Shepherd. By degrees I was sufficiently raised up to attend Meetings, visit some prisons, and see many persons, and we concluded our general visit to Ireland, to my relief, peace, and satisfaction. The Yearly Meeting crowned all, as to our ministerial services in our own Society. We left Waterford on the 11th of Fifth Month, after visiting Wicklow and Wexford, at that time remaining at Waterford a few hours only. We entered the steam-packet, slept on board, and left the harbour about three o'clock in the morning.

On arriving at Plashet she writes—

Although far from well, yet able to enjoy the sight of my beloved family and sweet home. I find things going on to my comfort and satisfaction; for this I desire to be humbly thankful.

The week following was much occupied by the interests of London Yearly Meeting.

A dispensation of most afflictive bereavement was now impending over the family circle, in the decease of Rachel Gurney, whose health had long been gradually declining. She had been, for some weeks, at Brighton; her anxious relatives having cherished the hope that a temporary residence there might recruit her enfeebled frame. At that place she was visited by Elizabeth Fry, to whom she had, from early childhood, been united in the tenderest affection. The depth and fidelity of Rachel Gurney's attachment to her sister had, in truth, been "wonderful." Self-sacrificing, considerate, and protecting—most sensitively alive to her interests, her cares, and her joys; but there were distresses approaching, from which this devoted friend and sister could not have shielded her; and the mercy was apparent, when little more than a year had passed by, of Rachel Gurney's having been taken hence, without seeing one, so greatly beloved, borne down by many sorrows.

Whilst engaged in sedulously attending on this precious invalid, the following entry was penned by Elizabeth Fry.

Brighton, Seventh Month, 20th.—When I arrived here, I found my beloved sister Rachel exceedingly ill, with a fresh attack of illness, and no sister with her; so that I was greatly needed, and much as I had feared, that seeing this beloved one in a low and suffering state, would be almost more than I could support, I have been wonderfully shielded, and I trust enabled to be a real help and comfort to her, in a time of deep trouble. This I feel cause for humble and renewed thankfulness, to be able, however feebly, to return the unbounded kindness of one, who has been so much to me. May I continue strengthened in this most interesting engagement, and minister to the spiritual and temporal wants of this tenderly beloved sister.

Plashet, Eighth Month, 2nd.—At Brighton, I had a meeting with the members of the District Society, which was humbling to me, as such exposures always are, more or less, and a real effort of duty; but I desired only to do it as such, and was very much helped to keep my point, and go steadily on with the business, to my satisfaction and I trust to the benefit of the institution; which appears to have done much good to the poor of the place. Nothing of the kind appears to me to effect so much, as forming and helping these public charities, because so many are assisted by them. I understood that this Society last year induced the poor to lay by amongst them, about £2000. Numbers of the distressed had been relieved, and visiting the poor appears to have been blessed, both to the visitors and the visited. I also called at one of the Blockade Service stations, and found that the libraries I had sent to the Coast Guard Stations, after my illness, three years ago, continued to be very useful to the men and their families. Out of deep distress, I formed these institutions, (if I may so call them) little thinking that an illness that appeared to myself, as if it would almost take away all my powers, should be the means of producing good to so many—surely out of weakness I was made strong. May it be a lesson to myself and others to bow under the Mighty hand of God, however mysterious His dispensations may be.

I was enabled to attend to my beloved sister, during the remainder of her stay at Brighton, and then brought her home here; she left us for Earlham, on Second-day, the 30th.

Whilst on her journey home, Rachel Gurney wrote to her sister Fry:—

"The quiet travelling has only been a luxury; both morning and evening have been delightful to me, as to weather and scenery. I have felt soothed and comforted, more than anything else. I am most deeply sensible of the blessing thou hast been made to me; I think it seems to have put me more in the right way of taking, bearing and feeling, my present allotment; above all, I trust it has strengthened me in my *best desires;* and endeavours to walk humbly with my God!"

We return to the journal.

Dagenham, Eighth Month, 15*th*.—My feelings have been much excited, by the very serious account of my beloved sister Rachel, implying a sensible decline of power and health, which touches me in a most tender place. I may say, in the prospect of losing her, that I shall lose the person that has (taking life through) been more to me, than any other mortal, in constant, faithful love, and kindness, and in ministering to all my wants, according to her ability. Oh! gracious Lord! grant her a full reward here, and above all, hereafter; but, I desire to return thanks for her prepared state of soul, (as far as we can judge, one of another), and the many alleviations granted her. If she be taken,—my companion, my friend, near my own age,—I think it will in no common degree, bring death home to my view, and may it lead me to have my heart really more placed on things above, less on things below.

In reference to her husband and children, she makes the following touching remarks:

22nd.—It is hard, very hard, a most difficult matter, to know how to help those, whose welfare and salvation are past expression near to us. We can only go to Him, who is willing and able, not only to hear our prayers on our own account, but on account of those most tenderly beloved; and who does, in His tender mercy, so bear our griefs and carry our sorrows, that our souls can rest on Him. Oh! may I ever have the encouragement of seeing those nearest to me walking closely with God; not doing their own pleasure, or walking in their own ways, but doing His pleasure and walking in His ways. I believe it would bring unspeakable joy, refreshment, and consolation to my soul; and may I never cease to commend them to Him, who can work with or without human instrumentality.

I went on Second-day to Lord Lansdowne (Secretary of State) and the Under-Secretary, T. Spring Rice, on prison matters, and was received with the utmost kindness and attention. The prison cause appears prosperous. On Third-day, I attended the Monthly Meeting, and, much in the cross, with great fear, weakness, and nervousness, I was enabled to minister consolation to others. Peace and refreshment followed to myself, and although trials have since attended me, I feel the sweet balm remain—that balm which heals the wounded heart.

25th.—I am, at times, reminded of these words in Job, chapter xxxiv., 29th verse—"When he giveth quietness, who then can make trouble? and when he hideth his face, who then can behold him? whether it be done against a nation, or against a man only?"

How striking a proof of the truth of the Scriptures, and that of which they testify, is the way in which they speak to our individual experience. Oh, may I dwell nearer to the source of all good, and live in a more devoted, quiet, humble, watchful, dependent and resigned spirit.

Earlham, 30*th*.—On Seventh-day, the 20th, my son John came with an express from town, to say that the accounts from Earlham were so much worse, that it was thought desirable that I should go as quickly as possible to Upton, to fix whether to set off that day or not; this agitated me and brought me very low, but on reading the different letters, and seeking for a quiet mind, I believed that there was no such hurry, and concluded to wait until after Meeting on First-day, and an early dinner with my family, before setting off. I find it very important in such cases as these, not to act upon impetuous feelings, but upon quiet and sober consideration; hurried movements rarely answer to ourselves or others.

We set off, and were favoured with a quiet journey, and a hopeful one, as I could not believe that we should find any very great change had taken place, and so it proved. Our much-loved invalid was certainly sunk, since we were last together, and in many things gone some steps lower; but there appeared to me so strong a vital principle remaining, that I think weeks, rather than days, are likely to be her portion here below. Her mind is in a most favoured state; she appears to feel it wonderful how easy her circumstances are made to her; her fear of death seems to be removed from her, she talks of it with ease, almost pleasure. Last night she said, that she wished not to be in other circumstances than she was, the way in which she had found the fulness of the power was quite beyond her expectation, and even her trials only appeared now to fit her for greater joys. At times her sinkings are great and also her sufferings, but in these states, though naturally low, faith always appears more than sufficient to sustain her, and she receives them only as a part of the present work of preparation. She said they led her to desire to depart; but her wish was, to say from her heart, "Not my will, but Thine be done."

Surely, this is a fresh proof of the wonderful work and power of grace, and Christian redemption—what consolation it brings! and how much we see, even in these times of deep trial, the mercy of a kind Providence, in granting so many mitigations and alleviations. Surely, His tender mercies are over all His works.

I think, I never am brought into contact with many of my beloved brothers and sisters, without a very humbling feeling of my own infirmity, and short-comings; I find them such examples to me, and am ready to say within my heart—though I have come so publicly forward—though I have preached righteousness in the great congregation, what will become of me, and of my house? and where are there amongst us the same fruits of the Spirit?

Passing through many domestic sorrows, and plunged into deep baptisms of spirit, how dark, at times, were the clouds of discouragement that concealed, from her mental view, those rays of "the Sun of righteousness," that had so graciously guided her in her path of devotedness to her God and Saviour! Yet, in all her distresses He was her refuge; and, in His own time, He again arose upon her soul "with healing in His wings," proving Himself her "light" and her "salvation," her "strong Tower" and her "Deliverer."

My merciful father has helped me, cared for me, sustained and provided for me, and in many ways blessed me; but I still see many hidden evils in my heart, and as for my family, fears often get hold of me, and for myself also, lest I should not walk worthy of my high and holy calling. I can only intercede for us all, that, for the sake of Him who came to seek and to save that which was lost, our gracious God would have mercy on us. Oh, dearest Lord! Thou hast granted the petition of Thine handmaid, for her brothers and sisters; she now sees in them, in a great measure, the travail of her soul, and is satisfied. Reject not her prayers, for her husband and children; bring them by any ways, or by any paths, that Thou mayst see meet, but let them also come to the knowledge of the ever-blessed truth, as it is in Jesus, that they may be saved with an everlasting salvation. And oh, gracious Lord, be with Thy poor servant to the end; and through the continued extension of Thy grace, Thy help, and Thy mercy, let nothing ever be permitted to separate her soul from Thy love in Christ Jesus, her beloved Lord, and all-sufficient Saviour.

We pause to contemplate her affecting petition on behalf of her husband and children. "By any ways, or by any paths, that Thou mayst see meet; but let them come to the knowledge of the ever blessed truth as it is in Jesus."

The eternal well-being of every immortal spirit, was, in her view, a subject of infinite importance; in comparison with which, all temporal considerations were lighter than the small dust in the balance. Who then can estimate the unutterable anxiety of her soul, that these most tenderly beloved objects of her conjugal and maternal affection, might yield to the visitations of a Redeemer's love, and become "heirs of salvation?" She had cherished an intense desire that her children might, from conviction, become "Friends,"—that they might be brought to a *saving* knowledge of the truth, under that form of Christian communion, which had been so eminently blessed to herself, and that they might adhere to the principles which, from having *experimentally* found their inestimable value, she had earnestly laboured to implant and enforce. Deep was her grief when she perceived that, as years added to their mental and physical growth, they appeared less inclined to walk in that path in which she had found the "pearl of great price."

There was, amongst her brothers and sisters, much of the fruit of the Spirit, in dedication of heart and labours of Christian love,—produced, in some of them, under an administration of religious truth differing from her own. It is probable that an association with these excellent persons might tend to strengthen the predilections of some of her own family, and to encourage their eventually becoming detached from the

Society in which they had been educated. There was, however, other influence, which yet more powerfully led them from "Friends;" an influence which Elizabeth Fry watchfully endeavoured to counteract, but which was not within her power to control; and many were the sorrows which she had to endure from the diversity, in the modes of worship and practice, consequent on her children becoming thus separated from her: but these sorrows did not abate her strong parental affection, or her solicitude that each might be brought unto Christ. In the deep fervour of her soul, her prayers were continually poured forth that those most dear to her—her husband and her children—might be made the blessed partakers of the rest that Jesus gives.

Her journal proceeds—

Earlham, Ninth Month, 2nd, First-day.—My sisters Catherine, Rachel, Richenda and I have had a very remarkable morning. I thought it better to stay at home from Meeting, to be with my beloved, suffering sister. I had a desire for some religious time with her. After she was dressed and removed into the dressing-room on her couch, we read in the Bible; but so overcome was she, from weakness and sleepiness, that she could not keep awake; however, we went on, till I knelt down in prayer and thanksgiving for her and us; this appeared more than to revive her; she prayed beautifully and powerfully for us then present, for all her sisters, for my children, and for me and my dearest husband. Afterwards, she sent a particular message to some of the absent, her "dear love, and that they should be told, what a rich blessing she had found there was in seeking, *first*, the kingdom of God and his righteousness." The consoling effect of this time lasted for many hours, so that our beloved invalid remained in a delightful state all day.

10*th*.—My beloved sister appeared much sunk last evening, but awoke early, greatly refreshed, quite clear, and even very bright in her mind, and relieved from suffering.

In the night I went to her, and seemed unable to endure witnessing her conflicts of body; but to my help and consolation, I found her thus relieved this morning. So it is, things too hard for us are not permitted; and my humble trust is, that as trials come, so strength will be given to endure them. My strong confidence for my beloved sister is, that for her, way will, in tender mercy, be made "through the valley of the shadow of death," and support granted to us also; though from the weakness of the flesh, fears, at times, overwhelm me on this subject. On seeing her so comfortable, I said to her, "brooks are granted us by the way;" she replied, "yes, and more of them the nearer we approach the journey's end."

Her brother, J. J. Gurney, wrote of their beloved dying sister. "On ——'s throwing out a hint respecting the 'Sacrament,' she disclaimed any wish or intention to partake in that ceremony; acknowledged that, in days past, she had received benefit from the services of the Church of England, but that she was now feeding exclusively on the substance, and did, indeed, eat the flesh and drink the blood of the Son of man. I am truly thankful for her being brought to this experience. Indeed, her abstraction from all dependence on human help is wonderful."

15th.—Sitting opposite to my most beloved sister in the blue-room:—She appears to be gradually sinking into death, and may we not humbly trust, and confidently believe, into the arms of her God and Saviour. Grant Lord, I pray Thee, if consistent with Thy holy and blessed will, that she may fall asleep in Thee, and that no painful struggles may attend her change; that quietly and imperceptibly she may cast off this mortal tabernacle, (having already testified to us her faith and her hope,) and be landed on the other side of Jordan, awaking to joy and glory unspeakable. And do Thou, Oh Lord! sustain us also, in this time of trial, and enable us in our low estate, to rejoice in Thee, our God and our Saviour, who yet giveth the victory over death, hell, and the grave.

I have been alone, and quiet a little while, and I find in this awful time, that "help is laid on One who is mighty;" for that, which ever since I came to an age of understanding, has appeared almost impossible to bear, even the loss of *this* sister, who has been like "flesh of my flesh, and bone of my bone," *now* I am enabled to receive, and bow under the dispensation with peace. I believe that she has done her work, and that we have nearly finished our work for her; but, is there not an all-sufficient Helper near, who is holding up her head above the waves of Jordan, that they overwhelm her not!

17*th.*—About three o'clock this morning, our most tenderly-beloved sister departed this life. Late in the evening she fell asleep, from which sleep she never appeared to awake. They came to let me know, about twelve o'clock, how she was going on; but, at first, I felt unequal to going to her, and she did not want me; but, gradually, I found my tribulated, tossed spirit, calmed, animated, and strengthened, so that I joined the company round her bed, where I remained until the solemn close. We sat some time in deep silence; then I knelt down, and asked that mourning and lamentation might not be the garment of our spirits, but thanksgiving, inasmuch as the warfare was accomplished, the conflict over, and, through the unmerited mercy of God, in Christ Jesus, an entrance was granted through the gates of the City, whose walls are salvation and whose gates are praise. Then I prayed for ourselves, that the loss of such a sister, who had, in so remarkable a manner, ministered to some of our necessities, might be made up to us by an increased portion of *spiritual* blessings, and that her various labours of love, to us and to our children, might receive such a blessing, as to produce an increase to our lasting good. After returning to bed, natural weakness much overcame me; the death of the body, and its terrors, got hold of me, and the heavenly Inheritance appeared hidden from my view, for a time. To-day, I feel able to partake of the repose now granted us, in no longer having to travel through "the valley of the shadow of death," with one so beloved; and, in a measure, to partake of her rest, as I believe I did, in no common manner, of her sufferings, as if one with her in them.

19*th.*—Blue-room—with my beloved sister's remains. All quietness, rest in comparison—over my own mind a solemn feeling of peace, and this truth impressed upon me, "There is a rest for the people of God." Several important lessons, I think, I have learnt by attending this most beloved sister. 1st, That persons are apt to dwell more on the means of grace, about which they differ, than its simple, pure operation, leading out of evil into good. This I have long believed; but, seeing one who united, as she did with the good in all, and could hardly be said to be of any sect or body of Christians, so grounded in the Christian life and practice, proves experimentally, that being united fully to any set of people, is not essential, and all minor points of difference of comparatively little value. 2ndly, I learn to trust more, and be less afraid. She, like myself, was liable to many fears, particularly in her nervous sinking states—how little cause had she for these fears, and how were the things that she most dreaded remarkably averted; also, That the last part of a death illness gradually appears to diminish, rather than increase, in conflict, as with natural life and power, sensibility to suffering lessens. In short, the lesson taught us is, to seek to serve and follow our Lord, and He will be with us, and make a way for us, even to the end. 3rdly, That in passing through life, patience should have its perfect work, that we should seek for a more willing mind to suffer, as well as to do, the will of God, looking for daily help in this respect; above all, that we should endeavour, in all things, for an upright, circumspect walk before the Lord, speaking the truth in love; that we should seek after full understanding of, and reliance on, the work of salvation through Christ, and obtain (if possible) more knowledge of the Scriptures, and a better acquaintance with religious books.

The remains of Rachel Gurney were interred in "Friends" Burial Ground at Norwich, on the 23rd. It was a solemn and favoured time—Elizabeth Fry ministered to the assembly with much power.

On the 24th, she went to Lynn, and the following evening wrote to announce the birth of a little grandson, thus rapidly passing from the last, to the first scene in "man's eventful history." She had been anxious to come to her child, and yet could scarcely leave Earlham sooner. To her family at home she says, "I cannot but thank a kind Providence for bringing me here in the needful time, and thus guiding my steps aright."

Plashet, First Month, 3rd, 1828.—This year commenced with many interests. On the morning of the new year, we assembled almost all our large household, and many guests, principally young people. Before we began reading, I mentioned some of the striking marks of Providential care and mercy shown to us during the last year. We then read, and afterwards had a solemn time, in which I returned thanks "for mercies past, and humbly craved for more." My dearest brother Joseph joined us, and under a serious, yet cheerful influence, our large party sat down to breakfast. This is often to me a most agreeable time of the day, after the repose of the night, and often some spiritual refreshment in our readings. I can hardly say how much I enjoy my family circle, and thankfully receive the blessings conferred on us.

31*st.*—During this month, my beloved family, husband and children, have occupied most of my time and attention. . . . In our own Society, I have had one important call to Birmingham, to attend a funeral; a very serious and weighty occasion it proved; numbers of the children and grand-children of the deceased, of various descriptions, were present. There was a crowded Meeting, and few ministers, so that the weight of the service appeared to devolve on me, there, and at the house. The help granted me was marvellous in my eyes; and I was enabled, at these different times, to preach the glad tidings, the liberty and the peace of the gospel of Christ. So it is, out of weakness, we are, when dependent on our Lord alone, made strong, and fear is removed in the most remarkable manner—my dearest brother Samuel accompanied me—who has such brothers as I have, to help in the needful time? I think, as it respects the ministry, I am never so much helped as when without other ministers to look to, my dependence being then singly on my Lord, and on His anointing. I yesterday went to see one of my sons at school, and attended Epping Meeting, which I thought a satisfactory time. I tried to make my visit pleasant to all the boys, by taking them a walk, and giving them oranges; I like that the instruments, who communicate religious instruction to the young, should be pleasant to them. I have had interesting, and encouraging communications from Ireland; as if in some parts particularly, our labours there had not been in vain. I have been to see my sister Hoare, and have felt the value of the near union between us; my dearest sister Rachel is often present with me, the way in which I have been enabled to support this inexpressible loss, is surprising to myself; surely it is only the tender mercy of my God, that has thus healed my wound, and upheld me under it. Indeed, at the close of this month, I may raise up a fresh Ebenezer, and say—the Lord be magnified, for His loving-kindness to me, His poor unworthy, yet dependent one! Oh! may He see meet to keep me in the way that I should go, and preserve me from right hand, and from left hand errors.

Second Month, 2nd.—Yesterday, was a full day, and one humbling in its effect. In the first place, I earnestly desired preservation, that I might keep my eye single to God, and not bow to man in spirit. I then went to town, and to Newgate, under a feeling of rather deep concern, where I unexpectedly found numbers of persons ; a magistrate, foreigners, a Jew, a clergyman, many ladies, some Friends, and my brother Samuel. Before I began to read, I, in secret, asked for preservation, at least it was my earnest desire to have my eye kept single to my God. But either the fear of man got too much hold of me, or the "unction" was not with me, for I did not feel the power of Truth over us, as it very often has been at such times. I am ready to believe, that if I had not looked at man, but dwelt yet deeper in spirit, I should have openly called upon the Lord, and should have found help and power in so doing. I went away humbled. I then went with my beloved brother Samuel to the Bishop of London, to talk to him about religious services with prisoners, to inform him of our situation respecting it in Newgate, and the extreme care necessary in the appointment of chaplains for gaols; also to speak to him of the state of our parish. I spoke, I trust, to the point, and that good, and not harm, will result from the visit; but I always fear, after such times, lest I should have said too much. We then made a call, where I pretty boldly spoke my opinions of theatres and public places; and in reply to the question, *How I went on, in reforming the world?* I replied that my zeal was strong, in my declining years, to do what little I could towards reforming things. Afterwards I feared that I might have said too much. We went to the Secretary of State's Office, and saw the Under-Secretary; there again, I had to speak my mind fully on many things, prisons especially.

Now during this day, my services were numerous—some of an important nature, and such as might by some persons be supposed exalting, to be admitted, although a woman, to represent things of consequence to persons of influence and power, and to be received as I am by them; but He who searcheth the heart, only knows my humiliation, and how, in these services, fears for myself get hold of me, lest I should bow to man, and not to God; lest any thing but the simple object of promoting "the thing that is good," should influence me. This I certainly know, that such engagements often bring me into deep exercise of spirit before the Lord, that I may be kept, as a clean instrument ready for His service, and not become contaminated by the spirit of self, nor the spirit of the world. Truly, my desire is, to walk humbly, faithfully, circumspectly, before my God in the first place, and, secondly, before my fellow-mortals; but ever, and in all things, to seek to serve my Lord, doing His will and His pleasure, before serving myself or others, or doing my own will or the will of man. Lord, continue to be my help, my strength, my glory, and the lifter up of my head; and if consistent with Thy holy will, bless my labours and the labours of others, in these works of charity, and keep us, the unworthy instruments employed in them, so as to be fitted to perform them, or any other service Thou mayst see fit to call us into. Amen.

Third Month, 5th.—May I not say to Him, who seeth in secret, Thou hast known my soul in adversity! but amidst these dispensations, is not the "Lord known by the judgment which he executeth?" What peace, what blessing, what fulness of help and consolation, have I also experienced. How have gospel truths opened gradually on my view, the height, the depth, the length, the breadth, of the love of God in Christ Jesus, to my unspeakable help and consolation.

27th.—On Second-day, I attended the select Quarterly Meeting, and was appointed representative to the Yearly Meeting. The next day the Meetings were satisfactory. How striking to me, and how humbling—here am I, that used to be one of the last, least, and lowest in this Quarterly Meeting, now obliged to be one of its foremost members in the Meetings of Discipline; partly from so many vacant places being left amongst us, partly from my long experience of its ways, and many years in its service; and last of all, truly, deeply unworthy as I am, because it has pleased a kind Providence to grant me the unity of my beloved friends, and thus to raise me up. My spirit, notwithstanding my outward cheerfulness, was much bowed down within me, in earnest cravings to be washed, renewed, and more fitted for my Master's service.

In the Fourth Month, Elizabeth Fry accompanied her husband on a short journey. To visit some meetings of Friends, and several Prisons formed her chief inducement, but she also was glad to avail herself of the change of scene and travelling for some of her family.

She writes to her children:—

From Matlock, *Fourth Month, 19th*, 1828.

The beauties of this delightful place, even amidst pouring rain, are such, as to make me long to have you all around us, to admire them. I am sitting in a bower window; a sweet little garden, cut out of the side of a high hill on one side, a deep valley on the other, the river Derwent at the bottom, full with the late rains, flowing over rocks; and very high rocky hills, covered with trees, beyond. We feel the comfort of quiet and rest the more, because we have had such a very full time, almost as much so as in Ireland. At Leicester, Nottingham, and Derby—Meetings, Prisons, Friends, other people, forming Prison Associations, and various engagements. My dear brother Joseph and I went forward to attend the Quarterly Meeting at Nottingham, which we were favoured to get well through. We then proceeded to visit three Prisons and a Lunatic Asylum.

From Uttoxeter, *Fourth Month, 21st.*

Yesterday was very interesting. We went eleven miles to sit at Meeting with some persons of the lower class, in a stocking-weaver's room; a very striking scene it was, and very pleasant afterwards to see these poor people. Two Friends sitting, during the Meeting, on the stocking-loom for want of chairs, and we believed that those chairs we had, were lent by the neighbours to help the party out. It is a very remarkable case—a poor man, a wheelwright, in a little out-of-the-way place called Cowhouse Lane, about ten miles from Matlock, became convinced of the principles of Friends at a public meeting, and it has spread to several of his neighbours, who sit down in silence together on First-days. We were all much pleased and interested by them. We returned to Matlock about four o'clock, and spent a quiet, pleasant evening.

Plashet, Fifth Month, 7th,—I am once more settled at home; after a journey to Lynn, and into the midland counties. In the course of it, I visited thirteen prisons, also some Meetings; often to my wonder, that so unworthy an instrument should be so honourably made use of, to minister to the spiritual state of others, and to visit, and be the means of assisting, so many in prison, and in bonds. Surely the hand of Providence is in some of these things, small and great! It was strikingly manifested in many instances on this journey; I was enabled to form three new Committees for visiting prisons, and to re-organise others, in a way that I hope will prove useful. Where my lot was cast among Friends, I also found the best help to be near. I attended the Derby and Nottingham Quarterly Meeting, as well as several other Meetings, and met my dearest brother Joseph at Leicester, where I was enabled to assist him in the needful time; it appeared almost providential. I walked into the Meeting where he was at Leicester; he did not expect me, neither did I know he was in that town. He appeared greatly in need of help, being fatigued and very unwell. Since my return home, the British Society Meeting has much occupied my attention. It was on the last day of last month; it was a very numerous assemblage of ladies, many of them of high rank. I had much to do in it from time to time, when the different reports were read; I explained a little, and at other times poured forth much of my mind on the subject. However, I went away low and humbled at the conspicuous part I had to take, not doubting that it would bring me into evil report, as well as good report. The general impression I hear was satisfactory, and I trust good was done: but I may set my seal to this—that public services are fearful services, and none but those engaged in them, know how much those are spared who do good privately. Still, if the Master calls us into public duties, it is not only well, but honourable, and in them much more good is accomplished, because so many are concerned; still, I would have no one seek for them, but if rightly brought into them, preservation will, I believe, be granted. A watchful, humble spirit is called for; one that is not exalted by the undue approbation of fellow-mortals, nor too much cast down by disapprobation or evil reports. There must also be willingness to commit all these works to Him, who can prosper them or not, according to His own good pleasure.

Plashet, Fifth Month, 12th.—Last Sixth-day, we had a very interesting visit to Newgate. Numbers were there; clergy, some of the nobility, the sheriff, many ladies, gentlemen, and Friends. It was a solemn time; the fear of man much taken away. After the reading, I had to speak to them, and pray for them. I have, of late, been surrounded by my family, and deep cravings of spirit have been my portion for them. Through all, I have, at times, almost panted for a surer and better resting-place, more particularly where there will be no more sin, or responsibility. I see much to enjoy here; but the temptations that are in this world, at times make me feel, if not weary of it, at least longing for a Heavenly inheritance; although the fear of the passage to it always makes me flinch from this great change, as well as the knowledge of my unutterable unworthiness.

Since I last wrote my journal, death has been brought closely home to me. I was unexpectedly called to attend my dear Aunt C——, in a violent illness, which ended in her death. I went to her on Seventh-day, and for some hours every day afterwards, and one night till she died. I fully believe her state was a blessed one, and that in her trial she knew the Rock to be her stay. Still, as far as I can judge from observation, death is, even to the righteous, an awful conflict, generally attended with distress of body, reduction of spirits, some obscurity of mind, and great difficulty in communicating to others, either the wants or the feelings. My aunt seemed, in her distress, to depend much upon me; I appeared to be a comfort to her, and was enabled, in measure, to minister to her bodily and spiritual wants. The day after all was over, and after having had a very solemn time with the family, I became ill myself; much as I had been at Waterford, hardly able to hold up my head, or go on my way. On Sixth-day I was worse. It was a sudden unexpected loss of strength, being brought down as to the ground, when I was anticipating, with no common degree of pleasure, the Yearly Meeting, and, after it, my child's wedding, looking for rather prosperous days. As usual in my illnesses, I was greatly cast down at times, and wonderfully reduced in a short time. In the midst of my conflict and distress, I still thought I could see the hand of God in it, to keep me low; may it be at *His footstool.* I abounded also with outward comforts and mitigations. My husband, my sister Buxton, my children, my sister Elizabeth Fry devoted to me, I wanted no outward thing; but was plunged under a deep feeling of my infirmity, and great unworthiness before God. I am now much relieved, very thankful, full of love, may I not say to all; sweetly in unity with my beloved Friends at the Yearly Meeting; in degree overflowing towards them all, still abundantly sensible of my unworthiness before the Lord. Oh! may he see meet further to fit me, to suffer as well as to do His will.

20th.—I think I am better, but am remarkably reduced for so short an illness. If during such times of trial, or in the end,—I am supported, the whole glory must be given to God; for I think it impossible for any one to be more naturally distressed or overset by bodily illness. Even if my sun sets under a cloud, all must be laid to my great natural infirmity in this respect. With God all things are possible, but if He should see meet, at that awful hour, to hide Himself from me, may none be discouraged; but all look upon it as a dispen. sation permitted, in some way for good. In times of health, also, at times, in sickness, I have had to rejoice in His salvation, and frequently, when most favoured with clearness of judgment, have perceived the wisdom and mercy of all His dispensations, particularly some of these afflictive ones. Why he saw meet to permit sin to come into the world is not for us, poor, frail, finite mortals, to comprehend; but that we have an enemy to buffet us, I cannot doubt. May we look to that blessed day, when God shall be "all in all," and shall "put all enemies under His feet," even Death itself. Dearest Lord, increase my faith more firmly, more fixedly establish me upon the Rock of Ages; that however the winds blow, the rains descend, or the floods beat against me, I may not be greatly moved; and let not any of the hindering or polluting things of this world lessen my love to Thee and to Thy cause; or prevent me from going steadily forward in heights and in depths, in riches and in poverty, in strength and in weakness, in sickness and in health; or prevent my following hard after Thee in spirit, with a humble, faithful, watchful, circumspect, and devoted heart. Amen.

At this time her daughter Richenda was married to Foster Reynolds. Two days after this event, she writes in her journal:—

The day before yesterday the wedding was accomplished. The Meeting was solemn and satisfactory. Our bride and bridegroom spoke well, and with feeling. My dearest brother

Joseph prayed for them and ministered to them, as did others; I prayed at the close of the Meeting most earnestly for them, for the other young people, and ourselves further advanced in life. After a short, solemn silence, the certificate was read and signed. In the morning we had a satisfactory reading with our children.

Thanks be to our Heavenly Father, there was, I think, throughout the day a great mixture of real solemnity with true cheerfulness. It was certainly no common day. Through everything, order, quietness, and cheerfulness were remarkably maintained. After dinner I returned thanks for our many blessings, and could, with a few present, feel how many outward deliverances we had experienced; that we had had our heads kept above the waters, spiritually and temporally, and were able to have such a day of rejoicing. Our dear bride and bridegroom left us in the afternoon. The evening was fine, and our lawn looked really beautiful, covered with the large and interesting party. In the evening we assembled together, and had a solemn religious time; giving, I trust, the praise that was due alone to Him, from whom all good and blessings flow.

It was remarkable that, during this cheerful evening, one of Elizabeth Fry's daughters alluded, in conversation with her mother, to the prosperity that surrounded them, to which Elizabeth Fry returned this striking reply;—"but I have remarked that when great outward prosperity is granted, it is often permitted to precede great trials." There is an old rhyme which says,

"When joy seemeth highest
Then sorrow is nighest!"

Surely this was verified, in the contrast between that day, and the events which so shortly followed.

Plashet, Eleventh Month, 4th.—I have been favoured to partake of very sweet feelings of peace, and refreshment of soul,—that which I am ready to believe, in the most unmerited mercy, is something of the "Well of water springing up unto eternal life." But I find outwardly, and about me, there are *storms;* not, at present, so much in my very own borders, as close to them.

5th.—The storm has now entered my own borders—once more we are brought into perplexity and trial—but I have this consolation, "He will regard the prayer of the destitute, and not despise their prayer." To whom can I go in this time of emergency, but to Him who hitherto has helped me, and provided for me and mine in a marvellous manner—made darkness light before me, and crooked things straight? Lord! Thou who remainest to be the God of my life, above all things, in this our sorrow and perplexity, cast us not out of Thy presence, and take not Thy Holy Spirit from us; keep us from evil and from the appearance of it, that through the help of Thy Spirit our conduct may be kept upright, circumspect, and clean in Thy sight, and amongst men! that, in all things, at all times, and under all circumstances, we may show forth Thy praise. Keep us in love and unity with those with whom we have to act, even if they do contrary to our wishes and judgment. But, oh, dearest Lord, if it be Thy holy will, make a way of escape for us, from the calamity we so much dread, and continue in Thy unmerited mercy to provide for Thy unworthy servant, her family and all concerned in this trial, that we may not want what is good and needful for us, and that others may be kept from suffering through us. If it be possible remove this bitter cup from us; yet, if it be Thy will that we drink it, enable us, through the grace and spirit of Him who suffered for us, to drink it without repining,—yet trusting in Thy love, Thy mercy, and Thy judgment.

It was not, at this time, the will of God to remove "the bitter cup" from His servant, but rather to grant strength and grace to drink of it, as coming from His holy hand.

The failure of one of the houses of business, in which her husband was a partner, though not that which he personally conducted, involved Elizabeth Fry and her family in a train of sorrows and perplexities, which tinged the remaining years of her life. Nature staggered beneath the blow—but the staff on which she leaned could not fail her, and she fell not.

Eleventh Month, 25th.—I have been brought at times, into little short of anguish of spirit; not I think so much for what we must suffer ourselves, as for what others may suffer. The whole thing appears fraught with distress. When I look at this mysterious dispensation, permitted by Almighty wisdom, I am ready to say, How is it, Lord, Thou dealest thus with Thy servant, who loves Thee, trusts in Thee, and fears thy name?—and then, I say this is my infirmity, thus to query. Need I not chastisement? Do I not deserve it? May it not be a mysterious dispensation of deep and sore affliction, laid not only upon us, but upon others, to draw us all more from the things of time, and to set us more on the enduring riches of Eternity. I cannot reason upon it, I must bow, and only bow, and say in my heart, which I believe I do, "Not as I will, but as Thou wilt." Well, if it be of the Lord, let Him do as seemeth Him good. Lord, let Thy grace be found sufficient for us, in this most awful time; and grant that we faint not when Thou rebukest us!

On the following First-day, the question was much debated, as to whether she, and her family generally, should attend their Meeting for worship, or not; but *she* was firmly decided that it was right to go, and of course she was accompanied by her husband and children. She took her usual seat, bowed down and overwhelmed, with the bitter tears rolling down her cheeks—no common thing with her.

After a very solemn pause, she rose with these words, her voice trembling with emotion; "Though He slay me, yet will I trust in Him;" and testified, in a few beautiful and impressive sentences, that her faith and love were as strong in the hour of adversity, as they had been in the time of prosperity. Her friends were deeply instructed and affected, marking, by their manner, and by their tears, their tender sympathy and love.

To her only absent child she wrote, on the 27th of Eleventh Month—

I do not like to pour out my sorrows too heavily upon thee, nor do I like to keep thee in the dark, as to our real state. This is, I consider, one of the deepest trials to which we are liable; its perplexities are so great and numerous, its mortifications and humiliations so abounding, and its sorrows so deep. None can tell, but those who have passed through it, the anguish of heart at times felt; but thanks be to our God, this extreme state of distress has not been very frequent, nor its continuance very long. I frequently find my mind, in degree, *sheathed* to the deep sorrows, and am enabled not to look so much at them—but there are also times, when secondary things arise—parting with servants, the poor around us, schools and our dear Place. These things overwhelm me; indeed I think, *naturally*, I have a very acute sense of the sorrow. Then, the bright side of the picture rises. I have found such help and strength in prayer to God; and highly mysterious as, in some points of view, this dispensation may be, yet I think I have frequently, if not generally, come to be able to say, "Not as I will, but as Thou wilt," and to bow under it. All our children, and children-in-law, my brothers and sisters, our many friends and servants, have been a strong consolation to me; and above all, a little refreshment to my tribulated spirit has been granted me at times, from what I trust are the well-springs from on High.

To Her Sister, Buxton.

Plashet, *Twelfth Month, 2nd.*

My dearest Hannah,

I have received your valuable and excellent letters; and the advice, as well as consolation in them, I trust will do us all good. My desire is, that we may entirely, and altogether, bow under our circumstances and the various pains attached to them. I feel with thee, and have felt all along, that a still greater pain and trial might, in many ways, have been permitted us; but one of its deepest stings is from the peculiar and perplexing nature of it. It abounds with temptation, as my dear friend, Mary S——, so deeply felt under similar circumstances; but there is a power that can preserve amidst them all, and in this power I trust. I see that I have many blessings left, and do earnestly desire to estimate them as I ought. Your very kind offer for Hannah, I do not at present think it right to accept; I think it better for her to drink the cup with us for a time, but I may be glad, before long, gratefully to accept it. I feel all your kindness, and trust I shall never be a burden to any of you. I expect our way will open—we must commit it in faith.

The tide of sympathy flowed in from all quarters. Many letters conveying the expression of most deep and tender interest in her afflictions, were now received by Elizabeth Fry, not only from near connections, intimate friends, and members of her own religious community, but also from individuals of every class, whose hearts had been impressed by her piety and benevolence—from distinguished nobles and senators, and from persons of the humblest walks of life.

Whilst this precious servant of God was thus passing through the furnace of adversity, the Compiler of this volume was privileged to belong to the Meeting (that of Gracechurch-street) which, when her state of health permitted, Elizabeth Fry constantly attended. The opportunities of public worship, as well as many of a more private character, at which this afflicted handmaid of the Lord was united in worship with her endeared friends, were often favoured with a solemnity, of which, perhaps, no adequate idea could be conveyed in words; and the offerings in prayer, as well as, at seasons, of devout thanksgiving, which she was enabled to dedicate to her Almighty Sustainer, were accompanied by a heavenly power and unction, that cannot, even now, be remembered without a reverent and affecting sense of that mercy and Fatherly loving-kindness, which thus strengthened her to glorify God in this furnace of adversity. The sweetness of her disposition, and the remarkable wisdom with which she was endowed, shone, in this time of trial, with increased brightness. She had a quality, difficult to describe, but marked to those who knew her well, the power of rapidly, and by a process of thought that she could herself hardly have explained, arriving at the truth, striking the balance, and finding the just weight of a doubtful question; no natural gift could be more valuable than this, under such circumstances.

Joseph and Elizabeth Fry resolved upon, at once, leaving Plashet, and seeking a temporary home in Mildred's Court, then the residence of their eldest son. One great mitigation attended this calamity, that the mercantile business, formerly their grandfather's, and conducted by their father, remained to the young men of the family, who were enabled, by the important assistance of their mother's brothers, to carry it on, and, by this means, aided by their uncles, to re-establish their parents in comparative comfort. With quitting Plashet came much that was sad—uprooting habits, long-formed tastes and local associations, parting with servants, and leaving many old pensioners and dependants.

Elizabeth Fry had, for many years, displayed singular wisdom and economy in her household arrangements, as well as in her charities and benevolent objects, varying according to the circumstances in which she had been placed. To "be just before generous," was a maxim often expressed to those around her. On this occasion, these powers were called into full action.

From some circumstances, connected with the impartial exercise of the discipline amongst Friends, her husband and children allowed their attachment to their own religious society to become weakened.

As the winter advanced, her health greatly failed. Truly the sorrows of her heart were enlarged. She exclaims in her journal, (which was very irregularly kept,) that her "soul was bowed down within her, and her eyes were red with weeping." In addition to domestic trials, her tender feelings were at times grievously and unnecessarily wounded, and, from without, there was much of bitterness infused into her daily cup, which can only be appreciated by those, who have had to endure a similar calamity; but the meekness and resignation of her spirit are evident from her entries in her journal.

Plashet, Twelfth Month, 16th.—I have had some quiet peaceful hours, but I continue in the low valley, and naturally feel, too much, leaving this sweet home, but not being well makes my spirits more weak than usual. I desire not only to be resigned, but cheerfully willing to give up whatever is required of me, and, in all things, patiently to submit to the will of God, and to estimate my many remaining blessings. I am sorry to find how much I cleave to some earthly things —health, ease, places, possessions. Lord, Thou alone canst enable me to estimate them justly, and to keep them in their right places. In thine own way, dearest Lord, accomplish Thine own work in me, to Thine own praise! grant that, out of weakness I may yet be made strong, and through Thy power, wax valiant in fight; and may I yet, if consistent with Thy holy will, see the travail of my soul, and be satisfied, as it respects myself and my most tenderly beloved family. Amen!

Mildred's Court, First Month, 19th, 1829.—My first journal in this year! What an eventful one was the last! prosperity and adversity were peculiarly our portion. It has been, in no common degree, a picture of life comprised in a small compass. However, through all, in prosperity and in adversity, however bright, or cloudy, my present position or my prospects may be, my desire for myself, and all whom I love is this, so strongly expressed by the Psalmist, "I will hope continually, and will yet praise Thee more and more!" So be it, saith my soul, and if it be the Lord's will, may light rise in our present obscurity, and our darkness become as the noonday, both as to temporal and spiritual prospects!

The deep discouragement passed through by Elizabeth Fry at this period, is evidenced by the following letter from her kind and faithful friend, Wm. Wilberforce, to whom it would appear, by the reply, that she had expressed some doubts of the propriety of resuming her labours in the prisons.

"Highwood Hill, Middlesex, *30th January*, 1829.

"My dear Friend,

"Though my eyes are just now so indifferent that I must be extremely sparing in the use of my pen, yet I cannot forbear or delay assuring you, that I do not see how it is possible for any reasonable being to doubt the propriety, (that is a very inadequate way of speaking—let me rather say, absolute duty,) of your renewing your prison visitations. A gracious Providence has blessed you with success in your endeavours to impress a set of miserables, whose character and circumstances might almost have extinguished hope; and you will return to them, if with diminished pecuniary powers, yet we may trust, through the mercy and goodness of our Heavenly Father, with powers of a far higher order unimpaired, and with the augmented respect and regard of every sound judgment, not merely of every Christian mind, for having borne with becoming dispositions, a far harder trial, (for such it is) certainly than any stroke which proceeds immediately from the hand of God. May you continue, my dear madam, to be the honoured instrument of great and rare benefits to almost the most pitiable of your fellow-creatures.

"Mrs. Wilberforce desires to join with me in saying, that we hope we shall again have the pleasure of seeing you, by and by, at this place. Meanwhile, with every kind regard, and friendly remembrances to Mr. Fry, and your family circle,

"I remain, with cordial esteem and regard,

"My dear friend, very sincerely yours,

"W. WILBERFORCE."

Mildred's Court, Third Month.—It appears late to begin the journal of a year; but the constant press of engagements, and the numerous interruptions to which I am liable in this place, prevent my having time for much writing. We are remaining here with our son and daughter, and their children, until there is some opening for having a settled home. However, my desire is, that we may, in faith and in humility, entirely bow. I have of late not visited the prisons, and been much occupied at home; but I trust that I may be permitted to enter this interesting work again, clothed as with fresh armour, both to defend me, and qualify me for fresh service, that my hands may be taught to war, and my fingers to fight; and that if consistent with the will of my God, I may, through the help of the Captain of my salvation, yet do valiantly.

During that mournful winter in London, there were periods of peculiar suffering and anxiety. Elizabeth Fry's own health being so shaken by her severe mental distresses, as nearly to confine her to her room, with a bad cough. Her beloved son William was on the bed of sickness, from oppression of the brain, the result of an overstrained and exhausted mind. Shortly afterwards, her daughter-in-law was, in the same house, in an alarming state of illness, and a friend who came to assist in nursing, was taken ill with the measles. The measles in a grown-up family becomes a serious disease. They were driven from London in consequence, though too late to escape infection, and took shelter in the vacant house at Plashet, which, for many weeks, became a scene of anxious nursing.

Thence they removed, early in the Sixth Month, to a small, but commodious dwelling, in Upton Lane, immediately adjoining the Ham House grounds, the residence of her brother Samuel Gurney.

Upton, 10*th.*—We are now nearly settled in this, our new abode; and I may say, although the house and garden are small, it is pleasant and convenient, and I am fully satisfied, and I am thankful for such a home. I have, at times, been favoured to feel great peace, and I may say joy, in the Lord, —a sort of seal to the important step taken; though, at others, the extreme disorder into which our things have been brought by all these changes—and the difficulty of making new arrangements, has harassed and tried me. But I trust it will please a kind Providence to bless my endeavour, to have and to keep my house in order. Place is a matter of small importance, if that peace, which the world cannot give, be our portion, even at times, as a brook by the way, to the refreshment of our weary and heavy laden souls. Although a large garden is not now my allotment, I feel pleasure in having even a small one; and my acute relish for the beautiful in nature and art, is, on a clear day, almost constantly gratified by a delightful view of Greenwich Hospital and Park, and other parts of Kent, the shipping on the river, as well as the cattle feeding in the meadows. So that in small things and great, spiritual and temporal, I have yet reason to raise up my Ebenezer, and praise, bless, and magnify the name of my Lord.

Sixth Month, 23*rd.*—I little expected to attend the Yearly Meeting, having of late appeared to be so much taken out of such things and such services, but, contrary to my expectation, way opened for me to attend every sitting, and to take rather an active part in it, to my real consolation, refreshment, and help. The unity of Friends was remarkable. I certainly felt very low at its commencement. After having, for so many years, received dear friends at my house, and that with such heartfelt pleasure, it tried, not to say puzzled me, why such a change was permitted me. But I rest in the weighty import of the words, "That which I do thou knowest not now, but thou shalt know hereafter."

Chapter Eighth.

1829–1833. Summons to the death-bed of an aged friend—Of a youth—Prepares her Text-book—Anecdote—Religious visit to Norfolk and Suffolk—Meeting of the British Society—Visit to Sussex and Surrey—Death of Robert Barclay—Of a grandson and nephew—Death of her uncle Joseph Gurney—Goes to his funeral at Norwich—Kent Quarterly Meeting—Interview with the Duchess of Kent and Princess Victoria—Yearly Meeting—Interview with Queen Adelaide—Convict ship—Dagenham—Public Meetings—Journey to Isle of Wight, &c.—Events at Ilfracombe—History of Samuel Marshall—Death-bed of a converted Jew—Cholera—Yearly Meeting—Meeting of the British Society—Visit to Wales and Ireland—Domestic interests—Sojourn in Jersey—Visit to Guernsey, &c.—Returns home—Illness of one daughter—Letter to another.

As we proceed with the journal of Elizabeth Fry, we perceive how deeply the sense of sorrow and of heavy trials was impressed upon her heart.—The following entry is calculated to renew our tenderest sympathy.

Eighth Month, 29th, 1829.—Our wedding-day! twenty-nine years since we married! My texts for the morning are applicable:—"Our light affliction which is but for a moment, worketh for us a far more exceeding and eternal weight of glory."—"We walk by faith, not by sight." As far as we can judge from external appearances, mine has not been a common life. He who seeth in secret, only knows the unutterable depths and sorrows I have had to pass through, as well as, at other times, I may almost say, joys inexpressible and full of glory. I have now had so many disappointments in life, that my hopes, which have so long lived strong, that I should see much brighter days in it, begin a little to subside, and my desire is, more entirely to look beyond the world, for that which can alone fully satisfy me; and not to have my heart so much set upon the things of this life; or even on those persons nearest me; but more set upon the life to come; and upon Him who is faithful, and will be *all in all* to His dependent ones. At the same time I desire faithfully to perform all my relative duties: and may my heart be kept in tender love to all near to me.

Upton, Tenth Month, 21st.—On First-day, we were rather suddenly summoned to Plashet House, to attend Anna Golder (aunt to my faithful Chrissy) who had charge of the house. She was one of the lowly, retired, humble walkers before the Lord; she was suddenly taken very ill, and died in half-an-hour after her niece got there. It was apparently a departure without sting, to mind or body; as far therefore, as it respected her, all was peace. But to myself it was different. I arrived there after dark, drove once more into the dear old place—no one to meet me but the poor man who lived in the house, no dog to bark, nor any life nor sound, as used to be. Death seemed over the place, such was the silence—until I found myself up stairs in the large, and once cheerful and full house; when I entered the bed-room, there lay the corpse. Circumstances combined to touch some very tender feelings, and the inclination of my heart was, to bow down upon my knees before the Lord; thankful, surely, for the release of the valued departed—but deeply and affectingly impressed with such a change! that once lively, sweet, cheerful home, lef desolate—the abode of death—and two or three watchers. It brought, as my visits to Plashet often have done, the hymn to my mind,—

"Lord, why is this? I trembling cried?"

Then, again I find I can do nothing, but bow, trust, and depend upon that Power, that has, I believe, thus seen meet to visit us in judgment, as well as in mercy!

31*st*—Since I last wrote, I have been called to another death-bed scene; our old and valued Roman Catholic friends, the Pitchfords, have lost their eldest son, a sweet, good boy. I felt drawn in love, I trust I may say, Christian love, to be much with them during their trial; I felt it right to leave my family, and spend First-day evening with them, when all hope of the child's life was given up. I had not only to sympathize with them in their deep sorrow, but to pour forth my prayer on their behalf. The next day I was with the poor child when he died, and was nearly the whole day devoted to them. We had a deeply interesting time after his death—my dear friends themselves, all their children, their mother, sister, and old nurse. My mouth was remarkably opened in prayer and praises, indeed, all day at their house something of a holy influence appeared to be over us. A fresh, living proof that what God had cleansed, we are not to call, or to feel, common nor unclean. It surely matters not by what name we call ourselves, or what outward *means* we may think right to use, if our hearts are but influenced by the love of Christ, and cleansed by his baptism, and strengthened by His spirit, to prove our faith by love and good works. *With* ceremonies, or *without* ceremonies, if there be but an establishment upon the Rock of Ages, all will be well. Although I am of opinion, the more our religion is pure, simple, and devoid of these outward forms, the better and the safer for us; at the same time, I do earnestly desire a more full union amongst all Christians, less judging one another, and a general acknowledgment, in heart, judgment, and word, of the universality of the love of God, in Christ Jesus our Lord.

Amidst Elizabeth Fry's numerous avocations, she found time to select a passage of Scripture for every day in the year. She endeavoured to combine in it, that, which is "profitable for doctrine, for reproof, for correction, for instruction in righteousness;" and, in a little preface, she urged the importance of so seeking to appropriate the truths contained in it, with a heart uplifted, that the blessed Spirit might apply the word; and concludes, "The rapid and ceaseless passing away of the days and weeks, as well as the months of the year, as numbered at the head of each day's text, it is hoped may prove a memento of the speed with which time is hastening on, and remind the reader of the importance of passing it as a preparation for eternity, in the service of God and for the benefit of mankind." As soon as her little work was finished and printed, she began its distribution; many thousands of copies did she give away, being amply supplied, from the stores of affluence, with the right means of dispersing them. Great numbers were otherwise circulated. Where have not these little text-books penetrated, from the monarch's gilded hall to the felon's dungeon?

Many instances of their usefulness came to light. The following narrative will interest the reader:—

"Two or three years after their publication, a text-book, bound in red leather, which she had given to a little grandson, fell out of his pocket at the Lynn Mart, where he had gone to visit the lions. He was a very little boy, and much disconcerted at the loss of his book, for his name was in it, and that it was 'the gift of his grandmother,' written by herself. The transaction was almost forgotten, when nearly a year afterwards, Richardson Coxe, the clergyman of Watlington, a parish about eight miles from Lynn, gave the following history of the lost book. He had been sent for to the wife of a man living on a wild common on the outskirts of his parish, a notorious character, between poacher and rat-catcher. The message was brought to the clergyman, by the medical man who attended her, and who after describing her as being most strangely altered, added, 'you will find the lion become a lamb,'—and so it proved; she, who had been wild and rough, whose language had been violent, and her conduct untamed, lay on a bed of exceeding suffering, humble, patient, and resigned.

"Her child had picked up the text-book, and carried it home as lawful spoil. Curiosity, or some feeling put into her heart by

Him without whom a sparrow falleth not to the ground had induced her to read it; the word had been blessed to her, and her understanding opened to receive the gospel of truth. She could not describe the process, but the results were there. Sin had, in her sight, become hateful; blasphemy was no longer heard from her lips. She drew from under her pillow, her 'precious book,' her 'dear little book,' which had been the means of leading her soul to Him, who 'taketh away sin.' She soon afterwards died in peace and in joyful hope."

Elizabeth Fry believed it to be her religious duty to lay before her Monthly Meeting, a concern, which had for some time rested upon her mind, to pay a religious visit to parts of Suffolk and Norfolk, and attend the Quarterly Meeting at Ipswich. Doing this, involved many pains and much effort. It was with fear and trembling, that she set forth on this errand of Christian love. She was accompanied by her sister-in-law, Elizabeth Fry, and their valued friend Joseph Foster.

She wrote while on this little journey, to her children at home, upon their being invited to attend, what is called, the "consecration of a Church," and to be present at a party afterwards.

Earlham, *Third Month, 23rd,* 1830.

My most beloved Children,

The information received to-day, that you should, any of you, have admitted a serious thought of attending our kind friend's party on the 31st, surprises and pains me; not but that I am also fully sensible of your willingness fully to be guided by my judgment in it. With respect to those over whom I have authority, I feel it impossible to leave them, in any degree, at liberty about it—it is a thing that *must not be.* I look upon it, not only as perfectly inconsistent with our views as Friends, but perfectly so for *all* religious professors, because, if I *did* approve of *consecrating* a church for the worship of the Almighty, I could not possibly conceive it an occasion for amusement or gaiety, but one of real seriousness. I see the thing to be *altogether* inconsistent with religious truth, both as to *the thing itself*, and this *commemoration* of it, and I trust that none of you will be present. I am sure it was, in the first instance, your own view of the case, therefore do not, my dearest children, be shaken in your judgments about it; I believe it will be a cross that you will never repent taking up, but on the contrary, be glad that you have done so; for sacrifices must be made to duty.

Upton, Fourth Month, 26th.—My arrival at home was clouded by a party, to which my children were invited, and rather wished to go. We had some pains about it—my path is a very peculiar one; and, as to bringing my family up consistent Friends, a most difficult one. My husband not going hand in hand with me, in some of these things, and my children, in no common degree, disliking the cross of the minor testimonies of Friends, and, from deeply sorrowful circumstances, often having had their faith in them tried, also their being exposed unavoidably, to much association with those, who do not see these things needful. My desire is, only to do what is for the real good of my children, and for the good of the cause which I love, and leave *myself* altogether out of the question, whether it bring me into evil report, or good report. I have often been brought by these things, especially of late, into deep conflict of spirit, and out of the very depths can only cry, Lord, help and guide me! and give us not over to the will of our spiritual enemies.

Sixth Month, 7th. I had a difficult path to tread during the Yearly Meeting. I did not, of course, receive Friends, but went as I was kindly asked, to various houses. I could not but, at times, naturally feel it, after having, for so many years, delighted to entertain my friends, and those whom I believe to be disciples of Christ, and now, in considerable degree, to be deprived of it. But, after relating my sorrows,

I must say, that through the tender mercy of my God, I have many blessings, and what is more, at times, such a sweet feeling of peace, that I am enabled to hope and trust, that, through the unbounded and unmerited mercy of God in Christ Jesus, my husband, my children, and myself, will eventually be made partakers of that salvation, that comes by Christ. The state of our Society, as it appeared in the Yearly Meeting, was satisfactory, and really very comforting to me; so much less stress laid upon little things, more upon matters of greater importance, so much unity, good-will, and what I felt, *Christian* liberty amongst us—love appeared truly to abound, to my real refreshment. I am certainly a thorough Friend, and have inexpressible unity with the principle, but I also see room for real improvement amongst us; may it take place: I want less love of money, less judging others, less tattling, less dependence upon external appearance. I want to see more fruit of the Spirit in all things, more devotion of heart, more spirit of prayer, more real cultivation of mind, more enlargement of heart towards all; more tenderness towards delinquents, and above all, more of the rest, peace, and liberty of the children of God!

I lately paid an interesting visit to the Duchess of Gloucester. Our British Society Meeting has been well got through. There is much yet doing in this cause. Oh! for a right, and diligent, and persevering spirit in it, and may the grace of our Lord Jesus Christ be with all those who are engaged in it.

The accounts received at this Meeting from various Com mittees for visiting female prisoners in Great Britain, were very encouraging. The following letter was at this time addressed to Elizabeth Fry:—

"Liverpool, *Sixth Month, 23rd,* 1830.

"The Ladies' Committee who visit the House of Correction at Kirkdale, near Liverpool, beg Elizabeth Fry's acceptance of a counterpane worked by the female prisoners, and trimmed with a fringe of their making. This memorial of a class of her unhappy fellow-creatures, so eminently benefited, and tenderly felt for by Elizabeth Fry, will, the Committee believe, be peculiarly grateful to her, as well as being a proof of their own affectionate regard.

"Signed, on behalf of the Committee, by

"REBECCA CHORLEY, *Secretary*."

A counterpane, elaborately embroidered, accompanied this letter.

From Hamburgh, Elizabeth Fry received an application that a copy of her likeness might be engraved for an Almanack published by Beyerink, entitled, "For that which is Beautiful and Good."

With this was sent to her the following translation of some lines, inserted in the "Almanac for the Beautiful and Good."

"1830.—Though faithful to her duty, as a wife and mother, into the night of the prison Elizabeth Fry brings the radiance of love—brings comfort to the sufferer, dries the tear of repentance, and causes a ray of hope to descend into the heart of the sinner. She teaches her that has strayed, again to find the path of virtue, comes as an angel of God into the abode of crime, and preserves for Jesus's kingdom that which appeared to be lost. Is not this, indeed, what may be called, loving our neighbour more than one's self?

"Leeuwaarden, *September*, 1829."

From Berlin, Elizabeth Fry had received letters from the Countess Von der Grœben, giving encouraging details of the results of Ladies visiting Prisons; and there, and at Potsdam also, of the establishment of places of refuge for such liberated prisoners, as seemed anxious for amendment.

The effect of kindness, and patient instruction, even on the most abandoned creatures, was beautifully described in a letter from "Madame Potemkin née Galitzin," addressed to Elizabeth Fry, from Petersburg.

Upton, Ninth Month, 11th.—I felt it right, yesterday, to lay before the Monthly Meeting, a view that I have had of attending the Quarterly Meeting of Sussex, and some of its particular Meetings. My sister Elizabeth Fry felt disposed to join me. It appeared to meet with rather unusual unity, therefore we are likely to go forward in it.

Tenth Month, 12th.—We, (my sister E. F., my brotner Samuel Gurney, and myself,) returned home from our journey on Seventh-day evening, after being out a week and two days. We were, in the first place, outwardly cared for by our dear friend Joseph Foster, who is truly a helper, spiritually as well as naturally; he accompanied us to Horsham, where, as usual under such circumstances, I felt ready to query, why I was there, and fears got hold of me. Friends received us with much kindness and apparent openness.

At Brighton, Elizabeth Fry attended the Meeting for Friends on the First-day morning, and in the evening held a large Meeting with persons of different persuasions. She had, at the Pavilion, an interview with the Countess Brownlow, and through her, communicated a message of serious import to Queen Adelaide; the substance of which is recorded in her journal as follows:

My prayer for the King and Queen was, that a blessing might rest upon them; that they might be strengthened by the spirit of God, to do His will, and live to His glory, (or to that purpose); then, for the Queen, I felt the great importance of her situation, that she was indeed like a city set upon a hill, amongst women; and my desire for her was, that her light might so shine before men, that they, seeing her good works might glorify our Father who is in Heaven. I expressed my desire that, for the good of the community, she might promote the education of the poor, the general distribution of the Scriptures, and the keeping the Sabbath seririously, by discouraging parties, &c., &c., on that day amongst the higher ranks, as I was sure the tendency of them was very injurious to the lower classes, and to the community at large. Then I touched on the anti-slavery subject, and the abolition of capital punishment; and presented to the Queen, my brother Joseph's Essays, also his Peculiarities of Friends, and my little book on visiting Prisons.

On Fourth-day morning, after several calls, and attending a Bible Meeting, we dined with some Friends very agreeably, and, in the evening, met about seventy persons on account of the District Society. It was truly encouraging to me, to hear what wonders it had done for that place. We had a delightful Meeting, a great variety of Christians present, and so much good-will and unity felt, that it comforted my heart At its close, our dear and valued friends Charles Simeon and Joseph Hughes gave us some sweet religious counsel; I felt the power such, that I could not help following them, and found that "out of the fulness of the heart the mouth speaketh"—giving glory to the Lord.

On fifth-day, several of the higher classes were invited to Meeting, and to my own feelings, a remarkable time we surely had; it appeared as if we were over-shadowed by the love and mercy of God our Saviour. The ministry flowed in beautiful harmony, I deeply felt the want of vocal prayer being offered, but I did not see it my place upon our Meeting assembling together, when, to my inexpressible relief, a friend powerfully and beautifully offered up thanksgiving and prayer, which appeared to rise as incense, and as an acceptable sacrifice. After a time of silence, I rose with this text: "There are diversities of gifts, but the same Spirit; differences of administration, but the same Lord; diversities of operations, but it is the same God who worketh all in all." In a way that it never did before, the subject opened to my view, whilst speaking; how did I see, and endeavour to express, the lively bond of union existing in the Christian Church, and that the humbling, tendering influence of the love and power of Christ, must lead us not to condemn our neighbours, but to love all. I had to end the Meeting by praying for the King, Queen, and all their subjects every where; for the advancement of that day, when the knowledge of God and His glory would cover the earth as the waters cover the sea; for those countries in Europe that are in a disturbed state, and that these shakings might eventually be for good. After a most solemn feeling of union, the Meeting broke up.

I have been thus full in the account of this journey, because it is, I think, well, in this way, to leave some memorial of the tender dealings of my gracious Lord and Master with me, when engaged in His service.

Upton, Eleventh Month, 3rd.—We returned home yesterday from Bury Hill, where my brother Samuel and myself went on Seventh-day, in consequence of the death of my dear uncle Barclay, whose funeral we attended the preceding Sixth-day, when thirteen of his children and children-in-law attended. It was to me very affecting, following the remains of this dear uncle to the grave, who was such a kind, generous friend, and helper to me. It is very striking to see one generation so nearly gone; so many of us, now entering the evening of our day, and our children and children's children coming up after us. Life thus passing away, "as a tale that is told."

Twelfth Month, 7th.—May I be enabled so to give an account of the various dealings of the Almighty with me and mine, that it may be useful to some, at least to my most beloved children and children's children. I have to begin with rather a melancholy tale:—My beloved children, Foster and Richenda Reynolds, lost their sweet baby upon the 4th of last month, after a few days' severe illness. Death is awful and affecting, come as it may! and this I truly felt, when seeing the sweet babe in its coffin, still retaining its beautiful colour. I could not but feel the uncertainty of all our possessions, yet the comfort, that death had only entered our family and taken one for whom we could feel no fear for the future. At her grave, the desire was very strong within me, that we might all become like little children, fit to enter the kingdom of God, being washed and made white in the blood of the Lamb. Since then, my dear nephew Harry Buxton has been called hence. His end appeared, in no common degree, peace, if not joy, in the Lord. He was about seventeen years of age—a remarkable instance of the care and religious instruction of parents being blessed; he was greatly protected through life, from any evil influences, and carefully and diligently instructed by his dear mother, particularly in all religious truth. He was a child, who in no common degree, appeared to be kept from evil, and to live in the fear and love of the Lord; he was cheerful, industrious, clever, very agreeable, and of a sweet person—a very deep trial it is to his dear parents to lose him. Still I feel, as if I could give up all my sons to be in such a state; but I may be mistaken in this, and perhaps my Lord may yet be pleased, to raise them up to His service here below, which would be a greater blessing, than having them taken in the morning of the day.

First Month, 11*th*, 1831.—When dressing, last First-day fortnight, A—— came in to tell me, that my dear and valued uncle Joseph Gurney had suddenly dropped down dead, at his house at the Grove, near Norwich, my aunt only with him at the time. It exceedingly affected me, for he was very dear to me, and more like a father than any one living; he was one in whom the religious life was beautifully manifested, more particularly in his humility, in his cheerfulness, and in his obedience. He was a lively minister of the gospel, a valuable and a delightful man, and his loss is indeed very great to those nearest to him, as well as to many others. I had a painful struggle, to know whether I ought to go to his funeral, or not. However, I decided to go, in which I felt peace, and then could leave it all comfortably. I have seldom, of late, felt more discouraged from a deep sense of the evil of my own heart, than when I first arrived at Earlham. There are times, when with my brothers and sisters particularly, the contrast of *my* circumstances with *their's* pains me; the mode of my feeling these things oppressed me. I walked alone through some beautiful parts of Earlham, and how did it remind me of days that are past! The sun shone brightly, and hardly a tree, a walk, or a view, but brought interesting remembrances before me; how many gone! how many changes! and then how far was I ready for my great change? It was New Year's Day; little did I expect to keep it there. I returned to the house, wrote to my husband and children, and poured out a little of my heart to them. I went to the Grove—felt my much loved uncle *really gone* —all changed there. I went to Norwich to call on a few sick, &c.; the place the same, but again how changed to me! However as my dearest family assembled, I became more comfortable.

Upton, Third Month, 19*th.*—I went on Second-day to attend the Kent Quarterly Meeting, accompanied by my dear sister Elizabeth Fry, and by Joseph Foster. I was much engaged from Meeting to Meeting, laboured to encourage the low, the poor, and the sorrowful; to lead to practical religion, and to shake from all outward dependencies, and to show that our principles and testimonies of a peculiar nature, should not be maintained simply as a regulation amongst us, but unto the Lord, and in deep humility, in the true Christian spirit, particularly as to tithes, war, &c. I felt much peace afterwards, and in going from house to house, breaking, I trust, a little bread spiritually, and giving thanks. It appeared *very* seasonable, though long delayed, as I have had it on my mind many months, but hitherto have been prevented by various things; yet this appeared to be the right time; and I take the lesson home, quietly to wait for the openings of Providence, particularly in all religious services, and not to attempt to plan them too much myself.

The kindness of Friends was great, and I received much *real* encouragement from them; some from the humble ones, that did my heart good. Indeed I cannot but acknowledge, in humiliation of spirit, however any may reason on these things, and however strange that women should be sent out to preach the gospel, yet I have, in these services, partaken of joy and peace, that I think I have never felt, in the same degree, in any other.

Fifth Month, 14*th*.—About three weeks ago, I paid a very satisfactory visit to the Duchess of Kent, and her very pleasing daughter, the Princess Victoria. William Allen went with me. We took some books on the subject of slavery, with the hope of influencing the young princess in that important cause. We were received with much kindness and cordiality, and I felt my way open to express not only my desire that the best blessing might rest upon them, but that the young princess might follow the example of our blessed Lord, that as she "grew in stature, she might grow in favour with God and man." I also ventured to remind her of King Josiah, who began to reign at eight years old, and did that which was right in the sight of the Lord, turning neither to the right hand nor to the left, which seemed to be well received. Since that, I thought it right to send the Duke of Gloucester my brother Joseph's work on the Sabbath, and rather a serious letter, and had a very valuable answer from him, full of feeling. I have an invitation to visit the Duchess of Gloucester next Fourth-day; may good result to them, and no harm to myself, but I feel these openings rather a weighty responsibility, and desire to be faithful, not forward. I had long felt an inclination to see the young princess, and to endeavour to throw a little weight in the right scale, seeing the very important place that she is likely to fill. I was much pleased with her, and think her a sweet, lovely, and hopeful child.

The Yearly Meeting begins next week; I am rather low in the prospect, having no house to receive my dear friends in London continues to be a pain to me. I desire to attend it in all humility, looking to my Lord, and not unto man; I desire to be kept in the unity of those with whom I am in religious communion, for I am one with them in principle· but we must forbear with each other in love, and endeavour, through every trial of it, "to keep the unity of the Spirit in the bond of peace." Be pleased, oh Lord! to be near to Thy most unworthy servant, defend her with Thy own armour from the various shafts of the adversary, keep her safely in Thy "pavilion from the strife of tongues." If Thou see meet to call her into Thy service, be a light unto her feet, and a lamp unto her path.

Sixth Month, 3rd.—The Yearly Meeting has concluded this week. I was highly comforted by the good spirit manifested in it by numbers. I think I never was so much satisfied with the ground taken by Friends, leading us to maintain, what we consider our testimonies, upon a scriptural and Christian ground, rather than because our forefathers maintained them. My opinion is, that nothing is so likely to cause our Society to remain a living and spiritual body, as its being willing *to stand open to improvement;* because, it is to be supposed that as the Church generally emerges out of the dark state it was brought into, its light will shine brighter and brighter, and we, as a part of it, shall partake of this dispensation. My belief is, that neither individuals, nor collective bodies, should *stand still* in grace, but their light should shine brighter and brighter unto perfect day. My dearest brother Joseph had a valuable Meeting for the youth, further to instruct them in Friends' principles, which delighted me; he was so clear, so sound, so perfectly scriptural and Christian, and so truly in the spirit of charity and *sound* liberality, *not laxity.*

25*th.*—I must give an account of the British Society Meeting. It was, I trust, well got through, and I feel the way in which its objects prosper, cause for humble thankfulness. Surely, the result of our labour has hitherto been beyond my most sanguine expectation, as to the improved state of our prisons, female convict ships, and the convicts of New South Wales. I desire to feel this blessing and unmerited mercy towards us, and those poor creatures, as I ought, in humility, and true thankfulness of heart.

There was, at this time, a bazaar, or sale, to replenish the funds of the hospital ship in the river Thames, so often greatly needed to assist mariners, &c., disabled by accident or disease. Elizabeth Fry was interested in its success, and was inclined to go. She was the more induced to do so, from finding that Queen Adelaide and several others of the reigning family were likely to be present. She had, for a considerable time, been desiring to obtain introduction to the Queen, because until this was accomplished, the etiquette of the court forbade Elizabeth Fry's bringing before her any of those important subjects on which, in her exalted and responsible station, she might, if her feelings could be interested in them, become a powerfully efficient helper, and thus be rendered a special blessing to the community over which, in the ordering of Providence, she was so conspicuously placed. Elizabeth Fry, after having, as she says, "seriously weighed it by night and by day believed it right to go." She was accompanied by her sister Catherine Gurney. On arriving, she was "discouraged at the gaiety of the scene, and was disposed to retreat"—her sister, however, believed it best to proceed, and they were quickly recognized by Captain Young, who led them to a private apartment, to which the Queen and her party soon afterwards repaired. Some of them respectfully noticed Elizabeth Fry, the Duke of Sussex met her with much kindness, and introduced her to the Queen, who was evidently gratified by the interview. This opened the way for subsequent communications, from which good resulted in various directions; and it became strikingly manifest that there was, in the heart of this estimable Queen, a sentiment that responded to the suggestions of benevolence. Her charities were diffusive, and her pious devotion and love to her Redeemer instructive and consoling; the termination of her earthly course being marked by the resignation, and true peace, of the humble believer in Christ.

Elizabeth Fry speaks of this interview as a remarkable opening; and adds, "my desire is, that it may please the Most High to bless it, that good may result from it."

I lately have had a deeply interesting visit to a female convict ship; surrounded as I am, at such times, by poor sailors and convicts, it is impossible not to feel the contrast of the circumstances in which I am placed. The last time I was in the ship *Mary*, there was such a scene around me—parting from them, probably for ever. So many tears were shed, so much feeling displayed—and almost all present of the low and the poor. Then, within a few days, to be in such a scene of gaiety; though the object in view was good, surrounded by royalty and the great of this earth. The contrast was striking and instructive. I ought surely to profit from the uncommon variety that I see, and the wonderful changes that I have experienced in being raised up, and cast down. Oh! may it not prove in vain for myself and others.

Dagenham, Seventh Month, 6th.—I have now before me, some deeply weighty family matters respecting my children. May the Lord in His tender mercy, be pleased to direct me in my conduct towards them. May I be enabled truly, faithfully, and humbly to do my duty towards them. Oh Lord! be Thou my helper and their helper, my guide and their guide, my defence and their defence, and whatsoever is right for them bring to pass; whatsoever wrong, prevent by Thy power and Thy providence. Amen!

At our last Monthly Meeting, I proposed to Friends to hold a Public Meeting at Maldon in Essex; and some Meetings among the lower classes around Barking and Dagenham. This is a weighty service; may the Lord be with me in it, to my own help, and the comfort and real edification of those I am thrown with; and may my beloved family partake of it.

Eighth Month, 1st.—Last evening we finished our Public Meetings in barns. I passed a humbling night—even in our acts of obedience and devotion, how evident is the mixture of infirmity, (at least so it appears to me,) and we need to look to the great offering for sin and for iniquity, to bear even these transactions for us. I apprehend, that all would not understand me, but many, who are much engaged in what we call works of righteousness, will understand the reason, that in the Jewish dispensation *there was an offering made "for the iniquity of their Holy Things."* Humiliation is my portion, though I may also say peace, in thus having given up to a service much against my inclination, and I hope, thankfulness for the measure of power at times granted in them.

Notwithstanding many family cares, and the weighty objects in which Elizabeth Fry was engaged, the summer of this year, which was passed at Dagenham, proved a peaceful one.

But in this quiet retreat (as in more public and busy scenes) some striking events chequered her course; but her lamp was so continually kept burning, that, in every exigency, a light shone upon her path, and afforded the guidance needful to direct her in the right performance of duty, and to convert each passing circumstance to a purpose of usefulness. No portion of human society was so elevated in worldly rank, or so much sunk in poverty and wretchedness, as not to raise in her heart emotions of deep Christian solicitude, or to induce her to follow the impulse of heavenly love, which led her to invite *all* to the *one* fold of eternal rest and peace.

Dagenham, Eighth Month, 24th.—Upon my return home to Dagenham this day week, in the pony chair, with little Edmund Gurney, there was a severe thunder-storm the greater part of the way, but I felt quite easy to persevere through it. But when I arrived at the Chequers Inn, I thought another storm was coming, and went in. We had been there but a few minutes, when we saw a bright flash of lightning, followed instantaneously by a tremendous clap of thunder. Upon being asked whether I was alarmed, I said that I certainly was, and did not doubt that an accident had happened near to us. My dear husband who was out in the tempest, arrived safely, but in a few minutes, a young man was carried in dead, struck with the lightning in a field close by. I felt our escape—yet still more the awful situation of the young man, who was a sad character; he had been at our Meeting at Beacontree Heath. This awful event produced a very serious effect in the neighbourhood; so much so, that we believed it right to invite all the relations of the young man, (a bad set,) and the other young men of the neighbourhood, to meet us in the little Methodist Meeting House, which ended in one more rather large Public Meeting. The event and circumstances altogether, made it very solemn, it appeared to set a seal to what had passed before in our other Meetings. My belief is, they have had a stirring effect in this neighbourhood, but they have been very humbling to me; the whole event, of this young man's awful death, has much confirmed me in the belief, that our concern was a right one, and tended to prepare the minds of the people to profit by such a lesson. My dear brother and sister Buxton, and their Priscilla, were with us at many of our Meetings.

27th.—We are just about leaving this place. I have endeavoured to promote the moral and religious good of the people since the Meetings, by establishing libraries of tracts and books at different places, and my belief is, that my humble labours have not been in vain, nor I trust will they be. I have felt so strikingly the manner in which the kindness and love of the neighbourhood has been shown to me, after thus publicly preaching amongst them; and as a poor, frail woman, advocating boldly the cause of Christ, I expected rather to be despised; whereas, it is apparently just the reverse. The clergyman and his wife almost loading us with kindness, the farmers and their wives very kind and attentive, the poor the same; I felt how sweet it is to be on good terms with all—one day drinking tea at the parsonage, abounding with plate, elegancies, and luxuries, the next day at the humble Methodist shoemaker's, they having procured a little fresh butter, that I might take tea under their roof; the contrast was great, but I can indeed see the same kind Lord over all, rich to all, and filling the hearts of His servants of very different descriptions with love to each other.

In the autumn, Elizabeth Fry accompanied her husband into some of the South-Western Counties. She writes from—

Sand Rock Hotel, Tenth Month, 9th.—This is the place in the Isle of Wight, where my most beloved sisters Rachel and Priscilla spent a winter. I may truly say, since coming to this beautiful and interesting spot, my heart has been much tendered, in remembering those so inexpressibly dear, feeling deeply, that their places here know them no more; it has revived a very strong feeling respecting the past. Their course finished, mine not yet fully run; and as I am deeply sensible that I cannot keep alive my own soul, oh may He, who remains to be our light and our life, keep me alive unto Himself, until He may fit me, by His own Almighty power and unmerited mercy, to enter a new life with all His saints in glory.

Barnstaple, 23rd.—First-day morning.—My distress is great this morning, owing to the steam-packet, with our dear son Gurney, not arriving as we expected, last evening. I have passed a conflicting night; my husband is gone to Ilfracombe, in hope of hearing something of the packet, and seeing after our dear boy, if he arrives; I stayed, because I thought that duty pointed out attending the little Meeting here, but I feel nervous, afflicted, and desolate. I believe it well, to be, now and then, brought to these trials of faith and of patience—may I not say, like the disciples formerly, "help Lord, or I perish!" may my experience be this day, that I cried unto the Lord in my trouble, and He delivered me out of my distresses. Oh, gracious Lord! quiet my troubled mind, increase my hope, trust, and full reliance upon Thee, upon Thy wisdom, Thy love, and Thy mercy, both as it respects myself, and my most dear children, particularly this beloved boy—give me faith to do Thy will this day, and even to prove a helper to those amongst whom my lot may be cast, and, if Thou seest meet, give me help from trouble, for vain is the help of man, in these extremities.

Linton, 27th.—I heard before I went to Meeting, (at Barnstaple,) that the people of Ilfracombe were not much alarmed for the packet. How far my mind was influenced by this, I cannot say, but I was favoured with a sweet calm in Meeting, and was enabled, I trust faithfully, to attend to the openings of duty there, to my own relief and peace, and I hope to the comfort and edification of those present. I had hardly entered the Friend's house afterwards, when the glad tidings came of my dearest Gurney's safe arrival. I have not, for some time, felt so much joy, I might almost say, that my heart rejoiced and leaped for joy; and I was enabled not only in heart, but on sitting down to dinner with my friends, to return thanks to Him, who, in His tender mercy, granted me this deliverance.

Shortly after this anxiety, when at Ilfracombe, a woman asked me if I should like to see a poor man, who was wrecked, and had had a very wonderful escape, the night before Gurney was on the sea; of course I assented, and Gurney, the woman and I, set off to see him. When we arrived at his cottage, we found a very fine, rather tall young man, who appeared to have been much bruised, shaken, and wounded, with a nice looking young woman, his wife; the house very clean, and a few books—but one particularly struck our attention—a Bible, with an inscription upon it in gilt letters, to this effect, "In commemoration of the courageous conduct of Samuel Marshall, in saving the lives of two women (who had been out on a Sunday party, a third was drowned) off the pier at Ilfracombe." It appeared, by the short history of this young man, that he had, from his great courage, good swimming, and kindness to others, been, at different times, the means of saving eight lives, at least; he had gone out to ships in danger near Ilfracombe, where, from the rocky nature of the coast, there often are shipwrecks. His own simple story about himself, on his recent shipwreck, was as follows:—

"He was fishing in a small boat with two other men; about twelve o'clock at night, a sudden squall or land wind blew from between the hills; he called out to his companions, 'we are lost'; the boat capsized, they, poor fellows, prayed for mercy, and sank. Marshall, knowing his great powers of swimming, would not give himself up, but caught hold of an oar, which proved to be a good one, nearly new; and although he knew that he was a mile from the shore, and the sea, in consequence of this land wind, very boisterous, he felt it right, at least, to make the effort to reach land. He soon found that, with all his clothes on, it would be impossible, but how to take them off, was the difficulty; his presence of mind appears to have been wonderful; he first got off his jacket, then his trowsers with extreme difficulty, because they became entangled in his feet, but by a violent effort he succeeded; he then found he could not well get rid of his shirt, nor swim with it on. He was driven to great extremity, his shirt being a new, stout, cotton one—he therefore, once more, made a violent effort, and tore it down in front, but the hem was so strong, that he there stopped, this he put to his mouth and bit it through; he then swam on until he nearly reached the shore, where the breakers ran so high that he lost his oar; once more, he almost entirely gave up hopes; but resolved on one last effort, and found himself thrown upon a rock very seriously bruised; he climbed beyond the reach of the water, and laid himself down, cold, hungry, and exhausted, either to perish, or to rest. He told me that, it being quite dark, he could not tell where he was cast ashore, but he was fully sensible that it must be where the rocky, high cliffs could be only here and there, climbed by man—his anxiety was consequently great, till day dawned, when he saw some sheep feeding up the cliff side. He was sure that wherever sheep could go, he could climb. As his poor feet were sadly cut, he took his stockings (which he still had on) and bound them round his feet with his garters; with this exception, he ascended the rough cliff, naked; his exhaustion and fatigue great indeed. After walking awhile, he arrived at a farm-house; the farmer took him for a lunatic, and, at first, spoke to him sharply, but soon finding his real case, he took him in, and treated him with the utmost hospitality. The farmer's wife prepared him a bed."

I now stop my narrative to say, that from my conversation with Samuel Marshall, I took him to be a man actuated by religious principles, but not possessing an enlightened understanding on these subjects; one who endeavoured to do, as far as he knew it, his duty; which he had so remarkably shown, in risking his own life to save the lives of others, particularly in the instance of the women, who were poor, and unable to remunerate him. I was strongly reminded, in hearing of his deliverance, of these words of Scripture, "with the merciful Thou wilt show Thyself merciful." The poor man said, also, that he prayed constantly when the salt water was not in his mouth, which showed on the one hand, his value for prayer, and on the other, his ignorance in supposing that when he could not speak, he would not be equally heard by Him, who knoweth the most secret desire of the heart. However, as I doubt not his prayers were offered in sincerity, they appear to have been accepted and answered. He was carried home to his sorrowful wife, who had heard of the boat being lost, and did not know that her husband was saved.

The mother of one of the other men, I found in the deepest distress, almost out of her mind. I tried to pour a little balm into her deep wounds, by endeavouring to lead her to look to Him, who can alone heal and help in our greatest trials.

Upton Lane, Eleventh Month, 16*th*.—I felt greatly helped in the quiet performance of my duties yesterday, up to a certain time, when, I believe, I gave way a little to natural infirmity about a trifle, and found how soon a cloud may be brought over the best principle, and what care and watchfulness is needed; and if there be the *least* fall, how necessary immediately to have recourse to the justifying principle of faith, that no further separation take place from good. I fully believe, that our spiritual enemy remains the accuser of the brethren, and endeavours, when he sees those, who desire to serve the Lord give way, even in a trifle, to take advantage of it to discourage them, and further to insinuate himself into their hearts. It is, I believe, one of the most important points in the Christian life, if we find ourselves tripping in thought, word, or deed, immediately to fly to the fountain that is set open for the unclean, that we may at once be cleansed, and obtain peace with God, through our Lord and Saviour Jesus Christ. Oh! for a little help this day to come to the living fountain, that I may be fitted for my Master's service, and enter it with a quiet mind. Lord, let it be so!

Twelfth Month, 20*th*.—I am once more favoured, after being far from well, with a renewal of health and power, to enter my usual engagements, public and private. Yesterday I went to town,—first attended the Newgate Committee, then, the British Society, which was very encouraging to me; there were many present, of different denominations of Christians, and a sweet feeling of love and unity pervaded the whole. Elizabeth Dudley spoke in a lively manner, and I had to pray. There is still much ground for encouragement in the prison cause, I believe a seed is sown in it, that *will* grow and flourish, I trust, when some of us are laid low. It is a work that brings with it a peculiar feeling of blessing and peace; may the Most High continue to prosper it! Afterwards, I went to Clapham to visit a poor, dying, converted Jew, who had sent a letter to beg me to go and see him; my visit was highly interesting. I often wish for the pen of a ready writer, and the pencil of an artist, to picture some of the scenes that I am brought into. A man of a pleasing countenance, greatly emaciated, lying on a little white bed, all clean and in order, his Bible by his side, and animated, almost beyond description, at seeing me; he kissed my hand, the tears came into his eyes, his poor face flushed, and he was ready almost to raise himself out of his bed. I sat down, and tried to quiet him, and by degrees succeeded. We had a very interesting conversation; he had been in the practice of frequently attending my readings at Newgate, apparently with great attention; latterly, I had not seen him, and was ready to suppose, that, like many others, his zeal was of short duration; but I had lately heard that he had been ill. He is one of those Jews, who have felt perfectly liberated from keeping any part of the Law of Moses, which some other converted Jews yet consider themselves bound to observe. I found, when he used to come so often to Newgate, that he was a man of good moral character, seeking the truth. But to go on with my story—in our conversation, he said, that he felt great peace, no fear of death, and a full reliance upon his Saviour for salvation; he said that his visits to Newgate had been to him beyond going to any church—indeed, I little knew how much was going on in his heart. He requested me to read a Psalm that I had read one day in Newgate, the 107th. This I did, and he appeared deeply to feel it, particularly as my dear friends and I made our little remarks, in Christian freedom, as we went along, truly, I believe, in the life. The poor Jew prayed very strikingly; I followed him, and returned thanks; what a solemn, uniting time it was! The poor Jew said, "God is a spirit, and they that worship Him, must worship Him in spirit and in truth," as if he felt the spirituality of the Christian administration. His countenance lightened with apparent joy, when he expressed his undoubted belief that he should soon enter the kingdom, and that I should, before long, follow him; then he gave me his blessing, and took leave in much tenderness, showing every mark he could, of gratitude and love. He did not accept any gift of money, saying that he wanted no good thing, as he was most kindly provided for by serious persons in the neighbourhood. After about two weeks I received an account of the peaceful end of this poor Jew.

Upton, Second Month, 21*st,* 1832.—We have lately been brought to feel very seriously the approach of the cholera to our own borders, as it is said to have been as near as Limehouse. I have not generally felt any agitating fear, but rather the weight of the thing, and desirous that it should prove a stimulus to seek more diligently after eternal things, and to be ready, spiritually, for whatever may await us; and outwardly to use all proper precautions. I have desired earnestly, that we should do our very utmost to protect our poor neighbours, by administering to their many wants. This led me to make some efforts with some of our women Friends, also with some other kind and influential people, and although perhaps, thought by some a busybody in it, yet more has been already accomplished, than I could have looked for. In such works of charity, I always desire to be preserved from a forward spirit, or an over active one, yet on the other hand, when I feel any thing laid upon me, as I did in this instance, I feel much bound to work in it, even through some discouragement and opposition; I mostly find in such cases, that way has been made for me, as if He, who called me to the work, was indeed with me in it.

It was a remarkable trait in the character of this highly gifted woman, that, when once she had undertaken to perform what she believed to be her duty, no discouragement deterred her from pursuing it; no obstacle appeared to her to be insurmountable. She laboured on with a quiet, patient perseverance, until she saw it accomplished—yet she trusted not in her own strength—she committed herself and her cause to the disposal of the Lord.

Third Month, 21*st.*—To-day is proclaimed a "fast-day" on account of the cholera; it is one of those occasions, in the observance of which we must each follow our own consciences. If the government of a country could make a people keep a day *really* holy unto the Lord, in real fasting, penitence and prayer, much good would result; but this, no government can do; and I fear that the present will rather be made a day of lightness and recreation. However, those wno do keep it seriously, I trust will be blessed in so doing, and their prayers answered, and that this awful disease may be (if right for us) checked in its progress.

I rather feel having to go before the Committee of the House of Commons, on the subject of prisons. May any good to this important cause be done by it, and may I be helped to do my part with simplicity, as unto God, and not unto man!

The object of this Committee, was to ascertain the best mode of Secondary Punishment, so as to be the most effectual in repressing crime.

We proceed with extracts from the journal.

Upton Lane, Sixth Month, 3rd.—We have just concluded the Yearly Meeting. It has been, in some respects, a marked one, and I hope an instructive one. . . . . . I had to speak twice in the Meetings; once in the first Meeting, acknowledging the loving-kindness and tender mercy of our God as manifested to us during the year that was passed, and what an inducement it should be to love and faithfulness. I had particularly to make allusion to the cholera not having made further devastations amongst us. I had, in another Meeting, in a similar manner to return thanks, and pray for us, as a Society, and for the Universal Church. I also had, from a deep feeling of duty, to express my thankfulness, that the Christian standard had been upheld amongst us, so much encouragement given to read the Scriptures, and attend to their holy precepts; but I felt a fear, whether the influence of the Holy Spirit, as our guide, had been quite enough dwelt upon, which, as a fundamental part of our principles, I trusted we should ever maintain. I also expressed my desire, that the fruits of the Spirit should be more manifest amongst us, not only in our peculiar testimonies, but in the subjection of our tempers and wills, which I thought to be much wanted, fearing that some maintained our testimonies, more from expediency than principle, which produced great inconsistency of conduct. I then added my earnest hope, that individually and collectively, we should stand open to improvement, making this our prayer: "That which I see not, teach Thou me;" that we should be willing to be taught of God immediately and instrumentally, that our light might shine brighter and brighter to the perfect day.

9th.—I yesterday was favoured to get through the British Society Meeting. It was, to me, a very serious occasion; our different reports were highly satisfactory and encouraging; but I felt it laid upon me to speak so decidedly on some points, that I could not fully enjoy it. After the British Society report was read, I first endeavoured to show the extreme importance of the work in which we were engaged, and the best means of producing the desired effect, of reforming the criminal; but what most deeply impressed me was, considering the awful extent of existing crime, and the suffering and sorrow produced by it—how far the conduct of the higher classes may influence that of the lower, and tend in many ways to the increase of evil, by ladies not setting a religious example to their servants, nor instructing them in the right way; by not keeping the Sabbath strictly,—by very late hours, and attending public places,—by vanity in dress, and by hurrying mantua-makers and milliners, and so causing them to oppress and overwork their young women—by not paying their bills themselves, or through some confidential person, but trusting them to young or untried servants, thus leading to dishonesty on their part, or that of the tradespeople,—by allowing their maid-servants or char-women to begin to wash at unseasonable hours, and consequently to require ardent spirits to support them. Then I represented how much they might do to promote good and discourage evil, by educating the poor religiously, in infant and other schools, by watching over girls after they leave schools, until placed in service, and by providing for them suitable religious, instructive, and entertaining books; also by forming libraries in hospitals, and workhouses, and by preventing the introduction of irreligious and light books. I also urged the establishment of district societies. These things I had forcibly and freely to express, showing the blessings of promoting good, and the woe of encouraging evil.

In the Seventh Month, Elizabeth Fry, together with her sister-in-law, visited, with certificates from their Monthly Meeting, the Half-year's Meeting in Wales, and some places in Ireland.

In the retrospect she writes:—

Ninth Month, 18th.—We returned home from our journey last Sixth-day evening, having been absent just five weeks. We visited several places in the south of Ireland, a good many in Wales, and some in England. I think I never remember taking a journey, in which it was more frequently sealed to my own mind, that we were in our right places; through much difficulty, our way was opened to go, and to continue out. Though I believe we have scripture authority for it—still further confirmed by the internal evidence of the power of the Spirit, and its external results,—yet, I am obliged to walk by faith, rather than sight, in going about as a woman, in the work of the ministry; it is, to my nature, a great humiliation, and I often feel it to be "foolishness," particularly in large Public Meetings, before entering upon the service; but generally, when engaged in the ministry, I find such an unction, and so much opening upon Christian doctrine and practice, that after a Meeting, I mostly say in my heart, "It is the Lord's doing, and marvellous in our eyes. Such was often the case in this journey. I felt amongst Friends in Ireland, as if my service was to lead them from all external dependence, either on their membership in the Society, their high profession, or their peculiar testimonies, and to show, that these things are only good as they spring from simple Christian faith and practice, and avail nothing, unless the heart be really changed and cleansed from sin, though I believed that these things would follow as the result, to those who fill the important place in the church, that in my opinion, Friends are called to occupy. Above everything else, I endeavoured to lead all to the grand foundation of Christian faith and practice. My dear sister was much led in the same line of ministry.

Dagenham, Tenth Month, 3rd.—Here am I sitting in solitude, keeping silence before the Lord; on the wedding-day of my beloved son William. As I could not conscientiously attend the marriage, I believed it right to withdraw for the day. Words appear very inadequate to express the earnestness—the depth of my supplication for him and for his—that the blessing of the Most High may rest upon them.

The notice of this day concludes as follows;—

As for myself, I sit solitary, in many things, but I thought to-day (from this wedding bringing these things home to me)—Have I not my Lord as my friend and my comforter? and is He not as a husband to all the members of His church? and am I not often satisfied and refreshed by His love?

Several months of the summer and autumn of 1833, were passed by Elizabeth Fry and her family, at a quiet retreat in the island of Jersey. She needed rest, and her health had suffered from the pressure of care and anxiety. The genial climate—the beauty of the scenery—the luxuriance of the productions—the prosperity of the inhabitants—the refinement and intellectual cultivation of the upper classes—combined with simplicity of habit, and, in many instances, with true piety and active benevolence, rendered the period of her residence in Jersey one of peculiar refreshment and pleasure. With her husband and children, and a few of her intimate friends, she would often spend the day in the remote parts of the island, amongst the secluded and romantic bays of its northern coast. The little party would picnic in the open air, or, as was then a very common practice, in one of the empty rooms of the small barracks scattered round the coast; left under the care of some old invalided soldier and his family. On these occasions, the tract bag was not forgotten—whilst the rest of the party were sketching or walking, she would visit the cottagers, and making herself as well understood as their antique Norman dialect permitted, would give her little French books, and offer the kind word of sympathy or exhortation. Alive to the beautiful, especially to the picturesque, the peculiarities of the Jersey Cottage and its inmates were all observed and enjoyed by her.

Amidst these scenes, the summer passed away, but higher and more important objects were not unheeded. There was in the island, a little band of persons, in very humble life, who professed the principles of Friends, one or two only, however, being members of the Society. They assembled for worship on the First-day morning, in the cottage of Jean Renaud, an old patriarch, residing on the sea shore, about a mile from the town of "St." Heliers. There was a quaint, old-fashioned effect about the low large room in which they assembled, whilst from large bundles of herbs, suspended from the beams to dry, a flower or a leaf would occasionally drop upon those sitting below.

The appearance of the congregation was in keeping with the apartment, seated on planks, supported by temporary props. An antique four-post bedstead stood in one corner; when the mistress of the house died, which occurred during their sojourn in Jersey, she was there laid out, a circumstance which did not prevent the Meeting assembling as usual; the drawn curtains screening the corpse from view. High-backed chairs were prepared for the seniors of the assembly, the younger members of Elizabeth Fry's family appropriating to themselves the window-seat. The novelty of the occasion was increased by the English ministry having to be interpreted, to render it comprehensible to the greater part of the hearers.

Nor were the Afternoon Meetings much less peculiar. They also were held at a private house, situated in the suburbs of the town; but the heat in-doors being considerable, the congregation not unfrequently moved to the small walled garden, and sat beneath the shade of some evergreens. This, however, was found practically so inconvenient, that a room in the town was engaged for the purpose, and properly fitted up. There, until Elizabeth Fry left the island, large congregations assembled, including many of the gentry and principal inhabitants; these meetings were exceedingly solemn and instructive. She was greatly helped by the company of her sister-in-law, Elizabeth Fry, with her friend and companion, Rebecca Sturges. Philanthropic objects also presented themselves to her notice, especially the state of the Hospital, including the Workhouse and Lunatic Asylum, and the Prison. Acts of the British Parliament have no power in the Channel Islands; as part of the ancient Duchy of Normandy, they are governed by their own laws and customs. None of the recent improvements in Prison Disipline had been effected in Jersey. After repeatedly visiting the Prison, and communicating with the authorities—she believed it the best course to have a letter which she had addressed to them printed for circulation. This document was very remarkable for its evidences of her wisdom and experience.

Eighth Month, 12th.—We feel much at home in this lovely island, and in rather a remarkable manner, our way opens in the hearts of those amongst whom we are residing. A very extensive field of service appears before us, in many ways. To try thoroughly to attend to the prisoners—to strive to correct evils in the hospital—to assist, in various ways, the Friends and those who attend Meeting—to visit several in Christian love, and try to draw them nearer together—oh! gracious Lord, grant Thy poor unworthy servant the help of Thy Spirit, to do Thy will, and let not her labour be in vain in Thee, her Lord and her God; but through Thy unmerited mercy in Christ Jesus, grant that her way may be made *very* clear before her, and ability given her to walk in it, to Thy praise, her own peace, and the real edification of those among whom her lot may be cast. Amen!

How wonderfully did the capacious mind of this extraordinary woman embrace every object that appeared to require assistance, or to need amelioration; and how instructive was the deep humility and holy fear in which she was preserved, as well as her dependence on divine direction and help.

To a daughter and son-in-law preparing to leave England for Madeira, in consequence of the latter* being in delicate health, she writes from Jersey, as follows:—

Eighth Month, 25th, 1833.

My much loved Children,

I fully expect one more opportunity of writing to you, before you leave England, but as our communications are now likely to be very seldom, I mean to take every opportunity to pour out my heart to you. I am, I hope, thankful to say, though truly and deeply touching to me, peaceful and satisfied about your proposed very important step. I remember Cecil's remark, "we are to follow, and not to force Providence," and as far as we can tell, the openings of Providence for you appear to be quietly, hopefully, and trustfully, to go forward in your proposed plans. I live much under the feeling that we are poor, impotent creatures, that we cannot save each other, spiritually or naturally; and though nothing, I believe, can,

*Since deceased from pulmonary consumption.

in feeling, exceed a mother's love or lively desire to serve her children, yet how little can she do! in short nothing, but as she is helped from above to do it, and the same power that can help her, can also work with, or without His instruments; this I most sensibly feel, therefore to Him, who is the keeper of His dependent ones, (which I believe you are) I entirely commit you, body, soul, and spirit. May He "do more abundantly for you, than we can either think or ask!" I desire for you, amidst the ups and downs, the storms and calms, the joys and sorrows, that may attend your course, that your hearts may be fixed, trusting in God. It is most important to seek for this fixedness of spirit, which sustains in trouble, and sanctifies our enjoyments. I have suffered from too deeply and acutely feeling things, and from much undue fearfulness—I wish my children to guard against these weaknesses, and to live more constantly in the quiet and trustful spirit. You must expect some little trials and difficulties in the voyage, but I trust they will not be great. Pray try to be of use to the crew, have tracts, testaments and psalters, to be got at for them; it might be of real use to the men, and a nice object of interest for you.

That grace, mercy, and peace, may be with you both, is the earnest desire and prayer of your most loving mother,

ELIZABETH FRY.

Jersey, Ninth Month, 10*th.*—I have much enjoyed and valued the pleasant retreat we have here. I desire, in deep gratitude, to acknowledge the renewed capacity to delight in the wonderful works of God. The scenery, and feeling fully at liberty to spend part of many days in the enjoyment of this beautiful country and weather, and my beloved husband and children, has been very sweet to me! What has not religion been to me! how wonderful in its operation! None but He, who knows the heart, can tell. Surely it has brought me into some deep humiliations; but how has it raised me up! healed my, at times, wounded spirit; given me power to enjoy my blessings, in what I believe an unusual degree, and wonderfully sustained me under deep tribulations. To me, it is anything but bondage, since it has brought me into a delightful freedom; although I had narrow places to pass through, before my boundaries were thus enlarged; so that from experience, I wish to be very tender over those still in bonds.

Since the time of rest on first arriving, my way has remarkably opened to a tide of service, of various kinds, as a minister of the gospel, and in philanthropic concerns. The prison, hospital, and the formation of a District Society, take up much of my attention, and visiting religiously the families who attend the Friends' Meeting. I have very much felt the weight of these meetings; duty alone, and what I believe to be the help of the Spirit, would carry me through such services, for which I am so totally unfit and unworthy. My dear sister and Rebecca Sturges have lately been with us, and I have valued their company.

Elizabeth Fry spent a few days in Guernsey, closely employed as usual in doing good.

The most important work which she accomplished in that island, was establishing "the St. Peter's Port Provident and District Society." It is spoken of, at the present time, in Guernsey, as being "a real blessing to the poor of the community, not only in having administered to their temporal wants in sickness or accidents, but also in having greatly improved their domestic comforts and moral character, by inculcating frugal and temperate habits."

On her return to Jersey she writes, under feeling of much sorrow—

25th.—On Seventh-day evening, in the midst of a very large party, our letters arrived; some from our dearest Hannah of a very touching nature; she had suffered so extremely on her voyage (to Madeira) as to bring on her confinement on board ship. Her child died, and her sufferings appear to have been extreme. The whole account was exceedingly affecting to me. But I desire to look above the agency of man, to Him, without whom not a sparrow falls to the ground, who orders all things in love, as well as in wisdom. My trust must be complete, my reliance entire, my hope continual. Lord, as all my springs are in Thee, I pray Thee daily, hourly, minutely, increase and renew my faith, patience, reliance, and hope, that I may never cast away my confidence, but that my soul may follow hard after Thee, even unto the end.

The time had now arrived to return home. She received accounts from England that called forth much anxiety. Several of her children required her attention. Her daughter Cresswell was seriously ill.

Lynn, Eleventh Month, 12th.—I left Jersey in the steamboat for Southampton. Parting, with many beloved friends there, I felt much. It is a place and people in which I have taken great interest: I also felt the uncertainty of the prospect before me, and in what state I should find my beloved child. I was much cast down, the wind rather high, and evidently rising. My maid and child quickly became ill, as did even our little dog. The passengers, one after another, almost all in the same state. The day gloomy, only now and then a ray of sunshine to enliven us. I remained, through mercy, quite well. We stopped at Guernsey, where I found, to my encouragement, some of my objects really prospering, and I was much pleased to hear that the School was established in the island of Herm. We dined whilst in the harbour there. Afterwards the weather became so boisterous, my cold so indifferent, and my poor boy so ill, that I remained in the cabin the whole evening, and a low time it was; fears got hold of me that I should never see Rachel again alive; but on the other hand I knew that I had a merciful Lord to deal with, who heard my prayers, knew my weakness, and I believed would not permit so overwhelming an affliction to overtake me. I desired humbly and patiently to trust. I felt the seriousness of our situation in the high wind, but was enabled entirely to leave it to Him, who orders all things well. We arrived at Southampton the next morning; I was much cast down and overdone, and during the journey to London, I had almost an inexpressible feeling of fatigue. I found rather a better account from Lynn, to my unspeakable relief.

From the accounts continuing better, Elizabeth Fry was, for a day or two, able to rest in the neighbourhood of London.

Then she pursued her way to Lynn, where, for six weeks she remained, devoted to her daughter, and to that devotion, guided by singular skill, and blessed by the providence of God, was apparently to be attributed her child's gradual restoration to health. From Lynn she wrote to her youngest daughter, then with the others of the party just returned home.

Lynn, *Eleventh Month*, 1833.

My dearest Louisa,

I feel inclined to write thee a few lines of salutation on thy return home. Thy sister and thyself have very important places to fill, although they may differ; and as I have told her my mind, I mean to do the same to thee—remember these words, "be sober, be vigilant." At thy important age much depends on not letting the mind *out*, if I may so express myself: it is a period of life when this is natural—various prospects in life may float before the view; but how infinitely important to know the heart to be staid upon God, and to find it meat and drink to be doing His will—how important to attend to *present* duties; this is the best preparation for the future, whatever that future may be.—I see that much devolves on thee; thou hast not only to look to thy own soul, but younger ones are looking up to thee, whom, I believe, thou mayst be the means of winning to Christ.

To the daughter whom she had so long nursed, she wrote, after her return home :—

The better accounts of thee are certainly very encouraging, and set me more at rest about thee ; still, my beloved child, I feel thou needest my sympathy and prayers: there is much to feel, even if it pleases Providence quite to raise thee up again: there is much to go through. I have often found, in recovering from long and severe illness, and entering life again, that our enemies spiritually are yet lively and strong, and even, we may say, after the "Beast has had a deadly wound, it still lives:" I know this by my own experience.

Chapter Ninth.

1834-1838. Visit to Dorset and Hants—Isle of Wight—Journey to Scotland—Death of the Duke of Gloucester—Letter—Coast Guard Libraries—Examination before the Committee of the House of Lords—Journey along the Southern Coast of England—Crosses to Jersey and Guernsey—Libraries for Packet Ships at Falmouth—For Shepherds at Salisbury Plain—Death of a sister-in-law—Religious engagements in Sussex—Visit to Dublin—Unpleasant Voyage to Guernsey—Illness and death of her sister Louisa Hoare—Death of King William IV.—Of a sister-in-law—Departure of her brother J. J. Gurney for America—Visits Paris—Meeting in Westminster—Journey to Scotland—Religious engagements in Surrey, Essex, &c.—Renewed prospect of visiting France.

Fourth Month, 1st, 1834.—I am likely to leave home to-day for religious service in Dorset and Hants. Oh, Lord! I pray Thee be with me, and anoint me for Thy work, that it may be fully to Thy praise, the edification of those I go amongst, and to my own help and peace; and be pleased to keep my children and family during my absence. Grant this, dearest Lord, for Thine own name sake. Amen.

12th.—I returned yesterday from my expedition, which I may thankfully say, proved very satisfactory.

She was accompanied on this journey by her friend William Forster, and her nieces Priscilla Buxton and Priscilla Gurney. Her aunt's address and manner on that occasion, and the impressions made upon her own mind, are admirably described by one of them; being at the time, in very delicate health, she was, perhaps, the more sensitively alive to her aunt's peculiar powers of soothing.

"There was no weakness, or trouble of mind or body, which might not safely be unveiled to her. Whatever various or opposite views, feelings, or wishes, might be confided to her, all came out again, tinged with her own loving, hopeful spirit. Bitterness of every kind died, when entrusted to her; it never re-appeared. The most favourable construction possible was always put upon every transaction. No doubt *her failing* lay this way; but did it not give her and her example a wonderful influence? Was it not the very secret of her power with the wretched and degraded prisoners? She always could see hope for every one; she invariably found, or made some point of light. The most abandoned must have felt that she did not despair for them, either for this world, or another, and *this it was that made her irresistible.*

"At Southampton, time and opportunity were rather unexpectedly afforded for an excursion to the Isle of Wight. I think she undertook it chiefly for the sake of pleasing Priscilla Gurney and myself; but it had important consequences. We travelled round by Shanklin, Bonchurch, and the Undercliff. She was zealous as we, in the enjoyment of the scenery and the wild flowers; but the next day, on reaching Freshwater, she was fatigued and remained to rest, whilst we went to see Alum Bay. On our return, we were told she had walked out, and we soon received a message, desiring us to join her at the Coast Guard Station We found her in her element; pleased and giving pleasure to a large group, who were assembled around her. She entered with the greatest sympathy into their somewhat dreary position, inquired into their resources for education for their children, and religious improvement for themselves—found them much in want of books; and from this visit originated *that great undertaking*, of providing libraries foı *all* the Coast Guard Stations in Great Britain—an undertaking full of difficulties, but in which her perseverance never relaxed till it was accomplished."

On a review of this journey, Elizabeth Fry writes:

Upton, Fourth Month.—At Portsmouth, we paid an interesting visit to the Haslar Hospital, the Hulks Hospital Ship, and some prisons; we also paid a delightful little visit to the Isle of Wight I felt more able to enjoy the great beauties of nature, from having been owned by my Lord and Master, in my religious services. What a relish does true religion give for our temporal, as well as spiritual blessings!

21*st.*—Yesterday (First-day) I attended Meeting, rather oppressed in body and mind. Ministered to by dear Elizabeth Dudley, but had such heaviness of body as to hinder spiritual revival. In the afternoon, I went, accompanied by Elizabeth Dudley, Rebecca Sturges, and some others, to visit the female convict ship; the sun shone brightly, the day delightful, the poor women rejoiced to see us, but my spirit was in heaviness, from the difficulty of leaving my family, even for a few hours, on that day. It was a fine sight to see about one hundred and fifty poor female convicts, and some sailors, standing, sitting, and leaning round us, whilst we read the Scriptures to them. I spoke to them, and Elizabeth Dudley prayed. Surely, to witness the solemn effect, the tears rolling down many cheeks, we must acknowledge it to be the Lord's doing; still I felt flat, though the others thought it a very satisfactory time; but in the evening I became more revived, and comforted, and thankful that it has pleased the Lord to send me to the poor outcasts, although, at times, feeling as if I went more as a machine moved by springs, than in the lively state I desire; but at other times it is different, and there is much sense of light, life, love, and power. To-day, I expect to go to the Duchess of Gloucester, and amongst some of the high in this life. May the Lord be with me, that my intercourse with these, may not be in vain in Him. I feel it no light responsibility, having the door so open with the Government of our country, and those filling high places; I am often surprised to find how much so; and yet the Lord only knows the depth of my humiliations, and how it has been out of the depths, that I have been raised up for these services. At the Admiralty, I have lately had important requests granted; at the Home Office, they are always ready to attend to what I ask; and at the Colonial Office, I expect that they will soon make some alterations in the arrangements for the female convicts in New South Wales.

Who has thus turned the hearts of those in authority? Surely it is the Lord. May He grant me wisdom and sound discretion, rightly to use the influence He has given me. Be near to Thy servant, this day, gracious Lord, in every place; and so help her by Thy Spirit, that she may do Thy will, and not bow to man, *but alone to Thee, her God;* doing all to Thy glory!

24th.—We dined at Lord Bexley's, and met Captain Mangles, the great traveller, several clergymen, and others. I desired to maintain the watch, but the company of serious, intellectual, and refined persons, is apt to draw me a good deal forth in conversation and mind, and often leads me to many fears afterwards, lest there should imperceptibly be any thing of showing off, and being exalted by man; but I may truly say, inwardly, I mostly feel reduced and humbled after such times, and fearful, lest I should have a cloud over me, so as to hinder my near communion with my Lord.

Upton, Seventh Month, 25th.—To-morrow I expect to set off on a journey into Scotland. I have taken an affecting leave of my family, praying, that we might again (if the will of God) be refreshed together; and my way has satisfactorily opened to go.

Her husband, and two daughters preceded her, and awaited her coming at Birnam Inn, near Dunkeld.

She arrived there on the 5th of the Eighth Month, and after giving her a few days' rest from her journey, the party set off for Loch Tay. At Kenmore, they enjoyed a quiet First-day, and tolerable Highland accommodation. In the evening, anxious to turn the day to some good account, Elizabeth Fry invited the servants of the inn, to attend the reading which she intended to have with her own family. A pretty large congregation assembled.

By Loch Tay, Eighth Month, 9th, First-day.—Not having a Meeting to go to, and not believing it right for me to attend any other place of worship, I desire to spend a time in solemn searching of heart before the Lord, and may I be enabled to hold communion with Him in spirit. On the morning of the 1st, the day appointed for the liberation of all the slaves in the British dominions, and on which my dear niece, Priscilla Buxton was to be married, I poured forth my soul in deep supplication before my heavenly Father, on behalf of the poor slaves, that a quiet spirit might be granted them—that their *spiritual* bonds might also be broken—that the liberty prepared for the children of God might be their portion. I also prayed for my beloved niece and her companion in life, that the Lord would be with them, keep them, and bless them.

Edinburgh, Eighth Month, 28th.—I left my dearest husband and two daughters in the Highlands, as I wished to accompany my boy on his way to England, and above all, to attend the Meetings, see the Friends, and visit the prisons here. I came under the belief that duty called me to do so. We experienced some danger in our journey, from an accident in a steam-boat, but the Lord protected us. I feel it to be a fearful thing to be here; there are many ministers besides me. Lord, be near to Thy servant, who is here without one relation or companion, and has left all, for what she apprehends to be the call of duty. Guide, guard, and keep her, qualify her for Thine own service, of whatever kind it may be, to Thine own glory; keep her eye very single to Thyself and to the direction of Thy Spirit.

Of her engagements in Edinburgh on this occasion, she writes, on returning to her family at Tarbet:—

I had much to be thankful for, in the help granted to me in such religious services, as I believe I was called into, in Meetings, families, and institutions. I had very solemn religious times in the Gaol and large Refuge, also shorter ones in the Bridewell and another Refuge. The hearts of many appeared to be peculiarly opened towards me, and entire strangers wonderfully ministered to my wants, and upheld my hands. Our dear friends who knew me before, were abundantly kind to me. May the Lord, in his love and mercy, reward them for all their great kindness to me, His very unworthy servant; and may He still soften and enlarge their hearts towards me, until the work that he gives me to do amongst them, be accomplished. I find a field for much important service for the poor, and to make more arrangements for the ladies who visit the prisons. I desire, and earnestly pray to be preserved from an over-active spirit in these things; and on the other hand, faithfully, diligently, humbly, and watchfully, to do whatever my Lord gives me to do, that may be to His glory, or the good of my fellow-creatures.

We have passed through very lovely country; but the sun has not shone much upon us, and the atmosphere of my mind has partaken of the same hue, which is not so pleasant as more lively colouring over the mind, but I am ready to think more profitable, and perhaps more likely to qualify me for the weighty duties before me.

After visiting other scenes of natural grandeur and beauty, and some hospitable friends, the travellers retraced their steps through Dumbarton and Glasgow to Edinburgh, where Elizabeth Fry was again received with affectionate kindness by her friends and fellow-labourers; her time and energies being devoted to the completion of those objects that had claimed her particular attention on her former visit.

But whilst many institutions of great importance owe their existence, either directly or indirectly, to her skill and exertions—and she sowed the seed of many a noble tree—she did not omit to avail herself of those small opportunities of benefiting others, that are presented in the occurrences of each passing hour. It was her unvarying practice, both at private dwellings, and at the inns where they passed their First-days, to invite the servants to attend the evening scripture readings; many of the visitors, who, like themselves, were only for a short time sojourners there, also joined them on these solemn and interesting occasions. Her's was a constant endeavour to leave some savour of good on all with whom she had any communication. The chambermaid and the waiter received the word of kindness and counsel, and a little tract or text-book to impress it upon their memories. The postilion at the carriage window, or the cotter at the road side, met with appropriate notice, and this mingled with the most unaffected enjoyment of the country, and spirit in all the incidents of travelling.

The result of her observations on the state of the Scotch Prisons, she forwarded to the proper authorities after her return home.

The close of the year 1834 was marked by the death of the Duke of Gloucester. He had been highly esteemed by Elizabeth Fry, from the time when, quartered at Norwich, in the latter part of the last century, he was amongst the few, who addressed words of friendly caution and sound advice, to the young and motherless sisters at Earlham. To the Princess Sophia of Gloucester, she wrote upon the occasion—

Upton Lane, *Twelfth Month*, 13*th*, 1834.

My dear Friend,

I hope thou wilt not feel it an intrusion, my expressing my sympathy with thee in the death of the Duke of Gloucester. To lose a dear and only brother is no small trial, and for a while makes the world appear very desolate. But I trust, having thy pleasant pictures marred in this life, may be one means of opening brighter prospects in the life to come, and of having thy treasure increased in the heavenly inheritance.

The Duchess of Gloucester kindly commissioned a lady to write to me, who gave me a very comforting account of the state of the Duke's mind. I feel it cause for much thankfulness that he was so sustained through faith in his Lord and Saviour, and we may humbly trust, through His merits, saved with an everlasting salvation. It would be very pleasant to me to hear how thy health and spirits are, after so great a shock, and I propose inquiring at Blackheath, where I rather expect to be next week; or, if thou wouldest have the kindness to request one of thy ladies-in-waiting to write me a few lines, I should be much obliged.

I hope that my dear and valued friend, the Duchess of Gloucester, is as well as we can expect, after her deep affliction.

With desires for thy present and everlasting welfare,
I remain, thy attached and obliged friend,
ELIZABETH FRY.

Upton Lane, First Month, 27th, 1835.—I yesterday went, *by appointment,* to visit the Duchess of Gloucester, after the death of the Duke. She gave a highly interesting account of his death. He appeared to depart in the full hope of a Christian. This I felt satisfactory and comforting, after having traced him from his youth up, and seen his conduct, and known his principles when a young man. I observe how gently the Lord deals with His people, and how, under the most varied circumstances, He visits all, and how He bears with those that fear Him. It appeared to me that the Duke desired to act up to the light received, and his faith was strong in his Saviour, which proved his stronghold in the day of trouble.

Second Month, 8th.—The way appears opening with our present Ministers to obtain libraries for all the Coast Guard Stations, a matter I have long had at heart. My desire is, to do all these things with a single eye to the glory of God, and the welfare of my fellow-mortals, and if they succeed, to pray that He, who alone can bless and increase, may prosper the work of my unworthy hands, and that I may ever wholly give the glory to Him to whom it is due, even my Lord and my God.

The beneficial effects of the libraries introduced, through her influence, into the Naval Hospitals at Haslar and Plymouth, and the testimony borne to their utility by Sir William Burnett, the highest medical authority in the navy, had confirmed her desire to extend this advantage to all the Coast Guard Stations, without further delay. It was brought under the notice of Sir Robert Peel, then first Lord of the Treasury, by means of a letter addressed by Elizabeth Fry to his brother Lawrence Peel, who had already ably seconded her views in the Brighton District Society. This application met with the approbation of Sir Robert Peel, by whom it was referred to Sir Thomas Freemantle—from him an assurance was received, that there existed a strong disposition on the part of the Board of Treasury to give effect to this object, and that, as soon as the proposed plan was matured, it should receive all the assistance in his power.

Seventh Month, 21st.—I have been very busy, trying to obtain libraries for all the Coast Guard Stations, and have had to see men in authority, who received me in a way that was surprising to myself.

Her projected plan of thus forming libraries for all the Coast Guard Stations throughout the United Kingdom, involved a vast undertaking, there being about five hundred of these, divided into twenty-four districts, and comprising upwards of 21,000 persons, including the wives and children of the men.

Government allowed a grant of £500. Large private subscriptions were obtained through Elizabeth Fry's exertions.

The details of the arrangement were almost entirely her

own, and remarkably adapted to meet the requirings of those whom she desired to benefit; having made herself mistress of the subject, and of the nature of the service, with surprising rapidity and correctness.

Besides contributions in money, many liberal donations of books were received from some of the most eminent booksellers; which, with the grants from the Society for Promoting Christian Knowledge, the Religious Tract Society, and other similar institutions, amounted in value to upwards of a thousand pounds.

The libraries, for the stations alone, amounted in all to 25,896 volumes. Fifty-two different works were prepared for each station, whilst a still larger and more important collection was to be attached to every one of the seventy-four districts, in order to afford the needful variety and change. The packages of books, the greater part carriage-free, were dispatched in the course of the summer from the Custom House, in Government vessels to their different destinations. But all this was not done without much fatigue and exertion, many wearisome journeys to London, and a great deal of writing; in the latter she was much assisted by a dissenting minister, who undertook the office of Secretary, and proved an efficient and useful agent to herself, and those gentlemen who acted with her.

On the 22nd of Fifth Month, Elizabeth Fry was ordered to attend the Select Committee of the House of Lords, appointed to inquire into the present state of the several Gaols and Houses of Correction in England and Wales. She was accompanied by Elizabeth Pryor, Jane Pirrie, and Catherine Fraser, who were likewise to be examined. Sir T. Fowell Buxton was with Elizabeth Fry. She and her companions were conducted by him to an ante-room, where they found the Duke of Richmond and Lord Suffield; the Duke of Sutherland came in shortly afterwards. The Duke of Richmond, as Chairman of the Committee, presided; the government short-hand writer was seated at the corner of the table, and Elizabeth Fry, Elizabeth Pryor, Jane Pirie, and Catherine Fraser at the right-hand of the Duke. There might be from twelve to fifteen noblemen present.

An eye-witness writes:

"Never, I should think, was the calm dignity of her character more conspicuous. Whatever her inward feelings might have been, nothing like excitement was visible in her manner—nothing hurried in her language. Perfectly self-possessed, her speech flowed melodiously, her ideas were clearly expressed, and if another thought possessed her, besides that of delivering her opinions faithfully and judiciously on the subjects brought before her, it was, that she might speak a word for her Lord and Master in that noble company.

"Beyond all topics, did she urge the vast importance of scriptural instruction for poor, fallen ones. Warmed by her subject, with her voice a little raised, and a look of solemn earnestness, she went on to say, after replying to one of the questions addressed to her—

"'I believe the effect of religious and other instruction is hardly to be calculated on—and I may further say, that notwithstanding the high estimation and reverence in which I held the Holy Scriptures before I went to the prisons, as believing them to be written by inspiration of God, and therefore calculated to produce the greatest good, I have seen (in reading the Scriptures to those women) such a power attending them, and such an effect on the minds of the most reprobate, as I could not have conceived. If any one wants a confirmation of the truth of Christianity, let him go and read the Scriptures in prison to poor sinners; you there see, how the gospel is exactly adapted to the fallen condition of man. It has strongly confirmed my faith, and I feel it to be the bounden duty of the Government and the country, that those truths should be administered in the manner most likely to conduce to the real reformation of the prisoner; you then go to the root of the matter—for though severe punishment may, in a measure, deter them and others from crime, it does not amend the character and change the heart, but if you have altered the principles of the individuals, they are not only deterred from crime, because of the fear of punishment, but they go out and set a bright example to others."

The quiet self-possession with which she delivered her opinions, won confidence and consideration; and she had the satisfaction to believe, that some points of importance were forwarded by the information which she furnished.

Her communications with persons who possessed worldly power were not rendered subservient to the gratification of self, to the indulgence of any principle of vanity, but, in the openings for usefulness to her fellow creatures; and, as she walked onward in the path of duty, she was preserved in watchfulness and humility. Her guileless simplicity of heart, the serious dignity of her deportment, and the unaffected polish of her manner, (divested as it was of all the ceremony of mere worldly politeness), inspired beholders with respect and reverence, whilst her modest, beaming smile of calm benignity impressed them with a consciousness of the love that influenced her.

Some business now required Joseph Fry's attention in the South of England: his wife accompanied him, with one of their daughters.

She almost always called at the Coast Guard Stations, and conversed with those whom she found there; frequently the officers would follow her to the inn for further communication. At Portsmouth, she visited Haslar Hospital, speaking kind and pitying words to the sick and deranged. Admiral Garrett and his family paid her the most hospitable attention; with his daughter she visited the Penitentiary at Portsea. While they went over the house, the unhappy inmates were assembled in the parlour, where they were all standing when Elizabeth Fry, and her young companion, returned to the room. The latter describes Elizabeth Fry, as "sitting down, laying her bonnet on the table, and making some inquiries as to the arrangements of the place, and the conduct of the young women there. Two were pointed out to her as being peculiarly refractory and hardened—without noticing this, she addressed some words of exhortation and advice to all, but when she arose to go away, she went up to these two, and extending her hand to each of them, said, in a tone and manner quite indescribable, but so touching—'I trust I shall hear better things of thee.' The hearts that had been proof against the words of reproach and exhortation, softened at those of hope and kindness, and both burst into tears."

The travellers made a three days' tour of the Isle of Wight; but at Cowes Elizabeth Fry separated from her husband and daughter, believing it her duty to cross to Jersey, in the hope of effecting something towards remedying the crying evils which still existed in the prison there. She was accompanied by her young friend, Lydia Irving, from London, who had kindly agreed to go with her; they went in the "*Ariadne*," Captain Bazin's steam-vessel. They had a rough passage, but a warm reception at D'Hautrée, Colonel (now General) Touzel's. By him and his family were they treated, not merely with hospitality, but with true Christian affection, as "beloved for their works' sake."

She laboured diligently during her stay on the island—her objects being the prison, district society, &c. She passed a few days in Guernsey, being similarly occupied—thence crossed to Weymouth—spent a short time at Plymouth, visited the Coast Guard Stations, &c., and, joined by her husband and daughter, proceeded to Falmouth, where they were warmly welcomed by her valued relatives of the Fox family, to whom she was much and justly attached.

Here she heard various particulars of the packets continually sailing from that port; she wished to have libraries for them also. In this she was assisted by Captain Clavell, and by many of the commanders of the packets; and she did not relax in her efforts until they were well supplied with Bibles, Testaments, religious tracts, &c. She received, a few months afterwards, a letter from one of Capt. Clavell's family, dated "Falmouth, January 27th, 1835," which says:—

I am sure you will be glad to hear our library is getting on with much success. The men appear more anxious than ever to read. · · · · · I cannot tell you how much we all feel indebted to you for your great kindness, and benevolent exertions; but particularly our poor sailors."

A few days were passed among the romantic beauties of North Devon. Thence they turned their steps homewards; but at Amesbury she paused long enough, to make arrangements for a library being established, for the use of the shepherds of Salisbury Plain. An excellent individual undertook the care of the books, and their circulation. After a few months' trial of the plan, he wrote to her—

"Forty-five books are in constant circulation, with the additional magazines. More than fifty poor people read them with attention, return them with thanks, and desire the loan of more, frequently observing, they think it a very kind thing indeed, that they should be furnished with so many good books, free of all cost, so entertaining and instructive, these long winter evenings.

From the different officers of the Coast Guard Stations, she received letters that gladdened her heart; all breathing the same spirit, expressing their cordial approbation of the plan, and the pleasure felt by the men and their families. But something beyond pleasure was desired by her, with whom the idea originated—that spiritual advantage and edification should accrue, to those who read. The seed that she sowed has, in truth, been in many instances remarkably blessed.

On arriving at home from this western tour, an afflicting event was impending, which she thus records:—

Upton, Tenth Month, 13th.—I returned home yesterday with my dear husband, from a very affecting and unexpected visit into Norfolk, in consequence of the severe illness and death of my beloved sister, Mary Gurney, my brother Joseph's amiable, devoted, and superior wife. She was in the prime of her day, only thirty-two years of age, a spiritually-minded and lively minister, a very intellectual person, and highly cultivated, generous, and remarkably cheerful, a wonderful helper to my brother, adapted to his wants. When I heard how ill she was, I could hardly believe she would die, she had such an apparent call here below, but our ways are not the Lord's ways, nor our thoughts, His thoughts. He took her, thus early, to Himself, but we apprehend, as the shock of corn fully ripe. Our dearest Joseph's resignation and patience are great indeed, and his even cheerful acquiescence with the will of his God, is instructive. The funeral was deeply affecting. After dinner we had an extraordinary time. Our dear brother Francis Cunningham prayed—his dear Richenda spoke. Joseph, in the most striking manner, enlarged on the character of the departed, on his loss, and his consolation; the day went on and ended well, in a reading with the poor neighbours; but words fail me, to tell of the solemn, holy, loving feeling over us. Oh! what a blessing is family unity in the Lord—my children who were present, and many others, were deeply and powerfully impressed. May it be lasting—may the same spirit that has so remarkably rested upon us, rest on them; the same love, the same peace, the same unity of spirit, the same freeness of spiritual communication. Such a day is almost like being raised above the things of this world; all appeared sanctified, all blessed, even the very beauties of the place. How did I feel called upon to entreat, and to warn, how did I seek to bear testimony to the very truth—and how did dearest Joseph, in his affliction, beseech all to come to Christ, for salvation.

23*d*.—Since my return home, I have had very satisfactory letters from the island of Jersey, saying that great alterations and improvements are taking place in the Hospital. The Prison Committee have also acted upon many of my suggestions. In our home prison cause, it is really marvellous to me to observe the openings of Providence, in the good effected by the members of the Ladies' British Society. I feel rather bound to record these things—not by way of boasting, but as a proof that all comes from the Lord, who blesses in the labour, and who strengthens for the work.

Upton Lane, Second Month, 25th, 1836.—On the 23rd instant, I thought it right to lay before my Monthly Meeting, my belief, that it was my duty to have some religious services in Sussex, Kent, and my own Quarterly Meeting. I can hardly express the sweetness and peacefulness I felt, in making this small sacrifice, to what I believe to be, the call of duty. The near unity and sympathy expressed with me by my friends, was also very encouraging and comforting. My dearest brother Samuel offering to take this expedition, was quite a help and comfort.

Third Month, 13th.—I returned from my journey on Sixth-day last, having been out a week. I felt low, in fact, almost ill, with the serious weight of the prospect of the Public Meetings. The first Meeting I wished to have, was at Hastings, the second at Rye; a curious interesting place, towards which I had felt much attracted in my last journey. We found a Meeting-house there. Grover Kemp, a valuable young minister, joined me at my request, which was a great satisfaction to me.

At Hastings, several of the Coast Guard men and officers were at the Meeting. I had many proofs of the use and value of the libraries sent to them, to my comfort and satisfaction; proving it not to have been labour "in vain in the Lord." Real kindness, almost affection, as well as gratitude, was shown to me, by several of the men and officers and their families. We hope a Bible Society will be formed at Rye in consequence of our visit, and a Prison Society at Dover. But to come to one of the most interesting parts of our expedition, we went to Sheerness, to visit the women and children in the ships in ordinary. Captain Kennedy had them collected at my request; it was a fine sight, in a large man-of-war, instead of bloodshed and fightings, to see many naval officers, two chaplains, sailors, soldiers, ladies, numbers of women and children, all met to hear what two Quakers had to say, more particularly a woman, and to listen to any advice given by them. We examined the children, as to their knowledge, then gave them advice, afterwards we addressed their parents, and lastly those present generally—we were received with great cordiality by Captain Kennedy, and his wife.

23*rd.*—I laid before our Monthly Meeting on Third-day, my belief of its being my duty to go to Ireland, and to take Liverpool and Manchester in the way. I had the unity of my friends—I say in my heart—unless Thy presence go with me, take me not up hence. May my Lord answer this prayer in His tender mercy.

Fourth Month, 14*th.*—Just about leaving home for Ireland—oh dearest Lord! bless, I entreat Thee, this act of faith, to my family, myself, and those amongst whom I go, and be, I most humbly pray Thee, my Keeper, their Keeper; my Helper, their Helper; my Strength, their Strength; my Joy and Peace, and their Joy and Peace, Amen! Grant this for Thine own name' sake, oh, most gracious Lord God! cause also, that we may meet again, in love, joy, peace and safety.

Upton Lane, Fifth Month, 13*th.*—I returned home safely yesterday afternoon. I think I never had so happy and so prosperous an arrival. I wept with joy; the stream appears to be turned for a while, my tears have often flowed for sorrow, and now my beloved husband and children have caused them to flow for joy. I found not only all going on well, and having done so during my absence, but to please, comfort and surprise me, my dearest husband had had my rooms altered, and made most comfortable, and my children had sent me nice presents to render them more complete. Their offerings of love quite gladdened my heart, though far too good for me; I felt utterly unworthy of them, I may say peculiarly so. I have seldom returned home more sensible of the hidden evils of my heart. Circumstances have unusually made me feel this. I fully believe in this going out, much help has been granted me, in various ways; my understanding has appeared to be enlightened, more fully to see and comprehend gospel truth, and power has been given me to utter it boldly, beyond what I could have supposed.

The preceding extract depicts what was, under all circumstances, the striking characteristic of this remarkable woman —her deep humility and lowly estimate of herself. She, who was continually devoting every energy of mind and body to promote the happiness of the human family, and whose self-sacrificing love assumed a concentrated form of tenderest attachment towards each member of her own immediate circle, calling forth, in every hour of need, the most assiduous exertions in their service, is yet found to be so acutely affected by tokens of kind attention from her husband and children—tokens which might naturally be expected by every affectionate wife and mother—that the tears of grateful joy are shed, and *her heart is gladdened* by offerings of love, which *she feels herself "utterly unworthy" to receive.* This incident pourtrays her mind, in lines more vividly defined than the pen can describe.

My desires and prayers are strong, that being returned home, I may profit by the deep experience of this expedition. May my holy Redeemer cause me by His Spirit to walk very closely to Himself, keeping to the truth in His Spirit, and, by His power, preserving me from impetuous zeal in holy things. In this Yearly Meeting, may very sound discretion be my portion. As for my home duties, my longings are indescribable that I may perform them in deep humility, godliness, holy fear, and love; that I may be a preacher of righteousness, in all things, and in all ways.

Sixth Month, 12th, (First-day morning.)—We, yesterday, had our British Society Meeting, and it was striking to me to observe, how much our various labours had been blessed, and to hear how many poor women, from various parts, have been induced to forsake their evil courses, and are now either leading good lives, or have died happy Christian deaths.

18*th.*—I have felt a good deal pressed in spirit, during these last few days. The day before yesterday I counted twenty-nine persons who came here, on various accounts, principally to see me; there are times, when the tide of life is almost overpowering. It makes me doubtful, as to our remaining much longer in this place, which, from its situation, brings so many here. I have several things which rather weightily press me just now. I desire to lay my case before the Lord, trusting in Him, and casting myself and my whole care upon Him. Dearest Lord, help: supply all our needs, through the riches of Thy grace, in Christ Jesus! Amen.

In the Sixth Month, Elizabeth Fry had the satisfaction of receiving the printed Report of the Committee acting under the sanction of the Government, for furnishing the Coast Guard of the United Kingdom with libraries of religious and instructive books; announcing the completion of the project, with a short account of what had been effected.

The Report is as follows:—

"The committee, acting under the sanction of His Majesty's Government, for furnishing the Coast Guard of the United Kingdom with Libraries of religious and instructive books, and also with school books for the families of the men employed on that service, having, by the blessing of Divine Providence, completed that object, it becomes their pleasing duty to lay before the subscribers a Report of their proceedings.

"In the commencement of this duty, it is proper gratefully to acknowledge, that the idea of furnishing these libraries first suggested itself to the benevolent mind of Mrs. Fry, whose active and charitable exertions, on all occasions affecting the benefit of mankind, are too well known, and too highly estimated, to need further remark on the present occasion, and who having previously succeeded in inducing his Majesty's Government to establish libraries for the use of the patients in the naval hospitals, was induced by the observations she had made on the subject, to endeavour to extend the same beneficial measure to the Coast Guard Service, and after several unsuccessful efforts, arising from the expense which it would occasion, a sum of £500 was obtained in 1835, from the First Lord of the Treasury (Sir Robert Peel) for this purpose, which munificent donation has since been followed by subscriptions from many charitable individuals, and grants from several public book societies, but as the whole of these funds were not sufficient to meet the object in view, the present Chancellor of the Exchequer (Mr. Spring Rice) kindly granted two further sums amounting together to £460 to effect its completion.

"The means thus so liberally afforded, have enabled the committee to provide and forward to the coast,—

498	Libraries for the Stations on shore, containing	25,896	vols.
74	Ditto Districts	12,880	
48	Ditto Cruisers	1,867	
	School books for the children of the crews of Stations	6,464	
	Pamphlets, Tracts, &c.	5,357	in Nos.
	Makin a total of	52,464	vols.

and thereby to furnish a body of deserving and useful men and their wives and families, (amounting to upwards of 21,000 persons,) with the means of moral and religious instruction, as well as profitable amusement, most of whom, from their situation in life, have not the means of procuring such benefits from their own resources, and who in many instances, are so far removed from places of public worship and schools, as to prevent the possibility of themselves or their families deriving advantage from either."

To have been enabled to accomplish this great undertaking, so fraught with vast and important consequences, was indeed a source of inexpressible relief and satisfaction to the mind of Elizabeth Fry.

Having now completed her onerous task in reference to the establishment of these libraries, her mind was much impressed with an apprehension that it was her duty again to visit Jersey and Guernsey, in order to promote some important reforms which, through her instrumentality, had been begun, but which, to render them effectual, required her assistance and direction. One difficulty presented itself in the indisposition of Louisa Hoare, and Elizabeth Fry felt deeply the seriousness and the trial of leaving the vicinity of London, at a time when the health of her sister indicated that she was sinking under the influence of disease. She earnestly sought for the guidance of her heavenly Father, and she believed it to be her duty to go to Jersey, at any sacrifice of personal feeling, and this view was confirmed, by knowing that by her suffering sister she was not needed ; every thing that love or skill could effect, being done for the beloved invalid, by her own family, and her other sisters. Another circumstance tended to satisfy her mind as to the rectitude of her decision : her sister-in-law Elizabeth Fry, then in very delicate health, having been again advised to visit the Channel Islands, where she had before derived much benefit from the mild sea air, she with Joseph and Elizabeth Fry, and their daughter, embarked at Southampton, on a calm fine evening, with every prospect of a good voyage, but these favourable appearances were not of long duration. About four o'clock in the morning, all on board were roused by the sudden stopping of the vessel. A dense fog had come on, when passing through the intricate passage between the Caskets and the island of Alderney. They remained many hours entangled amongst rocks, with the fog so thick, that it was not always easy to see the length of the vessel; much apprehension was entertained by many on board, in which Elizabeth Fry partook, though preserving her wonted calmness of demeanour. Providentially, there was, as passenger in the steamer, the old Guernsey pilot, who had, with remarkable skill, steered some vessels through a passage, generally considered impracticable. Of his advice and assistance, the Captain, himself an experienced pilot, took advantage, and after a time of careful navigation, the joyful tidings spread among the passengers, that the jeopardy was over, that they were through the channel, and once more in the open sea. The spirit of Elizabeth Fry's mind was exemplified by her remark to her daughter, when, as they approached Guernsey, the clouds passed away, and the sun shone forth in brightness.

It was First-day. She said, in a solemn manner, I have felt it very doubtful whether this was not to be, for us, the dawn of the eternal, instead of the earthly Sabbath; I thought it rather the Church above, than the Church below, we were to join to-day.

But we turn to her own interesting account of the excursion:—

Jersey, Eighth Month, 6th.—My husband and I have been here rather more than a week. I left home on Fourth-day, the 27th, accompanied by my dear sister Gurney, leaving my husband and the rest of the party to follow on Sixth-day, because I believed it to be my duty to attend the Quarterly Meeting at Alton, in my way to Southampton. In tender mercy, I was permitted to part from my beloved family in peace, in love, and in good hope that our Heavenly Father would bless and protect them. On Second-day, before leaving home, we had our dear children and grandchildren, for a sweet cheerful evening, drinking tea and having strawberries, in the garden, a little farewell frolic—it was a lovely sight. From Alton I proceeded to Southampton, where we all met, and were favoured with a favourable passage till early in the morning, when so awful a fog came on, just as we were in the midst of the rocks, between Alderney and Guernsey, that the Captain and the crew appeared to be much alarmed. We all felt it very seriously, and I experienced something of my own infirmity and fearful nature, still I was quiet, and I think trustful. It was delightful once more to see land, and to have the sun shine upon us. I can hardly express the feeling. We were detained about four hours in this fog. I must describe our arrival, the sun breaking out, showing us the islands of Guernsey, Herm, and Sark. Castle Carey, the place of our destination, on the top of the hill, surrounded by trees, looking beautiful: we met with the most cordial reception from our friends and their children—the place delightful—my room commanding the finest view of the sea and islands, our comforts abundant, far above our deserts. I had apprehended, previously to leaving home, that I should feel it a duty to visit the island of Alderney, but I became discouraged, the danger of the sea having been so much brought home to me, and the passage being very difficult. But I found upon weighing the subject, that I was not satisfied to omit it, and therefore, if a favourable opening occurred, resolved to make the effort, and to go on Fourth-day, the 11th. We tried for a conveyance in vain, till the very morning, when we found a vessel going. The sun shone brilliantly, the wind fair; every thing prospered our setting off, and we appeared to have the unity of all our party. My beloved husband, Edmund Richards, Sophia Mourant, and myself. We had a very favourable voyage, though these little sailing vessels are unpleasant to me, and give me an uncomfortable sensation. We arrived at this curious island, which is rocky, wild, not generally cultivated, covered in parts with a carpet of lovely wild flowers, and scantily inhabited by an interesting people. No inn, of course, but we had a very nice lodging, where we might truly say, we wanted for no real comfort: so the Lord doth provide. I was low and poorly, during the first part of our visit; but like the fog on the voyage, my cloudy state was suddenly dispersed, as from a ray of the Sun of Righteousness. We held some meetings, we also formed a Ladies' Charity to visit the poor, we proposed sending a library, and Edmund Richards formed a temperance society. We were received with great kindness, by numbers of the people, and by Major Baines the Governor, and his wife. We found no opportunity for our departure at the time we had proposed leaving Alderney, and were literally confined there, until the end of the following week, when the way appeared to be as clear to return, as it had been to go. A vessel to take us—the wind fair, and the sun bright. We arrived safely at Castle Carey, on the evening of the 24th of the Seventh Month, and found good accounts from home, and from the party who had preceded us to Jersey; thanks be to my Heavenly Father! My too anxious and fearful mind having been disposed to much anxiety. I had not much public service in Guernsey. Meetings as usual on First-day. I went to see many families of Friends and others, and besides some of the poor, visited the Hospital, and urged the great need of a Lunatic Asylum. The evening before our departure, I had a very solemn Public Meeting, with many interesting persons; afterwards several joined us at Castle Carey, where we had a time of much interest, pleasantly partaking of natural friendship; afterwards we were read to by a clergyman, and then I had a very solemn occasion of thanksgiving and prayer, greatly doubting my ever seeing most of their faces again. The next morning, John and Matilda Carey, their children, the clergyman, and our friends E. Richards and family, all accompanied us to the shore, some went with us in a boat to the ship, which I entered in peace and comfort, under the belief, that I had been in my right allotment in that island, and Alderney. We had a beautiful passage here, calm, and lovely weather, and had the blessing of finding the party well.

Jersey, 19*th*.—In this place I find much to occupy me, in the Hospital, the District Society, and in the Prisons. We receive much kind attention from the inhabitants of the island. I had much to say in a large District Society Meeting, yesterday—I hope usefully. I entered it prayerfully, but not enough so. I have enjoyed some delightful expeditions into the lovely country, where we have sometimes taken our cold dinner, and spent the day in the rocky bays. We have also joined two large parties of the same kind, which were pleasant to me; my nature leads me to be social, and rather like general society; but I wish all to be done in the right spirit. Innocent recreation, I believe, is profitable as well as pleasant. Our Lord desired His servants to rest, and He evidently felt for them when they had hardly time to eat; (6th chapter of Mark, 31st verse;) but this rest was after labour. I believe our recreations are right, as far as they fit us for our Master's service, and wrong, if they enervate and disqualify us for it. I have deeply felt my sister Hoare's state. I may say, in measure, I bear her burdens with her,—she has my frequent prayers, and my tears often rise in remembrance of her. My heart is also much at home, most tenderly interested for all my children, more particularly my boys. I think I have cause for much thankfulness in the accounts from them.

23*rd*.—The letters on First-day brought us the affecting intelligence that my much-loved sister Hoare was worse; her decline has been rapid the last week or two. My sister Cunningham wrote to me, to beg me to set off to her directly; this proved a stunning blow—the low estate of this tenderly beloved sister, the difficulty of getting to her, the doubts as to what I ought to do, all upset me, as I say, stunned me. What could I do, but pray, in this emergency, to be helped and directed aright; that I might faithfully do my duty to all, and that my poor, dear, afflicted sister might be so helped immediately by her Lord Himself, that no other help might be really needful to her, yet the infirmity of my heart led me to pray also, that if right for us, I might see her again, and be some little help and comfort to her in her last hours.

On calmly weighing the subject, Elizabeth Fry believed it to be her duty to remain in Jersey, until the important objects that had led her thither were accomplished. She was enabled to attend to each one, and to leave with peace.

A Committee of Ladies was established for visiting the Hospital in Jersey, with the wife of the Lieutenant-Governor, General Campbell, at its head. The District Society was increasing in usefulness, the new House of Correction was likely to be established on the best principles; and she had the comfort of knowing, that all these objects were left under the skilful and efficient superintendence of her kind friend

Major-General Touzel, who had been, with other Jersey gentlemen, faithful coadjutors in her various labours. Her visits to Alderney and Guernsey had, as we have seen, been accomplished to her own satisfaction.

Jersey, Eighth Month, 25th.—Since I last wrote, I have passed through much conflict—indeed I have been strongly drawn two ways. I now expect to cross to-morrow; but some discouragement attends it. I am about going to a Public Meeting of importance, to finish, as I suppose, such services here. Be pleased, most gracious Lord, to be with me in this straitened place, help me through this service, by Thine own Spirit, to glorify Thee; edify, comfort, and help this people, and those dear to me. Show me, I pray Thee, for Thy dear Son's sake, this token for good in my low estate—and if it please Thee, make my way quite clear before me; if I am called to my beloved sister, oh, dearest Lord, be Thyself with me, and all of us, that we may part in peace, love, and joy, in Thee. Amen. In Thy love and pity in Christ Jesus, hearken to my unworthy cry.

Upton Lane, Ninth Month, 13th.—I was favoured to get through this Meeting well. By the close of that day, I had very much concluded the various duties that I was called to perform in that island. I felt peace in going at that time. * * * * * We then set off, found a comfortable small vessel, and a good captain. * * * * We had altogether a pleasant and prosperous voyage.

On arriving at Hampstead she found her sister Hoare extremely ill and at times unconscious; but she had a return of some degree of brightness, and Elizabeth Fry writes:—

I had the inexpressible comfort of being permitted a few days with her, and she evidently liked my company. I particularly observed, how gently I was dealt with, by her reviving a little after I arrived, so that I had not the bitterness of seeing her at once sinking. The affliction was thus mitigated to me; I was enabled to show her some marks of my deep and true love, and to be with and earnestly pray for her, in the hour of death. I was helped to be some comfort to many of her family, (and utterly unworthy as I know I am of it) I believe in my various ministrations, I was enabled to prove the power of the Spirit to qualify for his own work; and amongst them all, particularly with my dear nephew, who has just entered the "Church," deeply to impress the necessity of the work of the Spirit being carried on in the heart; and of having Christian charity towards others of every denomination. My beloved sister Hoare's death has made a deep impression on me. I do not like to enter life or its cares, or to see many, or to be seen. I like to withdraw from the world, and to be very quiet. I have naturally much felt the event, though supported and comforted under it.

Tenth Month, 2nd, (First-day.)—On Second-day morning, when going into the select Quarterly Meeting, with my brother Samuel, my son William came to tell us, that a serious accident had happened to my husband and daughter in Normandy. They had been thrown down a precipice, the carriage broken to pieces, and although they had experienced a very Providential deliverance, in their lives being spared, and no dangerous wound received, yet Katharine was so much hurt, and my dearest husband so much shaken, that they wished me to go to them immediately. I gave up the Quarterly Meeting of course, and set off with my much-loved son William to Dover, so as to cross by the first packet to France. I remember my sorrow, and perhaps undue disappointment, in not accompanying them to France. It seemed almost as if my Heavenly Father had heard my murmurings, as He heard the children of Israel in the Wilderness, and had taken me to France, when I did go against my inclination, alas! I received it also as a lesson to have but one prayer and desire in all things, "that the Lord's will be done on earth as it is in Heaven." The accident was most serious; such an escape

I think I never heard of; the carriage, in the first instance, fell with one horse (the driver and the other horse being separated from them) about four yards perpendicularly: then the carriage was dragged down about twenty-six yards more. The poor peasants came to assist, and fetched the village doctor for the body and the priest for the soul.

To one of her sons she writes from Calais:—

Ninth Month, 26th, 1836.

William and I reached Dover soon after twelve o'clock last evening. We were settled by one o'clock, and off about half-past seven this morning. Our journey was an anxious one, until, as the evening advanced, I became more quieted, and trustful that all was ordered for us in mercy and wisdom. We had a very favourable passage of three hours; and to our great satisfaction, found your father looking for us on the quay. We found our dearest Kate exceedingly bruised, and very grievously hurt altogether. Your dear father looks, I think, shaken and aged by all that he has gone through. Mary has been a very attentive nurse. She looks also jaded, but from her excessive fright, when they were going down the hill, she knelt down and put her head on Katherine's lap, by which means her face was perfectly saved. And so I have, at last, touched French ground. William and I have not been idle; we have already visited the Prison and Hospital. We hope it may please Providence, in tender mercy, to permit us all to arrive at home next Seventh-day, probably by a packet that leaves this place that morning for London.

Upton Lane, Tenth Month, 15*th.*—William and I went one day to "St." Omer, and stayed till the next. We had a very interesting expedition; his company was sweet to me.

I was a good deal instructed, as well as interested, in visiting the Roman Catholic charities. The sacrifice that must be made to give up the whole life, as the Sisters of Charity do, to teach and bring up the poor children, and attend to the sick in their hospitals, is very exemplary; and the slackness of some Protestants, and coldness of too many, led me to think that, whilst the meritoriousness of good works may be unsoundly upheld by the Roman Catholics, yet, that it stimulates to much that is excellent; and a fear arose in my mind, that the true doctrine that teaches that we have no merit in anything that we do, is either so injudiciously represented, or so misunderstood, that, in too many cases, it leads to laxity, or to sin, and a want of diligence in works of righteousness and true holiness. I was much interested in witnessing the Mass, but here I thought I saw something of the work of true religion, under what appeared to me, the rubbish of superstition and show. But I also thought, that much of the same thing remained amongst Protestants. I long to see true religion in its purity and simplicity, spread more and more, to the glory of God and the peace of men.

Eleventh Month, 6th, (First-day.)—It has pleased our Heavenly Father to permit much trial within the last two or three weeks. My dearest Richenda has had a very serious, I may say dangerous illness; one of great suffering. This day week her medical attendants were much alarmed, and wished to have a third called in; I deeply felt her state, but very earnestly desired to have no will in it, seeing I knew not what was best for her. My prayer was most earnest for her salvation, that whenever taken hence, she might be ready, being washed and made white in the blood of the everlasting covenant.

During Chenda's illness, I had very affecting accounts from Lynn, of dearest Rachel; her little Willy and his nurse; all in the scarlet fever; the little boy very dangerously ill.

On the 17th of the following month, Elizabeth Fry, accompanied by some of her associates in the labours of the prisons, met by appointment a Committee of Gentlemen, at the Great Millbank Penitentiary, and she says:—

We found to our great satisfaction, that through the Secretary of State, Lord John Russell, our way was fully open to visit this prison, which we had long desired to do, but never before had gained access to it. Now, I think, every criminal prison in London is visited by us. I see much encouragement and cause for thankfulness, in our way thus continuing to be made in this work of Christian love. I went to Hampstead in the evening, truly affecting it was to find the real, great loss in that dear family. I felt much love towards them, but did not see religiously or naturally, that I was very likely to be able to help them.

Twelfth Month, 31*st*.—Late in the evening, alone.—I feel it rather a solemn close to this year; not a time of brightness, though abounding with causes for thankfulness—which I desire more deeply to feel. May my Lord grant, for His dear Son's sake, that the Holy Spirit may more abundantly rest upon me, and mine, as our Guide, Sanctifier, and Comforter. May I more faithfully, watchfully, and humbly, perform all my duties to my Lord, my family, my friends, the church generally, and the world, and to myself. In afflictions may my soul be possessed in patience and watchfulness! and may every day draw us nearer to God and His kingdom!

Upton Lane, First Month, 25*th*, 1837.—My heart and mind have been much occupied, by my brother Joseph's writing to inform me, that he apprehends it will be his duty to go to America this year, upon religious service. The subject is deeply important and weighty; yet I desire to rejoice in his willingness to give up all for the service of his Lord. Though some fears have arisen, from a sort of floating apprehension I have had for many years, that I ought, or might, go with him, if ever he visited that land. Upon viewing it, as it respects myself, I believe I may truly say, I do not, at present, see any such opening. As far as I can see, *home* has my first call of duty; what the future may produce, I leave; but as far as I know my own heart, I very earnestly desire to feel, continually, that I am not my own, but bought with a price; therefore, I am my Lord's servant, and must do as I am bidden, even if the service called for appear to *me* unreasonable. But I must further observe, that in condescending mercy, I have generally found in services *really called for*, there has been a *ripeness*, that may be compared to the fruit come to maturity. For this service, for the present, I see no way.

Second Month, 11*th*.—Yesterday, when I went to town to visit Newgate, I was stopped by Foster Reynolds, saying, that he had sad tidings for me—which proved to be, that my beloved sister Harriet was most suddenly taken, leaving eight young children and my poor dear brother. Still, I trust not "left," because surely the Lord will be near, to help him in this very deep sorrow. Of course we are brought very low by this fresh family affliction. Deeply do I desire, that it may be sanctified to us all. The same post brought yesterday, the account from my brother Joseph, that he had laid his concern to visit America before his Monthly Meeting. So one brother is called to do, the other to suffer;—may our Lord's will be done, by and through them both.

15*th*.—The funeral of my much beloved sister takes place today. What a scene of unutterable sorrow at Runcton, where a few days ago, all was, in no common degree, joy, peace, and great prosperity. Oh! what occasions are these, where families meet together, for the affecting and solemn purpose of committing the remains of a beloved one, to the silent grave.

May the Lord Himself lift up the light of His countenance upon them, bless them, and keep them in a sound mind, and sound faith. Be pleased, oh gracious Lord! to help, pity, and comfort these afflicted ones this day.

How touching—how affecting an event was this! bringing home the solemn truth that no circumstances, neither talent, wealth, beauty, nor earthly rank, can avail anything when the pale messenger is sent with the awful summons. Lady Harriet Gurney had entered the family, when many of the elder members had reached the meridian of life. She had come, not alone to gladden her own domestic hearth, but to diffuse of her bright loving, hopeful spirit amongst her husband's relatives. For fourteen years she had, in an exemplary manner, fulfilled the duties of wife and mother, friend and mistress.

Her brother-in-law, T. F. Buxton, wrote on the day of her funeral:—"In seeing her coffin committed to the vault, I could not but feel, that it contained all that remained of as much beauty, and true loveliness of mind, body, and spirit, as we ever saw removed from this world!"

Elizabeth Fry still laboured diligently in her works of mercy, and was most kindly assisted by members of the government.

Upton Lane, Third Month, 12th.—I yesterday, went to the Colonial Office to meet Sir George Grey, on subjects respecting New South Wales, and the state of the female convicts; to the Irish Office, and saw Lord Morpeth respecting National Schools and Prisons, and then to the Home Office, about Jersey Prisons, &c. In every one I met with a most cordial reception. So the Lord yet makes way with those in power.

Sixth Month.—The King died last Third-day, the 20th. Our young Queen was proclaimed yesterday. My prayers have arisen for her, that our Heavenly Father would pour forth His spirit upon her, guide her by His counsel, and grant her that wisdom which is from above. I have received a long letter from the Duchess of ——, containing a very interesting account of her, and the death of the late King.

Seventh Month, 20th.—I returned home yesterday evening from Lowestoft, after having accompanied my brother Joseph to Liverpool, on his way to America. Our time at Earlham was very interesting; I believe I was helpful to my brother in a large Meeting that he held, to take leave of the citizens of Norwich. It was a highly interesting occasion, and I trust edifying to many. I am very sorry to say, my mind has too much the habit of anxiety and fearfulness. I believe this little journey would have been much more useful to me, but from an almost constant cloud over me, from the fear of being wanted by some of my family. I think it would be better for myself, and for them, if they did not always cling so closely round my heart, so as to become too much of a weight upon me.

My beloved brother's leave-taking of Earlham and the family there, was very affecting; still there was peace in it, and joy in the Lord, inasmuch as there is delight in doing what we believe to be His will. Of this, I think we partook with him. We went from Earlham to Runcton; there we dined. Shall I ever dine with my three brothers again? the Lord only knows—my heart was tendered in being with them.

I rejoice that I proceeded with Joseph, for I did not, before that, feel that I had come at his mind, he had been so much engaged, but, on the journey, I did so very satisfactorily. Samuel, Elizabeth, Joseph and myself, thus had a time together, never to be forgotten. We had much interesting conversation respecting things spiritual and things temporal, ourselves and our families. We proceeded to Manchester, where we met our dear Jonathan and Hannah Backhouse, their children, and Eliza P. Kirkbride; also William Forster. We were a very united company. That evening, William Forster read the 54th chapter of Isaiah, expressing his full belief, that our dearest Joseph would experience the promises contained in the last few verses. The next day we went to Liverpool, and spent much of the morning in his very comfortable ship; we felt being in it, for it was very touching parting with one so tenderly beloved. We made things comfortable for him, I attended to the books, and that a proper library should go out for the crew, passengers, and steerage passengers. However occupied or interested, I desire never to forget any thing that may be of service to others. We had a delightful morning with Joseph, but the tears often rose to my eyes; still, I desire to be thankful more than sorrowful, that I have a brother so fitted for his Lord's service, and willing to give up all for His name's sake.

That evening, again we had an interesting religious time in prayer. The next morning there was a solemn calm over us—the day of parting was come. After breakfast we all assembled, with some of our friends. We read the 4th of Philippians, our spirits were much bowed and broken, but the chapter encouraged us to stand fast in the Lord, to help one another in Christ, even the women who laboured in the gospel, and, to be careful for nothing, for that the Lord would supply all our need.

After her brother had ministered to them, and prayer had been offered, she adds:—

Soon afterwards we went to the ship. I saw the library arranged, with some others to help me; then devoted myself to my beloved brother, put sweet flowers in his cabin, which was made most comfortable for him. It was announced that the ship was going—we assembled in the ladies' cabin—I believe all wept. William Forster said, the language had powerfully impressed him—"I will be with you always, even to the end of the world;" therefore we might trust our beloved ones to Him who had promised. I then knelt down with these words—"Now, Lord, what wait we for, our hope is in Thee," and entirely committed him and his companions in the ship, to the most holy and powerful keeping of Israel's Shepherd; that even the voyage might be blessed to him, and to others. In short, our souls were poured forth before and unto the Lord, in deep prayer and supplication. Joseph almost sobbed, still a solemn quiet and peace reigned over us. I believe the Lord was with us, and owned us at this solemn time. We left the ship, and walked by the side of the Pier, until they were towed out; then we went away, and wept bitterly—but not the tears of deep sorrow, far from it; how different from the grief for sin, or even disease, or the perplexities of life.

Upton Lane, Eighth Month, 6th.—I am much occupied about the great Female Prison in Ireland, also the one at Paramatta. Government is wonderfully kind, and I believe much good is likely to be done by the steps now being taken.

18*th.*—I have believed it right to have the poor invited, to attend the Evening Meeting at Ratcliffe to-morrow. These are weighty engagements; may the Holy Spirit be poured forth, for the comfort, help, and encouragement of the hearers, and to my own peace.

Second-day, 20*th.*—Yesterday, we were favoured to get well through the Meeting, the people were very attentive, and some appeared in tears. Christ was preached as the "Way" to the Kingdom of Heaven, the sacrifice for our sins, and the healer of our wounds. He appeared to me to be exalted, through the power of the Spirit. May I be faithful in every call of duty, trusting in Him who can qualify me by His own power.

Ninth Month.—Since this Meeting, the interest that others have taken with me in the poor of Ratcliffe, has led us to look into their deplorable condition. We have formed a committee to visit them at their houses, see their state, provide a library for their use, and probably an infant school. So one thing springs out of another!

Last Seventh-day, my brother and sister Gurney and I went to Crawley, to attend the little Meeting at Ifield, and to go to William Allen's at Lindfield. My brother said, that any serious persons who liked to attend the Meeting might do so, and to our surprise, we found a large congregation of the labouring classes; I should think nearly a hundred men in smock-frocks; it was quite a sight. I felt low, empty, unworthy, and stripped in spirit, but my Lord helped me. We certainly had a solemn Meeting, the people were very attentive; we also had a very satisfactory reading with the people at the inn. In the evening we attended another Meeting at Lindfield, in which William Allen very acceptably united. Other Friends were there. We also called upon some poor, sorrowful, destitute ones. This little excursion appeared blessed to our comfort, refreshment, and peace, and I believe had the same effect on those whom we visited. I observe, with those who may think they differ in sentiment, there is nothing like bringing them together; how often is it then found, that the difference is more in expression than reality, and that the spirit of love and charity breaks down the partition walls.

I have, for many months past, deeply felt the wish for more religious intercourse with my children, and more uniting with them upon important and interesting subjects. I have turned it in my mind, again and again, and at last have proposed making the experiment, and meeting this evening—first, to consider different subjects of usefulness in charities, and then to close with serious reading, and such religious communication as way may open for.

Thou, Lord, only knowest the depth of my desire, for the everlasting welfare of my children! If it be Thy holy and blessed will, grant that we may be truly united to Thee, as members of Thy Militant Church on earth, and spiritually united amongst ourselves, as members of one body, each filling his different office, faithfully unto Thee. Grant that this little effort may be blessed to promote this end, and cause that in making it, we may experience the sweet influence of Thy love shed abroad in each of our hearts, to our real help, comfort, edification, and unity!

To her children she writes on the subject of the preceding paragraph:—

Upton Lane, *Ninth Month*, 15*th*, 1837.

My dearest Children,

Many of you know that, for some time, I have felt and expressed the want of our social intercourse, at times, leading to religious union and communion amongst us. It has pleased the Almighty to permit, that by far the larger number of you no longer walk with me in my religious course. Except very occasionally, we do not meet together for the solemn purpose of worship, and upon some other points, we do not see eye to eye. There are times when, in my declining years, I seriously feel the loss of not having more of the spiritual help and encouragement of those I have brought up, and truly sought to nurture in the Lord. This has led me to many serious considerations, how the case may, under present circumstances, be in any way met.

My conclusion is, that believing, as we do, in one Lord as our Saviour, one Holy Spirit as our Sanctifier, and one God and Father of us all, our points of union are surely strong, and if we are members of one living Church, and expect to be such for ever, we may profitably unite in some religious engagements here below.

The world and the things of it occupy us much, and they are rapidly passing away—it would be well if we occasionally set apart a time for unitedly attending to the things of Eternity. I therefore propose that we try the following plan, if it answer, continue it, if not, by no means feel bound to it. That our party, in the first instance, should consist of no others than our children, and such grandchildren, as may be old enough to attend. That our object in meeting, be for the strengthening of our faith, for our advancement in a devoted, religious, and holy life, and for the object of promoting Christian love and fellowship.

That we read the Scriptures unitedly, in an easy, familiar manner, each being perfectly at liberty to make any remark or ask any question; that it should be a time of religious instruction, by seeking to understand the mind of the Lord, for doctrine and practice, in searching the Scriptures, and bringing ourselves and our deeds to the light, that it may be made manifest if they are wrought in God. That either before, or after the Scriptures are read, we should consider how far we are really engaged for the good of our fellow-men, and what, as far as we can judge, most conduces to this object. All the members of this little community, are advised to communicate any thing they may have found useful, or interesting, in religious books; and to bring forward any thing that is doing for the good of mankind, in the world generally.

I hope that thus meeting together, may stimulate the family to more devotion of heart to the service of their God, at home and abroad to mind their different callings, however varied; and to be active in helping others. It is proposed that this meeting should take place once a month, at each house in rotation.

I have now drawn some little outline of what I desire, and if any of you like to unite with me in making the experiment, it would be very gratifying to me, still, I hope that all will feel at liberty, to do as they think best themselves.

I am indeed,

Your nearly attached mother,

ELIZABETH FRY.

To comment on the preceding letter may be unnecessary, and it would be difficult to do so with sufficient delicacy. The reader will doubtless be impressed with the deep humility which led her to feel herself as *needing* the "*help* and *encouragement* of those" whom she "had brought up;" and will be tenderly touched with sympathy, in tracing the indications of the severe trial entailed on her by the departure of her children from union with her in religious profession, and consequently not affording her an opportunity of manifesting ner fervent solicitude for their spiritual welfare. The plan that she proposed opened the way for some advantages; and her sons were disposed to exert themselves to remedy several serious evils. These little family meetings were always concluded by reading a portion of Scripture.

Twelfth Month, 20th.—I have laid before my Monthly Meeting my prospect of visiting France, and obtained the concurrence of Friends. Oh! for help, daily, hourly,—and may a sound mind, love, and power, be granted to me and to others, to our own peace, and the glory of God.

First-day Afternoon, 24th.—An accident about carriages keeps me from Meeting, which I much regret. The Morning Meeting was solemn. After it, my certificate was read in our adjourned Monthly Meeting, which was exceedingly encouraging to me, it expressed great unity with me as a minister, and much concurrence in my concern to go to France. It appeared to be signed by nearly the whole of the Meeting.

Upton Lane, First Month, 6th, 1838.—I yesterday returned from a visit to Norfolk. Before going there, I laid my concern to go to France, before our large Quarterly Meeting, and had the very great encouragement of such a flow of unity, as I have seldom heard expressed upon any occasion.

24*th.*—I expect to leave home to-morrow for France. My spirit has been very much brought down before the Lord; some causes of anxiety have arisen; still in this my going out, love abounds in no common degree, and a portion of soul-sustaining peace underneath. These words comforted me this morning, 2 Timothy i. 12. "I know whom I have believed, and am persuaded that He is able to keep that which I have committed unto Him against that day." I therefore, in this going out, commit myself, and my all, to my most blessed and holy Keeper, even to the Lord God of my salvation, my only hope of real help and defence, and of eternal glory.

She was accompanied in this journey, by her husband, their valued friend Josiah Forster, and by Lydia Irving, the same young Friend who had gone with her to Jersey in 1835.

She wrote to her family from—

Abbeville, *First Month*, 28*th*.

We left Boulogne yesterday morning, in a very comfortable French carriage, we enjoyed our reading and conversation, until we arrived at Montreuil, where we were refreshed by a little bouillon; and then proceeded to this place; but the cold was bitter, and neither French fires, nor tea, nor any other means proved sufficient to warm us. As the following morning advanced, my sense of mercy and peace was great. I remembered that some devoted Christian expressed, "where the God of peace is, there is home." After breakfast we read as usual, then Josiah Forster went out; but he could hear of no Protestants, nor of any place of worship for them; nor of any place desirable for us to visit, excepting one hospital, one convent, and one prison. These we visited, after having had a very solemn and sweet meeting in our own room. That text was feelingly brought to our minds, "where two or three are met together in my name, there am I in the midst of them."

I find my small knowledge of the language very valuable, I can read to the *fille de chambre*, and in some degree convey my feelings and sentiments, enough to produce sympathy and interest. In our visit to the prison, convent, and hospital, I found this to be the case.

To go now to minor points: picture us,—our feet on some fleeces that we have found, generally wrapped up in cloaks, surrounded by screens, to keep off the air; the wood fire at our feet. We have just finished an interesting reading in French, in the New Testament, with the landlady, her daughters, and some of the servants of the hotel, they appeared very attentive, and much interested.

Farewell, my dearly beloved ones. May the Lord be with you, and keep you, and bless you!

Your tenderly attached,

E. F.

In Paris, comfortable and commodious apartments were prepared for them at the Hotel de Castille, by the kind attention of F. Delessert. They arrived there very tired and very cold, on the 30th of the First Month. The morning of the 31st was opened with solemn prayer, in which E. Fry besought wisdom from on High to direct, and strength to perform whatever might be called for at their hands. Then came a visit from their kind friend Delessert, two notes from Lord Granville, the English Ambassador at Paris: a call at the Embassy, and in the evening the company of M. de Pressensé, the Secretary of the Bible Society, with his wife.

Second Month, 1st, they attended the small Friends' Meeting held in the Faubourg du Roule, and afterwards called on La Baronne Pelet de la Lozere. In her, Elizabeth Fry found a friend and sister in Christ. They then paid a visit to Count Montalivet, Minister of the Interior, by whom they were most kindly received, and promised all needful admissions to the different prisons.

Afterwards, at the Hotel, they received visits from the Duchess de Broglie and other ladies. The following day found Elizabeth Fry oppressed and feverish, and evidently suffering from the cold which she had endured on her journey. Her new friends all displayed lively sympathy, whilst the Baroness Pelet, in particular, neglected no kindness or attention that appeared likely to add to her comfort.

The 3rd, though too unwell to go out, she received in the evening M. de Metz, Conseiller de la Cour Royale, and had much important conversation with him on the subject of Prisons, in which he was greatly interested. On First-day, she and her companions visited a school conducted by M. de Pressensé, for two hundred children; a cheerful and delightful sight. At twelve o'clock they attended Friends' Meeting: there were assembled French, English, a Pole, and Americans. Among this motley group might be found Roman Catholics, Presbyterians, Episcopalians, various Dissenters, with Friends.

On Second-day, the 5th, they visited the "St." Lazare Prison for women, containing nine hundred and fifty-two inmates; a very melancholy sight. An American lady invited the party to her house in the evening, where she received about fifty individuals, mostly English and Americans. The conversation turned upon the general state of society in Europe, but especially in France, and what would be the most likely means of benefiting its polished, refined, but dissipated and irreligious capital. The fearful writings of the day, "many too bad to read," were discussed, and what might be the root of a tree, the branches of which bore fruit of such deadly nature. There was present, on that occasion, a young medical student, who addressed himself to Elizabeth Fry on the fearful contamination to which young men in his position were exposed—no domestic home to retire to, none of that indefinable, but potent influence around them, of public opinion in favour of virtue and morality, their studies all tending to materialism, and to the lessening of that dependence upon an unseen superior Power, which lingers even in the unregenerate heart of man; and above all, little or no opportunity afforded them for the commonest religious advantages. This large gathering concluded by solemn exhortation and prayer.

On the 6th, accompanied by M. F. Delessert, the travellers visited a French Protestant school, for two hundred children, on the British and Foreign system, admirably conducted by a valuable committee of ladies. They dined at M. de Pressensé's, where was a large party afterwards. Many of them active members of the Societé Evangélique. Elizabeth Fry entered deeply into their labours of love, and spoke of this occasion as very encouraging to her, when she compared it with the state of things in France during her youth, and how unlikely it then seemed, that such a dawn of better things would ever appear there.

The 7th, they received many guests both morning and evening, and in the course of the day, accompanied the Duchess de Broglie to the Prison des Jeunes Détenus, a good, new building, the inmates well ordered, but still capable of improvement.

The following day was occupied by attending their Meeting in the morning, and in the evening receiving a number of ladies to consider how they might, in the best manner, promote good in the city, in Prisons, Schools, District Societies, and similar objects. The evening was finished by reading the 15th chapter of Luke.

On the 9th, the Prison for men (La Force) was visited.

The 10th, they inspected the Military Prison at St. Germains, which appeared to them to be, upon the whole, well conducted and in tolerable order; books they found to be greatly wanted. Afterwards they saw the Central Prison at Poissy; whilst they admired its good order, they considered it not sufficiently penal, too much like a large manufactory for different trades, instead of a place of punishment.

The following day—the First of the week—was indeed welcome, for its Sabbath was greatly needed by Elizabeth Fry. She desired that it might be free from company, and prove a season of refreshment, the press of people being so great, and the subjects for consideration so many and so exceedingly important. The Meeting was not a very large one, in it their certificates were read. They appeared much to interest those who heard them, and opened the way for a little explanation of Friends' principles. There were a few callers in the evening, amongst others, a gentleman interested about prisons, who remained during their Scripture reading, at which some of the servants of the Hotel were also present.

On the 12th, they visited the Prison of the Conciergerie.

There they saw the room where the unhappy Marie Antoinette had been confined. They took tea at the Methodist minister's, and passed an interesting evening with a large party of his congregation. At this time and in her subsequent visits to France, Elizabeth Fry's sympathies were much drawn forth towards the French Methodists, who appeared to her to be an earnest and spiritual people.

The next morning they went to some schools; one, an Infant School, was particularly attractive; the superintendents appearing well adapted for their important post; money was given to purchase the little creatures each a bun, which highly delighted them, their happy faces showing how pleased they were. Also an Hospital, and the Enfans Trouvés, were visited. Elizabeth Fry's maternal tenderness and experience, led her to give some advice about the poor babies' dress, that it might be less complicated, and afford them more liberty of movement. The nuns appeared kind. The Hospital they found very close, and wanting ventilation. The evening was passed at M. Lutteroth's, where between fifty and sixty persons were present, "many amongst them truly serious."

On the 14th, another visit was paid to the Women's Prison of "St." Lazare. There, after going over the building, the women were collected at Elizabeth Fry's request, that a portion of Scripture might be read to them. She chose the parable of the prodigal son. It was beautifully read by a French lady, from the Roman Catholic Prayer Book. A pause ensued, then Elizabeth Fry commented upon it, the same lady translated for her, sentence by sentence. It was exceedingly well done, losing little or nothing of its solemnity. The women were touched and impressed. She then asked them whether they would like ladies to visit them, read to them, and sympathize with them. The offer was eagerly accepted. "Oui, oui," "Eh, moi, aussi!" came from all sides; nor was it only these poor outcasts, and those accompanying Elizabeth Fry who wept, the jailor and turnkeys who had entered the room, contrary to her wishes, were so affected that tears ran down their cheeks.

They saw on the 15th, a school for about forty-five Protestants, many of them training for servants. To find attention paid to this class gave them much satisfaction. The next day some more "delightful schools" were inspected, and a prison for debtors.

In the evening, the meeting of persons interested in the promotion of philanthropic objects, which had been adjourned the preceding week, again assembled; much interesting conversation took place. As on the previous occasion, it was concluded by reading a portion of the Holy Scriptures and solemn silence.

On the 17th, Elizabeth Fry had an interview with the prison officers, and obtained much information respecting the state of the "St." Lazare Female Prison. The Baroness Pelet and a lady named Mallet interpreted for her. They saw M. Toase on the subject of fitting up a room, as a library, for the benefit of English and American students, and in the evening they went to the American clergyman's to meet some of the students, who are invited there once in every week to read the Scriptures, &c., &c. A young Englishman present expressed himself strongly; warning his contemporaries; first, on the awful prevalence of taking the sacred name in vain, secondly, the desecration of the Sabbath, and thirdly, against the literature of modern France, poisoned, as it is, with infidelity and licentiousness.

On the 20th, they visited the Salpêtrière, an Hospital for the old, infirm, epileptic, idiotic and insane.

A third visit was paid on the 21st to the "St." Lazare, in company with Lady Granville, Lady Georgiana Fullerton, and two other ladies. From what was witnessed in these visits, it was obvious, that great good would result from the regular attendance of a Ladies' Committee, though it was no easy matter to arrange it.

Elizabeth Fry visited the King and Queen and the Duchess of Orleans.

Before leaving Paris she addressed a memorial to the King, touching on the subjects that so deeply occupied her thoughts, but beyond every other thing, urging a more extended circulation of Holy Scriptures, and their free use in all public institutions in France.

From "St." Germains she wrote to her children.

Third Month, 5th, 1838

We arrived here last evening, after quitting the most deeply interesting field of service, I think I was ever engaged in. My first feeling is, peace and true thankfulness for the extraordinary help granted to us; my next feeling, an earnest desire to communicate to you, my most tenderly beloved children, and others nearest to me, the sense that I have of the kindness, and goodness, and mercy, of my Heavenly Father, who has dealt so bountifully with me; that it may lead all to serve Him fully, love Him more, and follow more simply the guidance of his Spirit.

After a full detail of their labours in the capital, she proceeds:—

Our visit to the King and the Queen was interesting; but alas! what, in reality, is rank? The King I think, in person, like the late Lord Torrington, the Queen a very agreeable and even interesting woman. I expressed my religious interest and concern for them, which was well received, and we had much conversation with the Queen and the Princess Adelaide, before the King came into the room. We strongly expressed to the Queen our desire to have the Sabbath better kept, and the Scriptures more read. She is a sweet-minded, merciful woman. There were present Madame Adelaide, the King's sister, one of the young Princesses, and the Marchioness of Dolomieu, principal Lady of Honour to the Queen.

We then proceeded to the Duchess of Orleans'; there we had a delightful visit, the sweetest religious communication with her, and other interesting conversation. We found her an uncommon person—my belief is, that she is a very valuable young woman.

The Queen appeared much pleased with my Text-book; and the Princess Adelaide said, she should keep it in her pocket and read it daily. Indeed no books have given the same pleasure as the Text-books, both in French and English. I think we have given away many hundreds of them, and next, in number, my sister Louisa's books on education; they delight the people; also a great many of Joseph's Letters to Dr. A——.

Her fatigues had been frequent and severe, and she was at times really ill; yet she concludes her report as follows:

Through all I must say, He, who I believe put me forth, has, from season to season, restored my soul and body, and helped me from hour to hour. This day week I sat down upon my chair and wept, but I was soon helped and revived. I long for every child, brother, sister, and all near to me, to be sensible how very near my Holy Helper has been to me; and yet I have exceedingly and deeply felt my utter unworthiness and short coming, and that all is from the fulness and freeness of unmerited mercy and love, in Christ Jesus. I can hardly express the very near love I have felt for you all. My prayers very often have risen for you, and if any labour I have been engaged in, has been accepted *through the Beloved*, may you, my most tenderly beloved ones, partake of the blessing attendant upon it.

I forgot to say, I think the few Friends in Paris have been greatly comforted and stimulated by our visit.

I end my account by saying what I trust is true, "The Lord is my Shepherd, I shall not want." We are now quietly at "St." Germains. We hear most interesting accounts of the state of Normandy, and have many letters of introduction to the places where we propose to go; if not wanted home, I shall be glad to go there. We propose being at Rouen to-morrow. I am,

Your most tenderly attached,

ELIZABETH FRY.

At Rouen they were much interested by meeting with a respectable woman in humble life, who had lived nurse fifteen years in a gentleman's family, a Roman Catholic, but his wife a Protestant. There she had been so much impressed by religious truth, (though still a Roman Catholic herself) that she felt it her duty, where she resided, to circulate the Scriptures and religious tracts. Her master told them, it was surprising the great influence she had obtained in the neighbourhood. Elizabeth Fry supplied her with six Testaments and a Bible, from the Bible Society Depot. From the same Society she obtained a number of copies for the school in the prison, where the Testament was habitually read, but the supply very inadequate. This school was under the care of the Abbè Gossier, Du Hamel, and other religious gentlemen, who themselves daily instructed the young prisoners.

At Caen, they found some excellent and devoted Methodists amongst the French; and learned that, through the efforts of one young English woman, (an orphan residing in a gentleman's family as governess)—many copies of the Scriptures had been purchased: and at the shop of a Roman Catholic, more than a hundred of de Sacy's Testaments sold since the beginning of the year.

The Prison of Beaulieu near Caen was visited by them with much satisfaction; nearly a thousand prisoners were confined there; they found it admirably regulated, and a serious Roman Catholic clergyman devoted to the good of those under his care. He gladly welcomed the gift of fifty Testaments.

At Havre, the Ladies' Bible Society had sold, during the

former year, four hundred and twenty-six Testaments, and thirty-three Bibles, and had given fifty Testaments to soldiers, who were in the habit, every evening, of reading them to their comrades in barracks

At Boulogne, they made arrangements for the sale of the Holy Scriptures, and took a lively interest in the District Society, thence crossed to Dover, and on the following day Elizabeth Fry had the comfort of reaching home.

Upton Lane, Fourth Month, 27th.—Yesterday was the largest British Society Meeting I ever remember, partly collected to hear my account of our French journey; there must have been some hundreds of ladies present, many of them of rank. In the desire not to say too much, perhaps I said too little upon some points, although I do not feel condemned, yet I am ready to think if I had watched and prayed more, I should have done better—my prayers have arisen, that, however imperfectly or unworthily sown, the seed scattered yesterday, may be so prospered by His own free power, life, and grace, that it may bear a full crop to His praise!

Fifth Month, 8th.—I have just had a serious faintness for a short time; at times, I think I may be suddenly taken off in one of these attacks—they appear to have so much to do with the heart. If perfectly ready, by being washed and made clean in the blood of the Everlasting Covenant, then, I think that a rapid translation, from time to eternity, may save much pain and sorrow. But all these things, I am disposed to leave wholly to the Lord, who has, through his unutterable mercy, been remarkably with me in life, and will, I believe, be with me in death. So be it, Lord Jesus! when Thou comest, even if it be quickly, through Thine own merits receive me unto Thyself!

20th.—To-morrow I am fifty-eight, an advanced period of, what I apprehend to be, not a very common pilgrimage. I now very earnestly desire and pray that my Lord may guide me continually, cause me to know more of the day of His power, that I may have my will subjected to His will. What He would have me to do, that may I do, where He would have me to go, there may I go—what He may call me to suffer for His name sake, may I be willing to suffer. Further, may He keep me from all false fears and imaginations, and ever preserve me from putting my hand to any work, not called for by Him. Be pleased to grant these my desires and prayers, for Thine own Holy and Blessed Name's sake!

Seventh Month, 8th.—This day I enter with much fear and trembling, as we are looking forward to a very important Meeting, to be held at the Westminster Meeting House, at the request of Hannah Backhouse, to which foreigners of rank, and our own nobility, are invited. The weight is great—very great, from various causes.

14*th.*—The Meeting was attended by many high in rank. Soon after we assembled, William Allen spoke for some time, then I knelt down, and felt much unction and power in prayer for the Queen, &c. After Hannah Backhouse had spoken, in a lively, simple, powerful manner, preaching the truths of the gospel, several went out. I then rose, first endeavouring to show that truth must not be despised, because it came through weak instruments. I mentioned how Anna in the Temple spoke of our Lord to all who looked for redemption in Israel, how the women first told of our Lord's resurrection, and that their fellow-disciples called it "idle tales." After thus showing that the Lord might see right to use weak instruments, I expressed my feelings towards those present. First, from Scripture, I showed that God is no respecter of persons, that from the palace to the very dungeon, I continually saw this. Then I showed the important and responsible situation of those who fill high places in the world. Either they would be blessed themselves and be a blessing to others, as a city set on a hill, their light shining before men; or they would be of the number of those, through whom offences come, and therefore with the "curse of the Lord" resting on them. I showed them some of their peculiar temptations, in being clothed in purple and fine linen, and faring sumptuously every day; and warned them, seeking to lead them to Christ, and to eternal glory, through Him. At the close, I had a few words to express in the way of exhortation, as to their example in their houses, amongst children and servants, reading the Holy Scriptures, family worship, and other points.

In the Eighth Month of this year, Elizabeth Fry entered on another visit to Friends of Scotland; for which, as well as for any other service that might open as a duty to be performed, she was liberated and cordially encouraged by the Monthly and Quarterly Meetings to which she belonged.

She was accompanied by her sister Elizabeth Fry, and by her esteemed friends William Ball and John Sanderson. Proceeding by Birmingham to Carlisle, thence to Edinburgh, Perth, and Forfar, they reached Aberdeen on the 18th. The two following days were devoted to the attendance of the General Half-year's Meeting, and to visits to the Friends of that district. Amongst others, one a very old and valued friend, John Wigham. He had been to her as a "nursing father" in the early part of her religious course.

The intercourse with him is thus described by one of her travelling companions:

"It was much like the meeting and interchange of parent and child, after long separation and many vicissitudes; and these last, as they had affected our dear friend in the interval, were freely spoken of by her, with that deep feeling, chastened into resignation, which so remarkably covers her subjected spirit, in relation to these affecting topics.'

The same Friend—giving a sketch of her varied engagements—remarks that she

"Visited the prison of Aberdeen, in company with A. and M. Wigham, the Provost, Sheriff, Town Clerk, and Bailie Blackie. The Bailie is a valuable man, who has done a great deal for the improvement of the gaol, which Elizabeth Fry finds very materially mended; in fact, in excellent order. The authorities here, are most anxious to facilitate Elizabeth Fry's inspection, and to forward her views, well knowing them to be the result of the enlarged observation, and long experience of a practical, judicious mind, as well as of close and heartfelt interest in the subject.

"A meeting has been held with the ladies of Aberdeen this evening, at our Hotel, when prison matters were discussed, and things put in train for forming a regular association, ere we leave the city. Elizabeth Fry's capacity for various successive engagements, all of an important nature, is astonishing. Surely, it is because she dwells mentally in the 'quiet habitation,' to which she continually resorts, for the renewal of that calming influence of the Spirit, which purifies the heart, clears the understanding, and rectifies the judgment, bestowing upon the truly devoted follower of the Lamb, 'the spirit of love, and of power, and of a sound mind.' She is both lovely and wonderful on close acquaintance; such energy, combined with meekness, and so much power with entire teachableness, are rarely found."

We continue to extract from the narrative of her companion William Ball.

"*Edinburgh, First-day, 26th.*—Our little party sat together after the manner of Friends this morning. Dear Priscilla Johnston joined us. I felt afresh, that it is a privilege to know that the worship of God, is in spirit and in truth; and may be rendered acceptable wherever contrite hearts are reverently turned towards Him, in dependence on the mediation of His beloved Son, who is ever near to those, if only 'two or three,' who are met to offer this worship in His name." * * * "Elizabeth Fry and her sister had desired to meet with the fishermen about Anstruther this evening; but we were all taken by surprise on going down to the town, to find that this simple, religious gathering, turned out to be a very large and crowded Meeting. The room we had arranged for, not having proved nearly capable of containing the people, they had flocked to a chapel near, the service of which (and of some others I believe) was put off to give place for a Public Meeting of Friends. We had expected to sit down with the poor fishermen, in a much more private way. John Sanderson stated to the asssemblage that we began with a pause of silence. Then Elizabeth Fry explained our views on worship, rather in the way of an affectionate introductory address. Her sister E. Fry bent the knee in prayer. After which, Elizabeth Fry was strengthened, in a very striking manner, to proclaim the glad tidings of the gospel of life and salvation—truly an awakening ministry! Her sister followed, enlarging on the nature and fruits of true repentance!—then Elizabeth Fry addressed the sea-faring men, most appropriately and feelingly, warned the sinners emphatically, and was afterwards engaged in fervent prayer. At the close of this memorable Meeting, Andrew Johnston briefly addressed this large assembly of his neighbours, acknowledging the kindness of the minister and attention of the people, and enforcing, with great seriousness, his desire, that the novelty of the occasion, might in no degree be suffered to divert solemn attention, from the infinite importance of the Gospel truths delivered.

"After primary attention to religious engagements among Friends in Edinburgh, on the 28th, 29th, and 30th; there was a party assembled to meet Elizabeth Fry, at the house of our valued and hospitable host, the late Alexander Cruikshank, on the evening of the 30th, when her conversation on the important subject of the condition and care of prisoners, greatly interested a large company, including some distinguished individuals, and some foreigners."

Many very important engagements occupied them at Edinburgh.

"On the evenings of the 2nd and 3rd of the Ninth Month, large Public Meetings for religious worship were held; the former at Edinburgh, the latter at Leith, in which Elizabeth Fry was greatly strengthened to declare the truths of the everlasting gospel of our Lord and Saviour Jesus Christ. Many calls were made on distinguished persons, and some visits also received, on the 3rd; especially one from the late Dr. Abercrombie, which will long be remembered with interest."

On the 4th they proceeded to Glasgow, and were similarly employed there. On the 7th they held a large Meeting for worship in the Seaman's Chapel.

On being favoured to reach home, she writes,—

Upton, Ninth Month, 26th.—We arrived home last Seventh-day, and, to my great comfort, I found all my family going on well and comfortably. I ventured to ask, or at least to desire, that if my goings out were acceptable to the Lord, and, if I were to be called to further, and perhaps still more weighty service, I might find the blessing of preservation extended to those most dear to me at home, as well as to myself in going. Through mercy, this sign has been rather unusually granted to me. What can I render unto my Lord for his tender and unmerited mercies?

Tenth Month, 28th.—I have paid a satisfactory visit with my husband, and partly accompanied by Peter Bedford and John Hodgkin, to Croydon and Ifield. Our Meeting in Sussex was a very satisfactory one; and a reading that we had the next morning at a cottage on a Common, belonging to a dear Friend, where we had been before. The libraries that we established, appear to have been much read and valued. It is cause for thankfulness, to find that our labour has not been in vain in the Lord. How sweet are His mercies! May all become His servants saith my soul!

I also left home accompanied by my beloved husband and my sister Elizabeth, to visit a few Meetings in Essex.

Twelfth Month, 6th.—This morning I felt deeply the seriousness of laying before my Monthly Meeting, my belief that it may be my duty again to visit France, and some other parts of the continent of Europe. It is after much weighty consideration, that I have come to the conclusion, that it is right to do this. I have long thought that this summer my course might be turned either to my dearest brother Joseph in America, or to the Continent of Europe; after much weighing it, I have believed the latter to be the right open ing for me. I laid my prospect before the Friends of our Monthly Meeting, this morning. Several Friends were there, not members of it. We had a very solemn Meeting—for worship first. My sister and I returned our certificates for visiting Scotland, and then I asked for one for Europe; having very earnestly prayed for help, direction, and protection. When under a fresh feeling of its being right to do it, I simply informed Friends that I looked to paying a visit to Paris, then to the Friends in the South of France; and should probably, in returning, visit some other parts of Europe. Much unity and sympathy were expressed with this prospect of religious duty by our own members and those who visited us. There certainly appeared to be, in no common degree, a seal set to this serious prospect of religious service.

I now desire to leave all to the further openings of Providence, as to when to go, who is to go with me, and where to go. I desire to leave it all to my most holy and gracious God. Although I am very deeply sensible that it is only through the fullness and freeness of unmerited mercy, love, and grace, that I dare call, or feel, my Lord thus to be my Head and Helper. I may acknowledge in faith, my belief that, through the help of the Holy Spirit, my Lord has been and is unto me "Wonderful, Counsellor, the Mighty God, the Everlasting Father, and the Prince of Peace."

After receiving from her Quarterly Meeting a certificate of cordial unity, and concurrence with her prospect of again visiting the Continent, she passed a few days in Norfolk.

Chapter Tenth.

1839-1841. Journey on the Continent—Paris—Lyons—Nismes—Avignon—Toulouse—The Pyrenees—Grenoble—Geneva—Zurich—Frankfort—Return home—Goes into Norfolk—Letter to a religious acquaintance—Audience of the Queen—Meeting in London—Leaves home for the Continent—Ostend—Brussels—Antwerp—Amsterdam—Zwolle—Minden and Pyrmont—Hanover—Berlin—Leipzic—Dusseldorf—Return home—Yearly Meeting—Establishment of "Nursing Sisters."

First Month, 12*th*, 1839.—I returned from Lynn last evening. I was a good deal with my beloved sister Catherine, who was there. Before parting, we had a deeply interesting time together, when the spirit of prayer was remarkably poured forth upon us. I prayed for them each separately, and believe that access was, in mercy, granted to the Throne of Grace. My dearest sister offered a solemn prayer for us before we rose from our knees. I felt, as I have often done, an earnest desire, that we may none be in spiritual bonds. I think Satan, in hardly any way mars the Lord's work more, than in putting persons in the stiff bonds of High Churchism. He attacks all professors in this way, and leads them to rest in their sectarianism, rather than their Christianity. I do not mean that this is the case with those I was amongst, but I see it a frightful bait, thrown out at all professors of all denominations. Few things I more earnestly desire, than unity in the church of Christ, and that all partition walls may be broken down. Lord, hasten the coming of that day, for Thy own name's sake!

16*th*.—On Second-day, I laid my concern to go to France before the Morning Meeting. I feel encouraged by all the testimonies from the Lord's servants, and from the real help and excellence of the arrangement, that we should thus, in such weighty and important duties, have the sanction of that section of the Church to which we belong.

I have received very encouraging accounts from Scotland as to the results of our last journey. Several refuges are likely to be formed, and women prisoners to be visited. The accounts from France have also been, in many ways, encouraging. My dear and valued friend, the Duchess de Broglie, who died some little time ago, expressed that her faith had been strengthened by our visit. Many important alterations have taken place in the prisons; the New Testament is now circulated in some of them, and in the hospitals. So I may take courage, and return God thanks.

Previous to our departure, I had the servants of our different families to meet me at Meeting; it proved quite a large number, almost filling our Meeting House. I believe it was a time of real edification and comfort to some who were there.

Her former kind companion, Josiah Forster, became again her attendant on this journey. His sympathy, his watchful care, and sound judgment, were very important in aiding her throughout her weighty engagements. She was also accompanied by her husband, who evinced an increasing desire to strengthen her in the pursuit of those objects which she believed it to be her duty to accomplish. One of her daughters also attended her.

Almost immediately after their landing at Boulogne, many persons came to seek Elizabeth Fry, and to welcome her to their shores.

She visited the prison there, which was in a very deplorable state; and in the evening received about forty at the Hotel, chiefly the members of a little District Society, which she had been instrumental in forming on her previous visit. The results of their labours were very satisfactory; many of the poor French were subscribing for, or buying New Testaments, as well as eagerly reading the tracts circulated amongst them. The state of the resident English poor was also considered as decidedly improved, through this means.

The servants of the Hotel earnestly solicited to be supplied with Testaments; it appeared that they lent them to their friends, who carried them into the country, where they were so eagerly read and re-read, that it was difficult for the rightful owners to regain possession of them.

On the 14th, *en route* to Abbeville, the party stopped at Samer for an hour, to give Elizabeth Fry the opportunity of visiting a poor sick Englishman in great affliction. At Montreuil-sur-Mer, she gave a tract to a man whilst changing horses; the carriage was soon surrounded by people begging for books; it was very striking to see their energy to obtain them. The same thing occurred at the Hotel at Abbeville, where those, to whom she had given them on her previous visit, begged for more, and came creeping up to her apartment to prefer their request. Her Text-books, "Les petits livres de matin," were the decided favourites. In the morning, the people of the Hotel again gathered round her. The First-day that she had spent there on her former visit to Paris—the reading they had in the evening—the prayer she offered for them, had made a deep impression. They beguiled her into the Kitchen, where she told them in broken French, which however they contrived to understand, a little of her wishes for them as to faith and practice; then all would shake hands with her. On reaching the capital, she writes:

Paris, Third Month, 17th.—How earnestly do I desire and pray, that my Lord would clearly point out my work in this place; that he would enable me, by His own Power and Spirit, to perform it in simplicity to His praise, the good of others, and my own peace.

Lord, regard Thy servant in her low estate, and if it be

Thy holy will, give some token, by Thy presence, Spirit, and Power that Thou art with us; and more abundantly fit and prepare for Thine own work, as Thou hast often blessed and abundantly increased that which may appear small in the eyes of man, to the help of numbers: so, oh Lord! bless, prosper, and increase the weak labours of Thy unworthy servant, to the good of numbers, and the promotion of Thy cause in this place; where "the world, the flesh, and the devil," appear so powerful. Answer this cry, I beseech Thee, and give Thy poor servant a quiet, patient, trustful spirit, only dependent upon the fresh pourings forth of Thy Spirit, and the incomings of Thy love. Amen.

24*th*.—In mercy my cry was heard. We went to our little Meeting, where were some seeking minds; and to my own feelings, we were remarkably bound together by the presence of our Lord. I also may thankfully say, that I was enabled to preach the word, and to pray. I felt it an encouraging, edifying time, and an answer to prayer. After Meeting, we called at our Ambassador's, and met with a very cordial reception.

On Sixth-day, we visited a large French Methodists' school; it was a very encouraging sight: there were about a hundred children, who appeared well taught. I had a good deal of advice to give them and their parents, and felt peace in the service; but the place was so exceedingly cold, that I left it with severe tooth-ache, which lasted all day, and brought me down in body and spirit.

Having invited a large company for philanthropic and religious objects for the following evening, I felt anxious: but when the time came, I was enabled, though the party was very large, to speak a little on the subject of Negro Slavery: and Josiah Forster expressed himself very agreeably upon the subject. We finished with a short, lively Scripture-reading, and to my own feelings, strength was, in a remarkable manner, given me in the needful time.

During the morning, I paid a most interesting visit to a

Roman Catholic lady,—a young widow,—her little children, and her friend. I have seldom seen the Christian life more exemplified. So we see and "perceive that God is no respecter of persons; but in every nation, he that feareth Him, and worketh righteousness, is accepted with Him."—Acts x. 34, 35.

Thus began this second sojourn in Paris; the same friends gathered round her, the same institutions were revisited, with some others which she had not seen before; the same objects of interest occupied her attention. The mornings were thus spent: the evenings generally at the houses of their many kind friends, or in receiving guests at the Hotel. Perhaps no one was more capable than Elizabeth Fry of appreciating the enjoyment of social intercourse or society, such as these occasions offered, but it was not from this motive that she united in them. She considered it her duty to avail herself of the opportunities thus afforded, for the diffusion of knowledge on those subjects which had brought her to Paris, the introduction of topics of a philanthropic and religious character.

Third-day.—Visited an hospital, and dined at Lord William Bentinck's, I trust to some good purpose, but I fear for myself in many ways, on such occasions.

Fifth-day.—A very solemn Morning Meeting, numbers there, mostly women, some ladies of rank, some very interesting persons. I was afresh enabled to pray and t minister.

Her ministry is described, by some who, on different occasions throughout this visit, were privileged to attend her meetings, as being of a powerfully impressive and instructive character, and peculiarly consoling to many afflicted ones.

Fourth Month, 7th (First-day).—One day we dined at our dear friends the Mallets', where we met a large family party, and had much interesting conversation. There was a sweet feeling of the love of God over us; I believe this service was called for, and was blessed to many present. Last evening about a hundred persons spent the evening with us. The subject of prisons was brought forward; Newgate, &c., I endeavoured to show the state of prisons formerly, and many of their improvements. But above all, to inculcate Christian principle as the only sure means of improving practice. I sought in every way, in the cases brought forward, to uphold the value of the Scriptures, and to show the blessed results of faith and repentance. We finished by reading in a solemn manner the 15th of Luke, as the chapter so greatly blessed to poor prisoners. I made little comment, there was very great solemnity over us. There were Catholics and Protestants, and I believe some of the Greek Church. There were Greeks, Ionians, Spaniards, a Pole, Italians, Germans, English, Americans and French. Several of the English and French, persons of rank; the Marquis de Brignolles, Sardinian Minister, and Prince Czartorinski. Thus this week has run away! may it have been for the real good of others, and the glory of God. Most merciful God, I perfectly know that I am unworthy to present myself before Thee on the bended knee of my soul. But I come boldly to the throne of grace, through the merits of Thy dear Son, our Mediator with Thee, our God. Grant, Holy Father, that the iniquity of my holy things may be blotted out, and that in my efforts to serve Thee, and promote the cause of truth and righteousness, my infirmities and the unworthiness of the instrument may not have cast a blemish on Thy truth. Grant also, Holy Father, that the word spoken may, through Thy blessing, comfort, strengthen, and edify Thy followers, and be a means of bringing many to repentance, and faith in Thy beloved Son, Christ Jesus our Lord. Dearest Lord, be near to keep, to help, and to direct all my steps, as I go on in this cause, for Thy glory, the good of others, and my own edification and peace. Permit Thy servant also to commend to Thy special keeping, all most near to her, left in her own land, and all everywhere, beloved by her, and for whom she travails in spirit, and spread the knowledge of Thyself, and of Thy Son, and Thy righteousness, through the Holy Spirit, everywhere on this earth. Amen!

Paris, 21st.—I feel that, under a lively sense of peace and rest of soul, I may record the mercies of the Lord this last week.

Our First-day was very satisfactory, a large Meeting; five of our children with us.

(Several of her family spent a few days in Paris at this time.)

I had a very serious, interesting, and intimate conversation with the Duchess of Orleans.

I visited and attended to some prisons, formed a Ladies' Society to visit the Protestants in prisons and hospitals, met a very influential company at dinner at Lord Granville's, much interesting conversation in the evening; the same twice at Baron Pelet's, and we had an agreeable dinner at Lord William Bentinck's. I have paid some very interesting private calls, spent one morning with my children; our great philanthropic evening largely attended, about a hundred and forty present. Josiah Forster gave a concentrated account of our former evenings, and added other things very agreeably. I strongly impressed upon them the extreme importance of the influence of the higher on the lower classes of society, by their example and precept; mentioned late hours, theatres, and other evils. Then advised; giving the poor Christian education, reading the Holy Scriptures in their families, lending Libraries, District Societies, and other objects; we finished with a very solemn Scripture-reading, the greater part of the third chapter of Colossians, and the 20th and 21st verses of the last chapter of the epistle to the Hebrews, "Now the God of peace, that brought again from the dead our Lord Jesus, that great Shepherd of the sheep, through the blood of the everlasting covenant, make you perfect in every good work to do His will, working in you that which is well-pleasing in His sight, through Jesus Christ; to whom be glory for ever and ever. Amen."

Previous to reading this, I had expressed some solemn parting truths, and our party broke up in much love and peace.

May the Lord of the harvest, Himself, cause that some of these may be gathered into His garner, and may He bless, prosper, and increase the seed so unworthily scattered.

On Fifth-day, we dined with some sweet, spiritual, and delightful people, the de Presensés and de Valcours; in the evening to Mark Wilke's, to meet a very large party of ministers from different parts of France, come to attend the Meetings of the various Societies.

Fontainbleau, 28th.—The day before our departure from Paris we visited the Prefét de Police, took in our report of the state of the Prisons, and obtained leave for the Protestant ladies to visit the Protestant prisoners; we had much interesting conversation. We have the great satisfaction of hearing, that a law is likely to pass for women prisoners throughout France to be under the care of women.

In the evening, and during the day, numbers came to take leave of us; a good many Greeks, who appeared to feel much interest in and for us, as if our labours with them had not been in vain.

On parting with my beloved children, (to return to England,) I could not refrain from many tears. Our beloved friend Emilie Mallet joined us very early in the morning, also our kind friend John Sargent, our friend de Béranger, and one or two others. My soul was particularly humbled within me, and, before parting, we assembled with our friends, and poured forth deep prayer and thanksgiving unto the Lord; thanks for the help granted to us, and for the kindness shown us by our Christian friends, and the love and unity we have partaken of with them; prayer that our labours might be blessed, and the seed scattered, prospered and increased, and that no reproach might have been brought by us upon the cause nearest to my heart; earnestly did I ask a blessing upon our friends, ourselves, the tenderly beloved ones just parted from, and those at home. After this we took an affectionate leave of all, including our host, hostess, and the Hotel servants.

Just before Elizabeth Fry left Paris, she was informed that the Archbishop was annoyed at her proceedings, that he had expressed dissatisfaction at the alterations which she had recommended in the "St." Lazare Prison, and had gone so far as to speak with regret, if not displeasure, of the Baron de Gerando, who had accompanied her in her visits to the hospitals. But the secret of the Archi-episcopal opposition lay not here—it was the more general knowledge of the Holy Scriptures which he dreaded. It was that the reforms which Elizabeth Fry recommended, were all based upon Scriptural authority, that it was to those sacred writings she referred, for rules of active obligation; and above all this, that she lost no opportunity in all companies, and on all occasions, where it could be done with propriety, to urge their perusal and general circulation.

She left Paris on the 27th of Fourth Month, and proceeded through Mélun to Fontainbleau. She had been furnished with a letter from the Minister of the Interior, granting her, Josiah Forster, and her husband, permission to visit all the prisons in France. This important document was first made use of at Mélun; and on this occasion, as on all succeeding ones, Elizabeth Fry was received with respect, and every facility afforded her and her companions, for inspecting the prisons.

She stopped at Auxerre and visited the prison there, and writes from Avignon—

Fifth Month, 9th.—We had no particular calls of duty, until we arrived at Lyons, where there was a great press of engagements—prisons and refuges to inspect, besides many schools, of which I had only time to visit one—a woman's adult school. We had a large company of the poorer French Protestants, on two different evenings, when we read with them. We also visited several of their houses; but it was more for serious conversation amongst them, than absolute religious engagement. We had one very important Meeting of influential people, in which I desired to speak the Truth in love. It was introduced by the Prison subject. I endeavoured to show, that change of heart could only be produced by Christian principles, as revealed to us in Holy Scripture, through the power of the Holy Spirit. This, I very boldly attested, and then strove to impress the importance of Christian example, and of religious duties being faithfully performed, both public and private. Then I entered upon useful societies, charities, and schools, with Christian instruction. We had much attention paid to us, much kindness shown to us, and I humbly trust, an impression made on many minds, and some humble, valuable Christians comforted by our visit.

To her children she writes from—

Nismes, *Fifth Month*, 12*th*, 1839.

We thankfully say, we feel peaceful, and in our right place, although separated from so many so very dear to us.

We paid a very interesting visit to Lyons, and found a good deal new in the Prisons and Refuges. An order of Catholics, called "the Brethren and Sisters of St. Joseph," believe it their duty entirely to take care of prisoners and criminals generally. They do not visit as we do, but take the entire part of turnkeys and prison-officers, and live with the prisoners night and day, constantly caring for them. I thought the effect on the female prisoners surprisingly good, as far as their influence extended. But the mixture of gross superstition is curious, the image of the Virgin dressed up in the finest manner, in their different wards. I feared that their religion lay so much in form and ceremonies, that it led from heart work, and from that great change which would probably be produced, did these sisters simply teach them Christianity. Their books appeared to be mostly about the Virgin; not a sign of Scripture to be found, in either prison or refuge. I felt it laid on me as a weighty, yet humbling duty, before I left Lyons, to invite Roman Catholics and Protestants, who had influence in the prisons, to come to our Hotel, and there, in Christian love, to tell them the *truth* to the best of my belief, as the *only* real ground of reformation of heart, and the means likely to conduce to this end. It was the more fearful, as I had to be entirely interpreted for. My heart almost sank within me as the time approached. It was about three o'clock in the day; about sixty people came, of the very influential Catholics and Protestants, and I was enabled through a most excellent interpreter, to show them, that nothing but the pure simple truth, as revealed in Scripture, through the power of the Holy Spirit, could really enlighten the understanding, or change the heart. My husband and Josiah Forster also, took a very useful and valuable part. *Much* satisfaction was expressed. We afterwards dined at a gentleman's, who lived in a lovely situation, on the top of a hill near Lyons. Our invitations began to flow in, and we should, I doubt not, had we stayed longer, soon have been in as great a current as at Paris, or greater. We met with some very interesting, devoted, Christian characters—a cousin of the Baroness Pelet's, almost like herself; her notes and flowers coming in every morning. The last day was most fatiguing; we had to rise soon after three in the morning for Avignon, to go a hundred and fifty miles down the Rhone.

We have passed through the most delightful country I ever saw. Lyons, with the Rhone and Saone, is, in its environs, beautiful, and the passage from Lyons to Avignon really lovely; mountains in the distance, (parts of the Alps,) their tops covered with snow; vegetation in perfection, the flowers of spring and summer in bloom at once, grass just ready to be cut, barley in the ear, lilacs, laburnums, syringas, roses, pinks, carnations, acacias in full bloom, yellow jessamine wild in the hedges. It is a sudden burst of the finest summer, combined with the freshness of spring. The olive groves, intermixed with abundant vineyards and mulberry groves, all beautiful from their freshness. The ancient buildings of Avignon, the ruins on the banks of the Rhone, the very fine and wonderful remains of the Roman aqueduct, called the Pont du Gard, really exceed description. This place also abounds in curious buildings. Here, or in the neighbourhood, we expect to remain some time.

We find the poor Friends delighted to see us, and the Protestants give us a hearty welcome.

From Avignon, they proceeded to Nismes. There, Elizabeth Fry made a longer tarriance than usual. For a week, she continued to be exceedingly interested by the various objects that presented themselves to her notice, and by the persons whom she met with. There exists at Nismes, and in the neighbouring villages, a scattered body of people, professing the principles of the Society of Friends. She and Josiah Forster visited, with much interest, all who resided at Nismes, and attended their Meetings. These simple, but valuable persons are the descendants of the Camisards, who took refuge in the mountains of the Cevennes, during the persecutions subsequent to the revocation of the Edict of Nantes.

Congenies was the next place visited by the travellers; it is a retired village, to the west of the road from Nismes to Montpellier, about four leagues from the former place. The inhabitants are almost all Friends; a kind and religious people. With her companion Josiah Forster, Elizabeth Fry regularly attended their Meetings for worship and discipline, by which she became exceedingly interested in their welfare. Their Meeting House was neat, and abundantly adequate to the needs of the congregation; she also visited them all in their families.

In all the villages round, there seemed to be a most eager, willing ear, to hear the truths of the gospel. The Meeting held at Congenies, on the last First-day evening, was crowded—the people clustered up to the top of the doors, in all the open windows, and on the walls outside, yet in perfect quietude and order. At Calvisson, on the following First-day, it was the same, the Meeting there was held in the Protestant Temple. The travellers left Congenies on the 27th, and after partaking of the abounding hospitalities of Doctor Pleindoux, at Nismes, proceeded by the ancient city of Arles to Marseilles. Before quitting Congenies, Elizabeth Fry wrote—

Fifth Month, 22nd.—Yesterday was my birthday, and it pleased my Heavenly Father, in His love and pity, to cause it to be a day of remarkable peace, from the early morning to the evening. I felt it was not for works of righteousness, that I had done, but of His grace and His mercy, that I have thus known my soul to be refreshed in the Lord. Lord, continue to be with us! lift up the light of Thy countenance upon us, and bless us all, absent and present; and particularly at this time, I ask Thee to bless our labours among this people, to their solid good, and Thy praise. Amen!

Sixth Month, 2nd.—We found a great deal of what was highly interesting in Congenies. A peculiar and new place to us. The country remarkable, much cultivated in parts, and planted with vineyards, mulberry, olive, and fig-trees, with but little corn. There is a very delightful air; the hills rather barren and singularly grey, with fine ruins upon some of them; and here and there a peep at the Mediterranean. The little dull villages, much strewed about, thickly inhabited, mostly by Protestants, who appear generally in a low, neglected state; we visited some of these villages, and had larger or smaller Meetings in them. We found a great inclination in the people to hear the truth, and I believe there is a real thirst after it. I humbly trust that the blessing of the Lord was with us, as I have seldom felt more peace, or more sense of this blessing, than when engaged in these labours of Christian love at Congenies, or a more clear belief that I was in my right place.

After visiting Marseilles, where many important objects called for attention, the travellers proceeded to Toulon, and there they visited the prisons and the galley-slaves; thence to Aix. This place was, on various accounts, interesting to the travellers: to Elizabeth Fry it was rendered particularly so, by her finding there a lively little Protestant congregation, under a zealous and apparently spiritual pastor. A great contrast to the scene which met her view, on turning into the Course on her arrival,—the procession of the Féte Dieu in all its tinsel finery.

From Aix, the travellers returned to Nismes. The subject of a District Society claimed attention. First-day, the 10th, was passed there: of this Elizabeth Fry writes:—

Sixth Month.—Our First-day at Nismes was aeeply weighty in prospect, so that I rested little at night, as I had ventured to propose our holding one Meeting in the morning, in the Methodist chapel, that whoever liked might attend it; and in the evening, to do the same in a very large school-room, that all classes might attend, as I believed that all would not come to a Methodist Meeting-house. I went, prostrated before the Lord, to this Meeting in the morning, hardly knowing how to hold up my head; I could only apply for help to the inexhaustible Source of our sure mercies; feeling that I could not do it, either on account of myself, or because it was the work in which I was engaged; but I could do it for the sake of my Lord, and that His kingdom might spread. Utterly unworthy did I feel myself; but my Lord was gracious. My dear interpreter, Christine Majolier, was there to help me in a very large Meeting, and I felt power wonderfully given me to proclaim the truths of the Gospel, and to press the point of the Lord Himself being our teacher, immediately by His Spirit, and through the Holy Scriptures, and by His Providences and works; and to show, that no teaching so much conduced to growth in grace, as the Lord's teaching. There was much attention; at the close, I felt the spirit of prayer much over us, longed for its vocal expression, and felt a desire some one might pray, when a Methodist minister, in a feeling manner, expressed a wish to offer something in prayer, to which, of course, we assented—it proved solemn and satisfactory.

We dined at our dear friend, the Pasteur Emilien Frossard's; he and his wife have been like a brother and sister to us; we were also joined by a Roman Catholic gentleman, who has, I think, been seriously impressed by our visit, and it has, led him to have the Scriptures read to his workmen. There were also Louis Majolier, his daughter, and a young English friend. I think I have very seldom in my life felt a more lively sense of the love of God, than at this table. I may say, our souls were animated under its sweetness; I think we rejoiced together, and magnified the name of our God.

In the evening, we met in a large school-room that would contain some hundreds, where numbers assembled, principally the French Protestants and some of their pastors. There, again, I was greatly helped, I really believe, by the Holy Spirit, to speak to them upon their important situations in the Church of Christ, and the extreme consequence of their being sound both in faith and practice. I also felt it my duty to show them, as Protestants, the infinite importance not only in France, but in the surrounding nations, of their being "as a city built upon a hill that cannot be hid." I showed them how the truth is spreading, and how important to promote it, being preachers of righteousness in life and conversation, as well as in word and doctrine. There was here also much attention; and our dear and valued friend and brother in Christ, Emilien Frossard, prayed beautifully, that the word spoken might profit the people, and particularly, that the blessing of the Lord might rest upon me. It was no common prayer on my behalf. Thanks to my Heavenly Father, the Meeting broke up in much love, life, and peace.

The next morning, Josiah Forster and I held a large Meeting, partly in the open air, at the village of Codognan. I was pleased to see many of our dear friends from Congenies and the neighbourhood, at this our last Meeting in this part. We separated from them under a lively feeling of true peace and much love, and concluded our services under a strong confidence that our feet had been rightly turned amongst them; a pastor—a stranger to us, closed the Meeting in a solemn and beautiful prayer.

After this, we proceeded on our journey to Montpellier, where important service opened for us. A Protestant Ladies' Committee was formed to visit the great Female Prison there; much important advice offered to the Governor upon the changes now being made in the prison, and female officers being appointed; we appeared to go in the very time wanted, and obtained the liberation of several poor women from their very sad cells. The Prefét was most kind to us, and thus, our way was easily made: the Mayor and all with us. Help was given me to speak religiously to the poor women, before all these gentlemen.

On the day that Elizabeth Fry left Montpellier, she diverged to Cette, and crossing the Lagune of Thon, in the boat of an English merchant vessel, rejoined her companions at Mézé, a little fishing village on its banks; the British Consul and his wife came with her, and the captain of the merchantman. It was a temperance ship, and the Captain a serious man. Whilst waiting at Mézé, to avoid the mid-day sun, Elizabeth Fry wrote to her friend John Carey, of Guernsey, to interest him on behalf of the British seamen frequenting the port of Cette, and to intreat him to obtain for them a supply of Bibles, Testaments, and Tracts.

Journal resumed:—

We proceeded from place to place until we arrived at Toulouse, on Seventh-day evening, the 16th of the Sixth Month. On First-day evening, we met a large number of Protestants at one of their Scripture-readings. At the close, a solemn prayer was offered for us by Francis Courtois, one of a very remarkable trio of brothers, (bankers there,) all three of whom are given up to the service of their Lord, and appear to have been instruments greatly blessed. Their kindness to us was very great. In Toulouse we visited two prisons; had one important Prison Meeting, and one exceedingly solemn and satisfactory Scripture-reading and time of prayer, with the Courtois family, one or two pasteurs, and other religious persons.

I left my husband, who was unwell from the heat, at Toulouse, and went in faith, and somewhat in the cross, to Montauban; the place where the ministers of the Protestant Church of France are educated; but I believed it right to go—Josiah Forster accompanied me.

To her Children in England.

Bagnères de Luchon, *Sixth Month, 23rd, First-day.*

Here I sit before breakfast, with a most lovely scene before me. On entering this solemn Sabbath morning—my soul and body refreshed, not only in admiring the wonderful works of the outward creation, and being revived by the delightful air, fresh from the snowy mountains before me; but what is more, my soul refreshed. I have been enabled to lift my heart to my Heavenly Father, for every brother, sister, and child individually, and for my dear husband; and collectively, for my many beloved ones; committing all to His holy keeping. *I feel rest.* And now, my beloved children, I will tell you a little how we go on.

My attraction homewards grows stronger and stronger, but I desire patiently to wait the right time; the openings for religious service are greater than I expected, more particularly amongst the Protestants, at Montpellier, Toulouse, and Montauban. At Montauban, without expressing any other wish, than to have an evening party at one of their houses, to meet some of the professors and students of the College, (the only one in France for educating Pasteurs for the Reformed Church,) we found, to our dismay, all arranged to receive us in the College; and on arriving there, imagine how I felt, when the Dean of the College offered me his arm, to take me into the chapel. There, I believe, the whole of the collegians were assembled, in all at least a hundred. It was fearful work. There were also numbers of the people of the town; we thought about three hundred. Josiah Forster spoke first, explaining our views at some length. Then I rose, with an excellent interpreter, one of their pasteurs; I first told them something of my Prison experience, and the power of Christian principle and kindness; then, I related a little of the state of their prisons in France; then, my ideas as to the general state of France; and afterwards endeavoured to bring home to them the extreme importance of their future calling, as pasteurs in their Church. I reminded them of that passage of Scripture, "the leaders of the people caused them to err." I endeavoured to show them how awful such a state of things must be, and the extreme importance of their being sound in doctrine and practice. Simple duty led me to Montauban. Josiah F. was my kind and useful companion. We were united in much Christian love to many there. I forgot to say, that at the close of the occasion, the pasteur who interpreted for me, prayed beautifully and spiritually, that the words spoken might profit the people; he also prayed for us; this has frequently occurred at the close of some of our interesting Meetings; a pouring forth of the spirit of prayer has been granted. My not knowing the language has obstructed my offering it, and it has appeared laid upon others instead. I have seldom felt sweeter peace in leaving a place than Montauban. At Toulouse we were deeply interested by the Courtois' brothers: they appear, body, soul, and spirit, devoted to the service of their Lord: quite a bright example to all of us. The world appeared as nothing to them. I have seldom seen men so wholly given up to good and useful objects: they were most kind to us. We had various calls of duty in that town, and I had a most excellent interpreter in François Courtois. We arrived here yesterday evening, after serious consideration, believing it the best to pursue this course. A certain time of quiet appears really needful to make representations to the French government, and to those in authority, of the various evils that want remedy in Prisons, &c. We understand there are many seeking, serious minds, to whom we may be of some comfort, which helps to reconcile us to the measure.

Elizabeth Fry's perseverance had surmounted every obstacle as long as her physical powers permitted; but from the effects of fatigue, and the heat of the climate, they were beginning to fail. Rest, and some cessation from mental and bodily exertion had become indispensable, and she yielded, though not without reluctance, to her husband's wish for a short tarriance in the cooler atmosphere of the Pyrenees. Speaking of this retreat, she says—

We went from Toulouse to Bagneres de Luchon, a most lovely place where we had a sweet, quiet lodging. I took two wonderfully fine excursions with my husband and children, (Josiah Forster partly with us,) which I rather enjoyed, particularly going into Spain.

One of these expeditions was to the Lake D'Oo Elizabeth Fry and her daughter were carried in chairs, each borne by four men, until they were about halfway up a steep ascent, on a little level of green sward, shadowed by a huge rock. They quitted their chairs for the carriers to rest themselves.

A group of wild-looking peasants were reposing near. Elizabeth Fry sat down by them, and entered into conversation; they assured her they "adored the Virgin in those parts;" she took out a French Text-Book;—the eight bearers joined the party. She read some words of Scripture, then drew attention to the wondeful works of God in creation, in the beautiful scene around them; then she spoke of His infinite mercy in sending the Lord Jesus Christ to redeem them. They listened with earnestness and respect, and thankfully received the little books she offered.

A day or two afterwards they ventured on a short excursion into Spain. A cool wet night, followed by a cloudy morning, gave hopes of less heat; after leaving Luchon, the party rode through the forest and valley of Beurbe, defiling along the most exquisite mountain pass; higher and higher it led them, till, on an elevated crest, the path turned suddenly downwards at a point called the "Postillion," where a small rock marked the boundary, and the guide exclaimed, "Nous voici en Espagne." They continued their descent for about half-an-hour, till they reached the boundary, where beech-trees and oaks again grew, amidst small patches of cultivation. Two Catalonian peasants were there, in their brown costume and scarlet sashes, and caps with long depending peaks. Elizabeth Fry, through the kind agency of Josiah Forster, was well supplied with extracts from Scripture in Spanish; to these men she gave several of them. Whilst the travellers dined on the grass, they observed one of the men reading attentively as he sat under the shade of a spreading chesnut, surrounded by his flock of goats. When rested and refreshed they continued their descent to a spot where they found several scattered cottages. Desiring to sow as "beside all waters," Elizabeth Fry left the little Scripture extracts at all these; in the manger of a cow-house, or on a nail of a door, for she had heard that the Spaniards, including the priests, were eager for books, and carefully preserved them.

During their little recess at Luchon, Elizabeth Fry, assisted by her companions, prepared a memorial of considerable length for the Minister of the Interior, and a shorter one for the Prefect of Police, embodying her observations on the state of the prisons which she had inspected, and her recommendations for their improvement.

From Bagnères de Luchon, they went to Bagnères de Bigorre, entering the gorge that heads to Luz and " St. Sauveur." They passed the ruined castle of " St. Marie," built by the English, the Templar's Fortress-church at Luz, and pursued their way to " St. Sauveur." There they remained some days, amidst the shadowy mountains which surround the town, and the rushing waters, not only of the Gaves, or rapid rivers of the district, but of the numerous little rivulets which feed them, tumbling and foaming from the rocks above.

The rest obtained here was beneficial to both body and mind ; and it is interesting to observe how, from the pressure of engagements of a most weighty character, the spirit of Elizabeth Fry was permitted, with a lively elasticity, to unbend and to repose itself in peace. She was endowed with a capacity for much enjoyment in the varied scenes of nature, and whether she beheld the grandeur of Alpine heights, or the rich foliage of the fertile valleys ; whether she gathered the shell on the beach, or the humble floweret by the roadside ; whether she surveyed the bright tints of a splendid sunset, or gazed on the wonders of the starry sky,—she saw in each, the impress of a Father's hand, graciously providing for His children, a store of blessing and a source of sanctified delight. She had also a nice, discriminating taste for the beauties of art. This gift, implanted in different degrees in every human mind, by the great Former of all things, was held by Elizabeth Fry in subserviency to the beneficient Giver. She felt pleasure in witnessing the products of genius and skill, when calculated to promote the convenience, or the innocent enjoyment of man.

How heart-saddening is the consideration that the artist, favoured by Heaven with surpassing talent, so frequently devotes it to the most unholy purposes—pandering to the evil propensities of our corrupt nature, instead of glorifying the Almighty Creator, in serving His creatures, by the exercise of some measure of a power to originate and construct that which is useful and beautiful—a power which in its infiniteness, framed the architecture of the heavens and the earth.

On their return, E. Fry writes:—

We left Toulouse last Second-day, and have been travelling rather hard through the South of France; the heat very oppressive. Little religious service opened on the way. But at Montpellier and Nismes, we again met some of our dear friends, and there appeared reason to believe that our labour had not been in vain in the Lord, particularly at Nismes and Congenies. Oh, may our Heavenly Father bless and prosper the seed scattered by us, His unworthy instruments; and may He, in His tender and unmerited mercy, guide and guard us to the end! Answer, I pray Thee, the deep cries of Thy servant for Thine own name's sake, and cause Thy love and peace to abound in our little circle, until we separate.

Bonigen, near Interlachen, Switzerland, Eighth Month. 11th.—I believe that my gracious Lord has guided our steps to this place; blessed be His name. Now to go on with my journal. At Grenoble, where I felt rather pressed in spirit, to spend a First-day, I had a curious opening for religious service, and I believe an important one with several enlightened Roman Catholics, several Protestants, and a school of girls. It was a time of spiritual refreshment, by which many appeared helped and comforted. The next day was occupied in important prison visits, and in the evening a Meeting with influential Roman Catholics.

Josiah Forster having left us to go by diligence to Geneva, we travelled alone through Savoy, and had a pleasant journey through a lovely country; but the darkness of the Roman

Catholic religion, and the arbitrary laws not allowing even a tract to be given away, were painful; we found that a Swiss gentleman had lately been imprisoned for doing it, and confined with a thief. We arrived at Geneva, the 25th of the Seventh Month, in the evening. Here we passed a very interesting time, from various and important openings for religious service, in large parties, in prisons, &c. My belief is, that we were sent to that place, and amidst some trials, from different causes, there was a pouring forth of spiritual help, and spiritual peace. Many of the pasteurs came to us, and not a few expressed their refreshment and satisfaction with our visit; before we left, several of the most spiritual, in a very striking and beautiful manner preached to us, particularly to myself, and prayed for us all: a time, I think, never to be forgotten by us. I believe the anointing was poured forth upon me, to speak the truth in love and power. I had an excellent spiritually-minded interpreter (Professor La Harpe): many appear to feel this occasion. A young English gentleman came up to me afterwards, and expressed his belief that it would influence him for life; and a lady came to me, and said, how remarkably her state had been spoken to. Much love was also shown to us, and unity. Indeed, I felt how our Lord permits His servants to rejoice together in love, and even to partake of the good things of this life, in His love and fear, with a subjected spirit, rejoicing in His mercies, temporal and spiritual. We had very great kindness also shown to us by many, among others, by our dear friend Mary Ann Vernet and her family, including her daughter the Baroness de Stäel, with whom we dined at Copet. The Duke de Broglie and his family were with her; we had a very interesting visit. We went from Geneva to our dear friend Sophia Delessert; her husband was out; they have a beautiful place on the banks of the Lake of Geneva, near Rolle; here we had the warmest reception, and were refreshed and comforted together; she is truly loved by me.

Of a very important and interesting occasion, where, at Beseinge, the beautiful residence of Colonel Tronchin, Elizabeth Fry met more than a hundred persons, we have some remarkable particulars, from the pen of a young student, since become the Secretary of the "Belgian Société Evangélique." He says:—

"We had half expected a philosophical discourse upon subjects of philanthropic and general interest, but every thing that fell from her lips was characterized by delicacy, extreme simplicity, and an ardent desire to draw our attention to our own happiness, in being permitted the opportunity for meditation on the one subject which seemed always present in her thoughts, Christ Jesus crucified for the expiation of our sins. At this distance of time I have an actual realization of the opening of her exhortation—'I think,' said she, 'it is impossible for us to be more profitably employed than by occupying the next few moments, with the contemplation of the love which the Lord Jesus has for us!' The rooms were full to overflowing; my fellow-students and I took up our places in the passage, on the stair-case, crowded round the open door, eagerly hanging on such parts of the beautiful exhortation, as we could catch by the most breathless attention; after she had concluded, she kindly came out amongst us, and expressed her regret that we should have been so inconvenienced. I can see her now, her tall figure leaning on Colonel Tronchin's arm, M. la Harpe at her side, her dignified, animated, yet softened countenance, bending towards us. I can never forget it. Such occasions are rare in life, they are very green spots in the garden of memory—more, they are opportunities given for improvement, solemnly increasing the responsibility of each who participates in them. May I never lose the impression of that day at Beseinge, nor the holy lessons I there heard and learnt."

On the First-day morning the travellers sat down in their room as usual, to worship after the simple manner of Friends. Some of the Vernet family, and a few others were present, and it proved a very solemn meeting. In the evening, their scripture-reading was attended by several pasteurs and a very numerous company, some belonging to the "evangelical" section of the "church," and others to that "national "church," which has become tinctured with vital error—the consequence of submitting the truths of divine revelation to the scrutiny and decisions of mere human reason.

On this occasion, Elizabeth Fry read the 58th chapter of Isaiah, and spoke at length on some parts of it. She prayed solemnly for those present; for the pasteurs, that they might be endued with wisdom and strength, for all who love the Lord, everywhere and of every name, and for the inhabitants of Geneva in particular.

At Lausanne, we met with a kind friend, Charles Scholl, whom we knew in England, a valuable pasteur. We visited the prisons; and with the women I had a religious time, one that appears to have made a considerable impression upon some of them. I have had very comforting accounts since I was there. A good many ladies and some gentlemen, met Josiah Forster and myself at a lady's house, where the subject of prisons was entered upon. In the evening we met a very large party, numbers of pasteurs, &c., at a gentleman's beautiful place on the banks of the lake; here again we had a deeply interesting time. I had to speak for some time, showing the effect of Christian principle and kindness on prisoners. I was well interpreted for, by my friend Charles Scholl. In conclusion, one valuable pasteur read, and another prayed for my preservation in my peculiar situation, and that I might not be entangled by the many snares that surrounded me. Much love and real unity we felt with many of these dear people. We then proceeded to Berne by Friburg; at Berne I again visited the Prison. These Penitentiaries at Geneva, Lausanne, and Berne interested me much, as excellent; still there are some things wanting At Berne, I had also a religious time with all the female prisoners. We visited the large and interesting institution of Dr. Fellenburg for boys, with which I was much pleased.

but I desired more reading of the Holy Scriptures, and spoke and wrote to him on the subject. We had a very hospitable reception to dinner, invited for half-past eleven, from a gentleman and his lady. At the prison, I was, at first, badly interpreted for, when a young lady, Sophia Werstemburger, came forward, as she has since told me, from believing it a duty, and offered to assist me. It was striking to me to observe, how remarkably she appeared helped to do it, and to convey my meaning.

The subject of this excellent and solemn address was afterwards published by Sophia Werstemburger in a German tract, and has been extensively used in Prisons

We resume the journal.

After this visit, we parted from our dear friend Josiah Forster, in love and unity, and I may add, grateful to him for his constant kindness, and faithful and industrious endeavour to help me in my various duties. May it please the Lord to grant him his reward, in a further knowledge of Himself, and of the rest, peace, and liberty, that He gives to His children and people.

From Berne the travellers went to Thun, and to Grindelvald and Brienz, being occupied at the different places with their varied pursuits; those of Elizabeth Fry were as usual, such as tended to promote the well-being of the inhabitants.

A First-day was passed at Brienz, where they had the unexpected pleasure of meeting some of Elizabeth Fry's valued friends of the Mackenzie family from Edinburgh, and of spending a quiet day together, concluded by a reading in the evening. The pastor of this place was also visited, and the condition of his flock inquired into. On a previous occasion, when on the Lake of Brienz, a poor boy who rowed the boat, had told her that his mother lay sick in a cottage that he pointed out. It rested on her mind, and in crossing the lake to return to Bönigen, she landed, not without difficulty, accompanied by the wife of the pasteur of Brienz. They found the poor woman very ill on a mattress, spread in the gallery of her cottage, with her Bible by her side; she was an afflicted Christian woman, to whom the few words of encouragement offered were very timely, to strengthen that which, through bodily suffering, seemed almost ready to die. The temporal wants were not forgotten, and the case was left under the care of the pastor's wife.

Whilst at Bönigen, Herr Mitchell, the landlord of the little inn, and his family, attended their First-day evening readings. On one of these occasions a peasant girl was with them who appeared pious and afflicted; her name was Madelina Kauss. She came from a neighbouring village to seek counsel of Elizabeth Fry. Madelina and her mother had joined themselves to a little body of serious people, Pietists, somewhat resembling Methodists, seceders from the National Church. The father, a coarse, ignorant man, vehemently threatened his wife, and turned his daughter out of doors to earn her own livelihood, which she did by weaving for nine French sous a day. Pious people from Berne had interfered on their behalf, but had only made matters worse. It so fell out that, about this time, a certain small, old-fashioned, black-letter German newspaper reached the little inn at Bönigen: the host and his household were startled on finding in it a long account of his guests, "a history of Mrs. Fry, her works and labours of love;" concluding with her visit to the Oberland of Berne, and residence at the Herr Mitchell's country inn. After careful perusal, it occurred to the worthy host, that in his inmates, he had found the very people to rectify the wrongs of poor Madelina, and restore peace in her parents' dwelling; persons, in his opinion, not to be resisted by Henrich Kauss, the peasant of Wildersewyl, to whom he advised that a visit should forthwith be made. When the carriage came to convey the party, he insisted on driving it himself, arrayed in his holiday costume. The interview with the family was quite pathetic. The father laid the fault of his violence and severity on the grandfather, and he on the schoolmaster; but a little kind and wise conciliation sufficed to bring them all to tears; they wept and kissed; and Herr Mitchell wept for sympathy. After which, Elizabeth Fry had a religious time with Madelina, her mother, and a few of their neighbours; leaving them with the thankful belief that they had been permitted to act the blessed part of peacemakers.

What a messenger of mercy was Elizabeth Fry! Varied and constant were the benefits conferred through her instrumentality. The query naturally suggests itself—*how* could it happen that *so many* calls on benevolence and christian sympathy could fall in her way?—the only reply to this must be the fact, that *she was appointed by the Most High to her remarkable vocation.* He it was, who, by the operation of His Holy Spirit, qualified her for the work that He ordained she should perform; He led her into it through a great diversity of channels,—and through paths that she knew not. Had not her mind been subjected to the divine will, waiting humbly before the Lord to receive direction from Him, the purposes of His wisdom and love would have been—at least by *her*—unfulfilled and unperceived.

After leaving Bönigen, Elizabeth Fry was met at Thun by Sophia Werstemburger, and in the evening Felemburgh, the chaplain of the prison at Berne, arrived there also; a few important hours devoted to prison subjects were concluded by a scripture-reading, and a time of worship.

Zurich, Eighth Month, 25th.—We left our sweet little home at Bönigen, on the banks of the Lake of Brienz, last Fourth-day. I felt refreshed by our visit to this lovely country. I think my prayers have been heard and answered, in its being a very uniting time with those most tenderly beloved by me. We have had some interesting communications with serious persons in the humble walk of life, who reside in that neighbourhood. We have desired to aid them spiritually and temporally, but the difficulty of communication has been very great, from want of suitable interpreters; still, I trust, that some were edified and comforted. I also hope our circulation of books and tracts has been useful, and the establishment of, at least, one library at Brienz, for the labouring classes. We have travelled along gently and agreeably by Lucerne, and through a delightful country.

On the morning of their departure from Zurich the venerable pastor Gesner, and many others, called to take leave. This apostolic old man pronounced a striking blessing on Elizabeth Fry, to which she replied in terms that caused the bystanders to weep aloud. They proceeded to Ludwigsburg for the First-day. Here she writes—

Ludwigsburg, (a few miles from Stuttgard,) Ninth Month, 1st.—On the evening of the day that I wrote at Zurich, we went with our dear friend the Baroness Pelet, afterwards joined by the Baron, to the house of an ancient, devoted pasteur, Gesner. His wife was the daughter of that excellent servant of the Lord, Lavater. We met a large number of persons, I believe generally serious. I had proposed to myself speaking on the Prison subject, but my way opened differently; to enlarge upon the state of the Protestant Church in France, to encourage all its members to devotedness; and particularly in that place, where deep trials have been their portion, from their Government upholding infidelity and infidel men. At the close of the Meeting, our venerable friend, Gesner, spoke in a lively, powerful manner, and avowed his belief that the Lord Himself had enabled me to express what I had done, it was so remarkably "the word in season." I paid, also, a satisfactory religious visit to the female prisoners in the afternoon. The next morning I visited the head magistrate, represented the evils I had observed, and saw some ladies about visiting prisons. We afterwards went a sweet expedition on the Lake, with our beloved friends the Baron and Baroness Pelet. Early in the evening, I set off with a dear girl—great grand-daughter to Lavater, and grand-daughter to Pasteur Gesner—Barbara Usteri, in a curious little carriage to pay some visits, and to spend an evening at the house of the aunt of Matilda Escher, another interesting young woman, with whom I had become acquainted, I believe providentially, at an inn near Interlachen. I had no one with me but strangers, as my dear family stayed with the Baron and Baroness Pelet at my desire; but I feel not among strangers, because those who love the Lord Jesus, are dear to me, and in our holy Head we are one. I can hardly express, on this journey, how much I have found this to be the case. The love, the unity, and the home-feeling, I have had with those I never saw before; and I have also found how little it matters where we are, for "where the God of peace is, there is home."

A letter to the resident Inspector of the Prisons at Ludwigsburg, was delivered, and half-past seven o'clock the next morning, appointed for her visit to that place. There a Swiss lad of eighteen years of age, was in waiting to act as interpreter. The women, though it was First-day, were engaged in needlework by order of the King,—a sad sight in a Protestant country! Elizabeth Fry also visited an Orphan Asylum; and in the evening again went to the prison. The women appeared in a tender, feeling state of mind, and a solemn reading of the Scriptures impressed them much. The travellers proceeded to Frankfort, where they met with much kindness from christian friends, visited the prisons, and had a stall opened in the town for the sale of Bibles and Tracts. A rapid journey from that place brought them to Ostend, whence they embarked for Dover on the 12th of the Ninth Month, and they were favoured to reach home in health and peace on the 13th.

About two months later, Elizabeth Fry visited Norfolk. Whilst staying at Lynn, with her son and daughter Cresswell, she found they contemplated placing their eldest son in the army. This was to her a most painful circumstance. Perhaps there could not be found a spirit to which war, in every shape, was more deeply abhorrent—its element a more absolute contrast with that atmosphere of love in which she was continually preserved.

From some members of her immediate family, the Compiler has received assurances that her utter disapprobation of this most evil system, and her grief that any of her descendants should be involved in it, continued to the close of her life to be unalterably strong. She says, on being apprised of the intention of her children in reference to this arrangement—

"My prayers were offered in secret, that my Lord would open some way of escape from a life, that I felt to be so unchristian and fearful a one. At first I said little, but kept my heart much lifted up on his account; but afterwards, I fully represented my views to him and to his parents, and I found they had great weight with them."

The plan for placing this beloved grandchild, who was but seventeen years of age, in this most unchristian profession, appeared to be abandoned; much to the relief and consolation of his dear grandmother.

At the commencement of the new year, Elizabeth Fry pours forth the desires of her soul in prayer, as follows:—

Under a sweet feeling of Thy merciful and providential care over us, and Thy gentle dealings towards us, most gracious Lord God, I humbly return Thee thanks, and ask Thee in faith, and in the name of our Redeemer, to continue to be with us, to keep us, and bless us, and more abundantly to bestow upon us the gifts of Thine own Holy Spirit, that we may faithfully fill the office Thou mayst call us into, to Thy glory, the good of others, and the spreading of the truth as it is in Jesus; also, be pleased, not only to bestow on us the gifts, but also the graces of Thy Spirit, that in meekness and deep humility, and much patience and long-suffering, we may walk worthy of Thee, who hast called us to Thy kingdom and glory. And now, Holy Father, under a fresh feeling of Thy love, Thy pity, and Thine unmerited mercy towards us, I commend my husband, myself, children, grandchildren, brothers, sisters, and their children, and all my beloved friends at home and abroad, and all who love Thy name and fear Thee, particularly the afflicted and tempted, to Thy most Holy keeping; and I also pray Thee, for the sake of Thy beloved Son Christ Jesus our Saviour, who tasted death for every man, to regard for good the world at large, especially those who yet sit in darkness. Lift up the light of Thy blessed and holy countenance upon these, and all wanderers, that they may behold Thy beauty and excellency, and come to the knowledge of Thyself and Thy dear Son. So be it, most merciful Lord God, that the day may hasten forward, when the knowledge of Thyself and Thy Christ, through the power of Thy Spirit, may cover the earth, even as the waters cover the sea! Amen.

Elizabeth Fry had, previously to her last visit to the Continent, believed it would be her duty to extend it to parts of Germany. The way thither did not, however, then appear fully to open. The attraction to that country was not lessened, and, with the concurrence of her friends at home, she prepared again to set out on this gospel mission. Her endeared friend and brother in Christ, William Allen, was impressed with a belief that he was required by his Lord to unite with her in the service. Before entering on their travels they were called on to perform several important duties in their own land, as will be shown by the following entries in the journal:

First Month, 1840.—An eventful time in public and private life. Our young Queen is to be married to Prince Albert. She has sent me a present of fifty pounds for our Refuge at Chelsea, by Lord Normanby. Political commotions about the country—riots in Wales—much religious stir in the "Church of England," numbers of persons becoming much the same as Roman Catholics—Popish doctrines preached openly in many of the churches—infidel principles, in the form of Socialism, gaining ground.

To a seriously-disposed person to whom Elizabeth Fry had been an instrument of religious edification, she wrote on the 15th of First Month of this year, from Upton :

My dear Friend,

Thy few lines gave me solid satisfaction, because they bespeak the real work of grace going on in thy heart. Does not our Lord say, "By their fruits ye shall know them?" What will any profession of religion avail us—however high —unless we have "put on the new man, which after God is created in righteousness and true holiness?" I am very deeply impressed with this most important truth, and much wish that those who profess Christ, every where, and of all denominations, felt it more; but Satan tries to turn them from it, and to have their religion consist in some outward form, and some peculiar views of doctrine, some exalted profession, rather than, in *deep humility* and *meekness of spirit*, acknowledging the Lord to be their Saviour, and the Holy Spirit to be their Guide, Comforter, and Sanctifier.

Farewell, thy affectionately interested Friend,

ELIZABETH FRY.

Upton, Second Month, 1st.—I am called to visit our young Queen to-day, in company with William Allen, and I hope my brother Samuel also.

We went to Buckingham Palace, and saw the Queen. Our interview was short. Lord Normanby, the Home Secretary, presented us. The Queen asked us where we were going on the Continent. She said it was some years since she saw me. She asked about Caroline Neave's Refuge, for which she had lately sent the fifty pounds. This gave me an opportunity of thanking her. I ventured to express my satisfaction that she encouraged various works of charity; and I said it reminded me of the words of Scripture, "with the merciful Thou wilt show Thyself merciful." Before we withdrew, I stopped and said, I hoped the Queen would allow me to assure her, that it was our prayer that the blessing of God might rest upon the Queen and her Consort.

I have for some time believed that duty would call me to have a meeting in London or the neighbourhood, previous to leaving home. I see many difficulties attached to it, and perhaps none so much, as my great fear of women coming too forward in these things, beyond what the Scripture dictates; but I am sure the Scripture most clearly and forcibly lays down the principle that the Spirit is not to be grieved, or quenched, or vexed, or resisted; and on this principle I act; under the earnest desire that whatever the Lord leads me into by his Spirit may be done faithfully to Him, and in His name; and I am of opinion, that nothing Paul said, to discourage women's speaking in the Churches, alluded to their speaking through the help of the Spirit, as he clearly gave directions how they should conduct themselves under such circumstances, when they prayed or prophesied.

In a letter written a few days afterwards, one who was present, not a Friend, described that Meeting in the following words:—

"It was really a most impressive occasion—the large, fine, circular building filled—not less, I should think, than fifteen hundred present. She began by entreating the sympathy and supplications of those present. I cannot tell you how mine flowed forth on her behalf. After her prayer, we sat still for some time, then William Allen spoke, and then she rose, giving as a text, 'Yield yourselves unto God, as those that are alive from the dead;' and uncommonly fine was her animated, yet tender exhortation to all present, but more especially the young, to present themselves as living sacrifices to the Lord,—to be made of Him new creatures in Christ—the old things passed away, and all things become new, as those alive from the dead. This change she dwelt and enlarged on much; its character, and the Power that alone can effect it; the duty demanded of us—'Yield yourselves;' and its infinite and eternal blessedness. I was astonished and deeply impressed; the feeling was, 'surely God is amongst us of a truth.'"

All now appeared clearly open for her leaving home, in order to proceed with the work that she believed was required on the Continent. She was accompanied, not only by her friend, William Allen, but also by her beloved brother, Samuel Gurney—his daughter Elizabeth and Lucy Bradshaw were enlisted in the service—being much needed, as helpers to their more aged friends, who, although possessing undiminished energy of mind and feeling, were evidently less vigorous in physical power than heretofore. Their valued friend, Josiah Forster, joined this little band, and rendered important assistance to them. They embarked for Ostend: on arriving there, Elizabeth Fry wrote to her family:—

Ostend, *Second Month*, 27*th*, finished Ghent, 29*th*.

We are favoured with a bright morning, and we may thankfully say that our spirits are permitted to partake of the same brightness. I have a sweet feeling of being in the right place. An order is come from the Belgian Government for us to visit their prisons. So the way opens before us; and though I give up much to enter these services, and feel leaving my most tenderly beloved ones, yet there is such a sense of the blessedness of the service, and the honour of doing the least thing for my Lord, unworthy as I am, that it often brings a peculiar feeling of health, (if I may so say) as well as peace, to my body, soul, and spirit.

My brother Samuel is a capital travelling companion, so zealous, so able, so willing, so generous; and I find dear Elizabeth sweet, pleasant, and cheering. Bruges is a delightful old town. Here we visited the English Convent, where to our surprise, we could only speak through a grating. We had a good deal of conversation with dear S. P——'s sister and the Superior. They appeared very interesting women. We talked about their shutting-in sys tem. I expressed my disapprobation of it as a general practice, and one liable to such great abuse. I sent them some books, and mean to send more. We also visited a large school; and to the great pleasure and amusement of the children, your uncle gave them all a present. They could not in the least understand our language, as they speak Flemish.

We have been much interested, this morning, in visiting the Maison de Force; it is a very excellent prison of considerable size, but wants some things very much. We have since been occupied with the numerous English here. They are without pasteur or school, and quite in a deplorable state. We propose having a meeting with them of a religious and philanthropic nature, and hope to establish some schools, &c., amongst them.

May the blessing of the Most High abundantly rest on you all.

From Brussels, *Third Month*, 1*st.*

We left Ghent on Seventh-day, about half-past two o'clock, after visiting a most deplorable prison, where we found a cell with the floor and sides formed of angular pieces of wood, so that no prisoner could stand, lie down, or lean against the wall, without suffering. We also visited a lunatic asylum, so beautifully conducted, that I more took the impression of how happy such persons may be made than I ever did before. They are cared for by the "Sisters of St. Vincent de Paul." After rather a slow journey, we arrived here to dinner, at six o'clock.

Ghent, Third Month, 3rd.—Here we are once more—we have visited another large prison for the military; and had a very interesting Meeting with the English workmen, their wives and children. I am glad to say, they conclude for us to send them schoolmasters. We had flocks after us last evening, English and Belgians—I suppose about seventy; they appeared to be touched by our reading. I observe how much the English appear impressed on these occasions. Our little party are very comfortable, and each has plenty to do

Antwerp, *Third Month*, 6*th*.

Upon our return to Brussels from Ghent, we visited the great prison of Vilvorde. We gave many of our little Scripture extracts to the prisoners. We got home to dinner, and spent the evening at the Baron de Bois', where we met several pleasant persons. A considerable number of Belgians, poor and rich, came to an evening Meeting at our hotel. The next day was one of no common interest. After some engagements in the morning, breakfasting out, &c., we visited the King. Our party were William Allen, my brother Samuel, J. Forster, and myself; and before we left, Lucy Bradshaw and dear Elizabeth were admitted to see him. We first had a very interesting conversation on the state of the prisons, and your uncle read the King our address to him upon the subject; when the part was read expressing our desire for him, the Queen and his family, he appeared to feel it much. We had open, interesting communication on many subjects. We remained nearly an hour. The Queen was unwell, and the children asleep, therefore I did not see them. We gave the King several books for himself and the Queen. We were invited by Count Arrivabene to dine with one of the first Belgian families. I felt it rather fearful, when, to my surprise after dinner, I was seated by the Dean of Brussels, surrounded by the company, and told that I was permitted to speak openly upon my religious views. Indeed, I think the wish was, that I should preach to them. This was curious, because I was warned on going to say nothing about religion. Preach I did not—as I do not feel that at my command; but I spoke very seriously about the Scriptures not being read in the prisons, and endeavoured to show, in few words, what alone can produce change of heart, life, and conduct, and the danger of resting in forms. We parted in much good-will, and we sent the Dean and the ladies some books. In the evening we had a philanthropic party at our hotel. The next morning, a large, very solemn and interesting religious Meeting at the hotel. We left

Brussels in much peace (*rejoicing* would not be too strong a word). In nearest love.

E. F.

Extract from a letter writen by her niece, Elizabeth Gurney:—

"*Brussels, Third Month, 6th.*—We expect to end our very interesting visit in this place to-day. A great Meeting is now assembling in the Table d'Hôte salon, fitted up by our landlord for the occasion. This is to be our farewell Meeting. We have had a very full morning, partly employed in distributing books. The servants at the palace sent an entreaty that they might not be overlooked.

"Yesterday began with a full tide of business. They were to see the King at twelve o'clock. He is a particularly pleasing-looking man, rather older than I expected. The Duchess of Kent had kindly written to the King, to say, that my aunt was likely to visit Brussels.

"I must tell you about our dinner at M. le Comte de——'s, the first Roman Catholic family here. We were taken there by our kind friend Count Arrivabene. The party consisted of fifteen persons, only two speaking English. Amongst them was the Dean, the head of the Church here, under the Bishop of Malines. Much that was interesting passed. The Dean and our aunt seated themselves in a corner of the room, and by degrees the whole party gathered round; the Count and Josiah Forster interpreting by turns. It was a critical thing to know what to say, as the conversation became more and more of a religious nature. She began on the prisons—prevention of crime—how much the upper classes are often the cause, by example, of the sins of the lower; related a few of her prison facts as proofs, and finally ended by saying, 'Will the Dean allow me to speak my mind candidly?' His permission being given, and that of the Count and Countess, she began by expressing the sincere interest that she felt for the inhabitants of this city, and how much she had been desiring for them, 'that as a people, they might each place less confidence in men, and in the forms of religion, and look to Christ with an entire and simple faith.' The priest said nothing; but turned the subject, and asked what the views of the Quakers were; upon which Josiah Forster gave them a short account in French, which appeared to interest them all."

The engagements in Rotterdam were numerous, as usual. But although many circumstances occurred to encourage her, Elizabeth Fry often went heavily on her way, feeling delicate in health, and oppressed in spirit. A letter from Dr. Bosworth, with whom she had become acquainted at Rotterdam, was very consoling to her. In it he says:—

"Before I answer your questions, let me discharge a debt of gratitude, which I and my wife owe to you and your friends, for your benevolent exertions in Rotterdam. You have excited amongst us, and have left, I trust, an abiding Christian affection. We feel we are brethren, united in the same good cause of our adorable Saviour, that of promoting 'peace on earth, and good-will to men.' How soon will the wood, hay and stubble of party be burnt up, and what is built on the Rock of Ages remain, &c., &c We are here in a parched wilderness, but your visit has brought a refreshing dew, and may it abide with us."

After spending some days at Amsterdam and Zwolle, where Elizabeth Fry had important service, holding Meetings, &c., the travellers went to Minden, to visit a small body of Friends resident there, as well as the larger congregation at Pyrmont.

Elizabeth Fry again writes to her family at home:—

Minden, Third Month, 28th.—We left Zwolle on Second-day, the 23rd, and slept at a true German inn—neither carpet nor curtain. Our night was disturbed, still we did well. The next day we set off in good time, and travelled until twelve o'clock; we did not settle till two in the morning. I think I have not yet recovered the fatigue, not having slept well one night since. We have been interested by the Friends, who are much like those of Congenies, but more entirely Friends; we have visited them in almost all their families, and had two Meetings with them. We have been brought into much sympathy with them, for they are a tried, and I believe a Christian people. We have this evening had three pastors with us, two of them I think spiritual men.

Our Meeting was largely attended this afternoon, and I can assure you my heart almost failed me, being interpreted for in German is so difficult, but we have in Auguste Mundhenck, a well educated young Friend, a capital interpreter. The Meeting ended well. In my wakeful nights I feel solitary, and have you very present with me; but I humbly trust He that sleepeth not is watching over you with tender care.

Pyrmont, 29*th*.—In our way here we visited, at Hameln, a large prison, under the King of Hanover, almost all the poor prisoners, upwards of four hundred in number, heavily chained. I told them a little of my deep interest for their present and everlasting welfare; they appeared to feel it very much; one poor man, a tall fine figure, with heavy chains on both legs, sat weeping like a child. I am just come in from visiting the families of Friends; they are really a very valuable set. I longed to take a picture for you of an old Friend with a plain scull-cap, either quilted or knitted, a purple handkerchief, a striped apron, and the whole appearance truly curious; but she was a sweet old woman, full of love. I am really amused, the old and young are as fond of me as if I could fully speak to them; the little ones sitting on my lap as if I were their mother, and leaning their little heads upon me. A little child about four or five said, what happy days they should have when we went to see them We expect a large party this evening.

30*th*.—We had our party, and understand there were present some of the first persons in the town, besides the master of the hotel, his wife, the doctor, the postmaster, the bookbinder, the shoemaker, &c., &c., &c.! We discussed the state of their poor, their not visiting them, or attending to them; for it appears that visiting the poor is not thought of here. I hope and expect our coming will be useful in this respect.

Hameln—ended Hanover, *Fourth Month*, 2*nd*.

Whilst stopping at a small inn, I mean to finish my account of our visit to Pyrmont. After I wrote, we went shaking on such bad roads from house to house to see the Friends, that I almost feared we must break down. We twice dined with them, in their beautiful spot at Friedensthal, (or the valley of peace,) surrounded with hills, and a river flowing through it. Roebucks wild from the woods abounding. We were very pleasantly received. Our visits were very satisfactory to these very valuable and agreeable people. Tears and kisses abounded at our departure. I must tell you of an interesting event:—I went to buy something for little John at a shop, where a very agreeable lady spoke to me in English, and I was so much attracted by her, that I requested her to accept a book, and sent a work on the rites and ceremonies of the Jews. I asked her to attend our Meeting on Second-day morning. She proved to be a Jewish lady of some importance; she came to Meeting with several other Jews, and truly I believe her heart was touched. I invited her to come and see us the next evening, when we expected several persons to join our party. The following day we agreed to form a District Society, to attend to the deplorable state of the poor. The Jewish lady capitally helped us, she then appeared in a feeling state; but this morning when the ladies met to finish our arrangements, and I felt it my place to give them a little advice, and my blessing in the name of the Lord, the tears poured down her face. I then felt it my absolute duty to take her into my room to give her such books as I thought right, and to tell her how earnest my desires were that she should come to the knowledge of our Saviour. I think in our whole journey no person has appeared to be so affected, or so deeply impressed; may it be lasting, and may she become a Christian indeed!

Hildesheim, *Fourth Month*, 6*th*.

We left Hanover to-day about five o'clock, after rather a singular visit. We arrived there on Fifth-day evening. On Sixth and Seventh day our way did not open quite so brightly as sometimes. We saw a deplorable prison; poor untried prisoners chained to the ground until they would confess their crimes, whether they had committed them or not, and some other sad evils. Several interesting persons came to see us. Seventh-day evening we spent at a gentleman's house, where we met some very clever and superior persons, and had much important communication upon their prisons, &c., &c. On First-day we had our little Meetings; such a tide on a Sabbath I think I hardly ever had; it was like being driven down a mighty stream; we had allowed persons to come to us, supposing it would be the last day there. I made some calls of Christian love. The principal magistrate came for an hour about the prisons, and very many other persons. In the evening we had also a party of a select nature to our Scripture-reading, and, after a very solemn time, we represented many things wanted in Hanover. I forgot to tell you, amongst other visitors, the Queen's Chamberlain came to say that the Queen wished to see our whole party on Second-day at one o'clock. We had proposed going that morning early, but put it off on this account. I think I never paid a more interesting visit to royalty—my brother Samuel, William Allen, and myself. In the first place we were received with ceremonious respect, shown through many rooms to a drawing-room, where were the Queen's Chamberlain and three ladies-in-waiting to receive us. . . . After some little time we were sent for by the Queen; the King was too ill to see us. She is a stately woman, tall, large, and rather a fine countenance. We very soon began to speak of her afflictions, and I gave a little encouragement and exhortation. She was much affected and after a little while requested us to sit down. We had very interesting and important subjects brought forward: the difficulties and temptations to which rank is subject—the importance of their influence—the objects incumbent upon them to attend to and help in, Bible Societies, Prisons, &c. We then read our address to the Queen, wishing her to patronize ladies visiting the prisons; it contained serious advice, and our desires for her, the King, and the Prince; then I gave the Queen several books, which she accepted in the kindest manner. . . .

At Berlin, the travellers found a cordial welcome from all ranks of persons, including the members of the reigning family. A wide field of usefulness appeared open before them, and in the Princess William, sister to the late King, Elizabeth Fry found a zealous co-operator in her labours on behalf of the prisons. This eminent and truly Christian lady had been as a mother to the younger children of the Royal Family, after the death of Queen Louisa, and in her exalted station, she was an example of every good word and work.

From a letter written by Elizabeth Fry's niece—

Hotel de Russie, Berlin

"Our dear aunt's first evening for philanthropic purposes took place on the 13th. There is a splendid room in the Hotel, capable of containing two hundred persons, where we have our réunions."

At one end of this large room was a platform, on which were seated Elizabeth Fry and her companions, with their valued friend, Professor Tholuck, as interpreter. E. F.'s niece adds,—

"It would be impossible to describe the intense interest and eagerness which prevailed when our aunt rose.

"The attention of the whole assembly seemed completely riveted by her address. William Allen had previously told them the object of their mission, and a little of what they had been doing since our arrival in Berlin.

"The Princess William has been very desirous to give her sanction, as far as possible, to the Ladies' Committee for visiting the prisons that my aunt has been forming; and to show her full approbation, had invited the Committee to meet her at her palace. The Princess had also asked some of her friends; so we must have been about forty. Such a party of ladies, and only our friend Count Gröben to interpret. The Princess received us most kindly. The Crown Princess arrived. The Princess Charles was also there; and the

Crown Prince himself soon afterwards entered. Our aunt sat in the middle of the sofa, the Crown Prince and Princess, and the Princess Charles on her right. The Princess William, Princess Marie, and the Princess Czartoryski on the left. Count Gröben sitting near her to interpret, the Countesses Bohlen and Dernath by her, I was sitting by the Countess Schlieffen, a delightful person, who is much interested in all our proceedings. A table was placed before our aunt with pens, ink, and paper, like other Committees, with the various rules that she and I had drawn up, and the Countess Bohlen had translated into German, and which she read to the assembly; our aunt then gave a clever, concise account of the Societies in England. When business was over, my aunt mentioned some texts, which she asked leave to read. A German Bible was handed to Count Gröben, the text in Isaiah having been pointed out, that our aunt had wished for, 'Is not this the fast that I have chosen,' &c. The Count read it, after which our aunt said, 'Will the Prince and Princesses allow a short time for prayer?' they all bowed assent, and stood, while she knelt down, and offered one of her touching, heartfelt prayers for them—that a blessing might rest on the whole place, from the King on his throne to the poor prisoner in the dungeon, and she prayed especially for the Royal Family. Then for the ladies, that the works of their hands might be prospered in what they had undertaken to perform. Many of the ladies now withdrew, and we were soon left with the Royal Family. They all invited us to see them again, before we left Berlin, and took leave of us in the kindest manner."

Amongst other most onerous concerns, Elizabeth Fry and William Allen felt it their duty to inquire into the actual state of the Lutheran Church, in the Prussian dominions, and whether it was still exposed to persecution. They found, that although its members were more leniently dealt with than they had been, great oppression still existed; confiscation of property and imprisonment being not unfrequently resorted to, to compel submission. Elizabeth Fry could not feel justified without endeavouring to bring the subject before the King. She had a strong inclination to consult the Crown Prince, when the unexpected meeting at the Princess

William's afforded her the desired opportunity. After earnestly petitioning for best Help, and wisdom from above, she opened the subject. The Prince gave her a most attentive hearing, and entirely encouraged her to act as she believed to be right. An address was beautifully drawn up by William Allen, this was translated into German, and presented through the official channel to the King. On the following day the King's Chaplain was the bearer of the delightful intelligence that the address had been graciously received, and that the King had said that "He thought the Spirit of God must have helped them to express themselves as they had done."

Elizabeth Fry writes from—

Frankfort, Fifth Month, 4th.—I felt very unwell yesterday, and low in spirits. My dearest brother and sweet niece were most kind to me; all that I required I had: so, "the Lord doth provide." I almost dreaded my night; but through tender mercy the Comforter was near to comfort and help my great infirmity, so that I rested in my Lord, and feel revived in body and soul this morning. This text has been present with me, "I am the Lord that healeth thee."—Exodus xv. 26. Such fears presented themselves. How could I get home? How could I bear the sea? should I not be much burdened, not having finished what I thought I ought to do? and so on; but now my most gracious and holy Helper delivers me from my fears. Thanks to His most blessed and holy Name.

From Düsseldorf the travellers visited the establishment of Kaiserswerth under the care of Pastor Fliedner for training Deaconesses, to tend and nurse the sick, and to aid their spiritual necessities, whilst providing for their temporal wants. At that time this admirable institution had existed only four years, but its utility was generally acknowledged, and information upon the subject earnestly desired. Pastor Fliedner, in furnishing his recollections of the visit, says:—

"The 8th of May, 1840, was a great holiday to us; Elizabeth Fry of London visited our institution. Of all my contemporaries none has exercised a like influence on my heart and life: truly her friendship was one of the 'all things,' which God, in sovereign mercy, has worked for my good. In January, 1824, I had had the privilege of witnessing the effects of Mrs. Fry's wonder-working visits among the miserable prisoners of Newgate. On my return to my father-land, my object was to found a society entitled the 'Rhenish Westphalian Prison Association,' having ramifications in all the provinces of Germany. In this I was greatly assisted by the advice and experience afforded me by this eminent servant of God. During my second stay in England, in 1834, I had the happiness, in common with Dr. Steinkopff, of spending a day with Mrs. Fry, at her own home, and also of accompanying her in one of her visits of mercy to Newgate. By this means, I was enabled to see and admire her, in her domestic, as well as public character. Thus may my happiness be estimated, when in 1840, Mrs. Fry, accompanied by her brother, her young niece, William Allen and Lucy Bradshaw, came in person to see and rejoice over the growing establishment of Kaiserswerth. She saw the whole house, going into every room, and minutely examining each detail, and then delivered to the inmates a deeply interesting discourse. Many were the tears shed, and I have a bright hope, not in vain. . . . . Truly God was in the midst of us, and the remembrance of that spirit of active, self-denying love, is one of the sweetest consolations which I possess, amid the trials and difficulties which every such institution must afford.

THOMAS FLIEDNER.

"*May* 26, 1848."

The following is Elizabeth Fry's touching and instructive record of their engagements at this time:—

Düsseldorf, Fifth Month, 10*th.*—Here we are, and thanks to my Heavenly Father I am much revived: my cough better; unfavourable symptoms subsided; sufficient strength given me for the various duties as they arise. I feel my prospect weighty; first, going to the prison to visit some prisoners whom I did not see yesterday. And then, we expect a large evening party to read the Scriptures and for worship, and this amongst strangers who know little or nothing of us, or our ways, and our interpreter not accustomed to us; but our holy Helper can, through His own unmerited mercy and Almighty power, really so help us as to touch the hearts of those who come to us, to their true edification. O gracious Lord! be with us, help us and bless us. Thy servants have come in much fear, much weakness, and under a belief that it is Thy call, that has brought them here. Now, be Thyself present with us, in this our last occasion of the kind, to our help, consolation, and edification! I can only cast myself on Thy love, mercy, and pity!

In the afternoon I visited the prison, accompanied by my dear brother, William Allen, and Lucy Bradshaw. We first collected a large number of men in a yard, and I was, in my low state of body, strengthened to speak to them in the open air. Unexpectedly, a valuable man, the Pastor Fliedner, met us, who interpreted beautifully for me. We then visited several wards, and the prisoners appeared to feel a great deal. May its effect long remain. I also visited a very valuable lady, a Roman Catholic, who has visited the prison many years. We partook of Christian love, and, I believe, of Christian unity. In the evening we had a very large party to our reading and worship; I should think nearly a hundred persons. My Lord and Master only knows what such occasions are to me, weak in body, rather low in spirits—amongst perfect strangers to us—not able to speak to them in their own language. To whom could I go? I could say, "With God all things are possible;" and so I found it. My brother Samuel read the 7th chapter of Matthew. One of the pastors read it in German. I soon spoke, and unexpectedly had to enlarge much on the present and past state of Germany: how it was that more fruit had not been produced, considering the remarkable seed sown in years past; the query, what hindered its growth? I expressed my belief—first, that it arose from a lukewarm and indifferent spirit; secondly, from infidel principles creeping in under a specious form; thirdly from too much superstition yet remaining; fourthly, and above all, from the love of the world, and the things of it, beyond the love of Christ. After showing the evil and its results—the seed obstructed, as in the parable of the Sower, bringing no fruit to perfection; I endeavoured to point to the remedy—to look at home, and not to judge one another; to ask for help, protection, and direction to walk in the narrow way: to be doers and not hearers of the word; and to devote ourselves to His service, who had done so much for us. William Allen followed with a satisfactory sermon. I then prayed very earnestly for them, and afterwards exhorted on reading the Scriptures, family worship, keeping the Sabbath, &c., and ended with a blessing—the attention was excessive; the interpretation excellent, by my dear friend, the Pastor Fliedner; hearts much melted, and great unity expressed by numbers. It was a very solemn seal, set to our labours in this land, and one not to be forgotten. So our Lord helped us, and regarded me, His poor servant, in my low estate; afterwards, peace was, in no common degree, my portion. Blessed be the name of the Lord. All my dear companions, William Allen, my brother, and the younger of the party, Lucy Bradshaw and my dear niece, appeared happy and cheerful. I returned thanks on sitting down to a refreshing meal, after the labours of the day: and I think I may say we ate our "meat with gladness and singleness of heart."

This very important journey was now nearly concluded—many religious Meetings had been held, which have not been particularly alluded to in this brief sketch—at Amsterdam, Brussels, the Hague, Zwolle, Hanover, Berlin, &c. The travellers had been much united in feeling one with another. William Allen's journal records, from place to place, the preciousness of Elizabeth Fry's gospel labours—the power and sweetness that attended them, and the reaching effect produced.

On arriving in England, she writes:—

We had a pleasant journey through Liege to Antwerp,

where we were cordially received by some of our dear friends in that place, who appeared to have been deeply impressed by our last visit. We had a solemn time after our reading in the morning, at Ostend, the last reading we had of this kind, in which I very earnestly and fervently prayed for my most tenderly-beloved brother, that the sacrifice he had thus made in his Lord's service, and all he had so liberally done for us, as His servants, might bring blessing to his own soul, and a large portion of the unsearchable riches of Christ. I prayed for his dear daughter, that the experience of this journey might be greatly blessed to her soul. I prayed for William Allen, that now, in his latter days, he might more and more be filled with, and spread the glorious truths of the Gospel, in their fulness, freeness, and universality. I prayed for Lucy Bradshaw also, and for the servants, that the journey might be blessed to them; and lastly, for my poor unworthy self, that I might be kept by the Lord, humble, faithful, trustful, and more devoted to Him and His service. It was as a spiritual farewell, and break up of this most interesting expedition. Our voyage was calm and beautiful. I return in a delicate state of health, and very weak in spirits, but deeply feeling my Lord's mercies towards me.

In reference to this parting and solemn hour, William Allen writes: "It was a most sweet and precious opportunity." "Dear E. J. F. prayed sweetly," and "gave utterance to a solemn feeling of thanksgiving."

In the course of this journey, Elizabeth Fry had experienced less difficulty than she anticipated from her entire ignorance of the German language, partly from the assistance of her companions, but even more from the efficient interpretation of like-minded persons, who arose for her help, as she passed on from place to place. She had also been furnished with a document, very useful to her, by the Chevalier Bunsen, at that time Prussian Minister at Berne. This truly excellent christian gentleman proved to her a very valuable and important helper in her arduous mission. But her dependence was not on man. She trusted in her God—she was preserved by her deep humility—she was strengthened by the spirit of constant and fervent prayer.

On their return from this Continental tour, both William Allen and Elizabeth Fry appeared considerably enfeebled in health, and the anxiety of their friends was consequently excited. They reached home two days previous to the Yearly Meeting.

Upton, 19*th*.—I attended the first sitting of the Select Yearly Meeting yesterday. My lot was to sit in silence. I saw many much loved by me. May my most gracious Lord help me by His own Spirit at this Yearly Meeting, fully, simply, and clearly to lay what I think and feel before this people; that which is right for the aged and more experienced, before them, and that which is for the youth, before them. Gracious Lord, help me to do it in faithfulness, in love, in truth, in deep humility and godly sincerity. Amen. We have had altogether a favorable reply to our letter from the King of Prussia; he justifies the measures pursued towards the Lutherans, but I believe our address will not be in vain. We have had satisfactory reports, of the Government already acting on our suggestions respecting the prisons in Prussia. The prisoners are to have more religious instruction, and more inspection. I have also had a very interesting letter from the Queen of Denmark, expressing real regret at our not going there, and not only great desire to see me there, but much unity with my views on many subjects.

She believed it her duty to unite with William Allen in having a Meeting with the youth of our religious Society, then in attendance at the Yearly Meeting.

25*th*.—Before breakfast—I am in a strait. O, my gracious Lord! be Thou my Helper, my Guide, my Counsellor, and my Defence: keep me, I pray Thee, from the most weighty service before me, unless it be really and truly Thy call, and if it be Thy call, fit me for it, by Thine own Spirit, and Thine own power; and touch my lips, as with a live coal from Thine altar; and may I be qualified to speak the word in season to those who need it. Anoint Thou the tongue to speak, and the ear to hear. Grant this prayer for Thine own sake.

Fifth-day morning, 28th.—The Yearly Meeting has cordially united in William Allen and myself having a Meeting for the young people. It is appointed for this evening, which I much regret, as my children cannot attend it, but I must commit all to my Lord.

Time did not admit of her absent children being informed of this Meeting. It proved a very solemn and favoured one—truly an answer to her humble, but fervent petitions.

Eighth Month, 6th.—There has been some fear of a war with France, which has been really sorrowful to me; I could have wept at the thoughts; so dear are the people of that country to my heart, and so awful is it to think of the horrors of war, whichever way we look at the subject, religiously, morally, or physically. The longer I live, and the greater my experience of life, the more decided are my objections to war, as wholly inconsistent with the Christian calling. O, may the Almighty grant, that through His Omnipotence, and unutterable love and mercy in Christ our Saviour, the day may not be very far distant, when the people shall learn war no more,—when peace and righteousness shall reign in the earth.

Earlham, Eighth Month, 21st.—My dearest brother Joseph is safely returned home, after his absence of three years, on his religious visit to America, and the West India Islands. I think I never saw any person in so perfectly peaceful a state: he says, unalloyed peace, like a sky without a cloud, and above all, enabled thankfully to enjoy his many blessings.

Twelfth Month, 31st.—I deeply feel coming to the close of this year, rather unusually so, it finds me in a low estate, and from circumstances, my spirit is rather overwhelmed, although I am sensible that blessings abound through unmerited mercy. I think the prison cause at home and abroad much prospering, many happy results from our foreign expedition, and much doing at home. Among other things, the establishment of a Patronage Society for prisoners, by which many poor wanderers appear to be helped and protected, and a Society for Sisters of Charity to visit and attend the sick.

Elizabeth Fry's habitual acquaintance with the chamber of sickness, and with scenes of suffering and death had taught her the necessity that exists for a class of women to attend upon such, altogether different from, and superior to, the hireling nurses that are generally to be obtained. Her communications with Pastor Fliedner, and all she learned from him personally, and by letter, of his establishment at Kaiserswerth, and above all her own visit to that remarkable institution, stimulated her desire to attempt something of the kind in England. Her own occupations being too urgent and numerous to allow of much personal attention, the plan was undertaken, and on a small scale carried into effect, by her sister, Elizabeth Gurney, with the assistance of her daughters, &c. The Queen Dowager kindly became Patroness, and with Lady Inglis as President, and an effective committee to conduct the management of the institution, it has steadily advanced and prospered.

Some misconception having arisen as to the nature of the plan, it was found desirable to change the designation of these "Protestant Sisters of Charity," and to appropriate to them the appellation of "Nursing Sisters." Their aid in sickness has been sought and greatly valued by persons of all classes, from Royalty to the most destitute.

One of Elizabeth Fry's sons was, during the spring of 1841, very seriously ill. As he recovered, her youngest daughter was becoming much indisposed.

During the Yearly Meeting, Elizabeth Fry writes:—

Upton, Fifth Month, 23rd, First-day.—The last week has been a serious one, attendance of the Yearly Meeting difficult, from Louisa's illness and other causes.

25th.—Yesterday, I accompanied Hannah Backhouse into the Men's Meeting. When she had spoken, I rose, saying, that I feared to make any addition, but that I had a few hints to offer. After expressing my earnest desire that they might all be washed and sanctified, and justified in the name of the Lord Jesus, and by the Spirit of our God, I began with my hints. I said my views of the state of the Society were not so discouraging as those of many others. I remembered, that our first Friends were gathered out of various religious denominations, and from the most spiritual of these, therefore, they were a spiritual and seeking people; but in our day, most were Friends from birth and education, and not conviction, though I believed there were really spiritual ones amongst us; but I saw much wanting, arising, partly from these causes, first, the tendency to be a formal people, resting in a high spiritual profession, like the foolish virgins, with lamps, but no oil in them; this did much harm. Then I feared, being so much a commercial people, that there were too many who bowed to the idols of gold and silver, and this hindered their serving only the living God; but above all, I apprehended that too many grieved, quenched, and resisted the Holy Spirit of God, and this was most injurious to us. I feared an unwillingness to be taught the first simple lessons of the Spirit, because humbling to the human heart, and that this hindered arriving at greater knowledge. I thought our deficiencies in faith and practice much to arise from this quenching the Holy Spirit. I believed if there was more faithfulness at all times and in all places—in the Market-place—in the Counting-house—they would be preachers of righteousness, and there would be judges raised up as at the first, and counsellors as at the beginning; that we should as a people, arise, shine, and show that the glory of the Lord had risen upon us, and that we should uphold our important testimonies in the spirit of wisdom and meekness. I also showed those who were young, how gently our Lord dealt with us, how He fitted us for His own work, how He gave us, not the spirit of fear, but of love, and of power, and of a sound mind. I also expressed my desire for all those engaged in the discipline, that their spirits might be covered with charity, that they might seek to restore the offender, remembering themselves, lest they should also be tempted, and that they might be enabled to strengthen the things that remain, that were ready to die. I concluded by expressing my desire, that all might fill their places in the militant Church on earth, and eventually join the Church triumphant in Heaven, in never-ending rest, joy and glory.

This visit to the Men's Meeting was a solemn and deeply instructive one. Both the dear friends were enabled to minister in the demonstration of the Spirit. But, although Elizabeth Fry's communication had been attended with much power and unction, she reviewed it with discouraging apprehensions; and, to a friend who had accompanied these two beloved sisters, she wrote some days afterwards: "I wish to have thy real opinion of H. C. Backhouse's and my visit to the Men's Meeting. I have sometimes feared about it lest any harm should have been done to the cause of truth and righteousness. Fears often creep in with me after weighty services, because I so abundantly know the weakness of the instrument through which the anointing flows. I feel encompassed with infirmity—a poor worm of the dust. Pray for my direction, as to my further going out, and coming in."

Sixth Month, 5th.—Our dearest Louisa decidedly mending. The query now comes closely home, Am I called again to the Continent or not? Gracious Lord, I earnestly pray Thee, for Thine own name' sake, to make my way plain before me, and through the power of Thine own Spirit, to make me perfectly willing to go, or to stay, to do or to suffer, to be something, or nothing, exactly as Thou mayst see good for myself, or on account of others. I do commit myself, my all, and Thy cause which I love, to Thy most Holy keeping and direction. Amen.

Chapter Eleventh.

1841-1843. Leaves home for the Continent—Rotterdam—The Hague—Amsterdam—Bremen—Hamburg—Copenhagen—Minden and Pyrmont—Hanover—Berlin—Silesia—Returns home—Lynn—Earlham—Winter at home—King of Prussia in England—Autumn at Cromer—Fishermen's Reading Room—Results of Christian efforts—Return by West Norfolk to Upton Lane—Death of a Granddaughter—Last visit to France—Female Prisons at Clermont, Paris, &c.—Interviews with many interesting Persons—Returns home—Meeting of "Ladies' British Society."

ALTHOUGH Elizabeth Fry had so repeatedly visited the Continent, and had so abundantly laboured in different nations, to spread the knowledge of the truth, and to encourage amongst the various classes of the people—especially those in most influential positions—a spirit of active benevolence, and efforts for the reform of many and serious evils, she did not feel that she had accomplished *all* that had been contemplated, as amongst the duties required of her. Her health had suffered much from a life of continuous exertion, and she shrunk from the fatigues that she well knew must be encountered in such a mission; and it was but too evident that her bodily powers were becoming greatly enfeebled. Yet it was not because the shades of evening were gathering around her, that she would slacken her labours for the good of others. Whilst it was yet day, she desired to work and to finish all that her great Master might have for her to do, before the night should come, in which no man can work.

(*Previous to Ratcliff Monthly Meeting,*) *Sixth Month*, she writes:—I most earnestly desire the direction of my Lord and Master, through the immediate teaching of His Holy

Spirit, that I may really know and do His will and His will only. For Thy Name' sake, O Lord! lead me and teach me. Am I once more to lay before the members of our little portion of Thy Church, my apprehended call of duty to go abroad? I earnestly pray Thee, if it be Thy call, make it very clear: if it be not, let me certainly know it, gracious Lord, that not my will, but Thine be done. Amen.

27th, First-day.—After most deeply weighing the subject, and after very earnest prayer for direction, I felt best satisfied to inform my friends of my belief that it might be right for me to accompany my dearest brother Joseph to the Continent, and to visit some of the more northern countries of Europe. I had very decided encouragement from Friends, particularly the most spiritual amongst them, which I felt helpful to me; but I was surprised at the degree of relief and peace that I felt afterwards, as from a voice before me, saying, "This is the way, walk in it."

Seventh Month, 28th, Second-day.—I had, on Seventh-day, letters from the Queen of Prussia, and the Princess William. The first expressing much satisfaction at our proposed visit; our way is clearly open in her heart, and that of the King.

My sister Gurney, and our dear friend Charlotte Upcher, went with me to the Bishop of London on Sixth-day, on the subject of the "Sisters of Charity." It has been a great pleasure to me, the Queen Dowager giving her name as Patroness.

Upton, Seventh Month, 30th.—All difficulties and obstructions, which have been serious and numerous, are removed, as far as I can see; the way is made plain and open before us, to set off to-morrow for our visit to Holland, Germany, Prussia, and Denmark. My brother Joseph, his daughter Anna, my dear niece Elizabeth Gurney, and my own maid go with me, with the prospect of every comfort this life can afford; and, I humbly trust, the Lord Himself calling us into His service that His blessing will be with those who stay, and those who go. Grant, gracious Lord, through the fulness of Thy love, that this may indeed be the case.

The travellers arrived at Rotterdam, on the 31st of Seventh Month, and passed a tranquil First-day there. In the evening, they held a large Meeting in an apartment of the Hotel; the following day visited prisons; and on the 2nd of Eighth Month proceeded to the Hague, whence Elizabeth Fry writes to her home circle:—

You will like to know that, through tender mercy, I was favoured to feel much rest, refreshment, and peace, at Rotterdam, and much evidence that I was in my right place. Our visits to the boys' prison at Rotterdam, and to the women's prison at Gouda, were highly interesting. I find a second visit to a place much better than a first. We had two Meetings—one philanthropic, one religious—both well got through, and a large attendance. I felt in leaving the place much comfort and satisfaction.

When we arrived at the Hague, our kind friend Lady Disbrowe, (the wife of the British Minister,) and Sir Alexander and Lady Malet, received us cordially. We divided our evening between Sir Edward Disbrowe's and our hotel, having a party for us by accident, in each place; on the whole both passed off very well, and many appeared to be very glad to see us again. We sent our letters to the King from Prince Albert. On Sixth-day, a message came to desire that we would wait upon the King and Queen the next day, at half-past one o'clock, accompanied by Lady Disbrowe.

We remained with the King and Queen, and their daughter the Princess Sophia, about an hour. As rather an interesting event in my life, I mean to tell you particulars of this interview. Before we went, we had a solemn, short Meeting for worship, with our dear and valued friends of this town; afterwards we prepared to go.

She had, just before leaving home, received from one of her sons, a present of a neat brown silk dress, and from another of her family a drab silk shawl. She shows her recognition of the kindness, by proceeding as follows—

I was decorated by my best garments outwardly, and I desired so to be clothed with better ornaments spiritually, as to render attractive that which I had to recommend. We all felt very weightily our serious engagement, as we had much to represent to the King respecting the West Indies, prisons, and religious education for the people in his own country. The King, a lively, clever, perfect gentleman, not a large man, in regimentals; the Queen (sister to the Emperor of Russia), a fine, stately person, in full and rather beautiful morning dress of white; the Princess much the same. After our presentation, the King began easy and pleasant conversation with me, about my visiting prisons. I told him in a short, lively manner, the history of it; he said, he heard I had so many children, how could I do it? This I explained; and mentioned how one of my daughters now helped me in the Patronage Society. He appeared much interested, as did the Queen. I then said, my brother had visited the West Indies, and would be glad to tell the King and Queen the result of his observations in those islands. This he did capitally, showing the excellency of freedom, and its most happy results; he represented, also, the sad effects of the Dutch enlisting soldiers on the Gold Coast, and how it led to evil and slavery, which so touched the King, that he said he meant to put a stop to it. I then began again, and most seriously laid before the King, the sad defect of having no religious education in their Government Schools, and the Bible not introduced. He said he really felt it; but what could he do when there was a law against it? We then endeavoured to explain how we thought it might be obtained. Our very serious conversation was mixed with much cheerfulness. I felt helped to speak very boldly, yet respectfully; so did my brother. I concluded by expressing my earnest desire that the King's reign might be marked by the prisons being so reformed, that punishment might become the means of the reformation of criminals; by the lower classes being religiously educated; and by the slaves in their colonies being liberated. The King then took me by the hand, and said he hoped God would bless me. I expressed my desire, that the blessing of the Almighty might rest on the King, Queen, their children, and their children's children. We gave them books, which they accepted kindly. It certainly was a very pleasant and satisfactory interview, that I humbly trust, will not prove in vain in the Lord.

On Sixth-day, with my brother, I visited the Princess of Orange. We had open, free, pleasant communication on many important points. The same morning, I visited the Princess Frederick, sister to the King of Prussia, just out of her confinement. I found her like the other members of that superior family. My brother, also, had very satisfactory intercourse with the Princess of Orange. The Ministers of the Interior and of Finance have been very kind, and we hope and expect that real good will result. The Princess of Orange has a lovely little boy about two months older than our Princess. The girls went to see him; they accompanied me to the Princess Frederick, who wished to see them, from her knowledge of us through the Prussian Court.

On the 7th, they reached Amsterdam, where they remained four days, visiting the prisons and various public institutions, and holding Meetings for philanthropic and religious objects. The Lunatic Asylum they found in a deplorable condition.

Among other miserable objects, one unhappy woman, unclothed, lay grovelling in straw. Whether the look of compassion, or the voice, attracted her, cannot be known; but she dragged herself, as near as her chains would admit, to her visitant, and endeavoured to reach her: the hand she desired to touch was yielded: she kissed it again and again, and burst into an agony of tears. How deeply affecting! Will any one venture to assert that this poor creature was past all touch of human feeling, or the reach of gentle control?

On the 14th, they arrived at excellent quarters, in the pleasant town of Bremen. The early part of First-day was spent in retirement, but in the evening there was a very large Meeting held in the Museum, a noble building near the hotel. Long before the appointed hour, well-dressed persons proceeded to secure places. Several of the pasteurs were present. One of them, at the close, arose and beautifully addressed *the missionary brother and sister;* expressing his desire that what had passed might be blessed to the people, and that they might be themselves blessed. To Elizabeth Fry he said, your name has long been to us "a word of beauty." A Christian gentleman wrote to them afterwards, "Now I am more than convinced that you are sent to us by the Lord, to be, and to become, a great blessing, and a salt to our city." The following morning they went to see the prison. Bremen is a Hanse Town. An address, embodying subjects of great importance, was afterwards prepared by Elizabeth Fry and her brother, and forwarded to the municipal authorities of the place.

When the carriage came to the Hotel door, for their departure, crowds of the lower classes surrounded it, wishing them a prosperous journey, "bon voyage," thanking them for the good Meeting they had had the evening before, and begging for tracts: whilst numbers could not be persuaded to move till Elizabeth Fry had shaken hands with them.

Their little transit across the Elbe would have been delightful, with a splendid setting sun, but for a mob of persons returning from Hamburg market, who having discovered Elizabeth Fry, and her tract bag, so pressed upon her that she was glad to take refuge in the carriage.

Whilst prisons and public institutions in Hamburg were visited during the mornings, the evenings were devoted by Elizabeth Fry and her companions to social intercourse, when subjects of a benevolent or religious character were discussed, or to appointed Meetings for worship. They held two of this nature, the last a very large one, in the Assembly Room, a splendid apartment, fully lighted, and well arranged with seats. Many of the authorities and principal inhabitants of Hamburg were present, the English Chargé d'Affaires, the French Chargé d'Affaires, Colonel F——, and others. They were conducted into the Meeting by the Syndic Sieveking, an eminently excellent man, who led them to a small platform. Great attention was paid to their communications, and the interpretation was excellent. At the conclusion, about fifty persons attended them to their apartment, when, after partaking of refreshments, they parted with regret and affection on all sides.

The following afternoon saw them embarked on the Baltic; they had a brilliant moonlight night, and an easy, pleasant voyage to Copenhagen, where they remained a week.

On board the packet after leaving Copenhagen, Eighth Month, 30th, Elizabeth Fry writes to her family:

We have been favoured to leave Denmark with peaceful minds, having endeavoured to fulfil our mission, as ability has been granted us; a more important one, or a more interesting one, I think I never was called into. On First-day morning, when we arrived in the harbour, we were met by Peter Browne, the Secretary to the English Legation, to inform us that the Queen had engaged for us apartments in the Hotel Royal. The appearance of the Hotel was, I should think, like the arrangements of one of our first-rate Hotels about a hundred years ago.

The next morning the Queen came to town, and we had a very pleasant and satisfactory interview with her. She certainly is a most delightful woman, as well as a truly Christian and devoted character; lovely in person, and quite the Queen in appearance. She took me in her carriage to her infant school, it really was beautiful to see her surrounded by the little children, and to hear her translating what I wished to say to them. After staying with her about two hours, we returned to our Hotel; and that evening took a drive to see the beautiful Palace of Fredericksburgh, in a most lovely situation, the beauties of land and sea combined, with fine forest trees around it. The following morning we regularly began our prison visiting; very sad scenes we witnessed in some of them. We saw hundreds of persons confined for life in melancholy places; but what occupied our most particular attention, was the state of the persecuted Christians. We found Baptist ministers, excellent men, in one of the prisons, and that many others of this sect suffered much in this country, for there is hardly any religious tolerance. It produces the most flattening religious influence, I think more marked than in Roman Catholic countries. We were much devoted to this service of visiting Prisons. Third and Fourth days, we received various persons in the evenings, but saw as yet but few Danes. On Fourth-day, we dined at Sir Henry Watkyn Wynn's, our ambassador, and here we became acquainted with several persons: they live quite in the country, and we saw the true Danish country-house and gardens. The King and Queen were kind enough to invite us all to dine at their palace in the country, on Fifth-day; this was a very serious occasion, as we had so much to lay before the King;—slavery in the West Indies—the condition of the persecuted Christians here—and the sad state of the prisons. I was in spirit so weighed down with the importance of the occasion, that I hardly could enjoy the beautiful scene. We arrived about a quarter past three o'clock; the Queen met us with the utmost kindness and condescension, and took us a walk in their lovely grounds, which are open to the public. We had much interesting conversation, between French and English, and made ourselves understood; when our walk was finished, we were shown into the drawing-room to the King, who met us very courteously; several were there in attendance. Dinner was soon announced: imagine me, the King on one side, and the Queen on the other, and only my poor

French to depend upon, but I did my best to turn the time to account. At dinner we found the fruit on the table; first we had soup of the country, secondly, melons, thirdly, yams, anchovies, cavia, bread and butter and radishes, then meat, then puddings, then fish, then chickens, then game, and so on. The fashion was to touch glasses; no drinking healths. The King and Queen touched my glass on both sides; when dinner was over, we all rose and went out together. The afternoon was very entertaining, the King and Queen took us to the drawing-room window, where we were to see a large school of orphans, protégés of the Queen. I took advantage of this opportunity, and laid the state of the prisons before the King, telling him at the same time, that I had a petition for him, which I meant to make before leaving the palace. After an amusing time with the poor children, my brother Joseph withdrew with the King into a private room, where, for about an hour, he gave him attention, whilst he thoroughly enlarged upon the state of their West India Islands. I stayed with the Queen; but after awhile went to them, and did entreat the King for the poor Baptists in prison, and for religious toleration. I did my best, in few words, to express my mind, and very strongly I did it. I gave also Luther's sentiments upon the subject. We slept at our friends the Brownes,' a beautiful place by the sea-side. An agreeable serious gentleman, Julius Schesteed, was our interpreter, and remained with us, helping us to prepare our document for the King; he has become our constant companion, and is now with us in the packet, going to Lübeck, to interpret for us there. On seventh-day, (one of our fullest days,) we drove into the country to visit the King's sister, the Landgravine of Hesse Cassel, the Prince, her husband, brother to the Duchess of Cambridge, and the lovely Princesses, her daughters. We endeavoured to turn these visits to account, by our conversation. In the evening, we held one of our very large Meetings. I trust that we were both so helped to speak the truth in love, on various and very important subjects, as to assist the causes nearest our hearts, for our poor fellow-mortals; it did not appear desirable to allude to the persecuted Christians: as we had laid their case before the King, we might have done harm by it; but I feel the way in which Protestant Europe is persecuting, to be a subject that cannot, and must not, be allowed to rest.

Where we now are, the same old Lutherans, whom we found persecuted in Prussia, are persecuting others. The way in which ceremonies are depended upon is wonderful, no person is allowed to fill any office civilly or religiously, until confirmed, not even to marry; and when once confirmed, we hear that it leads to a feeling of such security spiritually, that they think themselves at liberty to do as they like; sadly numerous are the instances of moral fall! These very weighty subjects so deeply occupying my attention, and being separated from so many beloved ones, prevent the lively enjoyment I should otherwise feel, in some of the scenes we pass through; but I see this to be well, and in the right ordering of Providence. I have the kindest attendants, and everything to make me comfortable.

On First-day morning, we had a very interesting Meeting with the poor Baptists. We then again went into the country, to lay all our statements before the King and Queen. I read the one about the prisons and the persecuted Christians; and my brother read the one about the West Indies: we had had them translated into Danish, for the King to read at the same time. After pressing these things as strongly as we felt right, we expressed our religious concern and desires for the King and Queen. I read a little to them in one of Paul's Epistles; after that I felt that I must commit them, and these important causes, to Him who can alone touch the heart. We had a very handsome luncheon, when I was again seated between the King and Queen. I may say their kindness was very great to me.

On Second-day morning, we formed a Society for attending to poor prisoners—gentlemen and ladies; and then paid a most delightful farewell religious visit, to the Queen and Princess. I forgot to mention a very interesting visit to the Queen Dowager.

We arrived at Lübeck, after a calm voyage; but I do not like nights in steam-packets. I believe that we were sent to Copenhagen for a purpose. May our unworthy labours be blessed to the liberation of many captives, spiritually and temporally.

May the God of peace be near to all of you, and to us, as our continual Keeper and Helper.

Farewell, in most tender and near love to all.

Yours indeed, and in truth,
ELIZABETH FRY.

By Lübeck they returned to Hamburg; thence Elizabeth Fry wrote to her family:—

Hamburg, *Ninth Month*, 3*rd*.

. . . .

We last night finished our labours in these Hanse Towns. We have laboured in them in various ways, particularly in this large and important town. We have boldly set our faces against religious persecution, and upheld religious toleration and Christian unity in the Church of Christ. We have also laboured about their prisons, and expect to have many evils mitigated. It is extraordinary, the good fellowship and love that we have enjoyed with numbers. In a spiritual sense, fathers, mothers, brothers and sisters given to us, and helpers most curiously and constantly raised up, from place to place.

. . . .

From Hamburg, by Minden and Pyrmont, they pursued their way to Hanover. At the latter place Elizabeth Fry writes to her youngest daughter.

Hanover, *Ninth Month*, 9*th*, 1841

I cannot express the fulness of my love and interest for my children in their different allotments, and how often I think f you and your families before the Lord, in my quiet meditations. We arrived here, after finishing our interesting and satisfactory visits to our dear Friends at Minden and Pyrmont. I felt it refreshing, being again with these dear simple-hearted people, and I do think they are useful in their allotment. How much I should like you to have seen us dining with them at Friedensthal; such a numerous family, grandmother, children, grandchildren, in a large room, and a beautiful and most hospitable German dinner. We not only were favoured with outward refreshment, but it reminded me of the disciples formerly, who went from house to house, breaking bread and giving thanks; and I desired that we might do as they did, "eat our meat with gladness and singleness of heart." I hope there was something of this spirit. The country lovely. I retired for rest on a little German bed, whilst my companions took a ride on horseback, over the beautiful hills. We had a very interesting Meeting, largely attended by the company who come here to drink the waters, and by the Pyrmontese. At Minden, the Friends are in more humble life. I could not but be struck with the peculiar contrast of my circumstances; in the morning traversing the bad pavement of a street in Minden, with a poor old Friend in a sort of knitted cap, close to her head, in the evening surrounded by the Prince and Princesses of a German court; for to our surprise, Dr. Julius's sister followed us to Minden, to inform us that in the town of Bückeburg, that we had passed through, there was a desire expressed that we should hold a Meeting, and that the reigning Princess wished us to go to the palace. After some consideration we agreed to go, and upon our arrival in the town, found a large Meeting of the gentry assembling; some time afterwards the Prince and Princesses and their family came in. They rule the state of Lippe Schonenburg, one of the small, rich German states. I endeavoured to speak the truth boldly in love, drawing results from my experience in prisons, and seeking, as ability was granted me, to bring it home to the hearts of those present. Your uncle also spoke to the same purpose. Afterwards we had a very agreeable visit to the palace, where we were most cordially received, and had tea at five o'clock; there were many to meet us. After this singular visit, we proceeded here, but did not arrive till past twelve o'clock at night, having had two Meetings at Minden, and one at Bückeburg. We were completely tired; almost too much so. To-day we are busy here, and I am delighted to find the dear late Queen really had the chains knocked off the poor prisoners at Hameln; it was a delightful sight to see their happy, grateful faces. They looked as if they knew that we had pleaded for them. I think it was one of the pleasantest visits I ever paid, and to find that the prisoners had behaved so well since, and that the kindness shown them had had so good an effect. We are now much occupied in answering an interesting letter from the King of Hanover to me, and as I have many weighty things to say to him, I fear I must leave off, being very tired, and expecting a large party this evening.

The evening proved particularly satisfactory. Elizabeth Fry and her brother, met both the gentlemen and the ladies' Committees for visiting prisons. A day of very hard travelling brought them to Magdeburgh, and a second, by railroad diverging to visit Wittenburg, to Berlin. Numerous objects awaited their attention in that city; not the less weighty to Elizabeth Fry, from having been there before and made so many acquaintances; besides the additional interest which she felt in Institutions already known to her.

The state of the prisons was, of course, her chief object of attention. She and her brother prepared recommendations to lay before General Thile, Minister of the Royal House, embodying their observations and opinions, and urging the necessity of many alterations before real improvement could be effected. The Prussian Royal Family were, at the time, in Silesia; thither the travellers had been invited to follow them, for there were those amongst them, who considered that the retirement of that district, would be well suited for the consideration of Elizabeth Fry's important objects. The prospect of going thither was weightily felt by her. She had, naturally, the fear of man deeply implanted in her character. Religion had changed its direction, but not eradicated it. It was no longer for herself that she was afraid: it was for the cause' sake to which her heart was given: for amongst these royal and noble personages she dreaded, in either herself or her companions, anything that might not adorn the doctrine of God her Saviour. She soon discovered that she had come amongst Christians, many of them devoted, like herself, to the service of their Maker. Amongst the members of the House of Brandenburg, she found many excellent persons.

No record of this time, singular and important as it was, exists of her own writing, excepting a letter to her grandchildren. But the deficiency is well supplied from the journal of one of her companions:—

"It was on the 10th of the Ninth Month that the travellers arrived at Hirschberg; a beautiful little village, inhabited by a clean and very respectable class of peasantry. It is situated about eight miles from the Royal residences of Ermansdorf, Fischbach, and Schildau; and is nearly equi-distant from Buchwald, the home of the Countess Reden, of whose Christian character and benevolence Elizabeth Fry had often before heard. The King and Queen were at that time residing at Ermansdorf. At Fischbach lived Prince and Princess William, (the uncle and aunt of the Queen,) with their sons Prince Waldemar and Prince Adelbert, and their daughter Princess Mary, now Queen of Bavaria. Prince Charles, brother of the King, was also on a visit to Fischbach. The sister of the King, and her husband, Prince and Princess Frederick of the Netherlands, with their daughter Princess Louisa, were then residing at Schildau.

"To many of the Royal family, Elizabeth Fry had been introduced in the previous year at Berlin, and the Princess Frederic of the Netherlands had been visited by her at her own beautiful home near the Hague some time before. It was a lovely spot in which Elizabeth

Fry now found her tent pitched for a while. To a mere passing traveller there was much to delight and to please; but still more of deep interest to those who could, in any degree, enter into the Royal domestic circles there assembled, and this Elizabeth Fry was privileged to do, with much enjoyment, and with an earnest desire to be permitted to be useful and faithful, in all her intercourse with them. The morning was usually passed in writing and preparing important documents on the Prison, Slavery, and other questions; and the afternoon in some visit to one of the palaces, which had been previously arranged. The First-day was replete with interest. In the early part of it, it was necessary to finish an address to the King on Religious Toleration, and on matters connected with Prisons.

"Elizabeth Fry was, at that time, suffering from great debility and fatigue; but a power, not her own, seemed granted her to rise above her infirmities, and to meet the various duties, which on that day were given her to fulfil. It is only those who held intimate communication with her at these times, who can, in any measure, understand the extreme nervousness of her constitution on the one hand, or on the other, the amount of strength granted her in every time of need. She prayed that in nothing might she seek herself, in all Christ Jesus; and that all which He laid upon her for His glory, and the good of her fellow-creatures, she might rightly and faithfully perform. The long and interesting papers which had been prepared for the King, were again perused during the drive to Princess William's Palace, which was reached about one o'clock, she having called on the way at Buchwald, for the excellent Countess, whose ever ready aid was given to support and help her, and who, in the present instance, interpreted Elizabeth Fry's words for the Princess. Many other ladies were assembled at the Palace, and after some conversation of a general nature, every one remained in silence, to listen to what she might have to say to them. This opportunity of addressing Gospel truth to such a company, she dared not pass by; every word appeared to be listened to, with the deepest attention, by all present. She spoke of the importance of upholding a religious standard in the world; of making a final and decisive choice in these important matters; of taking Christ as the only portion, and rejecting all besides. She impressed upon her hearers the duties, incumbent on persons of a higher class, of using their influence with others for good, and not for evil. She spoke of the privilege of possessing such means of usefulness. Very solemnly she urged upon all heads of large establishments, the vast amount of responsibility entrusted to them; the prevention of crime, and the good to be derived even by silent example, and by the daily reading of the Holy Scriptures to the assembled family. She added an account of the experience of many prisoners, as to the blessing of being placed in professedly religious families, and the awful temptations presented to the servants of those who take no care for their souls, and are neglecting their eternal interests. Many tears were shed on this occasion, and all seemed anxious to share her sympathy and love.

"During her stay in Silesia, Elizabeth Fry had opportunities of intercourse with the poor Tyrolese, who having fled from their native Zillerthal, on account of the religious persecution which they endured from the Austrian Government, had thrown themselves under the protection of the late King of Prussia; and, by him, had been placed under the care of the Countess Reden, who had proved herself indeed a nursing mother to them. It will be necessary to take a hasty review of the history of these Zillerthalians, in order rightly to estimate the deep interest excited in Elizabeth Fry's mind on their behalf."

These people had become, through reading the Bible and other religious books, converts from the Roman Catholic faith to Protestantism. After much patient suffering, they were commanded by the Austrian Government to quit their native land within four months. The late King of Prussia warmly sympathised with them, and gave permission for the emigration of the Zillerthalians into Prussia: he was willing to receive them all.

"The Zillerthalians hastened to complete their preparations; and fourteen days before the expiration of the four months, the first division of the wanderers commenced their journey; old age and infancy, manhood and gentle woman, alike leaving their beloved homes, and turning their faces to the asylum opened for them by the compassion of their noble protector. Very touching was the detail of their pilgrimage, most affecting and instructive their patience, their courage, their simple faith. Their new home lay in the domain of Ermansdorf, where each obtained a house and farm suitable to his means, and his former position in the Tyrol. The colony itself has received the name of their old home, Zillerthal. The Countess of Reden was appointed to attend to their necessities. She had cottages built for them in the true Swiss style, with large balconies and long roofs, and established for them schools, and, in every possible way, employed and instructed them. Ever thoughtful of their interests, the Countess invited them to come to Buchwald on that evening to receive encouragement and comfort from Elizabeth Fry; she having expressed her anxious wish to hold with them some communication in Christian love. A meeting was appointed for them on this First-day evening. The King and Queen and other members of the Royal family arrived to attend it. At length came the exiles from Zillerthal, forming a curious and picturesque group, dressed in the costume of their country. Both men and women in dark green cloth clothes, and high-pointed hats, many of the latter ornamented with garlands and nosegays of flowers. A long table was placed at one end of the room, at which the Zillerthalians sat, and in front of it was a Moravian brother, for whom the good Countess had sent forty miles, to act as interpreter. On the right hand of the table were seated the Royal family and others, and many persons stood crowding round the door. It would be scarcely possible to describe the deep interest of that whole group, or the solemn silence which prevailed when Elizabeth Fry began to speak.

"After J. J. Gurney had, in a few words, prepared the way for her, she rose with much solemnity and earnestness. Never did she address any assembly more beautifully, with more unction, or more truly from the depths of her heart, and no audience could have given more profound attention to every word she uttered. She invited them all to a close dependence upon Jesus Christ, and urged a full, firm, and constant trust in Him, as their Lord and their Saviour, their King and their God.

"With her usual clearness and power, each individual, each class present, seemed included in her address. It was the first occasion on which she had seen the King since his accession to the throne, and she knew, too, that it was the first time of his meeting many there present, as their sovereign. Her words of sympathy to him, on the death of his father, and her estimate of his present important position in Europe, which she spoke for herself, as well as for those about her, were beautifully adapted to the occasion. Joseph John Gurney added a few words; afterwards a hymn was sung, led by the Moravian Brethren; and then the Tyrolese departed. Every one flocked around her with a word of love or kindness, but none expressed more interest, or more gratitude, than the King himself."

How does the contemplation of such out-pourings of divine love, amongst the people of a strange language, composed of so great a variety of class and condition, raise in the heart the fervent glow of adoring gratitude to Him, with whom "there is no respect of persons"—in whose holy sight all merely external circumstances—all mere outward forms, with the differing shades of religious opinion, are but as the mist before the sun, and who regards, with equal acceptance, all those who fear Him and work righteousness. May He be graciously pleased to hasten the day, when His children, of every nation, kindred, tongue, and people, shall, as one household of faith, become united in Jesus; according to His sacred petition, "As Thou, Father, art in me, and I in Thee, that they also may be *one in us*."

On the following day, the travellers dined at Fischbach, where Elizabeth Fry again met the King, and then came the leave-taking, always so sad, when the probabilities of life afford little expectation of meeting again on this side the eternal world.

From this place she wrote to her Grandchildren:—

Fischbach.

Instead of my private journal, I am disposed to write to you from this very lovely and interesting place. I am not very well in health, but I may thankfully acknowledge, that although tried by it for a while, such sweet peace was granted me that I was permitted to feel it sleeping, as well as waking; so that I may say, my Lord restored my soul, and I fully expect is healing, and will heal, my body. I think a more interesting neighbourhood I never heard of, than the one we are in. These lovely mountains have beautiful palaces scattered about them. One belonging to the King, others to Prince William, Prince Frederick, and other Princes and Princesses, not royal; besides several to the nobility; but what delights my heart is, that almost all these palaces are inhabited by Christian families—some, of most remarkable brightness. Then we find a large establishment, with numerous cottages in the Swiss style, inhabited by a little colony of Tyrolese. They fled from Zillerthal, because they suffered so much on account of their religious principles, being Protestants. The late King of Prussia allowed them to take refuge in these mountains, and built them these beautiful cottages. We therefore rejoice in the belief, that in the cottages, as well as the palaces, there are many faithful servants of the Lord Jesus Christ. This evening we are to hold a Meeting for such as can attend, at the mansion of the Countess Reden, who is like a mother in Israel, to rich and poor. We dined at her castle yesterday. I think the palaces, for simple country beauty, exceed anything I ever saw; the drawing-rooms are so filled with flowers, that they are like greenhouses, beautifully built, and with the finest views of the mountains. We dined at the Princess William's with several of the Royal Family; the Queen came afterwards; she appeared much pleased at my delight on hearing that the King had stopped religious persecutions in the country, and that several other things had been improved since our last visit. It is a very great comfort to believe, that our efforts for the good of others have been blessed—may we be thankful enough for it. Yesterday, we paid a very interesting visit to the Queen, then to Prince Frederick of Holland and his Princess, sister to the King of Prussia; with her we had much serious conversation upon many important subjects, as we had also with the Queen. Dined early at the Countess Reden's. The Princess William, and her daughter the Princess Mary, joined us in the afternoon, with several others. How delighted you would be with the Countess and her sister; they show the beauty of holiness. Although looked up to by all, they appear so humble, so moderate in every thing. I think the Christian ladies on the Continent dress far more simply than those in England. The Countess appeared very liberal, but extravagant in nothing. A handsome dinner; but only one sort of wine, and all accordingly. To please us, she had apple-dumplings, which were thought quite a curiosity, and they really were very nice. The company stood still before and after dinner, instead of saying grace.

Afternoon.—We are just returned from Prince William's, where we have had a Meeting of a very interesting nature. Many ladies were assembled to meet us, that I might give them some account of my experience in prisons. Your uncle added some account of his journey in the West Indies. We expressed our desire that the blessing of God might be with them. Great love was shown us: indeed, they treat me more like a sister than a poor, humble individual, as I feel myself to be. On our return we met the King: we rather expect he will be at our Meeting at the Countess Reden's this evening.

Second-day morning.—We returned from our interesting Meeting at the Countess's about eleven o'clock in the evening. The Royal Family were assembled, and numbers of the nobility; after a while the King and Queen arrived. The poor Tyrolese flocked in numbers. I doubt such a Meeting ever having been held before, anywhere—the curious mixture of all ranks and conditions. My poor heart almost failed me. Most earnestly did I pray for best Help, and not unduly to fear man. The Royal Family sat together, or nearly so; the King and Queen, Princess William, Princess Frederick, Princess Mary, Prince William, Prince Charles, brother to the King, Prince Frederick of the Netherlands, young Prince William; besides several other Princes and Princesses, not royal. They began with a hymn in German. Your uncle Joseph spoke for a little while, explaining our views on worship. Then I enlarged upon the changes that had taken place since I was last in Prussia, mentioned the late King's kindness to these poor Tyrolese in their affliction and distress: afterwards addressed these poor people, and then those of high rank, and felt greatly helped to speak the truth to them in love. They appeared very attentive and feeling. I also, at the close of my exhortation, expressed my prayer for them. Then your uncle Joseph spoke fully on the great truths of the Gospel, and showed that the prince, as well as the peasant, would have to give an account of himself to God. In conclusion, he expressed his prayer for them. They finished with another hymn. It was a solemn time. We afterwards had interesting conversation for about an hour. When the King and Queen were gone, we were enabled to pray with the Countess, for herself and her sister, that all their labours in the Lord's service might be blessed. Now, my much-loved grandchildren, let me remind you that we must be humbled, and take up the cross of Christ, if we desire to be made use of by our Lord; "Him that honoureth me, I will honour." May you confess your Lord before men, and He will then assuredly confess and honour you. I can assure you, when surrounded by so many who are willing to hear me, I feel greatly humbled.

I wish dear Frank to read this, as my eldest grandchild, and one in whom I take so tender an interest. Indeed, my beloved grandchildren, you dwell very near my heart; may the same Holy Spirit who has helped and guided your grandmother, help and guide you!

May the Lord bless you and keep you, and raise you up for His own service; for it is a most blessed service. Dearest love to your fathers and mothers,

I am,

Your most loving grandmother,

E. F.

It was on this occasion the Princess William gave an account of the great prison at Jauer, and the King expressed a strong wish that Elizabeth Fry should see it, though considerably out of her route. This visit was afterwards accomplished. It proved one of mournful interest. In one cell was a murderer, in another a man of well-known desperate character; they were both most cruelly fettered, to prevent their escape through the window; each was fastened to an iron staple in the floor, with a heavy iron bar across the shoulder, to make any movement irksome. Their condition was afterwards represented by Elizabeth Fry to the King, who ordered their chains to be lightened, and commanded that immediate attention should be paid to their health, &c.

Many of the prisoners on this occasion were assembled in the chapel, when both J. J. Gurney and Elizabeth Fry spoke to them at considerable length. Their addresses were interpreted by the Moravian brother from Buchwald, whose attendance at the prison had been commanded by the King, for that purpose.

Extract from a letter to her youngest son—

Ermansdorf, *Ninth Month*, 20*th*.

This morning we visited the King and Queen, after our very interesting Meeting last evening which they attended, at the Countess Reden's; a Meeting never to be forgotten. We went with a long document to the King and Queen about the prisons, and various other subjects; we were received with the utmost kindness, and remained with them nearly two hours and a half. We also had a reading of the Holy Scriptures, and I prayed for them. We parted in love. . . . . . I wish I could fully describe the deep interest we have had in this journey, and how marked has been the kindness of Providence towards us, in many ways, and how blessed his service is. I certainly think the inhabitants of the mountains of Silesia the most interesting and curious assemblage of persons that I ever met with. We, from this place, see those beautiful mountains, the Reisenberg, in their splendour, the morning being very fine and bright; probably the last time I shall ever see them—though the King and Queen begged me to return; but this I never expect to do, for I find the roughs of the journey are, with all my numerous indulgences, far too much for me, and I often feel very nearly ill. I think through all, I have seldom had more reason to believe that I have been called to any service.

Elizabeth Fry's health, which had, for a considerable time appeared increasingly enfeebled, became more seriously affected; and it appeared right to proceed towards Ostend, whence they sailed to Dover on the 2nd of Tenth Month. There Elizabeth Fry was met by her husband, who was little prepared for the debilitated state in which she was brought back to him. At Ramsgate, where her eldest daughter awaited her, she remained, till she could be moved without material suffering. Her son William was at that time residing at Upton Lane, whilst his own house was undergoing some alterations. She stayed a few days with him and his family, and then, with great difficulty, she was conveyed into Norfolk, where, for many reasons, she was particularly anxious to go.

The state of her mind on returning from this Continental visit, during which she had been so much sought after by the great ones of this world, strikingly evinced, that she desired not "the honour that cometh from man," but that true honour which is the companion of humility, and which "cometh from God only."

In a letter to an intimate friend—referring to her indisposition—she wrote, shortly after her return home, as follows—

I desire for myself, and those who love me, that we may altogether leave my state of health to Him, who knows best what is best for me, and could immediately heal me, if He saw it best to do so. What a mercy I suffer so little, and have so many hours of rest, ease, and peace! It is good, now and then, to be taken from the bustle of life, and to rest a little beside the still waters: yet there are hours when, for the sake of the oppressed and the afflicted, I long to be strengthened to work. Then, again, I leave it to Him who can work as well without his unworthy instruments, as with them. I feel only an unworthy monument of the love, pity, mercy, and faithfulness of our Lord to one of His most undeserving servants.

The infirm state of Elizabeth Fry's health precluded at this period much active exertion; but her time was fully occupied, and her interest not at all diminished in those subjects to which she had so long devoted her attention. Her correspondence was extensive, both at home and abroad—the latter especially, much of it arising from her late journeys on the Continent. She had the great satisfaction of hearing of the beneficial results of her exertions in different places. From her beloved and valued friend, the Countess Reden, she received heart-cheering communications; the King of Prussia having urged upon General Thile, Minister of the Royal House, the necessity of effecting various reforms in prisons. The Countess Reden's letter enclosed an extract from a Prussian newspaper, giving an account of the striking effect of Elizabeth Fry's visit to the great prison of Jauer.

A few weeks later, an excellent letter was received from Pasteur Feldner—the chaplain of this prison—by which it was evident that Elizabeth Fry's christian ministrations had been blessed to the spiritual good of many. A hundred-and-three Bibles, and a hundred-and-twelve Prayer-books, had been purchased by the poor prisoners at the price of much self-denial, out of their small earnings; besides many copies of the Scriptures and tracts having been gratuitously distributed amongst them.

Elizabeth Fry had also a great number of letters, asking for assistance or advice, and requiring more time and thought than she had power to give. The liberality of her brothers, and some of her other relatives, enabled her to administer to the claims and distresses of many persons, in a manner which would have been otherwise impossible. She was, at this period, much with her own family, welcoming them to Upton Lane, or paying little visits at their respective houses. A small but commodious close carriage, given to her by her faithful brother Joseph John Gurney, and kept for her own particular use, afforded her the power of moving easily about, and greatly added to the comfort of her declining years.

She shortly afterwards visited Norfolk, and from Lynn she writes :—

Tenth Month, 21*st.*—I yesterday received a letter from my husband, saying that my dearest brother Joseph was married to Eliza P. Kirkbride, on Fifth-day the 21st. On the morning of their marriage, my heart was poured forth in prayers and tears on their behalf, that the blessing of the Most High might rest upon them.

About ten days afterwards, Elizabeth Fry visited Earlham. In reference to it, she wrote :—

Warley Lodge, 5*th.*—We had a most satisfactory visit, and parting from Earlham and my beloved brother Joseph. His dear wife met me as a sister, and was most kind to us all. We had a very interesting Sabbath. I accompanied them to Meeting in the morning, wishing to be with Eliza, at her first entry to Norwich as Joseph's wife. Our Meeting was very solemn, many very dear to us there. My brother spoke first, after I had knelt down and poured forth my heart in thanksgiving and prayer, for surely we had deep cause for thankfulness for his marriage, our remarkable journey, &c.; and indeed, we may say, our many great and wonderful deliverances. I also prayed for a continuance of blessing. Joseph's was one of his excellent and instructive sermons, particularly on the certain guidance of the Holy Spirit of Truth. Mine was rather a song of praise to our Lord, as "the Lamb of God who taketh away the sin of the world," the Physician of value who healeth all our diseases, our Guide through this wilderness, as a cloud by day and a pillar of fire by night, who had brought some of us through very dark places, so that through the fulness of His love, "the wilderness" had become at times as "Eden, and the desert as the garden of the Lord, joy and gladness being found therein, thanksgiving and the voice of melody." My sister Eliza followed in very solemn thanksgiving to the same purpose. In the evening we had another very interesting religious time together, in which our dear friend Robert Hankinson prayed for our brother and sister, and all of us.

Upton, Twelfth Month, 5th, (First-day morning.)—I have been favoured to be much better the last few days,—far more easy,—thanks to my Heavenly Father: though I suffer still at times. I look upon this late indisposition as a very privileged one, and have felt, and deeply feel, the mercy extended towards me, in all my wants being so wonderfully provided for.

The commencement of the year 1842, was marked by important engagements. Elizabeth Fry's health continued to manifest symptoms of decline, but the fervency of her zeal to procure relief to suffering fellow-mortals was unabated. During the preceding autumn, Sir John Pirie had been elected Lord Mayor of London. His wife had been one of Elizabeth Fry's most valuable helpers in the cause of prison reform; and now, that these estimable persons, who were remarkable for their devotedness to the spreading of true christian principle, were placed in so prominent a station, they were anxious, at every suitable opportunity, to promote an intercourse between Elizabeth Fry and such persons of influence and power, as would be likely to listen to her plans of benevolence, and to render them effective. On a public occasion, Sir John and Lady Pirie invited Prince Albert and the most prominent persons in the administration of government to dine at the Mansion House, and they earnestly solicited the company of Elizabeth Fry, in order to afford an opportunity for her bringing before those in authority some subjects of importance, on which, with her, they were mutually interested. To yield to this pressing invitation involved a serious responsibility. She fervently desired to act rightly; and she says, "I feel it a very weighty matter for my body, mind, and spirit: and do very earnestly crave direction and preservation in it, that if I go my way may be made very plain, and that my Lord may be with me there."

First Month, 17*th*.—Be pleased, oh Lord, to be very near to us this day, and help us to adorn Thy doctrine, and to speak the right thing in the right way, that the cause of truth, righteousness, and mercy, may be promoted!

18*th*, (*Third-day*.)—Through condescending mercy I may say I found this prayer answered. I had an important conversation on a female prison being built, with Sir James Graham, our present Secretary of State; upon the Patronage Society, &c. I think it was a very important beginning with him for our British Society. With Lord Aberdeen, Foreign Secretary, I spoke on some matters connected with the present state of the Continent. With Lord Stanley, our Colonial Secretary, upon the state of our penal colonies, and the condition of the women in them, hoping to open the door for further communication with him on these subjects. Nearly the whole dinner was occupied in deeply interesting conversation with Prince Albert and Sir Robert Peel. With the Prince, I spoke very seriously upon the Christian education of their children, the management of the nursery, the infinite importance of a holy and religious life; how I had seen it in all ranks of life; no real peace or prosperity without it. Then the state of Europe; the advancement of religion in the Continental Courts. Then prisons; their present state in this country—my fear that our punishments were becoming too severe—my wish that the Queen should be informed of some particulars respecting separate confinement, &c., &c. We also had much interesting conversation about my journeys, the state of Europe, habits of countries, mode of living, &c., &c. With Sir Robert Peel, I dwelt much more on the prison subject; I expressed my fears that gaolers had too much power, that punishment was rendered uncertain, and often too severe—pressed upon him the need of mercy, and begged him to see the New Prison, and to have the dark cells a little altered.

Elizabeth Fry availed herself of this opportunity to explain our religious principles in reference to worship, prayer, &c.; and the reasons for her not uniting, or rising, at the giving out of toasts, against which she bore a decided testimony.

The King of Prussia visited London during the first month of this year, and by his particular request, Elizabeth Fry met him at the Mansion House, between the times of public worship on First-day the 30th. They partook of a luncheon provided by the Lord Mayor, who, to prevent needless labour on that day, had chiefly a cold collation for his guests, and, by Elizabeth Fry's special request, allowed of no toasts. Of this important visit she writes as follows:—

30*th*, *First-day*.—I felt low and far from well when I set off this morning for London; but, through the tender mercy of my God, soon after sitting down in Meeting, I partook of much peace. I was humbled before my Lord in the remembrance of days that are past, when I used to attend that Meeting (Gracechurch-street), almost heart-broken from sorrow upon sorrow, and I remembered how the Lord sustained me, and made my way in the deep waters. He also raised me up, and then He forsook me not. I was enabled very earnestly to pray to my God for help, direction and preservation.

After this solemn and refreshing Meeting, we went to the

Mansion House. We waited some time in the drawing-room before the King arrived from "St. Paul's" Cathedral. I have seldom seen any person more faithfully kind and friendly than he is. The Duke of Cambridge was also there, and many others who accompanied the King. We had much deeply interesting conversation on various important subjects of mutual interest.

At the Mansion House, the King of Prussia arranged to meet Elizabeth Fry the following morning at Newgate, and afterwards to take luncheon at Upton Lane.

Second Month, 1st (*Third-day*).—Yesterday was a day never to be forgotten whilst memory lasts. We set off about eleven o'clock, my sister Gurney and myself, to meet the King of Prussia at Newgate. I proceeded with the Lady Mayoress to Newgate, where we were met by many gentlemen. My dear brother and sister Gurney, and Susanna Corder being with me, was a great comfort. We waited so long for the King that I feared he would not come; however, at last he arrived, and the Lady Mayoress and I, accompanied by the Sheriffs, went to meet the King at the door of the prison. He appeared much pleased to meet our little party, and after taking a little refreshment, he gave me his arm, and we proceeded into the prison and up to one of the long wards, where every thing was prepared; the poor women round the table, about sixty of them, many of our Ladies' Committee, and some others; also numbers of gentlemen following the King, Sheriffs, &c. I felt deeply, but quiet in spirit—fear of man much removed. After we were seated, the King on my right hand, the Lady Mayoress on the left, I expressed my desire that the attention of none, particularly the poor prisoners, might be diverted from attending to our reading by the company there, however interesting, but that we should remember that the King of Kings and Lord of Lords was present, in whose fear we should abide, and seek to profit by what we heard. I then read the 12th chapter of Romans. I dwelt on the mercies of God being the strong inducement to serve Him, and no longer to be conformed to this world. Then I finished the chapter, afterwards impressing our all being members of one body, poor and rich, high and low, all one in Christ, and members one of another. I then related the case of a poor prisoner, who appeared truly converted, and who became such a holy example; then I enlarged on love, and forgiving one another, showing how Christians must love their enemies, &c., &c. After a solemn pause, to my deep humiliation, and in the cross, I believed it my duty to kneel down before this most curious, interesting, and mixed company, for I felt that my God must be served the same everywhere, and amongst all people, whatever reproach it brought me into. I first prayed for the conversion of prisoners and sinners generally, that a blessing might rest on the labours of those in authority, as well as the more humble labourers for their conversion; next I prayed for the King of Prussia, his Queen, his kingdom, that it might be more and more as the city set on the hill that could not be hid, that true religion in its purity, simplicity, and power, might more and more break forth, and that every cloud that obscured it might be removed; then for us all, that we might be of the number of the redeemed, and eventually unite with them in heaven, in a never-ending song of praise. I only mention the subjects, but by no means the words. The King then again gave me his arm, and we walked down together; there were difficulties raised about his going to Upton, but he chose to persevere. I went with the Lady Mayoress and the Sheriffs, the King with his own people. We arrived first, I had to hasten to take off my cloak, and then went down to meet him at his carriage-door, with my husband, and seven of our sons and sons-in-law. I then walked with him into the drawing-room, where all was in beautiful order—neat, and adorned with flowers: I presented to the King our eight daughters and daughters-in-law, (Rachel only away,) our seven sons and eldest grandson, my brother and sister Buxton, Sir Henry and Lady Pelly, and my sister, Elizabeth Fry—my brother and sister Gurney he had known before—and afterwards presented twenty-five of our grandchildren. We had a solemn silence before our meal, which was handsome and fit for a King, yet not extravagant—everything most complete and nice. I sat by the King, who appeared to enjoy his dinner, perfectly at his ease, and very happy with us. We went into the drawing-room after another solemn silence, and a few words which I uttered in prayer for the King and Queen. We found a deputation of Friends with an address to read to him—this was done; the King appeared to feel it much. We then had to part.

The King expressed his desire that blessings might con tinue to rest on our house.

Throughout these engagements on this eventful day, the religious services, and the deportment, of this dedicated handmaid of the Lord, were truly such as adorned her high christian profession, and honoured the weighty truths that she was led to espouse.

Upton, Third Month, 15*th*.—My son and daughter Cresswell, and several of their children are staying here; their little Gurney just going into the navy. It greatly oppresses me in spirit, I so perfectly object to war on Christian principles; it is so awful in its devastating effects, naturally, morally, and spiritually.

The arrangement made for this grandson was a cause of great sorrow to Elizabeth Fry. She deeply disapproved of a warlike course, and its spirit was opposed to every feeling of her heart.

Upton, Fifth Month, 8*th*.—On Third-day, the Lady Mayoress and I paid interesting and satisfactory visits to the Queen Dowager, the Duchess of Kent, and the Duchess of

Gloucester. I went with my heart lifted up for help, and strength, and direction, that the visits might prove useful, that I might drop the word in season, and that I might myself be kept humble, watchful, and faithful to my Lord. I have fears for myself in visiting palaces, rather than prisons, and going after the rich, rather than the poor; lest my eyes should become blinded, or I should fall away, in any thing, from the simple, pure standard of truth and righteousness. We first called on the Duchess of Kent, and had interesting conversation about our dear young Queen, Prince Albert, and their little ones. We spoke of my foreign journey—the King of the Belgians, and other matters. I desired, wherever I could, to throw in a hint of a spiritual kind, and was enabled to do it. I gave the Duchess some papers, with a note to Prince Albert, requesting him to lay the suffering state of the Waldenses, from their fresh persecutions, before the Queen. We next visited the Queen Dowager, and met her sister, and the Duchess of Saxe Weimar, and her children. We had a very satisfactory time, much lively and edifying conversation upon the state of religion in Europe, particularly amongst the higher classes, and the great advancement of late years, in the conduct and conversation of the great of this world.

Through all these varied engagements, she maintained a close and jealous watch over her own spirit and conduct, as the following entry, made soon after these visits, evidences:—

"How blind are we to ourselves, so that neither nations, churches, nor individuals, see in themselves the symptoms of decay, visible to all around! the pride which leads to break the law of God, leads to this self-flattery." I have felt much warning and instruction in these words; they lead to the prayer, "O Lord, open Thou mine eyes, lest I sleep the sleep of death!" and lest the light that is in me become darkness!

Elizabeth Fry's health continuing in an infirm and suffering state, although better than during the winter, some change appeared necessary, with absence from the continual tide of London engagements. Her brother-in-law, Hoare, offered the loan of his house at Cromer, a commodious and agreeable residence on the top of the cliff, commanding fine sea views.

This offer was gladly accepted, and she was, amid various causes of sorrow, cheered by the kindness and affection of many whom she had long loved. Her sister, Catharine Gurney, was with them at the Cliff House; she saw much of the beloved residents at Northrepps Hall. Northrepps Cottage, Sherringham, and Cromer Hall, were also points of light on the landscape—two months thus passed away.

(*On the Journey*,) *Seventh Month.*—I have been poorly part of every night, or early in the morning, since I left Upton, so as to feel discouraged and flat at being so far from home; but I desire to trust entirely. I have sought to have my steppings directed by Him, who knows what is best for us. I have not felt a will in these arrangements, and I desire to leave all to Him who orders all things well. I at times feel, particularly at night, so sunk, that I am ready to apprehend my natural powers are really failing. I occasionally ask, in prayer, for passing revival from my states of suffering, which prayers are often remarkably granted; but I am not disposed really to ask for prolonged life, because I fear lest, like Hezekiah, I should live to transgress before the Lord. I have probably an undue fear of an imbecile or childish state, and becoming a burden to others; at the same time, the idea of life being continued to me is pleasant, and the fear of death and the grave, to my nature great; not that I fear for the everlasting state, although this confidence arises from no trust in any thing in myself, but faith in the mercy of God in Christ, who tasted death for every man; and a full belief that the tender mercy of my God is over all His works; and, unworthy as I am, that through His mercy, He will not cast me out of His presence, (which I delight in,) nor shut up His tender mercies from me.

Cromer, Seventh Month, 6th.—Here I am, in what was my dearest sister Hoare's little room, looking on the sea; but poorly after my journey; feeling the air almost too cold for me: but I am favoured to be quiet and trustful in spirit, and desire to leave all things to Him, who only knows what is best for me. My sister Catharine being with us, and my brother Joseph and his Eliza, and dear Anna, near to us, is very pleasant, and our dear brother and sister Buxton and Richenda being still at Northrepps.

Every week was marked by slow but steady increase in strength. But her amendment was retarded by anxiety on account of a daughter, then ill in the Isle of Wight. To this daughter, who was under much trial, she wrote:—

I am not very well to-day, but have not by any means lost the ground I had gained, though your trials appear to have brought me some steps back. If, in the ordering of Providence, things shall be brighter, I think I should rally again; but I desire to have my will given up to the will of Him who knows what is best for us all, and earnestly desire to be very thankful that our trials are not of a deeper dye; and being, as far as I know, brought on us by Infinite Wisdom, I do not feel them like those produced by the exquisite suffering of sin.

I am, thy loving, sympathizing, and yet hopeful mother

E. F.

The plan that had, in the winter of 1839, been projected for the placing of her eldest grandson in the army, to which, as before noticed, Elizabeth Fry had so strongly objected, was now again revived: it occasioned her much grief, but having used her utmost influence to prevent the arrangement, she felt she must leave the matter to those on whom the serious responsibility rested. In reference to it she writes:—

Seventh Month, 14*th* (*First-day*).—I have deeply and sorrowfully felt our grandson Frank's going into the army. I truly have tried to prevent it, but must now leave it all to my Lord, who can, if He see meet, bring good out of that which I feel to be evil.

Eighth Month, 14*th* (*First-day*). I have felt the weight of undertaking to establish a library and room for the fishermen, and something of a friendly society, as in my tender state the grasshopper becomes a burden. I was encouraged however in the night by these words, " Stedfast, immoveable, always abounding in the work of the Lord." In weakness and in strength, we must, as ability is granted, abound in the work of the Lord. May our labour not be in vain in Him! I have had very comforting accounts from Denmark—our representations attended to respecting the prisons, and likely to have much good done in them: also from Prussia. Surely our Lord has greatly blessed some of our poor efforts for the good of our fellow-mortals.

From the feebleness of the mortal tenement, and from various circumstances that severely tested her remaining bodily powers, Elizabeth Fry was often oppressed by the sinkings of nature. Yet her spirit was, at times, greatly revived by her continuing to receive these cheering tidings of the blessing that had rested on her labours of various kinds, both in her own and other lands. In Denmark, where the reader may have remarked how sad were the state and arrangements of the prisons, great and highly beneficial changes were, in consequence of her intercession, speedily effected with the express sanction of the King. New buildings had been added, by which a salutary classification was secured, employment had been provided, and apparatus supplied, by which the cells had been comfortably warmed during the winter season. In one great establishment, women had been placed over the female prisoners, and efforts were in progress to introduce the same mode of supervision in the other prisons, also fully to furnish all with Bibles, Testaments, Psalters, and other religious books. Committees of pious and devoted persons, who were willing to visit these receptacles of crime, and to labour for the reformation of their unhappy inmates, were organized with the cordial approbation of the King, who, in reference to them says, in reply to an address, "We have heard, with the greatest satisfaction, of the desire of benevolent individuals to unite together to form a Prison Committee, whose object should be the moral improvement of the prisoners, and their employment, and return to society on obtaining their freedom: therefore, we gladly give an opportunity to the members of this Committee, by means of visits and the distribution of religious and other fitting books, to exercise a good influence on the prisoners."

The Countess Reden transmitted to Elizabeth Fry a most gratifying account of the successful labours of her excellent christian friend, the Pasteur Feldner; through whose instrumentality, a most marked change had been wrought in many of the prisoners under his care. The erection of four new Penitentiaries had been commenced in Prussia; one in Berlin, another at Münster, a third in Silesia, and the fourth in Konigsberg. They were constructed on the most approved plans, under the special direction of the King.

From Dusseldorf, Elizabeth Fry received very satisfactory reports of the great improvements effected in the prison there; and of the establishment of an asylum, near that city, for young girls dismissed from the jail and evincing repentance, where, says the lady who addressed Elizabeth Fry on the subject, "under the guidance of an excellent monitor, they obtain instruction in every work required of a good servant." "This establishment," adds the lady, "is in such good repute, that as soon as they are qualified to go into service, the opportunity is never wanting for it. We hear many instances of their behaving well, and leading good lives. The best proof of the good effects of our asylum is, that in the two years of its existence, none dismissed from thence have been committed again."

The christian beneficence of the late excellent Queen of Hanover, who had so humanely listened to Elizabeth Fry's solicitations on behalf of the wretched prisoners at Hameln, as to mediate successfully with the King her husband, and to procure the release of several hundreds of poor creatures from the heavy irons and chains by which they were fettered, was also a source of encouragement and consolation to her compassionate spirit, which so tenderly sympathised with every form of human suffering. Her gracious Lord, to whose service she had, with steadfast faith, devoted herself and every faculty with which she was endowed, had thus evidently condescended greatly to prosper the work of her hands.

The indisposition that now prostrated her strength, and deprived her of the power to unite with her fellow-labourers of the Prison Committee, did not prevent her from cherishing an unabated interest in the work. The following note, addressed to the members of that association is so characteristic, that it deserves insertion.

I truly feel for you all, my beloved friends, who have now to bear the burden and heat of the day. May grace be granted you, and help from above, that you may be strengthened for your important work, and may your way be made plain before you; and may our Heavenly Father undertake for us in this weighty matter, and lead us to the right parties to send abroad, as matrons in the convict-ships, who may be a blessing to those they go amongst, and be kept and blessed themselves! I long to hear from thee, or one of you, again, and hope I may one day be enabled again to take a labouring oar. Farewell, in much true love and sympathy, to thyself and all thy fellow-labourers.

I am, very affectionately, thy friend,

ELIZABETH FRY.

This letter is dated Cromer, *Eighth Month*, 20*th*, 1842.

Two very suitable persons were subsequently recommended by the Committee, and appointed by Government, to the arduous and important office of matrons in the *Garland Grove.* Before their embarkation the following admirable letter was written by Elizabeth Fry to Catherine Fraser:—

Cromer, *Eighth Month*, 27*th*, 1842.

My Beloved Friend,

Thy note received to-day has been a real comfort to me; the post brought some sorrows, and thy note brought weight in the other scale; but I have sat at home weeping, as I did not feel much inclined to meet a delightful party of brothers, sisters, &c., at my brother Buxton's, but rather to sit alone, and look to my own vineyard, and my own very deep interests in my family and my beloved friends, and for the causes that are near my heart. I humbly thank our Heavenly Father, who has regarded our very unworthy prayers, and raised up those that we trust may be suitable in the convict-ship, and helpful in the colony; may grace and wisdom from above be poured forth upon them; may they remember that the servants of the Lord must prove their faith more by *conduct*, than word or profession; they must avoid anything like religious *cant*, if I may so express myself, and in an upright, holy, self-denying, and watchful deportment, be preachers of righteousness, and prove who it is that they believe in, serve, and obey. I am often inexpressibly bowed, and brought low in spirit, when I look at the standard and holy example of our blessed Lord, and then behold my own short-coming. I long for a closer walk with God, for myself, and all that I love; and that, through the help of the Holy Spirit, we should more constantly prove our love to Him who died for us and hath loved us with an everlasting love. Pray impress on these matrons, the extreme importance of their prudent and circumspect conduct, as it respects the gentlemen on board; and towards the women, the need of sound discretion, and the meekness of wisdom; and amongst all, to be wise as serpents, harmless as doves; and to be pitiful and courteous. I quite feel my indulgent life, and I am very ready to work when my Lord may enable me. I do not desire to save myself, unless duty calls me to do it: indeed, dear friend, I have always felt it an honour I have been unworthy of, to do any thing for my Lord, and to be made an instrument of good to my fellow-creatures. I have been thankful for thy letters, because they have encouraged me to hope that you are not discouraged, but that the Spirit of our God is poured forth upon my beloved friends, to help them in this weighty and important work, and to make them willing to labour in this service, and for the good of their poor fellow-mortals. My dear love to all our sisters in this service; and I am truly, in gospel bonds,

Thy attached Friend,

ELIZABETH FRY.

The appointment of these matrons was justly regarded by Elizabeth Fry, and her fellow-labourers as a step of the utmost importance. It mitigates most materially the evils attendant upon the transportation of females. Objections had been urged to the measure in former years, but now it was clearly admitted that none were so fit to have charge of these unhappy women, as persons of their own sex, if such could be found who, influenced by right motives, and possessing the requisite qualifications, were willing to encounter the privations and perils of a long voyage in such society.

Northrepps Hall, Ninth Month, 18th.—I exceedingly value the company of so many of my most tenderly beloved brothers and sisters, and other near and dear relations, so many nephews and nieces, and others also. How I wish that I upheld amongst these tenderly-beloved ones a more holy example. I do not often apprehend it my place to speak much of spiritual things; but I most truly desire constantly to uphold the christian standard, in an humble and watchful walk before the Lord, and before my fellow-mortals.

25th, (First-day.)—I have not enough dwelt upon the extraordinary kindness of our dear brother and sister Buxton and their children to us, at this time, truly humbling to me, a poor unworthy worm of the dust; also my dear brother Hoare, and all that family—such a sweet renewal of love amongst us. How blessed and how sweet is love, and how delightful to believe that it has, in measure, the Heavenly stamp upon it. Our dearest sister Catharine left Cromer yesterday,—quite a loss to us; her kindness has been great indeed.

Cromer, Tenth Month, 23rd.—Perhaps the last journal I may ever write in this place, as to-morrow we mean to depart for Lynn. Yesterday, I was very much affected and touched by something that occurred—it was almost overwhelming. We paid our farewell visit to Northrepps. My brother Hoare and his family went also; and at our beloved Fowell and Hannah's, were Andrew and Priscilla Johnston, Edward, and Catharine, and Richenda Buxton. After dinner, Gurney Hoare brought me a beautiful piece of plate, a silver ink-stand, and my husband a Testament, of fine paper and print, most beautifully bound. They gave these presents in the kindest way, expressing love and gratitude to us, and saying that dearest Anna Gurney and those absent of their families united in the present. I felt before receiving it, that I had been unduly loaded with gifts and kindness. My spirit was humbled, and really bowed within me, under a deep feeling of unworthiness at these proofs of love. My Lord only knows my sense of it; a poor, weak, unprofitable servant as I am, that He should thus put it into the hearts of His servants to show so much love and pity to me, in my poor, low, weak, and unworthy estate before Him. Gracious Lord! Thou knowest how little I can do for all these beloved ones. I pray Thee reward them with spiritual and temporal blessings; and if it be Thy will, let the sickly in body be more strengthened and restored, the sickly in soul healed; that all may be more filled and satisfied with the unsearchable riches of Christ.

On her way home, she stayed at Lynn for a few days, her last visit. In describing her state and habits whilst there, her daughter writes:—

"She was bright and lovely in spirit. She had a wise, kind word for all—children, servants, dependents. All loved her, all felt that her message was not from herself, nor of man's invention: but that in her Master's name she invited others to 'love and to good works.' She condescended to all; listening to the minutest details of their cares and pleasures, was ready in devising means for helping others, not merely in the great, but the little things of life; prompt in expedients, in the sick room, in the nursery with an unmanageable child, or a froward servant."

Elizabeth Fry reached home near the end of Tenth Month. A heavy family affliction awaited her return to Upton, in the illness and death of a lovely little grand-daughter, aged seven years. She was much with her children during their sorrowful nursing, sharing deeply in their grief. Her bereaved daughter keenly suffered under this chastening dispensation, but was favoured, in a striking manner, meekly to bow under it. Elizabeth Fry accompanied her afflicted child, when committing to their long home the precious mortal remains; and, when the mourners were about to quit the grave-side, her gentle voice was heard, uttering the words, "It is the Lord, let Him do as seemeth Him good." One of her family gives the following interesting details:—

"A family party gathered in the evening: after the fifth chapter of the 2nd of Corinthians had been read, Elizabeth Fry addressed a heart-searching exhortation to her 'children, grandchildren, and all the dearly beloved ones present,' to be ready 'when the next summons should come'—also 'thanksgiving that the lamb taken was a believing child, one rather peculiarly impressed with the fact of redemption, and forgiveness of sins through Christ; and in practice, an obedient, gentle-spirited creature; and according to the measure of so young a child, unusually full of good works and alms-deeds; for she gave much to the poor, whose tales of woe, (whether true or false, she did not stop to inquire,) always touched her; and her *good mark* money, which she saved till it amounted to a pound, she had given to the Ceylon Mission. Thus, even in so young a child, did the good tree bring forth little blossoms of good fruit, gone to mature and fructify in Heaven, through Christ who died for her, and in whom she truly believed.' Many other things were spoken by her in ministry on this occasion. Then she offered for all the three generations present, a soul-touching prayer."

Upton Lane, First Month, 1st, 1843.—Another year is closed, and passed never to return. It appears to me that mine is rather a rapid descent into the valley of old age.

Second Month, 6th.—I am just now much devoted to my children and all my family, and attend very little to public service of any kind. May my God grant, that I may not hide my talents as in a napkin; and on the other hand, that I may not step into services uncalled for at my hands. May my feeble labours at home be blessed. Gracious Lord, heal, help, and strengthen Thy poor servant, for Thine own service, public or private.

Third Month, 19th.—Met Lord Ashley to dinner at my son William's. . . . . . He is a very interesting man; devoted to promoting the good of mankind, and suppressing evil—quite a Wilberforce, I think.

Fourth Month, 2nd, (First-day.) I entered the last week very low in my condition, bodily and mentally, so much so, that some of my family could hardly be reconciled to my attending the Quarterly Meeting. In the select Meeting of Ministers and Elders, the subject of Unity was much brought forward; several spoke to it, and I had to express rather strongly, my belief that there is a great work going forward in the earth, and Satan desires to mar it, by separating the Lord's servants. I warned Friends upon this point, because there are diversities of gifts, differences of operation and administration; they should not sit in judgment one on another, or condemn one another, or suppose they are not of the same spirit, and one in the same Lord and the same God.

With somewhat of restored health, Elizabeth Fry believed it her duty once more to visit the Continent. Her attraction was peculiarly to Paris. Matters of importance that she earnestly desired to have completed, awaited her attention, and there appeared an opening beyond anything she had known before, for usefulness in that great capital. There were Christian and benevolent persons whom she desired to see again "in the flesh," and build them up, if enabled, in faith and hope. She had, with the unity of her friends, retained her certificates, granted her for her last journey. Her brother, Joseph John Gurney, also believed it his duty to visit Paris, as part of a more extended journey. His beloved wife accompanied him, and their valued friend, Josiah Forster, united in the engagement. In addition to these three participators and supporters in the various religious and philanthropic objects which might open before them, her eldest daughter went as her mother's especial attendant, to watch over and care for her health.

They landed at Boulogne. The voyage had been so trying to Elizabeth Fry, from a heavy rolling sea, and the weather being cold and unfavourable, that her fellow-travellers doubted the practicability of her pursuing her journey. By setting off late, and resting an hour or two in the middle of the day, she seemed revived, when at the end of two days they arrived at Amiens. Here the First-day was passed. In the evening they held a Meeting for worship, in the room used by the Protestants as their chapel, where a venerable pastor, eighty years of age, usually laboured among a small flock in the midst of a large Roman Catholic population. Many of these Protestants were present; their hearts appeared touched and animated by the ministry on this occasion, which tended to console the discouraged, and strengthen the feeble-minded.

At Clermont-en-Oise, the female part of the company visited the great central prison, containing more than nine hundred women. It is under the care of a Supérieure and twenty-two nuns. No men are ever allowed to enter.

On first arriving, Elizabeth Fry had expressed a great wish to see all the nuns, but the Supérieure considered it impossible, as they never leave the women; however, just before quitting the prison, she was conducted into an apartment, around which sat, some on chairs, some on extremely low seats, some apparently on the floor, the twenty-two nuns in their grey dresses, and the lay sisters in black; placed in the middle were Elizabeth Fry and her sister, E. P. Gurney, the Supérieure between them, holding E. Fry by the hand, whose daughter was requested by the Supérieure to interpret for them. It was no light or easy task to convey exactly her mother's address, on the deep importance of not only maintaining good discipline among the prisoners, but endeavouring to lead them, in living faith, to Christ, as the only Mediator between God and man, through whom alone they could be cleansed from the guilt and power of sin. At His name every head bowed. She then went on to tell of Newgate, and the effects of the Gospel there; many tears were shed at this recital. She concluded by a lively exhortation to these devoted nuns, whom she could "salute as sisters in Christ," to go forward in their work, but in no way to rest upon it, as in itself meritorious. Here the Supérieure interposed, "Oh non, mais il y a un peu de mérite, l'homme a quelque mérite pour ce qu'il fait:" an old nun, who understood English, rejoined, "Ma mère, Madame thinks that if the love of God does not sufficiently animate the heart to do it without feeling it a merit, or desiring reward, it falls short." "Ah, c'est bien! comme elle est bonne!" replied the Supérieure. Elizabeth Fry concluded by a few words of prayer in French. It was a striking scene, and a solemn feeling pervaded the whole.

Paris, (Hotel Meurice,) Fourth Month, 22nd.—We are favoured to be very comfortably settled here, and I may most thankfully say, feel in our right place, after a time of unusual conflict to my own mind.

I was little fit to enter Paris; the day was hot, and the rooms at the hotel oppressive; the noise of the street so great, that I feared, in my poor state, I could not support it, and was frightened about myself, and felt as if it were altogether too much for me, but I revived towards evening, was favoured with a peaceful night, and awoke much refreshed and comforted. Our beloved friend, the Countess Pelet has been a real helper to me, quite a spiritual comforter; so encouraging as to *the time of our visit*. She expresses her belief of our being surely guided by a spirit within, safely leading us to places at the right time. Others, really dear to me, show much faithful love, and they appear delighted to have us with them. On Fifth-day, we attended the little Meeting of Friends in the Faubourg du Roule. The next day, some of our serious friends came to us in the evening. And the following, we spent a very agreeable evening at the Mallets', where there was, to my feelings, a sweet sense of love and peace over us, with the numerous members of that interest ing family.

I may thankfully say, I now feel greatly healed, and helped, and encouraged, although it appears but little I have done for my Lord in any way; but I must wait His time and His putting forth, and not enter anything in my own way and time.

Lord! be pleased to grant, through Thy tender mercy in Christ my Saviour, that our visit to this place may be really profitable to ourselves, and to those we are come amongst, and that it may promote love and charity amongst Christians generally; help to remove dependence on the arm of man, and to have it placed on Thy arm of power, and stimulate many more diligently to seek Thy kingdom and Thy righteousness—that some worldly-minded wanderers may be led to return, repent, and live—that some that are dead may be made alive again—and that those that are lost may be found in Thy fold of peace and safety. Grant also, gracious Lord! that the great blessing of preservation may be with my tenderly beloved family at home.

On the 25th, Elizabeth Fry visited, by appointment, the Duchess of Orleans, at the Tuileries; but finding some difficulty in fully conveying her meaning, her daughter was sent for to interpret, who, in a letter to her sister, describes herself "ushered into an immense drawing-room," the size, and heavy crimson and gold magnificence of which, exceeded any room she had ever seen.

"On a sofa, about half-way up the room against the wall, was seated Elizabeth Fry; by her side a young lady, in deep mourning, over whose white and black cap, hung a large, long, crape scarf, or veil, that reached the ground on each side, her figure tall and elegant, her face and features small and delicate, her eyes blue, and her complexion very fair,—a lovely blush came and went as she spoke. Opposite to her, on a chair, was an elderly lady, the Grand Duchess of Mecklenburgh, her step-mother, who had brought her up from childhood. These three were the only occupants of that vast apartment. The conversation at first was upon the Duchess of Orleans' affliction. They had each a Bible in their hands. Elizabeth Fry read a few verses, and commented on them, on affliction and its peaceable fruits. They then spoke of the children of the House of Orleans, and the importance of their education, and early foundation in real Christian faith; the Grand Duchess of Mecklenburgh, an eminently devoted, pious woman, deeply responded to these sentiments. It was an hour-and-a-half before this interesting conversation came to a close."

The following First-day, after attending their own little Meeting, a large public one was held in the Methodist chapel; it was a very solemn one. J. J. Gurney spoke well in French, Elizabeth Fry through an excellent interpreter.

In the evening of the next day, they gathered round them a very singular party, about thirty persons of colour, chiefly from Hayti, the Isle of France, and Guadaloupe, principally students of law or medicine; one a painter, who had some good pictures in the exhibition.

The evening concluded with reading in the Bible. Elizabeth Fry addressed her auditory on the words of Peter, "I perceive that God is no respecter of persons;"—Acts x. 34—going on to that glorious passage in the Revelation, which tells of the company that cannot be numbered, gathered out of every nation, kindred, tongue, and people.

Speaking of the close of the day, she says: "I laid me down and slept in peace."

Fourth-day, a dinner at Count Pelet de la Lozère's; Fifth-day, at M. Guizot's: seated by their celebrated host, this dinner was felt by Elizabeth Fry to be an occasion of great responsibility. She was encouraged by his courteous attention, unreservedly to speak to him on the subjects which had so long been near to her heart. It was no common ordeal for woman, weak, even in her strength, to encounter reasoning powers and capabilities such as his. They spoke of crime in its origin, its consequences, and the measures to be adopted for its prevention; of the treatment of criminals; of education, and Scriptural instruction. Here Elizabeth Fry unhesitatingly urged the diffusion of Scriptural truth, and the universal circulation of the Scriptures, as the most potent means, within human reach, of controlling the power of sin, and shedding light upon the darkness of superstition and infidelity.

Elizabeth Fry again visited the Duchess of Orleans. She had also several interviews with the Grand Duchess of Mecklenburgh, their communications with each other being of a deeply religious character.

It was the period of the annual religious Meetings: many pasteurs were assembled in Paris; J. J. Gurney invited a considerable number to the Hôtel Meurice.

Paris, Fifth Month, 14th.—On Second-day, about thirty pasteurs came to breakfast: they are from different parts of France: a very interesting set of men. First we had a Scripture-reading; Joseph and myself had much to express to them at the time; a most weighty concern it was. My brother prayed, and one of the pasteurs spoke. We then breakfasted, and had really a delightful meal. I remembered that our Lord condescended to attend feasts, and this was a feast offered to His servants, of which we partook in love and peace. The pasteurs afterwards gave us an account of the religious state of the people around them; a good work certainly appears going on, amidst many obstructions. We then spoke to them. I particularly recommended religious unity with all who love the Lord, and kindness to the Methodists, as a valuable body of Christians.

Paris, Fifth Month, 21*st,* (*First-day.*)—My birth-day sixty-three! My God hath not forgotten to be gracious, nor hath He shut up His tender mercies from me.

The last week has been an interesting one. We were first sent for by the King. My brother, sister, and I, paid rather a remarkable visit to him, the Queen, and the Princess Adelaide. To my surprise and pleasure yesterday, there arrived from the Queen, a most beautiful Bible with fine engravings, without note or comment; given me as a mark of her satisfaction in our visit.

One evening, the Prime Minister Guizot dined with them. The topics before discussed were then resumed:—the state of Protestants in France, la liberté des cultes, and Negro Slavery. Elizabeth Fry entreated Guizot's attention to the state of the Sandwich Islands. She had, a few months before, received from Kamehameha III., the King of those islands, a letter, entreating her good offices to second his endeavours to prohibit the importation and use of spirituous liquors in his kingdom, the baneful and demoralizing effects of which, he stated to be lamentable.

Much had been done for the improvement of prisons since Elizabeth Fry's last visit to Paris. The importance of the subject had been fully recognized, and a bill brought before the Chamber of Deputies.

Boulogne, 28*th*.—Through the condescending mercy of our Heavenly Father we are safely and peacefully arrived here, after a quiet journey with my dearest Katharine. We were near meeting with a very serious accident, but through mercy, we escaped without injury. Our leaving Paris was no common occasion. The morning before, several of our beloved friends were with us; they literally loaded us with presents, indeed, it appeared as if they did not know how to show their love to us enough. Before we parted from each other, we had a most solemn time in prayer; little knowing whether we should see each other's faces more. I hardly knew how to accept all their generous kindness. What can we say, but that their hearts being thus turned to us must be "the Lord's doing, and is marvellous in our eyes?"

The previous evening many of our dear Friends, English and French, came to take leave of us; we read together the 121st Psalm. In the morning I visited a Roman Catholic Refuge, and finished well with the Greeks in the afternoon.

On Third-day, we visited the great military prison at St. Germain, accompanied by a French general, an English colonel, our excellent friend Count Pelt, and Moreau-Christophe. We were received very kindly by the Colonel, Governor of the Prison, and his wife, and took our *déjeûner* with them.

In the evening we went to a large Meeting in one of the Faubourgs, with the French Methodists in humble life. How curious the changes of my daily life!—what a picture they would make!—in the morning, surrounded by the high military, and the soldier prisoners—in the evening, in a Methodist Meeting-house, with the people and their pasteurs, and afterwards by poor little French children, hearing them read.

Another day I was at a large Prison Committee of Protestant ladies. I think they have been greatly prospered in their work of Christian love, in which they have persevered ever since my first visit to Paris: there have been many instances of great improvement in the prisoners under their care After prayer for them I left them.

On the afternoon of the First-day, she visited the "St." Lazare Prison; "such a scene of disorder and deep evil," she says, "I have seldom witnessed—gambling, romping, screaming. With much difficulty we collected four Protestant prisoners, and read with them." She afterwards "spoke to those poor disorderly women, who appeared attentive, and showed some feeling." She "represented to many in authority, the sad evils of this prison, and pleaded with them for reform, for religious care, and for Scriptural instruction." And she adds—

In the evening the dear Countess Pelet was with us, and we had a large assembly, mostly of English; it was thought ninety or a hundred. I was tried and poorly, my flesh and my heart ready to fail, but the Lord strengthened me, and I felt really helped by a power quite above myself. With this company I had a most satisfactory parting time, and a sweet feeling of love and unity with these servants of the Lord.

A quiet resting day was spent at Passy with her old and valued friends of the Delessert family, with whom she had some solemn religious communications on this, the last day she passed amongst them.

On returning home, she was able to attend one or two sittings of the Yearly Meeting in London, and for a short time, to encounter the current of life better than she had done before her journey.

Sixth Month, 25th.—A week of considerable occupation. Second-day, the British Society Committee; an interesting meeting with those beloved ladies; so much oneness in heart and purpose, a delightful evidence of the sweetness of Christian unity, and how those who differ in secondary points may agree in the most essential one, and be one in

Christ. We have cause for thankfulness in the excellent arrangements made by Lord Stanley for our poor prisoners in Van Diemen's Land; he appears so carefully to have attended to the representations we made respecting the evils existing there, and to have proposed good measures to remedy them.

Chapter Twelfth.

1843-1845. Attends the Quarterly Meeting at Hertford—Illness—Sandgate—Tonbridge Wells—Winter of great suffering—Removed to Bath—Returns home—Death of her sister-in-law, Elizabeth Fry—Death of a grandson—Stay at Walmer—Death of a Grand-daughter—Death of her son William—Of another Grand-daughter—Deep Affliction—Return from Walmer—Death of a Niece—Visit to her brother Joseph John Gurney—Parting with some of her children for Madeira—Death of Sir T. Fowell Buxton—Visit to Norfolk—Earlham—Northrepps—Yearly Meeting—"Ladies' British Society" Meeting—Marriage of her youngest Son—Removal to Ramsgate—Successive parties of her family—Sudden increase of illness—Death—Funeral—Concluding Remarks.

On the 21st of Sixth Month, Elizabeth Fry attended the Quarterly Meeting at Hertford, much to the comfort of Friends there. She was accompanied by her brother Samuel Gurney. This was the last time that she left home expressly on religious service. During the Seventh Month, she wrote :—

Last First-day was not one to be forgotten ; much of the morning without clouds. My dear brother and sister Buxton were at meeting. I felt it my duty to encourage the weary, and enlarged upon our foolishness, yet how the Lord is made unto His people wisdom, righteousness, sanctification, and redemption. There were some who appeared much impressed. Through the whole of that day and into the next, renewed peace rested on my spirit.

As the month passed on, Elizabeth Fry showed increasing symptoms of illness; the consequence, doubtless, of bodily fatigue and mental exertion; the effects of which were severely aggravated by a chill, from sitting one evening in the garden at Upton Lane.

In this state of indisposition she went to Sandgate, being additionally induced to go thither for the sake of her sister-in-law, Elizabeth Fry, whose declining health appeared to require the invigorating influence of the sea air. The following extract was penned soon after her settlement there:—

Sandgate, Seventh Month, 29th.—I have been permitted to pass through rather an unusual time of late, I think ——— (alluding to a painful circumstance), hurt me, bodily and mentally, and discouraged me. Our house was rather too full for me, and I got too anxious (my easily besetting sin,) about some nearest to me. . . . . . I find myself here in a lovely place by the sea, the air delightful, and the house pleasant. Thus the Lord provides for me in this my tried estate. If it please my Holy Helper, may He soon see meet to heal me.

First-day Afternoon.—No one of the family at home but myself; how very unusual a circumstance. I have at times, passed through a good deal of conflict and humiliation in this indisposition, and it is a real exercise of faith to me, the way in which I am tried by my illness. I suppose it arises from my extremely susceptible nerves, that are so affected when the body is out of order, as to cast quite a veil over the mind. I am apt to query whether I am not deceiving myself, in supposing I am the servant of the Lord, so ill to endure suffering, and to be so anxious to get rid of it; but it has been my earnest prayer that I might truly say, "Not as I will, but as Thou wilt." Lord! help me. I pray that I may be enabled to cast all my burthen, and all my care upon Thee, that I may rest in the full assurance of faith in Thy love, pity, mercy, and grace. I pray Thee help me, that my soul may be less disquieted within me, and that I may more trustfully and hopefully go on heavenward. Increase my faith in Thy faithfulness, gracious Lord! whilst I believe that those, who are *once* in grace, are not *always* in grace: yet help me ever to feel that faithful art Thou, O Lord! who hast called us out of darkness into Thy marvellous light; and Thou only canst do it; therefore be pleased to hearken to the prayer of Thy poor servant, increase her faith, and be Thyself, for Thine own name' sake, not only the author, but the finisher of it. Amen.

At Sandgate, she received the account of the death of a lovely niece: nine weeks before, a beautiful and blooming bride. In the state in which she then was, these tidings were deeply affecting to her, and very sorrowfully she writes respecting the event.

"In how many ways the Lord teaches us; surely the present is no common lesson."

To the bereaved family she wrote—"We live with you in spirit; and with all most dear to the beloved departed. It is sweet to remember that help is laid on One that is mighty, who, blessed be His holy name, is ever near to His dependent servants."

After several distressing weeks, Elizabeth Fry was moved to Tonbridge Wells, closely and faithfully nursed by her two youngest daughters.

Tonbridge Wells, Ninth Month, 10*th.*—We are favoured to be settled here in a comfortable house, where many accom modations abound; which, in my delicate state, I find a real help. I have been favoured to partake of sweet resting sleep; thanks to my Heavenly Father for His great mercy.

About two weeks later, she writes—My case has been rather increasingly distressing, from an almost total loss of appetite, and at times great lowness. Many fears creep in for my natural health, more particularly, as it respects the nervous system. Hitherto my Lord has said to the waves that would overwhelm me, "so far shalt thou go, and no further." And, merciful Lord, if it be Thy holy will, continue to keep them from overwhelming Thy poor unworthy servant, in this time of weakness and of frequent distress. Let not the waterfloods prevail. When my spirit is overwhelmed within me, enable me to look to the Rock that is higher than I, as a "refuge from the storm, a shadow from the heat, when the blast of the terrible one is as a storm against the wall." Her stay at Tonbridge Wells did not appear to be attended with any permanent benefit.

24th.—I desire, in this my sorrow and suffering, to cast myself and my whole care on the Lord. I know that I am poor, miserable, blind, and naked; and I look to my Lord for everything. The kindness of all around me is great, indeed wonderful to me, and their pleasure in being with me comforting, for I feel as if I must be burdensome to them. Most gracious Lord, if it be Thy will, let not this be the case, but bless this trying, humbling illness to them, as well as to myself; and may it please Thee to grant me grace, minute by minute, to hold fast my confidence, stedfast unto the end, that continuing faithful unto death, I may, through Thy merits, receive a crown of life!

She returned to Upton near the end of the Ninth Month, and very reluctantly relinquished the hope of spending part of the autumn in Norfolk. Her illness had its fluctuations, but she did not come down stairs after the 5th of Tenth Month. She, however, often told those around her, in her great bodily suffering—that the everlasting arms were always underneath her—that the under-current was peace and comfort, though the surface was so much tempest-tossed.

Upton, Tenth Month, 10th.—My God hath not forgotten to be gracious, or shut up His tender mercies from me; it appears to me that all of nature is to be brought low, for all that is of the Lord only, can stand the day of humiliation.

I may thankfully say, I am quiet and sustained in spirit, but do not often know peace to flow as a river, as at some former times; still help is constantly near from the sanctuary, though I abide under a sense of deep unworthiness before the Lord; but what can I do but wait in faith, until He be pleased fully to clothe me with the garments of His righteousness and His salvation? I feel I can do nothing for myself.

One afternoon, when some members of her family were reading with her, she was unable to attend to a very interesting religious biography, saying "it is too touching to me—too affecting." She added, after a pause, "How I feel for the poor when very ill; in a state like my own, for instance; when 'good' ladies go to see them.—Religious truths so strongly brought forward, often injudiciously." She went on speaking on this subject, and then dwelt on "the exquisite tenderness of the Saviour's ministrations;" "His tone and manner to sinnners!"

Soon afterwards she resumed, in the most impressive manner; saying, that "religious truth" was opened to her, and supplied to her "inwardly, not by man's ministration, but administered according to" her "need;" adding, "if I may so say, it is my life."

She frequently spoke of not being called to active service now, and that she had no desire as to recovery; on the contrary, she was "able quite to leave it." Frequently she repeated to those about her, "*I feel the foundation underneath me sure.*"

One evening she opened her heart on her deep and earnest desires for the good of her children. Of her "great sufferings"—"greater than any one knows"—that if they were to last, no one could wish for her life; but soon added "there is one thing I would willingly live for—the good of my husband and children, and my fellow-creaturers."

On the night of the 25th of Tenth Month, her spirit was remarkably strengthened to declare her faith and hope in God. She quoted many passages of Scripture, to prove that faith must work by love, and that faith, if true, must produce works. She said, "with the text, 'He that keepeth my sayings shall never see death,' take this one also, 'He that believeth on me shall never die.'" She afterwards expressed, in a tone of the deepest feeling, her "perfect confidence," her "full assurance, that neither life, nor death, nor angels, nor principalities, nor powers, nor things present, nor things to come, nor height, nor depth, nor any other creature, should be able to separate" her "from the love of God which is in Christ Jesus our Lord;" adding, "my whole trust is in Him, my entire confidence."—"I *know* in whom I have believed, and can commit all to Him, who has loved me and given Himself for me; whether for life or death, sickness or health, time or eternity."

In the course of the same day, she said very emphatically, to one of her daughters, "I can say one thing—since my heart was touched at seventeen years old, I believe I never have awakened from sleep, in sickness or in health, by day or by night, without my first waking thought being how best I might serve my Lord."

Elizabeth Fry had greatly wished to attend the marriage of her niece Anna, the only daughter of her beloved brother Joseph John Gurney; but as the time approached, all hope of accomplishing this passed away. With the promise of a family Bible, (her favourite wedding present,) she sent this note (dictated):

My dearest Anna,

I was very glad to receive thy note. I hope the Bible will be ready in a few days; the one I had ready for thee, I sent to Lady ——, hoping that it would induce Lord —— and her to have family reading. It is a great and unexpected disappointment to me, to see no probability of being able to attend thy wedding, but "it is not in him that walketh, to direct his steps;" the humiliation of my suffering may be better for me than going to the house of rejoicing, and if so permitted, we cannot doubt it. At all events, I think thou art sure that few more earnestly desire thy peace and prosperity than I do, in spirituals and in temporals—that thyself, and thy companion in life, may be enabled to serve the living God faithfully, through the power of His Holy Spirit; and that, through the faithfulness of the Saviour's love, His richest grace and peace may be with you, in heights and in depths, in sickness and in health, in riches and in poverty, in life and in death. My very dear love to my sister Catherine, thy father and mother, and the rest of your circle, also to thy dear intended husband. Thy much attached and well-wishing aunt,

ELIZABETH FRY.

On First-day the 6th of Eleventh Month, her son William and her youngest daughter being with her, a chapter in Job was read to her, also the 3d of John; after which she prayed, in a very striking manner, that when all the sorrows and fluctuations of time were ended, "We might behold His face in glory: that whilst here we might not deceive ourselves, but be true and decided followers of Him, who in His own good time would arise with healing on His wings, to deliver us from all our pain."

The following day, a very beautiful note being read to her, from one who preceded her to the heavenly mansions, a few days after writing it—in which, with reference to her, the three first verses of the 41st Psalm were quoted; she lay quiet for a short time, and then calling one of her daughters to her bedside, said, "May they not be deceived!" "One thing is certain, I have desired and sought to serve the Lord."

13*th*.—Her nephew, Edward Hoare, came to see her. He sat down by her sofa and said to her, "My dear aunt, what a consolation to know you to be of the church of God, which

He hath purchased with His own blood." After a little pause, she said with great humility, "But we must avoid false confidence." He replied, that there could be no false confidence, when our hope is fixed on Christ alone. She said with emphasis, "*There*, indeed, is no false confidence;" and added, that in this illness she had entirely felt without carefulness; so able to commit every person and every thing, and leave them in His hands; that she felt no service now called for from her, only to endure, "as seeing Him who is invisible."

She evinced a grateful feeling for every token of love and care: she spoke with earnestness of the affectionate attentions of her husband, and how kindly and patiently he assisted in nursing her throughout this protracted season of suffering.

To her children in Norfolk she addressed some very sweet sentences. After expressing (in her wonted humility) how deeply she felt their kindness to her, she adds,—

"I may thankfully acknowledge, I not unfrequently partake of hours of rest and peace, through the tender mercy of Him, who is touched with a feeling of our infirmities, and is our ever-living Advocate. Times of sore conflict are now and then permitted, but I have been sooner delivered out of them, than I was. As to outward help, (with regard to medicine,) I believe little can be done, but as it respects sympathy and care, much; but as I abound in these latter, in such a remarkable degree, I trust, if it be the will of my Heavenly Father, they may tend to raise up, if not that they may be blessed to my soul."

At this time, a lovely infant child of her nephew and niece Buxton was removed by death. Elizabeth Fry felt much on the occasion. On the following day, being First-day, Eleventh Month 26th, one of her sons, a daughter and a little grandson being by her bedside, she prayed nearly as follows, after the 18th chapter of Matthew had been read to her:—

Gracious Lord, grant that the promise to those, where two or three are gathered together in Thy name, may be fulfilled in our experience; and that Thou wilt look upon our whole circle, as well as the little group now present. Heal, as far as is consistent with Thy will, and grant patience and submission to whatever Thou mayest order. Lord, enable us to cut off the right hand, and pluck out the right eye, if they are likely to lead us into temptation. For ourselves, and those especially who are nearest to the little one whose spirit passed to Thee yesterday, enable us to give thanks, that he is among those innocent ones, whose angels, redeemed by the mercy of Christ Jesus, are for ever in Thy presence. And for all who are in affliction, we would ask Thy support.

One of the few remaining entries in her Journal is as follows:—

Upton, Twelfth Month, 7th.—Lord! undertake Thyself for me; Thy arm of power can alone heal, help, and deliver; and in Thee do I trust, and hope; though at times deeply tried and cast down before Thee; yet, O Lord! Thou art my hope, and be therefore entreated of Thy poor, sorrowful, and often afflicted servant, and arise for my help. Leave not my poor soul destitute, but through the fulness of Thine own power, mercy and love, keep me alive unto Thyself, unto the end! that nothing may separate me from Thy love, that I may endure unto the end; and when the end comes, that I may be altogether Thine, and dwell with Thee, if it be but the lowest place within the gate, where I may behold Thy glory, and Thy holiness, and for ever rest in Thee.

I do earnestly entreat Thee, that to the very last I may never deny Thee, or, in any way, have my life or conversation inconsistent with my love to Thee, and most earnest desire to live to Thy glory; for I have loved Thee, O Lord, and desired to serve Thee without reserve. Be entreated that through Thy faithfulness, and the power of Thy own Spirit, I may serve Thee unto the end. Amen.

Her agony, from violent spasm and cramp pervading all her frame, was frequently excruciating.

A few memoranda from the journal of her son William, are here introduced, not merely as illustrative of her state, but as descriptive of his communication with the tenderly-beloved mother, whom he was to precede, by so short a period, to the invisible world.

"The evening of the 29th, was one of the greatest suffering and distress; such as I never remember to have witnessed. But, through all, her faith was triumphant, and her confidence unshaken. I endeavoured to remember a few of her expressions, and have succeeded in calling to mind the following:—

"'I believe this is not death, but it is as passing through the valley of the shadow of death, and perhaps with more suffering, from more sensitiveness; but the rock 'is here;' 'the distress is awful, but He has been with me.'

"'I feel that He is with me, and will be with me even to the end. David says, 'why hast thou forsaken me?' I do not feel that I am forsaken. In my judgment I believe this is not death, but it is *as* death. It is nigh unto death.' She frequently expressed fears of being impatient. 'May none of you be called to pass through such a furnace; but still my sufferings have been mitigated through mercy and grace! fulness of grace! Now my dear William, be stedfast, immoveable, always abounding in the work of the Lord; and then thy labour shall not be in vain in the Lord. O! the blessedness of having desired to be on the Lord's side! (not that I have any merit of my own). I cannot express, even in my greatest trials and tribulations, the blessedness of His service. My life has been a remarkable one; much have I had to go through, more than mortal knows, or even can know; my sorrows at times have been bitter; but my consolations sweet! In my lowest estates, through grace, my love to my Master has never failed, nor to my family, nor to my fellow-mortals. This illness may be for death, or it may not, according to His will; but He will never forsake me, even should He be pleased to take me this night.'"

On the first of Second Month, her son William, her brother, Samuel Gurney, and two of her daughters, being around her bed, she prayed in a low voice, and at broken intervals, to the following purport:—

For help for this poor afflicted servant in her deep tribulation, that in passing through the floods they should not overflow her, and through the fire she should not be burned; that these trials in the hands of the great Refiner might tend to more perfect purification and refinement, and preparation for His service, whether in time or in eternity; but she wholly left this to His will. That if raised up, she desired it might only be to more entire devotedness to His service, and as an instrument to spread the knowledge of Christ and His truth amongst her fellow-mortals; and that mercy might be granted in body, soul, and spirit, to her husband, children, brothers, and sisters, and all beloved by her, even by Him whom she had steadily loved and desired to serve from childhood, though, through sore temptation and tribulation.

In the evening of the same day, she expressed her certainty of the truths of Revelation, saying, "I know my foundation to be sure, I feel the rock *always* underneath me."

The following morning, on her son William's reading an expression of love and sympathy from her eldest grandson, who had been placed in the army, and who, though so unfavourably circumstanced, was religiously inclined, she said, "My very dear love to him: tell him to be stedfast, immoveable, always abounding in the work of the Lord, for in *whatever circumstances*, it will not be in vain in the Lord."*

Her only absent daughter was at this time again summoned from Norfolk. Her mother had suffered, for some days before, with most painful neuralgic symptoms, but just then there was a degree of respite; the change, however, since she had seen her last, was sorrowful indeed to witness, and could but lead to the most alarming apprehensions. She spoke of her own recovery as a thing hidden from herself, and concerning which she had no desire. One day it was said to her, "that many a Christian had slept in this world, and to their own surprise awakened in glory;" she exclaimed directly, with most striking emphasis, "Oh! what a sweet thought." She spoke occasionally of her "timid nature;" of her "natural fear of death;" but on Second-day night, the 19th, when very low in body and spirit, she said emphatically, "should I never see the light of another morning, remember I am safe."

Her dependence on her Saviour, and utter rejection of every merit of her own, was entire. On one occasion, she said, when suffering extreme pain, "I am nothing, I have nothing; I am poor, miserable, naked, helpless. I can do nothing, but my Saviour is every thing, all-sufficient—my light, my life, my joy, my eternal hope of glory."

To one of the "nursing sisters" who was attending her, she thus expressed herself: "I am of the same mind as Paul, I can say, 'to me to live is Christ, but to die is gain.' What a grand thought it is! everlasting to everlasting, without trouble and without pain; to meet there, and together be for ever with Christ."

She was comforted, as were her attendants, by occasional visits from members of her own religious persuasion, and other Christian friends. Prayer was offered, from time to time,

* This young man, then twenty-two years of age, gave evidence of a decided christian principle, which greatly consoled his beloved grandmother. He soon afterwards left the army.

in her chamber. The visits of her sister Buxton were a true solace to her, she clung to her with inexpressible affection.

Her illness was a subject of tender interest and concern amongst all classes. To an intimate friend, who repeatedly visited her about this time, when she was with difficulty able to sit up during a few hours of the day, she dwelt, in a very clear and instructive manner, upon her own state, bodily and mentally. She expressed her belief that her illness was permitted for some special purpose, as it regarded herself, her family, and perhaps many others;—said she could not see what the termination of it was designed to be, adding, "I have had to look over all my life, and to review all the engagements which I have been led into." She spoke of her visit to the Mansion House, and of her meeting the King of Prussia there, and said she had never known a more deeply humiliating occasion; adding, "I cannot doubt that I was rightly led there, and none can think what I went through." Soon afterwards, she said to the same friend, "My life has been one of great vicissitude; mine has been a hidden path, hidden from every *human* eye. I have had deep humiliations and sorrows to pass through. I can truly say, I have 'wandered in the wilderness in a solitary way, and found no city to dwell in;' and yet how wonderful I have been sustained. I have passed through many and great dangers, many ways;—I have been tried with the applause of the world, and none know how great a trial *that* has been, and the deep *humiliations* of it; and yet I fully believe that it is not near so *dangerous* as being made much of in religious society. There is a snare even in religious unity, if we are not on the watch. I have sometimes *felt*, that it was not so dangerous to be made much of in the world, as by those whom we think highly of in our own Society: the more I have been made much of by the world, the more I have been *inwardly* humbled." She added, "I could often adopt the words of Sir Francis Bacon, 'When I have ascended before men, I have descended in humiliation before God.'"

To the same friend, who again visited her on the 27th of the following Month, and found her very ill and low, and who expressed a hope that she might yet be better, she said, "I have not yet seen how it will terminate—sometimes I have thought that perhaps I may be *partially* raised up, but I lay no *stress* on it." Afterwards she said with tears, "Oh, He is a covenant-keeping God! He keepeth covenant and mercy—Oh, may I ever *keep hold* of his mercy!" On the 29th, the same friend being again with her, and perceiving that she was much depressed, remarked, "I believe there is an open door set before thee, although thou mayst not always be able to *perceive* it open." The precious invalid wept much, and after a time said, "Oh yes! It *is* an open door." Presently she continued, "The Lord is gracious and full of compassion, I believe He will never leave me nor forsake me;" and after a solemn pause, she added, "I have passed through deep baptisms of spirit in this illness,—I may say, unworthy as I am to say it, that I have had to drink, in my small measure, of the Saviour's cup, when He said, 'My God! My God! why hast thou forsaken me?' Some of my friends have thought there was a danger of my being exalted, but I believe the danger has been on the opposite side, of my being too low." She afterwards said, with much sweetness, "I feel that He is gracious and full of compassion, and that He will not leave me destitute; and I trust He will never suffer me to dishonour His holy name." On the friend taking leave of her, she desired her dear love to several individuals, and added, "I love all my friends—I love every one."

As the spring advanced, there was a perceptible improvement, less severity of pain, and rather more appetite; she was moved now and then into another room, in a wheeled chair, and she began strongly to wish to be taken to Bath for the benefit of the waters. Her family feared to venture on such a trial of her little remaining strength; but, after many weeks of difficulty and doubt, it was decided that the attempt should be made, and her husband accomplished her removal to Bath. Her brother and sister Buxton were already there; and the closeness of the union, natural and spiritual, which subsisted amongst them, rendered their being near each other an important solace to them all. Various members of their families successively joined them; amongst others, her son William, and his little Emma.

How mercifully does the Almighty Disposer of events conceal, from His frail and feeble creatures, the knowledge of the future! Much of sorrow and infirmity oppressed some of this little band, but they could not foresee how soon the brightest of them were to be laid low.

Elizabeth Fry gained strength at Bath, and was unquestionably in better health on her return home. But she was closely touched by the rapid decline of her sister-in-law, Elizabeth Fry. They had been affectionately united for a long course of years. They had travelled together as ministers; they had, year after year, sat, side by side, in the Meeting-house at Plaistow, and now in her low and weakened condition, the severing of this tie was to her very painful.

Her sister died on the 2nd of the Seventh month in great peace.

There was an extraordinary weight upon Elizabeth Fry's spirit; she dwelt much, and often, on the invisible world; her sleep partook of these impressions. She dreamed that she saw, as she said, that "there were graves opened all around" her. Did not coming events cast their shadows before? And was not she thus, in some measure, prepared for the sorrows that were to follow? Her little grandson Gurney Reynolds, a very delicate child, was an especial object of interest to her; he was frequently with her, delighting in her gentle tenderness, and in the pursuits which she provided for him, so well suited to his feeble health. He left her not more unwell than usual. Tidings came of his being worse, and three days afterwards that his patient, lamb-like spirit, had departed as he lay upon the sofa in his mother's room. This was the 18th of the Seventh Month.

On the morning of his funeral she wrote to his parents:—

My dearest Foster and Chenda,

I deeply feel my separation from you this day; I long to be present with you to minister to your consolation. You have my earnest prayers that the best help may be with you, sustaining, healing, comforting you; enabling you to behold your beloved child at rest in Jesus; consequently that death has lost its sting, and the grave its victory. In the midst of this sore trial, may grace, mercy, and peace continue to be with you; and in His own time, may the Lord grant you "beauty for ashes, the oil of joy for mourning, and the garment of praise for the spirit of heaviness."

Your tenderly attached and sympathizing mother,

ELIZABETH FRY.

She had long and earnestly desired again to attend the Meeting for worship, at Plaistow It was proposed from one First-day to another; but the difficult process of dressing was never accomplished till after eleven o'clock, the hour when the meeting assembled. An attempt was made on the 28th of the Seventh Month, but it failed. Her disappointment was great, and the hold it took of her spirits so grievous, that it was resolved to make the effort, at any cost, on the following First-day. Her son William undertook to carry out her wishes—drawn by himself and a younger son, in her wheeled chair, she was taken to the Meeting, a few minutes after Friends had assembled, followed by her husband, her children, and attendants. Her son William seated himself closely by her side, and the rest near her. The silence that prevailed was singularly solemn. After some time, in a clear voice she addressed the Meeting. The prominent topic on which she enlarged was "the death of the righteous;" she expressed the deepest thankfulness, alluding to her sister Elizabeth Fry, for the mercies vouchsafed to "one, who having laboured long amongst them, had been called from time to eternity." She quoted that text, "Blessed are the dead who die in the Lord, for they rest from their labours, and their works do follow them." She dwelt on the purposes of affliction, on the utter weakness and infirmity of the flesh; she tenderly exhorted the young also, "the little children amongst us," referring to the death of little Gurney Reynolds. She urged the need of devotedness of heart and steadiness of purpose; she raised a song of praise for the eternal hope offered to the Christian, and concluded with those words in Isaiah,—"Thine eyes shall see the King in his beauty, they shall behold the land that is very far off." Prayer was soon afterwards offered by her, in much the same strain. *He* joined her in that solemn act, who never was to worship with her again, till, as we reverently trust, before the throne of God and the Lamb, they should unite in that ineffable song of praise, which stays not *day* nor *night*, for ever!

It being considered desirable that she should have the benefit of change and sea air, she was removed to Walmer: whence she wrote:—

I walk in a low valley; still I believe I may say the everlasting arm is underneath, and the Lord is near to me. I pass through deep waters, but trust, as my Lord is near to me, they will not overflow me. I need all your prayers in my low estate; I think that the death of my sister, and dear little Gurney, have been almost too much for me.

Thus was this servant of God permitted to go sorrowing on her way. But the storm had not blown over; again the thunder-clouds rolled up. On the 15th of the Eighth Month, the lovely little Juliana, the second daughter of her son William, one of the sweetest blossoms that could gladden the heart of a parent, was cut off after thirty hours' inexplicable illness. One day, however, but too fully sufficed to unfold the mystery: three of the servants at Manor House being attacked by scarlet fever. But all preceding sorrows seemed light in comparison, when the beloved head of that house was himself laid low by the awful malady. He had written on the death of his aunt shortly before: "Yesterday, we followed the remains of our dear aunt to the grave. We have the comfort of feeling assured, that she has entered into the joy of her Lord. May such be the case with us all! —but if we would 'die the death of the righteous,' *as* the righteous we must do our day's work in the day."

All stood aghast on hearing of his illness, and with distressful suspense awaited the accounts from hour to hour, and day to day.

"He surely will not be taken—so fearful an overthrow, so terrible a blow cannot be coming!" thus spoke hope and natural affection; but there was a response from the inmost heart of those who had watched his life and conversation, his increased religious thoughtfulness, the simple earnestness of his piety—and this response whispered—"is not the Master calling for him?"

The children were removed to Plashet Cottage, vacant from the death of Elizabeth Fry. As one and another showed symptoms of fever, they were carried back to Manor House. The servants continued to sicken successively, and were conveyed to a ward prepared for them at Guy's Hospital. The help of the "Nursing Sisters" became invaluable, two or three being in constant attendance. For about a week, strong hopes were entertained that the most precious life would be spared to his family, but such a result was not accordant with the divine will. On the day of the funeral of his little Juliana, he had asked to have his door open, that he might see the coffin as it was borne by, when, to the "Nursing Sister" by his side, he exclaimed, "I shall go to her, but she shall never return to me."

The fever ran its course, the excitement attending it came and went, but there was no recovering; all seemed to depend upon his powers of taking nourishment. He was calm, even cheerful; there appeared to be little, if any suffering; he perfectly knew his danger, he said that he "should like to recover, if it were right," but he was "quite willing to leave it in God's hand." When it was remarked to him, how great the mercy that sustaining patience had been granted him, he held up his hand with a great effort, and most emphatically replied, "God never has forsaken me, no, not for a moment, and He never will." As his last day commenced upon earth, his window wide open by the bed-side, and the sweet morning air blowing freshly in, he spoke of the fair view to be seen from it, and listened with interest, as the scene was described to him, the grey tints passing from the garden and terrace, and leaving them in light and sunshine. He spoke of his place, of his family, of his many blessings. Some little effort exhausting him, a stimulant was given; as he recovered, with a bright smile he exclaimed, "God is so good!" and they were his last words. Never, perhaps, was a dying bed more peaceful—more satisfactory the evidence that God was his refuge.

"Can our mother hear this, and live?" was the natural exclamation of her children. None need have feared her enduring the blow, for He who sent it bestowed His Holy Spirit with it. The Christian's faith proved stronger than the mother's anguish. She wept abundantly, almost unceasingly, but she dwelt constantly on the unseen world, and on those passages in the Bible which spoke of the happy state of the righteous. Her natural affections and interests were also, in no small degree, occupied for his widow and children, all his little ones having the fever.

The medical men insisted on the necessity of every one quitting the house. The little children were carried back to Plashet Cottage, where the others had become ill, and with the exception of three servants in one corner of the basement story, the house was deserted.

Elizabeth Fry was earnest to hear everything, and to have all particulars given her. The illness of her grandchildren occupied much of her thoughts; the accounts from them continued to fluctuate; but, Second-day, the second of Ninth Month, brought a more unfavourable report of Emma—the eldest. On the following morning she also was taken. She was a religious child, and no doubt rests in Jesus, whom she had loved and desired to obey. One grave contains the mortal remains of the father and his daughters.

The following First-day was a memorable one; the two last chapters of the Revelation were read, and then some memoranda concerning the beloved departed, and their closing hours upon earth. This was followed by solemn thrilling prayer, offered by their mother for those who remained, and for herself in her "low estate:"—for such as had fought the good fight, kept the faith, and obtained the victory, thanksgiving and praise!

Her own journal, written before the last blow fell, tells her feelings:—

Walmer, Eighth Month, 29th.—Sorrow upon sorrow! Since I last wrote, we have lost by death, first, my beloved sister, Elizabeth Fry; second, Gurney Reynolds, our sweet, good grandson; third, Juliana Fry, my dearest William and Julia's second daughter; and fourth, above all, our most beloved son, William Storrs Fry, who appeared to catch the infection of his little girl, and died on Third-day, of scarlet fever, the 27th of this month. A loss inexpressible—such a son, husband, friend, and brother! but I trust that he is for ever at rest in Jesus, through the fulness of His love and grace. The trial is almost inexpressible. Oh! may the Lord sustain us in this time of deep distress. Oh, dear Lord! keep thy unworthy, and poor, sick servant, in this time of unutterable trial; keep me sound in faith, and clear in mind, and be very near to us all—the poor widow and children in this time of deepest distress, and grant that this awful dispensation may be blessed to our souls. Amen. This tenderly beloved child attended me to Meeting the last First-day I was at home, and sat by me on the women's side.

Oh, gracious Lord! bless and sanctify to us all, this afflicting trial, and cause it to work for our everlasting good; and be very near to the poor dear widow and fatherless; and may we all be drawn nearer to Thee and Thy kingdom of rest and peace, where there will be no more sin, sickness, death, and sorrow.

The return home was sorrowful indeed; the void—the want so great, of a member of the circle, who, whilst he was the tried friend and faithful counsellor, was wont to bring with him an atmosphere of cheerfulness and love.

Another beloved son, William Champion Streatfield, had taken the fever, one of her "married children," as she designated those, not by birth connected with her. On the day of her return from Walmer, all hope of his recovery was abandoned.

It is possible that her intense anxiety, whilst the life of one so dear hung suspended as on a thread, and then the gradual deliverance from it, in some degree, tended to withdraw her thoughts from the afflictions which had preceded it. Her mind was also occupied in sympathy with her bereaved daughter-in-law.

In a letter, she wrote:—

Upton, Tenth Month, 13th.—We returned from Walmer on the 17th of the Ninth Month. We first went to my dear brother Gurney's, at Ham House, where I was received with every kindness. Our beloved daughter Julia was here when we came home, and stayed a few days afterwards. She was then removed to her sister's, where she (I may thankfully say) has since been confined. She has a sweet little girl, and is doing well. So we see that the Lord gives, and the Lord takes away, blessed be His holy name!

About six weeks after the decease of her son, she was again favoured with strength to attend the Meeting at Plaistow. The occasion was a *memorable* one. She was led, with great power and solemnity, to address the different classes then assembled; and perhaps few could remember a Meeting in which her gift in the ministry had been exercised with greater weight and clearness, or with a more remarkable appropriateness to the varied conditions of those who were present: and she afterwards supplicated with a degree of heavenly power and unction that deeply affected many hearts. From this time she continued frequently to labour amongst her friends in the ministry of the word; and her bodily strength gradually increased; so that, though very feeble, she was able, with some assistance, to walk a little.

To her sister Elizabeth Gurney, who had been from home, she wrote:—

Upton, *Tenth Month*, 21*st*.

My dearest Elizabeth,

I must thank thee before thy return home for thy sweet letter, but as we hope soon to meet, I will not say much. I also received one from our dear sister Eliza, which I hope to answer in a day or two.

I cannot give a very bright account of us, as I feel very poorly, very low and flat, and that we have many causes of deep sorrow—the effect of William's loss is hardly to be told. But I desire always to feel that our God is able to supply our needs, through the riches of His grace, in Christ Jesus our Lord.

I long to visit Earlham, but I fear that the season is too far advanced.

May you all feel for, and remember us, in our very low estate, and hoping soon to see your party home, I am with dear and tender love to all of you, including John and his sweet wife,

Thy much attached sister,

ELIZABETH FRY.

On the 1st of the Eleventh Month she addressed her last written communication to the Committee of the "Ladies' British Society."

My much-loved Friends,

Amidst many sorrows, that have been permitted for me to pass through, and bodily suffering, I still feel a deep and lively interest in the cause of poor prisoners; and earnest is my prayer that the God of all grace may be very near to help you to be steadfast in the important Christian work, of seeking to win the poor wanderers to return, repent and live; that they may know Christ to be their Saviour, Redeemer, and hope of glory. May the Holy Spirit of God direct your steps, strengthen your hearts, and enable you and me to glorify our Holy Head, in doing and suffering, even unto the end: and when the end comes, through a Saviour's love and merits, may we be received into glory and everlasting peace.

In christian love and fellowship,
I am affectionately your friend,
ELIZABETH FRY.

A new sorrow awaited her. On the 1st of Twelfth Month, Catherine Hankinson, the daughter of her late beloved sister Louisa Hoare, died—a few days after her infant son. Though young in years, she was not young in religious experience; devoted in heart and life, she was apparently ripe for glory, when it pleased the Lord to take her.

On this affecting event, Elizabeth Fry wrote:—

Eleventh Month, 2nd—The accounts of to-day are deeply affecting—to have the grave once more (and so soon) opened amongst us. What can we say but that "it is the Lord;" for the flesh is very weak, and these things are hard to our nature. I have felt the pain of this fresh sorrow, but desire that all most closely concerned may find Him very near to them, who "healeth the broken in heart, and bindeth up their wounds." My love and sympathy to all most nearly interested. We have our poor dear Julia and her children here, and very touching it is to be with them. I am, I think, just now very poorly, and much cast down, but I remember the scriptural words, "cast down, but not destroyed."

This "fresh sorrow" involved much personal loss and grief to one of her daughters, which occasioned her writing to her two days later, the following sweet and instructive lines:—

A few lines of most tender love to thee and thine. My spirit is so much broken within me, and bowed down, that I cannot write much. As the body so much affects the mind, I feel the more sunk under our trials from my state of illness; still the Lord sustains me in mercy and in love. I need all your prayers in this time of deep affliction, and you need mine. May our Lord sanctify our deep afflictions to us, that they may work for us here, the peaceable fruits of righteousness, and hereafter a far more exceeding and eternal weight of glory.

The increasing illness of her brother-in-law, Sir T. Fowell Buxton, occupied much of her thoughts, and excited her tenderest feelings, and she wrote the following to his eldest daughter, Priscilla Johnston:—

Twelfth Month, 1844.

My dearest Priscilla,

Thanks for thy kindness in writing to me at this time of deep sorrow; but strange to say, before thy note came, I had been so much with you in spirit, that I was ready to believe thy dearest father was sinking. I have felt such unity with him spiritually. My text for him, in my low state this morning, was, "The sun shall be no more thy light by day; neither for brightness shall the moon give light unto thee: but the Lord shall be unto thee an everlasting light, and thy God thy glory!" I believe this will be his most blessed experience, whenever our Lord takes him to Himself. I write with difficulty and in haste, but my heart is so very full towards you, that I must express myself. My dear love to every one of your tenderly beloved party, particularly thy mother. I feel as it respects thy dearest father, whether a member of the Church militant, or the Church triumphant, all is well—and we may, through all our tribulations, return God thanks, who giveth us the victory, through Jesus Christ our Lord! Most near and tender love to you all.

I am,

Thy much attached aunt,

E. F.

To the same, on the last day of the year:—

Upton, *Twelfth Month,* 31*st.*

My dearest Priscilla,

Thy mother's and thy letters have been truly consoling. I dwell much with you in spirit, and I feel near sympathy and unity with your beloved invalid, and with you all. How weighty to come to the close of this year, wherein so much has passed! "The Lord has given, and the Lord has taken away;" but through all we may say, "blessed be the name of the Lord!" I desire your prayers, (for my estate is a very low one,) for myself, for my husband and children; as we have all been brought very, very low before the Lord. May our afflictions be sanctified to us; not leading us to the world for consolation, but more fully to cast ourselves on Him who died for us, and hath loved us with an everlasting love. I write sadly, as it is difficult to do it, my hands are so much affected by my general state of health. With thy dearest father, I have felt in life no common religious bond. How sweet, how blessed to feel, that we have "one Lord, one faith, one baptism."

On the 19th of Second Month, her beloved brother Buxton was removed by death.

Though of a different character, another trial awaited her. Her son-in-law William Champion Streatfield, had not rallied from the effects of the fever, and he was now ordered, without further delay, to Madeira. To part from him, and especially from her daughter, was very grievous to her. It was not merely the pain and sorrow of losing the society of this beloved child, which she felt so acutely, but the peculiar and protracted nature of her own illness had rendered her exceedingly dependent on those who, like her daughter Hannah, had so largely shared in the attendance upon her. Two of their children remained near their grandmother, the others with their parents took their departure on the 16th of the First Month. She committed them in earnest supplication, to Him, whom winds and waves obey, and with whom are the issues of life;—and so they parted, never to meet again on earth.

There was one thing which rested upon her mind. A strong desire again to visit Norfolk, and stay once more at Earlham. With great difficulty it was accomplished; her husband and daughter Louisa taking her there. She remained at Earlham many weeks; often able to partake of enjoyment, and highly valuing the communion with her endeared brother Joseph John Gurney, his wife, and her beloved sister Catherine.

She went frequently to Meeting at Norwich. She was drawn up the Meeting, seated in her wheeled chair, and thence ministered with extraordinary life and power to those present; her memory in using Scripture, in no degree failing her, or her power in applying it.

She went forward to Northrepps, in order to mingle her sorrows with those of her much beloved and bereaved sister Buxton, and other mourners there. The last letter she ever addressed to her husband was from that place, dated Fourth Month, 10th, 1845:—

My dearest Husband,

I am anxious to express to thee a little of my near love, and to tell thee how often I visit thee in spirit, and how very strong are my desires for thy present and thy everlasting welfare. I feel for thee in my long illness, which so much disqualifies me from being all I desire to thee. I desire that thou mayst turn to the Lord for help and consolation under thy trials, and that, whilst not depending on the passing pleasures and enjoyments of this world, thou mayst, at the same time, be enabled to enjoy our many remaining blessings. I also desire this for myself in my afflicted state, (for I do consider such a state of health a heavy affliction,) independent of all other trials. I very earnestly desire for myself, that the deep tribulation I have had to pass through, for so long a time, may not lead into temptation, but be sanctified to the further refinement of my soul, and preparation for eternal rest, joy, and glory. May we, during our stay in time, be more and more sweetly united in the unity of the Spirit, and in the bond of peace. . . . . .

After she left Earlham, she went, for a few days, to Runcton, as it was thought better than her going to Lynn. Her children met her, and stayed with her there. Before she left Norfolk, she heard of the intended marriage of her youngest son. The prospect of this connection was peculiarly agreeable to her. Towards this, her last-born child, her motherly care had been specially extended. She was affectionately attached to her future daughter-in-law, and her being a member of the Society of Friends afforded her no small comfort. It was indeed a boon for all who loved her, to feel that she returned home under a ray of sunshine, and that the brightness of this event, to her feelings, was permitted a little to enlighten the last few months of her home life. The various arrangements and preparations connected with it, occupied, without wearying her mind, and her attention was, in some degree, withdrawn from dwelling upon her sorrows and deprivations. In her eldest grand-daughter, the first-born of her eldest son, and bearing her own name, she had, during this spring, a helpful, cheerful companion, who, with the elasticity of youth, (which is so pleasant to the infirm and declining,) cheered, whilst she cared for her grandmother. She had also many visitors, who came to her in their abundant kindness; for the hearts of all who loved her, were drawn out towards her in tender and affectionate interest, and many besides her own relatives and connections, with the excellent of the earth of various ranks and denominations, would drive down to Upton Lane, and sit awhile by her side, once again to partake of the sweetness and instruction derived from fellowship with her heavenly spirit.

In the latter party of Fifth Month, accompanied by her grand-daughter, Elizabeth Fry, she attended two sittings of the Women's Yearly Meeting of Friends in London: a Friend who was present thus narrates this occasion:—

"She had for many years, been regular in her attendance upon these Meetings, and had taken a lively interest in their proceedings. After an illness so critical, and still in a state of such great infirmity, to see her again amongst them, was scarcely less gratifying to many of the Friends there, than it was interesting to herself. On this occasion she spoke of the Saviour's declaration, 'I am the vine,—ye are the branches,—as the branch cannot bear fruit of itself, except it abide in the vine, no more can ye, except ye abide in me.' She alluded, in the course of her observations, to the day that is 'fast approaching to every one;' but urged the blessed truth on her hearers, that those 'who loved, served, and obeyed Him, who alone is worthy of all glory and praise, would find death deprived of its sting, and the grave of its victory.' The second Meeting she attended, was one when a Friend, Edwin O. Tregelles, gave a relation of his missionary labours in the West Indies. This recital drew from her, some account of her own travels on the Continent. She afterwards enlarged upon the various instruments, by which God accomplishes His own works in the world. She referred to the simile of the different living stones, which compose the temple of God. She addressed those of every age who heard her, especially such as might be compared to the hidden stones of the building. She encouraged them to go forward faithfully in the path of righteousness and good works; for, though they might not be so much seen and known, as the more polished stones in the orna mental parts of the structure—though perhaps not so fitted to shine, or to occupy a conspicuous situation—yet were their places equally ordered, equally important, and equally under the direction and all-seeing eye of the Divine Architect. She expressed her doubts, as to whether she should again be permitted to meet her beloved Friends in that place.—She offered prayer, her rich full voice filling the house; and concluded with that sublime passage, 'Great and marvellous are Thy works, Lord God Almighty, just and true are Thy ways, thou King of Saints.'"

On the 3rd of Sixth Month, Elizabeth Fry was present at the Annual Meeting of the "Ladies British Society." To spare her fatigue, the Committee kindly arranged to hold it in the Friends' Meeting-house at Plaistow, instead of the one at Westminster, which hitherto had been the place chosen.

At the Committee of the Society, held on the 3rd of the Eleventh Month following, there was drawn up by its members, a touching memorial of the feelings they entertained towards her.

In it they speak of this Meeting:—

"Contrary to usual custom, the place of Meeting fixed on was not in London, but at Plaistow in Essex; and the large number of Friends who gathered round her upon that occasion, proved how gladly they came to her, when she could no longer with ease be conveyed to them. The enfeebled state of her bodily frame seemed to have left the powers of her mind unshackled, and she took, though in a sitting posture, almost her usual part, in repeatedly addressing the Meeting. She urged, with increased pathos and affection, the objects of philanthropy and Christian benevolence, with which her life had been identified. After the Meeting, and at her own desire, several members of the Committee, and other Friends, assembled at her house. They were welcomed by her with the greatest benignity and kindness, and in her intercourse with them, strong were the indications of the heavenly teaching, through which her subdued and sanctified spirit had been called to pass. Her affectionate salutation in parting, unconsciously closed, in regard to most of them, the intercourse which they delighted to hold with her, but which can no more be renewed on this side of the eternal world."

On this occasion, when Elizabeth Fry attended, for the last time, the Meeting of the "British Ladies' Society," she had the satisfaction of knowing that Newgate, Bridewell, the Millbank Prison, the Giltspur Street Compter, White Cross Street Prison, Tothill Fields Prison, and Cold Bath Fields Prison, were all in a state of comparative order; some exceedingly well arranged, and the female convicts in all, more or less visited and cared for by members of the Committee. The prisons generally throughout England much improved, and in the greater number, ladies encouraged to visit the female convicts. She had, unquestionably, accomplished much, and above all had the joy of knowing, that the principles which she had so long asserted were universally recognized;—that the object of penal legislation is not revenge, but the prevention of crime; in the first place, by affording opportunity of reform to the criminal, and in the second, by warning others, from the consequences of its commission. But there was one thing which she was not permitted to see accomplished,—a refuge for every erring and *repentant* sinner of her own sex; the opportunity of reformation for all who *desired* to reform. There are those, who have striven to connect the memory and the name of Elizabeth Fry, with such a shelter for the outcasts of our great metropolis;—and they have had the satisfaction of seeing their benevolent effort, *to a considerable degree*, successful, in the establishment of the "Elizabeth Fry Refuge."

On the 26th of Sixth Month, her youngest son was married. She described the Meeting as "a very solemn one, something like a token for good;" and spoke of the connexion as a "ray of light upon a dark picture."

There was, (she wrote,) through all the real brightness of

the occasion, a deep feeling of the past; when dear Julia's children joined us in the afternoon, then the miss of dearest William was keenly to be felt. Champion and Hannah too so very far off, that there was much to cloud over the scene, as well as my poor state of health, making it more difficult to estimate my many present blessings, as I ought and desire to do.

As the summer advanced, sea air was considered desirable for her, and after some difficulty her husband obtained a house at Ramsgate, exactly suited to her necessities. She went for a week to see it, and to make her own arrangements, accompanied by her husband and her daughter Richenda. The day before leaving home, she wrote to her brother and sister Gurney:—

My dearest Samuel and Elizabeth,

I have rather longed to bid you farewell, before accompanying my husband to Ramsgate for a few days. My heart is much with you, and our dear brother Joseph also, just now. I particularly feel for you in your conflicts, as well as your joys. Humiliations we must expect to pass through, if we are to drink of the cup our Lord drank of, and be baptised with the baptism that He was baptised with; therefore we must not fear, but when our spirits are overwhelmed within us, we must look to the "rock that is higher than we, as a shelter from the storm, a shadow from the heat, when the blast of the terrible one is as a storm against the wall."

From Ramsgate, she wrote, for the last time, to her eldest daughter:—

Ramsgate, *Seventh Month, 5th.*

I much desire to be at our own Meeting on First-day, with dearest Harry and Lucy, and hope it may please a kind Providence to enable me to do so.

I have felt very poorly here in the morning, more so than usual, which has been rather discouraging. I much like the house as far as I have seen it, but I have not been up stairs. I have felt unusually low, and am sensible of my poor condition, as it is most feelingly brought home to me in almost every fresh effort. I desire in heart to say, "Not as I will, but as Thou wilt." I think none of my friends need fear (as I believe they used to do,) my being exalted by the good opinion of my fellow-mortals. I think my state is "cast down, but not destroyed." May my Lord, whom I have loved and sought to serve, keep me alive unto Himself, and may He clothe me with His armour that I may "stand in the evil day, and after having done all, stand."

The return of her son and his young bride, to Upton Lane, she wished to make as cheerful, as under existing circumstances, was possible; and in celebration of the event, a large family party was arranged for the garden. She asked the company of her brother and sister from Ham House.

My dearest Samuel and Elizabeth,

In true love, I advise your joining our simple evening party, which I humbly trust will be conducted on Christian grounds. The fact is, in my low estate, I felt much indisposed for a large dinner; I then wished for our dear little children to have some innocent pleasure, and also to show some mark of the deep interest we feel in the bride and bridegroom here, and in the bride and bridegroom elect. We wish to do it in the most simple manner. Remember, our most blessed Master attended the wedding feast.

She received her guests in a room, opening into the flower garden, and thence was wheeled to the end of the terrace; a very large family circle surrounded her, many connexions and others of her friends. It was a beautiful scene,—the last social family meeting at which she presided; and although infirm and broken in health, she looked and seemed herself.

In an easy chair, under the large marquee, she entered into animated discourse, on various and important topics, with the group around her, the Chevalier Bünsen, Merle D'Aubigné, Sir Henry Pelly, Josiah Forster, her brother Samuel Gurney, and others of her friends.

During the week following, she was moved to the house at Ramsgate, which had been prepared for her. A spacious bed-chamber adjoining the drawing-room, with pleasant views of the sea, in which she delighted, adding to her hourly comfort and enjoyment. She found objects there well suited to her tastes. She distributed tracts when she drove into the country, or went upon the Pier in a Bath chair. Seafaring men have a certain openness of character, which renders them more easy of access than others. They would gladly receive her little offerings, and listen to her remarks. She was also anxious to ascertain the state of the Coast Guard Libraries—whether they required renewing, and were properly used.

Soon after her settlement at Ramsgate, the family of her beloved son William came to her, and remained for several weeks. She delighted in them all; but little Willie Fry was something to her, almost beyond anything left in the world. He read the Bible to her every morning on her awakening. She strove to impress upon his young mind the value and beauty of the Christian life; she endeavoured to cultivate in him a taste for natural objects; she encouraged drawing and similar pursuits. Partly his name—partly his character, so much resembling his father's in early boyhood—excited her tenderest love.

Her prayer for her daughter and her children, on the evening before their departure, was beautiful, comprehensive, and touching; and so she commended them, whom she was to see no more on earth, to Him, who has declared Himself to be "a Judge for the widow, and a Father to the fatherless." Her eldest son, and her daughter Reynolds, with their families, were near her in the town; and the daily intercourse with them, was also a source of much comfort to her.

In a hand almost illegible, is this affecting entry in her journal:

Ramsgate, Eighth Month, 27th.—It still pleases my Heavenly Father that afflictions should abound to me in this tabernacle; as I groan, being burthened. Lord, through the fulness of Thy love and pity, and unmerited mercy, be pleased to arise for my help. Bind up my broken heart, heal my wounded spirit, and yet enable Thy servant, through the power of Thy own Spirit, in every thing to return Thee thanks, and not to faint in the day of trouble, but in humility and godly fear, to show forth Thy praise. Keep me Thine own, through Thy power to do this, and pity and help Thy poor servant, who trusteth in Thee. Be very near to our dear son and daughter, and their children in Madeira. Be with them, and all near to us, wherever scattered; and grant that Thy peace and Thy blessing may rest upon us all. Amen and Amen.

On the 13th of Ninth Month, she wrote to her son Joseph the following letter, which touchingly indicates the increased feebleness of the mortal tabernacle:—

First-day, Afternoon.

I am rather blanked to hear that we cannot see thee and thine this week. I rather particularly long to see a dear son again, as it feels long since John left us, and you are sure your beloved wives have also a true welcome. I feel myself *much* broken, and finding that neither sea air, nor any other thing appears much to raise me up; I do feel while *here*, (I mean in this life,) a great desire to be as much as I can with those most dear to me. My heart overflows with love, and most earnest desire for your present and everlasting welfare, particularly that all may be of the number of those who "die in the Lord," who "rest from their labours, and whose works do follow them."

The conclusion of this letter can scarcely be read without much mournful and tender emotion: it is as follows:—

I feel certainly very poorly, and unless there be some revival more than I now feel, I think that you cannot expect that you will very long have a mother to come to; but I know the Lord can raise me up again, and I should not be surprised if it should be His holy will; but into His hands I commit my body, soul, and spirit: humbly trusting that He will be my Keeper, Guide, and Guard, even unto the end; through the fulness of His love, pity, mercy, in Christ our Saviour! I know this is a low letter, may it lead to your sympathy, love, and prayers. I think I am low from parting with Julia and the children; my heart is so bound to you all. I am encouraged by remembering the 13th chapter of the First of Corinthians, because I feel that I may humbly trust that that love or charity there spoken of, lives in my heart, and is, as the apostle John says it is, a mark of having "passed from death unto life, because we love the brethren." (1 John iii. 14.)

The next day she wrote to her brother Samuel Gurney the following precious note:—

I was very low when I wrote to thee yesterday, therefore do not think too much of it. There is ONE only who sees in secret, who knows the conflicts I have to pass through. To him I commit my body, soul, and spirit; and He only knows the depth of my love, and earnestness of my prayers, for you all. I have the humble trust that He will be my Keeper, even unto the end; and when the end comes, through the fulness of His love, and the abundance of His merits, I shall join those who, after having passed "through great tribulation," are for ever at rest in Jesus, having "washed their robes, and made them white in the blood of the Lamb."

I am, in nearest love,

Thy grateful and tenderly attached sister,

E. F.

Pray remember the books for the poor old women; we must work whilst it is called "to-day," however low the service we may be called to; I desire to do so to the end, through the help that may be granted me.

On the 16th of the following month, she again, and for the last time, recorded her feelings in her journal, writing in a firmer hand, and with apparently more power.

Ramsgate, Ninth Month, 16th.—My dearest son Harry was married to dear Lucy Sheppard last Sixth Month, 26th. We had a very solemn Meeting; peace appeared to rest upon us at the Meeting, and at her father's house afterwards. My humble trust is, that the blessing of the Most High God is in this connexion. They spent some very satisfactory time with us before we left home. May grace, mercy, and peace rest upon them, and neither the fatness of the earth, nor the dew of heaven, be withheld from them, through the fulness of the love, mercy, and pity of our God, in Christ Jesus our Lord.

Our dearest niece Elizabeth was also married the latter end of the Seventh Month to my dear young friend Ernest Bünsen. May the blessing of the Most High God also rest upon them, naturally and spiritually. I pray the same for them as for Harry and Lucy.

Here the journal ends; the above being the last entry.

Her sister Buxton, with her daughter Richenda, visited her on the 17th of Ninth Month. They found her mind clear and powerful in spiritual things, enlarging upon them with comprehension of their import; her heart entirely in the things of God, choosing him and his service solely, with deep, earnest, constant desires (beyond words to express) for her husband and children, grandchildren, brothers and sisters, nephews and nieces, and all who were dear to her. After her sister went, her youngest son and his bride stayed a few days with her. Other members of the family came also to see her. Her son Joseph and his wife left with her one of their children.

The 14th of Ninth Month, with a large party of her family, she attended the small Meeting at Drapers, about four miles from Ramsgate. On this occasion, she preached a most powerful and remarkable sermon on the nearness of death, and the necessity of immediate repentance and preparation; adding, she believed to some of that small congregation it was the eleventh hour of the day. So it proved to more than one.

Her ministrations were much of the same character on the two following First-days. Her brother and sister Gurney stayed near her for some time, and several ladies from Zwolle were also there; and she valued the company of her kind friends, Sir John and Lady Pirie, who were then at Ramsgate.

On the 29th, the large family party dispersed. The Meeting of the preceding day had been one of great solemnity, and though little imagined at the time, well fittted to be a parting occasion with so many dear to her. For some days she was left with only her husband and eldest daughter, but the nursing was too arduous for them to bear alone, and it was a great relief to them when her daughter Rachel and her family arrived from Norfolk. At the Pier gate, awaiting them in the carriage, they found their mother. Her daughter had not seen her since her visit to Runcton, six months before; a great change was perceptible. There was a look of heaviness and weight; she rarely smiled, but on the other hand, far less often looked distressed; she walked rather better, her appetite was improved, and her nights not so disturbed; but there was a new symptom—occasionally severe pain in the head. It had first appeared ten days before, and had often been acute, but then was better.

The next First-day she went, as usual, to Meeting. On her return, she asked some of the family, who, from the distance, had been precluded from accompanying her, and had attended the public place of worship, if they had had "a comfortable church;" her general question when she met any of her children under similar circumstances. Then, without waiting for any inquiry respecting the worship in which *she* had united, she said, "we have had a very remarkable Meeting, *such a peculiarly solemn time*;"—that she had been so impressed by the "need of working whilst it was day, to be ready for the Master's summons, come when He might." Here the subject dropped, but she reverted to it more than once during the day. Those who were present described the occasion, as *a very peculiar and favoured one*. She had urged the question, "Are we all now ready? If the Master should this day call us, is the work completley finished? Have we *anything* left to do?" Solemnly, almost awfully, reiterating the question, "*Are* we prepared?"

Her habits, at this time, were apparently those of former days. She was a good deal occupied by writing. She arranged and sorted Bibles, Testaments, and Tracts. She had applied to the Bible Society for a grant of foreign Bibles and Testaments, which was liberally acceded to, and in the distribution of which, amongst the sailors of different nations in the harbour, she took great interest.

On Third-day, the 8th of Tenth Month, when driving out, her lively concern for the good of others appeared, if possible, greater than ever. Her natural character, acquired habit, and Christian duty, alike combined to strengthen this, but the judgment and power to direct it had, in measure, passed away.

On Fourth-day, the 9th, she was grievously distressed by her little grandson Oswald encountering a fearful accident, one knee slipping through the area bars of a window. It was at least ten minutes before help could be obtained to extricate him. The child's cries, and her knowledge of the fact, though at the time borne apparently well, occasioned a severe return of pain in the head at night, and she was very unwell the next morning, though through the day she had appeared but little the worse for it, and was perfectly self-possessed and judicious in giving directions. During the same morning, her friend Mary Fell paid her husband and herself a religious visit; she derived much comfort from it, as she had done, from the society of this long known and valued Friend, for some weeks preceding

Generally, whilst she dressed, one of her daughters sat with their mother. On one occasion, the Bible was opened at the text, "Beloved, think it not strange concerning the fiery trial which is to try you, as though some strange thing happened unto you." She entered, with lively interest, into the subject, and mentioned other passages of somewhat similar import which were sought for and read. The participation of the disciple in the sufferings of his Lord, was dwelt upon. She expressed herself with peculiar power, in a manner startling to the hearer. She had, through all her conflicts, seemed to cling to something, like the hope, almost expectation, that the western sky would be bright, that her sun would not set behind clouds; but now there was no allusion to any idea of the kind. The high privilege of suffering as a member of Christ, was the point she most dwelt upon. The world, even in the renewed, regenerated aspect which it bears to the Christian, appeared to have lost nearly all attraction.

There was another striking change. Her vigorous understanding and great capacity had given her the habit of control—she had been accustomed to power. During her long illness, this continued more or less to show itself, and it was not always easy to distinguish, how far her opinions about her own treatment and capabilites were-well founded or not. This feature of her character had disappeared. The will seemed wholly gone, the inclination even strongly to desire anything, had passed away; and she was content to leave things, whether little or great, to the direction of others. It was inexpressibly affecting to see her look of meek submission, to hear her plaintive answer, "Just as you like."

During one morning of acute suffering, the remark was made to her, How marvellous it was that she never seemed impatient to depart, believing, as there was good ground to do, that she had been fitted for the great change. She expressed her entire willingness to stay the Lord's time; that whilst there was any work for her to do, she wished to live, but beyond that, she expressed not the smallest desire for life. She added, that she had come to an entire belief, than any remaining dread would be taken away from her, when the time came, or that in tender mercy to her timid nature, she should be permitted to pass unconsciously through the dark valley.

On Fifth-day, she wrote to her youngest daughter:

Ramsgate, *Tenth Month*, 9*th*.

My dearest Louisa,

I think that a visit from thee and thy dear husband would be highly acceptable to us; but much as I should like to see the dear boys, I fear that the house is now too full, to take in more than we should have with Raymond and thyself.

I feel so shaken and so broken down, that I wish to see as much of my beloved children as I can; my love is very strong, and my flesh is very weak, I think increasingly so. I wish dear Christiana Golder to know how much I miss her. Pray tell Gurney and Sophia also how much I should like to see them; indeed, my heart is drawn very near to you all, and deep are my desires for your present, and above all, your everlasting welfare. . . . .

Thy tenderly attached mother,

ELIZABETH FRY.

On Sixth-day morning, Tenth Month, 10th, though very languid and feeling uncomfortable, she addressed this note to a friend to whom she had been long attached, not in religious profession with herself, with some texts for a young person, who desired to possess her autograph.

Ramsgate, 10*th*.

My dear Friend,

I have copied thee, these valuable texts, that prove salvation is open to all, through a Saviour's love and merits, who believe in Him, who no longer live unto themselves, but unto Him who died for them and rose again. May we all be of this blessed number. I should much like a nice long letter from thee. With true desires for thy present and everlasting welfare,

I remain,
Thy affectionate friend,
ELIZABETH FRY.

"We trust in the living God, who is the Saviour of all men, specially of those that believe." 1 Tim. iv. 10. "And I, if I be lifted up from the earth, will draw all men unto me." John xii. 32. "Therefore as by the offence of one judgment came upon all men to condemnation; even so by the righteousness of one, the free gift came upon all men unto justification of life." Romans v. 18.

After concluding this note, she brought out some sheets of Scripture selections, which she was preparing, with a view to eventually publishing another Text-Book, on the same plan as her former one. With this devout employment, was finished her work below. Strikingly, though unconsciously, did it exemplify the spirit and tenor of the life that was about to close!—fervently aspiring heavenward, and attracting others thither. A few hours succeeded—of suffering to the mortal frame—the soul being stedfastly anchored by faith upon the rock—and then her sun sank beneath its earthly horizon—setting in brightness, to rise on an eternally unclouded sphere!

It was remarked that she had, in selecting the texts, used no spectacles; and she said that her sight had become much better. This was a new and serious symptom.

Later in the morning, whilst driving out, she was strangely

oppressed—scarcely noticed the lovely views of the sea, which she generally so much enjoyed; but the most unusual thing was, that when her grandchildren were eager to give some tracts, she did not observe their request, till repeated two or three times. On passing some open country, where a ruddy farmer's boy was keeping cows, he told the children that he was there all day, that he had nothing to do, and should very much like to have "some reading." Their grandmother took no notice, nor until her tract-bag was put into her hand, did she attempt to choose any for him; then she did it with a slow and absent air, as if her thoughts were far away. That evening she was heavy and oppressed, and complained of suffering from the light.

These many circumstances, each trifling in itself, brought and weighed together, gave such cause for uneasiness, that her husband and daughters resolved the next day to send to Broadstairs, to learn if Dr. Paris were still there, for they had heard of his being at that place a short time before, and they wished to call in his assistance; but he was gone.

On Seventh-day morning the 11th, she awakened, suffering severely in her head. One of her grandchildren went to her at half-past seven o'clock: he read the 27th Psalm, which she asked for. Half an hour later, another went to her. She in no way referred to his brother having been there before, but again asked for the 27th Psalm. Her dressing was very slowly accomplished; she leaned her head upon her hand, and spoke very little. A text or two out of "Great and precious promises," (that excellent selection for the sick chamber,) seemed all that she could then receive. She had not asked for one of the children while she was dressing, the only morning she had omitted to do so, nor did she remark their absence. She had invited the children of Lady Arthur Lennox, to take their dinner at her luncheon. It was proposed that their coming should be deferred to another day, as she was so uncomfortable, but this she would not allow; when they came she was scarcely able to notice them, and sat looking very ill, leaning her head upon her hand. Afterwards Lady Lennox, and her sister, came for the children; she received them in the drawing-room and conversed a little, but they thought her unwell, and made a very short visit. They had been frequently with her before, they had paid her much kind attention, and their society had been very pleasant to her.

About five o'clock, whilst her husband and daughters were consulting as to the best method in which medical help might be obtained, her bell rang. She was in her own room, according to her usual custom in the afternoon, and had been lying on the sofa. She had nearly fallen, in being led from it to her chair by the fire, and help was wanted, to accomplish the movement. After being placed in her chair, she leaned on one side, as if unable to sit upright. Her attendant, who was accustomed to her, was alarmed and uneasy, but she was wheeled into the drawing-room, where it was proposed that she should dine, being nearer to her chamber than the dining-room. After her dinner, on attempting to move to the sofa, she twice sank to the ground, though entirely assisted by two persons. With extreme difficulty she was removed to her bed, where she lay with a calm, almost a torpid expression of countenance. She was quite willing to see a medical man, and answered his questions correctly. The attendance of one so kind and skilful was a great comfort, but her worn-out constitution forbade stringent remedies, so that little was attempted either by him or the physician, who repeatedly saw her in the course of the following day.

She soon became more alarmingly affected, and her limbs appeared wholly powerless. About six o'clock on First-day morning the 12th, she said to her maid, "Oh! Mary, dear Mary, I am very ill!" "I know it, dearest Ma'am, I know it," replied the servant. The precious invalid soon added, "*Pray for me—It is a strife—but I am safe.*" She continued to speak, but indistinctly, at intervals, and frequently dosed. About nine o'clock on First-day morning, the 12th, one of her daughters sitting on the bed-side had open in her hand that passage in Isaiah, "I, the Lord thy God, will hold thy right hand, saying unto thee, fear not, thou worm Jacob, and ye men of Israel, I will help thee saith the Lord, and thy Redeemer, the Holy One of Israel." Just then, her mother roused a little, and, in a slow, distinct voice, uttered these words, "*Oh! my dear Lord, help and keep thy servant!*" This was her last expression on earth: she never attempted to articulate again. A response was given by reading to her the above most applicable portion of Scripture; one bright look of recognition passed over her features, but it was gone as rapidly, and never returned. From this time, she became unconscious—no sound disturbed her—no light affected her—the voice of tenderness was unheeded—a veil was between her and all things here below, to be raised no more.

Difficulty of breathing ensued—and suddenly, about four o'clock in the morning of Second-day, the immortal spirit, which had so long reflected the bright rays of that heaven-inspired love which dwelt within it, passed away from the vicissitudes and sorrows of this earthly scene, to its eternal home in that "city, which hath no need of the sun, neither of the moon to shine in it; for the glory of God doth lighten it, and the Lamb is the light thereof."

Much affectionate respect for her memory, and sorrow for the termination of her eminently useful life, were evinced by the inhabitants of Ramsgate. A public manifestation of this feeling was proposed, but, from circumstances, necessarily declined by the family.

The funeral took place on the following Second-day, at Barking: and, after the mortal remains were committed to the dust, a large number of persons, who, in deep though silent sorrow, witnessed the affecting scene, assembled in a spacious tent erected for the occasion; in which a solemn Meeting was held. The sacred record was, with peculiar impressiveness, brought to remembrance, "And I heard a voice from heaven, saying unto me, Write, Blessed are the dead which die in the Lord from henceforth: yea, saith the Spirit; that they may rest from their labours; and their works do follow them." And from the grave, a call seemed to be emphatically uttered to survivors, "*Work ye also while it is day.*"

She, who had fulfilled her stewardship, and was gone to receive her eternal recompense, had bequeathed to each individual, and to all coming generations, a legacy involving a high responsibility. She had left behind her an example of unfaltering dedication in running with patience the christian race; her pious exhortations and her appeals of mercy had been uttered in the presence of thousands; their echo had passed on, and the sound had fallen on the ear of many thousands more; awakening in the bosom a holy sympathy with human suffering—animating to a heaven-directed effort to stem the overflowing current of sin and misery, and to point transgressors to an Almighty Deliverer, who "was manifested that He might destroy the works of the Devil."

Few will be found, especially among women, whose vocation may, in *all* points, resemble that of Elizabeth Fry. Perhaps, having been the appointed pioneer in the arduous path which unfolded to her view a vast variety of objects, each claiming the devotion of her christian benevolence and the energies of her powerful mind, *her* name may, in *some* respects, stand *alone* in the record of that peculiar mission to which she was ordained. But she had, from amongst the different classes and denominations of the religious world, many helpers in her works of faith and labours of love. More than a few of these have, like herself, been removed from their sphere of service on earth, to receive, as we may reverently trust, the hundred-fold of everlasting life. Others yet remain—pursuing under the influence of the same divine charity, the hallowed endeavour to reform the criminal, and to succour the indigent.

But may it be remembered, that every one, without distinction of sex or name, has an individual course of duty, which calls for the occupation of time, of talent, or of substance; and none can foresee how effectually *a faithful obedience* to this call, may tend to promote the glory of God, and the moral elevation of the human family. How inconceivable to the mind of Elizabeth Gurney, when, as a young and delicate girl, she first followed the impulse of a mysterious guidance that led her to visit the wretched inmates of a *Bridewell*, would have been the wondrous career which the unseen future was gradually to open before her; but, with her characteristic simplicity, she yielded her heart to the gentle touches of that heavenly Power, which, in a manner incomprehensible to herself, imbued her with a willing commiseration toward the abject and the outcast; and, whilst she sought to mitigate the distresses and to remedy the evils that, to a large extent, became continually more and more developed, as she pressed onward in her track of mercy, she was compelled to admit the conviction that a most serious responsibility rested on her own sex, in the efforts so greatly needed—yet by many still untried, but within the reach of most—to labour for the relief of the destitute, for the instruction of the ignorant, or for the reformation of the criminal.

She found, by experience, that devoted women—influenced by divine love—might become powerfully instrumental to check and to control the torrent of moral evil. By her own example she illustrated all that she enforced. And to a heart so acutely sensitive, so striving after a state of purity, so glowing with heavenly affections, the trial must have been great, indeed, of being thus brought into sympathy and frequent association with such accumulated forms of corruption and woe. Yet when—during a period of severe indisposition and near the close of her earthly pilgrimage—a near relative remarked to her that she had "made great sacrifices," she could reply, "I cannot call them *sacrifices*—it was my *delight*." Her delight it truly was to labour for the conversion and rescue of perishing sinners: and no toil was too arduous to be encountered, no suffering too great to be endured, to promote the welfare of immortal beings.

Like her great precursor, Howard, she "dived into the depths of dungeons," to bring into their gloom a ray of life, of love and hope. *His* monument records that, "in the unremitting exercise of christian charity, he trod *an open*, but *unfrequented* path to immortality." *He* travelled *alone* from land to land, pleading—but too often in vain—the cause of the agonized criminal, or the tortured victim of vengeance and tyranny; fearlessly encountering privation, danger, and difficulty. But such, happily, was not the experience of Elizabeth Fry. *Her* compassionate appeals on behalf of wretched convicts, groaning in fetters and laden with chains, were listened to with respect, and were generally successful. It was *her* lot also, to be often cheered by evidences, frequently little anticipated, that in different districts and countries, there were some bright christians of both sexes, who were willing to devote themselves, with self-sacrificing zeal, to the reform of the vicious, and to the relief of the sick and the destitute: and the mind that recognizes, in each individual of the human race, a brother or a sister for whom the Redeemer "gave Himself, a ransom" transcending all price, will contemplate, with grateful joy, the widening diffusion of active beneficence, and the kindred spirits that were prepared to catch, from the same holy altar, some portion of that flame of divine compassion, that glowed within the bosom of Elizabeth Fry.

Whenever a claim on her commiseration—whether small or great—was presented to her mind, with an impression that it required her attention, she shrunk not from the kindly impulse; and whatever obstacles might impede the accomplishment of her purpose, she steadily pursued it; and rarely did she ultimately fail: for she matured her schemes of philanthropy with a skill and discretion that almost invariably ensured success.

In every exigency she was sustained by *hope*—it was a principle so strong within her, that it animated and strengthened her in the execution of the most difficult designs. In her estimation of individual character, it sometimes induced anticipations that were not fully realized: it was on *this* point that the defect in her own was developed. On all the works of man, and on every phase of human existence, there is the stamp of imperfection: with *her* it sprang from an excess of that *charity* which "hopeth all things."

But as this faithful servant of God sought, with untiring energy, to complete her appointed task, she was often reminded of the truth, that, in the world's great harvest-field, where so much soil remains uncultivated, and from which so little of the heavenly fruit has yet been gathered, the labourers were comparatively few. Her own service was often toilsome, and the spiritual atmosphere in which she performed it most ungenial; yet cheerfully she fulfilled the duty of each passing hour: and the mental region into which, by this diligent occupation with the gifts bestowed on her, she was so remarkably introduced, was not *always* sterile from the blight of sin, not *always* tainted by the envenomed breath of the serpent. She was at times permitted joyfully to "walk in the light of the Lord," tasting the sweets of religious fellowship with minds assimilated to her own; beholding in the vineyard of the good husbandman, many a precious plant, flourishing beneath the rays of His love, and bringing forth fruit in its season, to the praise of His grace.

How is her memory embalmed with the fragrance of holy veneration, in the bosom of many a sincere disciple of the Lord Jesus Christ!—and most appropriately has the benediction been so often and so variously rehearsed, in reference to her abundant labours in His sacred cause, "Come, ye blessed of my Father, inherit the kingdom prepared for you from the foundation of the world: for I was an hungered, and ye gave me meat; I was thirsty, and ye gave me drink; I was a stranger, and ye took me in; naked, and ye clothed me; I was sick, and ye visited me; I was in prison, and ye came unto me." Matt. xxv. 34, 35, 36.

THE END.

www.ingramcontent.com/pod-product-compliance
Lightning Source LLC
LaVergne TN
LVHW021051110826
845150LV00001B/45

* 9 7 8 1 4 2 5 5 6 7 7 0 5 *